IN FULL FORCE AND VIRTUE

North Carolina Emancipation Records 1713-1860

William L. Byrd, III

HERITAGE BOOKS
2007

HERITAGE BOOKS
AN IMPRINT OF HERITAGE BOOKS, INC.

Books, CDs, and more—Worldwide

For our listing of thousands of titles see our website
at
www.HeritageBooks.com

Published 2007 by
HERITAGE BOOKS, INC.
Publishing Division
65 East Main Street
Westminster, Maryland 21157-5026

Copyright © 1999 William L. Byrd, III

Other Heritage Books by William L. Byrd, III:

Against the Peace and Dignity of the State: North Carolina Laws Regarding Slaves, Free Persons of Color, and Indians
Bladen County, North Carolina Tax Lists: 1768 through 1774, Volume I
Bladen County, North Carolina Tax Lists: 1775 through 1789, Volume II
For So Long as the Sun and Moon Endure: Indian Records from the North Carolina General Assembly Sessions, & Other Sources
In Full Force and Virtue: North Carolina Emancipation Records, 1713-1860
North Carolina General Assembly Sessions Records: Slaves and Free Persons of Color, 1709-1789
North Carolina Slaves and Free Persons of Color: Chowan County, Volume One
North Carolina Slaves and Free Persons of Color: Chowan County, Volume Two
North Carolina Slaves and Free Persons of Color: Pasquotank County
North Carolina Slaves and Free Persons of Color: Perquimans County
Villainy Often Goes Unpunished: Indian Records from the North Carolina General Assembly Sessions, 1675-1789

Other Heritage Books by William L. Byrd, III and John H. Smith:

North Carolina Slaves and Free Persons of Color: Burke, Lincoln, and Rowan Counties
North Carolina Slaves and Free Persons of Color: Hyde and Beaufort Counties
North Carolina Slaves and Free Persons of Color: Iredell County
North Carolina Slaves and Free Persons of Color: Mecklenburg, Gaston, and Union Counties
North Carolina Slaves and Free Persons of Color: McDowell County
North Carolina Slaves and Free Persons of Color: Stokes and Yadkin Counties

All rights reserved. No part of this book may be reproduced or transmitted in any form or by any means, electronic or mechanical, including photocopying, recording or by any information storage and retrieval system without written permission from the author, except for the inclusion of brief quotations in a review.

International Standard Book Number: 978-0-7884-1241-8

To the County Court of Perquimans now Sitting.

The Petition of the Subscriber Respectfully Sheweth —

That having under my care a Black man commonly known by the name of Edward Gerrish who for his faithful Services, honesty, Industry and good Oeconomy I am desirous should enjoy his freedom — do therefore request that you would take it into consideration and grant that his freedom may be Established under the act of Assembly in that case made and provided. —

Your Lenity therein will be acknowledged by your Petitioner. —

                                  Josiah White

We whose names are hereunto Subscribed being acquainted with the Honest Peaceable and Industrious Character of the above mentioned person are free that the Petition be granted. —

Caleb Winslow   Lawrence Perry
Jesse Rogerson   Joseph White
Josiah Jordan
Caleb Ettiff   Exum Newby
Uriah Hudson

Petition To Emancipate Edward Gerrish

No. Carolina ss.   For the Gen.ll Court

Henry Sheller & Patience his wife Complains of John Braveboy of Chowan prisoner in the Custody of the Marshall &c. For y.t whereas y.e Patience whilst she was the widow of one John Swaine Did at y.e special instance & request of the s.d John Braveboy on or about y.e 26.th day of August 1713 pay unto M.r James Ward of Chowan aforesaid the Sume of 28.£ Curr.t money &c. & also at the same time Did enter into one bill or obligacon to y.e s.d James Ward to pay him the further Sume of 27.£ like money Both w.ch s.d Sumes making together 55.£ was &c. in consideracon that the s.d James Ward should grant unto the s.d John his freedom he being a Slave And the s.d Henry & Patience further say that upon her y.e s.d Patience paying the s.d Sume of 28.£ & giving such bill or obligacon as aforesaid the s.d James Ward did free & sett at Liberty y.e s.d John from being a Slave And they further say that the s.d John &c. in consideracon of the premisses aforesaid did on or about y.e s.d 26.th day of August promise and assume to pay or cause to be paid unto the s.d Patience the aforesaid Several Sumes of 28.£ & 27.£ together with the further Sume of 10.£ making together the Sume of 65.£ Current money But the s.d John having no regard to such his promise & Assumpcon as aforesaid but fraudulently and deceiptfully intending to cheat & defraud the s.d Henry & Patience of the Sume of 65.£ hath not as yet paid or otherwise satisfyed unto the said Henry & Patience the s.d Sume of 65.£ tho' he the s.d John hath been in a friendly manner often requested thereunto but still refuses to pay the same from whence the s.d Henry & Patience say they have damage to the value of 150.£ And thereof this their suite is produced &c.

                                          Dan. Richardson att. pl.ts

How much we ask, bringing to you our pressing wants--come over and help us, for my people are in need of instruction, both spiritual and educational; and in thus aiding us you will accomplish a work of far reaching power, of which you now have no comprehension.   James L. Smith, a former slave.[1]

"Freighted with curses was the Bark that bore
The Spoilers of the West to Guinea's shore;
Heavy with groans of anguish blew the gales
That swell'd that fatal bark's returning sails."
"Loud and perpetual O'er the Atlantic waves,
For guilty ages, roll'd the tide of Slaves;
A tide that knew no fall, no turn, no rest,--
Constant as day and night from East to West,
Still wid'ning, deep'ning, swelling in its course
With boundless ruin and resistless force." --- Montgomery.[2]

"Men born and bred in slavery, are not men but children. Their faculties are never permitted to unfold themselves; and it is the aim of their masters, and the necessary effect of their condition, to keep them in a state of perpetual imbecility."[3]

---

[1] James L. Smith, *Autobiography of James L. Smith* (1881; reprint, New York: Negro Universities Press, 1969), vii.
[2] Ralph Randolph Gurley, *Life of Jehudi Ashmun* (1835; reprint, New York: Negro Universities Press, 1969), 101.
[3] Richard Hildreth, *Archy Moore: The White Slave* (1856; reprint, New York: Negro Universities Press, 1969), 101.

contents

INTRODUCTION .... **VII**

ACKNOWLEDGMENTS .... **XII**

CHAPTER 1 1
   Bertie County 1

CHAPTER 2 5
   Buncombe County 5

CHAPTER 3 7
   Caswell County 7

CHAPTER 4 9
   Chatham County 9

CHAPTER 5 11
   Chowan County 11

CHAPTER 6 37
   Craven County 37

CHAPTER 7 127
   Cumberland County 127

CHAPTER 8 135
   Duplin County 135

CHAPTER 9 137
   Edgecombe County 137

CHAPTER 10 143
   Franklin County 143

CHAPTER 11 149
   Gates County 149

CHAPTER 12 151
   Granville County 151

CHAPTER 13 157
   Guilford County 157

CHAPTER 14 167
   Halifax County 167

CHAPTER 15 171
   Lincoln County 171

CHAPTER 16 179
   New Hanover County 179

CHAPTER 17 185
ORANGE COUNTY 185
CHAPTER 18 191
PASQUOTANK COUNTY 191
CHAPTER 19 245
PERQUIMANS COUNTY 245
CHAPTER 20 263
RANDOLPH COUNTY 263
CHAPTER 21 267
ROCKINGHAM COUNTY 267
CHAPTER 22 269
STOKES COUNTY 269
CHAPTER 23 273
SURRY COUNTY 273
CHAPTER 24 275
WAKE COUNTY 275
CHAPTER 25 279
WARREN COUNTY 279
CHAPTER 26 285
WAYNE COUNTY 285
CHAPTER 27 289
WILKES COUNTY 289
CHAPTER 28 291
ACTS OF EMANCIPATION BY THE GENERAL ASSEMBLY 291
APPENDIX A 311
EMANCIPATION LAWS 311
APPENDIX B 319
QUAKER DOCUMENTS 319
INDEX 331

introduction

In 1860, almost all North Carolina counties retained on file a group of documents referred to as "slave papers." These papers were usually kept in the offices of the clerk of court or the register of deeds. The North Carolina State Archives maintain these records under the general headings of "slaves and free Negroes," or "slaves and free persons of color." Another specific group ("miscellaneous records") also contains papers relating to slaves and free persons of color. These documents are located in the North Carolina State Archives under the county collections.[4] It is from these time worn records that the emancipation papers in this book are derived. Rich and fascinating in content, they literally bring this forgotten era of history to life. Though numerous, they are by far not the majority of North Carolina's emancipation papers.

There are no abstracts in this volume. All the documents are complete transcriptions. Each record has been transcribed "as is" keeping preservation in mind for future generations of researchers. They may not be as fortunate as those of us who can still handle the originals. Whatever content the record contained, no matter how long, or how repetitive, was transcribed in full.

Every attempt has been made to be thorough in the search and transcription of these records. Many of the records pertaining to individual emancipation petitions were scattered throughout the files. In order to render them understandable, the papers relating to one another have been grouped together. This provides a clear and precise transcript of each individual emancipation record. The full emancipation process is available for many of them, but in other cases papers are missing. Not a few of them were deteriorated beyond reading.

These records are supplemented with the Acts of the General Assembly of North Carolina. These acts are comprised of private acts passed by the North Carolina General Assembly granting freedom to slaves whose masters had properly petitioned the court or general assembly for the emancipation of a slave or slaves. The private acts of emancipation cover the years from the late seventeen hundreds to the Civil War. The original source for each record can be found within this volume at the beginning of each county or individual record.

This book does not purport to contain a complete collection of North Carolina's emancipation papers. There are many more scattered throughout the North Carolina courts of pleas and quarter sessions and the superior courts of law. It should be observed that the majority of papers in this book are petitions to those very courts. To include the court records in this volume would lead to duplication of many of the petitions. Also not included in this volume are

---

[4] Thornton W. Mitchell, "Preliminary Guide to Records Relating to Blacks in the North Carolina State Archives," *Archives Information Circular* 17(June 1980): 3-4.

records from the North Carolina General Assembly, and records of Wills emancipating slaves. However, there are some petitions originating from Wills that are included. In addition, some of the petitions for emancipation in this book may not have been approved when presented to the general assembly. To include these other papers would increase the length of this book by a thousand pages. Work is, however, commencing with these additional sources. If it is feasible, they will be published at some future date.

Many of the petitions included contain information on North Carolina Indians who were either slaves, or were illegally held as such. One of the most pressing grievances of North Carolina Indians was the issue of the enslavement of their people. This was particularly true of Indian women and children. This practice was so common that the Pennsylvania Legislature enacted a law in 1705 against "...the further importation of Indian slaves from Carolina. "[5] During the Tuscarora War in 1712, Governor Hyde of North Carolina announced he had captured four hundred Tuscarora Indians. In the same war, James Moore, Jr. and John Barnwell of South Carolina carried off a thousand more into slavery.[6] The abolitionist Goodell stated as late as 1853 that "...the native Indians have also been enslaved, and their descendants are still in slavery."[7] It is quite common to find Indians listed as slaves or indentured servants in North Carolina records.

In one such case, included in this volume, there is a petition presented by an East Indian woman. She sued for her freedom based on the fact that she was descended from a free East Indian woman from Madagascar. She presented depositions from several states in her defense. A good number of cases similar to this one can be found in this book.

There is a wealth of information abounding in the petitions wherein masters expostulate to the court the reasons for wishing to free their slaves. The petitions reveal relationships between diverse cultures and races, and many of them depict those relationships on an intimate level. Long obscure, these records have mostly remained out of reach of the general public. The purpose of this book is to change that, and make them available to laymen and scholars alike.

One such narrative brought to light by John Hope Franklin is worth mentioning. In a petition sent to the North Carolina General Assembly in 1838, a White couple had taken in a slave girl while she was still an infant. They raised her "...as though she were their own flesh and blood, they being deprived of those common pledges of love and affection of parents, and ... said adopted coloured child became as near and dear to your petitioners as if she was borned of their bodies." Several years earlier the girl had been freed by the Wilkes County court. Mr. Franklin goes on to say "...it is safe to say that when the manumission was desired on the part of the master, but where the obstacles were practically prohibitive, the master relaxed his control on the slave and allowed him to go virtually free."[8]

This is not to say that everyone shared this philosophy. Kay and Cary, in *Slavery in North Carolina, 1748-1775*, explained that "In their eagerness to avert the loss of their human property, masters left no gates open -- including the pearly ones. Slaveholders who shaped the Fundamental Constitutions of 1669 explicitly asserted that conversion to Christianity would not qualify a slave for Freedom."[9] North Carolina's emancipation laws bore testimony to this fact. However, even with this mindset, more than two thousand slaves were emancipated between 1824 and 1826.[10]

It is generally accepted that North Carolina's emancipation laws were loosely enforced until after 1829. The pivotal change for more stringent laws were established in 1830. Several unexpected events helped pave the way for these new laws. In 1826 the Vermont legislature had sent a resolution to the North Carolina General Assembly. This resolution said, in explicit terms, that "...slavery is an evil to be deprecated by a free and enlightened people."[11] This document literally infuriated the general assembly. They were, however, unprepared for the crisis they were about to come face to face with.

David Walker was a black man born near Wilmington, North Carolina to a slave father and a free black mother. Under North Carolina law he was considered a free man. He eventually ended up in the city of Boston. In autumn of 1829 he privately published a pamphlet entitled *David Walker's Appeal, in Four Articles; To the Coloured*

---

[5] Hugh T. Lefler, *History of North Carolina*, v. 1 (New York: Lewis Historical Publishing Company, 1956), 70-71.

[6] J. Leitch Wright Jr., *The Only Land They Knew, The Tragic Story of the American Indian in the Old South* (New York: The Free Press, 1981), 143-144.

[7] Thomas D. Morris, *Southern Slavery and the Law, 1619-1860* (Chapel Hill: The University of North Carolina Press, 1996), 20.

[8] John Hope Franklin, "Slaves Virtually Free in Antebellum North Carolina," in *Race and History: Selected Essays, 1938-1988*, John Hope Franklin (Baton Rouge: Louisiana State University Press, 1989), 77. (*Hereafter cited as Race and History: Selected Essays, 1938-1988.*)

[9] Marvin L. Kay and Lorin Lee Cary, *Slavery in North Carolina, 1748-1775* (Chapel Hill: The University Press of North Carolina, 1995), 67.

[10] Alice D. Adams, *The Neglected Period of Anti-Slavery in America, 1808-1831* (Boston, 1908), 26.

[11] *Race and History: Selected Essays, 1938-1988*, 75-77.

Citizens of the World. The distribution of this pamphlet sent shock waves ringing throughout the Southern states because of its explosive nature. Within a few months after its publication, copies began to surface in ports of call from Virginia to Louisiana. The pamphlet delivered "...a furious indictment of American racism and slavery, coupled with a call to Southern Blacks to rise up and overthrow their masters." To worsen an already deteriorating situation, "...the author found ways to get his words into the hands of his primary audience." This audience consisted of the free colored citizens of the South. The startled North Carolina General Assembly reacted by implementing new restrictions on its slave population and the process of emancipation.[12]

The increasingly prohibitive laws in North Carolina induced the Quakers to invent schemes to circumvent the emancipation laws. Beginning in 1808 "The Yearly Meeting appointed a committee of seven to have under their care all suffering cases of people of color." In effect, "...the institution itself became a slaveholder." The aspiration of this custom "...was to give virtual freedom to the blacks when actual freedom was not recognized by the state; to ameliorate their conditions, and transport them to the free states." This strategy was legitimized by a law passed in 1796 entitled "An Act to secure property to religious societies or congregations of every denomination.[13] By 1822 there were four hundred and fifty slaves in possession of the Yearly Meeting. A report in 1830 declares that six hundred and fifty-two former slaves had departed to free governments.[14]

The *Raleigh Register* reported on May 30th, 1826 news concerning the annual meeting of the Society of Friends in North Carolina. In reference to the slaves sent to free governments, "...120 of the number are desirous of going to Hayti; 316 to Liberia, and about 100 wish to be sent to the non-slave-holding States of Ohio or Indiana." In addition to these slaves the "...Society have already sent off 64 persons to the State of Ohio, 47 by the Indian Chief, which lately sailed from Norfolk to Liberia, and 11 by another vessel which sailed about the same time to Africa."[15]

The very same year the North Carolina Manumission Society decided it would be an act of humanity to free their slaves, and send them to Hayti and Liberia without their consent.[16] This particular philosophy was supposedly not espoused by the American Colonization Society. This society was organized in Washington, D.C. in late 1816. Article II. of their constitution states that "The object to which its attention is to be exclusively directed, is to promote and execute a plan for colonizing (with their consent) the free people of color residing in our country, in Africa, or such other place as Congress shall deem most expedient."[17] The abolitionist William Jay suggested quite profusely that the intentions of the society may not have been as honorable as they pretended to be. At an address delivered to the Colonization Society in Virginia, one member described the free colored population as "A large mass of human beings who hang as a vile excrescence upon society." Another member portrayed them as "A horde of miserable people--the objects of universal suspicion--subsisting by plunder."[18]

The society itself was accused of pandering to the vested interests of slave owners, and enemies of the free colored population. Even the great abolitionist Wilberforce protested their actions. The opponents of the society proposed that the right of the free people of color to remain in America should be defended, as well as their right to emigrate.[19]

The first among many meetings by colored people opposing the Colonization Society was held in Richmond, Virginia in 1817. Thirty-five years later opposition to the society remained intact. A Philadelphia group resolved that "Whereas, our ancestors (not of choice) were the first successful cultivators of the wilds of America, we, their descendants, feel ourselves entitled to participate in the blessings of her luxuriant soil, which their blood and sweat

---

[12] Sean Wilentz, "Introduction," in *David Walker's Appeal, In Four Articles; to the Coloured Citizens of the World*, David Walker (New York: Hill and Wang, Inc., 1995), vii.

[13] Stephen B. Weeks, *Southern Quakers and Slavery: A Study in Institutional History* (Baltimore: The John Hopkins Press, 1896), 224-225. (Hereafter cited as *Southern Quakers and Slavery*.)

[14] *Southern Quakers and Slavery*, 227-228.

[15] Charles L. Coon, *The Beginnings of Public Education in North Carolina* (Raleigh: Edwards and Broughton Printing Company, 1908), 292-293.

[16] H.M. Wagstaff, ed., *The James Sprunt Historical Studies: Minutes of the North Carolina Manumission Society, 1816-1834* (Chapel Hill: The University Press of North Carolina, 1934), 118.

[17] William Jay, *Inquiry into the Character and Tendency of the American Colonization , and American Anti-Slavery Societies* (1838; reprint, New York: Negro Universities Press, 1969), 11. (Hereafter cited as *Inquiry*.)

[18] *Inquiry*, 18.

[19] G.B. Stebbins, *Facts and Opinions Touching the Real Origin, Character, and Influence of the American Colonization Society* (1853; reprint, New York: Negro Universities Press, 1969), 6-7. (Hereafter cited as *American Colonization Society*.)

enriched; and that any measure or system of measures, having a tendancy to banish us from her bosom, would not only be cruel, but in direct violation of those principles which have been the boast of the republic."[20]

"Appendix A" at the end of this volume contains the original text of all the emancipation laws enacted by the Colony and State of North Carolina. The only law excluded is the 1818 statute that transferred the power to receive petitions for emancipation from the North Carolina Courts of Pleas and Quarter Sessions to the North Carolina Superior Courts. Regarding the other laws, only those sections of the acts that pertain to emancipation are included.

"Appendix B" contains Quaker documents referred to in this introduction. There are other Quaker documents scattered throughout the General Assembly Session Records, and the North Carolina county records.

If there were any laws in force regarding emancipation prior to 1715, they are lost or missing. The first emancipation law to appear in North Carolina's colonial records is in the revised statutes of 1715. The 1715 statute restricted the freeing of "Runaways or Refractory Negroes." It allowed a master to set free his slaves as a "Reward for his, or their honest and Faithful Service." Slaves emancipated under this statute were required to depart the colony within six months after emancipation. The penalty for remaining was to be sold again into slavery for a period of five years. Many of these slaves left the colony for a short length of time, and returned declaring themselves as free residents. In consequence of these tactics the Government of North Carolina passed a law in 1723 empowering any person or persons to take up the former slaves and bring them before a magistrate. The Government then sold the said former slaves to the highest bidder for a term of seven years. Half the purchase money was paid to the person who apprehended the slave. (See Appendix A.)

In 1741 a statute was passed restricting emancipation for any reason whatsoever, "...except for Meritorious Services." The County Court now had jurisdiction over the process, and a license had to be granted giving permission to free any slave. Any slaves that were emancipated, contrary to this procedure, were to be taken up by the Church Wardens and sold at public vendue. This policy applied to Negro, Mulatto, or Indian slaves. (See Appendix A.)

In 1776 the Yearly Meeting of friends (Quakers) advised all who held slaves "...to clense their hands of them as soon as they possibly can." A committee was appointed to handle this issue. In 1777 the committee reported that a "...considerable number have been set free by those who had them in their possession, about forty of which have since been taken up and sold in consequence of an act of assembly passed at Newbern ...(which was after said negroes were manumitted.)"[21]

With the Revolutionary War raging, many slaves were defecting and fleeing to the British. One such British fleet dropped anchor at Cape Fear in 1776. A sizeable number of defecting slaves were organized into a company to support British soldiers. This action and the Quaker resolution contributed to the frustration of the North Carolina law makers. As a result of this situation the General Assembly enacted another law in 1777.[22]

The 1777 statute decried the "...evil and pernicious Practice of freeing Slaves in this State, ...at this alarming and critical Time to be guarded against by every friend and Wellwisher to his Country." This statute basically reconfirmed the 1741 law requiring meritorious services and nothing otherwise. The penalty was for the freed slaves to be taken up and sold to the highest bidder. To further curb the activities of the Quakers the General Assembly of North Carolina passed a harsh law in 1778 declaring that "...divers evil minded persons, intending to disturb the public peace, did liberate and set free their slaves, notwithstanding the same was especially contrary to the Laws of this State." This law was retroactive to the year 1775. The only exceptions to this law were freed slaves who had "...inlisted in the service of this or the United States previous to the passing of this Act. (See Appendix A.)

The Quakers protested this law in a petition in 1778 stating that some of the slaves taken up were emancipated before the 1777 law was passed. They petitioned the General Assembly again in 1779 requesting that the offending statutes should be repealed. Their request was bluntly denied by the General Assembly's legislative committee. Undaunted, the Quakers continued their protests, and filed petitions for years to come.[23]

In 1788, the General Assembly, still upset with the Quakers, amended the 1777 statute. In addition to meritorious services, and leaving the state within six months, they "...directed in what manner and for what purposes slaves illegally liberated shall be apprehended and sold." They targeted "...divers persons from religious motives, in violation of the said law," who "...continue to liberate their slaves, who are now going at large to the terror of the people of this State." This terror eventually manifested itself in 1795 when the Grand Juries of Pasquotank and Chowan

---

[20] *American Colonization Society*, 194-195.

[21] *Southern Quakers and Slavery*, 208-209.

[22] Jeffrey J. Crow, Paul D. Escott, and Flora J. Hatley, *A History of African Americans in North Carolina* (Raleigh: Division of Archives and History, Department of Cultural Resources, 1992), 34-35, 41. (Hereafter cited as *A History of African Americans in North Carolina*.)

[23] *A History of African Americans in North Carolina*, 42.

Counties censured the Quakers for their continuing efforts to emancipate slaves. Shortly thereafter, in 1796, the General Assembly strengthened and confirmed the powers vested in the county courts by requiring petitioners to obtain a license and entering it into record. (See Appendix A and Appendix B.)

In 1797 a petition from four slaves (supposedly emancipated illegally by the Quakers) was presented to the United States House of Representatives. A debate ensued as to whether or not to receive the petition. After voting "...on the question for receiving the petition being put, it was negatived -- ayes 33, noes 50."[24] Not willing to give up, in 1798 the Quakers sent a memorial to the House of Representatives. After reviewing the memorial, the committee in charge "Resolved, that the memorialists have leave to withdraw the said memorial and address."[25] (See also Appendix B.)

Added to the terror of the people was the problem of freed slaves who became a charge on the county. To eliminate this problem the General Assembly passed a law in 1801 requiring individuals desiring to liberate their slaves "...to enter into bond in the sum of one hundred pounds for each slave so liberated, with approved security." This action increased the difficulty of liberating slaves by placing a financial burden on the liberator. (See Appendix A.)

Until 1818 the power of emancipation was vested in the North Carolina Courts of Pleas and Quarter Sessions. An act passed in 1818 changed this policy and transferred the power to emancipate slaves to the North Carolina Superior Courts. The laws regarding emancipation did not change again until the year 1830. In that year North Carolina passed a general emancipation law. Persons desirous of freeing a slave were required to file a petition praying for emancipation. They were also required to state the name, sex, and age of each slave. In addition they were to give public notice of their intention to file a petition six weeks before the court hearing. A bond of five hundred dollars was required and filed for each slave destined for emancipation. This was to insure freed slaves would demean themselves honestly and correctly while in the State of North Carolina. Every freed slave had to leave the State within ninety days after emancipation. The rules differed slightly for slaves freed by last will and testament. The same process was followed, but it was stipulated that the slave or slaves could not be freed until two years after the decease of their master, and after probate was completed.[26] (See also Appendix A.)

The revised statutes of 1837 and 1854 reiterated and confirmed the 1830 statute. These laws remained intact until 1861. That year the General Assembly passed a law making it illegal to free a slave by last will and testament. (See Appendix A.)

---

[24] *Annals of the Congress of the United States*, 4th Cong., 2d sess., v. 6:2015-2024.
[25] *American State Papers*, From the 1st sess. to the 2nd sess. of the 10th Cong., v. 1:163-165.
[26] *Southern Quakers and Slavery*, 224.

acknowledgments

I found out early on there was no money available for publication of a work such as this. As important as it seemed, I was not able to draw attention to it. Unexpected resistance confronted me on several occasions, and has continued to haunt me for some time. Eventually, though, the book was completed, and hopefully it will serve as research tool for others interested in this subject.

The acquisition and transcription of the within emancipation records has taken nearly five years. Profound thanks are in order for the staff of the North Carolina State Archives. They tolerated me quite well considering the large amounts of loose papers that I requested to be copied, either on the spot, or to be sent to me. My special thanks to Russel Koonts, formerly of the North Carolina State Archives, for his help in procuring copies of the records. I especially would like to express my appreciation to Jennette Coleridge Taylor of the North Carolina State Archives. She went out of her way to look after my interests, and see to it that I received copies of all the records I needed to finish this project.

Acknowledgments are also deserving of the staff of the Southern Historical Collection at the University of North Carolina. They were always ready to help me with any problem. My thanks to Dr. Schrader for his help in finding sources that were difficult to locate.

Chapter 1: Bertie County Records

chapter 1

Bertie County

NORTH CAROLINA STATE ARCHIVES
BERTIE COUNTY RECORDS
MISCELLANEOUS RECORDS
C.R.010.910.1 BOX #1

To the Worshipful Justices of the County Court of Bertie
County the Petition of Jenny Ash

Humbly sheweth that your Petitioners Mother Nancy Ash was an Indian and Free born as this Petitioner is well informed and firmly believes she can Prove to the satisfaction of this Worshipfull Court That your Petitioner is now and for along time past hath been in the Possession of Mr John Gardner of this County who hath hitherto and still doth detain and [Faded] and her children as slaves and deprives her of that liberty which all free born persons are of right entitled to that she has two children who the said John Gardner also detains in Slavery for whom as well as her self she offers the Petition, That she is well informed and very believes that the said John Gardner intends to send her and her said children out of this State into the State of Virginia in order to prevent as far as [Faded] your Petitioner from making application to your Worships for her Just and Lawfull rights Your Petitioner therefore prays that your worships would Issue your Writ of summons Subpoena directed to the said John Gardner requiring and Commanding him to appear at the Next County Court to bee held for this County on the Second Monday in May next then and there to answer this complaint strictly injoining him to have the said Jenny Ash and her Children aforsd. before your worships at the same time and Place and further to compell him to give good and sufficient Security not to dispose of them or by any means convey them out of the State so as to prevent them from making their Personal appearance before your Worships at the next Court Afsd. and that your Worships would give your Petitioner Such further relief as your worships in your great wisdom shall think and your Petitioner as in duty bound will ever Pray &c
Jenny Ash

To the worshipful Justice of the County Court Bertie County
the Answer of John Gardner to the Petition of Jennie Ash

Answereth and saith That the said John Gardiner reserving to himself the advantage of the mannifold errors and Incertainties in the said petition saith that the said Jenny Ash is not an Indian nor is she free born but that she is a Mustee, and a slave, as he is ready to prove to the Satisfaction he verily believes of this worshipfull Court. the said John Gardiner denies that he ever did intend to carry the said Jenny Ash out of the County or State either into Virginia or South Carolina or her two children. The said John Gardiner further answereth and saith the said Jenny Ash was given by a Will as a Bequest to him by Samuel Cotton when she was of the age of Ten years reference being thereunto had may more fully and amply appear and by virtue of which bequest she has been in his possession as his Servant and Slave about fourteen years therefore he by virtue of the Laws of this State humbly conceives he is justly entitled to keep the said Jenny Ash as his property.
  Your Respondent therefore trusts this worshipful Court will order and decree that the said Jenny Ash be considered as his property and to his sole use and behoof and as in duty bound will pray
John Gardiner
Sworn before mee }
this 12: May 1785 } David Sutton

Know all men by these presents that we John Gardner, James Gardner & William Carter are held and firmly bound unto Simon Turner Esquire, presiding Justice of the peace for the County of Bertie and the others his brethren Justices also

Chapter 1: Bertie County Records

for the County aforesd. and their Successors in the Sum of one thousand pounds; to which paiment well and truly to be made unto them - We do hereby bind ourselves our Heirs, Executors, and admrs. jointly & severally firmly by these Presents sealed with our Seals and dated this 13th day of May 1785
The Condition of the above obligation is such that if the above bound John Gardner shall not remove or suffer to be removed out of the county of Bertie Jenney Ash, a Mulatto Woman whom the said John hath for many years kept in bondage as his Slave; but who by her Petition to the court of the county aforesd. alledges she is entitled to her Freedom & if the said John Gardner shall also perform relative to the said Jenny Ash, and shall regularly produce the said Jenny Ash at the next court and so from court to Court until the Court shall finally determine the complaint of her the sd. Jenny, by a decree for or against her then the above obligation to be void otherwise to remain in full Force & Virtue
Signed & sealed in presence of
                        John Gardner   (Seal)
                        James Gardner (Seal)
Stevens Gray   William Carter   (Seal)

****

North Carolina   }Pursuent to an order for that purpose
Bertie County   }This Day Came Susannah Grover

of Full Age; Sworn before me on the Holy Evangelist Deposeth and saith that she was well Aquainted with the family of Joseph Letchworth & was well Aquainted with Dorcas Letchworth and That her brother William Swain, Married Tabitha Letchworth who was a sitter to Dorcas Letchworth Which her husband Thomas Spencer Told her that Dorcas Letchworth was Married to Absalom Tootle some Time after they was Married Thos. Spencer her Husband Told her that Dorcas Totle had Got a Molatto Girl Child, by her fathers Negro fellow sesar, and That some few Days after she saw her brother & that she herself Asked her husband if she should Tell her brother & he said she might for he swore it was the Truth. And the Deponant further saith: That she Told him And he was Very Angry and said he would Go and see and Know the Truth: And after her brother Came back he Told her it was the Truth: And he was Threatening to leave his wife which was sister to this Dorcas Tootle: & This Deponant Saith That she understood by one of her sisters that Mr. Tootle Agreed with his wife that she should After it was Old Enough to Wean from her breast Transport it Away that it Shou'd not be Any Stain to his Childrens Carricter: this Deponant further saith that she & her Husband Moved Near Tar River And further saith that her husband Mr. Spencer Left his horse And in his looking for his horse he Calld in at one Mr. Griffith's where this Child was [?] My husband Come home he Told me That he had seen this Child and he said That he would Trace the Child and she should have her freedom when it Come of Age: And further saith that she was in Company with Elizabeth Letchworth And Elizabeth Letchworth Told her that she was at Dorcas Tootles and she told her that she had not Named the Child and she Named it Bettey. And as she was Married to Absalom Tootle; And this Deponant further Saith that the first Time she Ever saw the Molattoe Girl was at her own House: the wentch Come to see if she Could Tell her of her Mother And she Told her she Could And Did: Near about Thirteen or fourteen Years Agoe: And the Deponant further saith that some Time after Christmas Last past Mr. Joel Brown Came to her House with a Molattoe Child in his Lap which was a son to the sd. Betty Tootle And asked her if she had Any Spirits she Told him no: & she asked him what Negro he had been buying he Answered One a little way off The Deponant further saith That Near about Twenty Nine or Thirty year ago Her Husband Mr. Spencer Told her that Docter Seay Had Got the said Molattoe Child which he saw at Mr. Griffiths And further the Deponant saith not
Given under my Hand and Seal this 24th of July 1788
Wm. Horn (Seal)

North Carolina   }Pursuent to an order of Court for that
Bertie County   } purpose This Day Came Mary Harrell
of Full Age Sworn before me on the Holy Evangelist Deposeth and Saith That she has been well Acquainted with a Molatto woman by the Name of Bess Ever since she was a small Girl And upwards of Twenty seven years And further Saith that it was always Reported that she was free Born And The Deponant further saith that This woman while she lived with Docter James Seay A small Girl And went by the Name of Bess is the same which Now Goes by the Name of Betty Tootle The Deponant further saith that she has Been Acquainted with Docter James Seays family & with Docter Seay himself And Never Knew Docter James Seay to have Another Molatter Girl or Negroe Girl And That she knows that this Molatto by the Name of Betty Tootle is the same that went by the name of Bess when she was small and Lived

Chapter 1: Bertie County Records

with Docter James Seay And the Deponant further saith: that last faul was Twelve months Ago Joel Brown Came to her House And it Raised in Discourse Concerning this said Molatto woman and that she asked Mr. Brown what was the Reason that he had give her up her freedom so long That he wanted to make a Slave of Her now: and He Answered that He knew that she was free and that was the Reason that he Had And the Deponant further saith That Mary Harrell sister to Docter James Seay Sold Her that he had Returned the bill of Sale And had Received all his Money Back but five pounds and This Deponant further saith that this woman That goes by the Name of Betty Tootle is the very same which Docter James Seay always had And she Never Knew him to have Any Other And the Deponant further saith that some Time on the Last of December or the first of January last that one Night After she was Gone to bed that Reubin House And Joel Brown Came to her House And Reubin House to the Door And Calld And Joel Brown went into the Citching for to look for the wentch And this Deponant further saith That Mr. Brown said that his perticular Business was to look for the wentch And Reubin House Asked if there was Any straglers there Amd Mr. John Spencer Asked him what Straglers And Mr. House said Bess which Goes by the Name of Betty Tootle and further this Deponant saith that They had Besses Children Two from Thos. Whites one from Thos. Rhoades And there was Two Children at Jesse Browns he Likewise said that Jesse Brown said that he would give up them if he Got the Wentch And the Rest of the Children And further this Deponant Saith Not
Given under my Hand And seal this 24th July 1788
Wm. Horn (Seal)

North Carolina   } Pursuent to an Order for that purpose
Bertie County   } This Day Came Thomas Rhodes of full Age
Sworn before me on the Holy Evangelist Deposeth and saith that he formerly knew a Molatto Girl that Lived with Docter James Seay who went by the Name of Bess And That the said Girl some Time after Docter Seays Decease was at her Libertie And has Remained As a free woman for the space of about Eight years to the best of my Memory and has Gone by the Name of Elizabeth Tootle in Consequence of her passing As a free woman there has been three of the said Elizabeths Children bound out by order of Court And no Objection made by Any person And that the said Docter Seay never had Any other Molatto Child Since he bought the said Bess To the Best of My Knowledge which now Goes by the Name of Elizabeth Tootle And the Deponant further saith not Given under my Hand And Seal this 24th of July 1788
Wm. Horn (Seal)

State of North Carolina   }
Camden County   } Agreeable to a Command
to me directed from the Court of Bertie County in a Suite Elizabeth Tootle against Joel Brown & others, on the 13th day of May of 88 at the house of Mr. Henry Abbot of the County afsd. between the hours of 10 & 12 of the Clock I did proceed to take the Examination, Mr. Henry Abbot being of full age duly Sworn on the Holy Evangelist of Almighty god Deposeth and Saith that about Twenty four years agoe or upwards he Kept School in the uper eand of Bertie County Near Norflets ferry during that time he offen frequented the house of Doctr. Sea and the said Dr. Sea brought home a Meloto girl but dont Recolect the Name of her which girl Dr. Sea informed this Deponant that he had purchased her but of who he doth not Remember but Sometime after he had brought the sd. Girl home, the Doctor & his Wife did Express to this Deponent that they were Convinc'd that the Sd. Meloto Girl was free born and this deponent and the Wife of Dr. Sea advised him to Goe to the person he bought her of and Make him Selfe hole and the Sd. Dr. Sea did Inform this deponent that he had done as he & his Wife had Advised him to doe & this deponent understood by the Doctr. that he was made Hole Notwithstanding this deponent Saith that Dr. Sea was Sensured by many people for keeping her in Slavery and this deponent further Saith that he doth not Recolect that he has seen the said Meloto Girl for upwards of Twenty Years Neither doth he Know Wheather the Meloto girl that Dr. Sea bought & lived with him at that time is the same Elizabeth Tootle that is Plantiff against Joel Brown & Others -- and further this Deponant Saith Not
Sworn To before Me   Henry Abbot
Isaac Gregory

****

NORTH CAROLINA STATE ARCHIVES
BERTIE COUNTY RECORDS
MISCELLANEOUS SLAVE PAPERS

Chapter 1: Bertie County Records

C.R.010.910.1, BOX #3

An Act to emancipate certain persons therein named.

    Whereas sundry petitions have been presented to this General Assembly praying that Austin Curtis a Mulatto Slave belonging to Willie Jones, Grace and her Children to wit, Richard, Harriett, Samuel, Rebecca, and Elizabeth formerly the property of John Davis deceased, Absalom Spicer, formerly the property of Benjamin Rush, and Rachel, formerly the property of Sarah Rush, deceased, Richard, Dolly, and her son Nathan the property of George Marrick and Linney the property of John Spencer, and Richard and William the property of the estate of Thomas Prichard, deceased, be liberated and set free.

    Be it therefore enacted by the General Assembly of the State of North Carolina, and it is hereby enacted by the authority of the same, That the aforesaid Austin Curtis by and under the name Austin Curtis Jones, and the aforesaid Grace, Richard, Harriott, Samuel, Rebecca and Elizabeth by and under the names of, Grace Davis, Richard Davis, Harriott Davis, Samuel Davis, Rebecca Davis, and Elizabeth Davis, and the aforesaid Absalom Spicer, and Rachel Spicer by and under the names of Absalom Spicer, and Rachel Spicer, and the aforesaid Richard, Dolly, and Nathan, by and under the names of Richard Green, Dolly Green, and Nathan Green, and the aforesaid Linney, under the name of Linney Charlton, and Richard and William above mentioned, under the name of Richard Prichard Morris and William Prichard Morris, shall be and they and each and every of them are hereby declared to be free, by and under the names aforesaid and they and each and every of them shall from henceforward enjoy the protection of the Laws and the benefits of the Constitution of this State in the same manner as others of their colour who were born free.

    Provided nevertheless that nothing herein contained shall be construed so as to effect the title, or claim, of any person, or persons, other than the persons named in this Act.

Read three times and ratified in General }
Assembly the 17th day of January Anno } Wm. Lenoir S.S.
Domini - 1792 } S. Cabarrus Sp. H.C.
Wm. Britton, Esq.
Brittons X Roads

Raleigh, June 11, 1836
Dear Sir,
    Sir Outlaw being absent, I have opened your letter to him and attended to your requests. You will find on another part of this sheet, the Act required, properly authenticated; for which I paid the Secy. $2 out of your money, and the balance, **[Smudged]** dollars, is applied as you direct, and the receipt you will find below.
Very respectfully yours, &c
Thomas J. Lemay
Raleigh, June 11, 1836
    Received of Wm. Britton, Esq. three dollars in advance for the Star and N.C. Gazette, from June 16, 1836, to June 16, 1837.
Thomas J. Lemay

State of North Carolina
    Secretary of State's Office
I William Hill Secretary of State in and for the State aforesaid do certify that the forgoing is a true copy of An Act of the General Assembly of this State taken from the original which is on file in this Office.
Given under my hand this 11th day of June 1836
W. Hill
State of North Carolina
    Bertie county Court. May Term 1840
This paper writing was exhibited in open Court & ordered to be registered.
May 19th, 1840, This paper writing was registered this day in Book E.E. Pages 449, 50.
Thos. C. Watson Regr.

Chapter 2: Buncombe County Records

chapter 2

Buncombe County

NORTH CAROLINA STATE ARCHIVES
BUNCOMBE COUNTY RECORDS
MISCELLANEOUS RECORDS
C.R.013.928.8

Bond on Charles Coleman & others

N. Carolina

Know all men by these presents that We, Charles Coleman, Benjamin Richardson David McCassan William P Poore & Jesse Davis are held & firmly bound unto the Governor of the State aforesaid & to his Successors in Office in the Sum of Four Hundred dollars Currant Money of said State Which payment Well & Truly to be made & done we bind Ourselves Our Heirs Executors & Assigns Jointly Severally firmly by these presents Sealed with Our Seal & dated this 5th day of January 1830.

The Condition of the above Obligation is Such that if Charles Coleman a person of Collour do well & truly behave himself as a Peaceable Industrious Citizen during his Continuance in this State agreeable to the Act of Assembly In that Case made & provided Then the above Obligation to be Void Otherwise to remain in full force & Virtue In witness Whereof We have Hereunto Set Our hands and Seals this date above

Test	his	
Jno. Miller Clk.	Charles X Coleman	(Seal)
	mark	
	Benj. Richardson	(Seal)
	David McCassan	(Seal)
	Jesse Davis	(Seal)
	W.P. Poor	(Seal)

Chapter 3: Caswell County Records

chapter 3

Caswell County

NORTH CAROLINA STATE ARCHIVES
CASWELL COUNTY RECORDS
MISCELLANEOUS RECORDS
C.R.020.928.7

North Carolina }
Caswell County }
Know all men by these presents that we Solomon Parks, Solomon Groves, Romulus Sanders and Alexander Murphey all of Caswell aforesaid are held & firmly bound unto William Lea Esquire Chairman of the County Court of said County & his Successors in Office in the Sum of One Hundred pounds; for the which payment well & truly be made we & each of us jointly & severally bind ourselves our heirs Executors & administrators firmly by these presents sealed with our seals & dated this 15th day of October AD 1826 - The Condition of the above obligation is such that whereas the above bound Solomon Parks hath the day of the date hereof by & with the License Judgment & decree first had & obtained Set free & emancipated a Slave of the said Solomon heretofore called Rebecca & now known & called by the name of Rebecca Boling, Now if the said Rebecca shall never be chargeable to the Parish or to the said County, then this Obligation shall be void & of none effect, otherwise to remain in full force & virtue Signed Sealed & delivered

in presence of		
Thomas Ruffin	Solomon Parks	(Seal)
	Romulus Sanders	(Seal)
	Sol. Groves	(Seal)
	Alex Murphey	(Seal)

North Carolina } In the Court of Pleas & quarter
Caswell County } Sessions
To the Justices of the Worshipful Court of Pleas and quarter Sessions for Caswell County.
The Petition of Soloman Parks & his Slave Rebecca by her next friend & Master, the said Soloman -Humbly petitioning your petitioners Soloman Parks of Caswell County Planter & Rebecca of said County Slave (who petitions in this behalf by her Master & next friend the said Soloman) That your petitioner Rebecca is the Slave of your petitioner Soloman Parks by the consent, will & wish of her said Master she doth now apply to & petition your Worships to license her to be free & manumit & emancipate your said petitioner Rebecca, by the name of Rebecca Boling Your petitioner Soloman doth also pray your Worships to grant the prayer of the said Rebecca hereby declaring his full assent & satisfaction that she should be set free & emancipated - And your said Petitioner do humbly submit to your Worships, That the said Rebecca is a fit & proper object for the exercise of that legal discretion in her favor, which by the Law of the land is so wisely placed in the hands of your worships - She has always behaved & conducted herself uprightly, honestly, morrally, religiously & faithfully to her Master & Mistress, towards the fellow servants & the community at large - She is now between the years of Eighteen & Nineteen & hath ever served her Superiors meritoriously; having been engaged mostly near the persons of her Master & Mistress, whose good will & kindness, she is proud that her demeanor hath both [?] & obtain [**Torn**] her - She hath also been educated so as to be able both to read & write & such moral & religious instruction hath been bestowed on her as will enable her to see the value of a good reputation & dispose her to strive & attain it - She will well know her place & so carry & conduct herself as to be esteemed as she has hitherto been an honest Woman & humble Christian - Upon these facts your petitioners repeat their prayer herein before made - And Your petitioner Soloman Parks also shews that he is ready & hereby offers to enter into bond with approved Security that the said Rebecca if emancipated shall not become Chargeable to the Parish or to this County - and your petitioners as in duty bound will ever pray &c
    Soloman Parks

Chapter 3: Caswell County Records

Rebecca a Slave by her

State of North Carolina }
Caswell County }
  Soloman Parks maketh Oath that **[Torn]** Matter of Fact set forth in the forgoing Petition as of his Knowledge or true **[Torn]** the rest he believes to be true
      Solomon Parks
Subscribed & Sworn to
in Open Court

Exparte
Soloman Parks }
and   } Petition for Emancipation
Rebecca
  This Cause Coming on to be heard upon the petition & the proofs offered by the petitioners & It appearing to the Court that the said Petitioner the said Rebecca hath performed Many meritorious Services in sundry Respects & the said Petitioner Soloman in his said petition & also now in Open Court expressing his wish & desire that the said Rebecca Should be set free & emancipated - It is ordered & adjudged by the Court that the said Rebecca be set free & emancipated & she is hereby set free & emancipated by the name of Rebecca Boling & shall hereafter be & is entitled to all the privileges & Rights of a Free Woman and it is further ordered by the Court that the said Soloman give Bond in £100: - with Security to keep the said Rebecca from being chargeable to the Parish in which she resides or to this County: And the Soloman Parks accordingly entered into Bond with Solomon Groves, Alex. Murphey & Romulus Sanders in said Sum of £100: payable to William Lea Chairman of this Court & his Successors in office, conditioned that said Rebecca shall not be chargeable on the Parish or to this County

****

State of North Carolina }
Caswell County   } Jany. Sessions 1806
To The Worshipful the Court now Siting your Petitioner Joseph Bracken Humbly Sheweth that he is and has been owner of a Negroe Slave by the name of Amos and for divers good Causes is desirous the said Stated Shold be liberated agreeable to act of Assembly
  for it is stated & can be shewn that the said Amos has allways supported an honest character that his **[Torn]** service in sundry complaints**[?]** by the use of such medical aid as he has used in the neighborhood and is of as well disposed conduct as any slave Man   this Court make such examination as to **[Torn]** may **[Torn]** **[?]** and **[Torn]** accordingly your Petitioner being willing to comply with the act of Assembly in giving Bond &c & your Petitioner as in duty will pray

---

Know all men by these presents
  that we Joseph Bracken and Griffin Gunn are held and firmly bound unto Robert Parks Chairman of the County Court of Caswell in the Just and full sum of one Thousand pounds To be paid to the said Robert Parks or his successor in his office. To which payment well and truly to be made we bind ourselves our heirs Exrs. &c to the said Robert Parks Chairman as aforesaid or his successor in office. As Witness our hands and Seals, this 30th January 1806.
The condition of the above Obligation is such, That whereas the said Joseph Bracken, has this day Petitioned said County Court of Caswell now in Session, Under the Act of the General Assembly, that a certain Negroe Slave named Amos, the property of said Joseph Bracken may be liberated and become free, Which was accordingly granted, on his previously complying with the requisites of the Law in that case made and provided. Now should the said Negroe Slave named Amos, never become chargeable to the said County of Caswell and should the said Joseph Bracken, and Griffin Gunn bear harmless, and keep the said Negroe Slave named Amos from becoming chargeable at any time to the said County of Caswell, then the above obligation to be void or else remain in full force and virtue Signed Sealed and
In presence of   Joseph Bracken (Seal)
A. Murphy D.C.   Griffin Gunn (Seal)

Chapter 4: Chatham County Records

chapter 4

Chatham County

NORTH CAROLINA STATE ARCHIVES
CHATHAM COUNTY RECORDS
MISCELLANEOUS RECORDS
C.R.022.928.4

        Wm Brantly to Negro Dick - Manumission
            Feby 1801

State of North Carolina }
Chatham County   }

  I William Brantly of the State of North Carolina and County aforesaid, owner & possessor of a Negro Man Dick and Saly his Wife for and in consideration of his Meritorious Services and the further Consideration of two hundred dollars to me in hand paid by the said Dick, the receipt whereof I do hereby Acknowledge, I do for myself my heirs Executors & administrators Manumit set free, and further Quit claim the said Negro Man Dick and Saly his Wife and I do hereby Recommend them to the honorable General Assembly for their manumission Legaly. In Witness whereof I have hereunto set my hand and Seal the 13 day of October in the Year of our Lord 1800.
        William Brantly (Seal)
in presence of
William Guthrie
Thomas Harrington
Blake Brantley

****

          Mr Joseph Baker
          Pittsborough No Carolina

Fayaetteville March 24th 1823

Dear Sir
  I have given Harry an instrument of writing, and I wish you to examine it, and if possible have Harry Emancipated agreeable to law this week, as it is my sincere wish that he should be emancipated,
    I remain yours respectively
      Thomas Davis

Fayetteville January 1st 1823

State of North Carolina }
Cumberland County   }

  Know all men by these presents that I Thomas Davis of the State and County aforesaid, have this day set free from my service a certain male slave by the name of Harry; agreeable to my promise made said Harry in October 1815

Chapter 4: Chatham County Records

and I do most humbly pray that the Honorable Judge of the Superior Court of Chatham County would Emancipate the said Harry agreeable to law - as witness my hand and seal
Witness   Thomas Davis   (Seal)
Dolphus A. Davie

Thomas Davis Jr
vs
Exparte
Emancipation of
Harry Scerlock Decree

North Carolina   } Superior Court of law
Chatham County   } Spring Term 1823
Thomas Davis Jr. }
Exparte   } Decree

This Case Coming on to be heard upon the Petition of the Complainant, & the testimony of Witnesses & it appearing to the satisfaction of the Court that the allegations of the said Petition are true & that Negro Harry has been a Meritorious & faithful slave:

     It is therefore Ordered, adjudged & decreed by the Court that the said negro Harry be liberated & for ever set free from the Bonds of Slavery, & that he be known & called by the name of Harry Scerlock

Harry Scurlock
Joseph Scurlock
Will Rosser
to Gov. of the State
Bond for Good Behaviour

North Carolina   } Supr. Court of law
Chatham County   } Spring Term 1823
Thomas Davis Jr.   }
Exparte   } Decree

This Case coming on to be heard upon the Petition of the Complainant, & the testimony of Witnesses & it appearing to the satisfaction of the Court that the allegations of the said Petition are true & that Negro Harry has been a Meritorious & faithful slave:

     It is therefore Ordered, adjudged & decreed by the Court that the said negro Harry be liberated & for ever set free from the Bonds of Slavery, & that he be known & called by the name of Harry Scerlock

Thomas Davis Jr.
Exparte
Emancipation
of
Harry Scurlock

North Carolina   } Supr. Court of law
Chatham County   } Spring Term 1823
Thomas Davis Jr.   }
Exparte   } Decree

This Case Coming on to be heard upon the Petition of the Complainant, & the testimony of Witnesses & it appearing to the satisfaction of the Court that the allegations of the said Petition are true & that Negro Harry has been a Meritorious & faithful slave:

     It is therefore Ordered, adjudged & decreed by the Court that the said negro Harry be liberated & for ever set free from the Bonds of Slavery, & that he be known & called by the name of Harry Scerlock

Chapter 5: Chowan County Records

chapter 5

Chowan County

NORTH CAROLINA STATE ARCHIVES
CHOWAN COUNTY RECORDS
COLONIAL COURT RECORDS
CCR 192

No. Carolina Ss.   For the Genll. Court

  Henry Speller & patience his Wife Complains of John Braveboy of Chowan precinct in the Custody of the Marshall & For yt. whereas Sd. patience whilst She was the widow of Stephen Swaine Did at ye Special instance & request of the Sd. John Braveboy on or about ye 26th day of August 1713 pay unto Mr. James Ward of Chowan aforesd the Sume of 28: Currt. money also at the Same time Did enter into one bill or obligation to ye Sd. James Ward to pay him the further Sume of 27 of like money Both wch. Sd Sumes making together 55 was for & in consideration that the Sd. James Ward Should grant unto the Sd John his freedom from being a Slave And the Sd. Henry & patience further Say that upon her ye Sd. patience paying the Sd Sume 28 & giving Such bill or obligation as aforesd the Sd. James Ward did free & Sett at liberty ye sd. John from being a Slave And they further Say that the Sd. John for & in consideration of the promises aforesd. did on or about ye sd. 26th day of August promise and assume to pay or cause to be paid unto the Sd. patience the aforesd Several Sumes of 28 & 27 **[Torn]** with the further Sume of 10. making together the Sume of 65: Currant money But the Sd John having no regard to Such his promise & Assumption as aforesd but fraudulently and deceiptfully intending to cheat & defraud the Sd Henry & patience of ye Sd. Sume of 65 hath not as yet paid or otherwise Satisfied unto the Said Henry & patience the Sd Sume of 65. tho he the Sd. John hath been in a friendly manner often requested thereunto but still refuses to pay the Same from whence the Sd Henry & patience Say they have damage to ye value of 150 And thereof this their Suite is produced &C.

    Dan Richardson

****

NORTH CAROLINA STATE ARCHIVES
CHOWAN COUNTY RECORDS
MISCELLANEOUS RECORDS
C.R.X, BOX #4

       Negro Welcoms Petition for Emancipation
          To March Term 1800

State of North Carolina }
Chowan County   } March Term 1800
  To the Worshipful County Court of Pleas and Quarter Sessions for the County aforesaid.
Humbly Complaining Sheweth to your worships Your Petitioner Reuben Long. That your Petitioner is possessed of a Certain Negro man Slave Named Welcom, who has Served your Petitioner for many Years Past with great honesty, Fedelity, and Industry, and that his general Conduct has been highly Meritorious; Your Petitioner therefore In Consideration of the good Conduct and past Services of the said Slave Is desirous of having him Emancipated, and Prays that Your Worships will extend to him the benefits of the Act of Assembly in Such Case made and Provided
  And your Petitioner As in duty bound shall ever Pray &c
    Reuben Long

Chapter 5: Chowan County Records

John R M[?]

We whose names are hereunto Subscribed do Certify, That we have long Known Negro Welcome at Present the Property of Mr. Reuben Long, and that he has always as far as we know or believe Behaved himself as a faithful and Industrious Slave, and that his general Conduct has been highly Meritorious, we therefore Take the liberty to recommend him to the Worshipful the Justices of the County of Chowan as a proper Object of Emancipation, and which we Submit to their Consideration.

15 day of Februar 1800
Michl. Payne the oldest living in Edenton

Jas. Hathaway	Reuben Long	Thos Bissett
John Russel M[?]	Wm. Satterfield	Wm. Rombough
Chas. Roberts	John Little	Saml. Hoskins
Alexr Miller	John Fite	Saml. Tredwell
Fredr. [Smudged]	Myles Omalley	John Beasley
Flono[?] Niel	Geo. Wilkinson	Joseph Bozman
Thos. [?]	henry Cheshire	[?] Carter
Thomas [?]	Thos. Satterfield	Hend. Stand[?]
Jno Cheshire	J.B. Williams	Geo Morgan
Charles Sanders	John Luten	W. Slade
Edward Reiley[?]	Stephen Carpenter	Thomas [?]
Henry [?]	Peter P. Laurance	Francis Beasley
Sam Butler	Thos. Iredell	Edmd. Hoskins

****

Presentment
Grand Jury of Chowan
Emancipation of the Blacks 1795

North Carolina }
Chowan County } Decem Term 1795

The jurors for the State & County aforesaid present that the Country is reduced to a situation of great peril & danger in Consequence of the proceedings of the Society of people called Quakers - that the idea of Emancipation amongst Slaves is publickly held out to them & encouraged by the Conduct of the Quakers - that the minds of the Slaves are not only greatly corrupted & alienated from the Service of their Masters But run aways are protected, harboured & encouraged by them. Arsons are committed without a possibility of Discovery

    The Grand Jury are so Perfectly sensible of the infatuated enthusiasm of the Quakers as to partial & general Emancipation, that they see a present alarm amongst the minds of the people & forsee a prospect of imminent Danger to impend by the influence & [?] attempts of the Quakers to this purpose, which unless presented in due time, must [?] with destruction around the Citizens of the State.

    The Grand Jury reflecting upon the miserable havoc & Massacres which have lately taken place in the West Indies in Consequence of Emancipation; knowing the opinion of the Northern States; of the many hundred thousand slaves around them ; & of the infatuated enthusiasm of Men calling themselves religious, who are amongst them, conceive it a Duty which they owe to themselves, their familys & their Country to present this existing & alarming evil & to present the people called Quakers & their Abettors as the authors of the common Mischief in this quarter of the State where independent of foreign Opinion; emancipation is publickly held out by the Quakers to the Negroes & private funds established in support of it.

    The Grand Jury present that speedy & resolute Measures ought to be adopted by the good sensed Spirit of the people, in order to prevent that common appeal to arms in their own Defense which at present appears to be almost, if not altogether necessary.

John Little foreman	Masan Miller	James Bond
Josiah Herdell	Wm. Jones	JP [?]
Robert Egan	John Badham	Willis Wilder
James Woodward	Wm. Goodwin	Joshua White
Chs. Laughren		

Chapter 5: Chowan County Records

****

NORTH CAROLINA STATE ARCHIVES
CHOWAN COUNTY RECORDS
MISCELLANEOUS SLAVE RECORDS
C.R.024.928.4

Stephen Cabarrus
to   } Petition
               } for Freedom
The Court   } of Negroe Silvia

September Term 1800

To the Worshipful Justices of the Court ofthe County of Chowan.

    The Petition of Stephen Cabarrus Mo. respectfully Sheweth,

    That the deceased Wife of your petitioner has requested him to emancipate and Set free a Certain Negro Woman called Silvia, who during her life has rendered her the most faithful and meritorious services.
    That your petitioner conceives himself in duty bound, and most chearfully aquieses to pursue all legal measures to obtain the manumission of the said Slave.
    Your petitioner therefore requests that your Worships be pleased to take the Case into your Consideration, and grant the emancipation of the said negro Slave woman called Silvia under such rules and regulations as the Law directs, and your petitioner shall ever pray
S. Cabarrus
Chowan County March Term 1800

Stephen Cabarrus Esqr.
Bond of Indemnity
Septembr. Term 1800

State of North Carolina

Know all men by these Presents that we Stephen Cabarrus Esqr., Nath. Allen, & Auguste Cabarrus are held and firmly Bound unto Samuel Dickinson Esquire Chairman of the County Court of Chowan in the sum of Five hundred to be paid to the Samuel Dickinson Chairman his Successors or asigns, to the which payment well and Truly to be made & done we do bind ourselves Each of us, our & Each of our heirs Executors, administrators & assigns Jointly & Severally, firmly by these presents Sealed with our Seals & dated this 11th day of September in the year of our Lord 1800

The Condition of the above obligation is such that whereas at this Term of September, the above Named Stephen Cabarrus Esqr. hath Petitioned Agreeable to an Act of the General Assembly in such Case made & provided for the emancipation of a Certain Negroe woman Named Silvia Lorunt[?], the property Stephen Cabarrus and the said Court at this Term hath agreeable to the Petition of said Stephen Cabarrus, Granted the said Negroe Silvia Lorint her Liberty on the said Stephen Cabarrus giving Bond & Security to Indemnify the Parish: Now if the said Stephen Cabarrus, Nath. Allen, & Auguste Cabarrus do & shall Indemnify the said Parish & wardens of the poor of all Charges & Costs that may ever arise in Consequence of the Said Liberation of the said Negroe Silvia then this obligation to be Void else to remain in full Force & virtue.
Signed & Sealed in Presence of
Witness S: Dickinson   S. Cabarrus   (Seal)
                                        Nath. Allen   (Seal)
                                        A. Cabarrus   (Seal)

****

Chapter 5: Chowan County Records

NORTH CAROLINA STATE ARCHIVES
CHOWAN COUNTY RECORDS
MISCELLANEOUS SLAVE RECORDS
C.R.024.928.33

EMANCIPATION RECORD (NO DATE)

Ordered that a Commission issue to Jacob Jordan to take the Deposition of Evan Skinner in regards to what he knows Respecting the Title of Emancipation of two negroes Said to be the Property of John Smith & John Saunders.
        Jos. Blount Clk

Persuant to an order of Court I have taken the deposition of Mr Eaven Skiner Respecting the freedom of two [Torn] Negroes the property of John Smith and John Sanders   The Deponant Sayeth that he New the grand mother of the said Negroes to be a proper Slave which was an Indian woman taken and Sold as a Slave in the time [Torn] the Indian war and was all ways held and Deamed as [Torn] Slaves Ever Since and further the Deponant Sayeth Not

Sworn to be fore me   Jacob Jordan

****

Henry Eelbeck }
   to   } Petition
The Court   }

Filed September 1801[7?]

State of North Carolina
To the Worshipful the Justices of the County Court of Chowan

  The petition of Henry Eelbeck humbly sheweth that Major a mulattoe slave of your petitioner hath in consequence of his faithful services to Joseph Eelbeck decd. brother to your petitioner during his life and especially by his unremitted attention to him in his last illness and also by a similar conduct to your petitioner in a late indisposition so far Merited the affection of your petitioner; that your petitioner is desirous to reward him with his liberty and Sixty pounds. Your petitioner also begs leave to assure your Worships that the demeanor of the said Major has ever been highly meritorious & that no ill consequence will result from his emancipation. Your Petitioner therefore prays your Worships to emancipate the sd. Major and to confirm to him the name of Major Eelbeck -- and your petitioner as in duty bound will ever pray.
      Henry Eelbeck

****

King Luten & others to the Court
Petition
Prayer Granted June Term 1808

State of North Carolina }
Chowan County   } December Term 1807

To the Worshipful the Justices of the Court of Pleas & Quarter Sessions for the County aforesaid

The petition of King Luten, William Clark, William Hoskins, Nathaniel Hoskins, Zachariah Webb, William Hall and Reuben Symons, Humbly Sheweth unto your Worships that two Slaves named Mingo & Dolly his Wife the sole property of your Petitioners, have throughout life have always conducted themselves in a faithful, orderly and upright manner, that they have rendered to your petitioners, great & meritorious services, for which your Petitioners are desirous of remunerating them in an exemplary manner, so that it may conduce to the public good as well as gratify their own

Chapter 5: Chowan County Records

feelings, believing that by a due reward bestowed on merit, it may induce other slaves to act in the like exemplary manner -- Your Petitioners therefore pray your Worships to grant an order for the emancipation of the aforesaid Negro Slaves according to the several acts of Assembly in such cases made & provided & your Petitioners in duty bound shall ever pray &c.
King Luten, Nathl. Hoskins, William Hall, Zachariah Webb, Reuben Simons, William Hoskins, & William Clark

---

To the Court} Bond to endemnify
June Term 1808

State of No. Carolina
Know all men by these presents that we King Luten, Nathaniel Hoskins, William Hall, Zachariah Webb, Reuben Simons, William Hoskins, William Clark are held & firmly bound unto Stephen Cabarrus Esquire Chairman of the County Court of Chowan in the sum of two hundred pounds to be paid to the said Chairman his successors or assigns, to the which payment well and truly to be made and done we bind ourselves each of us, our and each of our heirs, executors, administrators & assigns, Jointly & Severally, firmly by these presents sealed with our seals and dated this 17th June 1808.

The Condition of the above obligation is such that whereas at this term of June, the above named King Luten, Nathl. Hoskins, William Hall, Zachariah Webb, Reuben Simons, William Hoskins, & Wm. Clark hath petitioned agreeable to an Act of Assembly in such case made & provided for the emancipation of certain negroes Mingo and Dolly (by names) the property of the said King Luten, Nathaniel Hoskins, William Hall, Zachariah Webb, Reuben Simons, William Hoskins and Wm. Clark and the Court at this term hath agreeable to the petition of said King Luten, Nathl. Hoskins, Wm. Hall, Zachariah Webb, Reuben Simons, Wm. Hoskins and Wm. Clark granted the said negroes Mingo and Dolly their liberty on the sd. King Luten, Nathaniel Hoskins, William Hall, Zachariah Webb, Reuben Simons, Wm. Hoskins and Wm. Clark giving bond & security to indemnify the parish, now if the said King Luten, Nathl. Hoskins, Wm. Hall, Zachariah Webb, Reuben Simons, Wm. Hoskins and Wm. Clark do and shall indemnify the said Parish Wardens of the Poor of all charges & costs that may ever arise in consequence of the said liberation of the said negroes Mingo and Dolly then this obligation to be void else to remain in full force and virtue. Signed & Sealed in Presence of King Luten (Seal), William Hoskins (Seal), Edmd. Hoskins (Seal), Nathl. Hoskins (Seal), William Hall (Seal), Reuben Simons (Seal), Wm. Clark (Seal), Zachariah Webb (Seal).

****

Auguste Cabarrus }
    to   } Petition
The Court   } Chowan

for liberation of Negro woman Rose: Granted June Term 1808

To the Worshipful the Justices of the Court of Pleas and Quarter Sessions in & for the County of Chowan.
The petition of Auguste Cabarrus Sheweth,

That your petitioner is possessed of a female negro slave by the name of Rose aged about thirty years who has eminently distinguished herself by a long and uniform course of honesty and fidelity in the discharge of her general duty as a Servant and by her meritorious Services. Your petitioner being therefore desirous of conferring liberty upon the said female Slave Rose which he cannot but consider as a reward due to her exemplary conduct prays that this Worshipful Court would in consideration of the premises grant its aid to your Petitioner for that purpose by making an order for her liberation.
    And your petitioner shall ever pray &c.
        Wm. A. Littlejohn Sol. pro Petr.

The petr. of Augt. Cabarrus praying the liberation of a female Slave by the name of Rose about 30 years of age, having been considered by the Court; It is ordered that the said Rose be liberated according to the prayer of the said

Chapter 5: Chowan County Records

petition on the said August Cabarrus first giving bond and security in the sum of £100 according to the Act of Assembly that the said Rose shall not become chargeable on the County or Parish.

Aug. Cabarrus's bond of Indemnity
June Term 1808

State of No. Carolina

Know all men by these presents that we August Cabarrus, Stephen Cabarrus and Honore Niel are held & firmly bound unto John Bond chairman and the rest of the Justices of Chowan County Court in the sum of one hundred pounds to be paid to the said John Bond &c chairman his successors or assigns to the which payment well and truly to be made & done we bind ourselves each of us, our & each of our heirs, executors, administrators & assigns Jointly & severally by these presents sealed with our seals & dated this [?]th day of June 1808.

The Condition of the above obligation is such that whereas at this term of June, the above named August Cabarrus hath petitioned agreeable to an act of Assembly in such case made and provided for the emancipation of a certain negro woman Rose (by name), the property of August Cabarrus and the Court at this term hath agreeable to the petition of said August Cabarrus giving bond & security to indemnify the Parish, now if the said August Cabarrus, Stephen Cabarrus and Honore Niel do and shall indemnify the said Parish & Wardens of the Poor of all charges & Costs that may ever arise in consequence of the said liberation of the said Negro Rose then this obligation to be void else to remain in full force and virtue.

Signed & Sealed in presence of   A. Cabarrus   (Seal)
                                      S. Cabarrus   (Seal)
                                      H: Niel   (Seal)

****

Petition of John Cunningham

State of North Carolina }
Chowan County   } June Term 1793

To the Worshipful the County Court of Please and Quarter Sessions for the County of Chowan the Petition of John Cunningham.

Humbly Sheweth
That your Petitioner's Father died when he was very Young leaving a Valuable but unproductive Estate for the Support of your Petitioner and his Mother, consisting principally of Young Slaves, among whom is a Mulatto Male Slave by the Name of James, the Profits of whose labour, has greatly if not principally contributed to the Maintenance & Support of your Petitioner thro a long Minority and an expensive course of Education. Your Petioner further Sheweth that the great profit which he has derived from the labour of the said Slave James has been owing as well to the great assiduity and attention of the said James in acquiring & Perfecting himself in the Trade or Mystery of a Barber & Hair Dresser as to his Industry sobriety and honesty Your Petitioner further Sheweth that during a Very dangerous and lingering Sickness last Spring (1794) the attention of the said James was such as cannot fail to inspire the highest gratitude in him in consideration whereof and as a reward for the past faithful Services of the said James, Your Petitioner is willing and desirous to Manumit or set him free conceiving that no less a reward will be commiserate to the Services Rendered, but to guard against the great injuries & inconveniences which might result from the indiscriminate Manumission of Slaves the legislature have Wisely provided that no Slave shall be Manumitted except for Meritorious Services to be approved of by the County Court, Your Petitioner is prevented from effecting his intentions without the aid and Assistance of Your Worships, May it thereof Please your Worships taking the past character and faithful and Meritorious Services of the said James into consideration to order & Decree that he May be Manumitted & Set free agreeable to the Directors of the Act of the General Assembly in Such Cases Made and provided And your Petitioner as in Duty bound shall ever pray &C

John Cunningham

Chapter 5: Chowan County Records

***

William T. Muse to the Court

Petn. for the liberation of negro George
Chowan June Term 1807
Prayer Granted

To the Worshipful the Justices of the Court of Pleas & Quarter Sessions for the County of Chowan at June Term 1807.

The Petition of William T. Muse Sheweth
That your petitioner owns a negro slave by the name of George, Commonly Called George Bonner by trade a house Carpenter and aged fifty five years or thereabout; that the said negro Slave from the time that he became the property of your petitioner, and always before that time as your petitioner has reason to believe, has distinguished himself by his willing & faithful discharge of his duty to his master as well as by his honesty & orderly Conduct. Your petitioner is therefore desirous to give the negro Slave George his freedom considering it as a reward due to his long and meritorious Services and prays this Worshipful Court to authorise and aid him in so doing.
And your Petitioner &c

       Wm. A. Littlejohn
       Sol. for Petr.

Wm. T. Muse Bond of Indemnity

September Term 1807
State of North Carolina

  Know all men by these presents that we William T. Muse & John B. Blount are held & firmly bound unto Stephen Cabarrus Esquire chairman of the County Court of Chowan in the sum of five hundred pounds to be paid to the said Stephen Cabarrus chairman his successors or assigns, to the which paymt. well and truly to be made & done we bind ourselves each of us, our & each of our heirs, executors, admrs. & assigns, Jointly & Severally, firmly by these presents Sealed with our seals & dated this 11th day of September in the Year of our Lord 1807.

  The Condition of the above obligation is such that whereas at this Term of September The above named William T. Muse hath petitioned agreeable to an Act of Assembly in such case made & provided for the emancipation of a certain negro man named George the property of Wm. T. Muse & the said Court at this term hath agreeable to the petition of said William T. Muse, Granted the said negro George his liberty on the said William T. Muse giving bond & Security to indemnify the Parish, Now if the said William T. Muse & John B. Blount do & shall indemnify the said Parish & Wardens of the poor of all charges & Costs that may ever arise in consequence of the said liberation of the said negro George then this obligation to be void else to remain in full force & virtue.
Signed & Sealed in presence of
Jas. Norfleet   Will: T. Muse (Seal)
       Jn. B. Blount (Seal)

***

Solomon Elliot }
  to   } Bound to produce A Certain Negroe Man
The Court } at September Term 1800

State of North Carolina} Chowan County Court June Term 1800

Know all men by these presents that we Solomon Elliot & John Blount are held & firmly bound unto Samuel Dickinson Esqr. Chairman & the rest of the Justices of the County aforesaid in the Just & full sum of onr hundred & fifty pounds Current money to be paid to the said Samuel Dickinson & we bind ourselves, our heirs, Executors & adminstrs. Jointly & Severally, firmly by these presents, Sealed with our Seals & dated this 14th day of June in the year 1800.

Chapter 5: Chowan County Records

The Condition of the above obligation is such that Whereas, the above Bounden Solomon Elliot, shall produce the Body of a Certain Negro man Slave Named Dick, said to be emancipated by the People Called Quakers, at the next County Court in the month of September next, then & there to deliver him to the Court, then this Obligation to be Void else to remain in full Force & Vertue.
Witness
J Norfleet   Solomon Elliot   (Seal)
                John Blount   (Seal)

****

Thomas Barnwell   } Pet.
     to   } for
The Court   } Manu.
Granted   June Term 1811
State of North Carolina Court of Pleas & Quarter Sessions
Chowan County   June Term 1811

To the Worshipful the Justices of the said Court
The Petition of Thomas Barnwell a free person of colour in the Town of Edenton humbly sheweth,

       That your Petitioner hath intermarried with one Asa a negro woman slave late the property of Henderson Standin Esquire & hath for a long time cohabited & still doth cohabit & live with her as his wife; that your petitioner hath by his said Wife two children, to wit, Thomas & Nancy; that Mr. Standin hath lately conveyed this woman & her children to your petitioner; that the said Asa hath always behaved as a peaceable, orderly, submissive & diligent slave & by her meritorious conduct during her servitude hath well entitled herself to the favor of this Worshipful Court - that your petitioner, impelled by the powerful feelings of a husband & father, & anxious to reward the faithful services of the said Asa, is desirous of manumitting her & the two above named infant children -- He therefore prays your Worships that in consideration of the premises, you would pass an order directing the manumission of the said slaves, upon his complying with the terms prescribed by the Acts of Assembly in such cases made and provided - And your Petitioner as in duty bound will ever pray &c.
          Ja. Iredell for Pet.

       The Subscribers have been long well acquainted with a negro woman named Asa, for whose freedom Thomas Barnwell has petitioned that the said negro woman has always conducted herself as a peaceable, orderly, obedient & well disposed slave -- and the Subscribers think from her maritorious conduct she is well entitled to the favor of the County Court - Edenton Sept. 1811.
Hendn. Standin
Sarah Etheridge
Anna Luten

                        Thomas Barnwell
              To   } Indemn. Bond
                         The Chairman

State of North Carolina Ss.
Know all Men by these presents that we Thomas Barnwell, Henderson Standin and James Norcom are held and firmly bound unto John Bond Esquire Chairman of the Court of Pleas & Quarter Sessions for the County of Chowan and his successors in office in the sum of One hundred pounds; to the payment of which well & truly to be made we bind ourselves, our heirs, executors and administrators, jointly & severally, firmly by these presents Sealed with our seals, and dated this second day of April in the year of our Lord One thousand, eight hundred and twelve.

       The Condition of the above obligation is such that whereas the Court of Pleas & Quarter Sessions for the County of Chowan at the Term of the second Monday of December One thousand eight hundred and eleven have manumitted & set free a certain negro slave named Asa -- late the property of the said Thomas Barnwell - Now if the said negro Asa - so liberated shall at no time hereafter become chargeable to the said County or any Parish therein, and

Chapter 5: Chowan County Records

if the said County shall at all times hereafter be indemnified and saved harmless from all charges and expenses which it may or might become liable to for the support & maintenance of the said negro Asa -- pursuant to the true intent & meaning of an Act of the General Assembly held at Raleigh in the year One thousand eight hundred & one, chapter twentieth, Then the above obligation to be void, otherwise to remain in full force & virtue.

Sealed & delivered In presence of   Thos. Barnwell
Witness   Hendn. Standin
Hendn. J. Standin   Ja. Norcom

Thomas Barnwell } Petr.
   To } for
The Court } Manu.
Granted June Term 1811

State of North Carolina Ss.

    Know all Men by these presents that we Thomas Barnwell, Henderson Standin and James Norcom are held & firmly bound unto John Bond Esquire Chairman of the Court of Pleas & Quarter Sessions for the County of Chowan & his successors in office in the sum of One hundred pounds; to the payment of which well & truly to be made, we bind ourselves, our heirs, executors, & administrators, jointly & severally firmly by these presents Sealed with our seals and dated this second day of April in the year of our Lord One thousand eight hundred & twelve.

    The Condition of the above obligation is such, that whereas the Court of Pleas & Quarter Sessions for the County of Chowan at the Term of the second Monday of December one thousand eight hundred & eleven have manumitted & set free a certain negro named Nancy late the property of the said Thomas Barnwell Now if the said negro Nancy so liberated shall at no time hereafter become chargeable to the said County or to any Parish therein, and if the said County shall at all times hereafter be indemnified & saved harmless from all charges or expenses which it may or might become liable to for the support & maintenance of the said negro Nancy, pursuant to the true intent & meaning of an Act of the General Assembly held at Raleigh in the year One thousand eight hundred & one, chapter twentieth; Then the above obligation to be void, otherwise to remain in full force & virtue.

Sealed & delivered In presence of   Thos. Barnwell
Witness   Hendn. Standin
Hendn. J. Standin   Ja. Norcom

Thos. Barnwell }
   To } Ind. Bond
The Chairman }

State of North Carolina ss.

    Know all Men by these presents that we Thomas Barnwell, Henderson Standin and James Norcom are held and firmly bound unto John Bond Esquire Chairman of the Court of Pleas & Quarter Sessions for the County of Chowan and his Successors in office in the sum of One Hundred pounds, to the payment of which well & truly to be made we bind ourselves, our heirs, executors & administrators, jointly & severally, firmly by these presents Sealed with our seals & dated this second day of April in the year of our Lord One thousand eight hundred and twelve.

    The Condition of the above obligation is such That whereas the Court of Pleas & Quarter Sessions for the County of Chowan at the Term of the second Monday of December in the year One thousand eight hundred & eleven have manumitted & set free a certain negro slave named Thomas late the property of the said Thomas Barnwell Now if the said negro Thomas so liberated shall at no time hereafter become chargeable to the said County or to any Parish therein, and if the said County shall at all times hereafter be indemnified and saved harmless from all charges & expenses which it may or might become liable to for the support and maintenance of the said negro Thomas pursuant to the true intent & meaning of an Act of the General Assembly held at Raleigh in the year One thousand eight hundred & one, chapter twentieth; then the above obligation to be void or otherwise to remain in full force and virtue. Sealed & delivered

In presence of   Thos. Barnwell
Witness   Hendn. Standin

Chapter 5: Chowan County Records

Hendn J. Standin   Ja. Norcom

****

Augustus Cabarrus
    to   } Petr. Emancp. negro Jim
The Court   } December Term 1811
State of No. Carolina }
Chowan County   } Decr. Term 1811

To the Worshipful County Court of Pleas and Quarter Sessions
    The petition of Augustus Cabarrus humbly complaining sheweth unto your Worships that he is the owner of a certain slave named James Williams, that the sd. negro James is an orderly, well behaved fellow, that he has paid your petitioner his full value and for his meritorious Services he is desirous of librating and setting him free -- may it therefore please your Worships to grant him his freedom upon his complying with the law, and as in duty bound, will ever pray &c
                A. Cabarrus

Auguste Cabarrus
    to   } Indemn.
Chairman   } Bond manumission of Jim Williams
State of North Carolina Ss.
    Know all men by these presents that we Aguste Cabarrus, James Norfleet and John Beasley are held and firmly bound unto Thomas Brownrigg Esquire Chairman of the Court of pleas and quarter Sessions for the County of Chowan and his Successors in office in the Sum of One hundred pounds, to the payment of which well and truly to be made we bind ourselves our heirs, Executors and administrators Jointly and Severally firmly by these presents, Sealed with our Seals and dated this 6th day of October in the Year of our Lord one thousand Eight hundred and twelve.
    The Condition of the above obligation is such that whereas the Court of pleas and quarter Sessions for the County of Chowan at the term of second Monday of September One thousand Eight hundred and twelve have manumitted and set free a Certain negro named Jim Williams, late the property of the said Auguste Cabarrus now if the said negro Jim Williams so Liberated shall at no time hereafter become chargeable to the said County or to any parish therein, and if the said County shall at all times hereafter be Indemnified and saved harmless from all charges and Expences which it may or might become liable to for the support and maintenance of the said negro Jim pursuant to the true Intent and meaning of an act of the General Assembly held at Raleigh in the year One thousand Eight hundred and one, Chapter twentieth, then the above obligation to be void otherwise to remain in full force and Virtue

Sealed and delivered   A. Cabarrus   (Seal)
in presence of   Jas. Norfleet   (Seal)
                                 Jn. Beasly   (Seal)

****

James Iredell   }
    To   } Petn. Emancp.
the Court   } Septr. Term 1812

State of No. Carolina   } Court of Pleas & Quarter Sessions
Chowan County   } June Term 1812

    To the Worshipful the Justices of the said Court The Petition of James Iredell Sheweth
    That your Petitioner is legally entitled to a certain negro Slave call'd Geoffrey, late the property of William Blair Esquire & is desirous of manumitting the said slave -- That this desire arises solely from an intimate knowledge of the integrity of the said Geoffrey, of his long & faithful services, of the affection & attachment he has always displayed towards his late master, & of his unremitted attention to him, while laboring as he has been for a few years past under

Chapter 5: Chowan County Records

almost continual bodily indisposition. Your Petitioner therefore Prays that on account of the honesty, fidelity and meritorious conduct of the said Geoffrey, Your Worships would be pleased to pass an order directing his manumission.

    Ja. Iredell

  The Subscribers are well acquainted with the above mentioned Geoffrey and believe the character there given him to be correct.

Edm Hoskins	L. McDonald	Geo Blair
Joseph Bozman	J.S. Crecy	Saml. Tredwell
Jas. Jones	Ja. Norcom	Jntn. Cheshire
Hendn. Standin	M.R.[?] Counts	W. Slade
John Norcom	J.W. Littlejohn	Jos. B. Skinner
Jas. Hathaway	John Popelston	H. [?]Kueg
Jn. Beasly	Nat. Bond	John [?]
Jackson [?]	L. Martin	Henry Wills
Andrew Knox	Charles Bissett	James R. [?]
[Faded]	[Faded]	Job Leary
Richd. Hoskins	John Skinner	

State of North Carolina Ss.

  Know all men by these presents that we James Iredell -- are held and firmly bound to Thomas Brownrigg Esquire Chairman of the Court of pleas & quarter sessions for the County of Chowan and his Successors in office in the Sum of One hundred pounds, to the payment of which well and truly to be made, we bind ourselves, our heirs Executors and administrators Jointly and severally firmly by these presents sealed with our Seals and dated this 6th day of October in the year of our lord one thousand Eight hundred and twelve.

  The Condition of the above obligation is such that whereas the Court of pleas and quarter Sessions for the County of Chowan at the term of the Second Monday of September one thousand Eight hundred and twelve have manumitted and set free a certain negro named Geoffrey late the property of said James Iredell Now if the said Negro Geoffrey so liberated shall at no time hereafter become chargeable to the said County or to any Parish therein and if the said County shall at all times hereafter be indemnified and saved harmless from all charges or Expences which it may or might become liable to for the Support and maintenance of the said negro Geoffrey pursuant to the true intent and meaning of an act of the General Assembly held at Raleigh in the year One thousand Eight hundred and one Chapter twentieth, then the above obligation to be Void otherwise to remain in full force and Virtue.

Sealed and delivered
in presence of   Ja. Iredell   (Seal)
          G.W. Blair   (Seal)

****

To the Worshipful Court of Chowan

  The petition of Wm. Righton of the Said County & State of North Carolina, most respectfully Sheweth that he is the owner of two Negro Slaves viz. Harry Commonly Called Harry Tredwell and his wife Jenny, both of which for meritorious Services rendered & their uniform good moral, and upright Conduct, he is desirous of liberating and Setting free. May it therefore please your Worships to grant this petition, and your petitioner as in duty bound will ever pray &c.

February 24th 1814   Wm. Righton

These are to Certify that we whose names are below are well acquainted with the Character of the within named negroes, Harry & Jinny and know them to be quiet peaceable orderly, well disposed people and have uniformly conducted themselves in an upright manner.

Febr. 1814   Ja. Iredell

Chapter 5: Chowan County Records

M. Sawyer	D. McDonald
John Popelston	Jno. Roberts
Hen. King	

Mr. Wm. Righton,
    If the emancipation of Harry & Jenny is obtained, I shall be willing to Join you in the Bonds required in such cases.

                              Yrs. respectfully
                              Saml. Tredwell

Feby. 21st 1814

Know all men by these presents that we William Righton and Samuel Tredwell are held and firmly bound unto Thomas Brownrigg Esqr. Chairman of the County Court of Chowan and his Successors in office, for the use of the poor of the said County in the Sum of Two hundred pounds which payment well and truly to be made to the said Thomas Brownrigg or his Successors in office we bind ourselves our heirs, Executors and administrators firmly by these present, Witness our hands and Seals this 14th Day of December 1814.

The Condition of the above obligation is Such that whereas upon the petition of William Righton exhibited to the County Court of Chowan at December Term 1814 The said Court proceeded to liberate Harry and Jinny therein named for their meritorious Services, Now if the said William Righton and Samuel Tredwell shall and will always save the said County of Chowan free from all charge or expense whatsoever in Consequence of the said Harry and Jinny being liberated as aforesaid, Then this obligation to be null and Void otherwise to remain in full force and virtue.

Witness

T. Creecy	Wm. Righton
Will. Norfleet	Saml. Tredwell

****

Petition of William Watts Jones to Emancipate Betty
Oct. 1822

State of North Carolina }
Chowan County   } Fall Term 1822
    To the Honble. the Judge of the Supr. Court of Law and Equity

The petition of William Watts Jones of the Town of Wilmington. Your petitioner respectfully represents, that in the month of May 1822 he intermarried with Elizabeth M. Littlejohn of the Town of Edenton; who was at that time possessed in her own right of a certain negro woman slave named Betty -- Your petitioner states that he has understood and believes, that said negro Betty, has always been an honest faithful and obedient servant and particularly attached to her Mistress, to whom, and to the family before she became her property, she repeatedly by her attention and fidelity both in sickness and health rendered the most meritorious services a slave could perform in dischargeing the common duties of a servant -- The said Slave Betty having also been the nurse of your petitioner's wife, she is also anxious to have her emancipated and to settle her with a suitable provision for life -- Your petitioner therefore prays the Court to grant him leave to emancipate said negro Betty, and your petitioner will ever pray &c.
Wm Watts Jones

State of North Carolina } In the Superior Court
Chowan County   } at Law Fall Term 1822

Know all men by these presents that we William Watts Jones, John W. Littlejohn and Joseph B. Skinner are held and firmly bound unto Exum Simpson Chairman of the Court of Pleas & Quarter Sessions of Chowan County and his Successors in office in the just and full sum of One hundred pounds for the true and faithful payment of which we bind ourselves and our heirs.

Chapter 5: Chowan County Records

The condition of the above obligation is such that whereas the above bounden William Watts Jones hath petitioned for and obtained an order of the Superior Court of Law of Chowan County at Fall Term 1822 to liberate and emancipate a certain negro woman Slave named Betty as by a reference to the proceedings thereon had will more fully appear Now if the said Betty shall not become chargeable as a pauper to the County aforesaid by such liberation and emancipation then this obligation to be void otherwise to remain in full force and virtue - Given under our hands & seals this 11th day of October 1822.

        Wm. Watts Jones   (Seal)
        J.W. Littlejohn   (Seal)
        Jos. B. Skinner   (Seal)

William Watts Jones   } Petition to emancipate &
     to   } liberate negro Slave Betty
The Court   }

On hearing the petition & it appearing to the Court by legal evidence that the said negro Betty has always been a true and faithful Servant and has done maritorious Services as stated in the petition -- and the petitioner having entered into bond with approved security as the Law in such cases directs it is ordered and adjudged that the said negro Betty for the causes aforesaid be and is hereby liberated and emancipated from all service as a Slave and that she be entitled to all the privileges and immunities of free people of Colour in this State -- And it is further ordered and adjudged that her said Master have leave to execute and deliver to said Slave such a deed of Emancipation as may be necessary to effect the same.

State of North Carolina }
Chowan County   }

     Whereas leave has been granted to me by the Superior Court of the County of Chowan to emancipate and set free a negro woman slave named Betty formerly the property of William Littlejohn and late the property of Elizabeth M. Littlejohn, now Elizabeth M. Jones - Now - Know all men by these presents that I William Watts Jones for and in consideration of the faithful and meritorious services performed by the said Betty, have emancipated and set at liberty and by these presents doth emancipate and set at liberty and absolve and discharge the said Betty from all service whatsoever giving and granting to her all the freedom of a free born negro as fully and amply as it is in my power to do. In witness whereof I have hereunto set my hand and seal this 11th day of October 1822.

Signed Sealed and   Wm. Watts Jones (Seal)
Acknowledged in
presence of J.W. Littlejohn

****

Petition of Augustus Johnson
April T. 1822
Granted

State of North Carolina } Superior Court of Law
Chowan County   } Spring Term 1822

     To the Honourable the Judge of the Superior Court of Law and Equity in and for the County aforesaid -- The Petition of Gustavus Adolphus Johnson, of the Town of Edenton, County and State aforesaid.
     Humbly complaining sheweth unto your honours that your Petitioner, a free man of Colour sometime in the year of our Lord 1814 purchased from James R. Bent Esquire, of said Town of Edenton, a woman of colour by the name of Betty or Elizabeth, with whom your petitioner had intermarried - that the said Betty or Elizabeth is now about twenty five years old and that your Petitioner hath continued to live with her ever since as his wife that your said petitioner and the said Betty or Elizabeth have by their said marriage three children, to wit, Mary about six years old, Ann about four years old and a boy Charles about nine months old -- all of whom are by reason of the purchase aforesaid the slaves of your Petitioner -- Your petitioner further sheweth unto your honour that the said Betty or Elizabeth hath always

Chapter 5: Chowan County Records

conducted and behaved herself to your Petitioner and to all other persons in an orderly and proper manner that she is a woman of correct deportment, dutiful to your petitioner and every way worthy of his bounty -- that the said children are of tractable and quiet dispositions -- And your Petitioner is desirous that the said Slaves should be emancipated, liberated and set free and admitted to such rights and privileges as by the Laws of the Land can be imparted to persons of colour -- Wherefore your petitioner gives his license therefore -- May it therefore please your honours to grant that these aforesaid Slaves may be emancipated, liberated and set free and capacitated for all the rights and privileges that free persons of colour are capable of receiving.

                      And as in duty bound your
                      Petitioner will ever pray &c.
                      G. A. Johnson

    Gustavus Adolphus Johnson maketh oath that the matters and things herein set forth are true to the best of his knowledge & belief.   G. A. Johnson
Sworn to in open Court
D. McDonald
Clk.

James R. Bent[?] Sheriff of the County of Chowan maketh oath that he is well acquainted with Gustavus Adolphus Johnson, the petitioner, who is as far as he knows, or hath ever understood a man of fair moral character and correct deportment and that his wife Betty or Elizabeth is properly described in the forgoing petition, that the said Gustavus & Betty with their children have always conducted and behaved themselves in a laudable[?] manner and have lived & continue so to live as this affiant believes in perfect harmony.
D. McDonald   J. R. Bent[?]
Clk.

Gustavus A. Johnson & als.   }
        To   } Indemnifying Bond.
Chairman of the Court   } Filed in Office August 29th 1822

State of North Carolina   }
Chowan County   }

    Know all men by these presents that we Gustavus Adolphus Johnson, James R. Bent**[Burt?]** and James Borritz are held and firmly bound unto Exum Simpson Esquire, Chairman of the County Court of Chowan in the just and full sum of one hundred pounds to be paid to the said Exum Simpson Esquire, Chairman of the County Court of Chowan, aforesaid, and his successors in office for the use of the poor of the County aforesaid for the true and faithful performance whereof we bind ourselves, our and each of our heirs, executors and administrators jointly and severally, firmly by these presents -- Sealed with our seals & dated the 22nd day of August AD 1822.

    The condition of the forgoing obligation is such that whereas, a certain woman Slave named Elizabeth, was at the last term of the Superior Court of Law holden for the said County of Chowan, pursuant to a petition of the said Gustavus Adolphus Johnson, set free, emancipated and liberated now if the said Elizabeth shall not become chargeable on the parish or county previous to his having the same effected or at any time hereafter then the forgoing obligation to be null and void, otherwise to be and remain in full force and virtue.

Signed, Sealed & delivered   G.A. Johnson   (Seal)
in presence of   J.R. Bent   (Seal)
Henry Wills   James Borritz   (Seal)

Gustavus A. Johnson & als.   }
        To   } Indemnifying Bond
Chairman of the Court   } Filed in Office August 29 1822
State of North Carolina   }
Chowan County   }

Chapter 5: Chowan County Records

Know all men by these presents that We Gustavus Adolphus Johnson, James A. Bent and James Borritz are held and firmly bound unto Exum Simpson Esquire, Chairman of the County Court of Chowan in the just and full sum of One hundred pounds, to be paid to the said Exum Simpson Esquire, Chairman of the County Court of Chowan aforesaid, and his successors in office for the use of the Poor of the County aforesaid: for the true and faithful performance whereof we bind ourselves, our and each of our heirs, executors and administrators jointly and severally, firmly by these presents Sealed with our seals and dated the 22nd day of August AD 1822,

The condition of the forgoing obligation is such that whereas, a certain boy child Slave named Charles, was at the last Term of the Superior Court of Law holden for the said County of Chowan, pursuant to a Petition of the said Gustavus Adolphus Johnson, set free, emancipated and liberated, now if the said Charles shall not become chargeable on the Parish or County previous to his having the same effected or at any time thereafter, then the forgoing obligation to be null and void, otherwise to be and remain in full force and virtue.

Signed, Sealed & delivered	G.A. Johnson	(Seal)
in presence of	J.R. Bent	(Seal)
Henry Wills	James Borritz	(Seal)

Gustavus A. Johnson & als. }
    To } Indemnifying Bond
Chairman of the Court } Filed in Office August 19th 1822
State of North Carolina }
Chowan County }

Know all men by these presents that We Gustavus Adolphus Johnson, James R. Bent and James Borritz are held and firmly bound unto Exum Simpson Esquire, Chairman of the County Court of Chowan in the just and full sum of One hundred pounds, to be paid to the said Exum Simpson, Esquire, Chairman of the County Court of Chowan aforesaid, and his successors in office for the use of the Poor of the County aforesaid: for the true and faithful performance whereof we bind ourselves, our and each of our heirs, executors and administrators jointly and severally, firmly by these presents Sealed with our seals and dated the 22nd day of August AD 1822.

The condition of the forgoing obligation is such that whereas, a certain Girl Slave named Mary, was at the last term of the Superior Court of Law holden for the said County of Chowan, pursuant to a petition of the said Gustavus Adolphus Johnson, set free, emancipated and liberated, now if the said Mary shall not become chargeable on the Parish or county previous to his having the same effected or at any time hereafter then the forgoing obligation to be null and void, otherwise to be and remain in full force and virtue.

Signed, Sealed & delivered	G.A. Johnson	(Seal)
in presence of	J.R. Bent	(Seal)
Henry Wills	James Borritz	(Seal)

Gustavus A. Johnson & als. }
    To } Indemnifying Bond
Chairman of the Court } Filed in Office August 29th 1822.
State of North Carolina }
Chowan County }

Know all men by these presents that We Gustavus Adolphus Johnson, James R. Bent and James Borritz are held and firmly bound to Exum Simpson Esquire, Chairman of the County Court of Chowan in the just and full sum of One hundred pounds, to be paid to the said Exum Simpson, Esquire, Chairman of the County Court of Chowan aforesaid, and his successors in office for the use of the Poor of the County aforesaid: for the true and faithful performance whereof we bind ourselves, our and each of our heirs, executors and administrators jointly and severally, firmly by these presents Sealed with our seals and dated the 22nd day of August AD 1822.

The condition of the forgoing obligation is such that whereas, a certain Girl Slave named Ann, was at the last Term of the Superior Court of Law holden for the said County of Chowan, pursuant to a Petition of the said Gustavus Adolphus Johnson, set free, emancipated and liberated, now if the said Ann shall not become chargeable on the Parish

Chapter 5: Chowan County Records

or County previous to his having the same effected or at any time thereafter then the forgoing obligation to be null and void, otherwise to be and remain in full force and virtue.

Signed, Sealed & delivered	G.A. Johnson	(Seal)
in presence of	J.R. Bent	(Seal)
Henry Wills	James Borritz	(Seal)

****

State of North Carolina } Superior Court of
Chowan County   } Law, April T. 1823

    To the Honorable the Judge of the said Court,
    The Petition of Henry King of the Town of Edenton herewith Sheweth,
    That he is the owner of a Negro woman Slave named Penny who has two infant children named Thomas and Charles, also Slaves of your Petitioner, that the said woman has been the property of your Petitioner for a number of years and has been a faithful & meritorious Servant, and your Petitioner being desirous of Emancipating her and her Children, as well on account of her meritorious Services, as because of his unwillingness to hold Slaves, prays you to grant him Permission to emancipate the Said Slaves upon his complying with the Conditions presented in the Act of assembly in such cases made and provided,

    On hearing the Petition and the evidence adduced to support it, it is Ordered & adjudged by the Court that the Petitioner Henry King have leave to emancipate the Slaves Penny and her two Children Thomas and Charles according to the Prayer of the Petitioner and that they be entitled to all the privileges and immunities of free people of Colour in this State.

Henry King and John Little }
        to   } Indemnifying Bond
Exum Simpson, Chairman   } June Term, 1823

State of North Carolina }
Chowan County   }

    Know all Men by these presents that we Henry King and John Little are held and firmly bound unto Exum Simpson Esquire Chairman of the Court of Pleas & Quarter Sessions of Chowan County in the sum of Three hundred pounds to be paid to the said Exum Simpson and his successors in office for the use of the poor of the said County, to which payment well and truly to be made we bind ourselves our heirs executors and administrators firmly by these presents Sealed with our seals and dated this 30th day of April 1823.

    The condition of the above obligation is such that whereas at the last Term of the Superior Court of Law for the County of Chowan permission was given to the above bound Henry King to emancipate three slaves to wit negro woman Penny & her two children Thomas & Charles Now if the condition of the above obligation is such that if the said slaves so emancipated shall never become chargeable to the said County or Parish then this obligation to be void - otherwise to remain in full force and virtue.

Sealed & delivered	Hen. King	(Seal)
In presence of	John Little	(Seal)
Henry Wills		

****

State of North Carolina } Superior Court of Law
Chowan County   } Fall Term 1825

    To the Honourable the Judge of said Court The Petition of Christopher Burkitt of said County a free man of colour,

Chapter 5: Chowan County Records

    Humbly sheweth unto your Honour that your Petitioner, sometime in the year of our Lord one thousand eight hundred and twelve purchased from Mr. William Righton of said County a woman of colour by the name of Charity with whom your Petitioner had intermarried -- that the said Charity is now between Fifty & Sixty years old and that your Petitioner hath continued to live with her ever since as his wife -- that your said Petitioner and the said Charity have by their said marriage two children, to wit, Peggy aged about fourteen years whom he purchased from the said William Righton a few months ago and Nancy aged about seven years born since the purchase of her said Mother Charity all of whom are by reason of the purchase aforesaid the Slaves of your Petitioner - Your Petitioner further sheweth unto your Honour that the said Charity hath always conducted and behaved herself to your Petitioner, and to all other persons in an orderly and proper manner, that she is a woman of correct deportment, dutiful to your Petitioner and every worthy of his bounty -- that the said Children are of tractable and quiet dispositions.

    And your Petitioner is desirous that the said Slaves should be emancipated, and set free, and admitted to such rights and privileges as by the Laws of the Land can be imparted to for persons of colour -- Wherefor your Petitioner gives his license therefore -- May it therefore please your Honour to grant that the aforesaid Slaves may be emancipated, liberated & set free and capacitated for all the rights and privileges that free persons of colour are capable of receiving -- And as in duty bound Your Petitioner will ever pray &c.

```
Sworn to in Open Court            his
12 October 1825         Christopher X Burkitt
D. McDonald Clk.                  mark
```

Christopher Burkitt maketh oath that the matters and things herein set forth are true to the best of his knowledge and belief.
```
Sworn to in open                  his
Court Fall Term 1825    Christopher X Burkitt
D. McDonald Clk.                  mark
```

William Righton and John Boush maketh oath that they are well acquainted with Christopher Burkitt, the Petitioner, who is as far as they know or believe, or ever understood, a man of fair moral character and correct deportment and that Charity the wife of the said petitioner is properly described in the forgoing petition, that the said Christopher and Charity his wife and their said two children have always these affiants believe conducted and behaved themselves in a laudable manner and have and continue to live as these affiants believe in perfect harmony.
```
Sworn to in open
Court Fall Term 1825    Wm. Righton
D. McDonald Clk.        William Bush
```

State of North Carolina }
Chowan County   }

    Know all men by these presents that we Christopher Burkitt, William Righton and William Boush are held and firmly bound unto Exum Simpson Esquire, Chairman of the County Court of Chowan and his successors in Office for the use of the Poor of said County in the sum of One Hundred Pounds Witness our hands and Seals the **[Blank]** October 1825.

    The condition of the forgoing is such that if negro woman Charity the wife of the said Christopher Burkitt, liberated at this term of Chowan Superior Court shall become chargeable on the Parish or County aforesaid previous to or after his having her liberated, then this obligation to be in full force and virtue otherwise to be null and void.
```
                                  his
Signed, Sealed & Delivered    Christopher X Burkitt
in presence of                    mark
Nat Haughton       Wm. Righton    (Seal)
                   William Bush   (Seal)
```

****

Chapter 5: Chowan County Records

Hannah Pritchit To The Court

Molly's freedom
Spring Term 1828
A.M.G.
To the Honorable Judge of the Superior Court of Law

  The petition of Hannah Pritchit humbly complaining Sheweth: That she lately purchased, the old faithful servant, named Molly, of Elizabeth Horniblow, and understanding that it was the last request of her sister Mrs. Horniblow, to req[?] the many meritorious services of the said Molly by granting unto her freedom. But the said Elizabeth Horniblow being suddenly called out of this world before she had time to make suitable provision for the said Molly on this behalf, your petitioner purchased her at the sale of the Executor of the said Elizabeth, for the purpose of fulfilling the works of her deceased sister. That your petitioner resided a long time in the family of her sister and is a witness to the many faithful and meritorious services of the said Molly to all the family but particularly to Mrs. Horniblow and being now desirous of emancipating the said Molly prays your Honor for an order for that purpose as the acts of assembly in such cases made and provided direct as in duty bound your petitioner will ever pray.

    A.M. Gatlin attorny
     for Petitioner

[Editor's Note: The following notation was found on the back of an endorsement.]
Mr. A.M.G. have you got the Paper containing Mr. Brougham's last
Speech in Past   WB Shepard

H. Pritchit, Affidavit

Hannah Pritchit being duly Sworn deposeth that Mrs. Horniblow, at the time of death, was considerably indebted to her (this affiant) and that the purchase of negro Molly was in part satisfaction of the debt - she further swears that there is no [?] understanding that the said Molly is to repay to her the amount of the purchase money but that she is anxious to liberate the said Molly for the reason set forth in her petition.

         her
Sworn to before me   Hannah X Prichard
this 10 April 1828   mark
Edm. Hoskins Clk of the County Court of Chowan

Hannah Pritchards Bond to save Harmless
Molly

State of North Carolina }
Chowan County   }
Know all men by these presents, that we Hannah Pritchard, John W. Littlejohn, Alfred M. Gatlin & James Moffatt are held and firmly bound unto Exum Simpson Chairman of Chowan County Court of Pleas & Quarter Sessions and his successors in office, in the sum of one hundred pounds, to which payment well and truly to be made we bind ourselves and each of our heirs, executors and administrators firmly by these presents sealed with our seals and dated this 10th April 1828.

  The condition of the above obligation is such, that whereas negro woman Molly lately the property of the above bounden Hannah Pritchard hath this day been emancipated and freed by the Superior Court of Law of Chowan County Now if the said Hannah Pritchard shall and will at all times save the County of Chowan harmless from any expense touching the support of the said Molly, then this obligation to be void otherwise to remain in full force & virtue.

Witness to the mark   her
of Miss Pritchard   Hannah X Pritchard   (Seal)
            mark
Jn Norwan[?]   A.M. Gatlin   (Seal)
         J.W. Littlejohn (Seal)
         James Moffatt (Seal)

Chapter 5: Chowan County Records

Hannah Pritchet } Petition of Emancipation of
To The Court } slave Molly

This case coming on to be heard on the petition of the petitioner and the testimony of Henry Flury[?] and Edmond Hoskins, it is ordered & decreed that the said negro slave Molly mentioned in the petitioners petition, for the causes therein set forth which are proved to the Court & believed be emancipated and set free from all service to the petitioner agreeably to the prayer of her petition; upon the petitioner Hannah Pritchet entring into bond with two securities to the Chairman of Chowan County Court of Pleas & Quarter sessions in the sum of one hundred pounds to save the County of Chowan harmless touching the support of the said Molly agreeably to the act of assembly in such cases made and provided -- which bond executed by said Hannah & Alfred M. Gatlin, John W. Littlejohn & James Moffatt as Sureties of said Hannah is now duly executed & delivered in open Court & filed with the Clerk of this Court.

****

Davy Dickinson
Petition for Emancipation
For Trial Spring Term 1847

North Carolina } Fall Term 1846
Chowan County } Superior Court of Law

To the Honble. the Judge of the said Court, The petition of Joseph D. Bond of said County, sheweth your Honor that he is the owner of a negro slave known by the name of "Davy Dickinson," who is now the age of fifty years. That the said negro slave has always maintained the character of a faithful, submissive and obedient Servant; and that besides this general performance of duty, he has rendered Meritorious Services.

He shews your Honor that he has not received in money or otherwise, the price or value, or any part thereof of said slave, or been induced to file this petition for the emancipation of said slave in consideration of any prior [?] or to be paid for him.

Your petitioner shews your Honor that he is desirous of emancipating and releasing from the bonds of Slavery said negro slave.

He therefore prays your Honor to order and decree said slave Davy Dickinson to be emancipated.

And your petitioner as in duty bound will ever pray.
Aug. N[?]
Sol. for petitioner

Joseph D. Bond makes oath that he has not received in money, or otherwise, the price or value, or any part thereof of the within mentioned slave, nor has he been induced to petition for his emancipation in consideration of any price paid or to be paid for
in by him.   Joseph D. Bond
Sworn to before me
Saml. T. Bond Clk.

In the matter of Joseph Bond's petition for the emancipation of Davy Dickinson

This cause coming on to be heard where the issues submitted to the jury and the finding of the jury of the same and the said petitioner having entered into bond according to law the Court doth order and adjudge and decree that the petitioner have leave to emancipate and free from the bonds of slavery his negro man slave Davy, commonly known as Davy Dickinson; and the said Davy being emancipated as aforesaid shall have the right to acquire property, and dispose of the same, and all other rights which free persons of colour are or should be permitted by the law of this State to exercise and enjoy. It is further ordered & [?] that the petitioner pay the costs.

State of North Carolina

Know all men by these presents that we Joseph D. Bond, Wm. C. Warren & Tho. D. Warren are held and firmly bound unto the State of North Carolina in the sum of five hundred dollars which payment well and truly to be

Chapter 5: Chowan County Records

made, we bind ourselves our heirs, executors and administrators. Sealed with our seals and dated this 9th day of April 1847.

The condition of the above obligation is such: That whereas by a decree of the Superior Court of Law of Chowan County rendered at this present term of said Court, the above bounden Joseph Bond hath obtained leave to emancipate his negro slave Davy Dickinson, now if the said Davy Dickinson shall honestly and correctly demean himself so long as he shall remain in the said State, & shall not be a parish charge, then the above obligation shall be null and void, otherwise to be and remain in full force and virtue.

                    Jos. D. Bond   (Seal)
                    W.C. Warren   (Seal)
                    Th: D. Warren   (Seal)

****

Benja. Sanders Man Taffeys Certificate

North Carolina

This may Certefy that the Bearer [?] of County Hereof a Negro man named Ben is a free Negro as he formerly belonged to Mr. Jonathan Sharrod Deceased who having Many Slaves & no Children alive not Desiering his Slaves Should Serve another Master Did in his will Generously give them freedom Which if disputed may be found on Record in the Court of the said County aforsaid & the aforenamed Negro Man having a Desier to travel to Virginia to Seek better imployment we the Subscribers do Certefy that the said Negro is a free man has Ever Since his working for himself behaved Very honest therefore we the Subscribers Do Recommend the Said Negro to Such Gentlemen as Shall imploy him.
Witness our hands this 21 January 1794   Ritchard Ratlieff

****

State of North Carolina   } February, 17th, 1844.
Chowan County   } Personally appeared
before me, Thomas V. Hathaway, Clerk of the Court of Pleas & Quarter Sessions, in and for said County, John Buchanan, a yellow man aged about thirty seven years, about five feet, six inches in height; & proved before me, by Duncan McDonald, of Edenton, that he was free born; that he was bound to said McDonald, until he arrived to the age of twenty one years, which time he served out: wherefore I do hereby Certify that the said John Buchanan hath made it satisfactorily appear, that he is a freeman & not a slave: & in testimony of his being a freeman & no slave, as proved on oath, by said Duncan McDonald of Edenton, North Carolina -- I have hereto set my hand & seal year aforesaid.

****

                              State vs Peter Cain
                              Ind. migrating into State
                                  Genl. Pros.
                            Chas Robinson Plntff
                                 Sworn & Sent
                               W.R. Skinner Clk.
                       A True bill Jos T. Waff[?] For.

State of N. Carolina   } Court of Pleas & Quarter Sessions
Chowan County   } Augt. Term 1859
     The Jurors for the State upon their oath present that on the first day of January 1859 a free negro named Peter Cain did migrate & move from the State of Virginia into the County of Chowan in the State of North Carolina and from that time up to the time of taking this inquisition has continuously resided in the said County of Chowan State aforesaid Contrary to the form of the Statute in such cases made & provided & against the peace & dignity of the State.
        Mr. S. Ha[?] Sol.
                               State vs Peter Cain

Chapter 5: Chowan County Records

Executed P.F. White Shff
by C.E. Robinson Dep. Shff

State of North Carolina }
Chowan County }
To the Sheriff of Chowan County you are hereby commanded to arrest the body of Peter Cain & bring him before me or some other justice of the peace of this County for migrating into this State agst. the statute made & provided in such cases.
Given under my hand & seal   [?] JP (Seal)

****

Testimonial

We the subscribers have had a knowledge this many years of Charles & Mary his wife Belonging to the estate of Francis Valet and do certefy they have been Faithful servants and conducted themselves with great propriety and have acted in a Meritorious Manner to their Master particularly in his last Sickness. Edenton Spt. 14th. 1807

Henry King	James Wills
John Popelston	Geo. Morgan
[?]C. Donaldson	J.W. Littlejohn
Hendn. Standin	Martin Norcom
H: Niel	Wm. Bombrough
Saml. Tredwell	King Luten
D. McDonald	Jas. Hathaway
Hen. King	B. Elliot
Edmd. Hoskins	John Dickinson
John W. Faslane[?]	John Cox
B[?] Hassel	[Torn]yler O'malley
Arthur Jones	

****

Mr. William Littlejohn
Edenton
Fbry. The 10th 1802

Wm: Littlejohn Esqr.
Sir,
I am informed by Mr. Dominick That Eli Wilkins a person of Coulour In the Town of Edenton hath been Taken up Under Some of the Acts of Assembly & bound for his apearance to Chowan County Court at March Term 1802 where he is to Stand his Tryal for to be sold as a Slave if My affidavit that I herewith forward to you is Not Sufficient to Extreicate the sd boy & for you to Give Up the Recognizance of the said Dominick & let the sd boy Stand Discharged I will forward any other proof that May be Deemed Necessary to that Efect as I am duly able So to do: & More Also bannd by the Laws of Nature & humanity.
I am with Submition
Your Hmb.Servt.   Tamer Wilkins

Tamer Wilkins affidavit

State of No. Carolina   } Personally apeared before
Martin County   } Mr. Ebenezer Slade one

of The Justices for the County aforesaid Tamer Wilkins & Made Oath In Dew form That on The Seventh of July one Thousand Seventeen Hundred & Eighty five She was Delivered of a Male Child which she Called Eli Wilkins a Natural

Chapter 5: Chowan County Records

Born & Child of Coulour which Child after Comeing of age to be bound She Bound as an apprentice to one John Edwards of Bertie County who Some Time Afterwards Removed to The then Cumberland Settlement & gave up the Indenture of sd. boy to his sd. Mother She then put the sd. boy with one John Acrey to Learn the Hatters Trade the Boy as She this Deponant Has Since Understood Runaway from sd. Acre Better than Three years ago & as She has been Informed hath been living with One Dominick Sine that Time in the Town of Edenton which sd. boy Hath been brought to Her by the sd. Dominick on the 10th Day of February one Thousand Eighteen Hundred & Two In the County & State aforesaid & She this Deponant Doth Acknowledge & Sware him to be the same boy In Testimony whereof She this Deponant Hath afixt her hand & Declared

the Same   Tamer
Test   her   X   Mark
E. Slade   Wilkins
JP for the County of Martin

Fbry the 10th 1802 This May Certify That I have Known the within Mentioned Tamer Wilkins for Several Years & Believe this is No Doubt of Her being free Born as will More fully apear By the Testimony of Many In the County of Bertie If is & should be Necessary given Under My hand and Seal the Day & Date above written.
         E. Slade (Seal)

****

Z. Webb & T. Vail
Petition of Sundry persons for the Emancipation of
Negroe Man Jack   March Term 1799
Granted

To the Worshipful the County Court of Chowan now Sitting
      The Petition of Zackariah Webb humbly sheweth That he your petitioner has A Negroe Man by the name of Jack who is now far advanced in years, and has been a faithful and orderly Servant ever since your petitioner was first acquainted with him which has been upwards of thirty years being raised with him. It being the wish of the said Negroe Jack to obtain his freedom, and having paid me a valuable consideration for his subsequent time, induces your petitioner to apply to your worships to set free the said Negroe Jack agreeable to the Law or Laws in that case made and provided. Altho your petitioner has it not in his power to point out any very meritorous Services yet he humbly conceives in submission to your superior Judgment that a servitude of upwards of sixty years being faithfully discharged, without once being accused of any misdemeanor whatever, to sully his character as A slave, may be deemed meritorious services sufficient for your worships to exercise your humanity and goodness in the manumission of said Slave.
      Zackariah Webb

We the Subscribers believe the facts stated in the above petition to be Just & true, we have for a long time been acquainted with the Said Negro Jack, & always understood that he demeaned himself as a faithfull, Sober, obedient, & orderly Servant. And we do most Chearfully Join the Petitioner in Petitioning your worships, to set free the Said Negro Jack.

E. Norcom	James Sutton
[?] Hasell[?]	Frederick Norcom
Wilson Webb	Joseph Standin
Geo. Wilkins	John Beaseley
Joshua Purkins	James Beasely
Thos. Rea	John Haughton
John Simons Senr.	Thomas Miers
Frederick Creecy	
Jonathan Haughton Junr.	
Job Pettyjohn	
Ann Blount	

Z. Webb   } Bond of

Chapter 5: Chowan County Records

    &   } Indemnification
T. Vail   } March 1799

State of North Carolina   } Ss. March Term 1799
Chowan County   }

     Know all men by these presents that we Zackeriah Webb & Thomas Vail of the County aforesaid are held & firmly bound unto Samuel Dickinson Esquire Chairman of the County Court aforesaid in the Just & full Sum of two hundred pounds Currant Money, to be paid to the said Chairman his Successors or assigns To which payment well & Truly to be Made we do bind ourselves, Each of us, our & each of our heirs Executors, administrators & assigns Jointly & Severally, firmly by these presents, Sealed with our Seals & dated this 12th day of March in the year of our Lord one thousand seven hundred & ninety nine.

The Condition of the above obligation is Such that whereas at this Term the above named Zackariah Webb hath Petitioned Agreeable to an act of the General Assembly in Such Case made & provided, for the Emancipation of a Certain Negro Man Named Jack formerly the property of Robert Donaldson and the Said Court at the above Term hath Agreeable To the Petitioned of the said Zackariah Webb, Granted the Said Negro Jack his Liberty on, the said Zackariah Webb giving Bond & Security to Indemnify the Parish   Now if the said Zackariah Webb & Thomas Vail Shall Indemnify the said Parish & wardens of the Poor of all Charges & Costs that may arrise in Consequence of the Said Liberation of Said Negroe Jack, then this obligation to be Void else to remain in full Force & Virtue.

Signed & Sealed in   Zackariah Webb   (Seal)
The Presence of   T. Vail   (Seal)
E. Norfleet

****

Dick Dingley to the Court} Petition
Elisha Norfleet Esqr.

Dr. Sr.
     Enclosed is a petition of Negro Dick Dingley for his Freedom. I intended to have New Modeled it but have not had time, will you be so Obliging as to Enter It, on the Appearance Dockett, I will on my return, see that proper Notice be given, to the Person Who Claims to hold him in Slavery.
                                I Am Sr.
                                Your Most
                                Obedt. Servt.
                                W. Slade

Deek Dingley   }
    vs   }
Jochabod Jordan   }

Petition &C.
To Septr. Term 1798
open Copy & Spa. Depont.
Chas. Roberts Sheriff

State of North Carolina   }
Chowan County Ss.   } June Term 1798.

To the worshipful Justices of the County Court of Pleas and Quarter Sessions for the County aforesaid.

Humbly Complaining Sheweth unto your WorshipsYour Petitioner Deek Dingley a free person of Colour Of the County of Chowan, That your petitioner formerly belonged to a Certain James Legett, of the County of [Blank] in the State

Chapter 5: Chowan County Records

aforesaid, and some Years ago entered into an agreement with Mr. Jochabod Jordan Of Chowan County by and with the consent of the said James Legett to purchase his time or Freedom of the said James, and It was further agreed by and between Your said petitioner and the said Jochabod Jordan, that your said petitioner should repay unto him, the amount of the purchase money which he should give to the said James Legett for your said petitioners freedom, and that upon so doing your Petitioner should be Emancipated and enjoy all the rights priviledges and emoluments Of a free Citizen, And your Petitioner In fact saith that pursuant to the said agreement, the said Jochabod Jordan did purchase him of the said James Legett for the sum of ninety five pounds Current Money, and that three years ago and upwards as well as your Petitioner now recollects he did repay unto the said Jochabod Jordan the full consideration money & Interest according to the said agreement whereupon the said Jochabod Jordan, did emancipate and Set at Liberty your said Petitioner, And your Petitioner expressly Charges that the original purchase by the said Jochabod Jordan, from the said James Legett was made under a Special Trust of Confidence, for his benefit and at his instance and request, And your petitioner further sheweth that he can produce indubitable proof of all the matter and things herein set forth, and also that he sustains a good Character and is of peaceable behaviour, and honest deportment, and well entitled to have and receive all the benefits, advantages and priviledges, Of which free persons of Colour in this State are intitled.

But now so it may please your Worships that the said Jochabod Jordan will knowing the premises but contriving unjustly to injure and agrieve Your Petitioner, hath Obtained a bill of Sale, from the said James Legett, and now sets up a Claim, to your petitioner as a Slave, and so harasses and disturbs him, that he cannot with safety pursue his lawful business. All which actings and doings of the said Jochabod Jordan are Contrary to Equity and Good Conscience, and manifestly and to the Injury and Oppression of your Petitioner. In Tender Consideration whereof, may it please your Worships to Grant your petitioner, a writ of Subpoena to be directed to the said Jochabod Jordan, commanding to be and appear before the next Court of Pleas and Quarter Sessions to be held for the County of Chowan on the 2d Monday in Septr. next then and there upon his Corporal Oath, true Just and perfect answer make to all and singular the matters herein Contained, as fully and amply as if the same were herein again repeated & he interrogated thereto, and that he may be compelled to deliver up to your said Petitioner, the aforesd. bill of Sale, and that your petitioners said emancipation may be confirmed, agt. the said Jochabod Jordan his heirs and assigns forever, and that he may have & act [?] Relief is the Premises is as the nature of his Case shall require, &C and he as in duty &c.

  W. Slade for the Petitioner

Depositions
To The Justices of the Court of Pleas and Quarter Sessions
for the County Court of Chowan held at Edenton

We the petitioners to The worshipfull County Court of Chowan
  Humbly Sheweth that a certain negro man named Deek Dingley of this County has bought his time of a certain Jochabod Jordan & has had his Liberty three years & has paid Said Jordan up agreeable to bargain but since of Late the Said Jordan has again Renewed his Clame to Said negro & want to Detain him in Slavery we the Subscribers Humbley pray that your worships will in your wisdom Redress the Said negro as he is a good Peaceable fellow & behaves himself orderly & to the Satisfaction of all his neighborhood & as in duty bound Shall ever Pray. March the 1st 1798

Jefrey White	Abner Hollowell
his	John Hollowell
Josias + Ward	Moses Hollowell
mark	Luke Hollowell
Joel Binum	Willis Griffin
William Winslow	Richard + Felton
James Ward	his
Daniel Taler	Miles + Stallings
Joseph Scott Senr.	mark
John Harval	Humphrey X Griffin
Samuel Parker	Brinkley Griffin
John Fullinton	Edward Welch
Jacob Ward	Isaac Biriam Senr.
Denby Ward	Isaac Byriam Junr.
Gabriel Elliot	Gabriel Chappel
James Byriam	Elias Stallings

Chapter 5: Chowan County Records

Samuel Perry	Tobi[?] Riddick
William Ward	Joseph Copeland Junr.
Seth Wood	Thomas Goodin
Harden Ward	Joseph Scott Junr.
thomas fourhand	Demsey Webb
Job Parker	John Parker
David Welch	Ruben Hoobs
Miles Ashley	Wiley Ming
John Perry	Thomas Soren[Toren?]
Joseph Jordan	Josiah Jordan
Moses Holls	Thos. Ward
Enuck Parker	Ser[?] garrett
[?]	John Sallings
Zachariah Stallings	

The Petition of negro Man Dick Dingley to the worshipful County Court of Chowan humbly Sheweth that a certain Jochabod Jordan of the County afore Said Reclaimd. the Said Petitioner of Mr. James Legett on Ronake for the Consideration of ninty five pounds & then the Said Petitioner made a bargain with Said Jchabod Jordan before witness that if the Said Petitioner paid him the Said Jordan the above Sum then the Said Petitioner was to be at full Liberty as will more fully appear the Said Petitioner has paid said Jordan his full Demand and Since that the Said Jordan has Let him have his Liberty for three years as agreed but so it is that of Late the Said Jordan has Renewed his Clame & has most Cruely Beaten your Petitioner & does all he Can to keep him the Said Petitioner in Slavery this therefore is Humbly to pray your worships that as your Petitioner is without Redress only through your worships that you will be please to Confirm the above bargain & Redress your Said Petitioner & as in duty Bound Shall Ever Pray.
March 1st 1798
    Dick Dingle

Dick Dingly }
 vs   } Subpn.
Jchabod Jordan } September Term 1798

Served on Jchabod Jordan
Chas. Roberts Sheriff

State of North Carolina
  To Jchabod Jordan for Certain Causes offered before our County Court of Pleas & Quarter Sessions for the County of Chowan, We Command you personally to be and appear before our said Court on the Second Monday in September Next then and there to answer the Petition of Dick Dingly, and abide by and perform Such Order & Decree therein as our Said Court Shall Seem Meet, Witness Elisha Norfleet Clerk of said Court at Edenton the 14th day June one thousand seven hundred & ninty Eight.
    E. Norfleet Clk.

Chapter 6: Craven County Records

Chapter 6

Craven County

**NORTH CAROLINA STATE ARCHIVES
CRAVEN COUNTY RECORDS
MISCELLANEOUS RECORDS
C.R.028.928.10**

Annapolis, 3d. April 1794

Gentlemen,
    Inclosed you will receive a Commission from the General Court of Maryland to take depositions in a Case depending there. The Copy of Mrs. Ridgeley's deposition which accompanies this, taken here, will explain the reasons why a Commission has been sent to Newbern in North Carolina. We are informed that the records of the County in which Newbern is, were destroyed by the Enemy during the late Revolution. If the fact be so, it is necessary that it should be proved in order to let in parish proofs; some of the Interrogatories under cover are accordingly founded to that fact; & it will readily occur to you that the Clerk of the County will be a proper person to prove that the records are wanting. If we have been misinformed, a Copy of the record of the trial & judgement of the Court under seal will be sufficient. I presume that the depositions were recorded, as is customary in such Cases in Courts of record. It is certainly a fact that there was a petition, as stated by Anne Ridgely in her deposition, at Newbern & that the petitioners were discharged from the service of Mr. Thomas their then Master by the judgment of the Court. That there was such a trial if the records are existing; or that the records are not to be had, if they were destroyed, is all that is expected to be proved by the Commission. I am with respect, your obedt.
Servt.   G. Duvall.

The State of Maryland
    To Joseph Taggart, Silas Cooke, Robert Donnell and Samuel Gerock Esquires of Newburn & State of North Carolina.
    Know Ye that we have appointed you, or any three or two of you, to be our commissioners to examine evidences in a cause depending in our General Court for the western shore of the said State, between William Dowrey Petitioner, and Francis Thomas, Defendant;
    We therefore request you, or any three or two of you, that at such time and place as to you, or any three or two of you, shall seem convenient, you cause to come before you, or any three or two of you, all such evidences as shall be named or produced to you, or any three or two of you, by either the plaintiff or defendant, and that you, or any three or two of you, examine them upon their corporal oaths, to be by you, or any three or two of you, administered, on the Holy Evangels of Almighty God, touching their knowledge or remembrance of any thing that may relate to the cause aforesaid; and that you, or any three or two of you, cause notice to be given to the parties, or their attornies, of the execution of this commission, before you execute the same; and having reduced the depositions of the witnesses, so taken by you, or any three or two of you, into writing, you send the same, with this our commission, closed under your, or any three or two of your hands and seals, to us, in our said court, with all convenient speed.
    Witness the honourable Samuel Chase Esquire, chief judge of our said court, the fifteenth day of June anno domini one thousand seven hundred and ninety three.
    Issued the twentieth day of September 1793.
G Duvall Esqr. Atty for Petitioner
B Johnson Esqr. for Defendt.   Jno. Gwinn Clk

William Dowry } Peto. for freedom in the General Court
    agt.   }

Chapter 6: Craven County Records

Francis Thomas } The deposition of Ann Ridgely of Anne Arundel County aged between fifty seven and fifty eight years being first sworn the holy Evangely of Almighty God, saith that she has seen William Dowry the petitioner but does not know much of him; that she knew Fanny who it is said, is Mother of the petitioner, very well; and this deponent also knew Mary Dove the Mother of Fanny ever since she knew her own Mother, and she knew Fanny who is about the age of the deponant from the time she was a child until she was a Woman; this deponent is the daughter of Eliazar Burkhead who was the Son of Abraham Birkhead, to whom Mary and Fanny both belonged when this deponent first knew them; And he gave Fanny to his daughter Frances Shekell the wife of John Shekell; this deponent further saith that Mary was a tall spare Woman, of a brown complexion, and was the grand daughter of the Woman, who came, or was imported into this Country and belonged to this deponants great grand Father as she has been informed and understood from her Mother and her Grand Father before mentioned: that her grand Father was the only child of his Father and possessed the whole estate; that this deponent has always understood that the Grand Mother of Mary Dove was a Yellow Woman and had long black hair; but this deponent doth not know whether she was reputed to be an East Indian or a Madagascarian, but she has understood that she was called in the family Malaga Moll, her name being Mary; and Mary Dove the Grand daughter claimed her Sirname from her said Grand Mother; this deponent further saith that the Mother of Mary Dove (whose name she does not remember) died before her Mother, and whilst her daughter Mary Dove aforesaid was a small girl; and this deponant saith after the death of her father, her Mother intermarried with Leonard Thomas and the aforesaid Mary Dove then lived in the family and belonged to this deponent's Brother James Birkhead, and upwards of forty years ago she sued for her freedom, and before any determination of the suit aforesaid Leonard Thomas moved with his family and effects to North Carolina, about twenty miles from Newburn and carried the aforesaid Mary Dove with him; this deponent's Brother James being then about five or six years of age: that the said Mary Dove prosecuted her claim to Freedom at Newburn in North Carolina soon after she was removed there, and obtained her freedom upon trial as this deponent understood, together with three of her Children and two of her Grand Children, Will and Sal; that this deponent has heard her father in Law Leonard Thomas say that a certain Alexander Sands, who was the Son of an East indian woman, and was commonly called Indian Sawony was a Witness for the said Mary Dove; and that he proved that the Grand Mother of Mary Dove was an East indian Woman; that this deponent does not recollect to have heard her father in Law mention any other Witness in particular who was sworn for the petitioner, but thinks he mentioned that one John Wells was sworn on her behalf; that the said Mary Dove had a brother named Dowry who belonged to this deponent's uncle, That the aforesaid Leonard Thomas removed back to Maryland in a few years and sometime afterwards returned to North Carolina near the Yadkin and died about a twelve month ago:

Sworn to in open Court [?] Octo. 1791.
    True Copy
    Jno. Gwinn[?]

William Dowrey	} Petition for freedom in the General Court
agt	}
Francis Thomas	} Petitioners Interrogatories

1. Do you know the parties in this Suit, and how long have you known them?

2. Do you know Mary Dove (grandmother of the petitioner) who lived in the family of Leonard Thomas late of the neighborhood of Newbern in North Carolina, deceased; and did you know the said Leonard Thomas, and how long?

3. Do you know that Mary Dove prosecuted her claim to freedom at Newbern in North Carolina against Leonard Thomas before mentioned, and did she obtain her freedom; if yes, when was it, & who were the witnesses sworn on the occasion, and what was the judgment of the Court?

4. Do you know that any of the descendants of Mary Dove, and how many, & what were their names, obtained their freedom of Leonard Thomas before mentioned?

5. Do you know that the Records of the County Court at Newbern were destroyed by the Enemy, and when were they destroyed, and if the whole of the said Records, or a part only, and what part, were destroyed during the late Revolution? relate your knowledge fully.

Chapter 6: Craven County Records

6. Have you any further knowledge of the Subject that will benefit the petitioner's claim to freedom; if you have relate it fully.
    G. Duvall

****

Craven

To the Justice of sd. County

       The petition of Euphronia Tinker
       Humbly Sheweth

  That she is possessed of a Mulatto Slave named Sylvester to whose industry she has for several Years been indebted for his support.
  That he has served her with fidelity for several years & has rendered her meritorious Services.
  That she wishes to reward him by granting him freedom & prays leave of the Court to emancipate him.
Dec. 15 1797   TN Martin
        att Petitioner

****

Know all men by these presents that we Adam Tooley James Tooley and John F. Smith are held and firmly Bound unto the chairman of the Court of Craven in the Sum of fifty pounds to be Levied on our Several Goods & chattels Lands and Tenements to the use of the said Chairman or his Successors in Office Signed Sealed and Delivered this 12th day of March 1799.

the Condition of the above condition is Such that Whereas Adam Tooly hath applied to the County Court of Craven to Emancipate and Sett free **[Faded]** slave the property of Sal **[Torn]** now in case the said Diner shall **[Torn] [Faded]** get a living so that become not chargeable on the Parish then and in that case the above Obligation to be Void otherwise to Remain in full force and Effect witness our Hands & Seals this day and date above written.
Test   Adam Tooley (Seal)
Ann Blinn Jams.Tooley (Seal)
      Jno. F. Smith (Seal)

****

Craven County Court of Pleas & Quarter Sessions

      To the Worshipfull the Justices of said Court

      The Petition of William Gibbes of the Town of Newbern
      Humbly Sheweth

  That your petitioner owns a negro man named Jerry, by whom he has been faithfully Served for great many years -- And who has been a principal instrument in the obtaining whatever property your petitioner has aquired.
  That the fidelity of that slave has been great, and his Care and attention to your petitioner, in sickness and in health, unremitted.
  That your petitioner is about leaving the State forever And Cannot Justify to himself to Carry the said slave from his Connections and native Country; nor to dispose of him in a manner which would take it out of your petitioner's power to reward the many & meritorious Services which he has rendered from said slave.
  Your petitioner therefore prays the assistance of Your worships, that he may be enabled to do Justice to the said negro Jerry, by rewarding his Services by granting him his freedom.

Chapter 6: Craven County Records

      Your petitioner is aware that when he solicits Your worships interposition, it is just he should Satisfy the Court of the propriety of granting it, by convincing them that said negro will not be likely to become, by his emancipation, a public charge.

      He therefore represents to Your Worships that altho' the said negro Jerry, is of a strong constitution & healthy of body, and is sufficiently expert in the baking business, not only to procure his livelyhood, but yet to gather some property -- Yet the petitioner has made a Sufficient provision for his further & better support, which justifies him in advancing that there is no reasonable Cause to apprehend that the said negro man will ever become a public burden -- Your petitioner having executed a deed Conveying to the said negro a house and Lot, in Newbern, which deed is ready to be delivered to said negro after his emancipation, it being useless to do so before. And your petitioner leaving to the said negro a sum of money & some other property as tools &c which said negro has aquired by his industry, While in his Masters Service.

      And your petitioner as in duty bound &c will ever pray.

Newbern March 5th 1796   Willm. Gibbes

***

Know all men by these presents that I Elizabeth Young of Craven County State of North Carolina for the many faithfull Services for a Number of Years and the Valuable Consideration of the Sum of Ninety Pounds Current Money of said State paid me by a Mulatto Man Named Moses therefore by these presents I Do Give the Said Moses his freedom on his paying a Ballance Which is Now Due me of the Sum of Eighteen pounds Six Shillings and Six pence, which when paid will be in full, of the sum of Ninety pounds, and the said Moses Cannot Obtain his freedom without the Approbation of the County Court of Craven My Desire is that the Worshipfull Court would be pleased to pass and Order for said Moses freedom the subscribing wittness Can Inform the Court of the Circumstances of the Case. Given under my hand Seal this 3rd January 1798

Wittness present

John Carney   Elisabeth Young   (Seal)
                Wallace Stiron
                Southy J Reece

Recd of Moses Eighteen pounds Six Shillings and Six pence In full for his service as a Slave, this 9th day March 1798
            Elisabeth Young

***

            Peto. of Alex. Stewart & Wife
      for Emancipation of John Alias Jno Stanly
                To March Term 1795
                    Granted

            To the Worshipful the Justices of
              the County Court of Craven

      The petition of Alexander Stewart & Lydia Stewart his wife of Newbern humbly sheweth that your petitioners have a mulatto boy slave named John of the age of 21 who has from his infancy faithfully & meritoriously served your petitioners and has demeaned himself with propriety. Your petitioners are therefore desirous to reward the faithful & meritorious Services of the said Mulatto boy by emancipating & restoring him to freedom.

      May it please your Worships therefore to grant Your petitioners license to Emancipate the said boy & your petitioner as in duty bound will ever pray.

March 12. 1795   Alexr. Stewart
                      Lydia Stewart

On hearing the petition of Alexr. Stewart & wife setting forth that they have a mulatto slave who has from his infancy faithfully & meritoriously served the said Alexander & his wife, And praying that they may have license of this court to reward that faithful & meritorious Services of said boy by Emancipating & setting him free. Ordered that they have

Chapter 6: Craven County Records

license Accordingly, reserving however the rights of all persons except the petitioners their heirs assigns & all claiming under them.

****

To the Worshipfull

The Justices of the County Court held for the County of Craven of the term of June AD. 1798

The Petition of Ann G. Daly Administratrix of the Goods & Chattels &C of John Daly esqr. decd. & Guardian of Ann G. Daly & Sidney Maria Daly, children of the said John Daly decd., Robert Donnell & Elisa. his Wife & Guardian of John Daly, son of John Daly decd. & John Sears, himbly Sheweth to your Worships that the said Administratrix has at present in her possession a certain Mullattoe Slave named Mary about the age of twenty years, which slave, in strictness of law makes a part of the personal estate of the said John Daly decd. Your Petitioners further shew that the said Mary has always been reputed to be the child of the said John Daly decd., and in that light trated & regarded by the said John in his life time.

Your Petitioners further state that it was ever the full determined and avowed intention & desire of the said John to give or Procure for the said Mary her freedom, and that to this effect the said John hath repeatedly & uniformly expressed himself during his life and at the hour of his death.

Your Petitioners further state that the said Mary is a Girl of excellent Character, that she is industrious sober & honest & has always behaved dutifully and affectionately towards the whole family. Your Petitioners fellt themselves bound to state that, John Daly, Ann G. Daly, & Sidney M. Daly, three of the Children of John Daly decd. are under age, & that to remove all objections that may arise on account of the interest they have in the said Mary, your Petitioners, Robert Donell & Jno. Sears, are ready to give any Security the Court may require either for their or the indemnification of the said Administratrix -- Your Petitioner therefore pray that taking the premises into consideration your worships would pass an order granting the said Ann G. Daly Administratrix as aforesaid a license to make free & emancipate the said Mullattoe female Slave named Mary.

And Your Petitioner in duty bound shall ever Pray
Ann G. Daly
Robert Donnell
Jn Sears

****

Craven County   June Term 1797

To the Justices of the Court of sd. County
The Petition of Margaret Moore, a free negro woman:

Humbly Sheweth, that Your petitioner has been possessed for seven years past of a negro man slave named Jack Fennel, with whom she has lived Several Years as a wife, & by whom she has had a number of Children.

That she has acquired, chiefly thro' the industry, labour & economy of said slave a plantation Containing two hundred Acres of land, on Which he has built her a good home & great many valuable improvements; that the said farm is stocked with cattle, hogs &c. That the said Slave has otherwise rendered her Several meritorious Services.

That her duty prompts her not to detain her said husband in bondage, & to endeavor if she can do it to prevent him from becoming on her death the property of his own children, or being otherwise Sold off from them.

She therefore prays that Your Worships would grant her a license authorising her to emancipate & set free the said negro Jack Fennell & as in duty bound &c

F X Martin
Att: Pet.

****

To the Worshipfull the Justices of Craven County Court

Chapter 6: Craven County Records

March Term 1785

The Humble Petition of Dorcas Brimson

Sheweth,
  That she is illegally held in Servitude by William Clark when she conceives she is intitled to her Freedom & the Liberty Which Free Persons in a Free Country are entitled to, and as her Complaint is returned to your Worships, she humbly hopes your Worships will take her case into Consideration and Discharge her from Servitude.
  And as in duty Bound she will ever pray &c.
Dorcas Brimson

****

Petition of Antonio for Freedom
December Court 1775
Read & Rejected

Craven County Ss.
To the Justices of the Peace constituting the Inferior Court of Craven County aforesaid
  The Petition of Antonio Muray (a free Negro) humbly Sheweth
That in the year one thousand seven hundred and Sixty nine your unhappy Petitioner, left a Wife & Children in the Havannah; Shiped himself on Board a Vessel Bound to Jamaica and Arrived at Jamaica & from thence to Carthagene, And back to Jamaica, And that he had lent one of the Sailors (John Taylor by Name) a Pistole while at Carthagene and on their return to Jamaica a Dispute happened between your Petitioner and the Said John Taylor, who refused to repay it, upon Which the Said John Taylor struck your Petitioner and he returned blows, and your Petitioner being A Black man was taken up at the Instance as Complaint of the Said John Taylor and committed to Goal for Which Assault he was not prosecuted, and after being Detained three months in the Said Goal untill as I understood five or Six pounds was due for the Fees of the Goal, when a certain Timothy Clear and Capt. Roberts came to the Goal & talked about purchasing some Negros that were in the Goal & at last Agreed with the Goaler to pay the Goal Fees & take Out your Petitioner & Another Free Negro which was in the same Goal Mr. Clear pd. the fees for me, & Capt. Roberts paid for the Others but before we left the Goal an Indenture was made for Six or seven years to the Said Clear who promised to set me at Liberty as Soon as I had earned the Value of the Money which he paid, And that Notwithstanding the fair promises of the said Timothy Clear, (that he wou'd use me Kindly & not detain me any longer than sufficient to reimburse him for about the Sum of Six pounds which was all he paid for me,) he hath treated me Cruelly, by unmercifull Whippings frequently for Six years, and not being Satisfied with my labour as a Slave during the Said Term, Sold me again to my present Master Thomas Parsons, who treats me Very Ill, Your Poor Petitioner Humbly prays that your Worships will take my unhappy Case into serious Consideration, and do what Justice and Humanity requires to be done in the premises.
  And your Petitioner Will ever pray

R Cogdell
for the Petitioner

****

Stephen Tinker
Bond respecting Free Negroe Tenah
June Term 1789

State of North Carolina }
Craven County   }
  Know all Men by these Presents that We Stephen Tinker, John Daly & William M Herritage all of the County & State aforesaid, are held and firmly Bound unto his Excellency Samuel Johnston Esqr. Governor & Commander in Cheif **[Faded]** in the sum of Five Hundred Pounds Sterling Money of Great Britain to be paid to the said Saml Johnston Esqr. Governor, or his Successors - Governors & Commanders in Chief for the time being. To the which payment well

Chapter 6: Craven County Records

and truly to be made & done We bind ourselves our Heirs Executors & administrators, jointly and severally, firmly by these Presents, Sealed with our seals & dated this 12th day of June Anno Dom. 1789

The Condition of the above Obligation is Such that Whereas, the above Bound Stephen Tinker hath imported into this State a Certain Negroe Woman named Lenah, alias Tenah and Phillis her Daughter and Caesar a Boy - her Childred and Sold them to William Shepard which Negroes have **[Bottom of page torn away]** shall Produce in an Authentic Certificate of his Performance thereof to the County Court aforesaid then the above Obligation to be Void, otherwise to remain in full force & Virtue

Sealed & Delivered	Stephen Tinker	(Seal)
in the Presence of	John Daly	(Seal)
Saml Chapman	Wm. M. Herritage	(Seal)

Whereas Stephen Tinker did import into this State a Certain Negroe Woman Named Tenah Alias Lenah and Phillis her Daughter and Caesar her Son which negroes he sold to William Shepard as Slaves and they having been by this Court heretofore Considered as intituled to her Freedom and accordingly so adjudged -- Whereupon Ordered that the said Stephen Tinker enter into Bond with two good and Sufficient Securities in the sum of Five hundred Pounds Sterling Payable to the Governor & Commander in chief and his successors for the use of the State, with Condition that that he shall and do within one year from this Time (if said Negroes choose) transport and **[Faded]** (dangers of the Seas & Life only excepted) such Negroes sold by him as Slaves as aforesaid in the State of Connecticut from whence he bought them - and that he Produce an Authentic Certificate of his performance thereof to the Court. Whereupon the said Stephen Tinker offered John Daly and William M. Herritage Esquires for his Securities, and they being approved of by the Court entered into Bond with the said Stephen Tinker Accordingly.

Clerks Office   Attest
June 13th 1789   Saml. Chapman

State of Connecticut Ss.
City of New Haven

Be it remembered that on this the twenty first Day of August in the year of our Lord one thousand Seven hundred and Eighty nine personally appeared before me Henry Daggett Esquire one of the Alderman of the City of New Haven in said State Captain John Clark of said City and being duly sworn, deposed declare & saith that at the City of New York in the County & State of New York at the instance and request of Stephen Tinker on the eleventh Day of August instant he received on Board the Sloop Catherine (whereof the said Clark is Master) a certain Negro Wench named Tenah alias Lenah and Phyllis her Daughter and Caesar her Son to transport into the State of Connecticut and that he the said Clark accordingly landed said three Negroes at the Port of New Haven in sd. Station on the thirteenth Day of August instant & from thence at the request of said Tinker send said Negroes to the Son of said Tinker residing in Lyme in the County of New London in said State.

Sworn to before me   John Clark

Henry Daggett Alderman

I Elizer Godrich Esquire Notary Public residing at the Port of New Haven in the State of Connecticut being duly appointed and Judge do hereby certify declare and make known to all whom it doth or may concern that Henry Daggett Esquire an Alderman of the City of New Haven in said State and as such is (in office) authorised to administer Oath that all faith & Credit is and ought to be given to his Certificate in said Capacity And further more I do hereby Certify that the said Henry Daggett subscribed to the Jurat of the other Affidavit are the proper hand writing of said Henry Daggett & that said John Clark the Deponant is well known to me the said Notary & is and ought to be esteemed a Gentleman of the strictest truth & veracity & that all faith is to be given to his said Deponant in witness whereof I have hereto Sett my hand & Seal of Office in said City on this Twenty first Day of August in the Year of our Lord one thousand Seven hundred & Eighty Nine.
Elizer Godrich Notary Plublic 1789

Chapter 6: Craven County Records

****

Hire of Slave

Lewis Bryan's Bond £500 Specie
regarding Negroe Girl Berry[Benny?]
June Court 1782

State of No. Carolina
    Know all men by these presence that We Lewis Bryan William Bryan & Nathan Bryan are held and firmly bound to His Excellency Alexander Martin Esqr. Governor and to his Successors in Office **[Faded]** sum of Five Hundred pounds Specie which payment whereof well and Truly to be made and we do bind our Selves Jointly and Severaly our Heirs Excrs and Admns firmly by these presence Sealed with Our Seals this 12th day of June 1782

    The Condition of the Above Obligation is Such that Whereas the Court of the County of Craven hath this day Made an Order that the Commissioners of Confiscated Property Should Forthwith put Lewis Bryan in possession of a Certain Negro Girl Called Benny which is Taken by the Said Commissioners the former property of William Russell **[Next two lines torn]** the said Lewis Bryan does **[Torn]** and Truly Account with the said Court of Craven for the future Hire of the said negro Girl and also deliver her up when Ever Ordered by the said Court thereto in case She Should be adjudged for **[Faded]** under the Laws of the State then the Above obligation to be Void otherwise to be and Remain in full force and Virtue

Sealed and Delivered	}	Lewis Bryan	(Seal)
in the presence of	}	Wm. Bryan	(Seal)
Chris Nealy		Nathan Bryan	(Seal)

****

North Carolina
Craven County

    To the Worshipfull the Justices of the Court of Sd. County

The Petition of Peter Thomejeaux of the town of Newbern , Mercht.

Humbly Sheweth
    That he owns a Mustee, or person of mixed blood, Martial, Whose faithful Services he is desirous of rewarding by granting him his freedom & emancipation.

    Your Petitioner finds himself precluded by An Act of Assembly passed in 1741 from emancipating his said slave, without the assistance of Your Worshipful Court in the premises.
    He therefore prays Your worships wd exert the authority vested in yr Court by the Law of the Land & Give him a license, permitting him to &c free & emancipate his Said Slave Martial
    & as in duty bound &c

F. X. Martin
Atto. for petitioner
Newbern Dec 16th 1791

Peter Thomejeux of the town of Newbern Merchant Maketh oath that his servant Martial is a mustee or person of mixed blood has during a period of years served him with uncommon faithfullness that he has during that time been intrusted with the Care of a Store in which were large quantities of goods & often sums of money & has ever withstood the temptation such trust gave use to That he has attended him with Care & affection during many long journies & Sicknesses -- that having been been Suffered to trade under his Master's eyes; he had loaded up a sum almost Sufficient to reimburse his Master his purchase money - Which property was destroyed by the late fire, altho' he might have saved

Chapter 6: Craven County Records

it had he not endeavoured to save his Masters goods in preference to his own. That for these Services this deponent pray a license to reward his said slaves fidelity by setting him free.

Sworn to in open Court　　　　　　　　　　　　　Thomejuex
this 16th Dc. 1791

****

The Petition of J.C. Stanly, Respectfully Sheweth, that he is the owner of a boy Slave named James whose meritorious Services he is desirous to reward by Emancipation - he prays a license from your Worships to emancipate & sett [free] the said boy [Torn]

June Term 1800　　　　　　　　　　　　　　　　J.C. Stanly
Craven County

****

To the Worshipfull the Justices of the County Court of Craven

　　　　The petition of Mary Carter begs leave to represent to your Worships, that she is the Owner of a Negro Man called Anthony formerly the property of aaron Brown of whom she purchased him by paying a valuable Consideration, that the said Anthony is her Husband, from which consideration, as also from the Knowledge she has of the upright conduct & manners of the said Anthony towards his fellow Citizens in general, She begs leave to intreat & Solicit of your Worships his freedom, to which she conceives him wntitled by the Laws of the Land & she as in duty bound will ever Pray &c.

　　　　　　　　　　　　[?] Martin Pro Petitr.

****

To the Worshipfull the Justices of the County Court of Craven

　　　　The petition of John C. Stanly of the Town of Newbern humbly sheweth that your petitioner is the executor of the last will of Richard Green Decd. who devised to your petitioner by his said will a certain Mullattoe Man Slave now about the age of twenty one years named John, by trade a barber, formerly the property of George Merrick & Brother to your petitioners wife. In Consideration of the good conduct of said John and of what your petitioner supposes to have been the desire of the said testator his his factor and various other good & lawful consideration your petitioner is desirous to liberate, emancipate & make free the said Slave John and prays your worships license for that purpose And your petitioner as in duty bound will ever pray.

　　　　　　　　　　　　　　　　　　　　　　　　Jno. C. Stanly

Upon readin the petition of John C. Stanly praying leave to make free a certain Mullattoe Man Slave John son of Richard Green Decd. and Brother to the wife of said petitioner formerly of the estate of George Merrick Decd. - now the property of said petitioner - Ordered that the petitioner have leave accordingly to comply with the laws in such case provided.

****

State of North Carolina
Craven County

Know all men by these presents that I Benners Vail of the said County planter am held and firmly bound to Joseph Leech Esquire Chairman of the Court of Common pleas and quarter Sessions of Craven County and to his successors in office in the full and just sum of two thousand Pounds currency of the state of North Carolina, to the payment whereof well and truly to be made I bind myself my heirs, executors and administrators firmly by these presents sealed with my seal and dated this eighth day of October in the year of our Lord 1801

Chapter 6: Craven County Records

The Condition of the Above Obligation is such that Whereas the said County Court, have passed an order for the purpose of declaring and setting free, the following slaves named Old George, Binah, Lanah, Stephen, and Lydia late the property of John Benners, and by his will &c desired to be set at liberty, which order requires that Security should be given for the good behaviour of said slaves and that said slaves should not become chargeable to said County for their maintenance Now therefore if the said slaves each and every of them should be and continue of good behaviour in all things, according to law, and if the said Benners shouls save the County of Craven harmless and free from all expence and charge for the maintenance of each and all of the said slaves, then the above obligation to be void, otherwise to be in full force

sealed & delivered in presence   Benners Vail   (Seal)
of Edward Graham

****

State of North Carolina   }
Craven County   } Know all men by these
Presents that We John C. Stanly & [Blank] are held and firmly bound unto his Excellency James Turner Esqr. Governor of the State aforesaid in the full and just sum of three hundred pounds Current money to be paid to his Excellency the Governor aforesaid his successors or assigns, to the which payment well and truly to be made We bind ourselves our heirs Executors & Adminstrators jointly & Severally firmly by these Presents. Sealed with our Seals & dated this [Blank] day of March AD 1805

The Condition of the above Obligation is such Whereas the above bound John C. Stanly hath obtained permission by license from the Justice of the County Court of Craven at March Term in the year aforesaid to emancipate and set free the following slaves Viz. Ketty his wife, and two children [Faded] Eunice Carruthers and Ketty Green Stanly Now in Case the Ketty, Eunice Carruthers & Ketty Green Stanly become not chargeable to any County or Parish in this State, then the above Obligation to be void, otherwise to be and remain in full force & Virtue.

Sealed & delivered   }   Jno. Stanly   (Seal)
in Presence of   }   Marcus C Hester[?]   (seal)

****

State of North Carolina   }
Craven County   } Know all Men by these presents
that We Jeffrey Sampson Benja. Borden & [Blank] are held and firmly bound unto his Excellency Benjamin Williams Esqr. Governor &c of the state aforesaid in the sum of two hundred pounds Current money to be paid to his Excellency the Governor aforesaid his successors or assigns to which payment well and truly to be made, we bind ourselves our Heirs Executors and Administrators, jointly & severally firmly by these presents Sealed with our Seals and dated this 27th day of October AD 1800

The Condition of the obligation is such that Whereas the above bounden Jeffrey Sampson hath obtained his freedom, upon the petition of his Master to the County Court of Craven now in case the said Negro man Jeffrey conducts himself in a peaceable orderly manner, and [Faded] Good behaviour and is not chargeable to any County or Parish in this State, then the above Obligation to be void, otherwise to remain in full force & Virtue

Signed, Sealed & Delivered   his
in the presence of   Jeffrey X Sampson   (Seal)
Saml. Chapman CC   mark
                                  Benja Borden   (Seal)

****

State of North Carolina   } Know all men by these
Craven County   } presents that we John
Howard and Richard Williams of the Said County are held and firmly bound unto Joseph Leech Esquire Chairman of the Court of Common pleas and quarter Sessions for Craven County and to his Successors in office in the full and Just Sum of four hundred pounds Currency of the State of North Carolina & to the payment whereof Will and truly to be

Chapter 6: Craven County Records

made We bind ourselves our heirs Executors and administrators [Torn] Sealed with our Seals and dated this 29th day of [Faded] 1801

The Condition of the above obligation Is such that Whereas the Said County Court have passed an order for the purpose of declaring and Setting free Peter Godett late the property of Said John Howard which order requires that Security Should be given for the good behaviour of Said Slave and that the Said Slave Should not become Chargeable to Said County for his Maintenance Now therefore If the Said Peter Godett Should be and Continue of good behaviour In all things according to law and if the Said John Howard and Richard Williams Should Save the County of Craven harmless and free from all Expence and Charge for the Maintenance of Said Peter Godett then the above obligation to be Null and Void otherwise to remain in full force and Virtue.

Signed Sealed & delivered }	John Howard	(Seal)
In presence of }	Richard Williams	(Seal)
[Faded] [Torn]		

***

State of North Carolina }
Craven County   } Know all men by these
Presents, that We Lydia Stewart & Thomas Webber are held and firmly bound unto his Excellency Benjamin Williams Esqr. Governor of the State aforesaid in the sum of Two hundred pounds Current Money to be paid to his Excellency the Governor aforesaid his Successors and Assigns to which payment well and truly to be made & done We bind ourselves our Heirs Executors and Administrators jointly & severally firmly by these presents, Sealed with our Seals and dated this 4th day of July AD 1801

The Condition of the above obligation is such that, Whereas the above bounden Lydia Stewart hath obtained permission from the County Court of Craven to emancipate a certain Negro[Marked Through] female Slave named Phillis - Now in Case it shall [Faded] appear [Faded]   hereafter that the said Phillis [Faded] chargeable to any County or Parish in this State then the above Obligation to be void otherwise to remain in full force & Virtue

Signed, Sealed & Delivered }		
in the Presence of }	Lydia Stewart	(Seal)
S Chapman CC	T Webber	(Seal)

***

State of North Carolina }   Common pleas and Quarter Sessions
Craven County   }   of March Term A.D. 1800; Of our
                       }   Independence the XXIV

To,
The Worshipfull the Justices of the Court
       The petition of Wilson Blount and Ann his wife of the County of Craven and town of Newbern, humbly sheweth, that your petitioners own and possess a certain mulattoe, female slave, named Hannah, of about the age of twenty six years, raised up from infancy under the eye and strict care, and in the family of your petitioners that, for sobriety, industry, and honesty the character of said Hannah has ever been and to this day remains truly exemplary; that she has in no instance within the knowledge of your petitioners betrayed principles or dispositions the free exercise of which her manumission could render inimical to society that on the contrary, though an humble and obscure yet in that event she would be a worthy and an useful member -- Your petitioners further beg leave humbly to suggest that to them, the whole life of the said Hannah has been one uniform display of meritorious services - of affection of their persons, zeal for their service, and attachment to their interests - Under the influence of these considerations, strengthened by the pressure of infirmities under which your petitioner Wilson labours your petitioners are desirous to remunerate the said Hannah with her freedom - But as this can only be effected by the aid and interdisposition of this worshipfull court Your petitioners therefore pray, that taking the premises under advisement, your worships would grant unto your petitioners a license to set free and discharge and forever liberate from slavery the said Hannah to the end that the said Hannah may be acquited of and from all manner of obligation of service to your petitioners their heirs executors and assigns, And that the same may be recorded - And Your petitioners as in duty bound shall ever pray
Wilson Blount & Ann Blount

Chapter 6: Craven County Records

Edward Graham their Attorney

The petition of Wilson Blount and Ann his wife praying that the petitioners may have a license to set free and liberate from slavery a certain female slave named Hannah owned by the petitioners, was preferred and read to the Court, and it being also certified to the Court that the said Hannah is of good and meritorious character; the Court after taking the same under mature consideration do allow the said petition, and do grant to the said Wilson Blount and Ann his wife, license to set free and liberate the said Hannah agreeably to the prayer of said petition.

****

To their Worships the Justices of Craven County towit

The Petition of Amelia Green Humbly Sheweth that your Petitioner having purchased of the Legal owners, her two daughters to wit, Nancy Green of William Howe and Princess Green of Bell Chapman to whom your Petitioner paid a valuable consideration and has Received two bills of Sale from them in which they convey all their Rights title and claim to the aforesd. Nancy and Princess and warrant and Defend the said Right to your petitioner

Now may It please your worships your Petitioner from maternal affection for her Said children as well as from their meritorious Services Rendered to your Petitioner by her children aforesaid for some years past Humbly prays that your Worships would take the Same into Consideration and Grant a License of Emancipation for her children aforesd. So that they may Injoy all the priviledges and Rights of Free persons of Like colour and your petitioner as in duty bound Will Ever pray &c &c

Amelia Green

State of North Carolina } September Term
Craven County Court } In the Year of our
Lord one thousand seven hundred and Ninety six,

To the Worshipfull the Justices of the County Court of Common pleas and Quarter Sessions held in and for the said County September Term A.D. 1796

The petition of Amelia Green of the said County and Town of Newbern humbly sheweth to Your Worships that She now is and for several years past has been a free Woman, that She is the Mother of a large family of Children all of whom except two daughters have been enabled as the fruits of their own industry and meritorious behaviour to acquire their freedom, Your petitioner further sheweth, that one of those two daughters not yet made free a mullatto of the name of Princess and about the age of Sixteen, was late the property of Isabella Chapman of New Hanover County in sd State, by the will of Ann Shaw, But that your petitioner (being induced thereto by her maternal affection towards her and a desire to see all her family on the same footing) with much toil and industry, has succeeded to raise a sum of money sufficient to purchase the said Princess her daughter from the said Isabella Chapman, and has there with actually purchased by fair bill of sale which She prays may be taken as part of her petition, the said Princess your petitioners daughter Your petitioners sole motion to the expence was that she might give freedom to her said daughter, Your petitioner further begs leave to Inform Your Worships that she is now far advanced in life and that she feels the infirmities of age growing upon her, and contemplates the awful event of her Death as at no very Distant period, an event (which, unless the goodness of Your worships prevent) might frustrate the pious intention of your petitioner towards her daughter and disapoint her of the reward of her labour. Your petitioner presumes to say with Confidence in behalf of Princess that she is a good Girl, a good daughter, that she possesses mild and peaceable disposition and industrious habits, which your petitioner will as is required make appear - Taking the premises therefor under your petitioners Your petitioner prays that your worships would please to grant her a license to set free and emancipate her said daughter the said Princess. And Your petitioner as in duty bound shall ever pray &c.

Signed in presence   her
of Edward Graham   Amelia + Green
                               mark

Chapter 6: Craven County Records

State of North Carolina }
Craven County } Ss. December Term 1799

The Worshipful the County Court of Craven The Petition of Nancy Handy a free person of Color humbly sheweth to this Worshippful Court, that during the Time she was a Slave and the property of Wm T Howe she conceived and did bear two children, to wit Louisa and Betsey And that she by certain Allowances and indulgences granted to her by her said Master did gather together & accumulate cash in sufficient quantity to purchase her self and said children and that the aforesaid Nancy did purchase from her aforesaid Master her aforesaid Children, and your Petitioner states that she has always endeavored to conduct herself as a peaceable citizen, And an useful one to the community by encreasing the number of good & valuable Citizens of the State, And your Petitioner therefore prays that this worshipful Court would grant the freedom of the said Children according to Act of Assembly in such case made and provided.
Benjm. Martin Atty
for the Children

State of North Carolina Court of Pleas & Quarter Sessions for the County of Craven December Term 1801

The Petition of Amelia Green humbly sheweth that Nancy Handy is her daughter and the property of whom is exclusively vested in your Petitioner by purchase from William T Howe as will fully appear reference being had to the deed of bargain & sale. Your Petitioner states that being aged & not long expecting to enjoy the pleasures of this world & to whom the womb of time is not open to inspect what may hereafter be brought forth or in what manner it may affect her daughter, should she be the Survivor wishes for license to liberate the said Nancy Handy. To the end therefore that your worships would grant to your petitioner license to manumit her said daughter agreeably to act of assembly in such case made and provided She represents & certifies to your Worships that her daughter is intitled to merit in always having conducted herself towards your Petitioner as a dutiful daughter. And your Petitioner as in duty bound will ever pray &c.

To the Worshipfull the Justices of the County Court

The Petition of Amelia Green and Nancy Handy, the Mother and Sister of Harriet Green a Woman of Colour, begs leave to Solicit and pray your Worships will take into your Consideration the Petition of the said Harriet Green - Your Petitioners state that they being the Mother and Sister of the said Harriet Green and so closely and nearly connected with her, they Purchased her of Mrs. Betsey Vail the Owner of the said Harriet for the express purpose of setting her free, they therefore humbly pray your Worships will liberate and Sett free the said Harriet and they as in duty bound will ever pray &c.

B H Martin
pro petr.

****

To the Worshipful the Court of Pleas & quarter Sessions of Craven

The Petition of Philip Neale Junr.
Humbly Sheweth,
That he is the owner of a negro Man named Ben, whose long meritorious Service he is desirous of rewarding
[Faded] emancipating
Wherefore he prays [?] permission
[Badly faded and damaged] FX Martin
[Damaged and faded]

Know all men by these Presents that we Benjamin Neale Philip Neale junior and Philip Neale Senr. & Wm Johnston all of Craven County and State of North Carolina are held and firmly bound unto his Excellency Benjamin Williams Esquire Governor of the State aforesaid in the just and full sum of two hundred pounds Current money of the State

Chapter 6: Craven County Records

aforesaid, for which payment well and truly to be made to the said Governor or his Successors in Office we bind ourselves our Heirs Executors and Administrators jointly and severally firmly by these presents Sealed with our Seals and dated this 18th day of September 1801

The Condition of the above Obligation is such that if the above bounden Benjamin Neale, take a negro Slave & on the **[Faded]** of his Master or Owners set free by **[Torn]** of the County Court of Craven made **[Faded & torn]** September Instant, shall well and truly **[Faded & torn]** according to the intent and **[Faded & torn]** Assembly in that Case made & provided **[Faded]** shall remain within the limits of the State aforesaid then the above obligation to be void, otherwise to remain in full force and virtue.

in presence of
John Bragg Jur.

                  his
Benjamin X Neale   (Seal)
   mark
Philip Neale Junr.   (Seal)
Philip Neale Sr.   (Seal)
Wm. Johnston   (Seal)

****

On hearing the petition on behalf of the Executors of James McKinley decd. praying license to emancipate a certain slave Dick belonging to the estate of the said James McKinley and the proof in support thereof - Ordered that the said Executors have license to emancipate and declare free the said slave Dick, on entering into bond for the good behaviour of the said slave and to indemnify the State against his maintenance with securities to the satisfaction of the clerk of this court and the parish of the courts of Craven agreeable to law.
        Ordered

****

State of North Carolina }
Craven County   } Know all Men by these Presents
that We Francis Louthorp & George Ellis are held & firmly bound unto his Excellency James Turner Esqr. Governor &c of the State aforesaid in the full and just sum of One hundred pounds to be paid to his Excellency the Governor aforesaid his Successors & Assigns to the which payment well & truly to be made & done, We bind ourselves, our Heirs Executors and Administrators jointly & severally firmly by these presents, Sealed with our seals & dated this 11th day of June AD 1803.

The Condition of the above Obligation is such Whereas the Court of pleas & quarter Sessions for Craven County have given permission to Jas. McKinley & William Good Executors of Thomas Thomlinson decd. to emancipate a Negro Woman Slave named June**[Juno]** the property of the said decd. agreeable to the directions of said Decd. in his Will Now in case the said Negro Woman June shall so demean herself that she be not chargeable to any Parish or County in this State then the above Obligation to be Void otherwise to remain in full force & Virtue.

Signed Sealed & delivered}   Fr. Louthorp   (Seal)
in the Presence of   }   Geo. Ellis   (Seal)
Saml Chapman CC   }

****

State of No. Carolina }
Craven County   } Know all Men by these Present, that
We Lydia Stewart and John C. Stanly, are held and firmly bound, unto his Excellecny Nathaniel Alexander Esqr. Captain General, Governor and Commander in Chief of the State aforesaid in the full sum of two hundred pounds, to be paid to the said Governor his successors in Office, to the which payment, well and truly to be made, We bind ourselves our Heirs Executors and Administrators, jointly & severally by these presents, Sealed with our seals, and dated this 10th June 1806

Chapter 6: Craven County Records

The Condition of the above obligation is such, that Whereas on the Petition of the above bounden, Lydia Stewart, the Justices of the Court of pleas and quarter Sessions held for the County of Craven, at June Term 1805, did grant permission to the said Lydia, to emancipate and set free, a Certain Negro Girl, slave named Bet, Now if the said Bet, shall afterwards be of good behaviour, then the above Obligation to be void, otherwise to remain in full force & virtue.

Signed Sealed & delivered}	Lydia Stewart	(Seal)
in the Presence of }	Jno. C. Stanly	(Seal)
Saml. Chapman CC		

State of North Carolina   }
Craven County   } Know all Men by these Presents that We Lydia Stewart, & John C. Stanly are held and firmly bound unto John Tillman Esqr. Chairman of the Court of pleas and quarter Sessions of Craven County, in the full and just sum of One hundred pounds, to be paid to the said Chairman or his successors in Office, for the use of the Poor of said County; to the which payment well and truly to be made & done, We bind ourselves, our Heirs, Executors and Administrators, jointly and severally, firmly by these Presents Sealed with our Seals, and dated this 10th June AD 1806

The Condition of the above Obligation is such, that Whereas leave is granted to the above bounden Lydia Stewart, to set free and emancipate, a negro girl slave named, Bet, now if the said Bet, shall not hereafter become chargeable to, or on the Parish or County, then the above Obligation to be void, otherwise to remain in full force & virtue

Signed, Sealed & delivered	}	Lydia Stewart	(Seal)
in the Presence of	}	Jno. C. Stanly	(Seal)
S Chapman CC			

****

Craven County

    To the Worshipful the Justices of the County Court of Pleas & Quarter Sessions of the County aforesaid.

The Petition of Elijah Calloway, of said County farmer

    Humbly Sheweth

    That your Petitioner is desirous to reward the faithful & meritorious Services of a negro slave of his named Reuben and humbly solicits the leave & Consent of Your Worships therefore

	FX Martin
June Sessions 1805	Atto. for Petitioner
	Elijah Callaway

The Subscribers, inhabitants of that part of the County of Craven, in which Reuben, the slave named in the annexed Petition was born & brought up, & has ever since resided beg leave to recommend him to the Worshipful Court of the County, as a proper object of the attention of their Worships. They are able from long acquaintance to bear testimony to his honest decent behaviour, & his industry and attention in honest pursuits: and his quiet deportment towards all persons.

Chas. Williams	Elijah Callaway
Isaac Willis	David Whitford
William Se[Smeared]rle	Aaron Ernul
Henry Warrin	Levi Rees
John Whitford	John Rees
Moses Ernul	David D. Dunn[?]
Joshua Willis	Ephraim Willis
Richd. Willis	Norman Willis

Chapter 6: Craven County Records

David Pearce   John Bright

Know all men by these presents that we Elijah Callaway and John Whitford & David Whitford are held & firmly bound to Lucas J. [?] Esquire Chairman of Craven County Court in the just & full sum of One hundred pounds (Say one hundred) to be paid to said Chairman or his successors in office for the use of the poor of said County, to the which payment well and truly to be made we bind ourselves, our heirs executors & administrators jointly & severally by these presents sealed with our Seals this 10th day of June 1805

The Condition of the above obligation is such that whereas leave is about to be granted to said Elijah Callaway to set free & emancipate Reuben a negro Slave of said Elijah now if the said Reuben shall not hereafter become chargeable on the parish or County - then the above obligation to be null & void otherwise to remain in full force & virtue

signed sealed & delivered   Elijah Callaway

Know all men by these presents that we Reuben Callaway, Elijah Callaway, John Whitford & David Whitford Are held & firmly bound to His Excellency James Turner Esq. Captain General, Governor & Commander in chief of the State of North Carolina, in the just & full sum of two hundred pounds to be paid to the said Governor Captain General & commander in chief of the State aforesd. or his successors in office to the which payment well & truly to be made We bind ourselves our heirs executors & administrators jointly & severally, by these presents Sealed with our seals & dated this 10th day of June 1805

The Condition of the above obligation is such that Whereas the above bounden Reuben has by Censure of the County Court been emancipated & set free Now if he shall afterwards be of good behaviour, then this obligation to be null and void otherwise to remain in full force & virtue

Syned & Sealed &	Reuben Callaway	(Seal)
delivered before	Elijah Callaway	(Seal)
FX Martin	John Whitford	(Seal)
[?] Williams	David Whitford	(Seal)

****

To the worshipfull the Justices of the County Court of Craven The Petition of Elizabeth Henry, respectfully sheweth, That she is the owner of two negro Slaves, Harry and Emanuel, whose long and meritorious Services, She is desirous to reward with emancipation, and prays the license of this Worshipful court for that purpose   June Term 1806
Granted   E. Henry

State of North Carolina }
Craven County   } Know all Men by these Presents, that
We, Elizabeth Henry and Saml Barrow are held and firmly bound, unto his Excellency Nathaniel Alexander Esqr. Captain General, Governor, and commander in chief of the State aforesaid, in the full and just sum of Two hundred pounds to be paid to the said Governor, or his successors in office, to the which payment, well and truly to be made, We bind ourselves our heirs executors, and Administrators, jointly & severally firmly by these presents sealed with our seals, and dated this 10th day of June 1806

Condition of the above Obligation is Such, that Whereas the Petition of the above bounden Elizabeth Henry, The Justices of the County Court of pleas and quarter Sessions held for the County of Craven at [Faded] Term in the year aforesaid, did grant a License to the said Elizabeth Henry, to emancipate and set free, a certain Negro man Slave named Emanuel, Now if the said Emanuel, shall afterwards be of good behaviour, then the above Obligation to be void, otherwise to remain in full force & virtue

| Signed, Sealed & delivered | E. Henry | (Seal) |
| in the presence of | Saml. Barrow | (Seal) |

Chapter 6: Craven County Records

State of North Carolina　}
Craven County　　　　} Know all Men by these Presents that We
Elizabeth Henry and Saml. G. Barrow are held and firmly bound unto John Tillman Esqr. Chairman of the Court of pleas and quarter sessions of Craven County, in the full and just sum of One hundred pounds, to be paid to the said Chairman or his Successors in Office, for the use of the poor of said County, To the which payment well and truly to be made and done, We bind ourselves our Heirs Executors and Administrators, jointly and severally firmly by these Presents, Sealed with our Seals and dated the 10th day [Faded]

The Condition of the above Obligation is such, that Whereas a License has been granted, by the Justices of the County Court aforesaid to the above bounden Elizabeth Henry, to set free and emancipate a negro Man slave, named Emanuel, now if the said Emanuel shall not at any time hereafter, become chargeable to, or on the Parish, or County of Craven, then the above Obligation to be void, otherwise to remain in full force & virtue.

Signed, Sealed & delivered　　　E. Henry　　　　　　(Seal)
in the presence of　　　　　　　Saml. G. Barrow
Saml. Chapman CC

State of North Carolina　}
Craven County　　　　} Know all Men by these Presents that
We Elizabeth Henry and Saml. G. Barrow are held and firmly bound unto his Excellency Nathaniel Alexander Esqr. Captain General, Governor and commander in chief of the State aforesaid, in the full sum of two hundred Pounds, to be paid to the said Governor, or his successors in Office, to the which payment well and truly to be made, We bind ourselves our Heirs, Executors and Administrators jointly & severally firmly by these Presents Sealed with our Seals and dated this 10th day June 1806

The Condition of the above Obligation is such, that Whereas on the Petition of the above bounden Elizabeth Henry, The Justices of the Court of pleas and quarter Sessions held for the County of Craven at June Term in the year aforesaid, did grant a License to the said Elizabeth Henry, to emancipate and set free, a certain Negro Man Slave named Henry, Now if the said Henry shall afterwards be of good behaviour, then the above Obligation to be void, otherwise to remain in full force & virtue

Signed, Sealed & delivered　　}　E. Henry　　　　　(Seal)
in the presence of　　　　　　}　Saml. G. Barrow　(Seal)
Saml. Chapman CC

****

State of North Carolina　}
Craven County　　　　}

　　Know all men by these presents that We John Daly and Charles Roach Jr. are held & firmly bound unto John Tillman Esq. Chairman of the Court of pleas and Quarter sessions of Craven County Court in the full and just sum of One hundred pounds [Faded] [Faded] said Chairman or his successors in Office for the use of the poor of said County, to the which payment well and truly to be made We bind ourselves our heirs executors and administrators jointly and severally firmly by these presents Sealed with our seals and dated this 28th day of July 1807

The Condition of the above Obligation is such that Whereas leave was granted to the Executor of Edward Griffith at June Term last past of Craven County Court to emancipate Alice a negro slave of the said Edward. Now if the said Alice shall not hereafter become chargeable on the Parish or County then the above obligation to be void

Signed Sealed and　　　　　}　JN. Daly　　　　　　(Seal)
Delivered in presence of　}　Charles Roach Jr　(Seal)
J G Stanly

State of North Carolina　}

Chapter 6: Craven County Records

Craven County } Know all men by these presents that We John Daly and Charles Roach Junr. are held and firmly bound unto his Excellency Nathaniel Alexander Esq. Captain General Governor and Commander in Chief of the State aforesaid in the full and just sum of One hundred pounds to be paid to the said Governor or his successors in Office to the which payment well and truly to be made, We bind ourselves our heirs executors and administrators jointly and severally by these presents Sealed with our seals and dated this 28th day of July AD 1814

The Condition of the above Obligation is such that Whereas on the petition of Lewis Fonville the Executor of Edward Griffith, the Justices of the Court of pleas & quarter sessions of Craven County at June Term AD 1814 did grant permission to the said Lewis to Emancipate and set free a certain negro woman Slave named Alice Now if the said Alice shall afterwards be of good behaviour then the above Obligation to be void

Signed Sealed and }	JN. Daly	(Seal)
delivered in presence of }	Charles Roach Junr	(Seal)

J G Stanly

****

To the Worshipfull the Justices of Craven County Court

The Petition of Elizabeth Henry respectfully sheweth, That she is possessed of the following Slaves whose meritorious services She desires to reward with the blessing of freedom, Vizt. Chelsea and her children Peter, Hannah, Abram, & Rosanna -: Tenah and her child Ben: Rose and Peggy - She prays that she may be permitted to emancipate the said slaves at such time as she shall think proper March 17, 1808   E. Henry

---

State of North Carolina }
Craven County }

Know all men by these presents that We Elizabeth Henry & John C. Stanly are held and firmly bound unto his Excellency Benjamin Williams Esquire, Captain General, Governor, and Commander in Chief of the State aforesaid, in the full sum of two hundred pounds, to be paid to the said Governor or his successors in office; to which payment well and truly to be made, we bind ourselves, our heirs, executors, and administrators, jointly and severally, firmly by these presents, sealed with our seals, and dated this 11th day of June A.D. 1808

The Condition of the above obligation is such, that whereas at the Court held for Craven County, at this day permission has been granted to E. Henry by the said Court, to emancipate and set free a certain negro slave named Chelsea. Now if the said negro so permitted to be liberated shall during her residence in the state of North Carolina behave herself as an honest and peaceable citizen, then the above obligation to be void.

Sealed and delivered }	E. Henry	(Seal)
in presence of }	Jno. C. Stanly	(Seal)

J G Stanly

State of North Carolina }
Craven County }

Know all men by these presents that We Elizabeth Henry & John C Stanly are held and firmly bound to John Tillman Esquire Chairman of Craven County Court, in the sum of one hundred pounds, to be paid to the said John or his successors in office, to which payment well and truly to be made we bind ourselves, our heirs, executors and administrators, firmly by these presents sealed with our seals and dated this 11 day of June AD 1808

The Condition of the above obligation is such, whereas at the Court held for Craven County, at this day permission has been granted to E. Henry by the said Court, to emancipate and set free a certain negro slave named Chelsea Now if the said negro so permitted to be liberated, shall not become chargeable to the parish of Craven County, or of any other County in this State, then the above obligation to be void.

Sealed and delivered }	E. Henry	(Seal)
in presence of }	Jno. C. Stanly	(Seal)

Chapter 6: Craven County Records

[Torn] Bright   Security   (Seal)
[Torn] by John C Stanly
[Torn]presence of
J G Stanly

State of North Carolina }
Craven County   }

Know all men by these presents that We Elizabeth Henry & John C Stanly are held and firmly bound unto his Excellency Benjamin Williams Esquire, Captain General, Governor, and Commander in Chief of the State aforesaid, in the full sum of two hundred pounds, to be paid to the said Governor or his successors in office; to the which payment well and truly to be made, we bind ourselves, our heirs, executors, and administrators, jointly and severally, firmly by these presents, sealed with our seals, and dated this 11th day of June A.D. 1808

The Condition of the above obligation is such, that whereas at the Court held for Craven County, at this day permission has been granted to E. Henry by the said Court, to emancipate and set free a certain negro slave named Peter Son of Chelsea. Now if the said negro so permitted to be liberated shall during his residence in the state of North Carolina behave himself as an honest and peaceable citizen, then the above obligation to be void.

Sealed and delivered   }   E. Henry   (Seal)
in presence of   }   Jno. C. Stanly   (Seal)
E. Bright   Security   (Seal)
signed by J.C. Stanly
in presence of
J G Stanly

State of North Carolina }
Craven County   }

Know all men by these presents that we Elizabeth Henry & John C Stanly are held and firmly bound to John Tillman Esquire Chairman of Craven County Court, in the sum of one hundred pounds, to be paid to the said John or his successors in office, to which payment well and truly to be made we bind ourselves, our heirs, executors, and administrators, firmly by these presents sealed with our seals and dated this 11th day of June 1808

The Condition of the above obligation is such, whereas at the Court held for Craven County, at this day permission has been granted to E. Henry by the said Court, to emancipate and set free a certain negro slave named Peter. Now if the said negro so permitted to be liberated, shall not become chargeable to the Parish of Craven County, or any other County in this State, then the above obligation to be void.

Sealed and delivered   }   E. Henry   (Seal)
in presence of   }   Jno. C. Stanly   (Seal)
E. Bright   Security   (Seal)
signed by J.C. Stanly
in presence of
J G Stanly

State of North Carolina }
Craven County   }

Know all men by these presents that We Eliz. Henry & John C Stanly are held and firmly bound unto his Excellency Benjamin Williams Esquire, Captain General, Governor, and Commander in Chief of the State aforesaid, in the full sum of two hundred pounds, to be paid to the said Governor or his successors in office; to the which payment well and truly to be made, we bind ourselves, our heirs, executors, and administrators, jointly and severally, firmly by these presents, sealed with our seals, and dated this 11th day of June A.D. 1808

Chapter 6: Craven County Records

The Condition of the above obligation is such, that whereas at the Court held for Craven County, at this day permission has been granted to E. Henry by the said Court, to emancipate and set free a certain negro slave named Hannah. Now if the said negro so permitted to be liberated shall during her residence in the State of North Carolina behave herself as a honest and peaceable citizen, then the above obligation to be void.

Sealed and delivered	}	E. Henry	(Seal)
in presence of	}	Jno. C. Stanly	(Seal)
E. Bright		Security	(Seal)

signed by John C Stanly
in presence of
J G Stanly

State of North Carolina }
Craven County }

Know all men by these presents that we E. Henry and John C Stanly are held and firmly bound to John Tillman Esquire Chairman of Craven County Court, in the sum of one hundred pounds, to be paid to the said John or his successors in office, to which payment well and truly to be made we bind ourselves, our heirs, executors, and administrators, firmly by these presents sealed with our seals and dated this 11 day of June 1808

The Condition of the above obligation is such, whereas at the Court held for Craven County, at this day permission has been granted to Eliza. Henry by the said Court, to emancipate and set free a certain negro slave named Hannah. Now if the said negro so permitted to be liberated, shall not become chargeable to the parish of Craven County, or of any other County in this State, then the above obligation to be void.

Sealed and delivered	}	E. Henry	(Seal)
in presence of	}	Jno. C. Stanly	(Seal)
E. Bright		Security	(Seal)

signed by John C Stanly
in presence of
J G Stanly

State of North Carolina }
Craven County }

Know all men by these presents that We Elizabeth Henry & John C Stanly are held and firmly bound unto his Excellency Benjamin Williams Esquire, Captain General, Governor, and Commander in Chief of the State aforesaid, in the full sum of two hundred pounds, to be paid to the said Governor or his successors in office; to the which payment well and truly to be made, we bind ourselves, our heirs, executors, and administrators, jointly and severally, firmly by these presents, sealed with our seals, and dated this 11th day of June 1808

The Condition of the above obligation is suc, that whereas at the Court held for Craven County, at this day permission has been granted to Eliza. Henry by the said Court, to emancipate and set free a certain negro slave named Abram. Now if the said negro so permitted to be liberated shall during his residence in the state of North Carolina behave himself as an honest and peaceable citizen, then the above obligation to be void.

Sealed and delivered	}	E. Henry	(Seal)
in presence of	}	Jno. C. Stanly	(Seal)
E. Bright		Security	(Seal)

signed by J C Stanly
in presence of
J G Stanly

State of North Carolina }

Chapter 6: Craven County Records

Craven County   }

Know all men by these presents that we Eliza. Henry & John C Stanly are held and firmly bound to John Tillman Esquire Chairman of Craven County Court, in the sum of one hundred pounds, to be paid to the said John Tillman or his successors in office, to which payment well and truly to be made we bind ourselves, our heirs, executors, and administrators, firmly by these presents sealed with our seals and dated this 11 day of June 1808

    The Condition of the above obligation is such, whereas at the Court held for Craven County, at this day permission has been granted to Elizabeth Henry by the said Court, to emancipate and set free a certain negro slave named Abram. Now if the said negro so permitted to be liberated, shall not become chargeable to the parish of Craven County, or of any other County in this State, then the above obligation to be void.

Sealed and delivered   }   E. Henry   (Seal)
in presence of   }   Jno. C. Stanly   (Seal)
E. Bright   Security   (Seal)
signed by JC Stanly
in presence of
J G Stanly

State of North Carolina   }
Craven County   }

Know all men by these presents that We Elizabeth Henry & John C Stanly are held and firmly bound unto his Excellency Benjamin Williams Esquire, Captain General, Governor, and Commander in Chief of the State aforesaid, in the full sum of two hundred pounds, to be paid to the said Governor or his successors in office; to the which payment well and truly to be made, we bind ourselves, our heirs, executors, and administrators, jointly and severally, firmly by these presents, sealed with our seals, and dated this 11th day of June 1808

    The Condition of the above obligation is such, that whereas at the Court held for Craven County, at this day permission has been granted to Elizabeth Henry by the said Court, to emancipate and set free a certain negro slave named Rosanna. Now if the said negro so permitted to be liberated shall during her residence in the state of North Carolina behave herself as an honest and peaceable citizen, then the above obligation to be void.

Sealed and delivered   }   E. Henry   (Seal)
in presence of   }   Jno. C. Stanly   (Seal)
E. Bright   Security   (Seal)
signed by JC Stanly
in presence of
J G Stanly

State of North Carolina   }
Craven County   }

Know all men by these presents that we Elizabeth Henry & John C Stanly are held and firmly bound to John Tillman Esquire Chairman of Craven County Court, in the sum of two hundred pounds, to be paid to the said John or his successors in office, to which payment well and truly to be made we bind ourselves, our heirs, executors, and administrators, firmly by these presents sealed with our seals and dated this 11 day of June 1808

    The Condition of the above obligation is such, whereas at the Court held for Craven County, at this day permission has been granted to Elizabeth Henry by the said Court, to emancipate and set free a certain negro slave named Rosanna. Now if the said negro so permitted to be liberated, shall not become chargeable to the parish of Craven County, or any other County in this State, then the above obligation to be void.

Sealed and delivered   }   E. Henry   (Seal)
in presence of   }   Jno. C. Stanly   (Seal)
E. Bright   Security   (Seal)
signed by JC Stanly

Chapter 6: Craven County Records

in presence of
J G Stanly

State of North Carolina   }
Craven County   }

Know all men by these presents that We Elizabeth Henry & John C Stanly are held and firmly bound unto his Excellency Benjamin Williams Esquire, Captain General, Governor, and Commander in Chief of the State aforesaid, in the full sum of two hundred pounds, to be paid to the said Governor or his successors in office; to the which payment well and truly to be made, we bond ourselves, our heirs, executors, and administrators, jointly and severally, firmly by these presents, sealed with our seals, and dated this 11th day of June 1808

The Condition of the above obligation is such, that whereas at the Court held for Craven County, at this day permission has been granted to E. Henry by the said Court, to emancipate and set free a certain negro slave named Tenah. Now if the said negro so permitted to be liberated shall during her residence in the state of North Carolina behave herself as an honest and peaceable citizen, then the above obligation to be void.

Sealed and delivered	}	E. Henry	(Seal)
in presence of	}	Jno. C. Stanly	(Seal)
E. Bright		Security	(Seal)

signed by JC Stanly
in presence of
J G Stanly

State of North Carolina   }
Craven County   }

Know all men by these presents that we Elizabeth Henry & John C Stanly are held and firmly bound to John Tillman Esquire Chairman of Craven County Court, in the sum of one hundred pounds, to be paid to the said John or his successors in office, to which payment well and truly to be made we bind ourselves, our heirs, executors, and administrators, firmly by these presents sealed with our seals and dated this 11th day of June 1808

The Condition of the above obligation is such, whereas at the Court held for Craven County, at this day permission has been granted to Elizabeth Henry by the said Court, to emancipate and set free a certain negro slave named Tenah. Now if the said negro so permitted to be liberated, shall not become chargeable to the parish of Craven, or of any other County in this State, then the above obligation to be void.

Sealed and delivered	}	E. Henry	(Seal)
in presence of	}	Jno. C. Stanly	(Seal)
E. Bright		Security	(Seal)

signed by Jno. C Stanly
in presence of
J G Stanly

State of North Carolina   }
Craven County   }

Know all men by these presents that We Elizabeth Henry & John C Stanly are held and firmly bound unto his Excellency Benjamin Williams Esquire, Captain General, Governor, and Commander in Chief of the State aforesaid, in the full sum of two hundred pounds, to be paid to the said Governor or his successors in office; to the which payment well and truly to be made, we bind ourselves, our heirs, executors, and administrators, jointly and severally, firmly by these presents, sealed with our seals, and dated this **[Faded]** day of June A.D. 1808

Chapter 6: Craven County Records

The Condition of the above obligation is such, that whereas at the Court held for Craven County, at this day permission has been granted to Eliza. Henry by the said Court, to emancipate and set free a certain negro slave named Ben. Now if the said negro so permitted to be liberated shall during residence in the state of North Carolina behave himself as an honest and peaceable citizen, then the above obligation to be void.

Sealed and delivered }	E. Henry	(Seal)
in presence of }	Jno. C. Stanly	(Seal)

E. Bright
signed by JC Stanly in
presence of
J G Stanly

State of North Carolina }
Craven County }

Know all men by these presents that we Elizabeth Henry & John C Stanly are held and firmly bound to John Tillman Esquire Chairman of Craven County Court, in the sum of one hundred pounds, to be paid to the said John or his successors in office, to which payment well and truly to be made we bind ourselves, our heirs, executors, and administrators, firmly by these presents sealed with our seals and dated this 11th day of June 1808

The Condition of the above obligation is such, whereas at the Court held for Craven County, at this day permission has been granted to Elizabeth Henry by the said Court, to emancipate and set free a certain negro slave named Ben. Now if the said negro so permitted to be liberated, shall not become chargeable to the parish of Craven County, or of any other County in this State, then the above obligation to be void.

Sealed and delivered }	E. Henry	(Seal)
in presence of }	Jno. C. Stanly	(Seal)

E. Bright
signed by JC Stanly in
presence of   J G Stanly

State of North Carolina }
Craven County }

Know all men by these presents that We Elizabeth Henry & John C Stanly are held and firmly bound unto his Excellency Benjamin Williams Esquire, Captain General, Governor, and Commander in Chief of the State aforesaid, in the full sum of two hundred pounds, to be paid to the said Governor or his successors in office; to the which payment well and truly to be made, we bind ourselves, our heirs, executors, and administrators, jointly and severally, firmly by these presents, sealed with our seals, and dated this 11 day of June A.D. 1808

The Condition of the above obligation is such, that whereas at the Court held for Craven County, at this day permission has been granted to Eliza. Henry by the said Court, to emancipate and set free a certain negro slave named Rose. Now if the said negro so permitted to be liberated shall during her residence in the state of North Carolina behave herself as an honest and peaceable citizen, then the above obligation to be void.

Sealed and delivered }	E. Henry	(Seal)
in presence of }	Jno. C. Stanly	(Seal)

signed in presence of
J G Stanly by Jno C Stanly

State of North Carolina }
Craven County }

Know all men by these presents that we Elizabeth Henry & John C Stanly are held and firmly bound to John Tillman Esquire Chairman of Craven County Court, in the sum of one hundred pounds, to be paid to the said John or his successors in office, to which payment well and truly to be made we bind ourselves, our heirs, executors, and administrators, firmly by these presents sealed with our seals and dated this 11 day of June 1808

Chapter 6: Craven County Records

    The Condition of the above obligation is such, whereas at the Court held for Craven County, at this day permission has been granted to Elizabeth Henry by the said Court, to emancipate and set free a certain negro slave named Rose. Now if the said negro so permitted to be liberated, shall not become chargeable to the parish of Craven County, or of any other County in this State, then the above obligation to be void.

Sealed and delivered }	E. Henry	(Seal)
in presence of }	Jno. C. Stanly	(Seal)

E. Bright
signed by Jno C Stanly in
presence of J G Stanly

State of North Carolina }
Craven County }

Know all men by these presents that We Elizabeth Henry & John C Stanly are held and firmly bound unto his Excellency Benjamin Williams, Captain General, Governor, and Commander in Chief of the State aforesaid, in the full sum of two hundred pounds, to be paid to the said Governor or his successors in office, to the which payment well and truly to be made, we bind ourselves, our heirs, executors, and administrators, jointly and severally, firmly by these presents, sealed with our seals, and dated this 11th day of June A.D. 1808

    The Condition of the above obligation is such, that whereas at the Court held for Craven County, at this day permission has been granted to Eliza. Henry by the said Court, to emancipate and set free a certain negro slave named Peggy. Now if the said negro so permitted to be liberated shall during her residence in the state of North Carolina behave herself as an honest and peaceable citizen, then the above obligation to be void.

Sealed and delivered }	E. Henry	(Seal)
in presence of }	John C Stanly	(Seal)

E. Bright
signed by John C Stanly in
presence of J G Stanly

State of North Carolina }
Craven County }

Know all men presents by these presents that we Elizabeth Henry & John C Stanly are held and firmly bound to John Tillman Esquire Chairman of Craven County Court, in the sum of one hundred pounds, to be paid to the said John or his successors in office, to which payment well and truly to be made we bind ourselves, our heirs, executors, and administrators, firmly by these presents, sealed with our seals and dated this 11th day of June 1808

    The Condition of the above obligation is such, whereas at the Court held for Craven County, at this day permission has been granted to Elizabeth Henry to emancipate and set free a certain negro named Peggy. Now if the said negro so permitted to be liberated, shall not become chargeable to the parish of Craven County, or of any other County in this State, then the above obligation to be void..

Sealed and delivered }	E. Henry	(Seal)
in presence of }	Jno. C. Stanly	(Seal)

signed by JC Stanly
in presence of J G Stanly CC

****

State of North Carolina }
Craven County }

Chapter 6: Craven County Records

Know all men by these presents that We Lovick Jones and Asa Jones are held and firmly bound unto his Excellency William Hawkins Esquire, Captain General, Governor, and Commander in Chief of the State aforesaid, in the full sum of two hundred pounds, to be paid to the said Governor or his successors in office; to the which payment well and truly to be made, we bind ourselves, our heirs, executors, and administrators, jointly and severally, by these presents, sealed with our seals, and dated this 24 day of March A.D. 1814

    The Condition of the above obligation is such, that whereas at a Court held for Craven County, at this day permission has been granted to Lovick Jones by the saidCourt, to emancipate and set free a certain negro slave named Jeoffrey. Now if the said negro so permitted to be liberated shall during his residence in the state of North Carolina behave **[Blank]** as an honest and peaceable citizen, then the above obligation to be void.

| Sealed and delivered | } | Lovick Jones | (Seal) |
| in presence of | } | Asa Jones | (Seal) |

State of North Carolina }
Craven County }

Know all men by these presents that we Lovick Jones and Asa Jones are held and firmly bound to John F. Smith Esquire Chairman of Craven County Court, in the sum of one hundred pounds, to be paid to the said John F. Smith or his successors in office, to which payment well and truly to be made we bind ourselves, our heirs, executors, and administrators, firmly by these presents sealed with our seals and dated this 24 day of March 1814

    The Condition of the above obligation is such, whereas at the Court held for Craven County, at this day permission has been granted to Lovick Jones by the said Court, to emancipate and set free a certain negro slave named Jeoffrey. Now if the said negro so permitted to be liberated, shall not become chargeable to the parish of Craven County, or of any other County in this State, then the above obligation to be void.

| Sealed and delivered | } | Lovick Jones | (Seal) |
| in presence of | } | Asa Jones | (Seal) |

****

State of North Carolina }
Craven County }

Know all men by these presents that We Stephen L. Ferrand Catharine Chapman and William P. Ferrand are held and firmly bound unto his Excellency David Stone Esquire, Captain General, Governor, and Commander in Chief of the State aforesaid, in the full sum of two hundred pounds, to be paid to the said Governor or his successors in office; to the which payment well and truly to be made, we bind ourselves, our heirs, executors, and administrators, jointly and severally, firmly by these presents, sealed with our seals, and dated this 20 day of March A.D. 1809

    The Condition of the above obligation is such, that whereas at the Court held for Craven County, at this day permission has been granted to H.L. Chapman by the said Court, to emancipate and set free a certain negro slave named Nathan. Now if the said negro so permitted to be liberated shall during his residence in the state of North Carolina behave himself as a honest and peaceable citizen, then the above obligation to be void.

Sealed and delivered	}	Stephn. L. Ferrand	(Seal)
in presence of	}	Catharine Chapman	(Seal)
		Will. P. Ferrand	(Seal)

State of North Carolina }
Craven County }

Know all men by these presents that we Stephen L. Ferrand Catharine Chapman & William P. Ferrand are held and firmly bound to David Stone Esquire Chairman of Craven County Court, in the sum of one hundred pounds, to be paid

Chapter 6: Craven County Records

to the said David or his successors in office, to which payment well and truly to be made, we bind ourselves, our heirs, executors, and administrators, firmly by these presents sealed with our seals and dated this 20th day of March 1809

The Condition of the above obligation is such, whereas at the Court held for Craven County, at this day permission has been granted to H.L. Chapman by the said Court, to emancipate and set free a certain negro slave named Nathan. Now if the said negro so permitted to be liberated, shall not become chargeable to the parish of Craven County, or of any other County in this State, then the above obligation to be void.

Sealed and delivered	}	Stephn. L. Ferrand	(Seal)
in presence of	}	Catharine Chapman	(Seal)
		Will. P. Ferrand	(Seal)

****

State of North Carolina }
Craven County   }

Know all men by these presents that We John Bragg Adam Bautz[?] are held and firmly bound unto his Excellency David Stone Esquire, Captain General, Governor, and Commander in Chief of the State aforesaid, in the full sum of two hundred pounds, to be paid to the said Governor or his successors in office; to the which payment well and truly to be made, we bind ourselves, our heirs, executors, and administrators, jointly and severally, firmly by these presents, sealed with our seals, and dated this 18th day of December A.D. 1809

The Condition of the above obligation is such, that whereas at the Court held for Craven County, at this day permission has been granted to Hannah Arthur by the said Court, to emancipate and set free a certain negro slave named John. Now if the said negro so permitted to be liberated shall during his residence in the state of North Carolina behave himself as a honest and peaceable citizen, then the above obligation to be void.

Sealed and delivered	}	John Bragg	(Seal)
in presence of	}	Adam Bautz[?]	(Seal)
		[Faded]	(Seal)

State of North Carolina }
Craven County   }

Know all men by these presents that we John Bragg Adam Bautz[?] are held and firmly bound to John Tillman Esquire Chairman of Craven County Court, in the sum of one hundred pounds, to be paid to the said John Tillman or his successors in office, to which payment well and truly to be made we bind ourselves, our heirs, executors, and administrators, firmly by these presents sealed with our seals and dated this 18th day of December AD. 1809

The Condition of the above obligation is such, whereas at the Court held for Craven County, at this day permission has been granted to Hannah Arthur by the said Court, to emancipate and set free a certain negro slave named John. Now if the said negro so permitted to be liberated, shall not become chargeable to the parish of Craven County, or of any other County in this State, then the above obligation to br void.

| Sealed and delivered | } | John Bragg | (Seal) |
| in presence of | } | Adam Bautz[?] | (Seal) |

****

State of North Carolina }
Craven County   }

Know all men by these presents that We John Arthur and Asa Arthur are held and firmly bound unto his Excellency William Hawkins Esquire, Captain General, Governor, and Commander in Chief of the State aforesaid, in the full sum of two hundred pounds, to be paid to the said Governor or his successors in office; to the which payment well and truly

Chapter 6: Craven County Records

to be made, we bind ourselves, our heirs, executors, and administrators, jointly and severally, firmly by these presents, sealed with our seals, and dated this 13th day of June A.D. 1814

The Condition of the above obligation is such, that whereas at the Court held for Craven County, at this day permission has been granted to Jacob Burt[?] by the said Court, to emancipate and set free a certain negro slave named Penny. Now if the said negro so permitted to be liberated shall during her residence in the state of North Carolina behave herself as a honest and peaceable citizen, then the above obligation to be void.

| Sealed and delivered | } | John Arthur | (Seal) |
| in presence of | } | Asa Arthur | (Seal) |

State of North Carolina }
Craven County }

Know all men by these presents that we John Arthur and Asa Arthur are held and firmly bound to John F. Smith Esquire Chairman of Craven County Court, in the sum of one hundred pounds, to be paid to the said John F. Smith or his successors in office, to which payment well and truly to be made we bind ourselves. our heirs, executors, and administrators, firmly by these presents sealed with our seals and dated this 13 June 1814

The Condition of the above obligation is such, whereas at the Court held for Craven County, at this day permission has been granted to Jacob Burt[?] by the said Court, to emancipate and set free a certain negro slave named Penny. Now if the said negro so permitted to be liberated shall not become chargeable to the parish of Craven County, or of any other County in this State, then the above obligation to be void.

Sealed and delivered}   John C Arthur (his mark)   (Seal)
                        Asa Arthur   (Seal)

****

State of North Carolina }
Craven County }

Know all men by these presents that We Benjamin Wallace & Benners Vail are held and firmly bound unto his Excellency Benjamin Smith Esquire, Captain General, Governor, and Commander in Chief of the State aforesaid, in the full sum of two hundred pounds, to be paid to the said Governor or his successors in office; to the which payment well and truly to be made, we bind ourselves, our heirs, executors, and administrators, jointly and severally, firmly by these presents, sealed with our seals, and dated this 10 day of July A.D. 1812

The Condition of the above obligation is such, that whereas at the Court held for Craven County, at this day permission has been granted to Benj Wallace by the said Court, to emancipate and set free a certain negro slave named **[Blank]**. Now if the said negro so permitted to be liberated shall during his residence in the state of North Carolina behave himself as a honest ans peaceable citizen, then the above obligation to be void.

| Sealed and delivered | } | Benjamin Wallace | (Seal) |
| in presence of | } | B Vail | (Seal) |

State of North Carolina }
Craven County }

Know all men by these presents that we Benjamin Wallace & Benners Vail are held and firmly bound to John F. Smith Esquire Chairman of Craven County Court, in the sum of one hundred pounds, to be paid to the said John F. Smith or his successors in office, to which payment well and truly to be made we bind ourselves, our heirs, executors, and administrators, firmly by these presents sealed with our seals and dated this 10 day of July 1812

Chapter 6: Craven County Records

The Condition of the above obligation is such, whereas at the Court held for Craven County, at this day permission has been granted to Benj Wallace by the said Court, to emancipate and set free a certain negro slave named **[Blank]**. Now if the said negro so permitted to be liberated, shall not become chargeable to the parish of Craven County, or of any other County in this State, then the above obligation to be void.

| Sealed and delivered | } | Benjamin Wallace | (Seal) |
| in presence of | } | B. Vail | (Seal) |

****

State of North Carolina }
Craven County }

Know all men by these presents that We John J McLin and James Luydam are held and firmly bound unto his Excellency William Hawkins Esquire, Captain General, Governor, and Commander in Chief of the State aforesaid, in the full sum of two hundred pounds, to be paid to the said Governor or his successors in office; to the which payment well and truly to be made, we bind ourselves, our heirs, executors, and administrators, jointly and severally, firmly by these presents, sealed with our seals, and dated this twelfth day of June A.D. 1812

The Condition of the above obligation is such, that whereas at the Court held for Craven County, at this day permission has been granted to John J McLin by the said Court, to emancipate and set free a certain negro slave named Sally Now if the said negro so permitted to be liberated shall during her residence in the state of North Carolina behave **[Blank]** as an honest and peaceable citizen, then the above obligation to be void.

| Sealed and delivered | } | Jno. J. McLin | (Seal) |
| in presence of | } | James Luydam | (Seal) |

State of North Carolina }
Craven County }

Know all men by these presents that we John J McLin and James Luydam are held and firmly bound to John F. Smith Esquire Chairman of Craven County Court, in the sum of one hundred pounds, to be paid to the said John F.Smith or his successors in office, to which payment well and truly to be made we bind ourselves, our heirs, executors, and administrators, firmly by these presents sealed with our seals and dated this 12th day of June 1812

The Condition of the above obligation is such, whereas at the Court held for Craven County, at this day permission has been granted to John J McLin by the said Court, to emancipate and set free a certain negro slave named Sally Now if the said negro so permitted to be liberated, shall not become chargeable to the parish of Craven County, or of any other County in this State, then the above obligation to be void.

| Sealed and delivered | } | Jno. J. McLin | (Seal) |
| in presence of | } | James Luydam | (Seal) |

****

State of North Carolina }
Craven County }

Know all men by these presents that We John Oliver and William W. Oliver are held and firmly bound unto his Excellency William Hawkins Esquire, Captain General, Governor, and Commander in Chief of the State aforesaid, in the full sum of two hundred pounds, to be paid to the said Governor or his successors in office; to the which payment well and truly to be made, we bind ourselves, our heirs, executors, and administrators, jointly and severally, firmly by these presents, sealed with our seals, and dated this second day of March A.D. 1814

Chapter 6: Craven County Records

The Condition of the above obligation is such, that whereas at the Court held for Craven County, at this day permission has been granted to John [?] Oliver by the said Court, to emancipate and set free a certain negro slave named Thomas [Faded] Now if the said negro so permitted to be liberated shall during his residence in the state of North Carolina behave [Faded] as a honest and peaceable citizen, then the above obligation to be void.

Sealed and delivered	}	Jno Oliver	(Seal)
in presence of	}	Wm. W. Oliver	(Seal)
Joseph Oliver			

State of North Carolina }
Craven County }

Know all men by these presents that we John Oliver and William W. Oliver are held and firmly bound to John F. Smith Esquire Chairman of Craven County Court, in the sum of one hundred pounds, to be paid to the said John or his successors in office, to which payment well and truly to be made we bind ourselves, our heirs, executors, and administrators, firmly by these presents sealed with our seals and dated this 12th day of March 1814

The Condition of the above obligation is such, whereas at the Court held for Craven County, at this day has been granted permission to John Oliver by the said Court, to emancipate and set free a certain negro slave named Thomas K Green[Greer?] Now if the said negro so permitted to be liberated, shall not become chargeable to the parish of Craven County, or of any other County in this State, then the above obligation to be void.

Sealed and delivered	}	Jno. Oliver	(Seal)
in presence of	}	Wm. W. Oliver	(Seal)
Joseph Oliver			

****

State of North Carolina }
Craven County }

Know all men by these presents that We Abner Hargett and Alfred Hargett are held and firmly bound unto his Excellency William Hawkins Esquire, Captain General, Governor, and Commander in Chief of the State aforesaid, in the full sum of two hundred pounds, to be paid to the said Governor or his successors in office; to the which payment well and truly to be made, we bind ourselves, our heirs, executors, and administrators, jointly and severally, firmly by these presents, sealed with our seals, and dated this tenth day of March A.D. 1812

The Condition of the above obligation is such, that whereas at the Court held for Craven County, at this day permission has been granted to Abner Hargett by the said Court, to emancipate and set free a certain negro slave named Peter Now if the said slave so permitted to be liberated shall during his residence in the state of North Carolina behave [Blank] as an honest and peaceable citizen, then the above obligation to be void.

Sealed and delivered	}	Abner Hargett	(Seal)
in presence of	}	Alfred Hargett	(Seal)
J G Stanly			

State of North Carolina }
Craven County }

Know all men by these presents that we Abner Hargett and Alfred Hargett are held and firmly bound to Jno F Smith Esquire Chairman of Craven County Court, in the sum of one hundred pounds, to be paid to the said John F Smith or his successors in office, to which payment well and truly to be made we bind ourselves, our heirs, executors, and administrators, firmly by these presents sealed with our seals and dated this 10th day of March AD 1812

Chapter 6: Craven County Records

The Condition of the above obligation is such, whereas at the Court held for Craven County, at this day permission has been granted to Abner Hargett by the said Court, to emancipate and set free a certain negro slave named Peter Now if the said negro so permitted to be liberated, shall not become chargeable to the parish of Craven County, or of any other County in this State, then the above obligation to be void.

Sealed and delivered }	Abner Hargett	(Seal)
in presence of }	Alfred Hargett	(Seal)
J G Stanly		

****

State of North Carolina }
Craven County }

Know all men by these presents that We John F Smith and Donum Mumford are held and firmly bound unto his Excellency Benjamin Smith Esquire, Captain General, Governor, and Commander in Chief of the State aforesaid, in the full sum of two hundred pounds, to be paid to the said Governor or his successors in office; to the which payment well and truly to be made, we bind ourselves, our heirs, executors, and administrators, jointly and severally, firmly by these presents, sealed with our seals, and dated this twentieth day of April A.D. 1811

The Condition of the above obligation is such, that whereas at the Court held for Craven County, at this day permission has been granted to John F Smith by the said Court, to emancipate and set free a certain negro slave named Douglas Now if the said negro so permitted to be liberated shall during his residence in the state of North Carolina behave himself as a honest and peaceable citizen, then the above obligation to be void.

Sealed and delivered	Jn. F. Smith	(Seal)
in presence of }	his	
	Donum X Mumford	(Seal)
	mark	

State of North Carolina }
Craven County }

Know all men by these presents that we John F Smith and Donum Mumford are held and firmly bound to Stephen Harris Esquire Chairman of Craven County Court, in the sum of one hundred pounds, to be paid to the said Stephen Harris or his successors in office, to which payment well and truly to be made we bind ourselves, our heirs, executors, and administrators, firmly by these presents sealed with our seals and dated this 20th day of April 1811

The Condition of the above obligation is such, whereas at the Court held for Craven County, at this day permission has been granted to John F. Smith by the said Court, to emancipate and set free a certain negro slave named Douglas Now if the said negro so permitted to be liberated shall not become chargeable to the parish of Craven County, or of any other County in this State, then the above obligation to be void.

Sealed and delivered	Jn. F. Smith	(Seal)
in presence of }	his	
	Donum X Mumford	(Seal)
	mark	

****

State of North Carolina }
Craven County }

Know all men by these presents that We Sacker Dubberly and Leonard Loftin are held and firmly bound unto his Excellency William Hawkins Esquire, Captain General, Governor, and Commander in Chief of the State aforesaid, in

Chapter 6: Craven County Records

the full sum of two hundred pounds, to be paid to the said Governor or his successors in office; to the which payment well and truly to be made, we bind ourselves, our heirs, executors, and administrators, jointly and severally, firmly by these presents, sealed with our seals, and dated this nineteenth day of March A.D. 1814

The Condition of the above obligation is such, that whereas at the Court held for Craven County, at this day permission has been granted to Sacker Dubberly by the said Court, to emancipate and set free a certain negro slave named Cannon Now if the said slave so permitted to be liberated shall during his residence in the state of North Carolina behave [Blank] as a honest and peaceable citizen, then the above obligation to be void.

| Sealed and delivered | } | Sacker Dubberly | (Seal) |
| in presence of | } | Leonard Loftin | (Seal) |

State of North Carolina }
Craven County }

Know all men by these presents that we Sacker Dubberly and Leonard Loftin are held and firmly bound to John F. Smith Esquire Chairman of Craven County Court, in the sum of one hundred pounds, to be paid to the said John F Smith or his successors in office, to which payment well and truly to be made we bind ourselves, our heirs, executors, and administrators, firmly by these presents sealed with our seals and dated this 19 day of March 1814

The Condition of the above obligation is such, whereas at the Court held for Craven County, at this day permission has been granted to Sacker Dubberly by the said Court, to emancipate and set free a certain negro slave named Cannon Now if the said negro so permitted to be liberated, shall not become chargeable to the parish of Craven County, or of any other County in this State, then the above obligation to be void.

| Sealed and delivered | } | Sacker Dubberly | (Seal) |
| in presence of | } | Leonard Loftin | (Seal) |

State of North Carolina }
Craven County }

Know all men by these presents that We Sacker Dubberly are held and firmly bound unto his Excellency William Hawkins Esquire, Captain General, Governor, and Commander in Chief of the State aforesaid, in the full sum of two hundred pounds, to be paid to the said Governor or his successors in office; to the which payment well and truly to be made, we bind ourselves, our heirs, executors, and administrators, jointly and severally, firmly by these presents, sealed with our seals, and dated this thirtieth day of August 1814

The Condition of the above obligation is such, that whereas at a Court held for Craven County, at this day permission has been granted to Sacker Dubberly by the said Court, to emancipate and set free a certain negro slave named Cannon Now if the said negro so permitted to be liberated shall during his residence in the state of North Carolina behave [Blank] as a honest and peaceable citizen, then the above obligation to be void.

| Sealed and delivered | } | Sacker Dubberly | (Seal) |
| in presence of | } | | |

State of North Carolina }
Craven County }

Know all men by these presents that we Sacker Dubberly are held and firmly bound to John F Smith Esquire Chairman of Craven County Court, in the sum of one hundred pounds, to be paid to the said John F Smith or his successors in office, to which payment well and truly to be made we bind ourselves, our heirs, executors, and administrators, firmly by these presents sealed with our seals and dated this 30th day of August 1814

Chapter 6: Craven County Records

The Condition of the above obligation is such, whereas at the Court held for Craven County, at this day permission has been granted to Sacker Dubberly by the said Court, to emancipate and set free a certain negro slave named Cannon Now if the said negro so permitted to be liberated, shall not become chargeable to the parish of Craven County, or of any other County in this State, then the above obligation to be void.

| Sealed and delivered } | Sacker Dubberly | (Seal) |
| in presence of } | | |

****

State of North Carolina }
Craven County }

Know all men by these presents that We Daniel Carthy and John C. Stanly are held and firmly bound unto his Excellency William Hawkins Esquire, Captain General, Governor, and Commander in Chief of the State aforesaid, in the full sum of two hundred pounds, to be paid to the said Governor or his successors in office; to the which payment well and truly to be made, we bind ourselves, our heirs, executors, and administrators, jointly and severally, firmly by these presents, sealed with our seals, and dated this twelfth day of June 1812

The Condition of the above obligation is such, that whereas at the Court held for Craven County, at this day permission has been granted to John C Stanly by the said Court, to emancipate and set free a certain negro slave named Bunyer Now if the said negro so permitted to be liberated shall during her residence in the state of North Carolina behave [Blank] as an honest and peaceable citizen, then the above obligation to be void.

Sealed and delivered }	Dan Carthy	(Seal)
in presence of }	P Kean	(Seal)
Elizabeth Carthy		
Catharine Carthy		

State of North Carolina }
Craven County }

Know all men by these presents that we Daniel Carthy & John C. Stanly are held and firmly bound to John F Smith Esquire Chairman of Craven County Court, in the sum of one hundred pounds, to be paid to the said John F Smith or his successors in office, to which payment well and truly to be made we bind ourselves, our heirs, executors, and administrators, firmly by these presents sealed with our seals and dated this 12th day of June AD 1812

The Condition of the above obligation is such, whereas at the Court held for Craven County, at this day permission has been granted to John C Stanly by the said Court, to emancipate and set free a certain negro slave named Bunyer Now if the said negro so permitted to be liberated, shall not become chargeable to the parish of Craven County, or of any other County in this State, then the above obligation to be void.

Sealed and delivered }	Danl. Carthy	(Seal)
in presence of }	P Kean	(Seal)
Elizabeth Carthy		
Catharine Carthy		

****

The Subscribers have been many years acquainted with Reuben Callaway, a free man of color and his wife Ruth. They are industrious, honest and sober people. Reuben has a freehold and considerable other property. His wife is his slave, and he is desirous to have her emancipated, We recommend her as a deserving woman and believe no injury will result

Chapter 6: Craven County Records

to the public from her emancipation. Ruth has no child by Reuben & has not had a child for twenty years. Craven County   March 1815

David Lewis	David **[Faded]**
Wm R Street	Norman Willis
Samuel Caspillis[?]	Major Willis
Adam Gaskin	Richd Willis
Elijah Callaway	Aaron Ernul
John Whitford	W. Handcock
Elijah Clark	Abner Pearce
Levi Rees	John Justice
M. E Stephens	R P Jones
John Green	

Reuben Callaway humbly begs permission of the Court to emancipate the woman Ruth named in the above recommendation for her meritorious services
Reuben Callaway by
J. Stanly his atto.

State of North Carolina }
Craven County   }

Know all men by these presents that We Reuben Callaway David Whitford and Abner Pearce are held and firmly bound unto his Excellency William **[Faded]** Esquire, Captain General, Governor, and Commander in Chief of the State aforesaid, in the full sum of two hundred pounds, to be paid to the said Governor or his successors in office; to the which payment well and truly to be made, we bind ourselves, our heirs, executors, and administrators, jointly and severally, firmly by these presents, sealed with our seals, and dated this thirteenth day of March A.D. 1815

The Condition of the above obligation is such, that whereas at the Court held for Craven County, at this day permission has been granted to Reuben Callaway by the said Court, to emancipate and set free a certain negro slave named Ruth Now if the said negro so permitted to be liberated shall during her residence in the state of North Carolina behave **[Blank]** as a honest and peaceable citizen, then the above obligation to be void.

Sealed and delivered	}	Reuben Callaway	(Seal)
in presence of	}	D Whitford	(Seal)
John Jones		Abner Pearce	(Seal)

State of North Carolina }
Craven County   }

Know all men by these presents that we Reuben Callaway David Whitford and Abner Pearce are held and firmly bound to John F Smith Esquire Chairman of Craven County Court, in the sum of one hundred pounds, to be paid to the said John or his successors in office, to which payment well and truly to be made we bind ourselves, our heirs, executors, and administrators, firmly by these presents, sealed with our seals and dated this 13th day of March 1815

The Condition of the above obligation is such, whereas at the Court held for Craven County, at this day permission has been granted to Reuben Callaway by the said Court, to emancipate and set free a certain negro slave named Ruth Now if the said negro so permitted to be liberated, shall not become chargeable to the parish of Craven County, or of any other County in this State, then the above obligation to be void.

Sealed and delivered	}	Reuben Callaway	(Seal)
in presence of	}	D. Whitford	(Seal)
John Jones		Abner Pearce	(Seal)

Chapter 6: Craven County Records

****

To the Worshipful Justices of Craven County Court
    The petition of Reuben Callaway humbly sheweth that he is owner of a woman slave named Judey, whose meritorious services he desires to reward by emancipation - He prays the license of your Worships to set her free upon her giving the bonds & Security required by law.

Sept: Term 1817
J Stanly for Petitioner

State of North Carolina   }
Craven County   }

Know all men by these presents that We Reuben Callaway Hezekiah Willis & Elijah Callaway are held and firmly bound unto his Execllency William Miller Esquire, Captain General, Governor, and Commander in Chief of the State aforesaid, in the full sum of two hundred pounds, to be paid to the said Governor or his successors in office; to the which payment well and truly to be made, we bind ourselves, our heirs, and administrators, jointly and severally, firmly by these presents, sealed with our seals, and dated this 12 day of September A.D. 1817

    The Condition of the above obligation is such, that whereas at the Court held for Craven County, at this day permission has been granted to Reubin Callaway by the said Court, to emancipate and set free a certain negro slave named Judey Now if the said negro so permitted to be liberated shall during her residence in the state of North Carolina behave **[Blank]** as an honest and peaceable citizen, then the above obligation to be void.

Sealed and delivered	}	Reuben Callaway	(Seal)
in presence of	}	Hezekiah Willis	(Seal)
Test Evan Jones		Elijah Callaway	(Seal)

Know all men by these presents that we Reuben Callaway Hezekiah Willis & Elijah Callaway are held and firmly bound to John F Smith or his successors in office, to which payment well and truly to be made we bind ourselves, our heirs, and administrators, firmly by these presents sealed with our seals and dated this 12 day of September 1817

    The Condition of the above obligation is such, whereas at the Court held for Craven County, at this day permission has been granted to Reuben Callaway by the said Court, to emancipate and set free a certain negro slave named Judey Now if the said negro so permitted to be liberated, shall not become chargeable to the parish of Craven County, or of any other County in this State, then the above obligation to be void.

Sealed and delivered	}	Reubin Callaway	(Seal)
in presence of	}	Hezekiah Willis	(Seal)
Test Evan Jones		Elijah Callaway	(Seal)

****

State of North Carolina   }
Craven County   }

Know all men by these presents that We William Holland & Joseph Brittain are held and firmly bound unto his Excellency William Miller Esquire, Captain General, Governor, and Commander in Chief of the State aforesaid, in the full sum of two hundred pounds, to be paid to the said Governor or his successors in office; to the which payment well and truly to be made, we bind ourselves, our heirs, executors, and administrators, jointly and severally, firmly by these presents, sealed with our seals, and dated this 11th day of September A.D. 1817

    The Condition of the above obligation is such, that whereas at the Court held for Craven County, at this day permission has been granted to William Holland by the said Court, to emancipate and set free a certain negro slave

Chapter 6: Craven County Records

named Caesar Now if the said negro so permitted to be liberated shall during his residence in the state of North Carolina behave [Blank] as an honest and peaceable citizen, then the above obligation to be void.

Sealed and delivered	}	William Holland	(Seal)
in presence of	}	Jos. Brittain	(Seal)
J G Stanly			

State of North Carolina }
Craven County }

Know all men by these presents that we William Holland & Joseph Brittain are held and firmly bound to John F Smith Esquire Chairman of Craven County Court, in the full sum of one hundred pounds, to be paid to the said John F Smith or his successors in office, to which payment well and truly to be made we bind ourselves, our heirs, and administrators, firmly by these presents sealed with our seals and dated this 11 day of Septr. 1817

  The Condition of the above obligation is such, whereas at the Court held for Craven County, at this day permission has been granted to William Holland by the said Court, to emancipate and set free a certain negro slave named Caesar Now if the said slave so permitted to be liberated shall not become chargeable to the parish of Craven County, or of any other County in this State, then the above obligation to be void.

Sealed and delivered	}	William Holland	(Seal)
in presence of	}	Jos. Brittain	(Seal)
J G Stanly			

****

State of North Carolina }
Craven County }

Know all men by these presents that We Asa Jones and Frederick Jones are held and firmly bound unto his Excellency John Branch Esquire, Captain General, Governor, and Commander in Chief of the State aforesaid, in the full sum of two hundred pounds, to be paid to the said Governor or his successors in office; to the which payment well and truly to be made, we bind ourselves, our heirs, executors, and administrators, jointly and severally, firmly by these presents, sealed with our seals, and dated this twelfth day of March A.D. 1818

  The Condition of the above obligation is such, that whereas at the Court held for Craven County, at this day permission has been granted to Asa Jones Exr. of Lovick Jones by the said Court, to emancipate and set free a certain negro slave named Robbin Now if the said negro so permitted to be liberated shall during his residence in the state of North Carolina behave [Blank] as an honest and peaceable citizen, then the above obligation to be void

| Sealed and delivered | } | Asa Jones | (Seal) |
| in presence of | } | Fredk. Jones | (Seal) |

State of North Carolina }
Craven County }

Know all men by these presents that we Asa Jones and Frederick Jones are held and firmly bound to John F Smith Esquire Chairman of Craven County Court, in the sum of one hundred pounds, to be paid to the said John F Smith or his successors in office, to which payment well and truly to be made we bind ourselves, our heirs, executors, and administrators, firmly by these presents sealed with our seals and dated this 12 day of March 1818

  The Condition of the above obligation is such, whereas at the Court held for Craven County, at this day permission has been granted to Asa Jones Exr. of Lovick Jones by the said Court, to emancipate and set free a certain

Chapter 6: Craven County Records

negro slave named Robbin Now if the said negro so permitted to be liberated, shall not become chargeable to the parish of Craven County or of any other County in this State, then the above obligation to be void.

| Sealed and delivered | } | Asa Jones | (Seal) |
| in presence of | } | Fredk. Jones | (Seal) |

****

State of North Carolina }
Craven County }

Know all men by these presents that We John C Stanley[Marked through] Tho. Mclin & Elijah Scott are held and firmly bound unto his Excellency William Miller Esquire, Captain General, Governor, and Commander in Chief of the State aforesaid, in the full sum of two hundred pounds, to be paid to the said Governor or his successors in office; to the which payment well and truly to be made, we bind ourselves, our heirs, executors, and administrators, jointly and severally, firmly by these presents, sealed with our seals, and dated this 11 day of June A.D. 1817

    The Condition of the above obligation is such, that whereas at the Court held for Craven County, at this day permission has been granted to John C Stanly & Elijah Scott by the said Court, to emancipate and set free a certain negro slave named Saphey Now if the said negro so permitted to be liberated shall during her residence in the state of North Carolina behave **[Blank]** as an honest and peaceable citizen, then the above obligation to be void.

| Sealed and delivered | } | Thomas Mclin[?] | (Seal) |
| in presence of | } | Elijah Scott | (Seal) |

State of North Carolina }
Craven County }

Know all men by these presents that we John C Stanly[Marked Through] Thomas McLin and Elijah Scott are held and firmly bound to John F Smith Esquire Chairman of Craven County Court, in the sum of one hundred pounds, to be paid to the said John F Smith or his successors in office, to which payment well and truly to be made we bind ourselves, our heirs, executors, and administrators, firmly by these presents sealed with our seals and dated this 11 day of June AD 1817

    The Condition of the above obligation is such, whereas at the Court held for Craven County, at this day permission has been granted to Jno C Stanly & Elijah Scott by the said Court, to emancipate and set free a certain negro slave named Saphey Now if the said negro so permitted to be liberated, shall not become chargeable to the parish of Craven County, or of any other County in this State, then the above obligation to be void.

| Sealed and delivered | } | Thomas McLin[?] | (Seal) |
| in presence of | } | Elijah Scott | (Seal) |

****

State of North Carolina }
Craven County }

Know all men by these presents that We Joseph Wallace Thomas Grace & Thomas Casey are held and firmly bound unto his Excellency William Miller Esquire, Captain General, Governor, and Commander in Chief of the State aforesaid, in the full sum of two hundred pounds, to be paid to the said Governor or his successors in office; to the which payment well and truly to be made, we bind ourselves, our heirs, executors, and administrators, jointly and severall, firmly by these presents, sealed with our seals, and dated this eleventh day of June A.D. 1817

Chapter 6: Craven County Records

The Condition of the above obligation is such, that whereas at the Court held for Craven County, at this day permission has been granted to Joseph Wallace by the said Court, to emancipate and set free a certain negro slave named Simon Now if the said negro so permitted to be liberated, shall during his residence in the State of North Carolina behave **[Blank]** as an honest and peaceable citizen, then the above obligation to be void.

Sealed and delivered	}	Joseph Wallace	(Seal)
in presence of	}	Thos Grace	(Seal)
		Thomas Casey	(Seal)

State of North Carolina }
Craven County }

Know all men by these presents that we Joseph Wallace Thomas Grace & Thomas Casey are held and firmly bound to John F Smith Esquire Chairman of Craven County Court, in the sum of one hundred pounds, to be paid to the said John F Smith or his successors in office, to which payment well and truly to be made we bind ourselves, our heirs, executors, and administrators, firmly by these presents sealed with our seals and dated this 11 day of June 1817

The Condition of the above obligation is such, whereas at the Court held for Craven County, at this day permission has been granted to Joseph Wallace by the said Court, to emancipate and set free a certain negro slave named Simon Now if the said negro so permitted to be liberated, shall not become chargeable to the parish of Craven, or of any other County in this State, then the above obligation to be void.

Sealed and delivered	}	Joseph Wallace	(Seal)
in presence of	}	Thos Grace	(Seal)
		Thomas Casey	(Seal)

****

State of North Carolina }
Craven County }

Know all men by these presents that We Donnum Montford are held and firmly bound unto his Excellency James Iredell Esquire, Captain General, Governor, and Commander in Chief of the State aforesaid, in the full sum of two hundred pounds, to be paid to the said Governor or his successors in office; to the which payment well and truly to be made, we bind ourselves, our heirs, executors, and administrators, jointly and severally, firmly by these presents, sealed with our seals, and dated this 29th day of February A.D. 1828

The Condition of the above obligation is such, that whereas at the Court held for Craven County, at this day permission has been granted to Donnum Montford by the said Court, to emancipate and set free a certain negro slave named Nelson Now if the said negro so permitted to be liberated shall during his residence in the State of North Carolina behave **[Blank]** as an honest and peaceable citizen, then the above obligation to be void.

Sealed an delivered	}	his	
in presence of	}	Donnum X Montford	(Seal)
Jno. Stewart Stanly		mark	
		[?]	(Seal)

State of North Carolina }
Craven County }

Know all men by these presents that we Donnum Montford are held and firmly bound to John F Smith Esquire Chairman of Craven County Court, in the sum of one hundred pounds, to be paid to the said John F Smith or his

Chapter 6: Craven County Records

successors in office, to which payment well and truly to be made we bind ourselves, our heirs, executors, and administrators, firmly by these presents sealed with our seals and dated this 29th day of February 1828

The Condition of the above obligation is such, whereas at the Court held for Craven County, at this day permission has been granted to Donnum Montford by the said Court, to emancipate and set free a certain negro slave named Nelson Now if the said negro so permitted to be liberated, shall not become chargeable to the parish of Craven County, or of any other County in this State, then the above obligation to be void.

Sealed and delivered	}	his	
in presence of	}	Donnum X Montford	(Seal)
		mark	
Jno Stewart Stanly		**[Faded]**	(Seal)

****

State of North Carolina }
Craven County }

Know all men by these presents that We John C Stanly & **[Faded]** are held and firmly bound unto his Excellency James Iredell Esquire, Captain General, Governor, and Commander in Chief of the State aforesaid, in the full sum of two hundred pounds, to be paid to the said Governor or his successors in office; to the which payment well and truly to be made, we bind ourselves, our heirs, executors, and administrators, jointly and severally, firmly by these presents, sealed with our seals, and dated this 28th day of October A.D. 1828

The Condition of the above obligation is such, that whereas at the Court held for Craven County, at this day permission has been granted to John C Stanly by the said Court, to emancipate and set free a certain negro slave named Peggy Now if the said negro so permitted to be liberated shall during her residence in the state of North Carolina behave **[Blank]** as a honest and peaceable citizen, then the above obligation to be void.

Sealed and delivered	}	J Stanly	(Seal)
in presence of	}	Jno C Stanly	(Seal)
[Faded]			

State of North Carolina }
Craven County }

Know all men by these presents that we John Stanly **[Faded]** are held and firmly bound to John F Smith Esquire Chairman of Craven County Court, in the sum of one hundred pounds, to be paid to the said John F Smith or his successors in office, to which payment well and truly to be made we bind ourselves, our heirs, executors, and administrators, firmly by these presents sealed with our seals and dated this 28 day of October 1828

The Condition of the above obligation is such, whereas at the Superior Court held for Craven County, at this day permission has been granted to **[Faded]** by the said Court, to emancipate and set free a certain negro slave named Peggy Now if the said negro so permitted to be liberated, shall not become chargeable to the parish of Craven County, or of any other County in this State, then the above obligation to be void.

Sealed and delivered	}	J Stanly	(Seal)
in presence of	}	Jno C Stanly	(Seal)
[Faded]			

****

State of North Carolina }
Craven County }

Chapter 6: Craven County Records

Know all men by these presents, that we Charles Gerock and John Snead are held and firmly bound unto his Excellency John Owen Esquire, Captain General, Governor, and Commander in Chief of the State aforesaid in the full sum of two hundred pounds, to be paid to the said Givernor or his successors in office, to the which payment well and truly to be made, we bind ourselves, our heirs, executors, and administrators, jointly and severally, firmly by these presents: Sealed with our seals, and dated this second day of November A.D. 1827[?]

The Condition of the above obligation is such, that whereas at the Court held for Craven County, at this day permission has been granted to Charles Gerock by the said Court to emancipate and set free a certain negro slave named Jenny Now if the said negro so permitted to be liberated, shall during her residence in the State of North Carolina, behave as an honest and peaceable citizen, then the above obligation to be void. Sealed and delivered in presence of

	Chas. Gerock	(Seal)
Abner Pasteur	Jno Snead	(Seal)

State of North Carolina }
Craven County }

Know all men by these presents, that we Charles Gerock and John Snead are held and firmly bound to John F Smith Esquire, Chairman of Craven County Court, in the sum of one hundred pounds, to be paid to the said John F Smith or his successors in office, to which payment well and truly to be made, we bind ourselves, our heirs, executors and administrators, firmly by these presents; sealed with our seals, and dated this 2nd day of November A.D. 1827[?]

The Condition of the above obligation is such, that whereas at the Court held for Craven County, at this day permission has been granted to Charles Gerock by the said Court, to emancipate and set free a certain negro named Jenny Now if the said negro so permitted to be liberated, shall not become chargeable to the Parish of Craven County, or of any other County in this State then the above obligation to be void. Sealed and delivered in presence of

	Chas. Gerock	(Seal)
Abner Pasteur	Jno. Snead	(Seal)

****

State of North Carolina }
Craven County }

Know all men by these presents that We John R Donnell are held and firmly bound unto his Excellency William Miller Esquire, Captain General, Governor, and Commander in Chief of the State aforesaid, in the full sum of two hundred pounds, to be paid to the said Governor or his successors in office; to the which payment well and truly to be made, we bind ourselves, our heirs, executors, and administrators, jointly and severally, firmly by these presents, sealed with our seals, and dated this 15th day of September A.D. 1816

The Condition of the above obligation is such, that whereas at the Court held for Craven County, at this day permission has been granted to Will. Blackledge Admnr. with will annexed of Mary Jones Spaight by the said Court, to emancipate and set free a certain negro slave named Sarah. Now if the said negro so permitted to be liberated shall during her residence in the State of North Carolina behave as an honest and peaceable citizen, then the above obligation to be void.

Sealed and delivered }	Jn Donnell	(Seal)
in presence of }		
B.C. Gillespie		

State of North Carolina }

Chapter 6: Craven County Records

Craven County   }

Know all men by these presents that we John R Donnell are held and firmly bound to John F Smith Esquire Chairman of Craven County Court, in the sum of one hundred pounds, to be paid to the said John F Smith or his successors in office, to which payment well and truly to be made we bind ourselves, our heirs, executors, and administrators, firmly by these presents sealed with our seals and dated this 15th day of September AD 1816

    The Condition of the above obligation is such, whereas at the Court held for Craven County, at this day permission has been granted to Will. Blackledge Admnr with will annexed of Mary Jones Spaight by the said Court, to emancipate and set free a certain negro slave named Sarah. Now if the said negro so permitted to be liberated, shall not become chargeable to the parish of Craven County, or of any other County in this State, then the above obligation to be void.

Sealed and delivered   }   Jn Donnell   (Seal)
B.C. Gillespie

****

State of North Carolina   }
Craven County   }

Know all men by these presents, that we John W. Guion, John R. Green are held and firmly bound unto his Excellency John Owen Esquire, Captain General, Governor, and Commander in Chief of the State aforesaid, in the full sum of two hundred pounds, to be paid to the said Governor or his successors in office; to the which payment well and truly to be made, we bind ourselves, our heirs, executors and administrators, jointly and severally, firmly by these presents; sealed with our seals, and dated this 28th day of November A.D. 1829

    The Condition of the above obligation is such, that whereas at the Court held for Craven County, at this day permission has been granted to John W. Guion by the said Court, to emancipate and set free a certain negro slave named Boston Fr[?]uson Now if the said negro so permitted to be liberated, shall during his residence in the State of North Carolina, behave as an honest and peaceable citizen, then the above obligation to be void.

Sealed and delivered in presence of   Jno. W. Guion   (Seal)
                                            John R. Green   (Seal)

State of North Carolina   }
Craven County   }

Know all men by these presents, that we John W Guion   John R Green are held and firmly bound to John F Smith Esquire, Chairman of Craven County Court, in the sum of one hundred pounds, to be paid to the said John F Smith Chairman or his successors in office, to which payment well and truly to be made, we bind ourselves, our heirs, executors and administrators, firmly by these presents; sealed with our seals, and dated this 28th day of November A.D. 1829

    The Condition of the above obligation is such, that whereas at the Court held for Craven County, at this day permission has been granted to John W. Guion by the said Court, to emancipate and set free a certain negro slave named Boston Fr[?]uson Now if the said negro so permitted to be liberated, shall not become chargeable to the Parish of Craven County, or of any other County in this State, then the above obligation to be void.

Sealed and delivered in presence of   Jno. W. Guion   (Seal)
                                            John R. Green   (Seal)

****

Chapter 6: Craven County Records

State of North Carolina }
Craven County   }

Know all men by these presents that We John C Stanly and John Clark Jr are held & firmly bound unto his Excellency Benjamin Williams Esq. Captain General Governor and Commander in Chief of the State aforesaid in the full sum of two hundred pounds, to be paid to the said Governor or his successors in Office to the which payment Well & truly to be made We bind ourselves our heirs executors and administrators jointly & severally firmly by these presents Sealed with our Seals & dated this 10th day of Decr. 1807

The Condition of the above obligation is such that Whereas leave Was granted to John C Stanly at December Term 1807 [Faded] Craven County Court to emancipate a Male Mulatto slave the property of said John C Stanly named John now if the said John shall hereafter demean himself in an orderly & peaceable manner then the above obligation to be void.

Signed Sealed &   }   Jno. C Stanly   (Seal)
delivered in presence of }   John Clark Jnr.   (Seal)
J G Stanly

****

To the Worshipfull the Justices of Craven County Court.
The Petition of Francis Hawks respectfully sheweth, That he is the owner of a negro woman slave named Pomona, formerly the property of Elizabeth Howard -- That he is desirous to reward the long & meritorious services of the said Pomona, with emancipation, & prays the license of this Worshipfull Court for that purpose.

June Term 1811
J. Stanly atto
for Petr.

****

To the Worshipfull the Justices of Craven County Court.
The Petition of Robert Lisbon a free man of color respectfully sheweth, that from the fruits of hard labor & honest industry he has been able to purchase his daughter Myrtylla his only child who was the slave of Frederick Divoux - He is anxious to secure to this daughter the blessing of liberty, which he confidently believes she will be found to deserve for her meritorious services & good conduct. For her character he fefers the Court to the accompanying testimonial & humbly prays he may be permitted to emancipate her upon giving the bond required by law.

Robt. Lisbon
granted   J. Stanly his atto

The Subscribers are acquainted with the girl Myrtilla the daughter of Robert Lisbon, whom he wishes to emancipate: they recommend her as industrious, honest & sober.   September 13. 1813

Fr. Divoux
Michl H. Lente
V Allen
Wm Laurence
Thomas Wadsworth
M.C Stephens
E. Henry
A. Ellis
John Jones
Stepn. B. Forbes

Chapter 6: Craven County Records

Jno. S. Mclin
John Justice

State of North Carolina }
Craven County }

Know all men by these presents that We Robert Lisbon Asa Jones and Frederick Divoux are held and firmly bound unto his Excellency William Hawkins Esquire, Captain General, Governor, and Commander in Chief of the State aforesaid, in the full sum of two hundred pounds, to be paid to the said Governor or his successors in office; to the which payment well and truly to be made, we bind ourselves, our heirs, executors, and administrators, jointly and severall, firmly by these presents, sealed with our seals, and dated this 31 day of December A.D. 1813

The Condition of the above obligation is such, that whereas at the Court held for Craven County, at September term last permission has been granted to Robert Lisbon by the said Court, to emancipate and set free a certain negro slave named Myrtilla Now if the said slave so permitted to be liberated shall during her residence in the State of North Carolina behave as a honest and peaceable citizen, then the above obligation to be void.

| Sealed and delivered } | Asa Jones | (Seal) |
| in presence of } | Frederick Divoux | (Seal) |

State of North Carolina }
Craven County }

Know all men by these presents that we Robert Lisbon Asa Jones & Frederick Divoux are held and firmly bound to John F. Smith Esquire Chairman of Craven County Court, in the sum of one hundred pounds, to be paid to the said John F Smith or his successors in office, to which payment well and truly to be made we bind ourselves, our heirs, executors, and administrators, firmly by these presents sealed with our seals and dated this 31 day of December 1813

The Condition of the above obligation is such, whereas at the Court held for Craven County, at September term permission has been granted to Robert Lisbon by the said Court, to emancipate and set free a certain negro slave named Myrtilla Now if the said negro so permitted to be liberated, shall not become chargeable to the parish of Craven County, or of any other County in this State, then the above obligation to be void.

| Sealed and delivered } | Asa Jones | (Seal) |
| in presence of } | Frederick Divoux | (Seal) |

****

To the Worshipfull the Justices of the Court of Pleas & Quarter Sessions for the County of Craven
    The Petition of John C. Stanly humbly sheweth that he is desirous to emancipate two negro women Sally and Sophia and he prays the permission of your Worships for that purpose He begs leave to say that the said women are honest & industrious & for their meritorious services are entitled to be liberated

Jno Stanly Atty

John Templeton }
Elijah Scott   } Securities

a Jonas
W. Gatlin
J. Brimer

****

To the Worshipfull the Justices of Craven County.

Chapter 6: Craven County Records

The Petition of John C Stanly respectfully sheweth that he is the owner of a woman slave named (Rachel & her children)[**Marked Through**] Rachael, & boy Kelsey, Hanneh Amy Ketty John & Alford whose meritorious services he is desirous to reward with emancipation. The said negros are of good moral character, sober & industrious, and are ready if emancipated to give the bond required by law that they shall not become chargeable to the parish -- Your Petitioner prays the license of your Worships to emancipate the said negroes, and as in duty bound he will ever pray   June 13. 1816

                Jno C: Stanly

State of North Carolina }
Craven County   }

Know all men by these presents that We Bacchus Simons and John Templeton are held and firmly bound unto his Excellency William Miller Esquire, Captain General, Governor, and Commander in Chief of the State aforesaid, in the full sum of fourteen hundred pounds, to be paid to the said Governor or his successors in office; to the which payment well and truly to be made, we bind ourselves, our heirs, executors, and administrators, jointly and severally, firmly by these presents, sealed with our seals, and dated this 16th day of June A.D. 1816

  The Condition of the above obligation is such, that whereas at the Court held for Craven County, at this day permission has been granted to John C Stanly by the said Court, to emancipate and set free certain negro slaves named Rachel & Kelsey Hannah, Amy Ketty John & Alfred Now if the said negroes so permitted to be liberated shall during their residence in the State of North Carolina behave as honest and peaceable citizens then the above obligation to be void.

		his	
Sealed and delivered	}	Backhaus ^ Simons	(Seal)
in presence of	}	mark	
		Jno. Templeton	(Seal)

State of North Carolina }
Craven County   }

Know all men by these presents that we Bacchus Simons & John Templeton are held and firmly bound to John F Smith Esquire Chairman of Craven County Court, in the sum of fourteen hundred pounds, to be paid to the said John F Smith or his successors in office, to which payment well and truly to be made we bind ourselves, our heirs, executors, and administrators, firmly by these presents sealed with our seals and dated this 16 day of June 1816

  The Condition of the above obligation is such, whereas at the Court held for Craven County, at this day permission has been granted to John C Stanly by the said Court, to emancipate and set free certain negro slaves named Rachel Kelsey Hannah Kitty & Alfred Now if the said negroes so permitted to be liberated, shall not become chargeable to the parish of Craven County, or of any other County in this State, then the above obligation to be void.

		his	
Sealed and delivered	}	Backhaus ^ Simons	(Seal)
		mark	
in presence of	}	Jno. Templeton	(Seal)

****

To the Worshipfull the Justices of the Court of

The Petition of Betty Horton

  Humbly sheweth that she owns a negro fellow named Will whom for meritorious Services she is desirous of obtaining license to emancipate & as in duty bound &c

Chapter 6: Craven County Records

F X Martin
Atto Petitioner

Craven Co. Court
June session 1807   Granted

***

State of North Carolina }
Craven County   }

Know all Men by these Presents that We Lydia Stewart, and John C. Stanly, are held and firmly bound unto his Excellency Nathaniel Alexander Esquire Captain General, Governor, and Commander in Chief of the State aforesaid, in the full sum of two hundred pounds, to be paid to the said Governor, or his successors in office, to the which payment well and truly to be made, We bind ourselves, our Heirs, Executors and Administrators, jointly and severally by these Presents, Sealed with our seals, and dated this 10th June AD 1806

The Condition of the above obligation is such, that Whereas on the Petition of the above bounden Lydia Stewart, the Justices of the Court of pleas & quarter Sessions, held for the County of Craven at June Term 1805, did grant permission to the said Lydia to emancipate and set free a certain negro boy Slave named Toney, Now if the said Toney, shall afterwards, be of good behaviour, then the above Obligation to be void otherwise to remain in full force & virtue.

Signed, Sealed & delivered	}	Lydia Stewart	(Seal)
in presence of	}	Jno. C. Stanly	(Seal)
Saml Chapman CC			

State of North Carolina }
Craven County   }

    Know all Men by these Presents, that We, Lydia Stewart, & John C. Stanly, are held and firmly bound unto John Tillman Esq. Chairman of the Court of pleas & quarter Sessions of Craven County, in the full and just sum of One hundred pounds, to be paid to the said Chairman, or his successors in Office, for the use of the poor of said County to the which payment, well and truly to be made and done We bind ourselves our Heirs Executors and administrators jointly and Severally, firmly by these Presents, Sealed with our Seals and dated this 10th June AD. 1806

The Condition of the above Obligation is Such, that Whereas leave is granted to the above bounden Lydia Stewart, to set free, and emancipate A negro boy named Toney a slave of the said Lydia, Now if the said Toney, shall not hereafter become chargeable in the Parish or County then the above Obligation to be void, otherwise to remain in full force & virtue

Signed, Sealed & delivered	}	Lydia Stewart	(Seal)
in the presence of	}	Jno. C. Stanly	(Seal)
Saml. Chapman CC	}		

***

To the Worshipfull the Justices of the County Court of Craven

    The petition of Lydia Stewart humbly sheweth unto your worships that your petitioner is the owner of a negro Woman slave named Amy who hath for many years past served Your petitioner with great fidelity and rendered her the most meritorious Services. That your petitioner is desirous of rewarding the said negro woman for serving and fidelity by emancipating her -- for leave and license to do which she humbly prays your worships
                      Lydia Stewart

Septr 14 1804

Chapter 6: Craven County Records

State of North Carolina }
Craven County }

Know all Men by these Presents that We Lydia Stewart and John C. Stanly, are held and firmly bound unto his Excellency Nathaniel Alexander, Esq., Captain General Governor & Commander in Chief of the State aforesaid, in the full sum of two hundred pounds, to be paid to the said Governor or his successors in Office to the which payment well and truly to be made, We bind ourselves our Heirs Executors and Administrators, jointly & severally by these Presents Sealed with our seals and dated this 10 June AD 1806

The Condition of the above Obligation is such, that Whereas the Petition of the above bounden Lydia Stewart, the Justices of the Court of pleas & quarter Sessions of Craven County, at September term AD 1804 Did grant permission to the said Lydia, to emancipate and set free a certain Negro woman Slave, named Amey -- now if the said Amey shall afterwards be of good behaviour, then the above Obligation to be void, otherwise to remain in full force & Virtue.

Signed, Sealed & delivered }	Lydia Stewart	(Seal)
in presence of }	Jno. C. Stanly	(Seal)
Saml. Chapman CC		

State of North Carolina }
Craven County }

Know all Men by these Presents that We Lydia Stewart & John C. Stanly, are held and firmly bound unto John Tillman Esq. Chairman of the Court of pleas & quarter Sessions of Craven County, in the full and just sum of One hundred Pounds to be paid to the said Chairman or his successors in Office for the use of the Poor of said County, to the which payment well and truly to be made and done, We bind ourselves, our Heirs, Executors and Administrators jointly & severally firmly by these Presents Sealed with our seals & dated this 10th June AD 1806

The Condition of the above Obligation is such, that Whereas leave is granted to the above bounden Lydia Stewart, to set free and emancipate, Amey, a negro Slave, of the said Lydia, Now if the said Amey, shall not hereafter become chargeable on the Parish or County, then the above Obligation to be void, otherwise to remain in full force and Virtue.

Signed, Sealed & delivered }	Lydia Stewart	(Seal)
in the presence of }	Jn. C. Stanly	(Seal)
Saml. Chapman CC }		

****

To the Honourable the Judge of the Superior Court of Law, for the County of Craven;
    The petition of negro Man Kelso, Most respectfully Sheweth unto your Honor, that he is unjustly detained in Slavery, by John C. Stanly. Your Petitioner further sheweth unto your Honor, that Mrs. Stewart of the town of Newbern in her lifetime to wit sometime in the year 1804 or 1806, filed her petition in the Court of Pleas and Quarter Sessions for the County of Craven, praying leave to emancipate and set free for Certain Causes therein Mentioned, her negro woman named Amy the Mother of your Petitioner, Your Petitioner further Sheweth unto your Honor, that the said was duly and legally emancipated according to the acts of Assembly in Such Case Made and Provided, and that sometime after said emancipation was there effected your Petitioner was born. Your Petitioner further sheweth unto your Honor, that the said Mrs. Stewart sometime in the year 182[Blank] departed this life leaving a last Will and testament, and therein appointed the said John C. Stanly her Executor, who lays claim by such authority to the Services of your Petitioner, none such having been given him by the said Will. Your Petitioner being Exceedingly poor, and feeling himself much aggrieved, is Compelled to resort to a Court of law to assert his just rights, & therefore Prays your Honor that he may be permitted to institute a Suit against the said John C. Stanly, and prosecute the same in forma Paupers.

Chapter 6: Craven County Records

Kelso or Kelcy Maketh oath that the matters of fact set forth in the foregoing Petition are true to the best of his Knowledge and belief, and that he is not Worth twenty five dollars, in any worldly substance saving and Excepting his wearing apparel and the matter in Contest in this Suit.

                         his
                     Kelcy X Davis
Sworn to before me   mark
this 3rd day of March 1832
Abner Pasteur Clk

I James W. Bryan Attorney &c do hereby Certify that I have Examined the papers and Matters of fact and Verily believe that negro Man Kelcy, has good Cause of action against John C. Stanly.
                 James W. Bryan

                               State of North Carolina

To The Sheriff of Craven County Greeting:
You are hereby commanded to summon James G. Stanly, to bring with him the record of the emancipation, of the mother of Kelcy Davis, late the slave of Mrs. Stewart personally to be and appear before the Judge of the Superior Court of Law, to be held for the County of Craven, at the Court House in Newbern, on the third Monday after the fourth Monday of September next, then and there to testify and the truth to say in behalf of Kelcy Davis in a certain matter of controversy before the said Court depending, then and there to be tried, wherein Kelcy Davis is plaintiff and Jno. C. Stanly is defendant. And this you shall in no wise omit under the penalty by law.
        Witness, Edward Stanly, Clerk of the said Court, at Newbern, the third Monday after the fourth Monday of March 1832

               Edw. Stanly

***

Know all Men by these presents that we Frederick Nash and George HB Burgwin are held and firmly bound unto John Tillman Esqr. Chairman of the court of Pleas and Quarter Sessions in the County of Craven and his successors in office in the Sum of one Hundred Pounds, for the payment whereof well and truly to be made we bind ourselves, our heirs, Executors & administrators firmly by these presents seal'd with our own hands this ninth day of June in the year of our Lord Eighteen hundred & Seven.

       The condition of the above obligation is such that whereas the above bounded Frederick Nash has this day by petition to the County Court of Craven procured an order for the emancipation of a Negroe man named Virgil. Now if the aforemention'd Virgil shall not at any time become burthensome or chargeable on the Parish or County then the above obligation to be null and void, Otherwise to be and remain in full force and effect.
               F Nash   (Seal)
               Geo. HB Burgwin   (Seal)

***

To the Worshipfull the Justices of Craven County Court.
       The petition no William Jesop humbly sheweth, That he is owner of the negro slaves named Isaac, Simon, Joshua, Higgins, George & Sinah whose long and meritorious services he is desirous to reward with emancipation - he prays that he may be permitted to do so. december term 1807

William Jesop
by owen Stanton
his attorney
granted for complying with requisite of law

Chapter 6: Craven County Records

State of North Carolina }
Craven County }

Know all men by these presents that We Isaac Luis Wm Physioc Joseph Physioc are held and firmly bound unto his Excellency Benjamin Williams Esquire, Captain General, Governor, and Commander in Chief of the State aforesaid, in the full sum of two hundred pounds, to be paid to the said Governor or his successors in office; to the which payment well and truly to be made, we bind ourselves, our heirs, executors and administrators, jointly and severally, firmly by these presents, Sealed with our seals, and dated this 15 day of December A.D. 1807

The Condition of the above obligation is such, that whereas at the Court held for Craven County, at this day permission has been granted to William Jessop by the said Court, to emancipate and set free a certain negro slave named Isaac Now if the said negro so permitted to be liberated shall during his residence in the State of North Carolina behave himself as an honest and peaceable citizen, then the above obligation to be void.

Sealed and delivered		his	
in presence of	}	Isaac X Luis	(Seal)
		mark	
Owen Stanton Lewes[?]		Wm. Physioc	(Seal)
		Jos. Physioc	(Seal)

Know all men by these presents that we Isaac Luis William Physioc Joseph Physioc are held and firmly bound to John Tillman Esquire Chairman of Craven County Court, in the sum of one hundred pounds, to be paid to the said John Tillman, or his successors in office, to which payment well and truly to be made We bind ourselves, our heirs, executors and administrators, ,firmly by these presents sealed with our seals and dated this 15th day of December 1807.

The Condition of the above obligation is such whereas at the County Court of Craven at this day permission has been granted to William Jesop by the said Court, to emancipate and set free a certain negro slave named Isaac **[Faded]** if the said negro so permittedto be liberated, shall not become chargeable on the parish of Craven County or of any other County in this State, then the above obligation to be void otherwise of full force and virtue

Sealed & delivered		his	
in presence of	}	Isaac X Luis	(Seal)
		mark	
Owen Stanton Lewes[?]		Wm. Physioc	(Seal)
		Jos. Physioc	(Seal)

State of North Carolina }
Craven County }

Know all men by these presents that We Joshua Lewes Lovick Jones & Gideon Jones are held and firmly bound unto his Excellency Benjamin Williams Esquire, Captain General, Governor, and Commander in Chief of the State aforesaid, in the full sum of two hundred pounds, to be paid to the said Governor or his successors in office; to the which payment well and truly to be made, we bind ourselves, our heirs, executors and administrators, jointly and severally, firmly by these presents, sealed with our seals, and dated this 4th March A.D. 1808

The Condition of the above obligation is such, that whereas at the Court held for Craven County, at this day permission has been granted to William Jesop by the said Court, to emancipate and set free a certain negro slave named Joshua Lewes Now if the said negro so permitted to be liberated shall during his residence in the state of North Carolina behave himself as an honest and peaceable citizen, then the above obligation to be void.

Sealed and delivered } his

Chapter 6: Craven County Records

in presence of	}	Joshua X Lewes	(Seal)
		mark	
Reuben P. Jones		Lovick Jones	(Seal)
		Gideon Jones	(Seal)

Know all men by these presents that we Joshua Lewes Lovick Jones G. Jones are held and firmly bound to John Tillman Esquire, Chairman of Craven County Court, in the sum of one hundred pounds, to be paid to the said John Tillman or his successors in office, to which payment well and truly to be made we bind ourselves, our heirs, executors and administrators firmly by these presents Sealed with our seals and dated this 15th day of December 1807

    The Condition of the above obligation is such Whereas at the Court held for Craven County at this day permission has been granted to William Jessop, by the said Court to emancipate and set free a certain negroe named Joshua Lewes: Now if the said negroe so permitted to be liberated, shall not become chargeable on the parish of Craven County or of any other County in this State then the above obligation to be void otherwise of full force and virtue.

		his	
Sealed & delivered	}	Joshua X Lewes	(Seal)
in presence of	}	mark	
Reuben P. Jones		Lovick Jones	(Seal)
		Gideon Jones	(Seal)

State of North Carolina }
Craven County }

Know all men by these presents that We Simon Luis Thomas Austin and Benjamin Borden are held and firmly bound unto his Excellency Benjamin Williams Esquire, Captain General, Governor, and Commandedr in Chief of the State aforesaid, in the full sum of two hundred pounds, to be paid to the said Governor or his successors in office; to the which payment well and truly to be made, we bind ourselves, our heirs, executors, and administrators, jointly and severally, firmly by these presents, sealed with our seals, and dated this 15th day of December A.D. 1807

    The Condition of the above obligation is such, that whereas at the Court held for Craven County, at this day permission has been granted to William Jessop by the said Court, to emancipate and set free a certain negro slave named Simon Now if the said negro so permitted to be liberated shall during his residence in the state of North Carolina behave himself as an honest and peaceable citizen, then the above obligation to be void.

Sealed and delivered	}	his	
in presence of	}	Simon X Lewis	(Seal)
		mark	
Geo Cooper		Thos. Austin	(Seal)
John Johnson		Benja Bordin	(Seal)

Know all men by these presents that we Simon Lewis Thomas Austin & Benjamin Borden are held and firmly bound to John Tillman Esquire Chairman of Craven County Court In the Sum of one hundred pounds to be paid to the Said John Tillman or his Successors in offis to which payment well and truly to be made, we bind our Selves our heirs Executors and administrators firmly by these presents Sealled with our Seals and dated this 15th Day of December 1807

    The Condition of the above Obligation is Such whereas at the County Court held for Craven at this day permission has been granted to Wm. Jessop by the said Court, to emancipate and Set free a certain negro Slave Named Simon now if the Said Negro so permitted to be Liberated Shall not become Chargible on the parish of Craven County or any other County in this State then the Above Obligation to be void

| | | His | |
| Sealed and delivered | } | Simon X Lewis | (Seal) |

Chapter 6: Craven County Records

In presence of	}	mark	
Geo Cooper		Thos. Austin	(Seal)
John Johnson		Benja Bordin	(Seal)

State of North Carolina   }
Craven County   }

Know all men by these presents that We Sinah Lewis George Cooper & Michael Ellis are held and firmly bound unto his Excellency Benjamin Williams Esquire, Captain General, Governor, and Commander in Chief of the State aforesaid, in the full sum of two hundred pounds, to be paid to the said Governor or his successors in office; to the which payment well and truly to be made, we bind ourselves, our heirs, executors, and administrators, jointly and severally, firmly by these presents, sealed with our seals, and dated this 15th day of December A.D. 1807

The Condition of the above obligation is such, that whereas at the Court held for Craven County, at this day permission has been granted to William Jesop by the said Court, to emancipate and set free a certain negro slave named Sinah Now if the said negro so permitted to be liberated shall during her residence in the state of North Carolina hehave herself as an hinest and peaceable citizen, then the above obligation to be void.

Sealed and delivered	}	[Faded]	(Seal)
in presence of	}	[Faded]	(Seal)
Attest			
Wm. Physioc		her	
Geo Cooper		Sinah X Lewis	(Seal)
		Mark	
		Michael Ellis	(Seal)

State of North Carolina   }
Craven County   }

Know all men by these presents that we Seniah Lewis George Cooper & Michael Lewis are held and firmly bound to John Tillman Esquire Chairman of Craven County Court, in the sum of one hundred pounds, to be paid to the said John or his successors in office, to which payment well and truly to be made we bind ourselves, our heirs, executors and administrators, firmly by these presents sealed with our seals and dated this 15th day of December 1807

The Condition of the above obligation is such, whereas at the Court held for Craven County, at this day permission has been granted to William Jessop by the said Court, to emancipate and set free a certain negro slave named Sinath[?] Now if the said negro so permitted to be liberated, shall not become chargeable to the parish of Craven County, or of any other County in this State, then the above obligation to be void.

		his	
Sealed and delivered	}	Peter X God[?]	(Seal)
in presence of	}	mark	
Attest		George Cooper	(Seal)
Wm Physioc		her	
Geo. Cooper		Seniah X Lewis	(Seal)
		mark	
		Michael Ellis	(Seal)

State of North Carolina   }
Craven County   }

Know all men by these presents that We George Luis Abner Whitehead Jno. Whitehead are held and firmly bound unto his Excellency Benjamin Williams Esquire, Captain General, Governor, and Commander in Chief of the State aforesaid,

Chapter 6: Craven County Records

in the full sum of two hundred pounds, to be paid to the said Governor or his successors in office; to the which payment well and truly to be made, we bind ourselves, our heirs, executors and administrators, jointly and severally, firmly by these presents, sealed with our seals, and dated this 24 day of February A.D. 1808

    The Condition of the above obligation is such, that whereas at the Court held for Craven County, at this day permission has been granted to William Jessop by the said Court, to emancipate and set free a certain negro slave named George Lewis Now if the said negro so permitted to be liberated shall during his residence in the state of North Carolina behave himself as an honest and peaceable citizen, then the above obligation to be void.

Sealed and delivered	}	his	
in presence of	}	George X Luis	(Seal)
Attest		mark	
		Abner Whitehead	(Seal)
Wm. Physioc		Jno. Whitehead	(Seal)

State of North Carolina }
Craven County }

Know all men by these presents that we George Luis Abner Whitehead and Jno. Whitehead are held and firmly bound to John Tillman Esquire Chairman of Craven County Court, in the sum of one hundred pounds, to be paid to the said John or his successors in office, to which payment well and truly to be made we bind ourselves, our heirs, executors and administrators, firmly by these presents sealed with our seals and dated this 24 day of February 1808

    The Condition of the above obligation is such, whereas at the Court held for Craven County, at this day permission has been granted to William Jessop by the said Court, to emancipate and set free a certain negro slave named George Luis Now if the said negro so permitted to be liberated, shall not become chargeable to the parish of Craven County, or of any other County in this State, then the above obligation to be void.

Sealed and delivered	}	his	
in presence of	}	George X Luis	(Seal)
Attest		mark	
Wm. Physioc		Abner Whitehead	(Seal)
		Jno. Whitehead	(Seal)

****

To the Worshipfull Justices of Craven County Court, The Petition of John C Stanly humbly sheweth That he is owner of a negro woman named Lydia and her children Virchey Mary Susan Virgil & Fred formerly the property of Virgil Crawford whose meritorious Conduct he wishes to reward by emancipation. He prays that he may be permitted to emancipate them upon giving the Bonds for their good behaviour required by law.
Jn. C. Stanly

State of North Carolina }
Craven County }

Know all men by these presents that We Bacchus Simmons & James York Green are held and firmly bound unto his Excellency William Miller Esquire, Captain General, Governor, and Commander in Chief of the State aforesaid, in the full sum of two hundred pounds, to be paid to the said Governor or his successors in office; to the which payment well and truly to be made, we bind ourselves, our heirs, executors and administrators, jointly and severally, firmly by these presents, sealed with our seals, and dated this seventeenth day of March A.D. 1815

    The Condition of the above obligation is such, that whereas at the Court held for Craven County, at this day permission has been granted to John C. Stanly by the said Court, to emancipate and set free certain negro slaves named

Chapter 6: Craven County Records

Lydia & her children Virchey - Mary - Susan - Virgil and Fred Now if the said negroes so permitted to be liberated shall during their residence in the state of North Carolina behave as honest and peaceable citizens then the above obligation to be void.

Sealed and delivered }	his	
in presence of }	Bacchus X Simmons	(Seal)
	Mark	
	James York Green	(Seal)

State of North Carolina }
Craven County   }

Know all men by these presents that we Bacchus Simmons & James York Green are held and firmly bound to John F. Smith Esquire Chairman of Craven County Court, in the sum of one hundred pounds, to be paid to the said John F. Smith or his successors in office, to which payment well and truly to be made we bind ourselves, our heirs, executors and administrators, firmly by these presents sealed with our seals and dated this 17th day of March 1815

The Condition of the above obligation is such, whereas at the Court held for Craven County, at this day permission has been granted to John C Stanly by the said Court, to emancipate and set free certain negro slaves named Lydia & her children, Virchy, Mary, Susan, Virgil & Fred Now if the said negroes so permitted to be liberated, shall not become chargeable to the parish of Craven County, or of any other County in this State, then the above obligation to be void.

	his	
Sealed and delivered }	Bacchus X Simmons	(Seal)
in presence of }	mark	
Jos. E. Sheffield	James Y. Green	(Seal)

****

To the Worshipfull the Justices of the Court of Pleas & Quarter Sessions of Craven

Humbly petitioning sheweth to your Worships Your petitioner William Conway, that Your petitioner is the legal owner of a certain Negroe Man Slave named Bachus, a Carpenter by trade, and also of his wife a negroe woman named Sukey both of them lately belonging Frederick Nash & George Burgwin Esqr. And your petitioner became the purchaser of said slaves under a trust that upon the performance of certain Conditions on their part your petitioner would release his claim upon the said slaves and assist them in an application to the Worshipfull Court for their freedom. And your petitioner states with confidence, that in industry fidelity and honesty & in all the qualifications of good citizens his Backus & Sukey will not suffer by a companion with any free persons of their colour Your petitioner therefore prays that upon conforming to the acts of the General Assembly in such case provided for Your Worships would grant him your license to emancipate & make free the said Slaves Bachus & Sukey And Your petitioner as in duty bound will ever pray &c

William Conway by
E. Graham his Attorney
petitioner

State of North Carolina }
Craven County   }

Know all men by these presents that We William Conway & William Mitchell are held and firmly bound unto his Excellency Benjamin Smith Esquire, Captain General, Governor, and Commander in Chief of the State aforesaid, in the full sum of two hundred pounds, to be paid to the said Governor or his successors in office; to the which payment well

Chapter 6: Craven County Records

and truly to be made, we bind ourselves, our heirs, executors and Administrators, jointly and severally, firmly by these presents, sealed with our seals, and dated this 23 March A.D. 1811

The Condition of the above obligation is such, that whereas at the Court held for Craven County, at this day permission has been granted to William Conway by the said Court, to emancipate and set free a certain negro slave named Bachus Now if the said negro so permitted to be liberated shall during his residence in the state of North Carolina behave himself as a honest and peaceable citizen, then the above obligation to be void.

| Sealed and delivered } | Wm. Conway | (Seal) |
| in presence of } | Wm. Mitchell | |

State of North Carolina }
Craven County }

Know all men by these presents that we William & William Conway are held and firmly bound to John F Smith Esquire Chairman of Craven County Court, in the sum of one hundred pounds, to be paid to the said John F Smith or his successors in office, to which payment well and truly to be made we bind ourselves, our heirs, executors and administrators, firmly by these presents sealed with our seals and dated this 23 day of March 1811

The Condition of the above obligation is such, whereas at the Court held for Craven County, at this day permission has been granted to William Conway by the said Court, to emancipate and set free a certain negro slave named Bachus Now if the said negro so permitted to be liberated, shall not become chargeable to the parish of Craven County, or of any other County in this State, then the above obligation to be void.

| Sealed and delivered } | Wm. Conway | (Seal) |
| in presence of } | Wm. Mitchell | (Seal) |

State of North Carolina }
Craven County }

Know all men by these presents that We William Conway & William Mitchell are held and firmly bound unto his Excellency Benjamin Smith Esquire, Captain General, Governor, and Commander in Chief of the State aforesaid, in the full sum of two hundred pounds, to be paid to the said Governor or his successors in office; to the which payment well and truly to be made, we bind ourselves, our heirs, executors and administrators, jointly and severally, firmly by these presents, sealed with our seals, and dated this 23 day of March A.D. 1811

The Condition of the above obligation is such, that whereas at the Court held for Craven County, at this day permission has been granted to William Conway by the said Court, to emancipate and set free a certain negro slave named Sukey Now if the said negro so permitted to be liberated shall during her residence in the state of North Carolina behave herself as a honest and peaceable citizen, then this obligation to be void.

| Sealed and delivered } | Wm. Conway | (Seal) |
| in presence of } | Wm. Mitchell | (Seal) |

State of North Carolina }
Craven County }

Know all men by these presents that we William Conway & William Mitchell are held and firmly bound to John F Smith Esquire Chairman of Craven County Court, in the sum of one hundred pounds, to be paid to the said John F Smith or his successors in office, to which payment well and truly to be made we bind ourselves, our heirs, executors and administrators firmly by these presents sealed with our seals and dated this 23 day of March 1811

Chapter 6: Craven County Records

The Condition of the above obligation is such, whereas at the Court held for Craven County, at this day permission has been granted to William Conway by the said Court, to emancipate and set free a certain negro slave named Sukey Now if the said negro so permitted to be liberated, shall not become chargeable to the parish of Craven County, or of any other County in this State, then the above obligation to be void.

Sealed and delivered }	Wm. Conway	(Seal)	
in presence of }	Wm. Mitchell		

****

To the Worshipfull the Justices of Craven County Court
The Petition of Wm. B. Green respectfully sheweth That he is the owner of a mulatto slave, called James York Green, whose faithful & meritorious services he is desirous to reward with the blessing of freedom. He prays the license of your Worships to emancipate the said slave upon his entering into the bonds required by law for the good conduct of the said James & to indemnify the Parish as required by law.

September 13, 1812
William B. Green
Tho A Green

The Subscribers respectfully certify to the Worshipfull County Court of Craven that they are acquainted with the above named James York Green he is a tolerable workman at the Carpenters trade, a sober, honest and industrious fellow and in their opinions would not disgrace the character of a free man

J. Mastin	Septr. 1812
M. E Stephens	M.E. Green
John Green	Tho A Green
	Wm. Mitchell
	Thomas Wadsworth

State of North Carolina }
Craven County }

Know all men by these presents that We William B Green and John Franklin are held and firmly bound unto his Excellency William Hawkins Esquire, Captain General, Governor, and Commander in Chief of the State aforesaid, in the full sum of two hundred pounds, to be paid to the said Governor or his successors in office; to the which payment well and truly to be made, we bind ourselves, our heirs, executors and administrators, jointly and severally, firmly by these presents, sealed with our seals, and dated this thirteenth day of September A.D. 1812

The Condition of the above obligation is such, that whereas at the Court held for Craven County, at this day permission has been granted to William B Green by the said Court, to emancipate and set free a certain negro slave named James York Green Now if the said negro so permitted to be liberated, shall during his residence in the State of North Carolina behave as an honest and peaceable citizen, then the above obligation to be void.

Sealed and delivered }	William B Green	(Seal)
in presence of }	John Franklin	(Seal)

State of North Carolina }
Craven County }

Know all men by these presents that we William B. Green & John Franklin are held and firmly bound to John F Smith Esquire Chairman of Craven County Court, in the sum of one hundred pounds, to be paid to the said John F Smith or

Chapter 6: Craven County Records

his successors in office, to which payment well and truly to be made we bind ourselves, our heirs, executors and administrators, firmly by these presents sealed with our seals and dated this 13th day of Septr. AD 1812

The Condition of the above obligation is such, whereas at the Court held for Craven County, at this day permission has been granted to William B Green by the said Court, to emancipate and set free a certain negro slave named James York Green Now if the said negro so permitted to be liberated, shall not become chargeable to the parish of Craven County, or of any other County in this State, then the above obligatiob to be void.

Sealed and delivered }	William B. Green	(Seal)
in presence of }	John Franklin	(Seal)

****

State of North Carolina }	SS County Court
Craven County }	March Term 1811

To the Worshipfull the Justices of the County Court of Craven the Petition of Bothwick Gillespie humbly sheweth That Mary Jones late of Craven County in and by her last will and testament directed your Petitioner who was Executor of the Said Mary's last will To emancipate and set free pursuant to law a Slave called John Downs belonging to the said Testratrix Mary in consideration of the faithfull and meritorious Services rendered by the said John Downs while in her Service a period of near fifteen years Your Petitioner wishing to yield obedience to the wishes of the said Mary and from a knowledge of the correct conduct and good behaviour of the said John Downs prays your Worships to grant a license to your Petitioner to emancipate the said slave called John Downs pursuant to the acts of Assembly in such cases made and provided.

B.C. Gillespie

State of North Carolina }
Craven County }

Know all men by these presents that We Borthwick C Gillespie   John Jones are held and firmly bound unto his Excellency Benjamin Smith Esquire, Captain General, Governor, and Commander in Chief of the State aforesaid, in the full sum of two hundred pounds, to be paid to the said Governor or his successors in office; to the which payment well and truly to be made, we bind ourselves, our heirs, executors and administrators, jointly and severally, firmly by these presents, sealed with our seals, and dated this fourteenth day of March 1811

The Condition of the above obligation is such, that whereas at the Court held for Craven County, at this day permission has been granted to Exr. of Mary Jones by the said Court, to emancipate and set free a certain negro slave named John Downs Now if the said negro so permitted to be liberated, shall during his residence in the state of North Carolina behave himself as a honest and peaceable citizen, then the above obligation to be void.

Sealed and delivered }	B.C. Gillespie	(Seal)
in presence of }	John Franklin	(Seal)
J G Stanly CC		

State of North Carolina }
Craven County }

Know all men by these presents that we Borthwick C Gillespie and John Franklin are held and firmly bound to John F Smith Esquire Chairman of Craven County Court, in the sum of one hundred pounds, to be paid to the said John F Smith or his successors in office, to which payment well and truly to be made we bind ourselves, our heirs, executors and administrators, firmly by these presents sealed with our seals and dated this 14 day of March AD 1811

Chapter 6: Craven County Records

    The Condition of the above obligation is such, whereas at the Court held for Craven County, at this day permission has been granted to Executor of Mary Jones by the said Court, to emancipate and set free a certain negro slave named John Downs Now if the said negro so permitted to be liberated, shall not become chargeable to the parish of Craven County, or of any other County in this State, then the above obligation to be void.

Sealed and delivered	}	B.C. Gillespie	(Seal)
in presence of	}	John Franklin	(Seal)
J G Stanly CC			

****

Daniel Nelson

To the worshipfull Court of Craven County
June Term 1811

    Daniel Former Slave of Benjamin Nelson deceased prays your Worships that an order may be made & a certificate granted him of hie emancipation agreeable to the Last Will of Benjamin Nelson who gave him thirty five Acres of Land during his life - he will give Security according to Law
Danl Nelson

This is to Certify that old Daniel is free Left So By my Brother Benjamin Nelsons Will and sence that time I have let him have His [?] he has not had his Freedom agreeable To Law as to the Priviledges of a free born Man of Color but, there is no person that hath Any Juris Diction over him but my self and I have none but to Defend him and keep him With in the bounds of the Law and on these terms He has Liberty to pass and repass Where he Pleases Given under my hand November 16th 1808
John S Nelson

The Court are of opinion that Daniel by giving Security may be free'd according to Law

****

Jno C Stanly prays of this Worshipfull Court permission to emancipate a negro woman Tempe He respectfully sheweth to this Court that the said Negro woman has ever conducted herself an orderly & discrete manner, that she has ever been remarkable for her honesty, her industry and her affection & attachment to her owners In particular he begs leave to state that in his late illness her diligence in watching, attending to & nursing him was such as merit from him thanks & praise & as to induce him to apply to this Worshipfull Court to have her liberated for her meritorious services.

Fredr. Jones &	}	Jno C Stanly
Wm Handcock	} securities	

Know all men by these presents that We Frederick Jones and William Handcock are held and firmly bound unto his Excellency William Hawkins Esquire, Captain General, Governor, and Commander in Chief of the State aforesaid, in the full sum of two hundred pounds, to be paid to the said Governor or his successors in office; to the which payment well and truly to be made, we bind ourselves, our heirs, executors, and administrators, jointly and severally, firmly by these presents, sealed with our seals, and dated this 15th day of December A.D. 1813

    The Condition of the above obligation is such, that whereas at the Court held for Craven County, at this day permission has been granted to John C Stanly by the said Court, to emancipate and set free a certain negro slave named Tempe Now if the said negro so permitted to be liberated, shall during her residence in the state of North Carolina behave as a honest and peaceable citizen, then the above obligation to be void.

Chapter 6: Craven County Records

| Sealed and delivered | } | Fredk. Jones | (Seal) |
| in presence of | } | W. Handcock | (Seal) |

State of North Carolina }
Craven County }

Know all men by these presents that we Frederick Jones and William Handcock are held and firmly bound to John F Smith Esquire Chairman of Craven County Court, in the sum of one hundred pounds, to be paid to the said John F Smith or his successors in office, to which payment well and truly to be made we bind ourselves, our heors, executors and administrators, firmly by these presents sealed with our seals and dated this fifteenth day of December 1813

    The Condition of the above obligation is such, whereas at the Court held for Craven County, at this day permission has been granted to John C Stanly by the said Court, to emancipate and set free a certain negro slave named Tempe Now if the said negro so permitted to be liberated, shall not become chargeable to the parish of Craven County, or of any other County in this State, then the above obligation to be void.

| Sealed and delivered | } | Fredk. Jones | (Seal) |
| in presence of | } | W. Hancock | (Seal) |

****

State of North Carolina } Court of Pleas & Quarter
Craven County } Sessions June Term 1815

    To the Worshipfull the Justices of the Court of Pleas & Quarter Sessions for the County of Craven
    The Petition of John C Stanly humbly sheweth that he is the owner of a negro man named Edmund who for his faithful & meritorious services has rendered himself worthy of the greatest kindness which this Petitioner can confer on him.
    Your petitioner therefore humbly prays that he may have permission to set free & liberate the said negro man Edmund for his many meritorious services - And your Petitioner as in duty bound will ever pray.
    W C Stanly Atty for Petr.

State of North Carolina }
Craven County }

Know all men by these presents that We John Jones and John Snead are held and firmly bound unto his Excellency William Miller Esquire, Captain General, Governor, and Commander in Chief of the State aforesaid, in the full sum of two hundred pounds, to be paid to the said Governor or his successors in office; to the which payment well and truly to be made, we bind ourselves, our heirs, executors, and administrators, jointly and severally, firmly by these presents, sealed with our seals, and dated this nineteenth day of June 1815

    The Condition of the above obligation is such, that whereas at the Court held for Craven County, at this day permission has been granted to John C Stanly by the said Court, to emancipate and set free a certain negro slave named Edmund Now if the said negro so permitted to be liberated, shall during his residence in the state of North Carolina behave as a honest and peaceable citizen, then the above obligation to be void.

| Sealed and delivered | } | John Jones | (Seal) |
| in presence of | } | John Snead | (Seal) |

State of North Carolina }
Craven County }

Chapter 6: Craven County Records

Know all men by these presents that we John Jones and John Snead are held and firmly bound to John F Smith Esquire Chairman of Craven County Court, in the sum of one hundred pounds, to be paid to the said John F Smith or his successors in office, to which payment well and truly to be made we bind ourselves, our heirs, executors and administrators, firmly by these presents sealed with our seals and dated this 19th day of June 1815

    The Condition of the above obligation is such, whereas at the Court held for Craven County, at this day permission has been granted to John C Stanly by the said Court, to emancipate and set free a certain negro slave named Edmund Now if the said negro so permitted to be liberated, shall not become chargeable to the parish of Craven County, or of any other County in this State, then the above obligation to be void.

| Sealed and delivered | } | John Jones | (Seal) |
| in presence of | } | John Snead | (Seal) |

***

To the Worshipfull the Justices of Craven County Court
    The Petition of John Downs humbly sheweth that he is the owner of a negro woman named Sarah, whose meritorious services he is desirous to reward with emancipation. The said Sarah is honest, industrious and sober, and if the humble prayer of this Petition be granted, Your Petitioner will give the bonds required by law that the said Sarah shall not become chargeable to the parish

                      June 1816
                      John Downs

The undersigned recommend the Petitioner John Downs as an industrious, honest & sober man and the woman Sarah deserves the good character given of her in the petition. June 1816

Asa Jones
John Jones
Jno. Oliver
Wm. Hollister
M. E Stephens
Saml. Oliver

State of North Carolina   }
Craven County   }

Know all men by these presents that We John Downs are held and firmly bound unto his Excellency William Miller Esquire, Captain General, Governor, and Commander in Chief of the State aforesaid, in the full sum of two hundred pounds, to be paid to the said Governor or his successors in office; to the which payment well and truly to be made, we bind ourselves, our heirs, executors, and administrators, jointly and severally, firmly by these presents, sealed with or seals, and dated this fourteenth day of June 1816

    The Condition of the above obligation is such, that whereas at the Court held for Craven County, at this day permission has been granted to John Downs by the said Court, to emancipate and set free a certain negro slave named Sarah Now if the said negro so permitted to be liberated, shall during her residence in the state of North Carolina behave as a honest and peaceable citizen, then the above obligation to be void.

		his	
Sealed and delivered	}	John X Downs	(Seal)
in presence of	}	mark	
		John Franklin	(Seal)
		Samuel Read	(Seal)

Chapter 6: Craven County Records

State of North Carolina }
Craven County }

Know all men by these presents that we John Downs are held and firmly bound to John F Smith Esquire Chairman of Craven County Court, in the sum of one hundred pounds, to be paid to the said John F Smith or his successors in office, to which payment well and truly to be made we bind ourselves, our heirs, executors and administrators, firmly by these presents sealed with our seals and dated this 14 day of June 1816

    The Condition of the above obligation is such, whereas at the Court held for Craven County, at this day permission has been granted to John Downs by the said Court, to emancipate and set free a certain slave named Sarah Now if the said negro so permitted to be liberated, shall not become chargeable to the parish of Craven County, or of any other County in this State, then the above obligation to be void.

Sealed and delivered }	his John X Downs mark	(Seal)
in presence of }	John Franklin	(Seal)
	Samuel Read	(Seal)

****

To the Worshipfull the Justices of Craven County Court
    Durant Hatch respectfully represents that he is the owner of a negro man Slave named Jacob commonly called Jacob McClure whose meritorious services he is desirous to reward with emancipation, the said Jacob is honest, sober & industrious, and Your Petitioner if permitted to set him free will give the bonds required by law that the said Jacob shall not become chargeable to the parish
June 1816   D. Hatch

State of North Carolina }
Craven County }

Know all men by these presents that We Durant Hatch and Thomas H Daves are held and firmly bound unto his Excellency William Miller Esquire, Captain General, Governor, and Commander in Chief of the State aforesaid, in the full sum of two hundred pounds, to be paid to the said Governor or his successors in office; to the which payment well and truly to be made, we bind ourselves, our heirs, executors, and administrators, jointly and severally, firmly by these presents, sealed with our seals, and dated this thirteenth day of June A.D. 1816

    The Condition of the above obligation is such, that whereas at the Court held for Craven County, at this day permission has been granted to Durant Hatch by the said Court, to emancipate and set free a certain negro slave named Jacob McClure Now if the said negro so permitted to be liberated, shall during his residence in the state of North Carolina behave himself as a honest and peaceable citizen, then the above obligation to be void.

Sealed and delivered }	D. Hatch	(Seal)
in presence of }	T.H. Daves	(Seal)
J G Stanly		

State of North Carolina }
Craven County }

Know all men by these presents that we Durant Hatch and Thomas H Daves are held and firmly bound to John F Smith Esquire Chairman of Craven County Court, in the sum of one hundred pounds, to be paid to the said John F Smith or his successors in office, to which payment well and truly to be made we bind ourselves, our heirs, executors and administrators, firmly by these presents sealed with our seals and dated this 13th day of June 1816

Chapter 6: Craven County Records

    The Condition of the above obligation is such, whereas at the Court held for Craven County, at this day permission has been granted to Durant Hatch by the said Court, to emancipate and set free a certain negro slave named Jacob McClure Now if the said negro so permitted to be liberated, shall not become chargeable to the parish of Craven County, or of any other County in this State, then the above obligation to be void.

Sealed and delivered	}	D. Hatch	(Seal)
in presence of	}	T.H. Daves	(Seal)
J G Stanly			

****

To the Worshipfull the Justices of Craven County Court
    The Petition of Donum Montford humbly sheweth that he is the owner of a mulatto boy called Abraham Moody Russell Allen whose meritorious services he is anxious to reward with freedom - that said boy contain a good moral character and is healthy & industrious He prays the license of your Worships to emancipate the said Abraham upon giving the bonds required by law

	Septr 1816
Signed in presence	his
of	Donum X Montford
John Green	mark
J G Stanly	

State of North Carolina }
Craven County }

Know all men by these presents that We Donum Montford and James Y Green are held and firmly bound unto his Excellency William Miller Esquire, Captain General, Governor, and Commander in Chief of the State aforesaid, in the full sum of two hundred pounds, to be paid to the said Governor or his successors in office; to the which payment well and truly to be made, we bind ourselves, our heirs, executors, and administrators, jointly and severally, firmly by these presents, sealed with our seals, and dated this twelfth day of September 1816

    The Condition of the above obligation is such, that whereas at the Court held for Craven County, at this day permission has been granted to Donum Montford by the said Court, to emancipate and set free a certain negro slave named Abram M. R Allen Now if the said negro so permitted to be liberated, shall during his residence in the state of North Carolina behave as an honest and peaceable citizen, then the above obligation to be void.

Sealed and delivered	}	his	
in presence of	}	Donum X Montford	(Seal)
J G Stanly		mark	
		James Y Green	(Seal)

State of North Carolina }
Craven County }

Know all men by these presents that we Donum Montford and James Y Green are held and firmly bound to John F Smith Esquire Chairman of Craven County Court, in the sum of one hundred pounds, to be paid to the said John F Smith or his successors in office, to which payment well and truly to be made we bind ourselves, our heirs, executors and administrators, firmly by these presents sealed with our seals and dated this 12th day of September 1816

    The Condition of the above obligation is such, whereas at the Court held for Craven County, at this day permission has been granted to Donum Montford by the said Court, to emancipate and set free a certain negro slave

Chapter 6: Craven County Records

named Abram M R Allen Now if the said negro so permitted to be liberated, shall not become chargeable to the parish of Craven County, or of any other County in this State, then the above obligation to be void.

Sealed and delivered }	his	
in presence of }	Donum X Montford	(Seal)
J G Stanly	mark	
	James Y Green	(Seal)

****

David Moore
Petition to emancpt
March 1817
read & granted

To the Worshipfull Justices of Craven County Court

    The Petition of David Moore humbly sheweth That he is owner of a mulatto girl slave named Alice, Whose meritorious services he desires to reward by emancipation - said girl is honest & industrious He prays the license of this Worshipfull Court to emancipate said girl upon giving the Bonds & security required by law in such case   March Term 1817

J. Stanly
for petitioner

Petition being read It is considered by the Court that the prayer of Petr. be granted & that he have license to emancipate said slave on entering into bond with security as required in such cases at such time

---

State of North Carolina }
Craven County }

Know all men by these presents that We David Moore and Valentine Richardson are held and firmly bound unto his Excellency William Miller Esquire, Captain General, Governor, and Commander in Chief of the State aforesaid, in the full sum of two hundred pounds, to be paid to the said Governor or his successors in office; to the which payment well and truly to be made, we bind ourselves, our heirs, executors, and administrators, jointly and severally, firmly by these presents, sealed with our seals, and dated this twelfth day of March A.D. 1817

    The Condition of the above obligation is such, that whereas at the Court held for Craven County, at this day permission has been granted to David Moore by the said Court, to emancipate and set free a certain negro slave named Alsey Now if the said negro so permitted to be liberated shall during her residence in the state of North Carolina behave as an honest and peaceable citizen, then the above obligation to be void.

Sealed and delivered }	his	
in presence of }	David X Moore	(Seal)
Jno S Green	mark	
	Valt Richardson	(Seal)
	Richd. Richardson	(Seal)

State of North Carolina }
Craven County }

Know all men by these presents that we David Moore and Valentine Richardson are held and firmly bound to John F Smith Esquire Chairman of Craven County Court, in the sum of one hundred pounds, to be paid to the said John F

Chapter 6: Craven County Records

Smith or his successors in office, to which payment well and truly to be made we bind ourselves, our heirs, executors and administrators, firmly by these presents sealed with our seals and dated this 12 day of March 1817

The Condition of the above obligation is such, whereas at the Court held for Craven County, at this day permission has been granted to David Moore by the said Court, to emancipate and set free a certain negro slave named Alsey Now if the said negro so permitted to be liberated, shall not become chargeable to the parish of Craven County, or of any other County in this State, then the above obligation to be void.

Sealed and delivered	}	his	
in presence of	}	David X Moore	(Seal)
Jno S Green		mark	
		Valtn Richardson	(Seal)
		Richd. Richardson	(Seal)

****

State of North Carolina
Craven County

Court of Pleas & Quarter Sessions March Term 1818
    The Petition of Jno. C. Stanly humbly sheweth that he is the owner of a negro woman slave named Mariah whose meritorious services has induced your petitioner to wish to liberate her. Your Petitioner therefore humbly prays that the Worshipfull Court will grant him permission to liberate said negro woman Mariah for her meritorious services aforesaid, & your petitioner will ever pray
Jno C Stanly

State of North Carolina   }
Craven County   }

Know all men by these presents that We Richard D Spaight are held and firmly bound unto his Excellency John Branch Esquire, Captain General, Governor, and Commander in Chief of the State aforesaid, in the full sum of two hundred pounds, to be paid to the said Governor or his successors in office; To the Which payment well and truly to be made, we bind ourselves, our heirs, executors, and administrators, jointly and severally, firmly by these presents, sealed with our seals, and dated this eleventh day of March 1818

The Condition of the above obligation is such, that whereas at the Court held for Craven County, at this day permission has been granted to John C Stanly by the said Court, to emancipate and set free a certain negro slave named Maria Now if the said negro so permitted to be liberated shall during her residence in the State of North Carolina behave as an honest and peaceable citizen, then the above obligation to be void.

Sealed and delivered	}	Richd Spaight	(Seal)
		Jn Donnell	

State of North Carolina   }
Craven County   }

Know all men by these presents that we Richard D Spaight are held and firmly bound to John F Smith Esquire Chairman of Craven County Court, in the sum of one hundred pounds, to be paid to the said John F Smith or his successors in office, to which payment well and truly to be made we bind ourselves, our heirs, executors and administrators, firmly by these presents sealed with our seals and dated this 11th day of March AD 1818

The Condition of the above obligation is such, whereas at the Court held for Craven County, at this day permission has been granted John C Stanly by the said Court, to emancipate and set free a certain negro slave named

Chapter 6: Craven County Records

Maria Now if the said negro so permitted to be liberated, shall not become chargeable to the parish of Craven, or of any other County in this State, then the above obligation to be void.

Sealed and delivered}   Richd D Spaight   (Seal)
                         Jn Donnell   (Seal)

****

To the Worshipfull the Justices of Craven County Court
    The Petition of John C Stanly respectfully represents, that he is the owner of a mulatto woman named Charlotte, and her son Richard whose faithfull & meritorious services he is desirous to reward with emancipation, the said slaves are persons of unexceptionable character for sobriety, honesty & industry and able to earn their livings by labor. Your Petitioner prays that on giving bond & security as required by law for the maintenance of said persons &c he may have the license of this Worshipfull Court to emancipate & set them free by the names of Charlotte Green, and Richard Green   March 1815

granted   Jno. Snead J.P.
                Wm. S. Spartan[?]
                [?] Cox

State of North Carolina   }
Craven County   }

Know all men by these presents that We Elijah Scott and John Templeton are held and firmly bound unto his Excellency William Miller Esquire, Captain General, Governor, and Commander in Chief of the State aforesaid, in the full sum of two hundred pounds, to be paid to the said Governor or his successors in office; to the which payment well and truly to be made, we bind ourselves, our heirs, executors, and administrators, jointly and severally, firmly by these presents, sealed with our seals, and dated this 11th day of March 1815

    The Condition of the above obligation is such, that whereas at the Court held for Craven County, at this day permission has been granted to John C Stanly by the said Court, to emancipate and set free a certain negro slave named Charlotte Green Now if the said negro so permitted to be liberated, shall during her residence in the state of North Carolina behave as a honest and peaceable citizen, then the above obligation to be void.

Sealed and delivered   }   Elijah Scott   (Seal)
in presence of   }   Jno. Templeton (Seal)

State of North Carolina   }
Craven County   }

Know all men by these presents that we Elijah Scott and John Templeton are held and firmly bound to John F Smith Esquire Chairman of Craven County Court, in the sum of one hundred pounds, to be paid to the said John F Smith or his successors in office, to which payment well and truly to be made we bind ourselves, our heirs, executors and administrators, firmly by these presents sealed with our seals and dated this 11th day of March AD 1816

    The Condition of the above obligation is such, whereas at the Court held for Craven County, at this day permission has been granted to John C Stanly by the said Court, to emancipate and set free a certain negro slave named Richard Green Now if the said negro so permitted to be liberated, shall not become chargeable to the parish of Craven County, or of any other County in this State, then the above obligation to be void.

Sealed and delivered   }   Elijah Scott   (Seal)
in presence of   }   Jno. Templeton (Seal)
Jonathan Price

Chapter 6: Craven County Records

****

James Y. Green
Petition for emancipation of Violet and Rigdon
Septr Term

State of North Carolina

To the Worshipfull the Justices of the Court of pleas and Quarter Sessions for the County of Craven - Humbly Petitioning sheweth unto your Worships your Petitioner James Y. Green that your petitioner aforesaid is the proprietor and owner by purchase of his the petitioners Mother named Violet, and Your petitioners brother named Rigdon Green both of whom are held in slavery by your Petitioner aforesaid, and your petitioner purchased the said Violet and Rigdon under a deep conviction that it was an act of duty and piety in your petitioner to make such purchase in order to redeem his Mother and brother aforesaid from the state of Slavery, & Your Petitioner further sheweth that the slaves Violet & Rigdon aforesaid have always sustained and still sustain, fair moral characters are industrious in their habits & peaceable in their deportment & meritorious for their services to their former owners   Your Petitioner is therefore desirous to set free the said Violet and Rigdon and to this end prays license of this Worshipfull Court, your petitioner first entering into bonds with security to be approved of by your Worships for the indemnity of the public against the maintenance of the slaves aforesaid and also for their good behaviour agreeably to the acts of the General Assembly in such case provided   And your Petitioner as in duty bound shall ever pray &cc

James Y. Green petitioner by
Edwd. Graham Atty

State of North Carolina }
Craven County   }

Know all men by these presents that We James Y Green and Jarvis B Brister[?] are held and firmly bound unto his Excellency John Branch Esquire, Captain General, Governor, and Commander in Chief of the State aforesaid, in the full sum of two hundred pounds, to be paid to the said Governor or his successors in office; to the which payment well and truly to be made, we bind ourselves, our heirs, executors, and administrators, jointly and severally, firmly by these presents, sealed with our seals, and dated this 18th day of September A.D. 1818.

The Condition of the above obligation is such, that whereas at the Court held for Craven County, at this day permission has been granted to James Y. Green by the said Court, to emancipate and set free a certain negro slave named Rigdon   Now if the said negro so permitted to be liberated shall during his residence in the state of North Carolina behave as an honest and peaceable citizen, then the above obligation to be void.

Sealed and delivered	}	James Y Green	(seal)
in presence of	}	Jarvis B Brister[?]	(Seal)
J G Stanly by			
Jas. Y York atty			

State of North Carolina }
Craven County   }

Know all men by these presents that we James Y Green & Jarvis B Brister[?] are held and firmly bound to John F Smith Esquire Chairman of Craven County Court, in the sum of one hundred pounds, to be paid to the said John F Smith or his successors in office, to which payment well and truly to be made we bind ourselves, our heirs, executors and administrators, firmly by these presents sealed with our seals and dated this 18 day of September 1818

The Condition of the above obligation is such, whereas at the Court held for Craven County, at this day permission has been granted to James Y Green by the said Court, to emancipate and set free a certain negro slave named

Chapter 6: Craven County Records

Rigdon Now if the said negro so permitted to be liberated, shall not become chargeable to the parish of Craven County, or of any other County in this State, then the above obligation to be void.

Sealed and delivered	}	James Y Green	(Seal)
in presence of	}	Jarvis B Brister[?]	(Seal)
J G Stanly by			
Jas. Y. Green atty			

State of North Carolina }
Craven County }

Know all men by these presents that We James Y. Green and Alexander Henderson are held and firmly bound unto his Excellency John Branch Esquire, Captain General, Governor, and Commander in Chief of the State aforesaid, in the full sum of two hundred pounds, to be paid to the said Governor or his successors in office; to the which payment well and truly to be made, we bind ourselves, our heirs, executors, and administrators, jointly and severally, firmly by these presents, sealed with our seals, and dated this eighteenth day of September A.D. 1818

    The Condition of the above obligation is such, that whereas at the Court held for Craven County, at this day permission has been granted to James Y Green by the said Court, to emancipate and set free a certain negro slave named Violet Now if the said negro so permitted to be liberated, shall during her residence in the state of North Carolina behave as an honest and peaceable citizen, then the above obligation to be void.

Sealed and delivered	}	James Y Green	(Seal)
in presence of	}	A. Henderson	(Seal)
Fran. Hawks			

State of North Carolina }
Craven County }

Know all men by these presents that we James Y. Green and Alexander Henderson are held and firmly bound to John F Smith Esquire Chairman of Craven County Court, in the sum of one hundred pounds, to be paid to the said John F Smith or his successors in office, to which payment well and truly to be made we bind ourselves, our heirs, executors and administrators, firmly by these presents sealed with our seals and dated this 18th day of September AD 1818

    The Condition of the above obligation is such, whereas at the Court held for Craven County, at this day permission has been granted to James Y Green by the said Court, to emancipate and set free a certain negro slave names Violet Now if the said negro so permitted to be liberated, shall not become chargeable to the parish of Craven County, or of any other County in this State, then the above obligation to be void.

Sealed and delivered	}	James Y Green	(Seal)
in presence of	}	A: Henderson	(Seal)
Frans. Hawks			

****

State of North Carolina } Court of Pleas and Quarter Sessions
Craven County } March Term 1818

    The Petition of Richard D Spaight to the Worshipful the Justices of the court of pleas and quarter sessions Your Petitioner humbly sheweth to your Worships that he is the proprietor of a mulatto man slave named John Green who hath conducted himself morally and with sobriety as far as your Petitioner knows. Your Petitioner also begs leave to inform your Worships that the said slave John has conducted himself generally and towards your petitioner meritoriously. In consequence of this meritorious conduct your Petitioner is desirous of emancipating him the said slave

Chapter 6: Craven County Records

John: And therefore Your Petitioner prays that he may be allowed to emancipate said John and your Petitioner as in duty bound will ever pray &c

                 R D Spaight

State of North Carolina   }
Craven County   }

Know all men by these presents that We Richard D Spaight are held and firmly bound unto his Excellency John Branch Esquire, Captain General, Governor, and Commander in Chief of the State aforesaid, in the full sum of two hundred pounds, to be paid to the said Governor or his successors in office; to the which payment well and truly to be made, we bind ourselves, our heirs, executors, and administrators, jointly and severally, firmly by these presents, sealed with our seals, and dated this 13th day of March A.D. 1818

  The Condition of the above obligation is such, that whereas at the Court held for Craven County, at this day permission has been granted to Rd D Spaight by the said Court, to emancipate and set free a certain negro slave named John Now if the said negro so permitted to be liberated, shall during his residence in the state of North Carolina behave as a honest and peaceable citizen, then the above obligation to be void.

| Sealed and delivered | } | Richd D Spaight | (Seal) |
| in presence of | } | Thomas H. Daves[?] | (Seal) |

State of North Carolina   }
Craven County   }

Know all men by these presents that we Richard D Spaight are held and firmly bound to John F Smith Esquire Chairman of Craven County Court, in the sum of one hundred pounds, to be paid to the said John F Smith or his successors in office, to which payment well and truly to be made we bind ourselves, our heirs, executors and administrators, firmly by these presents sealed with our seals and dated this 13 day of March 1818

  The Condition of the above obligation is such, whereas at the Court held for Craven County, at this day permission has been granted to Richard D Spaight by the said Court, to emancipate and set free a certain negro slave named Violet Now if the said negro so permitted to be liberated, shall not become chargeable to the parish of Craven County, or of any other County in this State, then the above obligation to be void.

| Sealed and delivered | } | Richd D Spaight | (Seal) |
| in presence of | } | Thomas H. Daves[?] | (Seal) |

****

To the Honourable the Judge of the Superior Court of Law for the County of Craven;
  The Petition of Stephen B Forbes of said County respectfully sheweth unto your Honors, that he is the owner of a negro woman Slave named Lettice, who is about fifty years of age, that said slave has during her long life of servitude been honest submissive and faithful to her owners. That her diligence & fidelity has been remarkable having been entrusted occasionally as a house keeper with the care of the house and keys and has never violated her trust, that during sickness in the family of her owners she has been devoted in her Care & attentions.

  In consideration of the premises, your Petitioner prays your Honors that he may be permitted to emancipate said slave agreeably to the Acts of Assembly in such case made and provided.

                 Jn H Bryan for Petr.

State of North Carolina   }
Craven County   }

Chapter 6: Craven County Records

Know all men by these presents, that we Spephen B. Forbes and Robert Primrose are held and firmly bound unto his Excellency John Owen Esquire, Captain General, Governor, and Commander in Chief of the State aforesaid in the full sum of two hundred pounds, to be paid to the said Governor or his successors in office; to the which payment well and truly to be made, we bind ourselves, our heirs, executors and administrators, jointly and severally, firmly by these presents; Sealed with our seals, and dated this 21 day of April A.D. 1829

The Condition of the above obligation is such, that whereas at the Court held for Craven County, at this day permission has been granted to Stephen B Forbes by the said Court to emancipate and set free a certain negro slave named Lettice Now if the said negro so permitted to be liberated, shall during her residence in the State of North Carolina, behave as an honest and peaceable citizen, then the above obligation to be void.

Sealed and delivered in presence of   Stepn. B. Forbes (Seal)
Abner Pasteur   Robert H Primrose (Seal)

State of North Carolina } Craven Superior Court
Craven County   } April Term AD 1829

Know all men by these presents, that we Stephen B Forbes are held and firmly bound to John F Smith Esquire, Chairman of Craven County Court, in the sum of one hundred pounds, to be paid to the said John F Smith or his successors in office, to which payment well and truly to be made, we bind ourselves, our heirs, executors and administrators, firmly by these presents; sealed with our seals, and dated this 21 day of April A.D. 1829

The Condition of the above obligation is such, that whereas at the Court held for Craven County, at this day permission has been granted to Stephen B Forbes by the said Court, to emancipate and set free a certain negro slave named Lettice Now if the said negro so permitted to be liberated, shall not become chargeable to the Parish of Craven County, or of any other County in this State then the above obligation to be void.

Sealed and delivered in presence of   Stephn. B. Forbes (Seal)
                Jn Street   (Seal)

****

To the Jailor of Craven County

You are hereby authorised & required to receive into your Jail a Certain Mulatto boy named Edward apprehended under suspicion of being a runaway

Wm G. Bryan   JP
Decr 10 1840
Jno B Daivrou[?]

State of North Carolina
   To the Sheriff of Craven County Greeting
We command you that you have the body of Edward Hammons detained under your Custody together with the day and cause of his being taken and detained by whatsoever name he may be called in the same before the Honourable Matthias E Manly one of the Judges of our Superior Courts of law at his office in Newbern on 8th day of June (9 oclock) to do and receive all and singular those things which our said Judge shall then and there consider of him in this behalf and have you then and there this Writ -- Witness the Honourable M.E. Manly one of our Judges of the said Superior Courts of law at Newbern the 4th day of June in the 65th year of our Independence
AD 1841
        Matthias E. Manly

Chapter 6: Craven County Records

You are hereby commanded to summon George Taylor & William H. Handcock
         M.E. Manly

I John B. Dawson Sheriff of Craven County return in this Writ that I have in my Custody & detain Edward Hammons by virtue of the process signed by William G Bryan Esq. a Justice of the Peace for Craven County which process is hereunto annexed -- I produce said Edward with, & [?] this Writ Newbern June 8th 1841

         Jno B. Dawson Shff

   To the Honourable Matthias E. Manly Judge of the Superior Court of law and Equity for the State of North Carolina

   The Petition of Edward Hammons humbly sheweth unto your honors that he is a free person of Colour free born and a Native of the State of North Carolina, that being in Chatham County in said State he on the first day of Novemb last past wished to come into the Eastern part of the State on a visit to his friends - That he procured from the Clerk of the County of Chatham N. A Stedman Esq. a Certificate of his freedom & he supposed that would be ample evidence of the fact, but [?] may it please your honours while in Novb.the Petitioner was Seized & Committed to the Jail of Craven County under suspicion as was alleged of his being a runaway Slave Petr. has been in said Prison now for six months & most unjustly illegally detained there by the Sheriff of said County - Petr. prays your Honors to grant him the benefit of the Writ of Habeas Corpus that his detention may be suspended of & he discharged from further imprisonment as in duty bound Petr. will ever pray

       his
    Edward --- Hammon
       mark

Edward Hammon maketh oath that the facts stated in the foregoing petition which are of his own Knowledge are true, and those which are not of his Knowledge he believes to be true

Sworn to Subscribed by }   his
the affiant this third   } Edward --- Hammons
day of June AD 1841 }   mark
before me   }
J.G. Stanly   }
Clerk of Craven County Court

The boy Edward Hammon having been brought before me in pursuance of the annexed writ, & the warrant for his detention hereto attached & other evidence produced having been considered, It is declared by me that there is no sufficient ground for the allegation of the warrant but that the said Edward is a free boy by the laws of the State & entitled to his dischargeIt is therefore ordered that he be discharged from custody & be allowed to go without day upon his paying his jail fees & taking the oath of insolvency provided in this behalf Given under my hand this the 8th day of June 1841

         Matthias E Manly

It further appearing that the boy is without the means of paying said fees & the sheriff being present & accepting notices[?] as tho it had been [?] given the said boy is admitted to take the oath of insolvency -- And it is accordingly administered
 Given as above M.E. Manly

To the Honourable the Judge of the Superior Court of Law for Craven County--

   The Petition of John T Lane of Craven County humbly sheweth unto your Honour that he is the owner of a Certain Male slave named Edward now fifty eight years old or thereabouts - that the said slave was the property of

Chapter 6: Craven County Records

Stephen Harris late of said County and come to this Petitioner as one of the next of kin of said Harris in the division of his slaves - Petitioner sheweth further unto your Honour that the said slave has been an old family servant that Petitioner has been well acquainted with for thirty years or more and that he has uniformly been a faithful and trusty servant and is well entitled as far as his behaviour extends to the boon[?] of freedom - That if honesty obedience, faithfulness and good conduct in a slave can Constitute much, then he has performed Meritorious services - and the petitioner believes his past life offers a sure guarantee of his future good behaviour Petitioner sheweth further unto your Honour that the former owners of said slave Edward expressed the most earnest Wishes that he should be emancipated and Petitioner under the circumstances is desirous to have their Wishes gratified - Petitioner further sheweth unto your Honour that he has not received in Money or otherwise the price or value or any part thereof of said slave or been induced to petitione for the emancipation thereof in Consideration of any price paid therefor or to be paid

Petitioner prays your honour that his said slave may be emancipated and set free from future Servitude and that he may have all further relief necessary in the premises - And as in duty bound petitioner will ever pray &c

AH [?] for petr.

John T Lane maketh oath that the facts set forth in the forgoing petition are true

Sworn & Subscribed   } John T. Lane
before me this 26   }
day of April 1848   }
Will T Blackledge   }

In the matter of Petr for the Emancipation of slave Edward
John T. Lane}

This case coming on to be heard & it being proved to the satisfaction of the Court that the petr has given Public Notice of his intention to file his said petition at the Court house in Craven County and in the Raleigh Register a newspaper printed in Raleigh the rest of Government as Prescribed by law, that the said slave is over the age of fifty years and it being further proved to the satisfaction of the Court & Jury empannelled for that purpose that the said slave has performed meritorious services, and the petitioner having made oath that he has not received in money or otherwise the Price or Value or any part thereof of said slave or been induced to petition for his emancipation in consideration of any price paid therefore or to be paid - it is ordered and adjudged by the Court that the said Petitioner John T Lane have license to emancipate and set free the said slave upon his entering into bond according to law, and the said John T Lane enters into bond accordingly in the sum of $500 with William W O[?]insbee Security which bond is accepted & entered to be filed Whereupon the said John T Lane now & forever relinquishes renounces releases & disclaims all right & title to said slave Edward & his future services and doth here manumit & set free the said Edward - Who is adjudged by the Court to be free and entitled henceforth to all the priviledges of a free man

It is further ordered & adjudged that the petr. pay all the Costs of this Proceeding

****

To the Worshipfull the Justices of the Court of Pleas & Quarter Sessions of Craven for March Term 1810

Humbly petitioning sheweth to your Worships Your Petitioner Owen Stanton, that your Petitioner is the owner of two negro Men slaves of About the age of twenty five & six Years named Silas and Peter, that your petitioner is desirous to emancipate & set free the said slaves for their meritorious services and orderly and moral conduct And your petitioner is ready to enter into and execute such bonds as in such cases are required by law - Your Petitioner therefor prays your Worships the premises considered & grant him a license to make free the above named slaves & your petitioner as in duty bound will ever pray &c Owen Stanton

Upon the petitioner executing with two sufficient securities to be approved of by the court the Bonds required by law, Ordered that the petitioner have leave to make free the slaves named in the petition Silas and Peter

---

State of North Carolina   }

Chapter 6: Craven County Records

Craven County   }

Know all men by these presents that We Silas Reed Gideon Jones & William Physioc are held and firmly bound unto his Excellency David Stone Esquire, Captain General, Governor, and Commander in Chief of the State aforesaid, in the full sum of two hundred pounds, to be paid to the said Governor or his successors in office; to the which payment well and truly to be made, we bind ourselves, our heirs, executors, and administrators, jointly and severally, firmly by these presents, sealed with our seals, and dated this 18 day of June 1810

The Condition of the above obligation is such, that whereas at the Court held for Craven County, at this day permission has been granted to Owen Stanton by the said Court, to emancipate and set free a certain negro slave named Silas Now if the said negro so permitted to be liberated shall during his residence in the state of North Carolina behaves himself as a honest and peaceable citizen, then the above obligation to be void.

Sealed and delivered }   his
in presence of   }   Silas X Reed   (Seal)
                                    mark
                             Gideon Jones   (Seal)
                             Wm Physioc   (Seal)

State of North Carolina }
Craven County   }

Know all men by these presents that we Silas Read Gideon Jones & William Physioc are held and firmly bound to John Tillman Esquire Chairman of Craven Court, in the sum of one hundred pounds, to be paid to the said John or his successors in office, to which payment well and truly to be made we bind ourselves, our heirs, executors and administrators, firmly by these presents sealed with our seals and dated this 18 day of June 1810

The Condition of the above obligation is such, whereas at the Court held for Craven County, at this day permission has been granted to Owen Stanton by the said Court, to emancipate and set free a certain negro slave named Silas Now if the said negro so permitted to be liberated shall not become chargeable to the parish of Craven County, or of any other County in this State, then the above obligation to be void.

Sealed and delivered }   his
in presence of   }   Silas X Read   (Seal)
                                    mark
                             Gideon Jones   (Seal)
                             Wm Physioc   (seal)

State of North Carolina }
Craven County   }

Know all men by these presents that We Peter Richard Gideon Jones & William Physioc are held and firmly bound unto his Excellency David Stone Esquire, Captain General, Governor, and Commander in Chief of the State aforesaid, in the full sum of two hundred pounds, to be paid to the said Governor or his successors in office; to the which payment well and truly to be made, we bind ourselves, our heirs, executors, and administrators, jointly and severally, firmly by these presents, sealed with our seals, and dated this 12 day of March A.D. 1810

The Condition of the above obligation is such, that whereas at the Court held for Craven County, at this day permission has been granted to Owen Stanton by the said Court, to emancipate and set free a certain negro slave named Peter Now if the said negro so permitted to be liberated shall during his residence in the state of North Carolina, behave himself as a honest and peaceable citizen, then the above obligation to be void.

Sealed and delivered }   his

Chapter 6: Craven County Records

in presence of	}	Peter X Richard	(Seal)
		mark	
		Gideon Jones	(Seal)
		Wm Physioc	(Seal)

State of North Carolina }
Craven County   }

Know all men by these presents that we Peter Richard Gideon Jones & William Physioc are held and firmly bound to John Tillman Esquire Chairman of Craven County Court, in the sum of one hundred pounds, to be paid to the said John or his successors in office, to which payment well and truly to be made we bind ourselves, our heirs, executors and administrators, firmly by these presents sealed with our seals and dated this 12 day of March 1810

  The Condition of the above obligation is such, whereas at the Court held for Craven County, at this day permission has been granted to Owen Stanton by the said Court, to emancipate and set free a certain negro slave named Peter Now if the said negro so permitted to be liberated, shall not become chargeable to the parish of Craven County, or of any other County in this State, then the above obligation to be void.

Sealed and delivered	}	his	
in presence of	}	Peter X Richard	(Seal)
		mark	
		Gideon Jones	(Seal)
		Wm Physioc	(Seal)

****

To the Honorable the Judge of the Superior Court of Law for the County of Craven
  The Petition of John C. Stanly humbly sheweth unto your Honor that he is the owner of negro slaves two negro men and two negro women - the Men Named Boston and Brister and the women named Betty & Money - These servants have each performed meritorious services for which it is the wish of your Petitioner to reward them by emancipation.
  They have each of them been dutiful and obedient servants, faithful and honest in the discharge of the various duties committed to their care - remarkable for their attention to the interest and wishes of your Petitioner & humble and respectful in their deportment to the Whites. The negro Man Boston is between thirty and forty years old - has been owned by your Petitioner more than thirty years and was the first - Man ever owned [by] your Petitioner -- The negro Man Brister is about the same age and has belonged to this Petitioner more than twenty years - They were purchased by your Petitioner to direct his attention to other matters, he left to the care of the two slaves the management of the said establishment -- During many years the establishment has been under the exclusive management of the aforesaid servants and they have faithfully collected and paid over to your Petitioner the money received by them from the Customers to the shop -- And your Petitioner is not informed and does not believe that a single instance exists in which they have wrongfully with held the money coming to your Petitioner -- These facts are stated more fully of establishing the honesty and fidelity of said slaves tho continually exposed to temptation
  Your Petitioner further sheweth that thru the agency of the Negro Man Brister he has recd such information as has enabled him to apprehend one of his slaves which had run away and to prevent the absconding of others who had manifested an intention of deserting. The same negro has at least once given such information to this Petitioner and thru him to the owner of a slave, which had run away and had reached the State of N. York, as enable the said owner to apprehend and recover his run away slave And this Petitioner believes but will not positively affirm that more than once he has recd. such intelligence which has been useful to the inhabitants of the town.
  Your Petitioner further states that during the period which he has owned the aforesaid negro men it has fallen to his lot to be afflicted with severe illness - twice at least your Petitioner's life was dispaired of and the office of nurse devolved on and by your Petitioner's family was committed to the said Negro Men Boston and Brister and that was the fidelity and tenderness with which they discharged the trust reposed in them that your Petitioner verily believes that (if his life was not preserved) at least his recovery was acellerated by their attentions.

Chapter 6: Craven County Records

    The Negro Women Betty is about Forty years old & Money is about nearly as old. They have been and are most faithful and honest and humble servants - attentive to the wishes and interest of your Petitioner and humble and respectful to the Whites.
    These Servants were the nurses of your **[Petitioner's]** wife during her last illness, which continued uninterrupted for ten years - the greater part of which time she was unable to render to herself any assistance and was dependant during all said time on the kindness of said negroes. The services which these slaves were called on to perform during all this time were arduous and menial and such as money could not have procured, yet they were performed with a cheerfulness and alacrity and kindness which demands to be rewarded by your Petitioner with emancipation.
    Your Petitioner therefore prays that he may have leave to liberate said slaves upon his complying with the requisitions of the law.

M. C. Stanly
for Petr.
Jn. C. Stanly

Affirmed to before me in open Court
Thos. G. Singleton Clk.

State of North Carolina

To the Sheriff of Craven County--Greeting:

You are hereby commanded to summon, George Wilson personally to be and appear before the Judge of the Superior Court of Law, to be held for the County of Craven at the Court House in Newbern on the fourth Monday after the fourth Monday of September present, then and there to testify and the truth to say in behalf of the State against the Petition of John C. Stanly for the liberation of slaves in a certain matter of controversy before said Court depending, then and there to be tried, wherein the State is plaintiff and John C. Stanly is defendant And this you shall in no wise omit under the penalty by law.

Witness, Thomas G. Singleton Clerk of the said Court, at New Bern the fourth Monday after the fourth Monday of Septr. 1828.
Thos. G. Singleton Clk

Mrs. Winney Wilson maketh oath that she is well acquainted with the two negro women slaves Named Betty & Mony the proper slaves of John C. Stanly - That they are obedient and humble servants and so far as this affiant knows they are honest - she has never heard them charged with dishonesty or disobedience or a want of and respect to their superior. That they were the nurses who attended on the wife of Jno. C. Stanly during her last illness which lasted for a very long time. This afft. has known the aforesaid slaves for more than ten years as ever as she can recollect.

                    her
             Winefred X Wilson
                   mark

Sworn to before me the 22nd
day of October 1828
Thos. G. Singleton Clk.

Elijah Scott maketh oath that he is well acquainted with Betty the slave of Jno. C. Stanly - that he believes her an obedient and humble and honest servant and has never heard her charged with dishonesty or improper conduct either towards her owners or towards the whites.

Elijah Scott

Sworn to before me the 22nd
day of October 1828

Chapter 6: Craven County Records

Thos. G. Singleton Clk

State of North Carolina }
Craven County }

Know all men by these presents that We John Stanly & John C. Stanly are held and firmly bound unto his Excellency James Iredell Esquire, Captain General, Governor, and Commander in Chief of the State aforesaid, in the full sum of two hundred pounds, to be paid to the said Governor or his successors in office; to the which payment well and truly to be made, we bind ourselves, our heirs, executors, and administrators, jointly and severally, firmly by these presents, sealed with our seals, and dated this 28 day of October A.D. 1828

The Condition of the above obligation is such, that whereas at the Court held for Craven County, at this day permission has been granted to John Stanly by the said Court, to emancipate and set free a certain negro slave named Money Now if the said negro so permitted to be liberated shall during her residence in the state of North Carolina behave herself as a honest and peaceable citizen, then the above obligation to be void.

Sealed and delivered	}	Jn C. Stanly	(Seal)
in presence of	}	J Stanly	(Seal)
G H Burgioyse			

State of North Carolina }
Craven County }

Know all men by these presents that we John C. Stanly and John Stanly are held and firmly bound to John F. Smith Esquire Chairman of Craven County Court, in the sum of one hundred pounds, to be paid to the said John F. Smith or his successors in office, to which payment well and truly to be made we bind ourselves, our heirs, executors and administrators, firmly by these presents sealed with our seals and dated this **[Torn]** day of October A.D. 1828.

The Condition of the above obligation is such, whereas at the Superior Court held for Craven County, at this day permission has been granted to John C Stanly by the said Court, to emancipate and set free a certain negro slave named Money Now if the said negro so permitted to be liberated, shall not become chargeable to the parish of Craven County, or of any other County in this State, then the above obligation to be void.

Sealed and delivered	}	Jn. C. Stanly	(Seal)
in presence of	}	J Stanly	(Seal)
G H Burgioyse			

State of North Carolina }
Craven County }

Know all men by these presents that We John C. Stanly and John Stanly are held and firmly bound unto his Excellency James Iredell Esquire, Captain General, Governor, and Commander in Chief of the State aforesaid, in the full sum of two hundred pounds, to be paid to the said Governor or his successors in office; to the which payment well and truly to be made, we bind ourselves, our heirs, executors, and administrators, jointly and severally, firmly by these presents, sealed with our seals, and dated this 28th day of October A.D. 1828

The Condition of the above obligation is such, that whereas at the Court held for Craven County, at this day permission has been granted to John C. Stanly by the said Court, to emancipate and set free a certain negro slave named Boston Now if the said negro so permitted to be liberated shall during his residence in the state of North Carolina behave himself as a honest and peaceable citizen, then the above obligation to be void.

Sealed and delivered }   Jn C. Stanly   (Seal)

Chapter 6: Craven County Records

in presence of   }   J Stanly   (Seal)
G H Burgu[Faded]

State of North Carolina   }
Craven County   }

Know all men by these presents that we John C. Stanly and John Stanly are held and firmly bound to John F. Smith Esquire Chairman of Craven County Court, in the sum of one hundred pounds, to be paid to the said John F. Smith or his successors in office, to which payment well and truly to be made we bind ourselves, our heirs, executors and administrators, firmly by these presents sealed with our seals and dated this 28th day of October A.D. 1828

     The Condition of the above obligation is such, whereas at the Superior Court held for Craven County, at this day permission has been granted to John C. Stanly by the said Court, to emancipate and set free a certain negro slave named Boston Now if the said negro so permitted to be liberated, shall not become chargeable to the parish of Craven County, or of any other County in this State, then the above obligation to be void.

Sealed and delivered   }   Jn. C. Stanly   (Seal)
in presence of   }   J Stanly   (Seal)
[Faded]

State of North Carolina   }
Craven County   }

Know all men by these presents that We John C. Stanly and John Stanly are held and firmly bound unto his Excellency James Iredell Esquire, Captain General, Governor, and Commander in Chief of the State aforesaid, in the full sum of two hundred pounds, to be paid to the said Governor or his successors in office; to the which payment well and truly to be made, we bind ourselves, our heirs, executors, and administrators, jointly and severally, firmly by these presents, sealed with our seals, and dated this 28th day of October A.D. 1828

     The Condition of the above obligation is such, that whereas at the Superior Court held for Craven County, at this day permission has been granted to John C. Stanly by the said Court, to emancipate and set free a certain negro slave named Brister Now if the said negro so permitted to be liberated shall during his residence in the state of North Carolina behave himself as a honest and peaceable citizen then the above obligation to be void.

Sealed and delivered   }   Jn. C. Stanly   (Seal)
in presence of   }   J Stanly   (Seal)
G H Burgioyse

State of North Carolina   }
Craven County   }

Know all men by these presents that we John C. Stanly and John Stanly are held and firmly bound to John F. Smith Esquire Chairman of Craven County Court, in the sum of one hundred pounds, to be paid to the said John F. Smith or his successors in office, to which payment well and truly to be made we bind ourselves, our heirs, executors and administrators, firmly by these presents sealed with our seals and dated this 28th day of October A.D. 1828

     The Condition of the above obligation is such, whereas at the Superior Court held for Craven County, at this day permission has been granted to John C. Stanly by the said Court, to emancipate and set free a certain negro slave named Brister Now if the said negro so permitted to be liberated, shall not become chargeable to the parish of Craven County, or of any other County in this State, then the above obligation to be void.

Sealed and delivered   }   Jn. C. Stanly   (Seal)

Chapter 6: Craven County Records

in presence of   }   J Stanly   (Seal)
G H Burgioyse

State of North Carolina   }
Craven County   }

Know all men by these presents that We John C. Stanly & John Stanly are held and firmly bound unto his Excellency James Iredell Esquire, Captain General, Governor, and Commander in Chief of the State aforesaid, in the full sum of two hundred pounds, to be paid to the said Governor or his successors in office; to the which payment well and truly to be made, we bind ourselves, our heirs, executors, and administrators, jointly and severally, firmly by these presents, sealed with our seals, and dated this 28th day of October A.D. 1828

      The Condition of the above obligation is such, that whereas at the Court held for Craven County, at this day permission has been granted to John C. Stanly by the said Court, to emancipate and set free a certain negro slave named Betty Now if the said negro so permitted to be liberated, shall during her residence in the state of North Carolina behave herself as a honest and peaceable citizen, then the above obligation to be void.

Sealed and delivered   }   Jn. C. Stanly   (Seal)
in presence of   }   J Stanly   (Seal)
G H Burgioyse

State of North Carolina   }
Craven County   }

Know all men by these presents that we John C. Stanly and John Stanly are held and firmly bound to John F. Smith Esquire Chairman of Craven County Court, in the sum of one hundred pounds, to be paid to the said John F. Smith or his successors in office, to which payment well and truly to be made, we bind ourselves, our heirs, executors and administrators, firmly by these presents sealed with our seals and dated this 28th day of October A.D. 1828

      The Condition of the above obligation is such, whereas at the Superior Court held for Craven County, at this day permission has been granted to John C. Stanly by the said Court, to emancipate and set free a certain negro slave named Betty Now if the said negro so permitted to be liberated, shall not become chargeable to the parish of Craven County, or of any other County in this State, then the above obligation to be void.

Sealed and delivered   }   Jn. C. Stanly   (Seal)
in presence of   }   J Stanly   (Seal)
G H Burgioyse

****

To the Worshipful Court of Craven County
The Petition of Ann Dowden, Executrix of William Dowden humbly sheweth, That her testator the said Dowden, intending to reward the meritorious services of a negro man named York his property, by his enjoined it upon your petitioner to emancipate the said York - Your Petitioner prays that she may be permitted by license of this Worshipful Court to emancipate and set free the said negro York, agreeably to the wish & directions of the said William Dowden.

Signed by the said Ann   }   Ann Dowden
Dowden, being first read }
to her, in our presence   }
Thos. Finley
S B Shannawoolf

Chapter 6: Craven County Records

State of North Carolina }
Craven County }

Know all men by these presents that We Ann Dowden John Templeton & William Tignor are held and firmly bound unto his Excellency David Stone Esquire, Captain General, Governor, and Commander in Chief of the State aforesaid, in the full sum of two hundred pounds, to be paid to the said Governor or his successors in office; to the which payment well and truly to be made, we bind ourselves, our heirs, executors, and administrators, jointly and severally, firmly by these presents, sealed with our seals, and dated this 28th day of December A.D. 1808

    The Condition of the above obligation is such, that whereas at the Court held for Craven County, at this day permission has been granted to Ann Dowden by the said Court, to emancipate and set free a certain negro slave named York Now if the said negro so permitted to be liberated, shall during his residence in the state of North Carolina behave himself as an honest and peaceable citizen, then the above obligation to be void.

Sealed and delivered }	Ann Dowden	(Seal)
in presence of }	Jno. Templeton	(Seal)
S B Shanawoolf	Wm Tignor	(Seal)

State of North Carolina }
Craven County }

Know all men by these presents that we Ann Dowden John Templeton & William Tignor are held and firmly bound to John Tillman Esquire Chairman of Craven County Court, in the sum of one hundred pounds, to be paid to the said John Tillman or his successors in office, to which payment well and truly to be made, we bind ourselves, our heirs, executors and administrators, firmly by these presents sealed with our seals and dated this 28 day of Octr. 1808

    The Condition of the above obligation is such, whereas at the Court held for Craven County, at this day permission has been granted to Ann Dowden by the said Court, to emancipate and set free a certain negro slave named York Now if the said negro so permitted to be liberated, shall not become chargeable to the parish of Craven County, or of any other County in this State, then the above obligation to be void.

Sealed and delivered }	Ann Dowden	(Seal)
in presence of }	Jno. Templeton	(Seal)
S. B Shanawoolf	Wm Tignor	(Seal)

***

To the Worshipfull the Justices of the Court of Pleas & Quarter Sessions for Craven

Humbly petitioning sheweth unto your worships your petitioner Thomas Newton, that your petitioner was the property of Benjamin Woods Esqr in his life time and that in conformity to the intention and desires of his said Master often times expressed the Executrix of Mr Wood was pleased to obtain leave from this Worshipfull Court to give your petitioner his freedom which has been confirmed to him accordingly - And your petitioner further sheweth that he has a wife named Sarah late the property of Mr John Devereaux, and that your petitioner has been enabled to purchase his said wife from Mr Devereaux by the fruits of his honest industry; And your petitioner presumes to say that his said wife bears an unexceptionable character for sobriety industry and orderly and peaceable conduct - And your petitioner being Master of the Carpenters business is able to maintain himself wife & children in [?] Your petitioner is therefore anxious to procure his wifes freedom And humbly prays your worships to grant him a license for this purpose upon your petitioner entering into Bond with securities agreeably to the acts of Assembly in such case provided for the good behaviour of his said wife and to indemnify the County against her becoming a County charge

And your petitioner as in duty bound &c
Thomas Newton by E Graham his Atto

Chapter 6: Craven County Records

State of North Carolina }
Craven County }

Know all men by these presents that We John Devereaux & Wm Hollister are held and firmly bound unto his Excellency David Stone Esquire, Captain General, Governor, and Commander in Chief of the State aforesain, in the full sum of two hundred pounds, to be paid to the said Governor or his successors in office; to the which payment well and truly to be made, we bind ourselves, our heirs, executors, and administrators, jointly and severally, firmly by these presents, sealed with our seals, and dated this 18th day of November A.D. 1808

    The Condition of the above obligation is such, that whereas at the Court held for Craven County, at September Term last past permission has been granted to Sarah Woods by the said Court, to emancipate and set free a certain negro slave named Tom Newton Now if the said negro so permitted to be liberated, shall during his residence in the state of North Carolina behave himself as a honest and peaceable citizen, then the above obligation to be void.

Sealed and delivered	}	John Devereaux	(Seal)
in presence of	}	Wm Hollister	(Seal)
M.E Stephens			

State of North Carolina }
Craven County }

Know all men by these presents that we John Devereux & Wm Hollister are held and firmly bound to John Tillman Esquire Chairman of Craven County Court, in the sum of one hundred pounds, to be paid to the said John or his successors in office, to which payment well and truly to be made we bind ourselves, our heirs, executors and administrators, firmly by these presents sealed with our seals and dated this 18 day of November 1808

    The Condition of the above obligation is such, whereas at the Court held for Craven County, at September Term last past permission has been given to Sarah Wood by the said Court, to emancipate and set free a certain negro slave named Tom Newton Now if the said negro so permitted to be liberated, shall not become chargeable to the parish of Craven County, or of any other County in this State, then the above obligation to be void.

Sealed and delivered	}	John Devereux	(Seal)
in presence of	}	Wm Hollister	(Seal)
M.E Stephens			

State of North Carolina }
Craven County }

Know all men by these presents that We Thomas Newton & Marcus C Stephens are held and firmly bound unto his Excellency Benjamin Smith Esquire, Captain General, Governor, and Commander in Chief of the State aforesaid, in the full sum of two hundred pounds, to be paid to the said Governor or his successors in office; to the which payment well and truly to be made, we bind ourselves, our heirs, executors, and administrators, jointly and severally, firmly by these presents, sealed with our seals, and dated this Eighteenth day of March A.D. 1811

    The Condition of the above obligation is such, that whereas at the Court held for Craven County, at this day permission has been granted to Thomas Newton by the said Court, to emancipate and set free a certain negro slave named Sarah Now if the said negro so permitted to be liberated shall during her residence in the state of North Carolina behave herself as a honest and peaceable citizen, then the above obligation to be void.

| Sealed and delivered | } | Saml. Oliver | (Seal) |
| in presence of | } | M. C Stephens | (Seal) |

Chapter 6: Craven County Records

State of North Carolina }
Craven County }

Know all men by these presents that we Thomas Newton & Marcus C Stephens are held and firmly bound to John F. Smith Esquire Chairman of Craven County Court, in the sum of one hundred pounds, to be paid to the said John F. Smith or his successors in office, to which payment well and truly to be made we bind ourselves, our heirs, executors and administrators, firmly by these presents sealed with our seals and dated this 18th day of March 1811

The Condition of the above obligation is such, whereas at the Court held for Craven County, at this day permission has been granted to Thomas Newton by the said Court, to emancipate and set free a certain negro slave named Sarah Now if the said negro so permitted to be liberated, shall not become chargeable to the parish of Craven County, or of any other County in this State, then the above obligation to be void.

| Sealed and delivered } | Saml. Oliver | (Seal) |
| in presence of } | M. C Stephens | (Seal) |

State of North Carolina }
Craven County }

Know all men by these presents that We Thomas Newton & William Hollister & John Justice are held and firmly bound unto his Excellency John Branch Esquire, Captain General, Governor, and Commander in Chief of the State aforesaid, in the full sum of two hundred pounds, to be paid to the said Governor or his successors in office; to the which payment well and truly to be made, we bind ourselves, our heirs, executors, and administrators, jointly and severally, firmly by these presents, sealed with our seals, and dated this 17th day of December A.D. 1818

The Condition of the above obligation is such, that whereas at the Court held for Craven County, at this day permission has been granted to Thomas Newton by the said Court, to emancipate and set free a certain negro slave named Macklin Newton Now if the said negro so permitted to be liberated shall during his residence in the state of North Carolina behave as a honest and peaceable citizen, then the above obligation to be void.

Sealed and delivered }	Wm Hollister	(Seal)
in presence of }	John Justice	(Seal)
JSM Brickell		

State of North Carolina }
Craven County }

Know all men by these presents that we Thomas Newton & William Hollister & John Justice are held and firmly bound to John F Smith Esquire Chairman of Craven County Court, in the sum of one hundred pounds, to be paid to the said John F Smith or his successors in office, to which payment well and truly to be made we bind ourselves, our heirs, executors and administrators, firmly by these presents sealed with our seals and dated this 17th day of December 1818

The Condition of the above obligation is such, whereas at the Court held for Craven County, at this day permission has been granted to Thomas Newton by the said Court, to emancipate and set free a certain negro slave named Macklin Newton Now if the said negro so permitted to be liberated, shall not become chargeable to the parish of Craven County, or of any other County in this State, then the above obligation to be void.

Sealed and delivered }	Wm Hollister	(Seal)
in presence of }	John Justice	(Seal)
JSM Brickell		

****

Chapter 6: Craven County Records

State of North Carolina }
Craven County   }

Know all men by these presents that We John C. Stanly John Templeton & John McLin are leld and firmly bound unto his Excellency William Hawkins Esquire, Captain General, Governor, and Commander in Chief of the State aforesaid, in the full sum of two hundred pounds, to be paid to the said Governor or his successors in office; to the which payment well and truly to be made, we bind ourselves, our heirs, executors, and administrators, jointly and severally, firmly by these presents, sealed with our seals, and dated this sixteenth day of June A.D. 1814

    The Condition of the above obligation is such, that whereas at the Court held for Craven County, at this day permission has been granted to Bob Lisbon by the said Court, to emancipate and set free a certain negro slave named Robert W Conway Now if the said negro so permitted to be liberated shall during his residence in the state of North Carolina behave as a honest and peaceable citizen, then the above obligation to be void.

| Sealed and delivered } | John J. McLin | (Seal) |
| in presence of   } | Jno Templeton | (Seal) |

State of North Carolina }
Craven County   }

Know all men by these presents that we John C Stanly John Templeton John J McLin are held and firmly bound to John F. Smith Esquire Chairman of Craven County Court, in the sum of one hundred pounds, to be paid to the said John or his successors in office, to which payment well and truly to be made we bind ourselves, our heirs, executors and administrators, firmly by these presents sealed with our seals and dated this 16 day of June 1814

    The Condition of the above obligation is such, whereas at the Court held for Craven County, at this day permission has been granted to Bob Lisbon by the said Court, to emancipate and set free a certain negro slave named Robert W Conway Now if the said negro so permitted to be liberated, shall not become chargeable to the parish of Craven County, or of any other County in this State, then the above obligation to be void.

| Sealed and delivered } | Jno. J. McLin | (Seal) |
| in presence of   } | Jno Templeton | (Seal) |

To the Worshipful the Justices of the Court of Pleas & Quarter Sessions for the County of Craven
    The Petition of Robert Lisbon humbly sheweth --
That your Petitioner was formerly a slave, and in consequence of his meritorious services was on the petition of his master emancipated under the license of this worshipful Court. Your Petitioner further sheweth that bein married to a negro woman slave the property of John C Osborne usually named Venus, your Petitioner purchased the said Venus and is now in law her master. Your Petitioner sheweth that the conduct of the said Negro woman Venus has been highly meritorious amd exemplary and that your Petitioner is anxious to be permitted to emancipate her. He prays that your Worships on being satisfied of these facts will graciously accord him a license to set her free - And your Petitioner will ever & gratefully pray.

Robt. Lisbon by
Will: Gaston

To the Worshipfull the Justices of Craven County Court
    The Petition of Robert Lisbon humbly sheweth that by honest industry he has obtained means to purchase his daughter Evelina, whose meritorious Services he is desirous to reward with emancipation. The said girl is honest, industrious, & healthy. He prays the license of Your Worships to emancipate the said Evelina upon giving the Bonds required by law

Chapter 6: Craven County Records

Septr. 1816
Robert Lisbon
by J. Stanly his Atto

The undersigned Certify that the Girl Evelina above named is a girl of honest character & industrious habits

Jno. Templeton
B.C. Good

State of North Carolina }
Craven County   }

Know all men by these presents that We Robert Lisbon Asa Jones Frederick Divoux are held and firmly bound unto his Excellency William Miller Esquire, Captain General, Governor, and Commander in Chief of the State aforesaid, in the full sum of two hundred pounds, to be paid to the said Governor or his successors in office; to the which payment well and truly to be made, we bind ourselves, our heirs, executors, and administrators, jointly and severally, firmly by these presents, sealed with our seals, and dated this thirteenth day of September A.D. 1816

    The Condition of the above obligation is such, that whereas at the Court held for Craven County, at this day permission has been granted to Robert Lisbon by the said Court, to emancipate and set free a certain negro slave named Evelina Now if the said negro so permitted to be liberated shall during her residence in the state of North Carolina behave as an honest and peaceable citizen, then the above obligation to be void

Sealed and delivered }	his Robert X Lisbon	(Seal)
in presence of }	mark	
	Asa Jones	(Seal)
	F. Divoux	(Seal)

State of North Carolina }
Craven County   }

Know all men by these presents that we Robert Lisbon Asa Jones and Frederick Divoux are held and firmly bound to John F Smith Esquire Chairman of Craven County Court, in the sum of one hundred pounds, to be paid to the said John F Smith or his successors in office, to which payment well and truly to be made we bind ourselves, our heirs, executors and administrators, firmly by these presents sealed with our seals and dated this 13th day of September A.D. 1816

    The Condition of the above obligation is such, whereas at the Court held for Craven County, at this day permission has been granted to Robert Lisbon by the said Court, to emancipate and set free a certain negro slave named Evelina Now if the said negro so permitted to be liberated, shall not become chargeable to the parish of Craven County, or of any other County in this State, then the above obligation to be void.

Sealed and delivered }	his Robert X Lisbon	(Seal)
in presence of }	mark	
	Asa Jones	(Seal)
	F. Divoux	(Seal)

****

To the honorable the Judge of the Superior Court of Law and Equity for the County of Craven
    The Petition of Stephen L. Ferrand respectfully sheweth, that your Petitioner is the owner of a coloured female slave usually called Caroline Lane whom he is very desirous of being permitted to Emancipate; that the said Caroline hath uniformly conducted herself with a propriety and decency far above her station in life and in the highest degree exemplary; that her services in every respect wherein they could be rendered have been singularly meritorious; that she

Chapter 6: Craven County Records

is strictly honest industrious modest; that she has been brought up in virtuous habits is scarcely distinguishable from a white person in complection, and is fitted to enjoy with propriety and to use with discretion the priveleges and rights which appertain to freedom.

Stephen L Ferrand by
Will: Gaston his atty

State of North Carolina }
Craven County   }

Know all men by these presents that We Stephen L Ferrand are held and firmly bound unto his Excellency Hutchins Burton Esquire, Captain General, Governor, and Commander in Chief of the State aforesaid, in the full sum of two hundred pounds, to be paid to the said Governor or his successors in office; to the which payment well and truly to be made, we bind ourselves, our heirs, executors, and administrators, jointly and severally, firmly by these presents, sealed with our seals, and dated this 24th day of April A.D. 1827

The Condition of the above obligation is such, that whereas at the Court held for Craven County, at this day permission has been granted to Stephen L Ferrand by the said Court, to emancipate and set free a certain negro slave named Caroline Lane Now if the said negro so permitted to be liberated shall during her residence in the state of North Carolina behave as an honest and peaceable citizen, then the above obligation to be void.

| Sealed and delivered | } | John R. Green | (Seal) |
| in presence of | } | Jno G Stanly | (Seal) |

State of North Carolina }
Craven County   }

Know all men by these presents that we Stephen L Ferrand are held and firmly bound to John F Smith Esquire Chairman of Craven County Court, in the sum of one hundred pounds, to be paid to the said John F Smith or his successors in office, to which payment well and truly to be made we bind ourselves, our heirs, executors and administrators, firmly by these presents sealed with our seals and dated this 24th day of April 1827

    The Condition of the above obligation is such, whereas at the Superior Court held for Craven County, at this day permission has been granted to Stephen L Ferrand by the said Court, to emancipate and set free a certain negro slave named Caroline Lane Now if the said negro so permitted to be liberated, shall not become chargeable to the parish of Craven County, or of any other County in this State, then the above obligation to be void.

| Sealed and delivered | } | John R. Green | (Seal) |
| in presence of | } | Jno G Stanly | (Seal) |

****

State of North Carolina } Spring Term 1829
Craven County   } Superior Court of Law

    The Petition of Nathaniel Smith of the town of Newbern respectfully sheweth unto your Honour, that he is the owner of a female slave Called Polly Aaron, about 25 years of age.

    Your petitioner sheweth unto your Honour that said slave has been remarkable for her obedience & fidelity to her owners and has always been noted for her honesty & industry, and that her Services have been uncommonly meritorious. In consideration of the premises he prays your Honour that he may be permitted to emancipate her agreeably to the acts of Assembly in such case made & provided.

Chapter 6: Craven County Records

Jn. H. Bryan
for Petr.

We the undersigned have been for a great many years acquainted with negro woman Polly Aaron, and knew her to be honest, & industrious in an unusual degree -- She has also according to the best of our information & belief been always obedient and faithful to her owners & respectful to white persons. We believe her services to have been uncommonly meritorious for a slave.

Apl. 21. 1829	Mary Harvey
	Amaryllis Ellis
	Rebecca Wallace

State of North Carolina }
Craven County }

Know all men by these presents, that we Ismael Aarons and Nathaniel Smith are held and firmly bound unto his Excellency John Owen Esquire, Captain General, Governor, and Commander in Chief of the State aforesaid, in the full sum of two hundred pounds, to be paid to the said Governor or his successors in office; to the which payment well and truly to be made, we bind ourselves, our heirs, executors and administrators, jointly and severally, firmly by these presents; Sealed with our seals, and dated this 12th day of May 1829

The Condition of the above obligation is such, that whereas at the Court held for Craven County, at this day permission has been granted to Nathaniel Smith by the said Court, to emancipate and set free a certain negro slave named Polly Aaron Now if the said negro so permitted to be liberated, shall during her residence in the state of North Carolina, behave as an honest and peaceable citizen, then the above obligation to be void.

Sealed and delivered in presence of

            his
Ismael X Aarons   (Seal)
   mark
Na Smith   (Seal)

State of North Carolina }
Craven County }

Know all men by these presents, that we Ismael and Nathaniel Smith are held and firmly bound to John F Smith Esquire, Chairman of Craven County Court, in the sum of one hundred pounds, to be paid to the said John F Smith or his successors in office, to which payment well and truly to be made, we bind ourselves, our heirs, executors and administrators, firmly by these presents; sealed with our seals, and dated this 12th day of May A.D. 1829

The Condition of the above obligation is such, that whereas at the Court held for Craven County, at this day permission has been granted Nathaniel Smith by the said Court, to emancipate and set free a certain negro slave named Polly Aaron Now if the said negro so permitted to be liberated, shall not become chargeable to the Parish of Craven County, or of any other County in this State then the above obligation to be void.   his

Sealed and delivered in presence of Ismael X Aaron (Seal)
          mark
         Na Smith   (Seal)

****

Know all men by these presence that I John C Stanly for and in consideration of five shillings to me in hand paid by Mary Sharp I have bargained Sold and delivered unto the said Mary Sharp a certain Negro woman Slave called Jenny & I do hereby agree warrant & defend the said Slave against the claims of all persons whatsoever - Octr 23d 1827

Chapter 6: Craven County Records

signed seald & delivered in   Jno C Stanly   (Seal)
presence of
Jno Stuart Stanly
Jn. H. Bryan

State of North Carolina   } Supr. Court of Law
Craven County   } October Term 1827

     The Petition of Mary Sharp humbly sheweth unto your Honour that [s]he is the owner of a female slave named Jenny, otherwise called Jenny Gaynor or Jenny Bryan - that said slave is about 60 years of age and is past the age of child bearing.

     Your Petitioner further sheweth unto your Honour that the said slave has been always faithful, honest, and humble, and has rendered highly meritorious Services to her owners - that she has been living for many years as a free person and has uniformly behaved with propriety & humility towards white persons, has been submissive to the laws and exemplary in her conduct.

     Your petitioner prays that the said slave may be emancipated agreeably to the Acts of Assembly in such Case made & provided.

State of North Carolina   }
Craven County   }

Know all men by these presents that We Mary Sharp are held and firmly bound unto his Excellency Hutchins G. Burton Esquire, Captain General, Governor, and Commander in Chief of the State aforesaid, in the full sum of two hundred pounds, to be paid to the said Governor or his successors in office; to the which payment well and truly to be made, we bind ourselves, our heirs, executors, and administrators, jointly and severally, firmly by these presents, sealed with our seals, and dated this 1st day of November A.D. 1827

The Condition of the above obligation is such, that whereas at the Superior Court held for Craven County, at this day permission has been granted to Mary Sharp by the said Court, to emancipate and set free a certain negro slave named Jenny Now if the said negro so permitted to be liberated shall during her residence in the state of North Carolina behave herself as an honest and peaceable citizen, then the above obligation to be void.

Sealed and delivered   }   Mary Sharp   (Seal)
in presence of   }   Jn. H. Bryan   (Seal)

State of North Carolina   }
Craven County   }

Know all men by these presents that we Mary Sharp are held and firmly bound to John F. Smith Esquire Chairman of Craven County Court, in the sum of one hundred pounds, to be paid to the said John F. Smith or his successors in office, to which payment well and truly to be made we bind ourselves, our heirs, executors and administrators, firmly by these presents sealed with our seals and dated this 1st day of November 1827

     The Condition of the above obligation is such, whereas at the Superior Court held for Craven County, at this day permission has been granted to Mary Sharp by the said Court, to emancipate and set free a certain negro slave named Jenny Now if the said negro so permitted to be liberated, shall not become chargeable to the Parish of Craven County, or of any other County in this State, then the above obligation to be void.

Sealed and delivered   }   Mary Sharp   (Seal)
in presence of   }   Jn H Bryan   (Seal)

****

Chapter 6: Craven County Records

To the Honorable the Judge of the Superior Court of Law of Craven County.

The Petition of Joshua Scott humbly sheweth - That he is the owner of a negro man slave named Moses, whose fidelity & valuable & meritorious Services he is desirous to reward with emancipation. Said Moses was once the property of Charles Sanders of Craven County who designed to emancipate him, for preserving his dwelling house & property from destruction by fire, occasioned by lightning but Sanders was embarrassed & the negro was sold for his debts. Your Petitioner has been & is still engaged in the butchering business, buying & selling Cattle - in which business he has had greatly to rely on the honesty & industry of Moses. Said negro is honest, sober, industrious, & is now nearly or quite sixty years of age. Your Petitioner prays that he may have the license of your Honor to emancipate said man Moses, on giving the bonds required by law - And he will ever pray

    Joshua Scott

State of North Carolina }
Craven County   }

Know all men by these presents that We Joshua Scott David Shackelford are held and firmly bound unto his Excellency Gabriel Holmes Esquire, Captain General, Governor, and Commander in Chief of the State aforesaid, in the full sum of two hundred pounds, to be paid to the said Governor or his successors in office; to the which payment well and truly to be made, we bind ourselves, our heirs, executors, and administrators, jointly and severally, firmly by these presents, sealed with our seals, and dated this 14 day of May A.D. 1824

The Condition of the above obligation is such, that whereas at the Superior Court held for Craven County, at this day permission has been granted to Joshua Scott by the said Court, to emancipate and set free a certain negro slave named Moses Now if the said negro so permitted to be liberated shall during his residence in the state of North Carolina behave as an honest and peaceable citizen, then the above obligation to be void.

Sealed and delivered }	Joshua Scott	(Seal)
in presence of }	D. Shackelford	(Seal)
J. S. Stanly		

****

To the honble. the Judge of the Superior Court of Law, for the County of Craven;

  The Petition of William Hollister respectfully sheweth unto your Honour that he is now the owner of two slaves by the name of Thomas, commonly called Tom Hollister, aged between forty six and fifty years, and another by the name of Mary aged about 28 (wife of Richard Smith a mulatto), that he is desirous of emancipating said slaves for their meritorious services, and he shows unto your Honour that the said Thomas has served him faithfully in various Capacities for near twenty years, that during that time he has made several voyages to the West Indies & New York where he might have easily obtained his freedom by absconding from his service that he has been always obedient, humble & respectful in his deportment towards the whites. That the slave Mary has been the property of your Petitioner for fifteen or sixteen years, that she has been much trusted in the management of his household, and as nurse to his children, and has proved herself to be faithful, humble & obedient - she has now been living to herself for five or six years as free, and has maintained a good character for orderly & decent Conduct, and industrious habits.

  In consideration of the premises your Petr. prays Your Honour that he may be permitted to emancipate said slaves agreeably to Act of Assembly &c
And your Petr. &c.

    Jn. H. Bryan for Petr.

State of North Carolina }
Craven County   }

Know all men by these presents, that we William Hollister & Saml. Oliver   Robt. V. O[?] are held and firmly bound unto his Excellency James Iredell Esquire, Captain General, Governor, and Commander in Chief of the State aforesaid,

Chapter 6: Craven County Records

in the full sum of two hundred pounds, to be paid to the said Governor or his successors in office; to the which payment well and truly to be made, we bind ourselves, our heirs, executors, and administrators, jointly and severally, firmly by these presents, sealed with our seals, and dated this 20th day of October A.D. 1828

    The Condition of the above obligation is such, that whereas at the Court held for Craven County, at this day permission has been granted to William Hollister by the said Court, to emancipate and set free a certain negro slave named Thomas Now if the said negro so permitted to be liberated, shall during his residence in the State of North Carolina, behave as an honest and peaceable citizen, then the above obligation to be void.

Sealed and delivered in presence of		
A Mitchell	Wm Hollister	(Seal)
	Saml. Oliver	(Seal)
	Robt. V. O[?]	(Seal)

State of North Carolina }
Craven County   }

Know all men by these presents, that we William Hollister & Saml. Oliver Robt. V. O[?] are held and firmly bound to John F. Smith Esquire, Chairman of Craven County Court, in the sum of one hundred pounds, to be paid to the said John F. Smith or his successors in office, to which payment well and truly to be made, we bind ourselves, our heirs, executors and administrators, firmly by these presents; sealed with our seals, and dated this 20th day of October A.D. 1828

    The Condition of the above obligation is such, that whereas at the Court held for Craven County, at this day permission has been granted to William Hollister by the said Court, to emancipate and set free a certain negro slave named Thomas Now if the said negro so permitted to be liberated, shall not become chargeable to the Parish of Craven County, or of any other County in this State, then the above obligation to be void.

Sealed and delivered in presence of		
A Mitchell	Wm Hollister	(Seal)
	Saml. Oliver	(Seal)
	Robt. V. O[?]	(Seal)

State of North Carolina }
Craven County   }

Know all men by these presents, that we William Hollister & Saml. Oliver & Robt. V. O[?] are held and firmly bound unto his Excellency James Iredell Esquire, Captain General, Governor, and Commander in Chief of the State aforesaid in the full sum of two hundred pounds, to be paid to the said Governor or his successors in office; to the which payment well and truly to be made, we bind ourselves, our heirs, executors and administrators, jointly and severally, firmly by these presents; Sealed with our seals, and dated this 20th day of October A.D. 1828

    The Condition of the above obligation is such, that whereas at the Court held for Craven County, at this day permission has been granted to William Hollister by the said Court to emancipate and set free a certain negro slave named Mary Now if the said negro so permitted to be liberated, shall during her residence in the state of North Carolina, behave as an honest and peaceable citizen, then the above obligation to be void.

Sealed and delivered in presence of		
A Mitchell	Wm. Hollister	(Seal)
	Saml. Oliver	(Seal)
	Robt. V. O[?]	(Seal)

State of North Carolina }
Craven County   }

Chapter 6: Craven County Records

Know all men by these presents, that we William Hollister Saml. Oliver Robt. V. O[?] are held and firmly bound to John F. Smith Esquire, Chairman of Craven County Court, in the sum of one hundred pounds, to be paid to the said John F. Smith or his successors in office, to which payment well and truly to be made, we bind ourselves, our heirs, executors and administrators, firmly by these presents; sealed with our seals, and dated this 20th day of October A.D. 1828

The Condition of the above obligation is such, that whereas at the Court held for Craven County, at this day permission has been granted to William Hollister by the said Court, to emancipate and set free a certain slave named Mary Now if the said negro so permitted to be liberated, shall not become chargeable to the Parish of Craven County, or of any other County in this State then the above obligation to be void.

Sealed and delivered in presence of	Wm. Hollister	(Seal)
A Mitchell	Saml. Oliver	(Seal)
	Robt. V. O[?]	(Seal)

****

State of No Carolina   } Court of Pleas & Quarter Sessions
Craven County   } December Term

The petn. of Jno C Stanly humbly sheweth that Margaret Haslin decd. was the owner of a negro woman Rachel who had rendered her many Meritorious services and that she Mrs. Margaret Haslin was anxious that the said negro woman Rachel should be liberated - And with a view to obtain the same she Mrs. Haslin bequeathed the said negro to your Petitioner with an injunction that he should procure the liberation - And your Petr. humbly pray that your Worshipful Court will direct and give permission for the liberation of said negro
    Jno C Stanly
                                Jno Petr.

****

State of North Carolina   }
Craven County   }

Know all men by these presents that We Margaret Haslin and Ann Nash are held and firmly bound unto his Excellency David Stone Esquire, Captain General, Governor, and Commander in Chief of the State aforesaid, in the full sum of two hundred pounds, to be paid to the said Governor or his successors in office; to the which payment well and truly to be made, we bind ourselves, our heirs, executors, and administrators, jointly and severally, firmly by these presents, sealed with our seals, and dated this 6 day of March A.D. 1809

The Condition of the above obligation is such, that whereas at the Court held for Craven County, at this day permission has been granted to Margaret Haslen by the said Court, to emancipate and set free a certain negro slave named Phoebe Now if the said negro so permitted to be liberated shall during her residence in the state of North Carolina behave herself as a honest and peaceable citizen, then the above obligation to be void.

Sealed and delivered	}	Margt. Haslen	(Seal)
in presence of	}	A Nash	(seal)
L Stewart			

State of North Carolina   }
Craven County   }

Know all men by these presents that we Margaret Haslen & Ann Nash are held and firmly bound to John Tillman Esquire Chairman of Craven County Court, in the sum of one hundred pounds, to be paid to the said John or his successors in office, to which payment well and truly to be made we bind ourselves, our heirs, executors and administrators, firmly by these presents sealed with our seals and dated this 6 day of March 1809

    The Condition of the above obligation is such, whereas at the Court held for Craven County, at this day permission has been granted to Margaret Haslen by the said Court, to emancipate and set free a certain negro slave named Phoebe Now if the said negro so permitted to be liberated, shall not become chargeable to the parish of Craven County, or of any other County in this State, then the above obligation to be void.

Sealed and delivered}	Margt. Haslen	(Seal)
L Stewart	A Nash	(Seal)

****

State of North Carolina   }   Superior Court of Law
Craven County   }   Spring Term 1827

    To the Honble. the Judge &C
The Petition of James W Bryan, respectfully sheweth unto your Honor; that a female negro slave by the name of Caty Commonly Called Caty Webber, has been from the time of her birth the slave of your petitioner, and his ancestors -- that she has rendered faithful and meritorious services of Various Kinds, mboth to your petitioner and his father & family, and is now advanced to an age exceeding fifty years.

    Your Petitioner has been informed & believes that she was a favorite slave of his father, and attended him with great fidelity & care through Various long & severe illnesses - and has also acted as nurse to several of the younger members of the family in all of which situations she has performed her duty, in a highly exemplary manner -- that her character for honest, correct & humble deportment is extensively Known & admitted.

    Your Petitioner is desirous that this faithful Servant should enjoy the remnant of her years in freedom & security & prays your Honor that she may be emancipated agreeably to the acts of Assembly in such Case made & provided.

                                    Jn. H. Bryan
                                    Jas W. Bryan
                                    pro. Pet.
I unite in this petition Jno C. Stanly

State of North Carolina   }
Craven County   }

Know all men by these presents that We James W Bryan and John H Bryan are held and firmly bound unto his Excellency Hutchins G. Burton Esquire, Captain General, Governor, and Commander in Chief of the State aforesaid, in the full sum of two hundred pounds, to be paid to the said Governor or his successors in office; to the which payment well and truly to be made, we bind ourselves, our heirs, executors, and administrators, jointly and severally, firmly by these presents, sealed with our seals, and dated this 24th day of April A.D. 1807.

    The Condition of the above obligation is such, that whereas at the Court held for Craven County, at this day permission has been granted to James W Bryan by the said Court, to emancipate and set free a certain negro slave named Caty Webber Now if the said negro so permitted to be liberated shall during her residence in the State of North Carolina behave as an honest and peaceable citizen, then the above obligation to be void.

Sealed and delivered }	James W. Bryan	(Seal)
in presence of }	Jn. H. Bryan	(Seal)
	Jno C Stanly	(Seal)

State of North Carolina   }
Craven County   }

Chapter 6: Craven County Records

Know all men by these presents that we James W. Bryan and John H Bryan are held and firmly bound to John F. Smith Esquire Chairman of Craven County Court, in the sum of one hundred pounds, to be paid to the said John F. Smith or his successors in office, to which payment well and truly to be made we bind ourselves, our heirs, executors and administrators, firmly by these presents sealed with our seals and dated this 24th day of April 1827

The Condition of the above obligation is such, whereas at the Superior Court held for Craven County, at this day permission has been granted to James W. Bryan by the said Court, to emancipate and set free a certain negro slave named Caty Webber Now if the said negro so permitted to be liberated, shall not become chargeable to the parish of Craven County, or of any other County in this State, then the above obligation to be void.

Sealed and delivered	}	James W. Bryan	(Seal)
in presence of	}	Jn H Bryan	(Seal)
		Jno. C. Stanly	(Seal)

****

| State of North Carolina | } Supr. Court of Law |
| Craven County | } Spring Term 1823 |

To the Honorable the Judge &C
The petition of Saml. Street respectfully sheweth unto your Honor; that he is now the owner of a negro woman slaved Called Delia aged about forty, whom for her meritorious services he is desirous to emancipate. Your petitioner alledges that the said slave acted as a faithful & attentive nurse to his oldest son & that from her breast his infancy was supported.

He further sheweth unto your Honor, that he has been in the habit for a number of years upon the occasion of any absence from home to confide to the sd slave the Custody of his household & domestic Concerns & has always found that the duties thereto annexed, have been discharged with the utmost fidelity & honesty. Influenced by these Considerations & prompted by a sense of Conscious obligation your petitioner respectfully prays your Honor that he may be permitted to carry his said desire into execution, by liberating said slave according to the Act of Assembly in such Case made & provided And yr petinr &C.

Jn. H. Bryan
for petionr.
Prayer granted

State of North Carolina }
Craven County }

Know all men by these presents that We Samuel Street & John S Morris are held and firmly bound unto his Excellency Gabriel Holmes Esquire, Captain General, Governor, and Commander in Chief of the State aforesaid, in the full sum of two hundred pound, to be paid to the said Governor or his successors in office; to the which payment well and truly to be made, we bind ourselves, our heirs, executors, and administrators, jointly and severally, firmly by these presents, sealed with our seals, and dated this 26th day of April A.D. 1823

The Condition of the above obligation is such, that whereas at the Court held for Craven County, at this day permission has been granted to Samuel Street by the said Court, to emancipate and set free a certain negro slave named Delia Now if the said negro so permitted to be liberated, shall during her residence in the state of North Carolina behave herself as an honest and peaceable citizen, then the above obligation to be void.

| Sealed and delivered | } | Saml. Street | (Seal) |
| in presence of | } | John S. Morris | (Seal) |

State of North Carolina }

Chapter 6: Craven County Records

Craven County }

Know all men by these presents that we Samuel Street & John S Morris are held and firmly boun to John F Smith Esquire Chairman of Craven County Court, in the sum of one hundred pounds, to be paid to the said John F Smith or his successors in office, to which payment well and truly to be made we bind ourselves, our heirs, executors and administrators, firmly by these presents sealed with our seals and dated this 26 day of April 1823

The Condition of the above obligation is such, whereas at the Court held for Craven County, at this day permission has been granted to Samuel Street by the said Court, to emancipate and set free a certain negro slave named Delia Now if the said negro so permitted to be liberated, shall not become chargeable to the parish of Craven County, or of any other County in this State, then the above obligation to be void.

| Sealed and delivered } | Saml. Street | (Seal) |
| in presence of } | John S Morris | (Seal) |

***

To the Honorable the Judge of the Superior Court of Law of the County of Craven.

The Petition of Frederick Jones of Newbern respectfully sheweth, that he is the owner of a negro man Slave named Peter, Commonly called Peter Reynolds, whose long and repeated meritorious services entitle him in the opinion of your Petitioner to the highest reward a master can bestow upon his Slave - the blessing of emancipation. The said Slave has not only uniformly proved industrious and sober, but has for a course of years, been entrusted by your Petitioner with the Cheif direction and care of a Turpentine distillery, in which a considerable capital was invested & several labourers employed - in which employment his fidelity and diligence have been highly meritorious.
Your Petitioner prays a license to emancipate the said Peter Reynolds upon the terms of giving the Bonds required by law.
April 26. 1822.

Frederick Jones maketh oath that the facts stated in the above petition are true.

Fredk. Jones
Affirmed the 26th April 1822
J.W. **[Faded]** by
J G Stanly

John Jones & Asa Jones make Oath, that they believe the Character & Services of the negro Peter mentioned in the above Petition are just & true

　　　　　　　　　　　　　　　Asa Jones
Sworn to 26th April 1822　　　John Jones
J.W. **[Faded]** by
J G Stanly

State of North Carolina }
Craven County }

Know all men by these presents that We Asa Jones and John Jones are held and firmly bound unto his Excellency Gabriel Holmes Esquire, Captain General, Governor, and Commander in Chief of the State aforesaid, in the full sum of two hundred pounds, to be paid to the said Governor or his successors in office; to the which payment well and truly to be made, we bind ourselves, our heirs, executors, and administrators, jointly and severally, firmly by these presents, sealed with our seals, and dated this 27th April A.D. 1822

Chapter 6: Craven County Records

  The Condition of the above obligation is such, that whereas at the Superior Court held for Craven County, at this day permission has been granted to Frederick Jones by the said Court, to emancipate and set free a certain negro slave named Peter Reynolds Now if the said negro so permitted to be liberated shall during his residence in the state of North Carolina behave as an honest and peaceable citizen, then the above obligation to be void.

| Sealed and delivered | } | Asa Jones | (Seal) |
| in presence of | } | John Jones | (Seal) |

State of North Carolina }
Craven County }

Know all men by these presents that we Asa Jones and John Jones are held and firmly bound to John F Smith, in the sum of one hundred pounds, to be paid to the said John F Smith or his successors in office, to which payment well and truly to be made we bind ourselves, our heirs, executors and administrators, firmly by these presents sealed with our seals and dated this 27th day of April 1822

  The Condition of the above obligation is such, whereas at the Superior Court held for Craven County, at this day permission has been granted to Frederick Jones by the said Court, to emancipate and set free a certain negro slave named Peter Reynolds Now if the said negro so permitted to be liberated, shall not become chargeable to the parish of Craven County, or of any other County in this State, then the above obligation to be void.

| Sealed and delivered | } | Asa Jones | (Seal) |
| in presence of | } | John Jones | (Seal) |

****

State of North Carolina } Superior Court of Law
Craven County } Spring Term 1829

To the Honorable the Judge of the Superior Court of Law for Craven County.

  The Petition of Silvester Brown Executor to the estate of Nathl Brown sheweth unto your Honor that as executor aforesaid he is in possession of and owner of a negro woman slave by the name of Edny. That with the consent of the legatees of the will of the said Nathl Brown he is desirous to emancipate the said negro woman slave. That she is about the age of fifty years, and that during a long period of 24 or 25 years that she was the property of his testator her conduct has been marked by the utmost propriety diligence and attention to the wishes of her late master.
  That during a long and protracted illness of her late master she was diligent and attentive sitting up with him with the utmoste diligence & care and by her diligence assisted in saving the life at one time of her late master. That during the infancy of the legatees of the said Nathl. Brown she was a careful and diligent nurse and during the infancy of one of said legatees who at that period of her life suffered very much from disease the said slave attended upon her with diligence night and day so carefully that it was thought that the preservation of her life was owing to the attentions of said slave. That during a period of illness of the **[Marked through]** of your petrs testator she attended with the utmost diligence & care, and indeed throughout the whole life of the said slave or since she has been the property of your petrs testator her conduct has been highly exemplary and she has been constantly rendering meritorious services for the benefit of her owners both in sickness and health. Your petr. therefore prays, that upon his complying with the requisites of the act of the Genl. Assembly in such case made & provided he may be permitted to emancipate said slave.
      Jno S Hawks atto for petr.

Mrs Chadwick maketh oath that she is the daughter of Nathl Brown and one of the legatees, that from her earliest recollection the negro woman Edny was a slave of her fathers and living in the family - that her conduct has always been extremely exemplary. That she knows that during a long and protracted illness of her father the said negro woman slave Edny was extremely attentive sitting up with him and nursing him - That she was the nurse of the children and confidential servant of her late mistress and that the attention and kindness she rendered the children were such as

Chapter 6: Craven County Records

would have been rendered by a mother. That during the infancy of this affiant she suffered very much from sickness and that during that time the slave Edny was her nurse and although at that time an infant she cannot recollect any particular services rendered yet she recollects having heard her mother say that at that time she was very serviceable - This affiant does state that at one period of the illness of her late father she verily believes that the said negro slave Edny by her diligence & care was incremental in saving his life - That during the sickness of her late mother the said slave was extremely diligent and attentive.

Sworn to before me   Cha[?] Chadwick
Abner Pasteur Clk

Miss Evelina Brown maketh oath that she is the daughter of Nathl Brown and one of the legatees. That negro slave Edny has been in the family since her earliest recollection and that her conduct has always been highly exemplary. That she was so young she has no recollection of the sickness of her father at the time spoken of. That she knows that negro slave Edny was her nurse and that during her infancy she was extremely kind & attentive to her as much so as this affiant thinks as if she had been her mother. That she was very attentive to her mother during her illness.

Sworn to before me   her
Abner Pasteur   Evelina X Brown
                                 mark

Chapter 7: Cumberland County Records

chapter 7

Cumberland County

NORTH CAROLINA STATE ARCHIVES
CUMBERLAND COUNTY RECORDS
MISCELLANEOUS RECORDS
C.R.029.928.14

                         Petition of Job Hazell
                      Praying for the Emancipation of Polly his wife
                          and his child Mary Ann
                            Superior Court Cumbl.
                               Spring Term 1821

North Carolina   }   Superior Court of Law
Cumberland County   }   Spring Term 1821

                     To the Honorable the Judge of this Court

       The Petition of Job Hazell of Cumberland County a free man of Colour praying for license to set free a certain negro woman slave named Polly, together with her daughter Mary Ann in consequence of and as a reward for meritorious services by her performed humbly sheweth

       That your Petitioner is the legal owner of the said Slaves Polly, and Mary Ann having purchased the same of the late John Winslow Esquire in 1817 - that the woman Polly now aged 56 years is the wife of the Petitioner having so continued since their intermarriage thirty years ago; that she was at that time a faithful and favourite Servant in the family of Francis Brice Esquire whom she served with fidelity until his death; - that she has since lived with this Petitioner, and by her exertions has assisted him in paying the wages for her hire to her former Master, besides the assistance she has rendered him in a long of Laborious domestic services; - that she has mean while reared a family of children in habits of sobriety and industry, who are now slaves, and are Valuable Servants to their respective owners; and that during all this time she has maintained in her neighborhood a character for good conduct and orderly deportment - all which statements your Honest petitioner is ready to substantiate by the testimony of respectable persons now in Court.

       Your Petitioner further states that the girl Mary Ann is the child of the said Polly, and is his daughter, & is now 13 years of age.

       Your Petitioner now humbly prays that license may be granted him to set free the said slaves, and that it be ordered by the Court that they be emancipated accordingly, and forthwith admitted to all the rights and privileges to which free persons of Colour in this State are by law entitled; - that hereafter they may be Known as free persons by the name of Polly Hazell, and Mary Ann Hazell; - and that your Honor in carrying the wishes of this Petitioner into effect, do make and further Order and decree in this matter as shall be considered meet and proper - And your

Petitioner as in duty bound shall ever pray &c

May 5th 1821   Job Hazell
by his Solicitor
Jno. D. Eccles

Chapter 7: Cumberland County Records

Ordered that the Petitioner have license to set free the negro slaves Polly and Mary Ann mentioned in the petition, according to the Acts of assembly and that they be admitted to the rights priveleges of which free persons of colour are entitled in this State, and that they be known by the names of Polly Hazell and Mary Ann Hazell.

****

Joseph Hostler's Bond
June 20th 1834

State of North Carolina }
Cumberland County   }

      Know all men by these Presents, that we Joseph Hostler, Edward L. Winslow, James Seawell and James Huske all of the County aforesaid, are held and firmly bound unto David L. Swain Esqr: Governor, Captain, General, and Commander in Chief, in and over the State aforesaid, in the Just and full Sum of Two Hundred Pounds, Currency of the said State, to be paid to his Excellency aforesaid or his Successors in Office: to which payment well and truly to be made and done, we bind Our Selves, our heirs, Executors and Administrators, jointly and Severally, firmly by these presents Sealed with our Seals and dated this 20th day of June A.D. 1834

The Condition of the above Obligation is Such that whereas the above bounden Joseph Hostler, a man of Colour, was by an Act of the General assembly passed A.D. 1833, emancipated and Set free, and Admitted to all the rights and privileges which are enjoyed by other free persons of Colour within the State, Now if the Said Joseph Hostler shall honestly and correctly demean himself as long as he shall remain in this State and shall save harmless, the parish of the Country, from all Charges or expenses on Account of him the Said Joseph, then the above Obligation to be void, Otherwise to be and remain in full force and effect

                his
      Joseph X Hostler   (Seal)
            Mark

      E.L. Winslow   (Seal)
      James Huske   (Seal)

Signed Sealed and delivered

in presence of
Archd. McLean Jr. Clk.

Joseph Hostler's Certificate etc:
June 20th 1834

State of North Carolina }
Cumberland County   }

Office of the Court of Pleas and Quarter Sessions of the said County of Cumberland

June 20th 1834

I Archibald McLean Jun: Clerk of the Court aforesaid do hereby Certify that Joseph Hostler, the identical Person named, and emancipated and Set free by the provisions of An Act of the Genl. assembly, passed A.D. 1833, Chapter 108 on the day above mentioned, appeared at the Office aforesaid, and entered into Bond in the Sum of two Hundred Pounds, payable to David L. Swain Esqr: Gov. & his Successors in Office, with Edward Lee Winslow, James Seawell and James Huske as Security, Conditioned for the honest & correct demeanor of the said Joseph Hostler, and also for the indemnity of the Parish according to the further provisions of said Act

Chapter 7: Cumberland County Records

In Testimony whereof I have hereunto Set my hand and affixed the Seal of my Office and of the Said Court at Fayetteville in the County aforesaid the day and date above written.

Archd. McLean Jr: Clk:

State of North Carolina } Court Pleas & Quarter Sessions
Cumberland County } March Term 1835

Then the Papers and Certificate relative to the emancipation of Joseph Hostler were produced in Court, approved by the Court, and on motion Ordered that a Record be made thereof From the Minutes

Test Archd. McLean Jr. Clk:

Bond
Mrs: Sophia L. Smith
John N. Huske
John Winslow
Under act of assembly emancipating Joseph Hostler
A.D. 1833 Chapt. 38
June 2d: 1835

State of North Carolina }
Cumberland County }

Know all men by these presents, that we Sophia L. Smith, John N. Huske and John Winslow, all of the County of Cumberland aforesaid, are held and firmly bound unto David L. Swain Esqr. Governor Captain General, Commander in Chief in and over the State aforesaid, in the Just and full Sum of Two hundred Pounds, Currency of the said State, to be paid to his Exellency aforesaid or his Successors in Office, to which payment well and truly to be made and done, we bind ourselves, our heirs, Executors and Administrators, jointly and Severally, firmly by these presents, Sealed with our Seals and dated this 2d. day of June Anno Domini 1835.

The Condition of the above obligation is Such, that whereas by an act of the General Assembly of the State of North Carolina passed A.D. 1833 Joe, a Slave belonging to the above bounden Sophia L. Smith, was, with the Consent and at the request of his said owner, the said Sophia L. Smith, emancipated and Set free and by the name of Joseph Hostler admitted to all the rights and privileges which are enjoyed by other free persons of Colour in this State; Now if the said Joseph Hostler, Shall honestly and correctly demean himself as long as he shall remain in this State, and shall have harmless the parish of the Country, from all Charges and Expenses on Account of him the Said Joseph Hostler, then the above obligation to be void otherwise to be and remain on full force and virtue.

Signed, Sealed and delivered
In the presence of   Sophia L. Smith (Seal)

****

Bond
Solomon W. Nash
to indemnify the Parish in the matter of emancipation of his
Children   June 9th: 1836

State of North Carolina }
Cumberland County }

Know all Men by these Presents that We Soloman W. Nash, James G. Cook, and Thomas C. Blake all of the County and State Aforesaid are held and firmly bound unto Richard Dobbs Spaight Esqr. Governor of the State of North Carolina

Chapter 7: Cumberland County Records

and his Successors in Office in the just and full Sum of Twelve hundred dollars for the payment of which Well and truly to be Made and done We bind ourselves and each of us and each of Our Heirs Executors Administrators and Assigns jointly and Severally firmly by these Presents. Signed Sealed and delivered this 9th day of June 1836

The Condition of the above Obligation is Such Whereas the above bounden Soloman W. Nash Petitioned the General Assembly of North Carolina at its last Session for the emancipation of his three Children, namely Lucy Ann Emiline and Priscilla and Whereas the said General Assembly passed an Act entitled "An Act to emancipate Lucy, Ann, Emiline and Priscilla of Cumberland County" Which provides for the emancipation and setting free the Children of said Soloman W. Nash above named, upon Condition that the said Soloman shall give Bond and good Security to the Governor And his Successors in Office in the County Court of Cumberland County, that the said Slaves Shall honestly and Correctly demean themselves as long as they shall remain in the State and shall not become a parish Charge Now therefore if the said Lucy, Ann, Emiline and Priscilla shall honestly and Correctly demean themselves and if they shall not at any time become a Parish Charge then this Obligation to be Void and of no effect Otherwise to remain in full force and virtue

Witness   Soloman W. Nash   (Seal)
                 Jas. G. Cook   (Seal)
                 Thomas C. Blake   (Seal)

Archd. McLean Jr. Clk:

****

Bond
Joshua Carmon
W.J. Anderson
for Abel Payne

State of North Carolina

Know all men by these presents that we Joshua Carmon and William J Anderson of the County of Cumberland and state aforesaid are held and firmly bound to William A. Graham Governor of the State of North Carolina and his successors in office in the sum of five hundred dollars - the which payment well and truly to be made we bind ourselves and our heirs. Sealed with our seals and dated this the 27th day of August A.D. 1847.

The condition of the above obligation is this - Whereas at the last session of the General Assembly of North Carolina it was enacted with the consent and at the request of Joshua Carmon that Abel Payne and Patsey his wife - two negro slaves - the property of the said Joshua Carmon should be emancipated and set free and by the names of Abel and Patsey Payne shall hereafter possess and Exercise all the rights and privileges which are enjoyed by other free persons of Color in this State and whereas further it was provided in said enactment that before said slaves shall be emancipated their said Master Joshua Carmon shall give bond and good security in the sum of five hundred dollars to the Governor and his successors in office in the County Court of Cumberland County - that the said slaves shall honestly and Correctly demean themselves as long as they shall remain in the State and shall not become a parish Charge

Now if the said Abel Payne and his wife Patsey Payne shall honestly and Correctly demean themselves as long as they shall remain in the State and shall not become a parish Charge then the above obligation shall cease to operate and be of no effect whatever but if otherwise it shall remain in full force and virtue.

Joshua Carmon   (Seal)
W.J. Anderson   (Seal)

Signed Sealed & delivered in presence of
A. McLean

****

Chapter 7: Cumberland County Records

Bond
John S. Pearson
John W. Wright
for Saml McKey

State of North Carolina

      Know all men by these presents that we John S Pearson and Jno W Wright of the County of Cumberland and State aforesaid are held and firmly bound to William A Graham Governor of the State of North Carolina and his Successors in Office in the Sum of five hundred dollars - the which payment well and truly to be made we bind ourselves and our heirs Sealed with our Seals and dated this the 8th day of September A D 1847

The Condition of the above obligation is this - Whereas at the last Session of the General Assembly of North Carolina it was enacted with the consent and at the request of John S Pearson that Samuel McKey a negro Slave the property of the said John S Pearson Should be emancipated and set free - and by the name of Samuel McKey shall hereafter possess and Exercise all the rights and privileges which are enjoyed by other free persons of Color in this State and whereas further - it was provided in said enactment that before said slave shall be emancipated the said Master John S Pearson shall give bond and good security in the sum of five Hundred dollars to the Governor and his Successors in Office in the County Court of Cumberland County - that the said Slave shall honestly and correctly demean himself as long as he shall remain in the State and shall not become a parish Charge Now if the Said Samuel McKey shall honestly and correctly demean himself as long as he shall remain in the State and shall not become a parish charge then the above obligation shall cease to operate and be of no effect whatever - but if otherwise it shall remain in full force and virtue

John S Pearson	(Seal)
J W Wright	(Seal)

Signed Sealed & delivered in the presence of
John W. Baker Jr

***

To the worshippful Court of Pleas and Quarter Sessions of the County of Cumberland.

The Petition of Thomas Grymes respectfully sheweth, that he has in his possession and is the owner of a certain female Slave named Maria; and that in consequence of the long faithful and meritorious Services of said Maria to her late Mistress Miss Elizabeth Winslow, he is desirous to emancipate said Maria from a State of Slavery: But as a license is necessary for this purpose from this worshippful Court the petitioner prays that the Court will take this Case into Consideration and allow him license to emancipate the said Maria. March Term 1814

Bela W. Strong   his
                     Thomas X Grymes
                          mark

The Petition of Thomas Grymes praying license to emancipate a female slave named Maria having been heard - and the Court being satisfied that her Services have been meritorious, it is ordered that the said Petitioner have license to emancipate the said slave by the name of Maria Grymes upon his entering into Bond with Security according to the act of 1801

Thomas Grymes &   }
David Ochiltree[?]   } Bond

for Maria Grymes
Emancipate
March Term 1814

Chapter 7: Cumberland County Records

State of North Carolina Ss

Know all Men by these presents that We Thomas Grymes and David Ochiltree both of the County of Cumberland State aforesaid are held and firmly bound unto John Dickson Esquire Chairman of the County Court of Cumberland aforesaid in the sum of One Hundred pounds Current money payable to the said Chairman or to his Successor or Successors in Office, to which payment well and truly to be made we bind ourselves jointly and severally our Heirs Executors and Administrators firmly by these presents sealed with our seals and dated this 10th day of March 1814

The Condition of the above Obligation is such that whereas the Justices of the County Court of Cumberland aforesaid hath this day, on the Petition of the said Thomas Grymes, Emancipated and set free a female Slave by the name of Maria Grymes

Now if the said Maria Grymes shall not hereafter become Chargeable on the Parish or County of Cumberland and shall at all times demean herself as an Orderly Citizen - then the above Obligation to be void Otherwise to be and remain in full force power and virtue

Signed and Sealed }   his
In presence of   }   Thomas X Grymes (Seal)
                                    mark
                           D. Ochiltree

****

Emancipation Bond
in Case of Louis Dunn

Filed in Office
8th May 1855

Know all men by these presents, that we, James Dunn, Jas. G. Cook, and A.J. O'Hanlan of the County of Cumberland, State of North Carolina, are held and firmly bound unto his Excellency, Thomas Bragg, Governor of the State of North Carolina, and his Successors in Office, in the Sum of Five hundred dollars, good and Lawful money of the United States, to be paid to the said Thomas Bragg, Governor &c. and his Successors in Office; to which payment well and truly to be made, we bind ourselves, our heirs, executors and administrators firmly by these presents
Sealed with our seals, and dated the 5 day of May 1855

The Condition of the above obligation is such, that whereas by an Act of Assembly of the State of North Carolina, in the Session of 1854 & '55 entitled "an Act to emancipate Louis, a slave, the property of James Dunn" it is enacted, "That Louis, a slave, the Property of James Dunn of Cumberland Co. be and is hereby with the consent and at the request of the said owner emancipated and set free and by the name of Louis Dunn shall hereafter possess and exercise all the rights and privileges which are enjoyed by other free persons of Color in this State   Provided nevertheless that before said slave shall be emancipated his said owner shall give bond with good sureties in the sum of five hundred Dollars, payable to the Governor of the State and his Successors in Office, that the said Slave shall honestly and correctly demean himself while he remains in this State and not become a County charge &c"

Now therefore if the said Louis shall honestly and correctly demean himself while he remains in this State and not become a County Charge, according to the true meaning and intent of the condition of his Emancipation, then this Bond to be void otherwise to remain in full force and virtue

In testimony whereof, we have hereunto set our hands and seals the day and year above mentioned
Witness
E.F. Hunt   his
                     Jas X Dunn   (Seal)

Chapter 7: Cumberland County Records

        mark
        Jas G Cook   (Seal)
        A.J. O'Hanlon (Seal)

****

Minutes
Spring Term 1820

Petition
of
Thomas Flowers

The Petition of Thomas Flowers praying for permission to emancipate his slave, Louisa, coming on to be heard, & satisfactory evidence having been adduced to the court, proving the good moral character of said slave & her performance of meritorious services, agreeably to the acts of the Genl. Assembly in such case made & provided; it is ordered, adjudged, & decreed that the prayer of the petition be granted, & that the petitioner have leave to emancipate said slave upon complying with the requisites of the law in such case made & provided.

chapter 8

Duplin County

NORTH CAROLINA STATE ARCHIVES
DUPLIN COUNTY RECORDS
MISCELLANEOUS RECORDS
C.R.035.928.8

Petition of Adam a Negroe Slave
Concurred and Adam Situated
April Term 1798

To the Worshipfull the Justices of the County Court of Duplin

The Petition of William Duncan begs leave humbly to Represent to your Worships that he is in possession of a Mulatto Slave called Adam, who has for a number of years past conducted and demeaned himself as a faithful, honest, and well deserving Servant. Your Petitioner conceives the said Negro Slave Adam from his meritorious Services & good conduct is justly entitled to the priveleges of a free Citizen he therefore prays your Worships will extend to him the Advantages which the Laws of the County extend to him & as in duty bound will ever pray.

                B.H. Martin pro petition
[The bottom half of this document is missing.]

Chapter 9: Edgecombe County Records

chapter 9

Edgecombe County

NORTH CAROLINA STATE ARCHIVES
GENERAL ASSEMBLY SESSIONS RECORDS
APR. - JUNE, 1784, BOX 3

EDGECOMBE COUNTY

House of Commons April 21, 1784

The Barer Hereof Edwin Griffin Soldiar in the North Carolina Battalion and in Captn. Millses Company having Served Twelve months Being the Term for which He was Ingaged is hearby discharged from the said Battalion in which we certifie that he has Behaved as a good & faithfull Soldiar

[?]

Given at Camp Near   3d N.C. Regt.
Bacons Bridge   [?] Musfee Lt Colton
1st July 1782   Maine

Edwd Griffin
Armstrong
Deposition

State of North Carolina }
Edgecombe County } Ss. August Term 1783

Personally appeared before me Coll. James Armstrong and being duly sworn deposeth and saith That on or about the first day of August in the year of our Lord one Thousand Seven hundred & Eighty one this deponent being at Martinborough in Pitt County and State aforesaid being appointed to Superintend the receiving of Draughts deserters and Substitutes for the Continental service from the district of Halifax and Newbern a certain William Kitchen who was then a deserter from the Continental Service haveing brought a certain Ned Griffin a Mollattoe or Mustee to this deponent as a Substitute in the room of the said Kitchen to Serve for the Term of Eighteen Months in the Continental Service the said Kitchen upon his delivering the said Griffin to this deponent (who ever mindful of his duty and determined strictly to adhere the Laws of this State particularly to the directions there injoined respecting the receptions of Draughts Substitutes &c I objected to the said Griffin upon his Principle that he was not perfectly satisfied of his being a freeman and the said Kitchen thereupon with the Strongest assurances declared that he the said Griffin was a free man and as such delivered him to this deponent declaring and positively affirming at the same time that he had Purchased the Service of the said Griffin and upon his Serving the said tour faithfully he the said Kitchen manumitted and totally discharged him from every speces of farther Services whatsoever. That upon those terms and Solemn assurances of Kitchen only he this deponent received and enroled him the said Griffin in the Continental service accordingly And farther this deponent saith that some time after the enrolement he met with William Griffin in these words; So says this deponent Kitchen has purchased of you a certain Ned Griffin (meaning the said Ned Griffin that he had received as a free man of Kitchen for a Substitute for him the said Kitchen upon which the said William Griffin answered yes, this deponent then demanded of him Cloathing for the said Ned Griffin upon which he the said William Griffin replied that he made no contract with Kitchen when he disposed of the Services of the said Ned Griffin so the said Kitchen therefore was under no obligation to comply with his requisition.
Sworn to before me
this 6th august 1783   } James Armstrong

Chapter 9: Edgecombe County Records

in Open Court   }
Isaac Sessums
A True Copy taken from the Original
Test Edward Hall

State of No. Carolina   }
Edgecombe County   }

  William Griffin an inhabiter of said County being first Sworn deposeth & Sayeth, that Some [time] in July in the year 1781 that he the said deponent did bargain & Sell a molatto man Slave Call'd by the Name of Ned Griffin, to a certain William Kitchen of said County to Serve in the Continental or State Service Twelve or Eighteen months at most, & he the sd. deponent saith that he Sold this sd. Ned for no other purpose nor intent, than to Serve as aforesd. & he this deponent did Expect that he the said molatto fellow Ned was to be a free man, & this deponent further saith that he heard the sd. Wm. Kitchen say that the sd. molatto fellow Ned was a free man, & that he the sd. Kitchen Never intended to Call upon the sd. Ned to Serve in any respect after he had Served the above said term of time & obtain'd a discharge from the aforesaid Servitude & further saith not.

The above deposition taken before me this 18th day of March 1784
     L Ruffin

State of N. Carolina   } H.C. April 21, 1784
Edgecombe County   } March ye 27th 1784

  This Day Joseph Fort voluntarily appeared before me, and being sworn on the holy Evangelist of Almighty God, Deposeth and Saith
  That in June or July in the year 1781 he was in company with William Griffis & William Kitchen of the County aforesd. & that the sd. Kitchen was bargaining With the sd. Griffis for a certain Mulatto man Slave named Ned whom the sd. Kitchen intended to put into the Continental service as a substitute in his own Room, and further this Deponent saith, that he heard the said Kitchen promise the sd. Mulatto Ned, that he shou'd be a free man provided he (the sd. Ned) wou'd enter into the Continental service and discharge him (the sd. Kitchen) from the same

      his
    Joseph I Fort
      Mark
Sworn before me Robt. Digges JP

To The General Assembly of The State of North Carolina
H.C. April 21, 1784

The Petition of Ned Griffin a Man of mixed Blood Humbly saith that a small space of Time before the Battle of Guilford a certain William Kitchen then in the service of his Country as a Soldier Deserted from his line for which he was Turned in to the Continental Service to serve as the Law Directs - Your Petitioner was then a Servant to William Griffin and was Purchas'd by the said Kitchen for the Purpose of Serving in His Place with a Solem Assurance that if he your Petitioner would faithfully serve the Term of Time that the said Kitchen was Returned for he should be a free Man - Upon which said promise and Assurrance your Petitioner Consented to enter in to the Continental Service in said Kitchens Behalf and was Received by Colo: James Armstrong at Martinborough as a free Man   Your Petitioner further saith that at that Time no Person Could have been hired to have served in said Kitchens behalf for so small a sum as what I was Purchased for and that at the Time that I was Received into Service by said Colo: Armstrong said Kitchen Openly Declared me to be a free Man - The faithful performance of the above agreement will appear from my Discharge - some Time after Your Petitioners Return he was Seized upon by said Kitchen and Sold to a Certain Abner Roberson who now holds me as a Servant - Your Petitioner therefore thinks that by Contract and merit he is Intitled to his Freedom   I therefore Submit my case to your Honourable Body hoping that I shall have that Justice done me as you in your Wisdom shall think I am Intitled to and Deserveing of & Your Petitioner as in duty bound Will Pray.

      his
   Ned X Griffin

Chapter 9: Edgecombe County Records

                                              mark

S N Carolina   }
Edgecombe County   }
April 4th 1784   }

State of N. Carolina   }
Edgecombe County   } April ye 6th 1784

     This Day Col. Henry Hart personally appeared before me, and being sworn on the holy Evangelist of almighty God, deposeth and saith,
     That about the Month of June or July in the year 1781 a certain William Kitchen & William Griffis met at his House, they being then on a Bargain for & concerning a certain Mulatto Man named Ned who was then held as a Slave by the said William Griffis, and that the sd. Kitchen then wanted to purchase the sd. Ned from the sd. Griffis intending to enlist him into the Continental service as a substitute in his own room & stead, the sd. Kitchen then being himself return'd a Continental soldier; & sometime after the aforesd. William Kitchen & William Griffis again met at the Chapel on Tar River, the afores'd Mulatto Ned being then present, where the Bargain for & concerning the sd. Ned was confirmed & Part of the Purchase Money paid, and this deponent further saith that he heard the sd. Mulatto Ned several different times say that he would not enter or enlist into the service unless he could thereby obtain his freedom, & that this deponent also heard the sd. William Kitchen say that if he (the sd. Ned) would fathfully discharge his duty in the room & stead of him the sd. William Kitchen that he the sd. Kitchen would never attempt or endeavour to hold him as a slave but that he should be a free man on his performing his duty in the aforesd. service, and further this Deponent saith not
                sign'd by Henry Hart
Sworn before
Robt. Digges JP

North Carolina
In the H Coms. 24 May 1784

Mr Speaker and Gentlemen

     On reading for the second time the Bill to enfranchise Ned Griffin we prepare the following amendments that the name William Griffis through every part thereof be deled and the name William Kitchen inserted
                Tho. Benbury S:S
By order
J Hunt CHC

North Carolina
In Senate 24th May 1784

Mr Speaker and Gentlemen
     We consent to the amendment by you proposed to be passed under the Bill for enfranchising Ned Griffin and have appointed Mr Battle and Mr Hill to see it made
                R Caswell SP
John Haywood ClK

****

NORTH CAROLINA STATE ARCHIVES
EDGECOMBE COUNTY RECORDS
MISCELLANEOUS SLAVE PAPERS
C.R.037.928.4

North Carolina   }

Chapter 9: Edgecombe County Records

Edgecombe County   }

To the Sheriff of Edgecombe County Greeting:
You are hereby Commanded that you Summon Thomas Hodges of your said County if to be found in your Bailiwic personally to appear before the Justices of the County Court of Pleas & Quarter Sessions, to be held for the same on the fourth monday in November next then & there to shew Cause by what Right title or claim he holdeth in Slavery, a Girl young Woman of mixed Blood named Bet (Elizabeth) who by Thomas Hall her Attorney Suggests that she is of free Parents & entitled to freedom -- And have then & there this Writ; Witness
Edward Hall Clerk of sd. Court the **[Blank]** Day of anno Dom. 1780, in the 5th year of Independence

Portess   }   Edwd. Hall C.C.
  agt.   }
Hodges }
Executed and returned

Henry Hart

****

Beck   }
  Vs   } Dep.
Sessums }

State of North Carolina   } In Obedience of and
Edgecombe County   } order of Court to me

Directed to take the Deposition of ann Bridgers in a suit Depending Between Beck plantiff and Alexander Sessums Defendant the said Ann Bridgers Deposeth and Sayeth --I no that the Indian woman that was Called [by] Christopher Guin I believe was a Indian

Question 1 What Resons had you to Believe they were Indians
Answer: because they ware Like all other Indians I ever see her Name was Jenny the Mother of Beck

Question 2 had you any other Reasons to believe they was Indians
only By her Looks
Answer: no I had not But her Looks was Sufficiant

Question 3 had she Long hair
Answer: Yes

Question 4 was She a Slave as Long as you new her
Answer: Yes

Question 5 Did Mr. Guin Call them Indians or Slavs
Answer: he Called them his Indians

Question 6 Do you Know whether Guing Ever said his wench Jene was Intitled to freedom or not
Answer: No

April 26 Day 1793   Jno. Batts JP

Becke a Woman of Colour}
     Vs   } Citation
Alexander Sessums   }

Chapter 9: Edgecombe County Records

The Court having heard &c answered the Testimony produced by the plaintiff to Support her claim to her freedom are of opinion that She is well entitled thereto from the said Testimony but not conceiving that her case comes up to the Act of Assembly in such cases made & provided do therefore determine that they cannot interpose to grant her the relief held out by the said Act & can take nothing by her motion as it now Stands.

****

To the Worshipfull The Justices of Edgecombe County,
The Petition of Limeric a Mullato Man held in Slavery by Samuel Collen Sheweth That his Mother was an Indian Woman and free, that in Consequence of such her Freedom he your Petitioner is entitled to a Liberation from Servitude he therefore Prays Your Worships to take this his Petition into Consideration & do therein what is agreeable to Law

Feby 11th 1782   Limeric (X)

****

State of North Carolina   }
Edgecombe County   } To the Sheriff of sd. County

greeting you are hereby commanded that you Summon James Williams if to be found in your Bailiwic to make his Personal Appearance at the next county court of pleas, to be held for the County of Edgecombe aforesd. on the first Monday in May next then and there to shew Cause why he keepeth in a State of Slavery, Sarah Rogers, who by her Petition to the Justices of the County court aforesd. alledgeth that she is a free woman And have you then and there this Writ -- Witness Edward Hall Clerk afsd. Court the 7th Day of Feby. -- 1785
            Edward Hall Clk.

****

State of No. Carolina   }
Edgecombe County Court   } May Term 1817
    To the Worshipful the Justices of the Court of Pleas & Quarter Sessions for the County aforesaid the Petition of Joel Battle humbly sheweth
    That Amos Johnson Late of the County aforesaid was at the time of his death the owner & possessor of a Negroe Man slave Named Jolly about 50 or 60 years of age - that the said Jolly was a faithful & deserving Servant and in his late Masters sickness nursed him with great attention and fidelity -- so much so that it was the dying request of the said Amos that the said Negroe Man Jolly sh'd be set free -- Your Petitioner further shews that in the division of the Negroes belonging to the Estate of the said Amos Johnson the said Jolly was allotted to your Petitioner who is desirous of carrying into effect the humane & benevolent intention of the said Amos -- he therefore prays that the said Jolly may be emancipated for meritorious services
            [?] for Petitnr.

****

Harry McClennan's Petition
To the Worshipful the Justices of the County Court of Edgcomb
The Petition of your Petitioner Harry McClennan humbly sheweth
    That your Petitioner is a freeman that for some time past he hath been held and claimed as a Slave by William Leigh late of this County that a suit is now depending in this Court before your Worships against George Brownrigg wherein the said George at the instance of your Petitioner hath pleaded that your Petitioner is a freeman & not a Slave.
    Your Petitioner further sheweth that he hath been informed that the said William Leigh apprehensive that the said issue will turn out against him designs to seize upon the body of your Petirioner & remove him to some foreign Country beyond the jurisdiction of this Worshipful Court By which means your Petitioner would be utterly deprived of the benefit of the law and of those natural & Civil Rights to which the Citizens of this Country are entitled.

Chapter 9: Edgecombe County Records

Your Petitioner further shews that impressed with the truth of the above design of William he is hampered and impeded in preparing himself in his defence and without the interposition of your Worships will be materially injured he therefor prays your Worships to take his Case into consideration & give such Relief as to you in your Wisdom may seem proper.

chapter 10

Franklin County

NORTH CAROLINA STATE ARCHIVES
FRANKLIN COUNTY RECORDS
MISCELLANEOUS RECORDS
C.R.039.928.9

1. Resolved, That the attempts now making by the Anti-Slavery Societies and abolitionists of the North, to procure an immediate & ultimate emancipation of the Slaves in the South, is an unauthorised, impertinent and mischievous interference with the rights and privileges of the Slave-holding States.

2. Resolved, as the firm and settled conviction of this meeting, That the project of the immediate or ultimate emancipation of the Southern Slaves, is wild, visionary and utterly impracticable; and that its advocates are so blinded by prejudice, or maddened by fanaticism as to be entirely incapable of viewing the subject with the eye of reason, or of true philanthropy.

3. Resolved, That the place adopted by the Anti-Slavery Societies and Abolitionists, of sending their emissaries, pamphlets and papers into the Southern States, has a direct and inevitable tendency to excite insubordination and insurrection among the Slaves, and of consequence to disturb the peace and endanger the Security of the lives and property of the Southern people.

4. Resolved, That the Anti-Slavery Societies and abolitionists, still persisting in their wild and wicked Schemes after having been warned of their fatal tendency, have forfeited every claim to the character of friends, and are to be considered and treated as our most inveterate foes.

5. Resolved, That towards that portion of our Northern fellow citizens, who are disposed to acknowledge our rights, and to respect our feelings, we cherish sentiments of the most friendly regard; and we shall confidently rely upon their patriotism, and their sense of Social obligation to procure the enactment of such laws in their respective States, as shall secure our lives and our property from the nefarious attempts of those who would deprive us of the one and rob us of the other.

6. Resolved, That for the purposes of bringing the grievances of the Southern people in a more authoritative and imposing form to the attention of their Northern Brethren, we cordially approve the Suggestion made at some of the numerous meetings recently held on this subject, that the Legislatures of all the Slave-holding States shall make proper representations and remonstrances to the constituted authorities of the non-Slave holding States, setting forth the wrongs of which they complain, and the redress which they have a right to expect.

7. Resolved, That We will unite heart and hand with our fellow citizens of the South, in all necessary and constitutional measures of protection and defence; and that relying upon the justice of our cause, and on Him whose arms has hitherto upheld and sustained us, we are prepared to resist even unto death every invasion of our chartered rights whether from open foes, or secret assassins.

8. Resolved, That it is expedient that committees of vigilance shall be appointed in every Captain's district of the County, whose particular duty it shall be to apprehend or cause to be apprehended and brought to justice all persons who are found, by means of writing, speaking or otherwise unlawfully disseminating the doctrines of the abolitionists; and

Chapter 10: Franklin County Records

also to cause to be taken up for examination all persons whatsoever who by their suspicious conduct, render themselves obnoxious to such a charge.

9. Resolved, That it is especially incumbent at this time upon all those who are charged with the execution of the patrol laws, to be unceasingly active and vigilant in the performance of their respective duties.

10. That the thanks and the lasting gratitude of the people of the Southern States are due, and are hereby tendered by us as a position of that people to the editor of Evening Star and the N. York Courier and Inquirer for their fearless and able defence of the Constitutional right of the Southern Slave holders.

****

James House
Petr., Spring Term 1820

State of North Carolina
Superior Court of Law, Spring Term 1820
The Petition of James House to the Honourable The Judges of the Supr. Court aforesaid Now Sitting -

    Your Petitioner humbly represents to your Honor that he is proprietor and owner of Negro Thomas and acquired title to him from the representatives of William Blackinal some short time Since - that for a number of years before he acquired title to the Said Slave he was well acquainted with him - that his conduct both before and Since his purchase has been strictly honest and in every respect exemplary - He has for a great number of years kept a Blacksmiths Shop in the neighborhood of your Petitioner and during the whole of his time had the entire management of the accounts and in no instance has he failed as this Petitioner verily believes to give entire satisfaction to his master and the customers that as a reward for his faithfulness and honesty his former master granted him liberty of trading and acquiring property; his punctuality in all his dealings has been so strict, that no man in my neighborhood is more to be relied on - or whose conduct is more approved of - That his behaviour is respectful, orderly and in every respect highly approved - so much so as to intreat in his behalf, the feelings of the Citizens of the County or a large portion of them, to aid and assist him in obtaining his freedom - That it was the intention of his former Master as often expressed before his death - and expressly expressed on his death bed to have him liberated if the laws of his Country would permit as a reward for his faithfull and Meritorious Services - That it is as with a view of rewarding the merit of said Thomas by having him liberated that your Petitioner acquired title as aforesaid, That your Petitioner is fully persuaded that no Slave is better entitled to the privilege of freedom than said Thomas that he will make a usefull and Valuable Citizen.

    That yr Petitioner is ready to verify the allegations in his petition of request - and will enter into such Bond as may be deemed by this Honorable Court & pray that the Said Thomas may be liberated according to the provisions of the act of Assembly in such case made & provided
    Well and pray &c
    Jas. House

This Petition being exhibited and by the Court here heard and examined and the meritorious Services and other facts therein stated having been proved by evidence satisfactory to the Court
    It is therefore ordered and adjudged by the Court that the Petitioner James House have leave to emancipate the said Negro Slave Thomas in the petition mentioned and that the said Thomas be emancipated liberated set free and have and enjoy all the rights of a free man by & under the name of Thomas Blacknall
    And thereupon the petitioner the said James House comes into Court here in his proper person and enter into Bond with James Yarbrough his Security in the sum of one hundred pounds as prescribed by the Act in such case provided When Whereupon the said James the Petitioner presents as aforesaid in Open Court declares that he doth freely absolutely and entirely emancipate and set free the said Thomas Blacknall and doth abandon and release all right whatever in and Over the person and services of the said Thomas - & pray the Court that the same may be entered of record which is ordered accordingly.

Know all men by these presents that we James Houser and James Yarborough of the County of Franklin State of North Carolina acknowledge ourselves, our Heirs &c justly indebted to John D. Hawkins esquire Chairman of the County

Chapter 10: Franklin County Records

aforesaid in the sum of One Hundred pounds - To which payment well & truly to be made we bind ourselves, our Heirs &c. Jointly & Severally firmly by these presents Sealed with our Seals and dated this 13th of April 1820

The Condition of the above obligation is such that whereas the above bound James Houser hath by a Judgment of the Superior Court of Law of Said County obtained Cause to liberate his Slave Thomas and Hath entered on the Records of said [County] that the said Slave Thomas is liberated and emancipated by the name of Thomas Blacknall Now in case the said James shall pay all such charges as the County aforesaid may have on account of said Thomas becoming chargeable to the County then the above obligation to be Void else to remain in full force

Signed Sealed	James House	(Seal)
in presence of	James Yarbrough	(Seal)
N. Patterson		

****

State of North Carolina }
Franklin County } Spring Term 1822

To the honourable the Judge of the Superior Court Now Siting for the County aforesaid

The Petition of Jesse Person humbly represents unto your honour that he is the owner of a Negroe man slave by the name of Mingo, formerly the property of Capt William Green late of this County -- who is now about Sixty years of age & who has served his late master in such a faithful manner and performed so many good, noble & meritorious acts through the whole time which he belonged to him - that the said Green for many years before he was Compeled to part with him - which was in consequence of Pecuneary embarrasments -- had determined to set him free.

Your Petitioner further represents unto your honour that the said Mingo is a preacher of the Gospel of the denomination of the Baptist persuasion, and has at this time; and has had for a great many years a Considerable Church in the neighborhood of Louisburg to the entire satisfaction of all the owners of Slaves who visit his meetings as well as others.

Your Petitioner further represents unto your Honour that at the time he purchased the said Negroe man Mingo, which was at a Sheriffs sale under an Execution against the said Capt Green that he paid only a very small part of the purchase money out of his own Pocket, the greater part having been paid to him by the members of the Church to which he was attached; and by the said Mingo himself.

Your Petitioner therefore prays your honour to grant an order Emancipating and seting free the said Negroe man Mingo upon your Petitioner Entering into such bond and Security as is required by the acts of the General Assembly in such cases made & Provided, and that the said Negroe in future bear the Name of Mingo Green &c And your Petitioner as in duty bound will ever pray &c

J. Person

Jesse Person to the Court
Petition for the Emancipation of Negro Mingo
Spring Term 1822   Decree

State of North Carolina } Supr. Ct. of Law
Franklin County } April Ss. 1822

On the Petition of Jesse Person Esqr. claiming to be the Proprietor of a Certain Negro Man by the Name "Mingo" of the age of Sixty years or thereabouts, late the property of Captain Wm. Green, praying that the said Negro Man by name "Mingo" may be emancipated and transferred from the Condition of Bondage to that of a Free Person of Color, upon the grounds of Meritorious Services alledged to have been done and performed by the said Mingo - The Court here taking into consideration the matter of said Petition and the prayer thereof, and after having heard the facts offered in evidence in support of the Meritorious Services alledged by the Petitioner and having duly considered the same doth adjudge & allow that the allegation of Meritorious Services on the part of the said Negro Man "Mingo" are well sustained by the

Chapter 10: Franklin County Records

proofs adduced from the hearing of the Petition filed in his behalf; and that the said Negro Man Mingo be emancipated and set free from all obligations of obedience to the commands of the Petitioner his late Master, and that Hence forth he be transferred to the Condition and priviledges of a free person of Color as established by law; and that the said Negro Man Mingo, be called & Known by the name of Mingo Green. This order and allowance is made to depend on the Petitioners entering into the Bond with Security as required by law in Cases of Emancipation.

Jesse Persons Obligation Bond
Spring Term 1822

Know all men by these presents that we Jesse Person, James C. Jones and John Person are held and firmly bound unto John D. Hawkins Esqr. Chairman of the County Court of Franklin and his Successors in office in the Just and full Sum of One hundred Pounds - to which Payment well and truly to be made and done we bind ourselves our heirs Executors Admrs &c - this 12th day of April in the year of our Lord AD 1822

The Condition of the above obligation is such, that whereas the above bounden Jesse Person hath at this time petitioned for the emancipation of a Certain Negro Man by the name of Mingo - And whereas the Court did Decree that the said Negro Man by Name of Mingo Should be emancipated & set free from all the Commands of his Master. Now therefore if the aforesaid Negro Man "Mingo" Shall not at any time hereafter become Chargeable on the Parish of the County of Franklin aforesaid, then the above obligation to be Void otherwise to remain in full force & effect

Signed Sealed in	J. Person	(Seal)
presence of	James C. Jones	(Seal)
J. Patterson	John Person	(Seal)

****

John Thomas - Bond

Know all men by these presents that we John Thomas amd Jordan Denson all of Franklin County are hald and firmly bound unto John D. Hawkins Chairman of the said County Court in the sum of one hundred pounds which payment well and truly to be made We bind ourselves our Joint and several Heirs Exrs. and Admrs. firmly by these presents seal'd with our seals and dated this 16th of Sept 1818.

The Condition of the above obligation is such that whereas a negro female Slave late the property of George Richards Dec'd has been liberated and set free for Meritorious Services Which Negro is by the name of Hicksy Now if the said negro Hicksy shall never become chargeable to the Parish or County then the above obligation to be Void else to remain in full force power & Virtue

Test	John Thomas	(Seal)
Henry Plummer	J. Denson	(Seal)

****

Jno. Mitchell
exparte
to Spring Term 1825

To the Honorable Judge of the Superior Court of Law and Equity for the County of Franklin; The Petition of John Mitchell of said County, humbly represents, That he is a free man of Colour resident within the aforesaid County of Franklin from the time of his birth to the present day, a Black Smith by Trade and from persevering industry and economy has acquired a Free hold estate and some other property That at an early period of his life he became attached to a woman Slave named Polly the property of Epps Moody Esquire late of this County but now residing in the State of Alabama, whom he made his wife and when Mr. Moody was about to leave the State become the purchaser of the said woman Polly with whom he had lived in great harmony ever since tho without having any Children. Your Petitioner begs leave further to represent that he has many relations residing in this part of the Country who he believes in the

Chapter 10: Franklin County Records

event of his death would claim the right of property by kinship and endeavor to sell his wife again contrary to the wishes of your petitioner, the law puting it out of his power to emancipate her by will, or making her heir to his little estate the joint earnings of their united industry, but he is informed the Honorable Court have the right vested in them by an Act of Assembly of this State to emancipate Slaves for Meritorious Services and if so he has no hesitation in believing that in asking the Court to emancipate his wife Polly, he asks only for an act of Justice which they will readily grant, for he flatters himself that her merits and Character are so well known in the neighborhood of her residence that among his neighbors there will not be one found however exalted or however humble but what would testify if necessary to her industrious moral & honest habits whilst your petitioner can aver that she is not only among the best of Slaves but among the best of wives Wherefore he prays your honor to take his case into Consideration and grant an order for the emancipation of his wife Polly and he as in duty bound will ever pray &c

Witness   John Mitchell
Willm. Burlingham

State of North Carolina   } We the undersigned residing in the
Franklin County   } neighborhood of John Mitchell the

aforegoing petitioner and being personally acquainted with him and his wife have no hesitations in Stating that we believe all the facts set forth in the aforegoing petition to be true - That the conduct of the said Polly on all occasions so far as has come within our knowledge is beyond the reach of Censure and we do most cordially unite with the said John Mitchell in praying the Honorable Court to grant the required relief - believing if merit is made the basis of emancipation that the said Polly is fully entitled to its benefits - Witness our hands this 15th day of March 1825

Tobs. Terrell, Francis Pugh, Wm. G. Jones, John Brodie, Willm. Burlingham, John Rowan, C. Foster, Wm. Ransom, A. Devaney, Joseph Bledsoe, Willis P. Ingram, Jeremiah Ingram, Hezekiah Terrell, John Terrell, C.A. Hill, James Maxwell, Nat Hunt, John Haywood, Willie Perry, A.T. [?], P.C. Person[?]

Jno. Mitchell to Chairman of the Court

Know all men by these presents that We John Mitchell & Tolliver Terrell are held & firmly bound unto John D. Hawkins Esqr. Chairman of the Court of Pleas & Quarter Sessions of Franklin County and his Successors in Office in the just sum of one hundred pounds to which payment we bind ourselves & our Heirs - Given under our hands & seals this 11th day of April A.D. 1825.

The Condition of the above obligation is such that whereas on the Petition of the said John Mitchell a negro named Polly the wife of said John has been this day duly emancipated by order of the Judge of the Superior Court for said County - Now if the said Polly shall not at any time hereafter become chargeable to the said County of Franklin in any respect whatever then the above obligation to be void, otherwise to remain in full force & virtue

Signed, sealed & deliv'd   John Mitchell   (Seal)
in presence of   Tobs. Terrell   (Seal)
G. Patterson

chapter 11

Gates County

NORTH CAROLINA STATE ARCHIVES
GATES COUNTY RECORDS
MISCELLANEOUS RECORDS
C.R.041.928.2

Affidavit of Miles Parker

Miles Parker maketh Affidavit that in the suit at the instance of Willis Hughes Agt. him he has understood from some of the Jury who sat on the above trial that they were dissatisfied with their Verdict and that some others of the said Jury were friendly to the emancipation of Negroes and their equality with the Whites that he was taken by surprise in the testimony of Sarah Daniel and that he can prove by two Witnesses that what she swore was untrue he can also prove by testimony that before he actually Struck or beat the said Negroe, he (the Negroe) had made at the Deponant to take a Stick from him & take his shirt[?] before he flogged him that the said Negroe conducted himself with great Impudence & sauciness to him, before he threatened to touch him

    Miles Parker

Sworn to in open Court
Test Law Baker CC

****

State of North Carolina }
Gates County } Know all men by these presents that we
Wiles Cowper, and Jethro Sumner are held and firmly bound unto William Goodman Esqr Chairman of the Court of Pleas and quarter Sessions for the county of Gates and his Successors for the use of the poor of the said County in the Sum of one hundred pounds To which payment well and truly to be made, we bind ourselves, our heirs Executors and Administrators Jointly and Severally, firmly by these presents, Sealed with our Seals And dated this 22d of May 1811.

  The condition of the above obligation is such that if the said Wiles Cowper shall indemnify, & keep harmless the wardens of the poor of said county from all costs and charges that they or any others may incur in consequence of a certain negro named Jack, liberated by said court on the petition of the said Wiles having become chargeable to said County previous to the same having been effected then the above obligation to be void otherways to be and remain in full force & virtue

    Wiles Cowper (Seal)
     J. Sumner

Signed Sealed &
executed in the presence of
Jas. Norfleet

****

State of North Carolina
Gates Ss } Feby Term 1805

Chapter 11: Gates County Records

The petition of Wiles Cowper to the Worshipfull the Justices of Court Aforesaid humbly prays the Negro Woman Sal the property of the petitioner may be set free and for ever liberated for and on account of Meritorious Services And your petitioners as in duty bound will ever pray &C

        Wills Cowper

The Prayer of the Petition granted on his giving Bond with
Approved Security agreable to Act of Assembly in the Sum of £200

State of North Carolina Gates County

Know all men by these presents that we Wiles Cowper & Thomas Ballard of the county and state aforesaid are held and Firmly bound to the Chairman of the Court & his successors in the just and full Sum of five hundred pounds current money for payment whereof well and truly to be made we bind ourselves our Heirs Executors & Administrators, firmly by these presents Sealed with our seal and dated this seventeenth day of Febuary 1805
    The condition of the above obligation is such that if the above bound Wiles Cowper shall at all times keep the county of Gates free from any and all charges & expences on account of a negro Woman named Sal then the above obligation to be void otherwise to remain in full force & virtue

test   Wiles Cowper   (Seal)
Hy Hudgins
Mills Eures   Thos. W. Ballard (Seal)

***

State of North Carolina
    Know all Men by these presents that We Henry Gilliam of the county of Gates are held and firmly unto: **[Blank]** to the which payment well and truly to be made unto the said **[Blank]** His Heirs Executors administrators and assigns, we bind our Selves heirs executors administrators Jointly Severally firmly by these presents Sealed with our Seals & dated this **[Blank]** of **[Blank]** 1821
The Condition of the above obligation is Such that whereas by an order of the Judge of the Superior Court of Law and equity for the County of Gates, in the Petition of Richard a Negro Slave the property of the said Henry Gilliam praying for emancipation and the prayer of said Petitioner Carried into effect. Now in case the said Richard shall well and truly behave himself as a good Orderly Citizen and if the said Henry Gilliam do & shall indemnify the Wardens of the poor for the County aforesaid from all Costs & Charges that may be accrued for an by reason of the said emancipation of the said Richard then this obligation to be Void else to Remain in full force & Virtue
        H. Gilliam   (Seal)

State of North Carolina   }
Gates County   } Supr Court of Law Fall Term 1821
To the honorable Judge of the Superior Court of Law
Your petitioner Henry Gilliam of the County & State aforesaid humbly shews that he is the owner of a Negro man named Dick Jones that he has owned him for three years that the said Dick Jones is a worthy Slave has done him great services and that he is a Slave of great merit, honesty and integrity and that for his meritorious services aforesaid he thinks the said negro Dick Jones well intitled to his freedom He therefore prays your honor to pas an order or decree to emancipate said Dick Jones from Slavery that he may be free for his meritorious services aforesaid And your petitioner will ever pray &c
        H. Gilliam

Chapter 12: Granville County Records

chapter 12

Granville County

NORTH CAROLINA STATE ARCHIVES
GRANVILLE COUNTY RECORDS
MISCELLANEOUS RECORDS OF SLAVES & FREE PERSONS OF COLOR
C.R.044.928.25

At a Court held for the county of Northampton the 10th day of February 1757.

Indian Sarah Pltf	}
vs	} In trespass Assault and Battery
Sarah Clarke deft	} False imprisonment

This day came the parties by their attornies & thereupon came also a Jury to wit Benjamin Williams &c who being elected tried & sworn to by the issue joind between the said parties as aforesd Miles Carey Gentn: attorney for the pltf to maintain the issue joind on the part of the sd. pltf gave in evidence to the said Jurors the deposition of Mary Hayes in these words to wit "That about fifty years past she knew an Indian wench called Moll belonging to Capt. Humphry Marshall of Isle of Wight County in Virginia &c she the said Moll had a female child called Sarah which child as she your deponent believes was afterwards the Slave of Thomas Whitfield of Nansemond County in Virginia aforesd. but your deponent does not know of what tribe of Indians the sd. wench Moll came from or of any pretensions she the said Sarah hath to freedom & further saith not." also the depositions of Cornelious Ratcliff, Rachael Norsworthy, John Sawyer & Mary Willson in the following words to wit "Cornelious Ratcliff aged eighty two or thereabouts saith that this deponent knew that the mother of the plaintif Sarah did belong to one Capt. Marshall & was always reputed to be his Slave & he this deponent saith that he heard that the said Moll came from Cape Fear & further this deponent saith not - "Rachael Norsworthy aged sixty nine or thereabouts saith she this deponent hath heard her mother say that her father bought the reputed mother of the plaintif and this deponent saith that she knows nothing of her being free and further saith not" - John Sawyer aged sixty six or thereabouts saith that he this deponent knew the Indian Moll the reputed mother of the plaintif Sarah and this deponent saith the said Moll was always a Slave as far as he knew for Capt. Marshall gave her away in his will as a Slave & further this deponent saith - Mary Willson aged forty years or thereabouts "saith that she this deponent has heard say that Moll the reputed mother of the plaintif Sarah was a Cape Fear Indian but she knows nothing of her being free & further saith not." Upon which the said Defendant by Alexander Elmesly her attorney says the several matters and things by the said plaintif given in evidence as aforesaid are not sufficient to maintain the said issue on the part of the said plaintif nor by the Law of the Land is she bound to give any answer thereto - Wherefore for want of sufficient evidence in this behalf the said defendant prays Judgment that the jurors aforesd. may be discharged from giving their Verdict & the said action of the plaintif against her the sd. defendant may be quashed &c

---

And at a Court held for the said County the 10th day of March 1757 This day came the parties aforesaid by their attornies aforesd. & the matter of Law reserved at the last Court to be argued being now fully debated by the counsel on both sides on consideration whereof it is the Opinion of the Court that the demurrer is good Therefore it is considered that the plaintiff take nothing by her bill but for her false clames be in Mercy &c And that she the said defendant go hereof **[Torn]** without day & recover against the said plaintiff her costs by her about her defence in this behalf expended &c

A true Copy   S. Kello C.

     Test. Sam Kello C.

Chapter 12: Granville County Records

Sir)
In Regard to Ben a boy John Clark sold John Potter I very well know & his mother before him - which was som talk of his Trying for his freedom - and was said that his mother Was a Indian but regard to his Being free I know nothing of, and I cant do him any manner of Service, But believe he has no Manner of Chance to Get free I'm Yr.   James Clark
29 Oct. 1781
To Mr. John Penn

Granvile County Court Augt. 7th 1782
A petition for freedom brought by Benja. Vicery[?] against Potters exrs. was heard & tried this day and the Court was of opinion that the petitioner had a right to his freedom from which Judgmt. the Defts. prayed an appeal.

    On the trial James Smith was examined as a witness who was upwards of sixty years of age and being unable to ride as far as Willsbgh on the motion of the pltf. his deposition was taken in open Court he being duly sworn deposeth And saith that he acted as an overseer for old Mr. Clark several years before his death & for some considerable time afterwards for his widow. That he knew the mother of the petitioner called Sarah that she was looked upon and understood to be the daughter of an Indian free woman, that she often said she had a right to be free, and he has frequently heard it said in the Family that she claimed her freedom, that there was some noise, that a certain person was about suing for her freedom at which time it was observed by the old Lady or some of her [Torn] that if she did not get her case tried before a certain old man died, whose name this deponent forgets, who lived a great distance from South Hampton from whence the said woman was brought, that she would not be able to prove her freedom, that the Family seemed very unwilling to talk publicly on this Subject, but rather inclined to keep it secret, that it was much talked of in the neighborhood that she ought to be free, that on the death of the old woman Mrs. Clark he was informed that the said woman Sarah & the petitioner were aloted to John Clark, that the said Sarah had long hair & he believes [Torn] descended from an Indian from her [Torn]Augt. Court 1782. Sworn to in open Court in Presence of Richd. Henderson

    Test.   Reuben Searcy C.C.

Vicory
 agt.
Potter &c
Executed
Thornton yancey[?]
not guilty & Jun [?]
J Penn

[Torn] of Granville County Greeting We Command you [Torn] Potter and Miles King [Torn] found in your bailiwick and them safely keep so [Torn] our County Court of Granville at the Courthouse [Torn] Answer Benjamin Vicory of [Torn] & Battery and False [Torn] two hundred pounds specie
Reuben Searcy Clerk of our said Court the sixth [Faded]
Reuben Searcy C.C.

State of North Carolina }
Granville County   } To Micajah Holliman & Henry Browne Gent. of Southampton County in Virginia esqr. Greeting we Command you that at such a certain day & place you cause to come before you Samuel Kello of your said County & him examine on oath as well on behalf of William Potters exrs. - as Benjamin Vickory - in a certain matter of controversy between the said parties in our County Court depending and such examination so taken under your hands & Seals you have before the Justices of our County Court on the first Monday in November next together with this writ.
Witness Asa Searcy Clerk of our said Court the 4th day of August -
A.D. 1783
Twenty days to the adverse party   Asa Searcy C.C.

Chapter 12: Granville County Records

a sufficient notice.

Potters Exrs.   }
   ads.   } dedimus
Vickory   }
To Nov. Term 1783

Nov: 1st 1783
The Execution of this Commr. appears by an attested Copy of the record of the Coty of Southampton in the suit Indian Sarah vs Sarah Clarke & by the deposition of Saml. Kello [Torn] Clerk of the sd. County hereto Annexed
        Micajah Holliman
        Henry Browne

Virginia Southampton County
Samuel Kello of full age being first sworn deposeth and saith that he hath been regularly appointed and sworn clerk of this County in which capacity he has served several years & that the original depositions of Mary Hayes of Northampton County No. Carolina & of Cornelious Ratcliff, Rachael Norsworthy, John Sawyer, & Mary Willson of the County of Isle of Wight in Virginia are lodged in his office & appear to have been properly taken and sworn to & that true Copies of them are inserted in the proceedings of the Court of the sd. County of Southampton in the suit Indian Sarah agst Sarah Clarke   hereto Annexed

Taken & Sworn to before us
this first day of Novr. 1783
Micajah Holliman   (Seal)
Henry Browne   (Seal)

****

To the Honbl. the Court of Granville

    We your petitioners (who are the only proprietors) do here humbly state to this Court that Jacob Fain, Thro' his Honest industry has procured Money suficient to our Satisfaction to purchase his freedom, which, together with his faithfulness as a servant, induces us to petition Your Worships that he may have his freedom, and do humbly desire that the Worshipful Court of Granville would emancipate the said Jacob, and your petitioners will ever be in duty bound to pray &c

1st May 1805   Elizabeth Bullock, Frances Boyd, William Boyd, James Maclin, Eliza Maclin, Wm.
Bullock

Know all men by these presents That we William Bullock and Leonard Henderson of the County of Granville & State of North Carolina do bind ourselves our Heirs Exrs. Administrators &c. to pay unto John Brodie Esqr. (Chairman) the full and just sum of one hundred Pounds Good & Lawful money of this State on or before the 1st day of August next ensuing As in witness whereof we have hereunto set our hands and affixed our Seals this Seventh day of May in the year of our Lord Eighteen hundred and five

The Condition of the above obligation is such Whereas the Worshipful Court of Granville has this day Emancipated A negroe man Called Jacob Fain by petition of the parties that owned the said Jacob. Now if the Above bound William Bullock & Leonard Henderson does well & Truly Prevent the said Man Jacob from becoming a charge to this County then the above obligation to become of no effect, Otherwise to remain in full force & Virtue
Witness
Jas. Sneed   Wm. Bullock   (Seal)
                                  L. Henderson   (Seal)

Chapter 12: Granville County Records

****

Petition for freedom
Jacob Fain

State of North Carolina }
Granville County }

To the honourable the Judge of the Superior Court for the County aforesaid

The Petition of Jacob Fain humbly sheweth unto your Honour, that having purchased Sally his wife of Sarah Smith & James his brother of William Bullock he prays your Honour that upon it being made appear unto your Honour that the aforementioned Sally & James have been faithful servants they may be liberated upon their meritorious services being proved to your Honour agreeable to act of Assembly
                        Jacob Fain

Exparte: Jacob Fain -
Upon the hearing of the petition in this court & the proofs offered of the truth of the allegations therein [?] & by the license & express assent of Jacob Fain, who is here present in Court, It is ordered & adjudged by the Court that Sally, a Slave of said Jacob, be & She is hereby emancipated & Set free by the name of Sally Fain & intitled to all the privileges rights & immunities of a free person of Color provided that the said Jacob shall enter Bond to keep her from being chargeable to Granville County, according to Law:-- And it is further ordered & adjudged &c. /the same as to James, by the name of James Fain/

Jacob Fain } Bond
Sally Fain
Filed in Office by Jno Bullock
the 6th day of Sept AD 1837
Tho H Willie Ck

State of North Carolina

    Know all men by these presents that we Jacob Fain principal and John Bullock & Thos S Williams Security all of the County of Granville and State aforesaid are held & firmly bound unto the State of North Carolina for the use of the Poor of the County of Granville [**Torn**] of Five hundred dollars to [**Torn**] payment well and truly to be made and done we bind Ourselves Our Heirs, Executors & Administrators jointly & severally firmly by these presents Sealed with Our seals & dated this **[Blank]** day of **[Blank]** AD 1837.
The Condition of the foregoing obligation is such that whereas Sally a slave the property of Jacob Fain of said County was after due proceedings had in the Superior Court of Law for the County of Granville by Judgment, sentence & decree had, given and pronounced by said Court at the Term thereof at September 1822[?] Emancipated and set free by the name of Sally Fain
    Now if the said Sally Fain Shall not in any wise be or become Chargeable to the County aforesaid, Then the above Obligation to be Void otherwise to be & Remain in full force & Virtue. Signed & Sealed by us this the day and date above written.

Witness		
	Jacob X Fain	(Seal)
Jno Lewis	Jno Bullock	(Seal)
Jno. L. Read	Thos Williams	(Seal)
Tho A Willie as to Bullock & Williams		

****

Pass Receipt.
from T Goss to

Chapter 12: Granville County Records

Negro Cambridge

State of North Carolina
Granville County
    To all Whom it May Concern
I Thomas Goss of the County and State aforesaid in Consideration of the many Services to me Rendered by my Negro Man and Woman Cambridge and Winny his wife do Clear them of being Commanded in My service & business of Labour or My heirs executors or administrators and do give them Priveledge to Continue on the Land Whereon they now Live during Life Nevertheless to be void in Case they or either of them Should Misbehave March 18th day 1816.

Test	his
Jno. Stephenson	Thomas T Goss
	mark

Elijah Goss & Fanny Goss
To } Bond
Wm M Sneed
August Court 1816

Know all men by these present that we Elijah Goss & Fanny Goss do acknowledge ourselves indebted to William M. Sneed Chairman of the County of Granville and to his Successors in Office in the sum of two hundred Pounds to which payment we bind ourselves our Heirs Executors and Administrators Jointly and Severally Sealed with our seals this 5th August AD 1816.

    The Condition of the above obligation is such that whereas the County Court Agreeable to the Last Will & Testament of Thomas Goss Decd. liberated Cambridge & Winney   now if they keep them off the Parish agreeable to Law then the above obligation to be void otherwise to remain in full force & virtue.

Witness
Step K Sneed   Elijah Goss   (Seal)
                           her
                        Fanny + Goss   (Seal)
                           mark

****

J. Somerville Bond
Somerville, John decd.

State of North Carolina }
Granville County   }

    Know all men by these Presents that I John Somervell am held and firmly bound unto Micajah Bullock Esquire or his Successors in Office the Just & full sum of two thousand Pounds for which payment we bind ourselves our Heirs Executors Administrators or assigns as Witness our Hands and Seals this 3d day of February AD 1807.

    The Condition of the above Obligation is Such that Whereas the County Court hath emancipated Hanson a Slave formerly the property of John Somervell Decd. Now if the said John doth ensure the said Hanson not to become chargeable to the County then the above to be void otherwise to remain in full force & virtue.

Witness
J Sneed   Tho. Somerville (Seal)

****

Harry & Rachel Cook
Harvey
Free Negroes

Torn   }

Chapter 12: Granville County Records

of Colo. Thomas Taylor   }
Exparte   }

Petition for the Emancipation of negroes Harry & Rachael
This petition coming on to be heard on the petitioner and evidence in support of it is ordered and adjudged by the court that the negroes Harry and Rachiel be Emancipated & set free from the bonds of slavery And that by the respective names of Harry Cook and Rachiel Cook they be entitled to all the priviledges and rights of free born negroes And it is further ordered and adjudged that the Petitioner Enter into bond and security for the good behaviour of said negroes and also that they shall not be chargeable to the County according to the acts of assembly to that effect made and provided which was accordingly done by giving William Hunt security accordingly.

I William Hunt of the County of Granville, and the State of North Carolina, Am held and firmly bound unto his Excellency G. Burton Governor of the State of No. Ca. and his successors in office in the just and full sum of four hundred pounds; to which payment well and truly to be made I bind myself my heirs Executors and assigns. Witness my hand and seal this 9th day of Sept. A.D. 1825

The condition of the above obligation is such that whereas Harry & Rachiel former slaves of Col. Thomas Taylor decd. have been manumitted and set free from the bonds of slavery by the honorable Superior Court for the County of Granville Holden on the first Monday of Sept. Ad. 1825 by the names of Harry Cook and Rachiel Cook Now if the said Harry Cook and Rachiel Cook shall continue to demean themselves as peaceable and orderly Citizens then the said obligation to be void; Otherwise to remain in full force and virtue.
                Wm Hunt

I William Hunt of the County of Granville and State of North Carolina am held and firmly bound unto William M. Sneed Chairman of the Court of Pleas and Quarter Sessions for the county of Granville and his successors in Office in the sum of Two hundred dollars to which payment well and truly to be made I bind myself my heirs Executors & assigns witness my hand and seal thid 9th day of Sept. AD. 1825.

The condition of the above obligation is such that whereas Harry & Rachiel former Slaves of Col. Thomas Taylor decd. have been Emancipate and set free from the bonds of slavery by the names of Harry Cook and Rachiel Cook Now if the said Harry & Rachiel shall continue solvent and not chargeable to the County this obligation to be void otherwise to remain in full force and virtue.
                Wm. Hunt

Chapter 13: Guilford County Records

chapter 13

Guilford County

NORTH CAROLINA STATE ARCHIVES
GUILFORD COUNTY
PETITIONS TO EMANCIPATE SLAVES
C.R.046.928.2

>William Burney
>Bond
>on which ordr
>come of the Court
>is to be entered
>on Docket of
>May Term 1816
>Bond executed at August Term 1816

Know all men by these presents that I William Burney of the County of Guilford and State of North Carolina am held and firmly bound unto William Miller Esqr governor and his successors in Office in the sum of two hundred pounds good and lawful money of the State aforesaid for which payment well and truly to be made I bind myself my heirs and executors and administrators firmly by these presents.

In testimony whereof I have hereunto set my hand and affixed my seal this the 23rd day of August 1816.

The Condition of the above Obligation is such that if a certain free man of Colour Commonly known by the name of Jeffery shall behave and demean himself as an honest and Orderly Citizen in the County of Guilford and elsewhere and shall refrain from all vicious practices whatsoever, then the above bounden William Burney shall be discharged and the above obligation shall be discharged and the above obligation shall cease and be void, otherwise it shall remain in full force and virtue.

Test   William burney (Seal)
J. Hanner CLK

****

>Jedediah Cusick
>Bond
>
>For the Good Behaviour
>of Will & Candis
>
>May Term 1818

[Torn]   May Term 1818
Know all men by these presents that I Jedediah Cusick of the County of Guilford and the State of North Carolina, am held and firmly bound to John Howell esqr Chairman of the County Court of Guilford in the penal Sum of Two hundred pounds good and lawful money of the State of North Carolina, for the payment of which Sum well and truly to be made, I bind myself, my heirs Exrs. &c firmly by these presents.

Chapter 13: Guilford County Records

The Condition of the above obligation is such that if Will and Candis, Persons of Color formerly the property of William Cusick dec'd and theretofore emancipated by order of the County Court of Guilford, shall behave themselves as peaceable and orderly Citizens, and shall be of good behaviour to the good Citizens of this State, during their residence therein, then this obligation to be void or else to remain in full force and effect.

Jno [?] Dick   J Cusick   (Seal)
J Hanner Clk

Jedediah Cusick
Bonds
To Keep Will & Candis
from Becoming a Charge
To the County
May Term 1818

Guilford County May Term 1819

Know all men by these presents that I Jediah Cusick of the County of Guilford & State of North Carolina am held and firmly bound unto John Howel[**Harvel?**] esquire Chairman of the County Court of Guilford and his Successors in office in the penal sum of one hundred pounds, for the payment of which sum well and truly to be made, I bind myself my heirs Exrs. &c firmly by these presents.

The Condition of this obligation is such that if the above bounden Jediah Cusick shall so keep or Cause to be kept Will and Chandis, Persons of Color formerly the property of William Cusick dec'd and heretofore emancipated by order of this Court, that they shall not brcome Chargeable to the County, during their residence therein; then this obligation to be null and void or else to remain in full force and effect.

Witness   J Cusick   (Seal)
J. H. Forrest
J Hanner Clk

***

The Petition of
Joseph Unthank   }
Josiah Unthank   } Exparte
Nathan Hunt   }

for the Emancipation of Scipio

State of North Carolina   } Superior Court of Law
Guilford County   } Spring Term AD 1820

To the Honorable the Judge of the Superior Court aforesaid: The Petition of Joseph Unthank Josiah Unthank & Nathan Hunt Senior by his Agent Nathan Hunt Junior, respectively sheweth unto your Honor that your Petitioners in or about the month of March AD 1814 contracted with Thomas Hussy for the purchase of a negro man called Scipio for the sum of four hundred Dollars, that the said negro man by the laws of this State is a slave, that the object of the purchase was not that of gain but your Petitioners knowing said negro man to be of good character honest and industrious in his habits & humble & inoffensive in his manners & well acquainted with the business of a Tanner That your Petitioners believing that he would repay them the purchase money intended and designed to effect his emancipation in the County Court according to the existing law. And your Petitioners further state that the said negro man has since faithfully repaid them the money given for his purchase, & that they understand and believe he has not only behav'd faithfully to his former Master Thomas Hussy & performed acts of a meritorious character towards him, but that since he has belonged to them his general conduct has been honest & correct & in many instances highly

Chapter 13: Guilford County Records

meritorious: they further state that the aforesaid Nathan Hunt Senior by whose agent Nathan Hunt Junior this Petition together with your other Petitioners is exhibited, has left this County for England & that the sole & only object of the said Nathan together with your other Petitioners was that of effecting the Freedom of the said negro slave as heretofore stated. Your Petitioners Further state that the said negro man Scipio has a wife and children & is about removing to the State of Indianna but are advised that if he is not legally emancipated he might be liable to be taken possession of by some evil or designing person & thus deprived of that liberty which your Petitioners wish to secure for him: And your Petitioners beg leave to aver that they are not apprised of neither do they believe there is any other pretension of claim to said negro except that alledged & set forth by your petitioners. And for the more entire satisfaction of your Honor as to the right of property in your Petitioners & more especially as to the good character & reputation of said negro Scipio your Petitioners beg leave to refer to the Annexed Bills of sale Certificate & Affidavits.

May it therefore Please your Honors to emancipate the said Negro Scipio agreeably to the act of Assembly in such Case made & provided & yr. Petitioners will ever pray.

Nathan Hunt Snr.
by his agent Nathan Hunt Jnr.
Joseph Unthank
Josiah Unthank

A bill of Sail for Sipo

State of North Carolina}
Rowan County   }

Receivd of Thomas Hussy four hundred Dollars in full for a Negro Man Named Scipio, The receipt Whereof We Jonas Leatherman, John Hampton & Wm. Keith Warrant the sd. Scipio to be Good Sound property unto the sd. Thos. Hussy his Heirs & Assigns   We the sd. Leatherman, Hampton & Keith do oblige ourselves by these presents forever Defend any Claim or Claims of any person or persons, in, & of the sd. Negro Man Scipio As in Witness our hands & seals, this 1st day of May in the Year of our Lord 1809.

Witness		
Nancy Leatherman	Jonas Leatherman	(Seal)
Abel Knight [?] 3rd	John Hampton	(Seal)
	Wm. Keith	(Seal)

North Carolina   Guilford County
Received of Nathan Hunt Joseph Unthank & Josiah Unthank four Hundred Dollars in full for a Negro Man Named Scipio, the Receipt Whereof I Thomas Hussey Will Warrant the sd. Scipio to be Good Sound property Unto the said Nathan Hunt Joseph Unthank & Josiah Unthank **[Rest of document missing]**.

State of North Carolina}
Richmond County   } To all whom it may Concern

This is to Certify that Scipio Leatherman a man of colour and a Tanner by trade has lived with us and Superintended a Tanyard for the last six years passed and has conducted himself to our satisfaction and has during the time Supported a good character.
April 6th day 1820

Eli Terry
James Pickett

State of No Carolina}
Richmond County   }

Chapter 13: Guilford County Records

    I Masten D Crawford Clerk of the Court of pleas & Quarter Sessions of the County aforesaid do hereby Certify that Eli Terry and James Pickett whose Signatures appear to the above Certificate, are men of respectability and that the utmost reliance should be placed on their Certificate.

    Given under my hand & seal of office at Rockingham the 8th day of April 1820.
Masten D. Crawford   Clk

Bond for Emancipation
of Scipio
Scipio: negro

Bond for Indemnification
April 7   1820

Know all men by these presents that we Joseph Unthank Josiah Unthank Nathan Hunt Jun. and George Swain are held and firmly bound unto the acting Wardens of the Poor in & for the County of Guilford in the sum of five hundred Dollars to be paid unto the said Wardens & their successors in Office to the which payment well & truly to be made we & each of us bind ourselves our heirs &c jointly & severally firmly by these presents seald with our seals & dated this 29th day of April AD 1820.

    The Condition of the above Obligation is such that whereas by an order & decree of the Superior Court of Guilford held on the fourth Monday after the fourth Monday in March AD 1820, the aforesaid Joseph Unthank Josiah Unthank & Nathan Hunt Junior Agent of Nathan Hunt Senior obtained a license to emancipate & set free a Negro slave named Scipio, now if the said Joseph Unthank Josiah Unthank & Nathan Hunt shall prevent the said Negro Scipio from at any time hereafter becoming chargeable to the Aforesaid County of Guilford & shall at all times hereafter indemnify the said County of Guilford against the maintenance of said Negro Scipio then the above obligation to be void otherwise to remain in full force & effect.

Acknowledged in Open Court	Joseph Unthank	(Seal)
(Tho. Caldwell CC)	Josiah Unthank	(Seal)
	Nathan Hunt Jnr.	(Seal)
	George Swain	(Seal)

****

Lewis Walton & others
Petition to Emancipate a Slave
Named Thomas Gossett
Decree filed & Ordered to be Enrolled

Fall Term 1858
Gil[?] & Shober Attos

State of North Carolina   }
Guilford County   }
Superior Court of Law
Fall Term 1858

To the Judge of Guilford Superior County
    Lewis Walton, Joseph Coltraine, John Coltraine, by Petition shew unto your Honor, that they are the owners of a negro man Slave named Thomas Gossett, who is over fifty years old, that he was raised by Abram Gossett, who willed to his **[Son?]** John O Gossett, who sold him to your Petitioners - that said Slave Thomas is a person of good character - has always conducted himself well, industrious, honest humble faithful - that he has been a most faithful Servant, reliable - They further shew that said Slave Thomas performed most Meritorious Services, and hath since been treated by his acquaintenances generally as a free man - that the house of your Petitioner John Coltraine caught fire, or was set

Chapter 13: Guilford County Records

on fire, at which time the said Thomas Exerted himself most meritoriously and risked his life - The House was locked when the fire was discovered and your Petitioner John Coltraine with his family was gone from the home that said Thomas then belonged to John O Gossett, and came in Sight - that he & James Pool and another commenced to work for your Petitioner John Coltraine - that the Said Slave Thomas, forced open the door, and at great peril carried out much of the valuable property that was in the House - the most of it Whilst the House was on fire and carried it out of the way of the fire - that he carried out as long as any thought by human Exertions could rescue any thing from the frightful flames - that he carried out the desk & papers in which the moneys & papers of said Petitioner John Coltraine were - that all that he by extraordinary Exertions goods amounting to several thousand dollars - the smoke house filled with [?] and well [?] were saved, much owing to the Exertions of said slave that this application would have been made sooner had he been over fifty years of age - that said boy Thomas has been a Servant at the New Garden Boarding School for the last 17 years, & and his conduct in all respects good & had been [?] with the keys - is certainly a faithful boy & in all things most worthy - is humble - & has no diffculties.

    Your Petitioners have not received in money or otherwise the price or value, or any part thereof of said Slave or been induced to Petition for his Emancipation in consideration of any price paid or to be paid therefore.

    Your Petitioners therefore pray your Honor to decree the Emancipation of said Slave Thomas Gossett, on the proper bond being given according to law and to grant the necessary orders & decrees to make the said Thomas a free man and grant all other & necessary [Indecipherable] - they with [?] will ever pray &c.

John A Gilmer
Sol for Petitioners

    The Petitioner Lewis Walton makes oath that the several matters of fact set forth in the forgoing petition as of his own knowledge are true, & those not of his own knowledge he believes to be true.
Subscribed & sworn to before me
WD Trotter CSC   Lewis Walton

State of North Carolina
Guilford County
Superior Court of Law
Fall Term 1858
Lewis Walton
John Coltraine
Joseph Coltraine
Ex parte

    Petition for the Emancipation a Slave named Thomas Gossett

    Aaron Stalker affirms that he is well acquainted with the slave Thomas Gossett & has known him a long time - that he arrived at the House of John Coltraine on the day that it was burnt - from what he learned then & has always understood the slave Thomas Gossett rendered meritorious Services on that occasion Substantially as stated in the Petition - that the said Thomas certainly deserves the Character given him in the Petition, & he conceives that he has earned & richly deserves his freedom - that said boy Thomas is a Servant at New Garden, and is certainly a faithful and deserving Slave.

Subscribed & Sworn
to before me
in open Court
WD Trotter CSC   Aaron Stalker

Guilford Superior Court of Law
Fall Term 1858

Lewis Walton, Joseph Coltraine & John Coltraine
    Ex Parte   }Petition to Emancipate a Slave named Thomas Gossett More than fifty years of age

    This Case Comeing on to be heard on the Petition, accompanying Affidavits, it is declared by the Court that the Slave Thomas Gossett is over fifty years of age of good and Excellent Character, and hath rendered Meritorious

Chapter 13: Guilford County Records

Services, such as subscribed and pointed out by the act of assembly & set forth in the Affidavits, & the Petitioners and the said Thomas Gossett now here in open Court, after his freedom & herein declared and decreed entered into bond payable to the State of North Carolina in the Sum of five hundred dollars with Aaron Stalker & Lewis Walton as Securities Condition that the said Thomas Gossett shall honestly & correctly demean himself so long as he shall remain in this State, and shall not become a County charge, which bond is accepted by the Court & ordered to be filed.

Ordered by the Court that this decree be entered & [?] on the Minutes of this Court - Ordered further that the Clerk of this Court furnish to the said Thomas Gossett a Certified Copy of this decree.

Ordered further by the Consent of parties that the said Thomas Gossett pay the costs of this Cert.

I William D. Trotter Clerk of said Court Certify that the above is a full true & perfect Copy of the decree in the above Case.
Witness W.D. Trotter Clerk of our said Court at Office in Greensboro on the fourth Monday after the 4th Monday in September 1858

W.D. Trotter Clk

North Carolina }
Guilford County }

The forgoing Bond and the Certificate thereto was duly Registered on the 11th day of January AD 1859
In Book D. No. 2 page 181   Ezre Willis Ck

Know all men by these presents that the undersigned are held and firmly bound unto the State of North Carolina in sum of five hundred dollars for the payment of which well and truly to be made we bind ourselves our heirs &C jointly & severally & firmly by these presents - Witness our hands & Seals this the 28th day of October 1858.

The Condition of the above Obligation is Such, that Whereas a negro slave the property of Lewis Walton, John Coltraine and Joseph Coltraine named Thomas Gossett, on Petition of his said owners hath by a decree of Guilford Superior Court decreed to be Emancipated and set free according to Act of Assembly - the said Slave Thomas Gossett being over fifty years of age.

Now if the said Thomas Gossett shall honestly and correctly demean himself so long as he shall remain in this State and shall not become a County charge then the above obligation to br null and void otherwise to remain in full force & Effect.

	His	
W.D. Trotter CSC	Thomas X Gossett	(Seal)
	mark	
	Aaron Stalker	(Seal)
	Lewis Walton	(Seal)

****

Henry Bevell
Petition
For Emancipation

State of North Carolina: To the Honorable the Judge of the Superior Court of Law & Equity for Guilford County Greeting:

Humbly petitioning sheweth unto your Honor your Petitioner Henry Beville of the County and State aforesaid That your petitioner is now possessed and claims title to a negro slave named Bridget; that said slave Bridget was once the property of your petitioner's father & continued in his possession for a number of years, that during her continuance in his family she performed many meritorious and praise worthy services towards your petitioner's father & family, that she raised your petitioner in a great measure & has in all instances contributed much to his welfare:

Your petitioner further states that the said slave was for some time out of his family but that he has lately got her into his possession, that he is now anxious to emancipate her for her meritorious and praise worthy services not only to your petitioner but to his family & that her course of service has uniformly been such as the Act of Assembly in such cases made and provided requires, To the end therefore that the said slave Bridget may meet with such requital from

Chapter 13: Guilford County Records

your petitioner as her meritorious and praise worthy conduct to him & his family entitles her to, & from the further consideration that your petitioner is unable to make such requital without the instance of this Honorable Court before which such matters are properly cognizable, your petitioner comes forward & ask the interference of this Honorable Court in his behalf in this - that he may be at liberty to emancipate said slave Bridget for the reason already mentioned and that by order of this Honorable Court she may be entitled to all such rights and priviledges as are vested in free born Black persons & your petitioner will ever pray &C
Henry Beville

We and each of us bind ourselves our heirs &c to pay to John Howel, Chairman, and his successors in office one hundred pounds for the payment of which well & truly to be made we bind ourselves jointly & firmly by these presents, Witness our hands & seals this 26th April 1823.
The Condition of the above obligation is such that whereas Henry Bevill has obtain'd a decree of the Honourable Superior Court this day to emancipate a certain negro slave Bridget, now if the said Henry shall keep the said Bridget from becoming a charge upon the wardens of the poor for Guilford County then the above obligation to be void otherwise to remain in full force & effect

Witness		
Jno Caldwell CC	his	
	Henry X Bevill	(S)
	mark	
	Edward Bevill	(S)
	[?]Bert Bevill	(S)
	John Walker	(S)

****

Petition of Adam Mitchell
for the emancipation of
Negro Philip

State of North Carolina   } Superior Court of Law
Guilford County   } Fall Term 1829

     To the Honourable the Judge of the Superior Court of Law for the County aforesaid the Petition of Adam Mitchell Sheweth to Your Honour that he is the Owner of a Negro Man Slave by the Name of Philip that he has owned said Negro for about seventeen years last past during all which time said Philip has Conducted himself well, and has sustained a fair Character for honesty & sobriety -- Your Petitioner further states that the said Philip has always been unusually industrious and attentive to the interest of Your Petitioner and for many years has had his entire Confidence -- Your Petitioner believes that if the said Philip was emancipated he would be a Sober, industrious & Orderly Citizen -- Your Petitioner prays that this able Court will permit him to emancipate the said Negro Philip -- The said Philip has (as Your Petitioner believes) performed meritorious Services within the meaning of the Act of the General Assembly -- And Your Petitioner is ready to enter into such bonds as are required to cause it be done by such Security as the law requires -- And to all such Other Acts as may be required of him for the purpose aforesaid.
     And Your Petitioner as in duty bound will ever pray &c
                                                              Adam Mitchell

---

Adam Mitchell   } Petition praying for License to Emancipate a negro man
Exparte   } Slave named Philip

This Cause Coming on to be heard ob the Petition of the Petitioner -- And Witnesses being examined in Open Court -- It was made Satisfactorily to Appear to the Court that the negro Slave Philip was unusually faithful in the discharge of his duties to his Master and had always sustained a good Character And it further Appearing to the Court that the said Philip hath performed Meritorious Services within the meaning of the Acts of the General Assembly -- It is therefore Ordered Adjudged and decreed by the Court -- That the Petitioner Adam Mitchell have leave to emancipate and set free the said Negro Philip and that the said Philip is hereby emancipated & set free & vested with all the rights and

Chapter 13: Guilford County Records

priviledges which belong to a free born negro -- upon bonds being given for the good behaviour of the said Negro Philip, and that he shall not become Chargeable to the County of Guilford.

NB   Bond is not filed -- nor deed of Emancipation

Bond

We acknowledge ourselves indebted to Joseph Gibson esqr Chairman of the County Court and his Successor in Office in the sum of One hundred pounds.
    To be Void on Condition that certain negro man named Philip lately emancipated or about to be emancipated in Guilford Superior Court by Adam Mitchell shall never become Chargeable on the County of Guilford -- Otherwise to remain in full force and effect Witness our hands and seals this 25th of Feby 1830.

	his	
Test	Philip X Mitchell	(Seal)
Jno Caldwell	mark	
	Adam Mitchel	

***

The Petition of Henry Humphrys
for the Emancipation of Kiziah

State of North Carolina   } Superior Court of
Guilford County   } Law Fall Term 1829

    To the Honourable the Judge of the Superior Court of Law for the County aforesaid
The Petition of Henry Humphrys Sheweth to your Honour that he is the Owner of a female Slave by the name of Kiziah & that he has been the Owner of the said Kiziah for the last twenty years during all which time the said Kiziah has Conducted herself with propriety and has always sustain'd a Character for Honesty -- Your Petitioner further states that the said Kiziah was for a number of years kept about the House of your Petitioner during all which time she discharged her duties with faithfulness and was unusually attentive to the interests of Your Petitioner & trust worthy in every situation in which she has been employed by Your Petitioner -- Your Petitioner believes that the said Kiziah has performed Meritorious Services within the Meaning of the Acts of the General Assembly & prays your Honour to permit him to emancipate the said Kiziah -- Your Petitioner is Willing & Ready to enter into the bonds required by law or cause it to be done -- And Your Petitioner as in duty bound will ever pray &c

                                                            Henry Humphrys

---

Henry Humphrys   } Petition praying for License
                            } to emancipate a Negro Woman
Ex parte   } Slave Named Kiziah

    This Cause Coming on to be heard in the Petition of the Petitioner -- And witnesses being examined in Open Court -- It appears to the Satisfaction of the Court that the said Kiziah was unusually faithful in the discharge of her duties to her Master and has always Sustained a good Character And it further appearing to the Court that the said Kiziah hath performed Meritorious Services within the Meaning of the Acts of the General Assembly -- It is therefore Ordered Adjudged and Decreed by the Court -- That the Prtitioner Henry Humphrys have leave to emancipate and set free the said negro woman kiziah and the said Kiziah is hereby emancipated and set free & invested with all the rights & priviledges which belong to a free born negro - upon bonds being given for the good behaviour of the said negro Kiziah, and that she shall not become chargeable to the County of Guilford.

NB   The Bond not now given nor the Deed of Emancipation.

Chapter 13: Guilford County Records

Bond for Kiziah
$100

We acknowledge ourselves indebted to Joseph Gibson Chairman of he County Court or his Successors in Oofice in thesum of one hundred Pounds.
    To be void on Condition that a Certain Negro by the name of Kiziah Mitchell lately emancipated in Guilford Superior Court by Henry Humphrys shall never Become Chargeable on the County of Guilford. Otherwise to remain in full force and effect -- Witness our hands & seals - this 15th of Frby Ad 1830.

	her	
Test.	Kiziah X Mitchel	(Seal)
Thos. Caldwell	Henry Humphrys	(Seal)

****

Jehu Ballinger
Petition for Emancipation
of Dave

Petition Granted

Noth Carolina } Fall Term 1829
Guilford County }To the Honourable Judge of

The Superior Court of Law for Guilford
    The Petition of Jehu Ballinger Humbly complaining Sheweth unto your Honour that **[Blank]** Mcleutad[?] late of this County the father in law of your petitioner, duly made and executed his last will and testament, which has been duly recorded in the proper Court, wherein and whereby, he requested and directed that a negro man then belonging to him by the name of Toby - or Tobias should be emancipated and set free after the death of the Testator, for the faithful and many meritorious services which said Tobias had rendered unto him and his aged wife, and for the careful manner in whic the said Tobias had taken care of his property and himself in his very advanced age.
    Your Petitioner shews that the estate of said testator was involved in debt, and hereby it became necessary to make sale of Tobias to raise money for the discharge of the debts: Your Petitioner, regretting to see the last will of his father in law, on thid subject, thwarted, purchased said negro Tobias about fifteen years ago, and has held him as his slave ever since.
    Your Petitioner shews that within a short time after the purchase of said tobias, your Petitioner had the misfortune to loose his wife, who died leaving infant children survivimg her: That your Petitioner was a man in very moderate circumstances, and his business, & employments, often made it necessary that he should be from house, and that the care of the children should be entrusted to Tobias. Your Petitioner not having married since the death of his wife.
    Your Petitioner shews that said Tobias has rendered him many and important meritorious services but more particularly in assisting him in raising his children; and from the kind attention and affectionate care which he extended towards them during their tender years: Your Petitioner's children are now all nearly grown and join your Petitioner in a prayer that he may be emancipated.
    Your Petitioner Preys your Honour to grant to him a License to emancipate and set free the said Tobias and that he may be decreed to be free, and to enjoy all the rights and privilidges that are enjoyed by a free negro under the Laws of this State and your Petitioner will ever prey
                                                                 Jehu Ballinger

---

Decree

The Petition of Jehu Bollinger for license to emancipate Tobias his slave coming on to be heard, and satisfactory evidence having been offered to the Court of the Meritorious Services of said Slave Tobias, and of his good moral Character: It is Ordered Adjudged and decreed that said Jehu Bollinger have License to emancipate & set free his said slave Tobias:and it is adjudjed and decreed that said Tobias be emancipated, and that the said Tobias is hereby

Chapter 13: Guilford County Records

manumitted and set free, and vested with all the rights and privileges of a free born negro and to be call'd and known for the future by the name of Tobias Bollinger Magellan

---

Bond for Tobias

We acknowledge ourselves indebted to Joseph Gibson Esquire Chairman of the county Court of Guilford and his successors in office in the sum of one hundred pounds.

    To be void on condition that that certain negro man named Tobias lately emancipated or about to be emancipated by Jehu Bollinger shall never become chargeable upon the County of Guilford - otherwise to remain in full force and effect. Witness my hand and seal This the 30 day of October 1829
Test

                                          Jehu Ballinger   (Seal)
                                          Jonathan Parkes   (Seal)
                                            Jacob Hubbard   (Seal)

Jehu Ballinger to Tobias
Deed of Emancipation
Fall Term 1829
Guilford Superior Court

To all whom these presents shall come Greeting
    Know ye that I Jehu Ballinger of the County of Guilford and State of North Carolina having obtained a License to emancipate my negro Slave Tobias, from the Superior Court of Guilford County -- do hereby give and grant unto the said Tobias his emancipation and freedom for life, and I the said Jehu do hereby quit claim to all further services of said Tobias and do release unto the said Tobias his freedom and all services for the balance of his lifetime, and I do hereby emancipate, manumit, and set free the saud Tobias forever and do vest him with all the powers rights and privileges of a free born negro: The said Tobias having assumed to himself and adopted the name of Tobias Magellan by which he is to be hereafter known
Witness my hand and seal This the 30th day of October 1829   Jehu Ballinger   (Seal)
Test
J.M. Morehead
Acknowledged in open Court
Thos. Caldwell   CC

Chapter 14: Halifax County Records

chapter 14

Halifax County

NORTH CAROLINA STATE ARCHIVES
HALIFAX COUNTY RECORDS
MISCELLANEOUS RECORDS
C.R.047.928.8

In the Matter of Julius H Zollicoffers Will
Transcript from Supr.& Supreme Co
1858

State of North Carolina }
Halifax County } Be it remembered that at the Superior
Court of Law begun & held for the County aforesaid at the Court House in Halifax Town on the fourth Monday after the fourth Monday in March AD Eighteen hundred & fifty five a Transcript from the Court of Pleas & Quarter Sessions in the following words & figures is filed in Office to wit

State of North Carolina }
Halifax County } Be it remembered that at a court of
Pleas & quarter Sessions held for the County of Halifax and state aforesaid on the third Monday of august 1854 at the Court House in the Town of Halifax being the 19th day of Said Month a paper writing reporting to be the last will & Testament of Julius Zolliecoffer was offered for probate and Jno D Weeks & wife Emily, Jerome B Zolliecoffer and George Zolliecoffer Entered their Caveat to said paper writing and thereupon an issue was made up, and the following Proceedings was had and taken which is in words & figures as follows

In the Matter of Julius H Zolliecoffer }
Will }

A Paper writing purporting to be the last will & testament of Julius H Zolliecoffer is brought into Court by James Simmons with whom the said was deposited by the supposed Testator and the Executer therein named declines to offer the same for Probate and it being suggested to the Court that Certain Slaves of the supposed Testator to Wit Lydia and her children Henry & Ritter also Tom & Dick and a child of Ritter whose name is not Known born since the date of the Will and directed to be emancipated by the said supposed Will the Court doth direct the same to be Propounded as the Last Will & Testament of the said Julius H Zolliecoffer and that the Solicitor of the County be appointed to appear on behalf of the Probate of said paper and that he be specially charged with representing the interest of the said slaves.

And therefore John D Weeks & his wife Emily Jerome B Zolliecoffer and George B Zolliecoffer Caveat the same Paper and deny that it is the last Will and Testament of the supposed Testator, whereupon the Court doth direct an issue to be made up to be tried by a Jury to Wit, Whether the said Paper writing or any part thereof be in fact the last Will & Testament of the said Julius H Zolliecoffer

Commission to take depositions in the County at ten days notice, notice on Jno D Weeks for the Caveators and on FNM Williams for the propounder of the Will deemed notice to Parties, respectfully.
A Copy of which said Paper Writing offered as aforesaid is in the words and figures as follows,

State of North Carolina }
Halifax County } I Julius H Zollicoffer of the County &
state aforesaid do hereby make and publish this my last Will & Testament

Chapter 14: Halifax County Records

    I desire that my slaves Lydia and her two Children Henry & Ritter, also my boys Tom and Dick with the Child or children of girl Ritter which it is now Probable will soon be born shall have their and to that end I direct that my Executor hereafter to be named shall as soon after my death as he can conveniently do so take the said slaves to some free State and Provide a settlement for them, and I hereby give to the said Executor One Thousand dollars to make said settlement and direct my estate be charged with the expence of carrying said servants and their increase to some free State as above directed,

    I give and bequeath my other slaves, Horace, Jesse, Julia, Mack, & Weldon to be equally divided between my three Children, Jerome B Zollicoffer, Emily Caroline Weeks, and George B Zollicoffer,

    I also give & bequeath my landed Estate to be Equally divided between my before named Children Jerome B., Emily Caroline & George B, to them and their heirs forever,

    It is my wish that my daughter Emily Caroline shall have my grey horse, buggy & Harness,

    I wish the remainder of my Property sold and all claims due me Collected and after paying the Charges herein made upon my estate for the benefit of the Slaves which are to be Liberated. The fund which remains is to be invested so as to pay an annual or semi annual interest which interest is to be equally divided and Regularly paid over to my before named Sons Jerome B & George B Zolliecoffer and my daughter Emily Caroline Weeks,

    It is my desire that the said fund remain invested among the Joint lives of my said three Children and in the event of the death of either of them then the one third is to descend immediately to the Child or Children of the one who may die, and in case either one of my said Children should die leaving no Child then I wish his or her Portion to remain in Common stock between the survivors to remain and descend as above provided,

    I hereby nominate and appoint my son Jerome B. Zollicoffer my Executor to this my last Will and Testament, In Witness whereof I hereto set my hand and affixed my seal this 14th day of October 1853,

    The word Joint interlined before signed

Witness   Julius H Zollicoffer (Seal)
James Simmons
Jesse Pittard

    This Case was then Continued to the following November Term of said Court. When being Called up it was ("Continued") to the Ensuing February Term of said Court,

    At the February Term of said Court the Case was Called up for Trial and the following Proceedings was taken and had to wit,

    Jury Sworn & Empanneled to Wit, Jas B Burgess, Wm H Shields, Wm H Smith Richd H Walker Thos W Grey WW Brickell Thomas Irby, Jesse Carter Wm E Fenner, Richd Carpenter Hyram Stock[?] Wm D Faucett Who find that the Paper offered as the last Will and Testament of Julius H Zollicoffer is in truth the last Will and Testament of the said Julius H Zollicoffer, Ordered by the Court that the said Paper be recorded as such last Will and Testament, Judgment against the defendant for the Costs, from this Judgment an appeal is Prayed to the Superior Court which is allowed by consent without security,

    I hereby Certify that the foregoing is a true and correct Transcript of all the proceedings had & taken in the Suit in the Matter of the Probate of Julius H Zollicoffers Will as appears of record in my office. In Testimony whereof I hereunto subscribe my Name and affix the seal of my office this the 11th day of Apl 1855
        W.W. Daniel Clerk

Issues in the case of Julius H Zollicoffers Will

1. The caveaters deny that any part of the writing propounded as the last will & testament of the supposed testator is such.

2. That so much of the said writing as in the following words (the fund which remains is to be invested so as to pay an annual or semiannual interest which interest is to be equall divided and equally paid over to by before named sons Jerome B & George B Zollicoffer and my daughter Emily Caroline Weeks -- It is my desire that the said fund remain undivided leaving the first [?] of my said two children and in the event of the death of either of them their one third is to descend immediately to the child or children of the one which may die, and in case either one of my said children should

Chapter 14: Halifax County Records

die leaving no child then I wish his or her portion to remain in common stock between the survivors to remain and descend as above provided) is not any part of the Will of said supposed testator

3rd. That so much of the said Writing as in the following words :I desire that my slaves Lydia and her two children Henry & Ritter also my boys Tom and Dick with the child or children of girl Ritter which it is now probable will soon be born shall have their freedom and to that end I direct that my Executor hereafter to be named shall as soon after my death as he can conveniently do so, take the said slaves to some free state and provide a settlement for them, and I hereby give to the said Executor one thousand dollars to make said settlement, and direct that my estate be charged with the expence of conveying said servants and their increase to some free state as above directed) is not any part of the last Will & Testament of the supposed testator.

Jury towit -- &c sworn & impannelled who for their verdict say that they find all the issues in favor of the caveators and that in part of the said writing is the will and testament of the supposed testator Verdict set aside and a new trial granted as to the third issue.

County Court Cost

Clerk D	5.20
Tax	1.00
Sheriff	4.90
Plaintiff Atto}	
M Williams }	4.00
J Pittard	19.84
M A Willcox	9.00
W Browning	10.20
Jas Simmons	10.10
AB Pierce	6.74
WS Johnson	5.77
TM Browning	5.77
Transcript Sol &c	1.85
MA Willcox	5.00
	$89.37

And Thereupon the Case is Continued to Fall Term 1855 Judge Caldwell presiding at Which Term the Case is still Continued to Spring Term 1856 where the following proceedings is had to Wit: Judge Dick, Esqr.

Jury Sworn and Empanneled to Wit, Eli Lewis John Hardee, Edwd Fell[?], Watkins Clark, James Leggett, Richd B Parker, EA Pearson Willis Weatherbee John H Carlisle, Hiram Scott[?], FH Whitaker, MW Pittman, who say that Julius H Zollicoffer was incapable of Making a Will at the time that the Will now bewfore the Court was made -- which verdict was set aside by his Honor Judge Samuel Person, and a new trial granted.

And afterwards at Fall Term 1856 the Case was Continued by Consent of Parties Judge Saunders presiding and at the Spring Term following which was held, commencing the 20th day of March 1857 the Case was also Continued by absence of Plaintiffs Atto B Moore

Judge Manly Presiding

And at the Fall Term following which commenced on the 26th day of Octr 1857 the Case was continued for Absence of Atto General, Judge Saunders Presiding

And afterwards at the Spring Term which Commenced the 19th day of March 1858 the following Proceedings is had to Wit: Judge Ellis Presiding,

The following Jury Sworn & Empanelled to Wit: M.S. Wiggins, John P. Turner, NM Long, John H Wood, JW Harris, Jas Butts, Jas V Allen, Leroy Pierce, John T Spivey, Wm C Ousby, ET Clark, WD Staten, who say they find the last issue in favour of the Propounders, that so much of the said Paper Writing as in the following words, I desire that my slaves Lydia and her two Children Henry and Ritter and my Boys Tom & Dick with Child or Children of girl Ritter which it is now Probable will soon be born shall have their freedom, and to that end I direct my Executors hereinafter to be named shall so soon after my death as he can conveniently do so take the said slaves to some free state and provide a settlement for them, and I hereby give to my Executor One Thousand dollars to make said settlement and direct that my Estate be Charged with the expence of Conveying said servants and their increase to some free state as above directed" is the last Will & Testament of Julius H Zollicoffer

Judgment against the Appellants and their Securities to the Appeal bond for cost,

Motion for new Trial. Rule discharged

Chapter 14: Halifax County Records

Appeal to the Supreme Court by giving Security

And afterwards at the Fall Term of the Superior Court of Law held for the County of Halifax commencing on the 25th day of October 1857 Judge Caldwell Presiding the following Certificate from the Supreme Court is filed,

North Carolina
Supreme Court June Term 1858
In re Julius H Zollicoffers Will
     This Cause Came on to be argued upon the transcript of the record from the Superior Court of Law of Halifax County upon consideration whereof this Court is of opinion that there is no error in the record & proceedings of the said Superior Court therefore it is Considered and Adjudged by the Court here that the said Judgement be & the same is hereby in all things affirmed, and it is ordered that this Judgement be Certified to the said Superior Court to the intent that all necessary Proceedings may be had therein according to Law, and it is considered that the State receive against John D Weeks, Jerome B. Zollicoffer & George B Zollicoffer the Caveators, and James S Snow and JW Doyal their Sureties for the appeal from the said Judgement as appears by the appeal bond sent up with the forming part of the record in this Court the cost in the said Superior Court incurred to be taxed in the same Court and also the sum of $14.66, the cost in this Court incurred & let execution issue.
               Certified by
               EB Freeman Clk

It is therefore ordered by the Court that the said Will remaining in this office as was established by the Verdict & Judgement of this Court be remitted to the Court of Pleas & quarter Sessions of this County with a Transcript of the Proceedings in this Court had to the end that the said Will may be duly recorded & filed in the said Court of Pleas & quarter Sessions, & that further Proceedings may be had thereon according to Law.

State of North Carolina   }
Halifax County   }
     I Jas M. Grigg and Deputy Clerk of the Superior Court of Halifax County do Certify that the foregoing is a true and correct Transcript of the Proceedings in the matter of Julius H Zollicoffers Will.

     In Testimony Whereof I hereunto set my hand and affix my seal of office this the [Blank] day of November AD 1855.
               Jas M. Grigg and D.C.

In the matter of Julius H Zollicoffers will -- It is ordered by the Court that the Attorney General Wm A Jenkins be allowed one hundred dollars for his service in representing the slaves directed to be emancipated & to be paid out of what is bequeathed to them.
Received from James H. Whitaker Esq. Clerk of the Court of Pleas and Quarter Sessions for the County of Halifax State of North Carolina, the sum of one hundred dollars, the same being my fee as One of the Counsel for the Slaves directed to be emancipated by the last will and testament of Julius H. Zollicoffer late of Halifax County Deceased - And is paid me out of the fund of two thousand dollars specified in the Compromise entered into on the 23rd day of February in the year 1859 by B.Y. [?] and Edwd. Conigland[?] in behalf of Jerome Zollicoffer George Zollicoffer and John D. Weeks & wife, and by W.A. Jenkins Attorney General of North Carolina in [Torn] of the negroes directed to be emancipated by said last Will & Testament.
Halifax N.C. July 2nd 1860
Witness   J.W. Lancaster

Chapter 15: Lincoln County Records

chapter 15

Lincoln County

NORTH CAROLINA STATE ARCHIVES
LINCOLN COUNTY RECORDS
MISCELLANEOUS SLAVE PAPERS
C.R.060.928.7

                              Jacob Ramsour &
                              Peter Mauney Exrs
                              of Christian Eaker
                              Petition to Emancipate
                              Hanna Violet & Dave
                              Negro Slaves

                                      Filed at Fall
                                      Term 1831

                                    Overruled by
                                the Court. Ordered
                                that Petitioners
                                  pay the costs.

North Carolina   Superior Court of Law
Lincoln County   Fall Term A.D. 1831

      To the honorable Judge of said Court the Petition of Jacob Ramsaur and Peter Mauney executors of Christian Eaker deceased late of said County in the State aforesaid showeth to Your Honour that their Testator Christian Eaker departed this life about the _____ day of _____ A.D. having made and published his last Will and Testament (which has been duly proved & recorded according to Law) by which he appointed your petitioners Executors and Trustees to execute the trusts therein contained and in said Will he the said Christian Eaker deceased disposed of all his estate both real and personal except three negroe slaves Viz Hanna and Violet negro women and Dave a negro boy & he made as to them the following bequest -

                        "secondly my will is that my three Slaves, Hanna
                        "about forty seven years of age. Violet forty two
                        "years of age Dave a Mulatto boy about ten years
                        "of age My Will is that they above Slaves be
                        "liberated and set free at my decease and that
                        "My Executors prepare a petition to the Superior
                        "Court of Lincoln Praying the said Slaves to be
                        "liberated and Set free for their meritorious ser-
                        "vices that they have done in taking more than
                        "usual Care of Me & My wife in our declining
                        "years and in bestowing more than usual
                        "kindness to myself & to my said wife
                        "both in sickness & in health and in taking

Chapter 15: Lincoln County Records

"More than usual care of my Stock & other things
"for our support"

Your Petitioners therefore prays that they may be permitted the trust reposed in them by the last will & testament of the said Christian Eaker and in consideration of the faithful & Meritorious services of them the said Slaves to their master & mistress rendered during their Masters life & in his last illness and their kind attention to their mistress since the death of the said Christian Eaker to Execute a deed of emancipation to each of the said Slaves upon their giving bonds with sufficient security according to the act of Assembly and Your Petitioners as in duly bound well ever pray.

J. P. Henderson
Atto. for Petitioners

****

Deed of Emancipation For
Negro Sally

Know all men by these presents that I Billy Friday a free man of color of Lincoln County in the State of North Carolina, have & by these presents, liberate, let free & emancipate, a certain negro woman by the name of Sally, my wife, formerly the property of John Fulenwider The Superior Court of Law of said County having first given leave, for that purpose and from this day she is at liberty to go as a free born person.

Witness my hand & seal April 23rd 1830

Test.

Lwn. Henderson   Billi Friday (Seal)

Now all men by these presents that we Billy Friday a free man of colour, Henry Fulenwider & David Dellinger are held and firmly bound unto Andrew Hoyle chairman of the County Court of Lincoln in the penal sum of five hundred dollars.

This condition of this obligation is such that whereas the above bounden Billy Friday, hath this day obtained leave of the Superior Court, & has executed a deed of emancipation for Sally his wife, Now if the said Sally shall conduct herself as a peaceable, orderly person & be of good behavior & shall never become a charge to the County, then this obligation to be void, otherwise to remain in full force & effect - Witness my hand & seal April 23rd 1830.

Test	Billi Friday	(Seal)
Lwn. Henderson	Henry Fulenwider	(Seal)
	David Dillinger	(Seal)

North Carolina   Superior Court of Law
Lincoln County   April Term 1830

To the Honorable the Judge of the Superior Courts of Law and Equity in & for said County. The petition of Billi Friday a free man of colour, Humbly showeth unto your Honor that he has purchased his wife Sally, and has a desire to liberate her. That she has been the wife of your petitioner for about twenty seven years, and has borne him eleven children - During all that time she has been an affectionate & kind woman of good character & is wife to your petitioner - That she is new about forty eight or forty nine years of age. That from having lived so long together & her meritorious services - He prays this leave of this Honorable Court, to liberate & set free his wife Sally, & your petitioner as in duty bound will ever pray to

Robt. H. Burton
for Billi

Chapter 15: Lincoln County Records

****

North Carolina } Whereas by an Act of the General
Lincoln County } Assembly of said Stat[e] Passed at

Raleigh in the year of our Lord one thousand Eight hundred & Eleven, Chapter 94th. Emancipating Two Negroes formerly the property of James Baird Deceast, named Prince, & Rose which before recited Act Requires Bond & Security of the Heirs or representatives of said James Baird to be given to the Chairman of the County Court of Lincoln - Therefore we James C. Baird & John Baird do own & Acknowledge ourselves Indebted to Peter Hoyle Chairman of Said Court in the sum of four hundred pound good & Lawful Money of Said State to be levied off our goods & Chattles Land & Tennements as all other Penal Bonds given under our hands & seals this 19th Day of April 1819

The Condition of the above obligation is such that if the said Negroes Prince & Rose do well & truely behave themselves as pieceable Citizens & never become a publick Charge, Then the above obligation to be void & of no effect otherwise to remain in full force & virtue as all other Penal Bonds given under our hands & Seals the day & year first above written

Witness   James Baird   (Seal)
I. Holland Jurat J. Baird   (Seal)

State of North Carolina }
Lincoln County   }   April Sessions 1819

The within bond was proven in open court by the Oath of Isaac Holland a subscribing witness thereto & recorded at length on the Minutes of Said Court
Witness   Vardry McBee   CC

****

Petition of Wm. J. Wilson
Exr of Wm. Berry
for Emancipation of Negro Milly
April Term 1829

State of No. Carolina }   Superior Court of Law
Lincoln County   }   April Term 1829

The petition of Wm. J. Wilson of said County petitioning represents to your Honour that a certain William Berry late of said County deceased about [Blank] in the year [Blank] having made and published his last will and testament by which he appointed your petitioner and his son William Berry the executor to his Will, that they both qualified, and that said William his executor eloped from this County some time ago leaving your petitioner to close the business of the estate himself.
That in said Will is stated following clause "Fourthly it is my will and I hereby direct my Executors to apply for and if possible to obtain the emancipation of my negroe woman Milly at the expiration of the year A. D. 1828 during which time I allow her to be hired at the direction of my Executors yearly or otherwise" = Your petitioner states that the meritorious services on which the petitioner founds his petition and which he has been informed and verily believes to be true and that the said slave Milly for the last 8-10 or 12 years of the life of his testator after the death of her testators wife, had the entire management and charge of the domestic affairs of the household to as great an intent as her mistress had during her life; and that she discharged her duty in a most faithful and meritorious manner = that the testator was frequently subject to spells of [?????] and said slave Milly would go in search of him, hunt him up, take him home and take care of him; and that her whole deportment and character were entirely meritorious and praise worthy - such as to induce the wish of her Master that she should be emancipated; (she is now about forty five years old) Your petitioner prays that he may be permitted in the fulfilment of the trust which he has applied and undertaken to include by the probate of the will and his qualification as an executor; that he may be permitted to execute to her a deed of emancipation, by complying with the legal requisites
William J. Willson

Chapter 15: Lincoln County Records

Executor of Wm. Berry
Dec'd.

State of No. Carolina
Lincoln County

  The petition of Wm. J. Wilson executor of Wm. Berry for the emancipation of a negroe woman slave foremrly the property of his Testator Wm. Berry coming in to be heard on the petition, a copy of the will and other testimony; and it appearing to the satisfaction of the Court that the prayer of the petition ought to be granted in consideration of the meritorious services of said slave Milly and her general honest character and good deportment for many years passed - and the said Wm. J. Wilson having sworn bond and security agreeable to the requisites of the act of assembly it is ordered adjudged and decreed that the saidWilliam J. Wilson is executor of William Berry be permitted and he is hereby authorised to emancipate the woman slave Milly mentioned in his petition - and she is hereby emancipated.

State of No. Carolina
Lincoln County

  Know all men by these presents that we Wm. J. Wilson executor of Wm. Berry deceased and Isaac Davis am held and firmly bound unto His excellency John Owens Governor of the State of No. Carolina and his successors in office for the use of the state in the sum of two hundred pounds which payment we bind ourselves and our heirs - Witness our hands & seals 21st April 1829. The condition of the above obligations is such that whereas the above bounden Wm .J. Wilson executor aforesaid hath this day petitioned for and obtained leave to emancipate a certain Negroe slave named Milly formerly the property of Wm. Berry deceased - Now if the said Negroe Woman Milly shall be of good behaviour during this time she may remain in the state then the above obligation to be Void or to remain in full force and Virtue

Witness   Wm J. Wilson   (Seal)
Lwn. Henderson

          His
        Isaac Davis   (Seal)
          mark
        Isaac Davis   (Seal)

             Bond of Wm. J. Wilson
               Exr of Wm. Berry
           dec'd respecting the liberation of
                Negro Milly

State of No. Carolina
Lincoln County

  Know all men by these presents that we Wm. J. Wilson executor of the late Wm. Berry and I. Davis am held and firmly bound unto Andrew Hoyle Chairman of the County Court for said County and his successors in office for the use of the poor of said County in the sum of one hundred pounds to which payment we bind ourselves and our heirs witness our hands & seals this 21st April 1829

  The condition of the above obligation is such that whereas the said Wm. J. Wilson executor as aforesaid hath this day filed his petition for the emancipation of a certain negroe slave Milly formerly the property of his testator Wm. Berry which is granted, an giving bond and security agreeably to law, Now if the same negroe slave Milly should not become a charge to the County, but shall support herself without any call on the wardens of the poor then this obligation to be void or to remain in full force and virtue

Chapter 15: Lincoln County Records

Witness   Wm J. Wilson   (Seal)
Lwn. Henderson

                      Isaac Davis   (Seal)

                        Deed of Emancipation
                         from Wm. J. Wilson
                          Exr. of Wm. Berry
                             dec'd - To

State of North Carolina
Lincoln County

     Know all men by these presents that I William J. Wilson of the County and state aforesaid as executor of the last will and testament of William Berry deceased by virtue of the authority given me by the said William Berry in his last will and by virtue of the authority given me by a judgement decree of the Honorable Superior Court of Law for Lincoln County at April Term 1829 - and for and in consideration of the meritorious services rendered by a certain Negroe slave Milly (formerly the property of my Testator Wm. Berry) to said Testator and in consideration of her uniform honest character and faithful deportment to her former Master = I do hereby by virtue of the aforesaid authority and for the consideration herein before recited emancipate and set free from slavery during her life the said Milly hereby declaring that she and her future increase are to be free from servitude to my self as executor as aforesaid or to any other person, Witness - my hand and seal this 22nd day of April 1829

Signed Sealed & delivered   William J. Wilson   Exr
in Presence of us   of Wm. Berry Dec'd (Seal)
A. M. Burton   Atto.
for Milly in open Court

Lwn. Henderson   Clk
Milly

****

State of North Carolina   }   Superior Court of Law
Lincoln County   }   October Term 1822

     To the Honourable the Judge of the Superior Court of law in and for said County. The petition of James Boyd executor of the last Will and testament of John Boyd deceased Humbly showeth unto your Honor that the said John Boyd departed this life, in the last month of July or first of August in the present year. That the said John Boyd duly executed & with which has been regularly proven in Lincoln County Court & admitted to record, a copy of which is hereunto annexed and prayed to be taken as part of this petition. Your petitioner states that John Boyd deceased appointed him his sole executor, that he has qualified as such, and taken upon himself the execution of said Will. By the last Will & Testament of the said John Boyd deceased, among other things is the following clause. "My Mulatto man servant York I will and bequeath to my son James until he can be liberated according to law; and I order & direct that my executor shall petition to the next Superior Court of law that may be held for Lincoln County after my decease of the same shall happen thirty days before the term of said Court, and if not at the next ensuing term of the same, praying for liberty, to emancipate the said York for the meritorious services he hath rendered to me & my family, and for which I feel myself concientiously bound to provide for his liberation agreeably to my promises made to him; and if liberty shall be granted him, that my executor shall liberate him accordingly." which will more fully appear by the annexed copy of said Will.

     Your petitioner represents unto your Honor that the said Mulatto man York has always conducted himself as a trust faithful servant, that he is of good character and by his conduct and meritorious services had obtained the confidence of the testator & all the family. Your petitioner further represents that in the emancipation of the said York, no person can be injured but himself, as no person has any right or claim to said York except your petitioner, for by the Will of said John Boyd, the said York is "willed & bequeathed to your petitioner until he can be liberated according to law."

Chapter 15: Lincoln County Records

Agreeably therefore to the directions of said John Boyd as contained in his last Will, and in accordance with his own wishes, your petitioner prays this Honorable Court, that he may have liberty to emancipate the said mulatto man York, and that henceforth he may be free from bondage and enjoy all the privileges of a free man, your petitioner first complying with the different acts of assembly in such cases made & provided; and your petitioner as in duty bound will ever pray to.

R. H. Burton for Petitioner

        James Boyd

State of North Carolina	}	We the Subscribers
	}	acknowledge Ourselves
Lincoln County	}	Indebted to the

Justices of Lincoln County Court & their Successors in office in the Sum of one hundred pounds which payment well & truly to be made & done we bind ourselves our heirs Executors Administrators & Assigns - Sealed & dated this 25th day of April 1821.
  The condition of the above obligation is such that whereas John Boyd Snr, hath this day obtained permission for a Certain Negro fellow named York to Carry a Gun on the plantation or any where on the land of the Said John Boyd to take Care of his masters Stock or Crop or even hunt or kill game on the land of his Said Master - Now if the Said York shall at all times hereafter under said privilege shall conduct himself in a harmless & orderly manner then this Obligation to be Void otherwise to Remain in full force & Effect

Witness   John Boyd   (Seal)
V. McBee

        James Boyd   (Seal)

Know all men by these presents that we James Boyd and Daniel Sullivan are held & firmly bound unto Gabriel Holmes, Governor of the State of North Carolina, for the use of the State in the penal sum of two hundred pounds to which payment well & truly to be made & done, we bind ourselves our & each of our heirs, executors & administrators
  The condition of the above obligation is such that whereas the above bounden James Boyd has emancipated a certain negro man by the name of York, formerly the property of John Boyd now deceased, by leave of the Superior Court of Lincoln County, now if the said negro man York shall be of good behaviour, during the time may remain within the state of North Carolina, then this obligation to be void and of no effect, otherwise to remain in full force - Witness our hands & seals October 23rd 1822

Test   James Boyd   (Seal)
Wallace A. Henderson
        Daniel Sullivan   (Seal)

Now all men by these presents that us James Boyd and Daniel Sullivan are held & firmly bound unto Peter Hoyle chairman of the County Court of Lincoln, and his sessessors in office for the use of the poor of the County of Lincoln, in the penal sum of one hundred pounds, to which payment well & truly to be made & done we bind ourselves, our & each of our heirs, executors and administrators. The condition of the above obligation is such that whereas the above named James Boyd, hath this [day] liberated & set free a certain negro man York, formerly the property of John Boyd now deceased, the leave of the Superior Court, having been first obtained, Now if the said negro man York shall now become chargeable on the parish or County, then this obligation to be void & of no effect, otherwise to remain, in full force. Witness our hands & seals October 23rd 1822

Test   James Boyd   (Seal)
Wallace A. Henderson
        Daniel Sullivan   (Seal)

****

Chapter 15: Lincoln County Records

State of North Carolina
Lincoln County

To the Honourable the Judge of the Superior Court of law & Equity, in & for said County The Petition of Alexander Dickey of said County hunbly showeth unto your Honor, that heretofore a certain Alexander Dickey the father of your petitioner had title to & the possession of a negro man slave by the name of Derry - That during the life of said Alexr Dickey the said Derry always conducted himself as a dutiful obedient servant towards his master & family and has the character of a peaceable orderly & moral man among all his acquaintance & neighbors. Your petitioner states that he has frequently heard his father Alexr Dickey the elder say that it was his intention to liberate said Derry at the age of thirty. But so it was the said Alexander Dickey died before the slave arrived at that age. Your petitioner states that the said Alexander Dickey died intestate about twelve years ago, that William Oats & Thomas Weir administered upon his estate; that the vendue of said administrators your petitioner purchased said negro man Derry & has paid for him, so that no person has any interest, title or claim to said negro, but your petitioner. Your petitioner represents unto your Honor that ever since his knowledge & acquanitance of & with said negro man slave Derry he has always supported the character of an honest, industrious, obedient, & moral man. That since your petitioner has owned him, he has hired him out to others & he was worked a great part of his time from home, during all which time he has uniformly supported his good character, that he has enquired of his conduct, & always heard a good report of him, & believes he can bring testimony to prove as good character of him as most of men. Your petitioner having a desire to fulfil the desires of his departed father, & knowing the meritorious services & conduct of said negro man slave Derry, prays leave of this Honorable Court, to emancipate & set free from slavery, the said negro man slave Derry, he first complying with the requisites of the acts of assembly in such case made and provided And you petitioner in duty bound will ever pray etc

Test.   Alexander Dickey
Lwn. Henderson

Bond of Alexr Dickey & Wm. Oats
To Keep the County Clear & free from
becoming chargeable to said Co.

Know all men by these presents that we Alexander Dickey & Wm. Oats are held & firmly bound unto Peter Hoyle Esq. Chairman of the Court of Pleas & quarter sessions for the County of Lincoln & his successors in office for the use of the poor of said County to which payment well & truly to be made they bind themselves & their heirs in testimony whereof thet have hereunto set their hand & seals this 27th day of October 1825

The above obligation to be void on condition a certain negro nam named Derry a liberated slave, shall not become chargeable on said County of Lincoln - Witness our hands & seals the day & date above written

Test.   Alexander Dickey   (Seal)
Lwn. Henderson Clk
                   William Oats   (Seal)

Bond of Alexr Dickey & Wm. Oats
for the good behavior of
Negroe Derry

Know all men by these presents that we Alexander Dickey & William Oats, both of the County of Lincoln and State of North Carolina, are held & firmly bound unto Hutchins G. Burton/Benton[???], Governor of the state of North Carolina & his successors in office in the sum of two hundred pounds, to which payment well & truly to be made & done, we bind ourselves, our & each of our heirs, executors & administrators sealed with our seals & dated 25th October 1825

The condition of the above obligations is such that whereas the above bounden Alexander Dickey, has this day petitioned & obtained leave of the Judge of the Superior Court of law & equity for said County at this Time, to emancipate & set free a certain negro man slave, by the name of Derry, & executed a deed therefor, Now if the said

Chapter 15: Lincoln County Records

Derry shall hereafter, while he remains in this State conduct & behave himself as a peaceable citizen then this obligation to be void, otherwise to remain in full force & effect - Witness our hands & seals the date above.

Test	Alexander Dickey	(Seal)
Lwn Henderson		
	William Oats	(Seal)

State of North Carolina
To the Sheriff of Lincoln County Greeting:

You are hereby commanded to summon Moses Stroup William Oats personally to appear before the Judge of our Superior Court of Law, at the present court to be held for the county of Lincoln at the court house in Lincolnton on the 4th Monday in October instant then and there to testify and the truth to say in behalf of Alexr Dickey in a certain cause then and there depending, and to be tried; concerning the emancipation of Slave Derry. And this you shall in no wise onit under the penalty prescribed by law. Herein fail not, and have you then and there this writ.

Witness Lwn Henderson Clerk of our said court at Lincolnton the 4th Monday in October and in the 50th year of our Independence.

Lwn Henderson

Chapter 16: New Hanover County Records

chapter 16

New Hanover County

NORTH CAROLINA STATE ARCHIVES
NEW HANOVER COUNTY
RECORDS OF SLAVES AND FREE PERSONS OF COLOR
C.R.070.928.3

Wm. A. Wrights Bond for Emancipation
of Isabella & Jane Allen

Filed June Term 1844

Teste LH Marsteller Clk

State of North Carolina
New Hanover County

 Know all men by these presents, that we William A. Wright and Alexander McRae, are held and firmly bound unto James T. Miller Esquire, Chairman of the County Court of Pleas and Quarter Sessions for the County of New Hanover, and to his Successors in Office, for the poor of the County aforesaid, in the sum of One hundred dollars, to which payment well and truly to be made, we bind ourselves our heirs, executors and administrators jointly and severally, firmly by these presents. Sealed with our seals, and dated the 14th day of June AD 1844.

 The Condition of this obligation is such, that whereas the two female slaves named Isabella Allen, and Jane Allen, have been emancipated and made free by An Act of the General Assembly of North Carolina, passed in the year eighteen hundred and twelve, upon Condition that bond with good and sufficient security is given that the said Isabella and Jane liberated by the said act, shall not become burdensome to the Parish in any County in the said State; Now if the said Isabella and Jane, emancipated as aforesaid, shall not become chargeable on the parish of St. James, or on any County of the State aforesaid, then this obligation to be null and void, otherwise to be and remain in full force and effect.

Signed sealed and	Wm. A. Wright	(Seal)
delivered in presence of	Alex MacRae	(Seal)
L.H. Marsteller Clk		

****

Emancipation Bond of Isaac Belden

State of North Carolina }
New Hanover County }

 Know all Men by these Presents that We Robert Belden of the County of Cumberland and **[Blank]** of the County of New Hanover are held and firmly bound unto his Excellency Edward B Dudly Governor of North Carolina and to his Successors in Office in the just and full sum of Five hundred dollars Current Money of the United States of America for the payment of which well and truly to be made and done We bind ourselves our heirs Executors and administrators jointly and severally firmly by these presents Sealed with our seals and dated this **[Blank]** day of June AD 1837

Chapter 16: New Hanover County Records

The Condition of the above Obligation is such that Whereas the petition of the above bounden Robert Belden the Legislature of North Carolina passed an Act to emancipate and set free a slave named Isaac the property of said Robert Belden On Condition that the said Robert should enter into Bond and Security that said slave Isaac shall honestly and correctly demean himself as long as he shall remain in this State and shall not become a Parish Charge. Now therefore if the said Isaac shall well, honestly and correctly demean himself so long as he shall remain in the State of North Carolina and shall not hereafter become a Parish Charge within said State, then the above Obligation to be Void and of no effect Otherwise to remain in full force and Virtue

Witness J.H. Brewster[?]	R.C. Belden	(Seal)
	Daniel Sherwood	(Seal)
	LH Marsteller	(Seal)

****

James G. Hostler
Bond required by the Act of the General Assembly
emancipating him

State of North Carolina }
County of New Hanover }

Know all men by these presents that we James G. Hostler, William A. Wright and James S. Green all of the town of Wilmington in the County and State above written, are held and firmly bound unto the State of North Carolina in the just and full sum of five hundred dollars, to the payment of which well and truly to be made we bind ourselves our heirs executors and administrators jointly and severally firmly by these presents   Sealed with our seals and dated this the 13th day of March A.D. 1855

The Condition of the foregoing obligation is such, that whereas the above bound James G. Hostler by an Act of the General Assembly of this State ratified the 16th day of February 1855, entitled "An Act to emancipate James G. Hostler a slave" is emancipated and set free; which said act contains the following proviso - viz - "Provided nevertheless that before the said slave shall be emancipated he shall give bond with good security in the sum of five hundred dollars payable to the State of North Carolina, conditioned that he the said James G. Hostler shall honestly and correctly demean himself, and shall not become a parish charge; which bond shall be approved by the Court of Pleas and Quarter Sessions of the County of New Hanover, and be deposited in the office of said Court and may be sued on to the use of any Parish or of any person injured by the misconduct of said James G. Hostler" - Now therefore if the said James G. Hostler shall honestly and correctly demean himself and shall not become a parish charge, then and in that event this obligation shall be void and of no effect, anything herein before contained to the contrary notwithstanding, but otherwise the same shall be and remain in full force and virtue

Signed sealed and delivered	JG Hostler	(Seal)
in the presence of	James S. Green	(Seal)
Saml R. Bunting	Wm. A. Wright	(Seal)

James G. Hostler tendered to the Court a bond with Wm A Wright and James S Green as his securities thereto payable to the State of North Carolina in the sum of $500, conditioned that he the said James G Hostler shall honestly and correctly demean himself, and shall not become a parish charge according to the proviso of an Act of the General Assembly of this State entitled "An Act to emancipate James G Hostler a slave" ratified February 16th 1855; which said bond was approved by the court and ordered to be deposited in the office of the court.

****

Bond for the Emancipation of Solomon Nash

State of North Carolina }
New Hanover County }

Chapter 16: New Hanover County Records

Know all men by these presents that we John Waddell, Francis N. Waddell, & John Waddell Jr. are held and firmly bound unto Edward B. Dudley Esqr. Chairman of the County Court of Pleas and Quarter Sessions, for the County of New Hanover, and to his successors in office, for the use of the poor of the County of New Hanover, in the sum of one hundred pounds to which payment well and truly to be made we bind ourselves, our heirs, executors and administrators, jointly and severally, firmly by these presents. Sealed in our seals and dated the 26th day of July - A.D. 1827

Whereas the above named John Waddell has obtained an order of the Superior Court of the County aforesaid for the emancipation of a certain negro slave named Solomon Nash, the condition of this obligation is such, that if the said negro slave Solomon Nash shall not, at anytime hereafter, become chargeable on the Parish of St. James, or on the County of New Hanover then this obligation to be void, otherwise to be and remain in full force and effect.

John Waddell   (Seal)
F.N. Waddell   (Seal)
John Waddell Jr.   (Seal)

***

Rich'd Green's Bond

Know all Men these presents that we Richard Green and John P. Williams are held and firmly bound unto James Foy James Moore and Richard Quince Justices assigned to keep the peace and the rest of Justices of the County aforesaid in the just and full sum of Two hundred Pounds current Money of the State aforesaid to be paid to the said Justices, the Survivor, or Survivors of them, their heirs, Executors and Administrators To which payment well and truly to be made We bind ourselves our heirs Executors & Admrs. jointly and severally by these presents. Sealed with our Seals and dated this eighteenth day of December 1800

The Condition of the above obligation is Such that whereas the above bounden Richard Green hath this day obtained an order of the Worshipful County Court of New Hanover County for the emancipation of a certain Mulatto Woman named Venus formerly the property of Richd Green. Now if the said Negro Woman named Venus shall not at any time become in any manner chargeable upon the State County or Parish Then the above obligation to be Void and to remain in full force & Virtue

Richard Green (Seal)

Signed sealed and
delivered in presence of
Thos F Davis   Pugh[?] Williams (Seal)

***

Bond of John McLellan
for the Emancipation of
Maria & her four Children
William Elizabeth Margaret & Mary

State of North Carolina } Court of Pleas & Quarter Sessions
New Hanover County   } June Term 1797

Know all men by these Presents that We John McLellan, George Hooper, Henry Urquhart and John Allan all of the County aforesaid, are held and firmly bound unto his Excellency Samuel Ashe esqr. Governor, Captain General and Commander in Chief in and over the State aforesaid in the just and full sum of One thousand Pounds, for the which payment well and truly to be made to his Excellency the Governor aforesaid his successors or assigns We do hereby, jointly and severally, firmly by these presents, bind our selves and each of us our Heirs Executors and Administrators, Sealed with our seals and dated as above

The Condition of the above Obligation is such, that Whereas, the Justices presiding in the Court aforesaid at the Term aforesaid have on the Petition of the aforesaid John McLellan, emancipated and sett free, as fully and amply,

Chapter 16: New Hanover County Records

as by the Law of this State they are enabled, a certain female Negro Slave, belonging to the said John McLellan named Maria and her four children named William, Elizabeth, Margaret and Mary; Now in case the said female Negro Slave Maria and her four Children William, Elizabeth, Margaret and Mary or either of them shall not in any manner whatsoever become chargeable to or on this or any other County within this State, then the above Obligation to be void otherwise to remain in full force and Virtue

Signed Sealed & Delivered   John McLellan   (Seal)
in presence of   G. Hooper   (Seal)
James W. Walker   Henry Urquhart   (Seal)
    John Allan   (Seal)

***

Bond that Page do not become
chargeable on this or any other Co.
Jno Telfair & Ben Blany
16th June 1797

State of North Carolina   }
New Hanover County   } Ss.

Know all men by these Presents that We John Telfair and Benjamin Blany both of the State and County aforesaid and of the Town of Wilmington are held and firmly bound unto William Green, William Cuttar and Robert Nixon esquires Justices assigned to keep the peace &c for the County aforesaid and to their Executors and Administrators in behalf of the rest of the Justices for said County in the just and full sum of One Thousand pounds, for which payment well and truly to be made, We do hereby bind ourselves and each of us our Heirs, Executors and Administrators jointly and severally, firmly by these Presents, as Witness our hands and seals this 16th day of June 1797

    The Condition of the above Obligation is such, that Whereas the Justices above named at the request and on the Petition of William E. Atkins now deceased, at the Term of March last past of the Court of Pleas and Quarter Sessions held at Wilmington for the County aforesaid, did Emancipate and sett free a certain Negroe Slave, a female, by the name of Page, the property of said William E. Atkins. Now in case the said female Slave Page do not, nor ever shall, in any wise, manner or form become chargeable to, or burthen on, the Parish of Saint James, the County aforesaid, or to or on any other Parish or County within the State aforesaid, then this obligation to be void and of no effect otherwise to remain in full force and Virtue.

Signed Sealed and acknowledged   John Telfair   (Seal)
in presence of   Bn. Blaney   (Seal)

James W. Walker

***

John McAustan

Bond for Emancipation of Tom

State of North Carolina   }
New Hanover County   }

    Know all men by these presents that we John Macauslan and William Watts Jones are held and firmly bound unto John Hogg Esquire, Chairman of the County Court of Pleas and Quarter sessions, for the County of New Hanover and to his successors in office, for the use of the poor of the County of New Hanover, in the sum of one hundred pounds, to which payment, well and truely to be made; we bind ourselves, our heirs, executors and administrators, jointly and severally, firmly by these presents. sealed with our seals and dated the 14th day of May A.D. 1818.

Chapter 16: New Hanover County Records

Whereas the above bonden John Macauslan has obtained an order of the county court aforesaid for the emancipation of a certain negroe slave named Tom the condition of this obligation is such, that if the said negroe slave, Tom shall not, at any time hereafter, become chargeable on the Parish of St. James, or on the county of New Hanover, then this obligation to be void otherwise to be and remain, in full force and virtue and effect.

Signed, sealed and delivered John Macauslan (Seal)
in presence of Wm. Watts Jones (Seal)
A.M. Hooper

Chapter 17: Orange County Records

chapter 17

Orange County

NORTH CAROLINA STATE ARCHIVES
ORANGE COUNTY SLAVE RECORDS
C.R.073.928.8

John Hogg
Petition for Emancipation of Frank
To August 1818

State of North Carolina }
Orange County } Ss.

County Court of Pleas and Quarter Sessions. August Sessions A.D. 1818.

To the Worshipfull the Justices of the said Court
The Petition ex parte of John Hogg

Your Petitioner John Hogg, of the Town of Wilmington in this State, sheweth to your Worships that he is possessed of a mulatto man Slave known and called Frank, as of his own proper goods and chattels; that the said Frank is an honest, industrious, sober and well disposed man, and is a good Carpenter. And your Petitioner further sheweth to your Worships that the said Frank hath performed for him sundry highly Meritorious services; in consideration whereof, your Petitioner is willing to set free and emancipate the said Frank, and by these presents doth emancipate the said Frank, and set him free, provided your Worships confirm the same by your decree or Judgement - Your Petitioner prays your Worships to execute and confirm by a Judgement or decree to be pronounced by you his wish and act aforesaid; And your Petitioner will ever pray &c.

John Hogg   (Seal)
by Wm. Norwood his Atto.

John Hogg, Petition ex parte -

This Petitioner coming in to be heard on this Petition, and the evidence offered by the Petitioner, It is ordered adjudged and decreed, according to this Petition and prayer of the Petitioner, that the Mulatto Man Frank mentioned in the said Petition be and he is hereby emancipated from the State of Slavery, and set free with all the rights and privileges of free people of Colour in the State of North Carolina: And that the said Frank be hereafter known and called by the name of Francis Hogg

****

August Term 1801
To the Worshipful Justices of the Court of Pleas & Quarter Sessions for Orange County now sitting, the Petition of Pomfrett Herndon of said County humbly sheweth that your Petitioner is now, and hath for some time previous to this date been possessed of a certain Negro Man Slave called and known by the name of Peter, who for Meritorious Services he is desirous to liberate and make free - Your Petitioner prays that the said Peter may be emancipated according to the provisions of the Acts of Assembly in such Cases made and provided and be called and known by the name of Peter Justus
And your Petitioner will pray -

Chapter 17: Orange County Records

Pomfrett Herndon

****

To the Worshipful the County Court of Pleas & Quarter Sessions for the County of Orange.
The Petition of Pleasant Henderson
respectfully represents

That he owns a certain negroe fellow known by the name of Abraham now about the age of forty one years, who your Petitioner is desirous shall be set free by an order of Your said Court - This application is made under a persuasion that when the Merits of the said person of colour is ascertained by your worships, no reason can exist against granting the prayer of Your Petitioner, more particularly where he is ready to render substantial security for his future good behaviour.

Your Petitioner, in the case of obtaining his wish, requests that the said negroe may be liberated under the name of Abraham
Manns
                        P. Henderson
Feby 1809

****

Affrica - Petition

State of North Carolina
Orange County Court of Pleas and Quarter Sessions A.D. 1799
To the Justice of the said Court now siting

William Cain, of the County aforesaid, sheweth unto your Worships, that he is possessed of Africa, a Negro Man Slave, as his property; And that the said Africa hath always been an industerous, honest and faithfull Slave; and hath rendered unto your Petitioner several Meritorious services of high importance to him. Amongst others hath taught and instructed your Petitioner, and one of his other Slaves, in the art and mistery of Malting, Brewing, and distilling grain, whereby your Petitioner hopes to derive great profit and gain. Your Petitioner therefore, in Justice to the Merits of a Dutiful Slave, prays that the said Africa may be emancipated, and henceforth enjoy his Freedom, & your Petitioner will ever pray

Wm. Cain   Wm. Norwood
by his Atto.

Gentlemen   I intended to Try to this day to have Africa emancipated & Set Free as I promised him when I bought him of William Courtney upon his paying the purchase money with Costs and learning my people the art of Stilling and Malting which he the said Africa hath Done and will do I Expect, however I wish him to be Set Free by the County Court of Orange this day if they please as its out of my power to be up as my wife is So indisposed I cant by no means leave her   your Obedient Hum. Servt. William Cain
                        March 1st 1799

Whereas William Cain of this County, hath Petitioned this Court to liberate and set free, Africa his Slave, a black man about 40 years of age and about 5' 8-1/2" Inches High, formerly the Slave of Wm. Courtney of Hillsborough Tavern Keeper; and this Court having heard the said Petition, and being satisfied as to the Meritorious Services rendered by the said Africa, do adjudge and allow the said services to be good and sufficient; it is therefore Ordered and Adjudged by the Court that the said Africa be henceforth discharged from Slavery, and be free; and the said Africa is hereby permitted and licensed from this time to go at large, unmolested, as a free man with all the privileges pertaining to a free man of his Colour and shall henceforth be known by the name of Africa Parker.
Africa

Chapter 17: Orange County Records

Order for Liberation

On the Petition of William Cain to liberate Africa, his Slave; The Court having heard the said Petition, and being satisfied as to the Meritorious services rendered by the said Africa, do allow the same; and thereupon and by, and with the assents of the said William Cain given here in Open Court, do liberate the said Africa and set him free; And that the said Africa may not hereafter be claimed or molested as a Slave, doth hereby permit and license the said Africa, henceforth to go at large as a free man.

***

State of North Carolina }
Orange County   } Feb Term 1825

Know all men by these presents that we Levy Whitted and James Webb are hereby firmly bound in the sum of one Hundred Pounds to Abner B. [?] Chairman of the County Court and his Successors in office Witness our hands and seals

  The condition of the above obligation is such that if the said Levi Whitted Ex of Jehue Whitted (Decd) Shall keep Fanny Whitted a Woman of Colour late a Slave of the said Jehu (Decd) but who was Emancipated by the County Court of Orange in the year 1814 from being chargeable on the County and indemnify the Wardens against all charge and expence for the support and maintenance of said Fanny then the above obligation to be void or remain in full force

Levi Whitted (Seal)
James Webb (Seal)

***

On the Petition of Frances Child and Mary Doherty Praying for the emancipation of Rachel Sukey and Billy Persons of Mixed blood and lately held as Slaves by Robt. Freeman of Warren County, Planter who it is alledged still claims the same Persons as his Slaves - it is ordered by the Court that a Copy of said Petition be served on the said Robert Freeman with notice to appear at the next Term of this Court to answer the Same and defend his right & title he may have - And that in the mean time and until the further order of this Court is the [?] the said Rachael Sukey and Billy be and remain in the possession care custody and power of Mary Doherty the Petr. who agrees to receive & keep them. And that she have full power and authority during the pending of this Suit or until the full direction of the Court to preserve and defend such Possession agst. the said Robt. or any other Person claiming possession on the said Rachel Sukey and Billy.

***

Know all men by these presents, that we Richard Henderson, and John Taylor of the County of Orange, and State of North Carolina are held and firmly bound unto his Excellency David Stone Esqr. Govr. of the said State, and his Successors in Office in the just and full sum of two hundred pounds, for the true and faithfull payment whereof, we, and each of us do hereby bind ourselves, our Heirs, Executors & Administrators firmly by these presents, In testimony whereof we have hereunto subscribed our names, and affixed our Seals this 30th day of August A.D. 1810 -

  The condition of the above obligation is such, that whereas a negro man by the name of Daniel formerly the property of the above Bounden Richard Henderson, hath been emancipated on the Petition of the said Richd. Henderson, by the Court of Pleas and Quarter Sessions for Orange County, now if the said negro man Daniel shall in all things demean himself in an honest, upright, and peaceable manner whilst he continues to reside in North Carolina, then the above obligation to be void, otherwise to remain in full force and virtue

     Richd. Henderson (Seal)
Isaac Holder   J. Taylor (Seal)

***

Zachariah Dicks

Chapter 17: Orange County Records

Petition for the Freedom of Patience
1801

state of North Carolina }
Orange County }

The Petition of Zachariah Dicks

Your Petitioner shews that he is possessed of a black negro Woman Slave known by the name of Patience about the age of twenty four years, as of his own proper Slave; that the said Slave has served him with unusual industry, honesty and integrity, and has by her labor, diligence, and Care, greatly assisted him in maintaining and providing for his family; and has rendered to him and them great and meritorious services. And he further sheweth that she has at all times behaved herself peacibly, honestly and well in every respect.

Your Petitioner moved by humanity, Justice, and a sense of the benefits received by the meritorious services of the said Slave; and being willing and desirous as a Compensation to her therefore, and as an encouragement to others to behave in a like manner; to emancipate and set her free: prays that she may be liberated and set free and known hereafter by the name of Patience Brawer[?]

Zachariah Dicks

****

Petition for the liberation of Jacob Johnston
filed August Term of Orange Court 1801
Petition allowed

To the Worshipful the Justices of the Court of Pleas and Quarter Sessions for Orange County now sitting the Petition of Ave Heathcock of said County humbly sheweth, that your Petitioner is now, & hath for a long Time previous to this date been possessed of a certain Negro Man Slave called and known by the name of Jacob, who for meritorious Services She is desirous to liberate and make free -- Your Petitioner prays that the said Jacob may be emancipated according to the provisions of the Acts of Assembly in such Cases made & provided, and be called & known by the name of Jacob Johnston

And your Petitioner will pray &c.

August Term} Ave Hathcock   John Saley[?] [Marked thru]

Dun. Cameron Atto.

****

Petition of John Newlin for the emancipation of Nathan

filed Sep: Term 1829

To the Honorable the Judge of the Superior Court of Law for Orange County.   The Petition of John Newlin

Respectfully sheweth,
That he is the Owner of a Slave named Nathan, whom he is desirous of emancipating for an on Account of his Meritorious Services. That the said Nathan has conducted himself in Such Way for many years as to entitle him to his Freedom in the opinion of those who have been well acquainted with him, as will, your Petitioner believes, make a good Citizen, if Set free -- Your Petitioner is prepared to lay before the Court Proofs of his Meritorious Services, and he prays that he may have License granted to him to emancipate Said Nathan: And he will ever pray

Chapter 17: Orange County Records

To Sep: Term 1829   John Newlin

    Your Petitioner further shews that the meritorious Services Referred to above are those of uncommon Fidelity to his Master, Humbleness of Behaviour, & Honesty & Diligence in the Discharge of his Duties for a great Number of Years

A.D. Murphy.
for John Newlin

Chapter 18: Pasquotank County Records

chapter 18

Pasquotank County

NORTH CAROLINA STATE ARCHIVES
C.R.075.928.9
RECORDS OF SLAVES & FREE PERSONS OF COLOR
1733-1866

John Overton Oct 30 - 1830
State of No Carolina   }
Pasquotank County   } Personally appeared before me Bartholomew Evans and being duly qualified Saith that John Overton son of Lamuel Overton and Roas his wife is to the best of his Knowledge a free born person and from my own Knowledge I do believe him to be a free man of Colour given from under my hand this 26th Octor. 1830
        Thos. L. Shannanhous JP

****

Braddock Overton -- 3rd Nov 1830
State of No Carolina   }
Pasqnt. County   } Personally appeared before me Benja. Powers and Saith that the bearer Braddock Overton is the son of Rose and Lamuel Overton and that he was free born to the best of his Knowledge given from under my hand the 1st Novr. 1830

        Thos. L. Shannanhous JP

****

This may certify that Thamas Jane, daughter of Jeffrey Overton of color is a free born person & is therefore entitled to her free papers

May 5th 1856   J.M. Pool

****

Harriet Turner is the daughter of Ann Turner a free Woman of Colour
Abner Williams Sep 1835

****

State of North Carolina

   Pasquotank County

I Benjamin Albertson hereby certify that girl Sarah Manley, daughter of Nancy Manley, aged 18 years, dark complected, about 5 feet high with no remarkable scars, is now living in my service. That said girl was born of free parents and has always had the full enjoyment of her freedom.
   June 6th, 1838   Benj Albertson

Chapter 18: Pasquotank County Records

****

Rachel Morris   May 38
I do hereby certify that I am & have been well acquainted with Rachel Morris wife of John Morris - that the said Rachel is the daughter of Lemuel & Jenny Hall free persons of color, Pasquotank County May 1838   Joshua A. Pool
} Henry
} By
} Hamett[**Harnett?**]

****

Notice to
   Vs.   }
James White   }Ss.

A Coppy Delivered James White on 23rd day of October
W Banks DS

Evan Evans Comes into Court & lays Claim to the within Named Negro Sarah

It is Ordered On Agreement that the within Named Negro Sarah be discharged

Mr James White Sir
       Sir, there is Negro woman Slave by the Name of Sarah now now in Custity said to be liberated by You and to be Sold during the Next Court to be Held for the County Pasquotank on the Court [**Torn**] This is to Notify you to attend and make Claim if any you have
Octob 22nd 1802
W Banks DS

****

Relfe, Pleasant -- Children
Sep 1835
State of North Carolina   }
Pasquotank County   }
I Ambrose Knox of the County aforesaid do hereby Certify that Stephen Relfe, Hen[?] Spence, Mary Relfe are the Children of Pleasant Relfe who is a free Person of Colour, Resident of this County

                                                                            Ambrose Knox

****

Abbey Overton
Oct 30 - 1830
State of No. Carolina   }
Pasqt. County   }
This may Certify that I believe Abby Overton Wife of John Overton and Daughter of Tully and Betty Bowe to be free born as I have been a long time aquainted with her father and Mother being free persons and have never heard anything to the Contrary given from under my hand the 26th Octob 1830

                                                                            Thos L. Shannonhouse

****

Molly Overton
3 Nov. 1830
State of No. Carolina   }

Chapter 18: Pasquotank County Records

Pasqt. County }
Personally appeared before me Mr Benja. Powers and Saith that Moly Overton the wife of Braddock Overton and the daughter of Lamuel and Jenny Hall was free born to the best of his Knowledge given from under my hand the 1st Novr. 1830.
Thos L. Shannonhouse

****

John Morris
Feb 1831
The Bearer, John Morris of Colour was proved to be a free man, by the Oath of John Starre[?] -- before me, the 9th day of September 1831

State of North Carolina   }Tho. Bell
Pasquotank County   }
Son of Betty Morris
5 feet 8/ inch high
37 years old
Light Black
Scar on left side forarm

****

State of North Carolina   }
Pasquotank County   } Ss.
    I William Templeman Muse Clerk of the County Court of Pleas & Quarter Sessions for the County Aforesaid, Do hereby Certify unto all Whom it may Concern. That the bearer hereof John Overton Who is about Twenty Years of Age, Six feet & half an inch high, black Complexion With a Scar cross ways on the back of his Wrist of the left hand, is the Son of Rachael Overton, a free Person of Colour and a Native Citizen of the County aforesaid, And that the said John Overton is entitled to enjoy all the rights and Priviledges allowed to free Persons of colour by the laws of the said State of North Carolina.

****

A bill of Sail of Samuel Sexton
Pd.
Regent

Registered in Book 1 page 340 May 31   1820 by
John C Ehringhaus

State of North Carolina   }
Pasquotank County   } December Term 1819
This Bill of Sale from Samuel Sexton to Wilson Sanderlin was exhibited & Acknowledged in Open Court - Ordered to be Registered.
Test.   Will: T. Muse   Clk

Received of Wilson Sanderlin the Sum of Nine hundred Dollars it Being in full Payment and Sattisfaction for four Negros by the Names of plesent and Lyda, Jane and Jack the Children of Negro woman Plesant Which Negros I promis to warrant and defend the Right and title unto the said Wilson Sanderlin his heirs or assigns against the Lawful Claims of all persons what Ever in witness Whereof I have hear unto set my hand and seal this the 4th of March 1819
Signed & delivered
In the Presents of   Samuel Sexton   (Seal)
Daniel McPherson
John Bell
****

Chapter 18: Pasquotank County Records

Manumission for Patience

I James Elliot of the County of Perquimon State No Carolina having under my care a Negro woman named Patience aged about twenty three years which I Manumit & Sett free and do for my Self my heirs Exors. & adms here by Release Unto her all my Right In trust or Clame as to her person or any Estate She now have or shall here after acquire & witness where of I have here unto Set my hand & Seal this 24th day of the 6th mounth 1788.

James Elliot

B: Albertson
(Coppy as fir as Relates to Patience)

****

Burges
Jeremiah } Peto.
To } for
The Court } freedom

State of North Carolina }
Pasquotank County } Decem Term 1793

    To the Worshipful County Court of Pleas & Quarter Sessions for the County of Pasquotank aforesaid
    The Petition of Jeremiah Alias Jeremiah Burges Sheweth
    That he was Born of the Body of Nancy Alias Burges a Free Woman of Colour late of the said County of Pasquotank, that some evil disposed person during the Infancy of your Petitioner removed him from the said County of Carteret into the said County of Pasquotank and sold him as he hath been informed to Edward Everigain late of the said County of Pasquotank Esquire deceased as a slave and that in whose service he has since remained and that David George Administrator &c of the said Edward Everigain since his death continues to hold Your Petitioner in Slavery all which Actings & doings are contrary to the Law of Land & of Equity & good conscience In tender consideration whereof may it please Your Worships to grant to your Petr. A Writ or Writs or Subp. Commanding the said David George Admr. As aforesaid to appear & Answer &c and to grant your Petr. Such other & further relief as under the Act of Assembly in such Case made & provided & in Equity **[Smudged]** he is entitled to receive & your Petr as in duty bound shall ever pray &c

Wm Blair Atto.

Joseph Hendley agrees to be Security for this Cort

****

Edenton Supr.
Court } Court
Agt } Writ
    } Certiora

Pasquotank County Court

November Sup Court }
Edenton District 1778 } State of No Carolina

On Motion that a Writ of Certiorari shoud Issue to the Justices of Pasquotank County, to remove all the Orders and Proceedings of the Court of the said County relating to the Sale and enslaving of the following Persons, or either of them Viz. Hannah, David, Charles, Toby, Pritchard, Nero, Prissilla, Rose, Judith, Jane, Albertson, Samuel, Hagai, Ann and Sarah, on suggestion that the said Persons, tho free Subjects of the State, were Sold and enslaved by Order of the said Court, in express Violation of the Constitution of this State, and contrary to Natural Justice, and that there are Manifest Errors and Irregularities in the said Proceedings.
    Ordered that a Certiorari Issue accordingly, unless Sufficient Cause to the Contrary be shewn within the three first days of the next ensuing Term.

Chapter 18: Pasquotank County Records

                                        Will Righton for Cha. Bondfield   C.S.C.

****

                             John & Anne
                                Symons
                                Petition
                                Granted

Pasquotank Sct.
            To the Worshipful Court
            Of Sd. Prct. Now Sitting

The humble Petion of Thos. Symons & Anne his Wife
Humbly Sheweth

      That yr. Petitioner Anne Symons before her Marriage to the Sd. Thos. Sold a Negroe Man to John Bundy deceased & she gave sd. Bundy her Bond for the same but the sd. Bundy, by Chance gott the Bond & Cutt his Name there from, So that Yr. Petitioner has never as yet been Satisfied for the Same, & now beggs an Order to Recover the Same Negroe out of the hands of Samll[?] Bundy Admr. Of the sd. John Bundy & also what Wages is due from his Work & Yr. Petr. As in Duty Bound Shall ever Pray.
Thos. Symons
Anne Symons
[Editor: A note gives the date for this document as 1735]

****

Negroe Toney
To   } Peto. For
The Court   } Manumission

State of North Carolina
        To the Worshipful the County Court of Pasquotank sitting The Petition of the subscribers Inhabit County
                Humbly Sheweth
        That a number of Negroe Slaves of Citizens of this State having entered into a com**[Torn]**
Run away and leave the State had actually ma**[Torn]**
With a certain **[Blank]** Sikes the owner & master of**[Torn]**
Crafts lying at Symon's Creek-Bridge to convey **[Torn]**
Of the Northern States – That a certain Negroe **[Torn]**
Toney ------------formerly the property **[Torn]**
[Blank] Symons now of Samuel White **[Torn]**
their intention immediately conveyed intelligence **[Torn]**
of the Neighbours who collected with an intent **[Torn]**
the said Negroes but a party having previously **[Torn]**
the information of the Master or Skipper of the sd. **[Torn]**
secured them.
        Your Petitioners further shew that **[Torn]**
Negroe Slave is advanced in years, that he has **[Torn]**
Character of an honest, faithful & industrious Servant **[Torn]**
Present Master Samuel White sensible of his **[Torn]**
Faithful Services is willing under the directio**[Torn]**
That he should receive his freedom as a reward **[Torn]**
Your Petitioners conceiving that the Zeal Displ**[Torn]**
Said Negroe Toney in support of the laws and **[Torn]**

Chapter 18: Pasquotank County Records

[Torn]on of property to the Citizens altho displayed proved only
[Torn]tention is a highly meritorious Service, and fully
[Torn] that such information from persons of his description
[Torn]th to receive every encouragement which the nature
[Torn] will admit do therefore pray Your Worships that
[Torn]t to the Powers vested in you by the Act of the
[Torn] Assembly in such Cases made and provided you
[Torn] pleased to manumit & set Free the said Negroe
[Torn]oney And Grant &c And Your Petitioners as in duty
[Torn]ill ever Pray &c

Nixonton Decemr. 6th   1792

[Torn] White
[Torn] Donald
[Torn] [?]
[Torn] lassey
[Torn] Metcalfe
[Torn] Davis
[Torn] Jackson
[Torn] White
[Torn] Charles
[Torn] [?]
[Torn]amin White
[Torn] Sikes

Jn Lane
J Banks
John Sawyer
Moses Jackson jur.

****

Petition Concerning
Negro Dave
X—10

To the Worshipful Cort now Setting at Nixonton

The Petition of Jeremiah Symons Humbly Sheweth, that under a Sence of Gratitude, for the many Servises, to him renderd by a Certain Negro Man by name Dave, aged about fifty Years, formerly the Property of Joseph McAddams Decd. Whome your petitioner purchased for a Considerable Sum of Money, which Sum of Money he the Said Negro Dave, by his Study applycation to business hath replaced to your petitioner, whereby your Petitioner humbly Conceives that he Merrits his freedom. And hope that the Honorable Cort in their Clemency will Grant that the said Negro Man Dave, may injoy his freedom under the restrictions that other free people of Cullor Injoy in this State. And your Petitioner in Duty bound shall ever pray &c   March Term 1798

Jeremiah Symons

We the Subscribers being acquainted with the above named Negro Man this Many Years, and believe him to be an Honest, Peaceable, and Orderly Person, & that we never in the Corce of our Knoled knew or heard to the Contrary.

John Price
Jno. McDonald
David Tatem

Jesse Symons
Wm Bru[?]

****

To the Worshipful Justices of the County Court of Pasquotank County now Siting
    The petition of James Nixon of the Said County Respectfully Sheweth

Chapter 18: Pasquotank County Records

Whereas your Petitioner under a sence of the many Services Rendered by a Certain Negro man by name Moses and a woman Named Easther Supposed to be about Sixty years of age   Each formerly the property of Thomas Pritchard Deceased Late of your said County which by the Dicision of the said deceased's Estate fell to your petitioner and Knowing the Intention of the said deceased – their former master, to whom I was nearly allyed by Marriage with his daughter

Whereby my mind being Impressed with Tenderness towards the aforesaid Moses & Easter with desires that they might Enjoy their freedoms the full Remaining days of their lives. They being under their former master found to be Trusty Honest & Carefull of his Intrest for which Merit their said master place great Confidence in their distinguishing manner.

Therefore it is the Cincear Request of your said Petitioner that your Worships might in your great Clemency grant that the said Negroes Moses & Easter might be freed under the Restrictions that other free negroes Enjoy in this State and Your Petitioner as in duty bound Most Cincearly prays &c

June 1797
Jas. Nixon

We the Subscribers being for a long time acquainted with the within Named Negroes Moses & Easter and never knew to our Knowledge or ever heard but what the said negroes bore a good Character they being of a peaceable Quiet and orderly disposition, therefore we the Subscribers do Join with the Petitioner for the Liberation of the within negroes &c

J Smithson	Wm Lane
Timy Trueblood	William Stott
Joab Jackson	W Keaton
Benjn. Symons	Saml Keaton
Jno Nicholson	John Banks
Hiram C. We[?]	John Pendleton
Robert Bailey	John Morris
Z Nixon Junr	Devotion Davis Sinr.
Benjamin White	Thomas Pritchard
J Lane	Fred. B. Sawyer
	Thos. Davis
	Devotion Davis
	John Manly
	Thomas Johnson
	Gabl. Bailey
	Cr. Nicholson

****

Petition for the
Liberation of Negro
Sam
Entd.
X—12

To the Worshipful the Justices of the Inferior Court of Pleas & Quarter Sessions for the County of Pasquotank
The Petition of the Subscribers Inhabitants of said County. Humbly Shew.

That your Petitioners having for a Number of Years been particularly Acquainted with the person mentioned in the Annexed Petition (Viz Negro Man Samuel) and believes him to be a peaceable person, so therefore pray Your Worships to grant the Said Samuel his freedom – Agreeable to the before mentioned petition, and your Petitioners as in duty bound will ever pray.

Devotion Davis	John Price
Briant Brothers	William Price
Durant Davis	David Tatem
Miles Davis	Joshua Brothers

Chapter 18: Pasquotank County Records

Bailey Davis   Wm Bru[?]
Abraham Boswell
Samuel **[Faded]**
John Brothers
Enoch Brothers
Mark Delon
Richard Brothers

****

Sylvester   }
To the   } Peto. For
Court   } emancipation

Pasq. County
June Term 1797
W Blair Atto

State of North Carolina   }
Pasquotank County   } June Term 1797

        To the Worshipful the County Court of Pleas & Quarter Sessions for Pasquotank County
The Petition of Thomas Sylvester a freeman of Colour Humbly Sheweth
        That he some years agoe took to Wife a Negroe Woman Slave by the Name of Joan the property of a certain Jeremiah Symons who hath bore him four Children, to wit, Abba, Nancy, Jerry and Annaretta.
        That by the Assistance, Industry economy & Prudence of his said Wife Joan he hath been enabled to raise a sufficient Sum to purchase her and her Children from their said Master.
May it therefore please your Worships taking your Petitioners Case under your consideration to pass an Order for the liberation & emancipation of the said Joan, Abba, Nancy, Jerry and Annaretta by the Names of Joan Sylvester, Abba Sylvester, Nancy Sylvester, Jerry Sylvester, and Annaretta Sylvester agreeable to the Power & Authority in your Worships Vested by the Act of the General Assembly in such Cases made and provided And Your Petitioner as in duty bound shall ever pray &c.
                       Will Blair for the
                       Petitioner

****

Sampson   }
To the   } Peto. For
Court   } emancipation

Pasq. County
June Term 1797
Will Blair Atto

State of North Carolina   }
Pasquotank County   } June Term 1797

        To the Worshipfull the County Court of Pleas & Quarter Sessions for Pasquotank County
The Petition of Lovey Sampson a Free woman of Colour Humbly Sheweth
        That she some years agoe took to Husband a Mulatto man Slave named David late the property of a certain Jeremiah Symons. That by the Assistance, industry, prudence and economy of her said Husband she hath been enabled to raise a sufficient Sum of Money to purchase her said Husband David from his said late Master. May it therefore please your Worships taking your Petitioners Case under your consideration to pass an Order for the liberation and emancipation of the said David by the Name of David Sampson agreeable to the Power & Authority in your Worships

Chapter 18: Pasquotank County Records

Vested by the Act of the General Assembly in such Cases made & provided And your Petitioner as in duty bound shall ever pray &c

                                  Will Blair for the
                                  Petitioner

***

                          March Term 1797

To the Worshipful the Justices, of the County Court of Pasquotank now Setting

    The Petition of Jacob Stevenson, a Slave, the property of Enoch Relfe, by and with the Consent of his said Master Humbly Sheweth, That the said Enoch Relfe Purchased him at Colo. Edward Evergans Vendue – And for no other Purpose and reason but that your said Petitioner should not fall into the hands of any person that might Abuse him – Knowing that he had done many Services to his former Masters that were Meritorious And as far as his Master believes, has always Conducted himself as well as any Person of his Colour.

    Your Petitioner therefore Prays that as it is done by the Consent of his said Master, that your Worships Will liberate him, Agreeable to the Act of the General Assembly in such Cases made and provided And your Petitioner will in duty bound ever Pray &c

                          Jacob Stephenson

Done by Consent
Enoch Relfe
March 12th 1797

We the subscribers have known the above Named Jacob Stevenson for many years past, And as he has always Conducted him self in a very Exemplary Manner – We therefore think him, highly deserving of Liberation

Jonathan Bundy		
John Pritchard	Thomas T Relfe	Danl. Shinley
[Torn]rd Davis	Wm Burrow	[Faded] Brother
[Torn] keaton		
John Stevenson	Archd. Davis	[Faded] Grifess[?]
Joshua Brother	John Crocker	William Wilson
Jas Cartwrite	J.A. Jordan	Stephen Barnes
Jos Pendlton	Jos: Scott	Wm Lane
J[?] Pendleton		
Jesse Ridding	William E. Wright	Joseph Brother
Jno Brother	Thomas Reding	
Lemuel Pendleton	Zachariah Jackson	Const. Luten
J McDonald	Fred. B. Sawyer	Jobe Carver
Thomas Jordan	Jas. L. Shannonhouse	Henry[?] Brother
	Joseph Relfe	
John Ferris	Demsey Nash	James Benton
Clem Cartwrite	John Baily	Samuel Cobb
Reub. Keaton	J Banks	Halld Lockwood
Adkins Massey	John Commander	Oney Dameron
Isaac Overman	Olliver Thackry	Thos Ackis
Devotion White	Durant Davis	
William Stott	Wm Gaskins	
Wm Banks	Benj Overman	
J Pendleton	[?] Hartness[?]	
J Lowry		

***

                          Petition
                          Henry Palin
                          For Liberation

Chapter 18: Pasquotank County Records

Of Negroes Aaron & Sarah

The Petition of Henery Palin son of Hennery Palin dcd
To the Respected Cort now Setting at Nixonton ~ March Term 1797

    Your Petitioner under a sence of gratetude for the many services rendered to my Dear Parents, by a Certain Negro Man and Woman named Aaron and Sarah upwards Fifty Years of age, whereby not only my Self but my nearest Connections in Life hath been benefited ~

And knowing that it was the Desire of my father towards the latter part of his days that the Sd. Negros might Injoy their Liberty who hath often been heard to Express him Self to that purpose

So Likewise it is the ernist request, and desire of Your Humble Petitioner that they may be free, and that the Respected Cort would from their Clemmency, grant the Request of their Humble Petitioner ~

    We whose names are hereunto Subscribed, being well acquainted with the above Said Negros this many Years can say on their behalf that they are Quiet Peaceable and orderly, they being also useful in the Neighbor hood, More Especialy the woman, who is a goodness in sickness and Scilful in Many Cases~

Fred B. Sawyer	J Trott
Jesse Riding	J Smithson
B Pritchard	Wm Barrow
	JA Jordan
	Elias Albertson
	[?]
	Jno. Nicholson
	Jno. McDonald

****

Jera. Symonds
Petition Conserning
Negro Amereto
Granted March '98
Test Will: T. Muse Clk

To the Worship Cort now Setting at Nixonton
    The Petition of Jeremiah Symons

Humbly Sheweth that under a Sence of Gratitude, for the long and Continued Servises of my Negro Woman by name Amereto who hath Served Me in the Station of House Servant, with Grate fidelity for Many Years, (My Situation in Life being Such) She the Said Negro woman having the whole care within Dors committed to her Care, wherein She hath behaved with the uttermost Care, and Honesty, To recompence her honist indevours, Your Petitioner is Desirous to Set her free, and hope that the Honorable Cort will in their Clemency Grant that the Said Negro Woman Amereto may Injoy her freedom under the restrictions that other free People of Collar Injoy in this State ~ And your Petitioner in duty bound Shall ever pray &c

March Term 1798   Jeremiah Symons

    We the Subscribers being acquainted with the above named Negro Woman this Many Years and believe her to be an Honest, peaceable and Orderly person, and that we never knew, or heard to the Contrary

John Price
Jesse Symons
David Tatem
Wm Brewer
Jno. McDonald

****

Jas. Nixon – Peto. For
Liberation of Negro David
March 98
Granted

Chapter 18: Pasquotank County Records

Test Will: T. Muse Clk

The Petition of James Nixon to the Respected Cort now Seting at Nixonton for September Term 1797, Respectfully Sheweth~

Whereas Your Petitioner under a Sence of Gratitude for the many Servises rendered, by a Certain Negroe Man by Name David aged near Sixty Years formerly the Property of Thos. Pritchard Decd. Which by Division of Sd Estate fell to me, and knowing the Intention of his former Master, to whom I was near by allyed by Marriage to his only Daughter where by my Mind being imprest with Tenderness towards the Sd Negro David with Desires that he might injoy his freedom the remainder part of his days, he being under his former Master found to be trusty, honest & careful of Sd Masters Intrest for which Merrit, he placed grate Confidence in him in a distinguishing manner Therefore it is the Ernist desire and request of Your Humble Petitioner that the Respected Cort now Siting might in there Clemmency grant that the Sd. Negro David might be free under the restrictions that other free Negros injoy in this State, which is the Sincere Desire and request of Your Humble petitioner

James Nixon

We the Subscribers being a long time acquainted with the above Sd Negro man David, and never knew to our knoledg or ever heard but that the Sd Negro bore a good Carrector, he being of peaceable, Quiet, and Orderly disposition therefore we the Sd Subscribers Joine with above Petitioner~~

Thomas Pritchard
Halld Lockwood
Abram Jordan
Robt B Jordan
John Pritchard
John Price

Jno. Smithson junior
Danl. Shinley
Thos Wilson
Thos Reding
[?] Morris Senr
[?] Palin
Benja Bailey
Archd Davis
Lemuel Jennings

****

To the Justices of the Court of Pasquotank County whereas A certain Negro Man Called Sam formerly the Property of my Father Josiah Bundy Deceasd. And at the Death of my Mother Elizabeth Symonds Deceasd. The Right of Said Negro Sam Decended to me agreeable to the Last will of my Said Father, Now it is my desire and Request that the said Negro Sam Shall be Liberated and Set free, , if the Court would Please to attend to a Petition on the Occasion and grant him Such benevolence as the nature of the Case or Petition may admit the Said Negro Sam residing Chiefly in Your County & under the Care of my Brother Josiah Bundy the Courts Attention to this my Request will much Oblige Their Friend

Joshua Bundy

Jones County the 25th day of
The 1st Month 1798

****

Jno. Commander
Petition for Freedom of Negro Jack
To March Term 1798
Granted
Test Will: T. Muse Clk
Granted
Jack Lane

State of North Carolina }
Pasquotank County } March Term 1798
To the worshipful County Court of Pleas and Quarter Sessions for the County aforesaid

Chapter 18: Pasquotank County Records

Humbly Sheweth unto your Worships Your Petitioner John Commander is the Owner of a Certain Negro Man slave known by the Name of Jack of the age of Fifty years or thereabouts, that the aforesd. Negro slave has always hitherto as far as Your Petitioner Knows or believes Conducted himself as Faithful Honest and Meritorious Slave, and your Petitioner in Consequence of his long and faithful Services, is desirous of rewarding him, in a Suitable manner, which he conceives he cannot sufficiently do, otherwise than by procuring to him his freedom.

      He therefore Humbly prays this Worshipful Court, to Grant him a License, to emancipate the said slave according to the directions of the Act of Assembly in Such Case made and Provided, and Your Petitioner as in duty Bound shall ever pray &c

W. Slade for the
Petitioner

****

Edmund White   } Petition for
      To   } Liberation of
The Court   } a Negro

Granted June 1799
Will: T. Muse Clk

To the Justices of the Inferior Court of Pleas & Quarter Sessions held for the County of Pasquotank
    The Petition of Edmund White an Inhabitant of said County --- Humbly Sheweth
    That Your Petitioner being possessed of a Negro Man by the Name Jonas, Who formerly belonged to Christopher Nicholson decd. & was some time ago taken up and sold as a Liberated Slave, Who thereupon advanced the purchase Money, to Enoch Relfe Esqr. Late decd. Who was the purchaser, and by the said Enoch Relfe Conveyed by deed of Gift to Your Petitioner, --- Your Petitioner therefore (after remarking that said Negro Man Jonas is of a general good Character in the County Wherein he is known) Humbly pray that you would Grant an Order that Said Man Jonas be Liberated under Such Restrictions as you shall see meet, and your Petitioner as in duty bound Will ever thankfully Acknowledge &c

                                                                               E White

6th Mo. 6th 1799

****

                                Saml. Jackson
                             Peto. For Ichabod

                              Granted June 1799
                                Will: T. Muse

                    The County Court of Pasquotank
The Petition of Samuel Jackson, Humbly Sheweth
    That he from Motives of Humanity & Gratitude humbly Solicits the favour of the Worshipful Bench to Liberate and set free his Negro Man Ichabod who hath ever Distinguished himself a faithful Servant & from the Meritorious services, of the Said Ichabod Your Humble Petitioner Considers he is intitled to his freedom for which Your Humble Petitioner Prays &c

7th June 1799
Sam. Jackson

****

Thomas Jordan
    To   } Petition

Chapter 18: Pasquotank County Records

The Court
Granted June 1799
Will: T. Muse Clk

To the Justices of the Inferior Court of Pleas & Quarter Sessions for the County of Pasquotank
    The Petition of Thomas Jordan an Inhabitant of said County
    Humbly Sheweth
That your Petitioner being possessed of a Negro Man by Name Luke Which Descended to him by Inheritance from the death of his father, Said Negro being then Very Young and for Many Years was hired out and the Monies arising thereupon applied to the Education of your petitioner, Your Petitioner therefore Humbly prays that you would grant him License to Emancipate Said Slave, as he thinks his Conduct in many Instances comes under the Meaning of the Act of Assembly as Meritorious ----- Your Petitioner would further Observe that Said Negro Man Luke is about 47 years of Age appears Sufficiently Capable of acquiring Comfortable Livelihood &c   Your Petitioner as in duty bound will ever thankfully Acknowledge &c
6 Mo. 4th 1799
                                                  Thomas Jordan

****

Devotion Davis Senr.
    To   } Peto. For Freedom
                } of Negro George
The Court
Granted March 1799

To the Worshipfull Court
The Petition of Devotion Davis Senr. Humbly Sheweth
    That My Negro Man George hath been a Faithfull Servant for Many Years, and Extrensic of his Servile duty hath Accumalated a Sum to Purchase his Freedom which I have received from him & in Consideration Whereof I do in Submission to the Court Consider His Services as Meritorious and Humbly request the Worshipfull Bench to imancipate the Said george for Which Your Humble Petitioner Will Ever pray &c
                                                  Devotion Davis

Devotion Davis Junr
Durant Davis
Jos Davis

****

John Nixon &als
To   } Peto. Emanc:
          } Negro George
The Court

Granted March Term 1799

    To the Worshipfull Court
The Petition of the Subscribers Humbly Sheweth
That Negro George (the Property of Thomas Nicholson & John Nixon) being a person of Good Character and always has distinguished himself an Honest industrious faithful servant, having in Many instances Merited the indulgence of imancipation for which your Petitioners Beg the favour of Granting to him the same as his Legal Masters desires it should be done.
Your Petitioners Shall Ever pray
March 1799   Jno Nixon
J Lane
Wm Br[?]
McMorine

Chapter 18: Pasquotank County Records

Cr Nicholson
Aaron Morris Junr

****

Jas. Nixon Peto.
For Pleasant

Granted March Term 1800
Will: T. Muse

State of North Carolina }
Pasquotank County   } Decr. Term 1799

To the worshipful the Justices of the County Court of Pasquotank
The Petition of James Nixon and others Humbly Sheweth, that Pleasant a Negro woman Slave the Property of James Nixon has for Many Years Past Conducted herselfe to her Present and former owners as a faithful Servant
    May it therefore Please your Worships to Emancipate her, the Said Pleasant as the Law in Such Cases Direct, and your Petitioners as in duty Bound Shall Ever pray &c
Will: T. Muse
Wm Lane
Hugh Knox
David Tatem
Wm Farange[?]
John Commander
Caleb Trueblood
Thos. Markam
Jno. McDonald

****

Bond, Thos. Nicholson
To save harmless the
Overseers of the Poor &c
June 1800

State of North Carolina }
Pasquotank County   }

    Know all Men by these presents that we Thomas Nicholson and Edward White are held and firmly bound unto the Justices of the County aforesaid in the Sum of Five hundred pounds, to be paid to the Said Justices, or their Successors in Office. To Which payment well and truly to be made, we bind ourselves our Heirs Executors and Admrs. Jointly and severally firmly by these Presents, Sealed with our seals, and dated this 6th day of June Anno Domini 1800.

    The Condition of the Above Obligation is such that Whereas Rose White Nicholson hath been this day by the Worshipful the County Court of Pleas and Quarter Sessions for the County aforesaid, liberated and set free from Slavery, in as full and ample Manner as the laws of the said State will admit, Now if the above named Thomas Nicholson his Heirs Executors or Administrators or any of them do and shall from time to time; and at all times hereafter Acquit discharge and save harmless, the Overseers of the Poor and inhabitants of the County aforesaid from all Costs, Charges and troubles whatsoever for and by reason of the liberation of the said Rose White Nicholson and of and from all suits Charges and demands whatsoever touching and Concerning her liberation, then the above Obligation to be Void, Otherwise to be and remain in full force and virtue.
Test.   Thomas Nicholson   (Seal)
Will: T. Muse   Edm. White   (Seal)
****

Chapter 18: Pasquotank County Records

Joseph Wilson } Petition for
To the Court } Liberation Rachael
               } & Children

Granted March Term 1800
Will: T. Muse Clk

To the Justices of the Inferior Court of pleas & Quarter Sessions for the County of Pasquotank now Setting
    The Petition of Joseph Wilson Inhabitant of the said County
Humbly Sheweth
    That your Petitioner having under his care or possession A Negro woman by the Name of Rachel Wife of Luke (formerly the property of Thomas Jordan Senr. & who hath been liberated by this Court by the name of Luke Howard) and her five Children (to wit) Jesse about 10 years of age, Keziah about 8 years of age, Ruth about 6 years of age, Rachel about 4 years of age, & John about 2 years old. ~
    Your Petitioner Humbly Request that you would please to grant an order that the said Rachel & her Children be liberated under Such Restrictions as other persons of Colour ~
    And your Petitioner as in duty bound will ever thankfully Acknowledge &c.
                                                                                             Joseph Wilson

---

                                    Bond
                          Joseph Wilson & Als to
                            Save harmless the
                        Overseers of the Poor &c

State of No. Carolina }
Pasquotank County   }

    Know all men by these presence that We Jos. Wilson, Thomas Jordan & Joseph Bundy are held and firmly bound unto the Justices of the County aforesaid in the sum of Five hundred Pounds, to be paid to the said Justices, or their Successors in Office: To the which payment well and truly to be made, We bind ourselves, our Heirs, Executors and Administrators, jointly and Severally, firmly by these presents, Sealed with our Seals, and dated this 6th day of March Anno Dom 1800.

The Condition of the above Obligation is such that Whereas Jesse about ten years of age, Keziah about Eight years, Ruth about six years of age, Rachel about four years of age, and John about Two years of age Children of Luke Howard who have been this day by the Worshipful the County Court of Pleas and Quarter Sessions for the County aforesaid, liberated and Set Free in as full and ample Manner as the laws of the said State will admit. Now if the above Named Joseph Wilson, Thomas Jordan & Joseph Bundy their Heirs Executors or Administrators, or any of them, do and shall from time to time, and at all times until the said Jesse, Keziah, Ruth, Rachael, & John shall Severally Arrive to the Age of Twenty one Years of Age, Acquit discharge, and save harmless, the Overseers of the Poor and inhabitants of the County aforesaid, from all Costs, Charges and Troubles Whatsoever for and by reason of the Liberation of the sd. Jesse, Keziah, Ruth, Rachael & John, and of and from all Suits Charges and demands Whatsoever touching and Concerning their liberation, then the Above Obligation to be Void, otherwise to remain in full force and Virtue.

Sealed and Delivered }	Joseph Wilson	(Seal)
In the Presence of }	Thomas Jordan	(Seal)
Will: T. Muse Clk	Joseph Bundy	(Seal)

****

William Robinson
To the   }
Court   } Petition

Chapter 18: Pasquotank County Records

Sept Term 1800
Granted Septr. 1800
Will: T. Muse

To the Worshipful the Justices of the County Court of Pleas & Quarter Sessions for the County of Pasquotank

The Petition of William Robinson humbly sheweth that he is at present the Owner of a certain Negro Woman Slave Named Hagar who for her faithful Services to Thomas Nixon her former Master, was liberated by him, but being contrary to law, she was taken up and Sold by order of the County Court of Perquimans Since that time she has by her care & Industry raised a Sum Sufficient to satisfy her present owner for the purchase money.

Mat it therefore please Your Worships to Order & decree that the said Negro Woman Hagar be Liberated & set free, for her Meritorious Services & Your Petitioner as in duty bound shall ever Gratefully Acknowledge &c.

Wm Robinson

The same as the Other Petition
Hagar Robinson

Bond
William Robinson, to
Save harmless the Overseers of
The Poor &c.
Sep. 1800

State of North Carolina }
Pasquotank County   }

Know all Men by these presents that We William Robinson and Benjamin Pritchard are held and firmly bound unto the Justices of the County Court of Pleas and Quarter Sessions for the County aforesaid in the Sum of Two hundred and fifty pounds Current Money of the said State, to be Paid to the said Justices, or their Successors in Office – To Which payment well and truly to be made, We bind ourselves our Heirs Executors and Administrators, jointly and Severally firmly by these presents, Sealed with our Seals and dated this 4th day of September 1800.

The Condition of the Above Obligation is such that Whereas Hagar Robinson hath been this day by the Worshipful the County Court, liberated and set free from Slavery, in as full and ample Manner as the laws of the said State will Admit – Now if the above named William Robinson his Heirs Executors or Admrs. Or every of them, do and shall, from time to time, and at all times hereafter, Acquit discharge and save harmless the Overseers of the Poor and inhabitants of the County aforesaid from all Costs Charges and trouble Whatsoever for and by reason of the liberation of the Said Hagar Robinson, and of and from all suits Charges and demands Whatsoever touching and Concerning her liberation – then the above Obligation to be Void, Otherwise to be and remain in full force and Virtue.

Sealed and Delivered }   Wm Robinson   (Seal)
In the presence of   }   Benjamin Pritchard (Seal)
Will: T. Muse Clk

****

J.S. Shannonhouse
    To   }
    The Court } Peto.

March Term 1800
Granted
Will: T. Muse Clk

State of North Carolina }
Pasquotank County   } March Term 1800

To the Worshipful the Justices of the County Court of Pleas and Quarter Sessions for the said County of Pasquotank The Petition of James S Shannonhouse

Chapter 18: Pasquotank County Records

Sheweth

That Your Petitioner hath a Mulatto or Boy of Colour of Two years of Age or thereabouts by the Name of Abner which for sufficient Causes & considerations he is desirous of emancipating and for whose future support and Maintenance he is ready and willing to enter into Bond with sufficient Securities agreeable to the directions of the Act of the General Assembly in such Cases lately made and provided   May it therefore Please your Worships to Pass an Order or Decree for the emancipation of the said Mulatto or Boy of Colour by the Name of Abner Relfe with such Rights and Privileges as are usually Granted to and enjoyed by The Persons of Colour &c   And Your Petitioner as in duty Bound shall ever Pray &c

                         Jas. S Shannonhouse

****

Aaron Morris
   To   } Peto.
The Court

                Granted June Term
                1800 See the Minutes
                Will: T. Muse Clk

Pasquotank County June Term 1800

  To the Justices of the County Court of Pleas & Quarter Sessions Now Setting
  The Petition of Aaron Morris respectfully sheweth that his Negro Woman Hannah has been brought up under his Perticular care as a House Servant, and has at all times behaved herself honestly and has served him faithfully; that she is now about Twenty five years of age and has three Children (Viz) William, Davis, & Jacob, - your Petitioner therefore Request for the reasons aforesaid that the Sd. Hannah and her three Children may be Emancipated according to the Act of Assembly in that Case made & provided, In duty bound your Petitioner will ever Greatfully acknowledge &c.

                             Aaron Morris

Hannah   }
William   } Morris
Davis   }
Jacob   }
                Granted

****

                Petition of
                Thos. Nicholson
                1800

               granted June Term 1800
               See the Minutes
               Will: T. Muse Clk

To the Justices of the Inferior Court of Pleas & Quarter sessions for the County of Pasquotank Now Sitting
  The Petition of Thomas Nicholson Humbly Sheweth
  That your Petitioner having under his care a Negro Man Named Thomas about 40 years of age which he is desirous to Liberate therefore pray that you would grant an Order that said Negro man Thomas be Liberated and set free by the Name of Thomas Nicholson Morris and your Petitioner as in duty bound will ever thankfully Acknowledge &c
6th Month 5th 1800   Thomas Nicholson

Chapter 18: Pasquotank County Records

We the Under Written being well Acquainted with the person mentioned in the foregoing Petition that he is a peaceable well disposed person having resided in this County a Number of Years and We think deserving the Clemency of the Court 5th June 1800 ~

[?] Shepherd
Thomas Jordan
Aaron Morris

Will: T. Muse
Jno. McDonald
Wm. Wilson
Mordecai Morris

****

1800 the 6th Mo. 3rd day ~

To the County Court of Pasquotank now Sitting Greeting &c

Whereas Your Petitioner hath a Certain Negro woman Named Rose, Residing in this County & the Wife of a Certain Jonah which Sd. Jonah was some time past Emancipated by order of sd. Court It is therefore the Request of Your Petitioner that an order be Granted for the Emancipation of sd. Rose she being about 50 Years of age and as far as I have Understood is of a peaceable & Quiet behaviour Your order for the above will be acknowledged &c

PS the Sd. Rose goes by the
Name of Rose White Nicholson

Thomas Nicholson

Granted on Giving Bond of Indemnity

****

James Nixons Peto.
For Negro James
Granted March Term 1800
Will: T. Muse Clk

To the Respected Cort now setting for March Term 1800

The Petition of James Nixon Respectfully Sheweth, that my Negro Man James whome I Perchased som time past ~ By his Industry hath replaced the Perchase Money Therefore Your humble Petitioner request that You in your Clemency will Grant that the Sd. Negro James may be free by Name James Robinson as other free People of Collar in this State ~ & Your Petitioner in Duty Bound Shall ever Pray &c.

Jas. Nixon

We the Subscribers Being Acquainted with the Sd. Negro James for a Considerable time & believe him to be Peaceable Quiet and Industerus Person & that we never heard any thing to the Contrary

Jacob Jackson
W ro by
Nathan Morris
John Bell

John Price
Cr Nicholson
A Morris Junior
Benjamin Symons
Bailey Davis
Thos. Ackess
J Lane
Thos. [Faded]
Wm Lane

****

The Petition of Hester
March Term 1800
Granted

Chapter 18: Pasquotank County Records

Will: T. Muse

The Petition of Hester formerly the Property of Colo. Edward Evergan Esquire late decd. To the Worshipfull Court of Pasquotank County Humbly Sheweth

That Whereas the said Evergan in his life time oft did express before a Number of Witnesses his desire to Emancipate and Set free his Negro Woman Hester at his Death in Case She should be the longest liver in Consequence of her Great Care of his Interest and her Uncommon Fidelity. Therefore we the Subscribers Willing that his Pious and Grateful Intentions shoud be put in Execution do with Submission, Petition Your Worshipfull Body to Emancipate & Set free the said Hester under such restrictions as the law Directs in Such Cases, & that she shall be Called by the Name of Hester Evergan --- and this Case with Great Submission your Petitioners Submits to your Worshipfull Body and as in duty bound will ever Pray, this 20th February 1800.

John McDonald	Sarah Symons	Jonathan Banks
Reub Keaton	John Sampson	T Freshwater
Wm. Wilson	William Symons	Wm Farange
Jas. L. Shannonhouse	J Keaton	Ben [?]
Thos T. Relfe	Sam. Overman	Jo. L. Brosher
Fred. B. Sawyer	N. Overman	
Thomas Nicholson	Jno. Brosher	
Peleg Pendleton		

****

Jos. Wilson   } Petition for
    To   }
The Court   } Liberation Aaron

Granted March Term 1800
Will: T. Muse

To the Justices of the Inferior Court of Pleas & Quarter Sessions for the County of Pasquotank now Sitting
The Petition of Joseph Wilson Inhabitant of the County aforesaid
Humbly Sheweth,
That your Petitioner having under his care or possession A Certain Negro Man Named Aaron about 40 years of age (formerly the Property of Robert Murden deceas'd) Which your Petitioner thinks himself in duty bound to Extricate from Slavery, yet knowing there are Acts of the General Assembly prohibiting the Emancipation of Slaves Excepting for Meritorious Services &c &c, Nevertheless your Petitioner being Willing & desirous as aforesaid to do all in his power towards the Above laudable purpose and at the same time Considering the Said Negro Man Aaron is well known to many of the Inhabitants of the County aforesaid, being his Native place, do therefore humbly Request that you would be pleased to grant an Order for the Liberation of the Said Man Aaron, and that he may henseforward Injoy the same, under Such Restrictions as other free persons of Colour.
And your Petitioner as in duty bound will thankfully Acknowledge &c.
Joseph Wilson

****

Jos. Wilson   } Petition for
To the Court   } Liberation London

Granted March Term 1800
Will: T. Muse

To the Justices of the Inferior Court of Pleas & Quarter Sessions for the County of Pasquotank now Setting,
The Petition of Joseph Wilson Inhabitant of the County Aforesd.
Humbly Sheweth, -- That your Petitioner having under his care or possession a certain Negro man named London about 40 years of age (formerly the property of Benjamin Leonard of the County aforesd. Decd. Which your Said Petitioner

Chapter 18: Pasquotank County Records

thinks himself in duty Bound (from the faithful and Meritorious Services of said Negro Man London in several Instances) to Extricate from Slavery, yet knowing there are Acts of the General Assembly prohibiting the Emancipation of Slaves Excepting for Meritorious Services &c &c, Nevertheless your Petitioner being Willing & desirous as aforesd. To do all in his power towards the above lawdable purpose, and at the same time Considering the said negro Man London is well known to Many of the Inhabitants of the County aforesd., being his native place, do therefore Humbly Request that you would be pleased to grant an Order for the Liberation of said Man London, And that he may henseforward injoy the same, under such Restrictions as other free persons of Colour.

And your Petitioner as in duty bound will thankfully Acknowledge &c.

Joseph Wilson

****

Granted March Term 1800
Will: T. Muse

To the Worshipfull Cort now seting at Nixiton for March Term 1800
Your Petitioner under a Sence of Duty as knowing that it was my Fathers Desire in his Life time to Emancipate and Set free a Negro Man by Name Davice aged about 30 Years, which Sd Davis hath behaved himself in an honest, peaceable, and Industrous Manner. Therefore your Humble Petitioner Earnestly requests, that in your Clemency you will Set free the Said Negro Davis, by name Davis Gipson as other free People of Collar in this State, and Your Petitioner in Duty Bound Shall Ever Pray, &c.

Henry Palin

We the Subscribers being a Considerable time acquainted With the above mentioned Negro Man Davis, and know him to be a Peaceable, Quiet, Industerus and Honest Negro and that we never heard any thing to the Contrary.
John Price
Joshua Morris Senr
Thomas Morris
William delon
Benjamin Sawyer
Thomas White
John Hankins

****

Peto. Negro Woman Ruth
Granted March 1800
Will: T. Muse

To the worshipfull the Justices of the County Court of Pleas and quarter sessions for the County of Pasquotank
The Petition of the Subscribers Humbly Sheweth that the Bearer negro Ruth Served the Late Colo. Evergan for many years & after his death Fell to David George as he being an Heir of the Said Evergain & Served the Said David George during his Life Time, after his death was Divided to John McDonald as he was an Heir of David George who Sold her to William Farang & the Said William to her Husband Jonas as will more fully appear by the Bill of Sale Hereunto annexed, That the said Negro Ruth Before and Since the Purchase of her Time by her Said Husband from William Farang Conducted her Selfe in a very Exemplary manner, may it therefore Please your worships to Liberate & set her the said negro Ruth free and that she may Hereafter pass & be known By the name of Ruth Evergain and be Entitled to Injoy all the Rights & Priviledges of other free Persons of Colour in as full and ample manner as the Laws of the State will Admit.

William Farange	Holld Sackwood[?]
John McDonald	Wm. Banks
Reub Keaton	Hugh Knox
Wm. Wilson	
Jas. L. Shannonhouse	
Andrew Knox	Joab Jackson

Chapter 18: Pasquotank County Records

Griffith Sawyer   [?]
Jonathan Dukais[?]   Wm. C. Browne
Jonathan Price

****

William Robinson
To the
Court Petition
Septr Term 1800

Granted Septr 1800
Will T. Muse

To the Worshipful Justices of the County Court of Pleas and Quarter Sessions for the County of Pasquotank
    The petition of William Robinson humbly sheweth that he is the present Owner of a certain Negro Man Slave named Tom formerly the property of Col. Edward Evergan decd. Who was a faithful slave to his former Master, and has Satisfied his present Owner for the purchase Money May it therefore please the Court to order & decree that the said Negro Man Tom be liberated & set free for his Meritorious Services and your Petitioner as in duty Bound shall ever Gratefully Acknowledge &c.

                                                              Wm. Robinson
The Prayer of the Above Petition Granted on Giving Bond to keep him Clear of the Parish
(Known by name of Tom Robinson)

****

Job Morris, Peto.
For Betty

Granted Septr 1800
Will: T. Muse

To the Worshipful the Justices of the County Court of Pasquotank
    The Petition of Job Morris
Humbly Sheweth

    That your petitioner having in his possession a negro Woman Slave Named Betty (Daughter to your said Petitioner) Which he purchased as may appear by a Bill of Sale from under the hand & Seal of John McDonald, and being desirous to Emancipate said Woman Betty, do therefore Humbly pray that your Worships would be pleased to Grant an Order for that purpose and your Petitioner as in Duty bound will ever pray &c

September   his
Thomas Jordan   Job XXX Morris
                                                                                                                   mark

****

Aaron Morris Peto.
For George entd.

Granted June Term 1800
Will T. Muse Clk

Pasquotank County June Term 1800
    To the Justices of the County Court of Pleas & quarter Sessions Now setting

Chapter 18: Pasquotank County Records

The Petition of Aaron Morris respectfully Sheweth that my Negor boy George hath been brought up Under my Care and hath behaved himselfe Orderly peaceably and is Industrous and is About twenty one Years of Age Your Petetioner therefore Requests for the reasons aforesaid that the said George may be Emancipated According to the Act of Assembly in that Case made and provided, In duty bound Your Petitioner will ever Gratefully Acknowledge &c.

Aaron Morris

Granted

****

Mary Nicholson
         } Peto. For
         } Liberation
To   }
The Court

Granted
Septr Term 1800
Will: T. Muse

To the Justices of the Inferior court of Pleas & Quarter Sessions for the County of Pasquotank Now Sitting
    The Petition of Mary Nicholson and others Inhabitants of said County.
Humbly Sheweth
    That your Petitioner the said Mary Nicholson having in her possession a Negro Man called Stephen aged about 40 Years, Which she Conceives is Justly entitled to his freedom from his upright Conduct and faithful Services – Therefore pray that you would take his Case into Consideration, and Grant an Order for his Liberation if you in Wisdom shall so see meet, and your petitioner as in duty bound will ever thankfully Acknowledge &c.

3rd of 9th Mo. 1800
                    Mary Nicholson
                    Henley Nicholson
                    William Nicholson
                    Wm. Wilson
                    James White
                    Thomas Nicholson
                    John Russell
                    Jonathan Price
                    Thomas Jordan

****

Peto. For the liberation
Of Negro James

X—74

Dr Sawyer security   } £500
Jona. Price   }

To the Worshipful the Justices of the County Court of Pleas & Quarter Sessions for the County of Pasquotank
    The Petition of John Conner, Humbly Sheweth
    That he purchased negro Man Slave named James at the Vendue of John A. Jordan Deceased – and in Consequence of the said Negro James's faithful Services to his former Owners, And to Your Petitioner since he Owned him – Your Petitioner is desirous that he should be liberated & set free. May it therefore please Your Worships to grant an Order for the liberation of the sd. Negro James, And that he may enjoy all the rights and priviledges of other free Persons of Colour in as full and ample manner as the laws of the State Will Admit
    And as in duty Bound &c.

Septr. Term 1799   John Conner

Chapter 18: Pasquotank County Records

We Whose Names are under Written have known the above named James for Several years, & as far as we know & believe, has Conducted himself well

Devotion Benton
Henley Nicholson

Will: T. Muse
Thos. T. Relfe
Thos. Jordan
Abram Jordin
[Faded]
[Faded]
Thomas Morris

***

Peto. For the Liberation
Of Negro Toney
X—72

Will T. Muse   } Securities
Jonathan Price }

To the Worshipful The Justices of the County Court of pleas and Quarter sessions for the county of Pasquotank
  The Petition of the Subscribers Humbly Sheweth
  That the bearer Negro Tony, Served the late Colo. Evergan for Many Years, that he was sold at the Vendue of the Said Colo. Evergan & purchased by the late Mr. George, of Whom the Said Negro Toney purchased his time, as will more fully appear by the Bill of Sale hereunto annexed – That the said Negro Toney before and since the purchase of his time from Mr. George Conducted himself in a very Exemplary Manner --- May it therefore Please Your Worships to liberate & set him the said Negro Toney free, and that he may hereafter pass & be known by the name of Tony Evergan, and be entitled to enjoy all the rights and priviledges of other free Persons of Colour, in as full and ample manner as the Laws, of the State will admit.

September Term 1799

      Wm Lane
      Hugh Knox

Will T. Muse

Wm Wilson
 his
James X Griffin
 Mark
James Carver
John Hankins
Jno. McDonald
Adkins Massey
Thos. Markam
Clement Cartwright
Reu Keaton
Thomas Pritchard

***

London Leonard } Petition
To the Court   } for
               } Liberation
               } of his wife

X-284
Granted June Term 1801
See the Minutes
Will: T. Muse Clk

To the Justices of the Inferior Court of pleas & Quarter sessions for the county of Pasquotank now Setting.

Chapter 18: Pasquotank County Records

The Petition of london Leonard (a person of color) Inhabitant of said County Humbly Sheweth.
That Your Petitioner having lately purchased his beloved Wife Edith, formerly the property of Ja[Torn] Leonard Deceas'd, ~
Your Petitioner Humbly Request that you would please to Grant an Order that said Edith be liberated under Such Restrictions as other persons of Colour and your Petitioner as in duty bound will ever thankfully Acknowledge &c
London Leonard

****

Jos. L. Brosher
Peto.

X-200
Granted March Term 1801
See the Minutes
Test. Will: T. Muse Clk

The Petition of Joseph L. Brosher unto the Court of Pasquotank Humbly Sheweth,
That whereas Your Petitioner Holds a Negro Man Slave by the Name of Pompy and a Negro Woman by the Name of Hannah and is desirous that your Worshipfull body would under the Act of Assembly Grant their Liberation, as it is your Petitioners Perticular desire and request, they being Usefull to the Community, Pompy is a Very Good Cooper and has always behaved himself in an Upright Manner and his Wife Hannah is a Midwife Well Approv'd of and has Practiced with Applause a Number of Years, if the Court Sees Cause to Grant this Petition my desire is that they in future Shall be known by the Name of Pompy Taylor & Hannah Taylor & shall have all the Priviledges that other People of Colour has in this State, and as in duty bound your Petitioner will ever pray
Given under My hand this 3rd March 1801
T Freshwater   Joseph L. Brosher
We the Subscribers do [Torn] the Petitioner in the within Petition and in [Torn] thereof have thereunto Set our hands

This Petition Granted on giving Security to Keep Clear of a Parish Charge

---

Bond
Joseph L. Brosher & als
March 1801

State of North Carolina }
Pasquotank County   }

Know all Men by these presents that We Joseph L. Brosher & Thads. Freshwater are held and firmly bound unto the Justices of the County Court of Pleas and Quarter Sessions for the County aforesaid, in Sum of Two hundred and fifty pounds Current Money of the said State; to be paid to the said Justices, or their Successors in Office, to which payment well and truly to be made and done, We bind ourselves our Heirs Executors and Administrators, jointly and severally firmly by these presents – Sealed with our Seals and dated this 4th day of March 1801.

The Condition of the above Obligation is such that whereas Pompy Taylor and Hannah Taylor, hath been this day by the Worshipful the County Court, liberated & set Free from Slavery, in as full and Ample Manner as the laws of the said State will Admit – Now if the above Named Joseph L. Brosher his Heirs Executors or Administrators or any of them, do and shall, from time to time, and at all times hereafter acquit, discharge, and save harmless the Overseers of the Poor and inhabitants of the County Aforesd from all Costs Charges and troubles whatsoever for and by reason of the liberation of the said Pompy and Hannah Taylor, and of and from all such Charges and demands whatsoever touching and Concerning their liberation, then the above Obligation to be Void, Otherwise to be and remain in full force and Virtue

Sealed and Delivered }   Jos. L. Brosher   (Seal)
In the presence of   }   T Freshwater   (Seal)

Chapter 18: Pasquotank County Records

Will. T. Muse Clk

****

Josiah Trueblood
Peto.

X 247

Granted March Term 1801
See the Minutes
Will T. Muse Clk

Pasquotank County March term 1801
To the Justices of the County Court of Pleas and Quarter sessions Now Setting
    Respectfully Sheweth that your Petitioner has two Negroes under his Care one by the Name of Cattron aged about 36 years and has behav'd herself Honestly and Industerously one by the Name of Ivey Aged about two year, therefore for the above resons your Petitioner Earnestly Request that the Cort May take their **[Torn]** Under Consideration and Order that the for said Cattron & Ivey be Emancipated Acording to the Act of Assembly in that Case Maid and Provided & as in duty Bound and your Petitioner Will ever Aknowledg

Prefer that their Names   Josiah Trublood
Be Cattron Roch
& Ivey Roach

The Prayer of this Petition Granted on giving Bond to Keep them Clear of the Parish

****

Durant Davis Peto.
For Freedom of Miriam
X-373

To the Worshipful the County Court of Pleas and Quarter sessions for the County of Pasquotank
    The Petition of Durant Davis, Humbly Sheweth – That he at present Owns a Certain Negro Woman Slave Named Miriam Who has conducted herself for some Years Past in a very Meritorious Manner – and your Petitioner is therefore desirous that she should be liberated from Slavery
    May it please your Worships, to order her liberation in as full and Ample Manner as the laws of the State will admit – and your Petitioner as in duty bound will ever pray

Decr. Term 1801   Durant Davis
Granted on giving the Usual Bond

****

Frs. White Peto.
Granted

X- 359
September term 1801
To the Justices of County Court of Pleas and Quarter Sessions held for the County of Pasquotank
    The Petition of Francis White Humbly Sheweth that his Negroe man Joe and his Wife Comfort has always Lived in the Neighborhood of Symons Creek and have never been Guilty of any misdemeanor what ever. And that the Said Joe has bought his wife Comfort and has nearly paid me for his price. And under these Considerations I pray your Worships that they both may be Emancipated under the Act of Assembly in that case made and provided and am willing

Chapter 18: Pasquotank County Records

to become bound that they shall not be chargeable to the Public, and in due Submission your petitioner will ever greatfully Acknowledge

Francis White

Granted by the Court   Mr. White Giving Sufficient Security
Charles Grice on the Bench
J Lane
Dems. Nash
Eb [?]

Bond
Frs. White & als
Sep. 1801

State of North Carolina   }
Pasquotank County   }

      Know all Men by these presents that we Francis White and Job Cartwright are held and firmly bound unto the Justices of the County Court of Pleas and Quarter Sessions for the County aforesaid, in the sum of Two hundred and fifty pounds Current Money of the said State, to be paid to the said Justices, or their Successors in Office, to Which Payt. Well and truly to be made and done, We bind ourselves, our Heirs Executors and Administrators, Jointly and Severally firmly by these presents, Sealed with our Seals and dated this 11th day of September Anno Dom 1801.

The Condition of the above Obligation is such that Whereas Comfort White hath been this day by the Worshipful County Court, liberated and set free from Slavery, in as full and Ample Manner as the laws of the said State will Admit; Now if the above named Francis White and Job Cartwright their Heirs Executors or Administrators, or any of them do and shall from time to time, and at all times hereafter, Acquit, discharge, and save harmless the Overseers of the Poor and Inhabitants of the County afsd. From all Costs and Charges and demands whatsoever for and by reason of the liberation of the said Comfort; & of and from all such Charges and demands whatsoever touching and Concerning her liberation, then the above Obligation to be Void, otherwise to be and remain in full force and Virtue.

Sealed and Delivered   }   Francis White   (Seal)
In the presence of   }   Job Cartwright   (Seal)
Will: T. Muse Clk

***

Emanuel Morris } Petition for
       To   }Liberation
The Court   }Fanny

To the Worshipful Court of Pasquotk. Now Sitting
      The Petition of Emanuel Morris Humbly Shews.
      That Your Petitioner, having lately made a purchase of his Wife Fanny (as will appear by the Annexed Bill of Sale) and Wishing her to have the Priviledge of her freedom, do therefore Pray your Worships to take the matter under your Notice, and grant the Said Fanny her Freedom as you have heretofore done in like Cases, and Your Petitioner as in duty bound will ever pray &c.

                                        his
December 8th 1801   Emanuel X Morris
                                        Mark

A Norris   Granted

***

Tho: Jordan   } Petition for

Chapter 18: Pasquotank County Records

    To   } Liberation
The Court   } Jenny & Child Gilbert

X – 381
Dec. 1801

To the Justices of the County Court of Pasquotank Now Sitting
    The Petition of Thomas Jordan
        Humbly Sheweth
    That Having in his Possession a Negro Woman named Jenny and Boy Child Gilbert formerly the Property of Benjn. Leonard Decd. And wishing to Emancipate them (Said Woman being a Serviceable person) do therefore pray that you would take the same into Consideration and grant an Order for that purpose, if you should so see meet, and Your Petitioner as in duty bound will ever thankfully Acknowledge &c.

12th mo.th, 8th 1801   Thomas Jordan

****

Thomas Jordan   } Petition for
    To   } liberation
The Court   } Isaac

X- 381

To the Justices of the County Court of Pasquotk. Now Sitting
    The Petition of Thomas Jordan
        Humbly Sheweth
    That Rebekah Pearson, Stephen Henley & Ann Henley of Randolph County, & William Pearson of Perquimons County, having in their possession a Certain Negro Man Named Isaac which they are Desirous to Emancipate on Acct. of his Fidelity & Services to them heretofore and on Acct. of the Inconvenience of the distance of their residence from each other, have requested Your Petitioner to Act for them (Said Negro having been raised in this County from his Infancy & now resident here) which said request will appear reference being had to the Annexed Letters of Attorney under their hands & Seals. Your Petitioner therefore prays that you will pass an Order for the same, as you may see meet, and Your Petitioner as in duty bound will ever thankfully Acknowledge &c.

12th Mo. 8th 1801   Thomas Jordan
Granted

****

Jon. Banks   The within Petition Granted
                     On Giving the Usual Bond

Jeremiah Willcox
Andrew Pendleton
Chris Cartwright
Jeremiah Palmer

X – 380

For Negro   }
James to   } Petition
The Court   }
To the Worshipfull the County Court of pleas and Quarter Sessions of Pasquotank, the petition of the Subscribers Humbly Sheweth

Chapter 18: Pasquotank County Records

    Your Petitioner Set forth that Negro James a Man of Colour (Formerly the property of Robert Palmer Esqr. Decd. But at Present the property of Thaddeus Freshwater) hath so Ingratiated himself in his said Masters favour that he is desirous of freeing the said James, and whereas we the Subscribers Petitioners having known the Said Negro for a number of years, and being Satisfyed that his life and Conduct hath been upright & hath Never been Impeach'd for any Misdemeanor and that he has been an Orderly faithfull Slave to his Master's therefore we pray your Worshipfull body will take his Case into Consideration and Sanction his Liberation as the law gives Liberty in such Cases, & your Petitioners as in duty bound will ever pray this 1st Decr. 1801.

Thomas Gaskins	T Freshwater
William Gaskins	W. Keaton
Charles Markham	Thos. Markam

****

James Tadlock
Peto.
X – 311

Granted June Term 1801
Will: T. Muse Clk
See the Minutes

Pasquotank County June the first 1801

To the Justices of the County Court of Pleas & Quarter Sessions Now Siting
    Respectfully Sheweth that your Petitioner having A Negro man under his Care named James aged about 45 years and has behaved himself Honestly and Industerously therefore for the above Resons your Petitioner Earnestly Requests that the Court may take this matter under Consideration and order that the Said James be Emancipated acording to the Act of Assembly in that Case Made and provided and provided as in Duty Bound and your Petitioner will Ever acknowledge.

Proposed that his Name be James Williams   James Tatlock

Granted on giving Bond & Security to keep him Clear of the Parish.

****

Peto.
Caleb White
For Freedom of Negroes
X - 402

To the Justices of the County Court of Pleas and Quarter Sessions held for the County of Pasquotank December Term 1801

The Petition of Caleb White humbly Sheweth that his Negro woman Venus aged about thirty five years with her four Children namely Charlotte, Cloe, Venus & Silva now living near the head of Pasquotank river having always behaved themselves in Such an orderly manner as to induce your Petitioner to believe they deserve their freedom – So your petitioner therefore humbly Prays that your honours may take the matter under concideration and grant that the above Said Negro woman with the above named Children shall be liberated under the Act of Assembly in that Case made and provided as your petitioner in duty bound will ever greatly acknowledge &c

                                                                                                        Caleb White

Granted on giving the Usual Bond

Bond
Caleb White

Chapter 18: Pasquotank County Records

Decr 1801

State of North Carolina }
Pasquotank County } Ss.

    Know all Men by these Presents that we Caleb White and James Carver are held and firmly bound unto the Justices of the County Court of Pleas and Quarter Sessions for the County aforesaid, in the Sum of Two hundred and fifty pounds Current Money of the said State, to be Paid to the Justices, or their Successors in Office, to Which Payment Well and Truly to be made and done, We bind ourselves our Heirs Executors and Administrators Jointly and Severally firmly by these Presents, Sealed with our Seals and dated this 9th day of December Anno Dom 1801.

The Condition of the above Obligation is Such that Whereas Venus, Charlotte, Chloe, Venus and Sylvia hath been this day by the Worshipful County Court, liberated and set Free from Slavery in as full and ample manner as the laws of the said State will admit – Now if the above Named Caleb White and James Carver – their Heirs Executors or Admnrs – or any of them do and shall from time to time and at all times hereafter Acquit, discharge and save harmless the Overseers of the Poor & Inhabitants of the County aforesaid from all Costs charges & Troubles Whatsoever for and by reason of the liberation of the said Venus, Charlotte, Chloe, Venus and Sylvia and of and from all suits charges and demands Whatsoever touching and Concerning the liberation then the above Obligation to be Void, Otherwise to be and remain in full force and Virtue.

Sealed and Delivered }	Caleb White	(Seal)
In the Presence of }	James Carver	(Seal)
Will: T. Muse Clk		

****

The Petition of
James L. Shannonhouse
X—303
Granted March Term 1801
Will: T. Muse Clk

State of North Carolina }
Pasquotank County } March Term 1801

    The Petition of James L. Shannonhouse Humbly Praying the liberation of a Molatto Girl which he has in his family now a Slave under him, who was formerly the Property of Enoch Relfe decd. And she having conducted her self as an Honest and faithful slave your Petitioner prays your Worships will liberate and sett free said Molatto Girl by the Name of Pleasant and that she may enjoy the Privileges granted by An Act of Assembly for such People of Colour to enjoy, and go by the name of Pleasant Relfe hereafter. Your Petitioner will ever Pray &c
5th March 1801
Jas. L. Shannonhouse

****

Benjamin Pritchard
   To } Peto.
The Court
Granted June Term 1800
See the Minutes
Will: T. Muse

    Your Petitioner under a Since of Gratitude for the Many Servises, as well as fervent Desire to eas my own Mind, Humbly request that You in Your Clemency may Grant the freedom of My Negro Man Richard about age of fifty Years under the same restrictions as other free People of Colour Injoy in this State, And that he may be Known by the Name of Richard Michell

Chapter 18: Pasquotank County Records

And Your Petitioner will ever thankfully Acnoledg and &c
                                            Benjamin Pritchard
We the Subscribers being for a long time acquainted with the above Negro Man Richard and know him to be a Very Peaceable, Quiet, Industerus, and Honest Person and that we never herd of any thing to the Contrary therefore join in the request of the Petitioner   John Price

                                            Benja Sawyer
                                            Micajah Chancey
                                            William Conner

****

George R. Henley
To} Pet: for Liberation of Moses
The Court
Granted
X--947

To the Worshipful the County Court of Pleas and Quarter Sessions for the County of Pasquotank.
    The Petition of George R. Henley and others praying for the liberation a Certain Negro Man Slave named Moses. Your Petitioner states that the said Negro Slave Moses is now Considerable Advanced in Years and has always supported a general good Character, he is generally known in the Neighborhood as a Skilful Pilot from Newbegun Bridge to the mouth of the Creek in which Capacity he has always, as well as every other given general Satisfaction from his Universal good Conduct and Meritorious Services -- Your petitioner is induced to believe that his liberation from Slavery will be granted by Your Worships -- Your Petitioner further states that he is ready to Comply with the requisitions of the Act of the General Assembly in such Cases made and provided -- And Your Petitioner as in duty bound will ever pray.

George R. Henley	Aaron Morris Senr.
Wm. Spencer	John Cooke[**Cocke?**]
Davd. Williams	Thomas Overman
William C George	Wm Wilson
Spephen Keaton	Will: T. Muse
Ambrose Knox	Jno. McDonald

Bond
George R Henley & als

State of North Carolina   }
Pasquotank County   }

    Know all men by these presents that we George R. Henley, Joshua Trueblood, Thos. Overman of the County of Pasquotank, are held and firmly bound unto David Pritchard Esquire Chairman of the County Court of Pleas and Quarter sessions for the County aforesaid or to his Successors in Office, in the Sum of one hundred pounds - To the which payment well and truly to be made and done, we bind ourselves our heirs Executors and Admrs. Jointly and severally firmly by these presents Sealed with our seals and dated the [?] day Decr 1812

    The Condition of the above Obligation is such that Whereas the above bounden George R. Henley hath with the approbation of the Court, liberated and set Free from slavery a Negro Man slave named Moses Now if the above bounden George R. Henley their Heirs Executors or Admrs. Or any of them do and shall from time to time and at all times hereafter Acquit discharge and save harmless the Overseers of the Poor and Inhabitants of the said County from all Costs charges and troubles Whatsoever for and by reason of the liberation of the said Negro Slave Moses and of and from all other suits charges and demands whatsoever touching and Concerning the same then the above obligation to be void, otherwise to remain in full force.
Registered

Chapter 18: Pasquotank County Records

****

John Brown }
    To   } Petition
The Court }
X--515
Granted
Thads. Freshwater
John McDonald
Securities

To the Worshipful the Justices of the County Court of Pleas and Quarter Sessions of the County of Pasquotank

    The Petition of John Brown   Carpenter   Man of Colour
        Humbly Sheweth
    That some time Prior to the 7th day of January 1801   That your Petitioner John Brown did intermarry with a certain negro woman Slave by the name of Rose the Property of Jesse Trueblood by Whom he had had two Children viz, John and George   And on the Aforesaid 7th day of January 1801, the Said Jesse Trueblood did by his deed of Bargain Sale and Conveyence Sale Sign and Sold over all his Right and title to the Said Negro Woman Rose and her Children John and George unto him the Said John Brown his Heirs & Assigns for Ever

    Your Petitioner John Brown further Shew to Your Worships that the Said Child by the Name of George has departed this life Since the Said 7th January 1801 And that the Said Woman Rose has been delivered of a Daughter Whose Name is Call'd Parthena
    Therefore Your Petitioner John Brown Humbly Pray your Worships to take into Consideration the Peculiar Situation of his having a Wife & Children Who under the Law are Slaves and that You in Your Wisdom will Liberate and Set at Liberty The Said Negro Woman Rose and her Children John and Perthena, And allow them the Same Priviledges that is allowed People of Colour in this State agreeable to Law -- And that they may be Call'd & Known by the name of Rose Brown, John Brown, and Perthena Brown -- And as in duty bound Your Petitioner John Brown Will ever Pray &c
        his
17th May 1804   John   X   Brown
                                                                                                                    Mark

We Whose Names are hereunder Written do Certify that We Live in the Neighborhood Where the Within mentioned John Brown & his Wife & Children Viz Rose, John, & Perthena Now lives and are Well Acquainted with the Manner in which they Conduct themselves in life as to their Honesty and Industry ---- Therefore We Join the Said John Brown in his Petition to the Justices of the County Court of Pleas and Quarter Sessions to be held at the Court House in Elizabeth City on the 1st Monday in June next for the County of Pasquotank To Liberate and Set free the Said Negro Woman Rose and her Children John & Perthena -- that they may have the same Rights and Priviledges that is allowed by Law to People of Colour in this State   And that they may be Call'd and Known by the Names of Rose, John & Parthena Brown
    And as in deauty Bound Your Petitioners Will ever Pray &c
17th May 1804

Christopher Cartwright	T Freshwater
Jonathan Banks	his
Fred Jennings	Richard X Madkins
Thomas Stott	mark
John Pool	[?] Luten
W. Keaton	Benjamin Palmer
John Jervis	his
Ozios Overman	Joshua X West[?]
Hezekiah Cartwright	Thomas Markham
Wm Saunders	Joshua Robarts
Wm Gaskins	Charles Markham

Chapter 18: Pasquotank County Records

Jno. Brosher
Robert Pool
William Stott
Jos. Fox
Benjn. Maddux
Nathan Overman
    His
Thomas X Man
    Mark
Charles Wooton
Robert Markham
William Fox
William Cartwright
Const. Luten
Joseph Cartwright
Joseph Lacy
Benjamin Meeds
W Sanders
John Meeds
John Berry
Hugh Knox
John McDonald
Enoch Bundy
Wm. Nicholson
Wm. Symons

John Keaton Junr.
Nehemiah Pendleton
Isaac Keaton
Simon Brosher
James Pool
Joseph B. Pool
J Robertson
Robt. Lowry
Demcey Jennings
Henry A Snowdon
Stephen Barns
Henry Keaton
Thomas Cartwright
Jesse Trueblood
Henley Nicholson
Stephen Keaton
John Palmer
Wm. Chalke
Benj Lowry
Thomas Wood
William Davis
Robert Avery
Wm Wilson
W Henly
Ch[?] Cartwright

****

Joseph Riddicks Bond

Know all men by these presents that We Joseph Riddick of Gates County & Col John Koen & Col John Hamilton of Pasquotank County, are held and firmly bound Unto the Chairman of the Court of please & Quarter Sessions, for the County of Pasquotank, and his Successors in office in the Sum of two Hundred Dollars, for the true payment of which we bind ourselves jointly & Severally firmly by these presents, sealed with our Seals and dated this Seventh day of Sept 1802.

The Condition of the above Obligation is Such, that Whereas the above bounden Joseph Riddick having prayed the Worshipful Court of the County of Pasquotank, for a Certificate or permit for a Certain Negro Man Sesar, the property of Sd. Riddick, to keep a Gun for the purpose of Hunting &c On Sd. Riddick Land and plantation, in Sd. County of Pasquotank, by the Name of Makeshift, Now if the Said Negro sesar Use his Gun With Care and fedility & Without injury to any of the Citizens of the County aforesaid, the above obligation to be Null & Void Otherwise to remain in full force & Virtue

Signed & Sealed the day and date above Said
Test W Banks

    Jo Riddick   (Seal)
    Jn Hamilton   (Seal)
    J Koen   (Seal)

****

Bond
John Boyd & als

State of North Carolina   }
Pasquotank County   }March Term 1805

Chapter 18: Pasquotank County Records

   Know all men by these presents that we John Boyd and William T Muse of the County aforesaid are held and firmly bound unto John Smithson Esquire Chairman of the County Court of Pleas and Quarter Sessions for the County aforesaid in the full & Just Sum of One hundred pounds to be pd. To the sd. Chairman or to his Successors in office, To the which payment well and Truly to be made and done, we bind Ourselves our heirs Executors & Admors Jointly and Severally firmly by these presents, Sealed with our seals and dated the 7th day of March 1805

The Condition of the above Obligation is such that whereas John Boyd by his Petition has liberated and set free from Slavery a negroe Woman named Betty, Now if the above bounden John Boyd and William T Muse their heirs Exors or Admors or any of them do and shall from time to time and at all times hereafter Acquit discharge and save harmless the Overseers of the Poor and Inhabitants of the County aforesaid from all Costs Charges and troubles whatsoever for and by reason of the liberation of the said negroe Slave Betty and of and from all other suits Charges and Demands whatsoever touching and Concerning the same then the above Obligation to be void otherwise to remain in full force and Virtue.

Sealed & Delivered }	John Boyd	(Seal)
In the presence of }	Will: T. Muse	(Seal)
Wm Spencer[?]		

****

William Muse Esquire

Hugh Knox respecting
The emancipation of Negro Woman
Fereba the Wife of Harey Knox

William Muse Esquire
   Dear Sir
      The Bearer hereof Harry has Call'd on me this Morning on his way to Court in Order to endeavour to get the Sanction of the Honorable Court for the freedom of his Wife Ferebee, and tells me that he should do Well to get some Instrument of Writing from Under My hand to that Purpose, I feel myself Perfectly at a loss for a form and cant see why it is necessary for me to Particularly as I have no More claim to him or his Wife than any other Person, The Court having Freed the Said Hary at my request & I have sold him his Wife since he has been a free Man Which Proceedings I Presume has been regularly recorded, But if my consent for the freedom of his Wife is only wanting I give it with Freedom
I am Dear Sir your Sincere friend   Hugh Knox
2d December 1806
Granted

Emancipation Bond
Ferebee Knox
Decr. Term 1806

State of North Carolina }	
Pasquotank County }	December Term 1806

Know all men by these presents that we Harry Knox, William T Muse & George AL Conner of the County aforesaid are held and firmly bound unto John Smithson Esquire Chairman of the County Court of Pleas and Quarter Sessions for the County aforesaid or to his Successors in Office in the Sum of one hundred pounds, To the Which payment well and Truly to be made and done, we bind ourselves our heirs Executors and Administrators Jointly and Severally formly by these presents, Sealed with our Seals and dated the 2d day of December 1806.

The Condition of the above Obligation is such that Whereas Harry Knox by his Petition has liberated and set free from Slavery a negro woman named Ferebee Now if the above bounden Harry Knox Wm T. Muse & George AL Conner their heirs Exors or Admors. Or any of them do and shall from time to time and at all times hereafter Acquit discharge

Chapter 18: Pasquotank County Records

and save harmless the Overseers of the Poor and Inhabitants of the County aforesaid from all Costs Charges and troubles whatsoever for and by reason of the liberation of the said negro Slave Ferebee And of and from all other suits Charges and demands whatsoever touching and Concerning the Same; then the above Obligation to be Void otherwise to remain in full force and Virtue

Sealed & Delivered
In the presence of

                his
              Harry X Knox (Seal)
                Mark

Will: T. Muse (Seal)
Geo AL Conner (Seal)

***

Emancipation Bond
John L Brosher & als
For Negro Judah & her
Child Weeks
June 1806

State of North Carolina }
Pasquotank County   } June Term 1806

Know all men by these presents that we John L. Brosher & McKeel Cartwright of the County aforesaid are held and firmly bound unto John Smithson Esquire Chairman of the County Court of Pleas and Quarter Sessions for the County aforesaid or to his Successors in office in the sum of **[Blank]** pounds, To the which payment well and truly to be made we bind ourselves our heirs Executors and Admors. Jointly and Severally firmly by these presents, Sealed with our Seals and dated the 5th day of June 1806

The Condition of the above obligation is such that whereas John L. Brosher by his Petition has liberated an set free from slavery a negro Woman named Judah & her Child Weeks Now if the above bounden Jno. L. Brosher & McKeel Cartwright their heirs Exors. or Admors. or any of them do and shall from time to time and at all times hereafter Acquit discharge and save harmless the Overseers of the Poor and Inhabitants of the County aforesaid from all Costs Charges and troubles whatsoever for and by reason of the liberation of the said Judah & Weeks And of and from all other Suits Charges and Demands whatsoever touching and Concerning the Same, then the above obligation to be void, Otherwise to remain in full force & Virtue

Sealed & delivered   John L Brosher (Seal)
In the presenc of   Mc. Cartwright (Seal)
Will: T. Muse Clk

***

Bond for Emancipation
John McDonald & als
For Ned & Rose
Decr 1807

State of North Carolina }
Pasquotank County   } December Term 1807

Know all Men by these presents, that we John McDonald William Wilson & John Boyd of the County aforesaid are held and firmly bound unto John Smithson Esquire Chairman of the County Court of Pleas and Quarter Sessions for the County aforesaid, or to his Successors in Office, in the sum of Two hundred pounds - To the Which Payment Well and truly to be made and done, We bind ourselves our Heirs Executors and Admnrs. Jointly and Severally firmly by these presents Sealed with our Seals, and dated the 9th day of Decr 1807

Chapter 18: Pasquotank County Records

The Condition of the above Obligation is such, that Whereas the above bounden John McDonald hath with the Approbation of the Court, liberated and set Free from Slavery a Negro Man & Woman named Ned & Rose   Now if the above bounden John McDonald, Wm. Wilson & John Boyd their Heirs or Admrs., or any of them do and shall from time to time and at all times hereafter Acquit discharge, and save harmless the Overseers of the Poor and Inhabitants of the said County, from all Costs Charges and troubles Whatsoever for and by reason of the liberation of the said Negro Slaves Ned & Rose   and of and from all other Suits Charges and demands Whatsoever touching and Concerning the same then the above Obligation to be Void, Otherwise to remain in full force and Virtue.

Sealed & Delivered	Jno. McDonald	(Seal)
In the presence of	John Boyd	(Seal)
Will. T. Muse Clk	Wm. Wilson	(Seal)

****

Bond
John McDonald & als for
Wm Farange**[Marked Through]**
Emancipation of Penny
March 1803

State of North Carolina   }
Pasquotank County   }March Term 1803

Know all men by these presents that we John McDonald, Charles Grice and William Templeman Muse are held and firmly bound unto John Smithson Esquire Chairman of the County Court of Pleas and Quarter Sessions for the County aforesaid, in the sum of One hundred pounds to be paid to the said Chairman or his Successors in office, To the which payment well and truly to be made, we bind ourselves, our heirs Executors and Administrators, Jointly and severally firmly by these presents, sealed with our seals and dated this 12th day of March 1803.

The Condition of the above Obligation is such that Whereas negroe woman Penny a slave lately belonging to the Estate of Sylvester Hosener deceased hath been this day on Petition of William Farange her present owner liberated and set free from slavery for meritorious services in as full and ample manner as the Laws of the said State will admit; Now if the above bound John, Charles, and William their heirs Executors or Administrators or any of them, do and shall from time to time and at all times hereafter Acquit discharge and save harmless the Overseers of the Poor and Inhabitants of the County aforesaid, from all Costs Charges and troubles whatsoever for and by reason of the liberation of the said Penny and of and from all suits Charges and demands whatsoever touching and Concerning her liberation then the above Obligation to be void otherwise to be and remain in full force and Virtue.

Sealed and Delivered	Charles Grice	(Seal)
In the presence of	Jno. McDonald	(Seal)
	Will: T. Muse	(Seal)

****

Bond
Benja. Pendleton & als
March 1803

State of North Carolina   }
Pasquotank County   } March Term 1803

Know all men by these presents that we Benjamin Pendleton, Joseph L. Brosher and James Jackson are held and firmly bound unto John Smithson Esquire Chairman of the County Court of Pleas and Quarter Sessions for the County aforesaid in the sum of one hundred pounds to be paid to the said Chairman or his Successors in office, To the which

Chapter 18: Pasquotank County Records

payment well and truly to be made, we bind ourselves, our heirs Executors and Administrators Jointly and severally firmly by these presents, sealed with our seals and dated this 12th day of March 1803.

The Condition of the above Obligation is such that Whereas negroe man Ben a slave lately belonging to the Estate of Sarah Pendleton deceased hath been this day on Petition of Benjamin Pendleton Executor of the last will and Testament of the said Sarah, liberated and set free from slavery for meritorious services in as full and ample manner as the laws of the said state will Admit; Now if the above bound Benjamin, Joseph and James their heirs Executors or Administrators or any of them do and shall from time to time and at all times hereafter Acquit discharge and save harmless the Overseers of the Poor and Inhabitants of the County aforesaid, from all Costs Charges and troubles whatsoever for and by reason of the liberation of the said Benjamin and of and from all suits Charges and Demands whatsoever touching and Concerning her liberation then the above obligation to be void otherwise to be and remain in full force and Virtue.

Sealed and Delivered	Benjamin Pendleton	(Seal)
In the presence of	Jos. L. Brosher	(Seal)
Wm Spence	Jas. Jackson	(Seal)

****

Bond
Richard P. Morris & als
Decr. 1806

State of North Carolina }
Pasquotank County } December Term 1804

Know all men by these presents that we Rd. P. Morris William Wilson and William T. Muse of the County aforesaid are held and firmly bound unto John Smithson Esquire Chairman of the County Court of Pleas and Quarter Sessions for the County aforesaid or to his Successors in office, To the which payment well and truly to be made and Done, we bind ourselves our heirs Executors and Administrators, Jointly and Severally firmly by these presents, Sealed with our Seals and Dated the 5th day of December 1804.

The Condition of the above Obligation is such that whereas Rd. P. Morris by his Petition has liberated and set free from slavery a negro Woman named Rose about Forty two years of age, Now if the above bounden Rd. Morris and Wm. Wilson & Wm. T. Muse their heirs Executors or Administrators or any of them do and shall from time to time and at all times hereafter acquit discharge and save harmless the Overseers of the Poor and Inhabitants of the County aforesaid from all Costs Charges and troubles whatsoever for and by reason of the liberation of the said negroe slave Rose and of and from all other suits Charges and Demands whatsoever touching and Concerning the same, then the above Obligation to be void otherwise to remain in full force & Virtue.

Sealed & Delivered }	Richard P. Morris	(Seal)
In the presence of }	Wm. Wilson	(Seal)
	Will: T. Muse	(Seal)

****

Bond
John Mitchell & als

State of North Carolina }
Pasquotank County }September Term 1804

Know all Men by these presents that we John Mitchell, William Proby and John McDonald of the County aforesaid Are held and firmly bound unto John Smithson Esquire Chairman of the County Court of Pleas and Quarter sessions for the County aforesaid or to his Successors in office, to the which payment well and truly to be made and done, We bind ourselves our heirs Executors and Administrators, Jointly and Severally firmly by these presents, Sealed with our Seals and dated the 7th day of Sepr. 1804

Chapter 18: Pasquotank County Records

The Condition of the above Obligation is such that Whereas John Mitchell by his Petition has liberated and set free from Slavery a Negro Woman named Jean about Forty five years of age, Now if the above bounden John Mitchell and Wm Proby & Jno McDonald their heirs Executors or Admors. or any of them do and shall from time to time and at all times hereafter Acquit discharge and save harmless the Overseers of the poor and Inhabitants of the County aforesaid from all Costs Charges and troubles whatsoever for and by reason of the liberation of the said negro slave Jean and of and from all other suits Charges and demands whatsoever touching and Concerning the same, then the above Obligation to be Void otherwise to remain in full force and Virtue.

Sealed and Delivered	}	John Mitchell	(Seal)
In the presence of	}	Jno. McDonald	(Seal)
Will: T. Muse Clk	}	William Proby	(Seal)

****

Bond
John Winslow & als
Sep. 1804
David Perry

State of North Carolina }
Pasquotank County } September Term 1804

    Know all Men by these Presents that We John Winslow Thos. Low & Benjamin White of the County aforesaid are held and firmly bound unto John Smithson Esquire Chairman of the County Court of Pleas and Quarter Sessions for the County aforesaid or to his Successors in Office - To the which payment well and truly to be made and done, We bind ourselves our Heirs Executors and Administrators, Jointly and Severally firmly by these presents Sealed with our Seals and dated this 6th day of September Anno Dom 1806.

The Condition of the above Obligation is such, that Whereas Josiah Perry by his Petition has liberated and set free from slavery named David about Fifty years of age, Now if the above bounden John Winslow Thomas Low and Benja. White their Heirs Executors or Admors or any of them, do and shall from time to time and at all times hereafter Acquit discharge and save harmless, the Overseers of the Poor and inhabitants of the County aforesaid, from all Costs Charges and troubles whatsoever for and by reason of the liberation of the said Negro Slave David, and of and from all other suits, Charges and demands whatsoever touching and Concerning the same, then the above Obligation to be void, otherwise to Remain in full force and Virtue

Sealed and delivered	}	John Winslow	(Seal)
In the Presence of	}	his	
Will: T. Muse Clk	}	Thos. X Low	(Seal)
		Mark	
		Benjn White	(Seal)

****

Bond
Hugh Knox & als

State of North Carolina }
Pasquotank County }

Know all Men by these presents that we Hugh Knox, Samuel Newbould, & Wm. Wilson of the County aforesaid are held and firmly bound unto John Smithson Esquire Chairman of the County Court of Pleas and Quarter Sessions for the County aforesaid or to his Successors in office in the Sum of One hundred pounds, To the which payment well and truly to be made and done, we bind ourselves our heirs Executors and Administrators Jointly and Severally firmly by these presents Sealed with our Seals and dated the 5th day of Septr. 1805

Chapter 18: Pasquotank County Records

The Condition of the above obligation is such that Whereas Hugh Knox by his Petition has liberated and set free from slavery a negroe Man named Harry Senr about Forty Seven years of age Now if the above bounden Hugh Knox **[Blank]** their heirs Executors or Administrators or any of them do and shall from time to time and at all times hereafter discharge and save harmless the Overseers of the Poor and Inhabitants of the County aforesaid from all Costs Charges and troubles whatsoever for and by reason of the liberation of the said negroe Slave Harry, and of and from all other suits Charges and Demands whatsoever touching and Concerning the Same, then the above obligation to be void otherwise to remain in full force and Virtue

Sealed & Delivered	Hugh Knox (Seal)
In the presence of	S Newbould (Seal)
Will: T. Muse	Wm. Wilson (Seal)

****

Bond
James Nixon & als

December Term 1805

The Within Bond not having been Signed at the last Term and it Appearing to the Court that Jas. Nixon is since dead it is Ordered that the Sd. Emancipation be Confirmed on the within Negro Isaac's giving Bond with Miles Jackson & Thos. Cartwright as Securities
Test
Will: T. Muse Clk
March 6. 1806

State of North Carolina   }
PasquotankCounty   } December Term 1805.

Know all men by these presents that we Miles Jackson and Thomas Cartwright of the County aforesaid are held and firmly bound unto John Smithson Esquire Chairman of the County Court of Pleas and Quarter Sessions, for the County aforesaid or to his Successors in Office, in the sum of One hundred pounds to the which payment well and truly to be made and done, we bind ourselves our heirs Executors and Administrators, Jointly and Severally firmly by these presents, Sealed with our Seals and Dated the 5th day of December 1805.

The Condition of the above Obligation is such that Whereas James Nixon by his Petition has liberated and set free from Slavery a negro Man Named Isaac - Now if the above bounden Miles Jackson & Thos Cartwright their heirs Exors or Admors or any of them do and shall from time to time and at all times hereafter Acquit discharge and Save harmless the Overseers of the Poor and Inhabitants of the County aforesaid from all Costs Charges and troubles whatsoever for and by reason of the liberation of the said Negro Slave Isaac and of and from all other suits Charges and Demands whatsoever touching and Concerning the Same, then the above Obligation to be Void, otherwise to remain in full force and Virtue

Sealed and Delivered }	his	
In the presence of }	Miles X Jackson	(Seal)
	Mark	
Will: T. Muse Clk	Thos Cartwright	(Seal)

****

Wm. T. Muse
To} Peto. For Freedom
The Court
X--836
Negro Woman Phillis
Granted Decr. Term 1810

Chapter 18: Pasquotank County Records

State of North Carolina }
Pasquotank County } December Term 1810

To the Worshipful the Justices of the County aforesaid, The Petition of William T. Muse Sheweth, That Negro Woman Phillis, Who belonged in the Family of the late Enoch Relfe Esqr. For many years, and to your Petitioner for more than eight years past, has as far as he hath always understood Conducted herself in a very Meritorious Manner, And in Consequence thereof, Your Petitioner is desirous that she should be liberated & set free from Slavery under the laws in such Cases provided & he submits the same to the Approbation of your Worships &c.

Jas. L Shannonhouse	Will: T. Muse
Thomas Davis	Jos. Parker
John Cook	Wm Spence

****

Bond
William T Brothers & als

State of North Carolina }
Pasquotank County } December Term 1810

Know all Men by these presents that we, William Brothers William T Muse and Thomas Davis of the County of Pasquotank are held and firmly bound unto David Pritchard Esquire Chairman of the County Court of Pleas and Quarter Sessions for the County aforesaid, or to his Successors in Office, in the sum of One hundred pounds, To the which payment well and truly to be made and done, We bind ourselves our Heirs Executors and Admrs. Jointly and Severally firmly by these presents Sealed with our seals and dated the 5th day of Decemr. 1810

The Condition of the above Obligation is Such that whereas the Above bounden William Brothers hath, With the Approbation of the Court, liberated and Set Free from Slavery a Negro Woman Slave named Molly. Now if the above bounden William Brothers, William T. Muse, and Thomas Davis their Heirs Executors or Admrs. Or any of them do and shall from time to time and at all times hereafter Acquit, discharge and save harmless the Overseers of the Poor and Inhabitants of the said County, from all Costs Charges and troubles whatsoever for and by reason of the liberation of the Said Negro Slave Molly and of and from all other Suits Charges and demands whatsoever touching and Concerning the same then the above obligation to be Void, otherwise to remain in full force and Virtue

Sealed and Delivered }	his	
In the presence of }	William X Brothers	(Seal)
Richard Muse	mark	
	Will: T. Muse	(Seal)
	Thomas Davis	(Seal)

****

Samuel Warren
To} Peto. For freedom of Doctr Jack
The Court
X--844
Granted Decr Term 1810

State of North Carolina
Pasquotank County Court Decemr Term 1810

To the Worshipful Court

Chapter 18: Pasquotank County Records

The Petition of Samuel Warren Humbly Sheweth That he is in possession of a Negro Man slave named Jack commonly called Doctor Jack which slave he has long owned & for whose faithful & meritorious services he wishes to remunerate him on exemplary manner and therefore Prays your Worships that the said Negroe Slave may be emancipated pursuant to Law & your Petitioner as in Duty bound will ever pray &c.

Will Blair for
The Petitioner

****

William Brothers
To} Peto. For Freedom
The Court
Of his Wife Molly
X--742
Granted Decr Term 1800

The within Granted on the Petition giving Bond agreeable to Law for the Court
Thos Nicholson

August 30th Day 1808 Recd. From William Brothers the sum of three Dollars and fifty Cents in full Pay for His wife Molly that he Bought at my Brothers Sale
Jesse Riding

State of No. Carolina   }
Pasquotank County   } March Term 1810

    The Worshipful the Justices of the County Court of Pasquotank aforesaid, The Petition of William Brothers, Humbly Sheweth, That some Years ago he was liberated by this Worshipful Court, Since then he has Purchased his Wife Molly that heretofore resided in the family of the late Colo. Riding, and as far as he believes always conducted herself in a Very Meritorious Manner, Your Petitioner therefore Prays that your Worships Would liberate & Set her free from Slavery under the Act of Assembly in Such Cases Provided - And your Petitioner Will &c.

Test. Will: T. Muse
Jas. L. Shannonhouse
Thomas Davis
Gabl. Bailey
HP [?]

                                                    his
                                      William X Brothers
                                           mark

****

William Jordan Per Agent
To} Pet.
The Court
X--753

Granted on giving Bond Security
Agreeable to law

To the Worshipful the Justices of the County Court of Pleas and Quarter sessions of Pasquotank County
    The Petition of William Jordan late a Citizen of the County aforesaid, and now a resident of the County of Isle of Wight in Virginia, Sheweth that he hath lately sold his lands in the County of Pasquotank aforesaid, and by the laws of the State in Which he resides, he is not permitted to remove his Slaves there, and having one among them called Tom otherwise Young Tom Who hath always Conducted himself Very Meritoriously toward Your Petitioner, and not being desirous in Consequence thereof of hiring him out as a Common Slave, begs that your Worships would liberate & set him free from Slavery under the Act of assembly in Such Cases Provided and your Petitioner &c

Chapter 18: Pasquotank County Records

Per Authority from
William Jordan
Will: T. Muse
March 3rd 1810.

We Whose Names are under Written, are Well Acquainted with the above Named Negro Tom & recommend the Worshipful Court to grant the prayer of the above Petition

	Hugh Knox	
Andrew Knox	Henry P. Overman	
	Thomas Jordan	
John Cook	Nehe. Pendleton	
	Jas. L. Shannonhouse	
Wm. Wilson	Nathan Overman	Wm Spence[?]
T. Freshwater	John McDonald	Jos Z. Keaton

****

Primus Knox
To} Petition
The Court
Granted
X--948

To the Worshipful the County Court of Pleas and Quarter Sessions for the County of Pasquotank

    The Petition of Harry Knox humbly sheweth unto your Worships, that Primus Knox the Brother and property of your Petitioner, is desirous of being liberated and set free from slavery   his former services, his upright, and Uniform good Conduct through life, he trusts will entitle him to some favor from your Worships, he has paid and fully satisfied your Petitioner the sum Advanced from him, he further shews unto your Worships that he is now sixty Years of Age and wishes to have permission to retire in peace with his Old companion, to spend the remainder of his days without injury to any person whatsoever, he is ready to Comply with the requisitions of the Law in such Cases made and provided ---
And Your Petitioner as in duty bound will ever pray

	his
William Spencer[?]	Harry X Knox
Richard Muse	mark
Ambrose Knox	Will: T. Muse
Thomas Davis	Andrew Knox
Hugh Knox	Wm Wilson
T Freshwater	John McDonald
Jos. L. keaton	George R. Henley
William Crutch[?]	William C George
Nehe. Pendleton	Jos. Blount

The prayer of the Petitioner is granted on Security being given that the Petitioner give Security against becoming a County Charge

Bailey Jackson
John Shaw
Josiah White

Bond
Harry Knox & als
For Primus

State of North Carolina   }
Pasquotank County   }

Chapter 18: Pasquotank County Records

Know all Men by these presents that we Harry Knox Hugh Knox and William T Muse of the County of Pasquotank are held and firmly bound unto David Pritchard Esqr. Chairman of the County Court of Pleas and Quarter Sessions for the County aforesaid, or to his Successors in Office, in the sum of one hundred pounds, To the which payment well and truly to be made and done we bind ourselves our heirs Executors and Admrs. Jointly and severally firmly by these presents sealed with our seals and dated the 10th day of Decemr. 1812

The Condition of the above Obligation is such that Whereas the above bounden Harry Knox hath with the Approbation of the Court, liberated and set Free from slavery a Negro Man Slave Named Primus Now if the above bounden Harry Knox & others their Heirs Executors or admrs. Or any of them do and shall from time to time and at all times hereafter Acquit discharge and save harmless the Overseers of the Poor and Inhabitants of the said County from all Costs Charges and troubles whatsoever for and by reason of the liberation of the said Negro Slave Primus and of and from other suits charges and demands Whatsoever touching and Concerning the same then this Obligation to be void otherwise to remain in full force and virtue

Sealed & delivered   }   his
In the presence of   }   Harry X Knox   (Seal)
Richd. Muse as to H. Knox   mark
                                                              Hugh Knox   (Seal)

****

Penelope Swann
To} Peto. Emancipation
The Court
X--987
March Term 1812
J.N. atto.

State of North Carolina   }
Pasquo. County Court   } March Term 1812

To the Worshipful the County Court of Pleas and Quarter Sessions for the County aforesaid
    The Petition of Penelope Swann respectfully sheweth unto Your Worships that she is the owner of a certain negro Slave, named Hannibal, who she is desirous should be liberated and set free, May it please Your Worships to grant and direct the Clerk to make the necessary orders, when the requisites of the Acts of Assembly for such cases made and provided shall be complied with, And Your Petitioner as in duty bound will ever pray &c.
Jas. Norfleet Atto Pet

Granted

****

Ruth Evergans Peto.
Granted

State of North Carolina   }
Pasquotank County   } June Term 1813

    To the Worshipful the County Court of Pasquotank   The Petition of us whose Names are under Signed humbly Sheweth unto your worships that Ruth Evergain has Purchased from Thomas R Stamp her Husband whose name is Jonas and has paid him the said Stamp the full amount of the Purchase money which will appear by a Bill of Sale now on your Records also that he the Said Jonas is now Considerable Advanced in years and that he has always Conducted himself in an orderly Manner to his Master as well as to us your Petitioners   Your Petitioners therefore Pray your

Chapter 18: Pasquotank County Records

Worships to grant him the said Jonas his liberty so that he may Injoy all the Rights and Priviledges which all Persons of Color are Intitled to and your Petitioners &c

If the Petitioner, Jonas, can give Security as the Law requires, I think it would be humanity in the Court to grant his prayer.
          Wm. Wilson

Thomas Banks	Stephen Scott
Ben Loury	William [Faded]
Hugh Knox	T Freshwater
Ambrose Knox	Beno Keaton
William Crutch	G.W. Pendleton
Stephen Keaton	Jas Jackson
Will T. Muse	Jno. McDonald

****

          Peto. For Emancipation
          Of Negro Joseph
          Granted
          X--1173

We the Undersigned do Approve of the within Petition and pray the Court to grant an Order for the Within purpose.
Will. T. Muse
Thos Shannonhouse
Je[?] Go[?]
Charles Grice
John Shaw
Saml Jones

State of North Carolina }
Pasquotank County   } 3rd Mo:3rd Day 1813

    To the County Court of Please & Quarter sessions now Setting

    Humbly Sheweth, that your Petitioners is now in possession of a Negro Man by the name of Joseph Formerly the Property of William Jordan of the State of Virginia, Who in his will give to the trustees of the Society of Friends of North Carolina on Purpose that they might procure unto him the said Joseph his freedom, Now what your aforesaid Petitioners Request is that the Court Order his Emancipation, and your Complying therein will Much Oblige Your Petitioners and Thankfull friends

Yearly Meeting Trustees }	Josiah Bundy
Agreed by the Court }	Thomas Jordan
	Joshua Trueblood
	Nathan Trueblood
	John Shaw

****

          Peto. For Emancipation of
          Negroes Tom & Tamer
          X--1173

We the Undersigned do Approve of the Within petition and pray the Court to grant on Order for the within purpose.
          Will: T. Muse
          Stephen Charles

Chapter 18: Pasquotank County Records

Thos Shannonhouse
JD G[?]
Charles Grice
John Shaw
Saml Jones

State of North Carolina }
Pasquotank County }3rd Mo 1813

To the County Court of Please and quarter Sessions now Setting

Humbly Sheweth that your Petitioner is now in Possession of two Negroes by the names of Thomas & Tamer formerly the Property of William Jordan of Virginia who in his Will give to the Trusteese of the Society of Friends of No. Carolina on Purpose that they might Procure unto them the aforesaid Thomas & Tamer, their freedom. Now what your aforesaid Petitioners Request is that the Court Order their Emancipation & your Complying therein will much Oblige your Petitioners and Thankfull Friends

Yearly Meeting Trustees }	Josiah Bundy
Agreed by the Court. }	Thomas Jordan
}	Joshua Trueblood
}	Nathan Trueblood

Bond
Joshua Trueblood
Tom & Tamer
March Term 1813

State of North Carolina }
Pasquotank County } Ss.

Know all Men by these presents That we Joshua Trueblood Isaac Overman & William T. Muse of the County of Pasquotank, are held and firmly bound unto David Pritchard Esquire, Chairman of the Court of Pleas and Quarter Sessions for the County aforesaid or to his Successors in Office in the Sum of Two Hundred pounds, To the which payment well and truly to be made and done, We bind ourselves our heirs executors and Administrators jointly and severally firmly by these presents, Sealed with our Seal and dated the 4th day of March 1813

The Condition of the above Obligation is such, That Whereas the above bounden Joshua Trueblood hath with the approbation of the Court liberated and set free from Slavery two Negroes named Tom & Tamer Now if the above bounden Joshua Trueblood & others their heirs Exors Admors or any of them do and shall from time to time and at all times hereafter, Acquit, discharge and save harmless the Overseers of the Poor and inhabitants of the said County from all Costs, Charges and troubles whatsoever from and by reason of the liberation of the said Negroe Slaves Tom and Tamer, and of and from all other Suits, Charges and demands whatsoever touching and concerning the same then the above obligation to be void, otherwise to remain in full force and virtue.

Sealed and delivered	Joshua Trueblood	(Seal)
In the presence of	Isaac Overman	(Seal)
Richard Muse	Will: T. Muse	(Seal)

****

Thomas Jordan Junr. & others
To} Petition for the Liberation of Negro Woman
The Court
X--1344

To the Worshipful the Inferior Court of Pleas and Quarter Sessions for the County of Pasquotank Now Sitting

Chapter 18: Pasquotank County Records

The Petition of Thomas Jordan Junier David Williams and others Inhabitants of the said County Humbly Shew Your Worships that having in his possession a Negro Woman named Tamar (the Widow of John Warner a free person of Colour,) well known in many parts of the County as a good Midwife, And the said Jordan being in particular manner desirous as a Compensation for her many faithful Services, to liberate her, Who with the other Subscribers hereto, do humbly pray Your Worships to grant an Order for the above laudable purpose -- And Your petitioners as in duty bound will ever pray &c

September Term 1813

             Thomas Jordan
             David L Williams
             Will: T. Muse
             Richard Muse
             W Carter
             Wm Gregory

***

Petition

To the Worshipful the Court of Pleas & Quarter Sessions held for the County of Pasquotank December Term 1814.

The Petition of Jenney Pearson having some time past purchased her Husband by the Name of Richard from James L Shannonhouse attorney of Robert McMorine Esquire, as per his bill of Sale Accompanying this may appear, and is now the whole and Sole property of your petitioner, And your said Petitioner being desirous that her said husband should enjoy every priviledge that herself is intitled to, Humbly pray your Worships to take the Matter into Consideration and grant an Order for the Emancipation of the said Richard by the Name of Richard Pearson, and Your Petitioner as in duty bound will ever pray &c

                              Jenney Pearson

We the undersigned being Well Acquainted with the within mentioned Slave by the name of Richard late the property of Robert McMorine & formerly that of Colo. Thos. Harvy and Colo. Edward Evergain, and believe him to be a person of an upright Character, and therefore hope the Worshipful Court may Consider him as an Object worthy of his freedom and enlargement, as other free persons of Colour, and grant the Same agreeable to the within Petition of his wife Jenny Pearson.

December 1st 1814.

Thomas Jordan	Thomas Davis
Natha Jackson	Briant Brothers
Bailey Davis	Asa Jackson
Frederick Fletcher	Jas. McAdam
Stephn. Mullin	Samuel Trueblood
John Pool Senr.	Adam[?] Davis
Benja. Bailey	

                 Bond
              Jenny Pearson & als

State of North Carolina }
Pasquotank County   }

Know All men by these presents that we Jenny Pearson, William T. Muse and Miles Davis of the County of Pasquotank are held and firmly bound unto David Pritchard Esquire Chairman of the County Court of Pleas and quarter Sessions for the County aforesaid, or to his Successor in office in the Sum of One hundred pounds, To which payment well and truly to be made and done we bind ourselves our heirs Executors and Administrators Jointly and Severally firmly by these presents Sealed with our Seals and dated the 7th day of Decemr. 1814

Chapter 18: Pasquotank County Records

The Condition of the above Obligation is such that Whereas the above Jenny Pearson hath with the approbation of the Court liberated and set free from Slavery a Negro Man Slave named Dick, Now if the above bounden Jenney Pearson & als their heirs Executors or Administrators or any of them do and shall from time to time and at all times hereafter Acquit discharge and save harmless the Overseers of the Poor and inhabitants of the said County from all Costs Charges and trouble Whatsoever for and by reason of the liberation of the said Negro Dick and of and from all Other Suits Charges and demands whatsoever touching and Concerning the same the above obligation to be void otherwise to remain in full force and Virtue

Sealed and delivered }		her
In the presence of }	Jenny X Pearson	(Seal)
Richard Muse	mark	
	Will: T. Muse	(Seal)
	Miles Davis	(Seal)

****

Simon L Brosher & others
To} Petn. For Emancipation
The Court
X--1419

To the Worshipful the Court of Pleas & quarter Sessions held for the County of Pasquotank Now Sitting.
  The Petition of Simon L Brosher, and others Inhabitants of said County, Humbly Sheweth
    That Your Petitioner having under him, a Certain Negro man Slave by the name of Caesar, which your said Petitioner is desirous of emancipating for and in consideration of his faithful Services hitherto rendered to your said Petitioner as an excellent Blacksmith he being a person well known as to his peaceable and Civil Department. Your Petitioners therefore Pray Your Worships to grant an Order to Liberate the aforesaid Caesar by the Name of Caesar Harvey and that he may be entitled to the Priviledges that other free persons of Colour enjoy under the Laws of the State in Such Cases -- And your Petitioners as in duty bound will ever pray &c

June 6th 1814

Simon L Brosher	Asa Sanderlin
Joshua Lowe[?]	Nat[?] Jackson
Ben Loury	W Carter
Thomas Knights	Wm Gregory
John Davis	Enoch Sawyer
Richard Muse	Thomas Davis
Jno. McDonald	Thos Pool
[?]	John Jennings

Bond
Wm. T. Muse & als
For Cesar Broshers
Emancipation

State of North Carolina }
Pasquotank County }

  Know all men by these presents that we William T Muse & John C Ehringhaus of the County of Pasquotank are held and firmly bound unto David Pritchard senr. Esquire Chairman of the County Court of Pleas and Quarter Sessions for the County aforesaid or to his Successors in office in the Sum of One hundred pounds. To the which payment Well & truly to be made and done, We bind ourselves our heirs Executors and Administrators Jointly & Severally firmly by these presents, Sealed With our Seals & dated the 9th day of December one thousand eight hundred and fourteen
  The Condition of the above Obligation is such that Whereas Simon Brosher hath with the approbation of the Court liberated and set free from Slavery a Negro man named Ceasar   Now if the above bounden William T. Muse &

Chapter 18: Pasquotank County Records

John C Ehringhaus their heirs Executors Administrators or any of them do and shall from time to time and at all times hereafter acquit discharge and save harmless the Overseers of the Poor and Inhabitants of the said County from all Costs Charges & Troubles whatsoever for and by reason of the liberation of the said Negro Cesar Brosher and of and from all other Suits Charges and demands whatsoever touching and Concerning the same, the above obligation to be void, otherwise to remain in full force and virtue

Sealed and delivered in }	Will: T. Muse	(Seal)
The presence of }	John C Ehringhaus	(Seal)

****

George Ott To the Court
Petition for Emancipation
X--1422

The within Petition is granted

State of North Carolina } September Term 1814
Pasquotank County } To the County Court

    Your Petitioner George Ott Humbly shews that he is the Proprietor of two negro Slaves one named Charles & the other Rose who is his wife, both of which he believes to be honest industrious and worthy of trust: And both of which from their honesty & fidelity and meritorious services he wishes to be emancipated in the manner provided under the provisions of our Acts of Assembly

    He further shews that he is willing to comply with the requisites of the law in such cases made and provided. He therefore prays that your Worships Emancipate the said negroes Charles & Rose his wife on your Petitioner complying with the requisites of the Law in such cases

For George Ott
John C. Ehringhaus: Agent

Bond
George Ott & als

State of North Carolina }
Pasquotank County }

    Know all men by these presents that we George Ott John C. Ehringhaus & William Carter of the County of Pasquotank are held and firmly bound unto David Pritchard Esquire Chairman of the County Court of Pleas and quarter Sessions for the County aforesaid or to his Successors in Office in the sum of two hundred pounds To which payment well & truly to be made and done we bind ourselves our heirs Executors and Admrs. Jointly and Severally firmly by these presents sealed with our seals and dated this 8th day of December 1814

    The Condition of the above obligation is such that whereas the above George Ott hath with the approbation of the Court liberated and set Free from Slavery a Negroe Man & Woman Slave named Charles & Rosa Now if the above bounden George Ott John C Ehringhaus & William Carter and als their heirs Executors or administrators or any of them do and shall from time to time and at all times hereafter Acquit discharge and save harmless the Overseers of the poor and inhabitants of the said County from all Costs Charges and troubles whatsoever for and by reason of the liberation of the said Negroes and of and from all other Suits Charges and Demands Whatsoever touching and and concerning the same then the above Obligation to be void otherwise to remain in full force and Virtue

Sealed and delivered }	John Ehringhaus as Agent	(Seal)
In the presents of }	for George Ott	
	John C Ehringhaus	(Seal)
	W Carter	(Seal)

Chapter 18: Pasquotank County Records

****

Willm. T. Muse's Peto.
For the Emancipation
of Negro Joe
X--1632
Decr Term 1816
Granted on giving Bond &c
Will: T. Muse
(Now Joseph Stevenson)

State of North Carolina

    To the Worshipful the Justices of the County Court of Pleas & Quarter Sessions for the County of Pasquotank. The Petition of William T. Muse of the said County, Humbly Sheweth, That Negro Joe, Commonly called Joe the Blacksmith a Slave belongs to him, Who has for many years past conducted himself in a Very Meritorious manner generally, as well as to the several Masters he has had, and especially so, to your Petitioner - Your Petitioner is therefore on that Account, desirous that he should be liberated & set free from Slavery - May it therefore please your Worships to grant him the said Joe his freedom or Emancipation under the laws in such Cases Provided - And your Petitioner as in duty bound &c.

Will: T. Muse
Decr. Term 1816

Ordered that the Petition of Negro Man Joe as Respects his freedom be granted on his Masters Consent, and his giving Security to be kept Clear of the Parish for life
Decr Term 1816
Agreed to

Bond
For the liberation of
Joseph Stevenson
December Term 1816

State of North Carolina   }
Pasquotank County   }

    Know all men by these presents that we William T. Muse and Richard Muse of the County of Pasquotank are held and firmly bound unto David Pritchard Esquire Chairman of the County Court of Pleas and Quarter Sessions for the County aforesaid or to his Successors in office in the Sum of one hundred pounds. To which payment well and truly to be made and done we bind ourselves our heirs Executors and Administrators Jointly and Severally firmly by these presents sealed with our seals and dated the 5th December 1816.

    The Condition of the above obligation is such that whereas the above bounden Wm. T. Muse hath with the approbation of the Court, liberated and set free from Slavery a Negro Man Slave Named Joseph - now if the above bounden Wm. & Richard Muse their heirs Executors Administrators or any of them do and shall from time to time and at all times hereafter acquit discharge and save harmless the overseers of the Poor and Inhabitants of the said County from all Costs Charges and troubles whatsoever for and by reason of the liberation of the said Negro Joseph and of and from all other suits charges and demands whatsoever touching and Concerning the same the above obligation to be void otherwise to remain in full force and virtue

| Sealed and delivered In } | Will: T. Muse | (Seal) |
| The presence of } | Richard Muse | (Seal) |

****

Aaron Morris Senr.
To} Petition

Chapter 18: Pasquotank County Records

The Court
X--675

To the Worshipful the County Court of Pleas and Quarter Sessions for the County of Pasquotank

    The Petition of Aaron Morris Senior Humbly Sheweth, unto Your Worships, that he is desirous of Liberating and setting free from Slavery A Certain Negro Man Slave by the Name of Jack, who has Served your Petitioner faithfully for many Years; and in consideration of his Obedience and good Conduct your Petitioner is willing (if Consistent with the Opinion of the Court) reward him with his freedom and hopes your Worships will grant the above Petition, on Complying with the requisitions of the Act of the General Assembly in such Cases made and provided, and Your petitioner as in duty bound will ever pray

Aaron Morris Senr.   John Cook
T Freshwater

Agreed to by the Court

Benjamin Pritchard   Thomas Banks
Will: T. Muse   Richard Muse
Francis Wilson   Adam[?] G Banks
Jos. Parker

Bond
Aaron Morris Senr
& als

State of North Carolina   }
Pasquotank County   }

    Know All Men by these presents that We Aaron Morris Senr. William T Muse and Frances Wilson of the County of Pasquotank are held and firmly bound unto David Pritchard Esqr. Chairman of the County Court of Pleas and Quarter Sessions for the County aforesaid, or to his Successors in Office in the sum of One hundred pounds - To the Which Payment Well and truly to be made and done We bind ourselves our heirs Executors and Admrs. Jointly and severally firmly by these presents Sealed with our Seals and dated the 4th day of March 1813

    The Condition of the above obligation is such that whereas the above bound Aaron Morris Senr. Hath with the Approbation of the Court liberated and Set Free from Slavery a Negro Man Slave Named Jack. Now if the above bounden Aaron Morris Senr. & als their heirs Exors or Admrs. Or any of them do and from time to time and at all times hereafter Acquit discharge and save harmless the Overseers of the Poor and Inhabitants of the said County from All Costs Charges and troubles whatsoever for and by reason of the liberation of the said negro Jack - And of and from all other Suits Charges & demands whatsoever touching and Concerning the Same then the above obligation to be Void otherwise to remain in full force and Virtue

Sealed & delivered in   }   Aaron Morris   (Seal)
The presence of   }   Will: T. Muse   (Seal)
Aaron White   Francis Wilson   (Seal)

****

Bond
Nathan Trueblood & als
March Term 1815

State of North Carolina   }
Pasquotank County   }

Chapter 18: Pasquotank County Records

  Know all men by these presents that we Nathan Trueblood, Joshua Trueblood Aaron Albertson of the County of Pasquotank are held and firmly bound unto David Pritchard Esquire Chairman of the County Court of Pleas and Quarter Sessions for the County aforesaid, or to his Successors in Office in the sum of One hundred pounds, to which payment Well and truly to be made and done we bind ourselves our heirs Executors and Admors Jointly and Severally firmly by these presents, Sealed with our Seals and dated the 8th day of March 1815

  The Condition of the above Obligation is Such that whereas the above Nathan Trueblood hath with the Approbation of the Court, liberated and set free from Slavery a Negro Man Slave Named Silas   Now if the above bounden Nathan Trueblood and others their heirs Executors and Admors. or any of them do and shall from time to time and at all times hereafter Acquit discharge and save harmless the Overseers of the Poor and Inhabitants of the said County from all Costs, Charges and troubles whatsoever for and by reason of the liberation of the said Negro Silas and of and from all other Suits Charges and demands whatsoever touching and Concerning the Same the above Obligation to be void otherwise to remain in full force and virtue

Sealed and delivered	}	N. Trueblood	(Seal)
In the presence of	}	Joshua Trueblood	(Seal)
Richard Muse DC		A Albertson	(Seal)

***

Certificate of Freedom
Feb. 1812

State of North Carolina }
Currituck County   }

  We whose names are hereunto Subscribed and our Seals Severally Affixed, being two of the acting Justices of the Peace for the county and State aforesaid, Do, certify that Rachel Patterson, the bearer hereof was born in the county of Currituck and State aforesaid, and of Free Parents, and that she Served her Apprenticeship with Mrs. Liddia Jarves in the Neighborhood of Powels Point, in the county and State afsd., and was Legally discharged from her said Mistress at twenty One years of Age, the said Rachel Patterson is a Mulatto or Woman of Colour, and of a Yellow complexion about twenty five Years of Age Short and well Proportioned thin Vissage a Small Scar in her left Eye Brow, Flat Nose, and is said to be Married to a free negro called Moses in Pasquotank county, and we further certifie that the Said Rachel Patterson has always Behaved herself as an Honest and Peaceable Citizen while she lived in our county of Currituck Given under our hands and Seals this 20th [Faded] Anno Domini 1812

                  L.W. [?] (Seal)
                   Jona. Lindsey (Seal)

State of North Carolina }
Currituck County   }

  I Jehu Hall D. Clerk of the county aforesaid do Certifie under my hand and seal of my Office that L.W. [?] and Jonathan Lindsey Esquires, are Acting Justices of the Peace for the county aforesaid and were so on the 20th of Feby. 1812 the day on which they Signed the Above Instrument of writing, and that all good faith and Credit is Given to their Judicial functions [Unreadable] Under my hand and Seal of my Office this 28 day of February 1812

                                      (Currituck Seal)

***

Negro Girl Milly
To} Petition for Freedom
The Court
To be Served on Solomon Pool
& Returned to Court
X--2855

Chapter 18: Pasquotank County Records

Pasquotank
June Term 1824
Executed
Wm. Guyer[?]

State of North Carolina }Court of Pleas & Quarter Sessions
Pasquotank County }March Term 1824

Mr. Solomon Pool,
    Sir, on motion it is ordered that you make your personal appearance at the next Court to be held for the aforesaid County, at the Court house in Elizabeth City, on the first Monday of June next, and shew Cause if any you have, why you should not give up your claim to the Services of Negro Woman Milly Bound to you, she claiming her freedom by age, otherwise the Court will direct her accordingly   Witness Charles Grice Clerk of the said County at Elizabeth City, the first day of March 1824
Charles Grice Clk
To the Sheriff of Pasquotank County Greeting

***

Thomas M Blount
To}Petition to Manumit a Negro
The Court
X--3110
Fall Term 1826

State of North Carolina }Superior Court of Law
Pasquotank County }Fall Term 1826

    To the Honorable the Judge of the Superior Court of Law & Equity in and for the County aforesaid,
    The Petition of Thomas M Blount of the town of Edenton in the State aforesaid Humbly Sheweth,
    That he is the owner of a negro man slave by the name of Frank Commonly Called Frank Goodman aged about 28 years, that the said Frank has always been a faithful & dutiful Servant not only to your Petitioner but to his former masters, your petitioner further sheweth that the said Frank is orderly and well disposed and conducts himself with becoming propriety to his superiors. Your petitioner therefore prays that your Honor will manumit the said Frank according to the Act of Assembly in Such Cases made & Provided, And your Petitioner as in duty bound will ever pray &c
Tho. M Blount

Order
For liberation
Of negro man
Frank
X--3110

On Petition of T M Blount praying for the liberation of a certain negro Slave called Frank (commonly called Frank Goodman) It is ordered, adjudged & decreed by the Court that the said Frank be liberated & set free from slavery - that he hereafter pass & be known by the name of Frank Goodman & be entitled to enjoy all the rights priviledges & advantages of other free persons of Colour Agreeably to Act of Genl. Assembly in such cases made & provided And that all such estate hereafter acquired by him, be held by him & his heirs forever to him & their only in behoof, so far first as the laws of this State will admit.

Bond

Chapter 18: Pasquotank County Records

Know all Men by these Presents that we Thomas M Blount & J.L. Bailey are held and firmly bound unto Owen Williams Chairman of the Court of Pleas and Quarter Sessions of Pasquotank County in the sum of One Hundred Pounds, payable to the said Owen Williams & his Successors in Office to which payment well & truly to be made we bind ourselves our & each of our heirs executors & administrators firmly by these presents Sealed with our Seals & dated at Elizabeth City this 26 day of October 1826

The Condition of the above obligation is such that whereas at the present term of the Superior Court of Law for the County of Pasquotank the above named Thomas M Blount hath obtained permission to liberate & manumit a certain slave belonging to him named Frank Goodman and hath manumitted the said Slave accordingly - Now if the said Slave Frank Goodman shall never become a Parish Charge or County Charge in the County of Pasquotank then the above obligation to be void - Otherwise to remain in full force & virtue

Sealed & delivered	Thos. M. Blount	(Seal)
In presence of	Jno. L. Bailey	(Seal)

****

Bond

Know all Men by these presents that we William W. Freshwater and John Cartwright are held and firmly bound unto Owen Williams Chairman of the Court of Pleas & Quarter sessions of Pasquotank County in the sum of One hundred pounds, payable to the said Owen Williams and his Successors in Office, to which payment well and truly to be made we bind ourselves, our & each of our heirs, executors and administrators firmly by these presents Sealed with our Seals and dated at Elizabeth City this 27th day of October 1825

The Condition of the above obligation is such that whereas at the present Term of the Superior Court of Law for the County of Pasquotank the above named William W. Freshwater hath obtained permission to liberate & manumit a certain slave belonging to him named Solomon & hath manumitted the said slave accordingly Now if the said Slave Solomon shall never become a Parish Charge or County Charge in the County of Pasquotank, then the above obligation to be void -- Otherwise to remain in full force & virtue

Sealed & delivered	W.W. Freshwater	(Seal)
In presence of	his	
Augustus Moore	John X Cartwright	(Seal)
	Mark	

****

Bond
Thos. R Cobb & als for
Emancipation of Mark Cobb
March Term 1818

State of North Carolina }
Pasquotank County   }

Know all men by these presents that we Thomas R Cobb & Samuel Matthews of the County of Pasquotank are held and firmly bound unto Anthony Markham Esquire Chairman of the County Court of Pleas and Quarter Sessions for the County aforesaid or to his Successors in Office in the sum of Two hundred pounds To which payment well and Truly to be made and done, we bind ourselves our heirs Executors and Administrators jointly and Severally firmly by these presents Sealed with our seals and dated the 5th March 1818.

The Condition of the above Obligation is such that whereas Mark Cobb hath with the approbation of the Court been Liberated and set free from slavery Now if the above bounden Thos & Samuel their heirs Executors or Administrators or any of them do and shall from time to time and at all times hereafter Acquit discharge and save harmless the Overseers of the Poor and Inhabitants of the said County from all Costs Charges and troubles whatsoever for and by reason of the liberation of said negro Mark and of and from all Other Suits Charges and demands

Chapter 18: Pasquotank County Records

Whatsoever, touching and Concerning the Same the Above Obligation to be void Otherwise to remain in full force and virtue

Sealed and delivered   }   Tho R. Cobb   (Seal)
In presence of   }   S. Mathews   (Seal)
Will: T. Muse Clk

****

Petition
Peleg
Negroe Woman

To the Worshipful the Justices of the County of Pasquotank

The Petition of Peleg, Negroe Woman formerly the property of Sarah Commander Sheweth that on an Exec of the Estate of John Commander her former Master, at the request of her Mistress at the time pushed with the Exetrx she did [?] & raise for her by hard work industry & saving a sum sufficient to discharge the same & to release her from the said Debt for which Consideration being fairly purchased, her said Mistress is willing & desirous that she may be liberated & she prays the same accordingly

In Respect whereof
J Hamilton
Sepr 1752[82?]

****

Aaron Morris} Petition for Emanuel
To the Court

Granted June Term
1800 See the Minutes
Will: T. Muse Clk

To the Justices of the Inferior Court of Pleas & Quarter sessions for the County of Pasquotank

The Petition of Aaron Morris Junr. Inhabitant of said County Humbly Sheweth That Your Petitioner having under his Care or possession a Negro Man by the Name of Emanuel, formerly the property of Ambrose Knox late of said County deceasd.

Your Petitioner Humbly Request that you would please to grant an Order that Said Emanuel be liberated Under such Restrictions as other persons of Color And your Petitioner as in duty bound will thankfully Acknowledge &c

Aaron Morris Junr.

****

George Bonners
Peto. For liberation
Of Charity or Chat.
X--1416

To the Worshipful the County Court of Pasquotank

The Petition of George Bonner, Humbly Sheweth, That his Wife Charity formerly the property of Wm. T. Muse, has for many years conducted herself in a Very Meritorious Manner, that she was Nurse to the late Mrs. Muse & for Services rendered to her family, she was given by the said William T. Muse several years ago to your Petitioner, Your Petr. Therefore prays that the Worshipful Court would liberate & set her free from Slavery on Complying with the requisites of the law, by giving Bond & Security &c. & Your Peto. Will ever pray.

Test   his
Will: T. Muse   George GB Bonner
                                                                              Mark

Chapter 18: Pasquotank County Records

I Certify the Contents of the foregoing Petition is Correct.
Will: T. Muse

****

                                        Betty Smith et als
                                        Bond

State of No Carolina   }
Pasquotank County   }

      Know all men by these presents that we Betty Smith, Thos. Banks & William James are held and firmly bound to fredk. Whitehurst County Trustee in the just & full sum of Two hundred Dollars for the well & truly paying of which we bind ourselves & our heirs, jointly & severally firmly by these presents

      The Condition of the above obligation is such that if negro man Jack late the property shall not become a Parish Charge then this obligation to be void otherwise to remain in full force power & virtue

Spencer Sawyer
                                        Betsy Smith   (Seal)
                                               X
                                        Her mark
                                       Thomas Banks   (Seal)
                                       William James   (Seal)

chapter 19

Perquimans County

NORTH CAROLINA STATE ARCHIVES
PERQUIMANS COUNTY RECORDS
MISCELLANEOUS RECORDS
C.R.077.928.2

To the Worshipfull Court now Sitting we the subscribers petition your Worshipfull body to take into Consideration the following petition (to wit) Samuel S. White became the purchaser of a Man of Colour Commonly Known by the name of Job Hurdle whom he is desirous of liberating by Complying with the Act of Assembly in that case Provided and to [?] [?] believe the sd. negro to be an honest industrious well disposed fellow and join in this petition which we hope may be granted and in duty bound we will pray &c
May 9th 1814

James Nixon	Joseph Scott	Jo Riddick Senr
H. H.	John A Toms	M Jordan
Abraham Hurdle	his	
Nathan Ward	Seth X Jones	Harmon Hurdle
	mark	Henry Hallings
	Benjnm. Toms	Rueben Riddix
	Josiah Bagley	Job Riddick
	Uriah Hudson	Isaiah Riddick
	John Tettor	John Bogue
	his	
	Aaron X Hill	Josiah Jordan
	mark	Ca[?] Elliot Jr

The prayer of the Petitioner granted unanimous by S.S. White Complying with the Act of Assembly in that Case made. In behalf of the Court Gab. White

Samuel S. White
Petition Granted

Saml. S. White
Emancipation Bond
for Negro Job
Aug Term 1814

State of No Carolina   }Know all men by these presents that
Perquimans County   }we Saml. S. White David White & Elias Albertson

of the County and State aforesaid are held & firmly Bound unto Isaac Barber Esqr. Chairman of the County Court aforesaid & to his successors In office in the Sum of one hundred Pounds Current money of the said State to the which payment well & truly to be made We bind ourselves And Each of us our & Each of our heirs Exetrs. Admrs. & Assigns Jointly severally & firmly by these presents, signed with our seals & Dated this the 9th Day of August 1814.

Chapter 19: Perquimans County Records

Condition of the above obligation is such that whereas The Above bounden Samuel S. White Hath Petitioned for & obtained the freedom & Liberation of a Certain negro Man slave by the name of Job -- And therefore if the said Samuel S. White shall save harmless & secure the Parish And Wardains of the poor of the said County from any Expence that may hereafter Incur with respect To support and Maintenance of the said Negro Job -- liberated & set free as aforesaid then this obligation to be Void - And of no Effect otherwise to be & remain in full force & Virtue.

signed seal'd & Delivered }	Samuel White	(Seal)
In presence of }	David White	(Seal)
John Wood	Elias Albertson	(Seal)

****

To the County Court of Perquimans
    The Petition of Your Petitioner humbly sheweth, that having under my Care two people of Colour, (To Wit) Mills aged about twenty six years, and Pleasant aged about twenty four years, and being continuously concerned to endeavor to obtain their freedom, do humbly request that you will be pleased to take the matter unto your serious consideration, and grant me relief by freeing the persons aforesaid - and your nobility therein will be gratefully acknowledged by your friend and well wishes.

2nd Mth. 11th 1811   Caleb Winslow

The above petition was granted in open Court unanimously by entering into bond agreeable to Act of Assembly in such Case made and provided Feby Term 1811
                                           Wm. Jones

Caleb Winslow & others
Emancipation Bond
February Term 1811

State of North Carolina   } Know all men by these presents
Perquimans County   } that We Caleb Winslow

    are held & firmly Bound unto the Chairman and other the Justices of the County Court aforesaid in the sum of Two Hundred pounds Current money to be paid to the said Justices or to their successors in office to the which payment well & truly to be made we Bind ourselves & Each of us our & Each of our Heirs assigns &c Jointly Severally & firmly by these presents Signed with our seals & Dated this the 12th of February 1811.

    Condition of the above is such that Whereas the said Caleb Winslow Hath petitioned for & obtained the freedom & Liberation of Two Certain Negro slaves under His Care by the names of Mills & Pleasant Now therefore if the said Caleb Winslow shall - Indemnify & save Harmless the Parish of said County from any Charge or Expence that may incur respecting the support & Maintenance of the said Negroes, Then the Above to be Void otherwise to Be & remain in full force & Virtue.

John Wood	Caleb Winslow	(Seal)
	Jesse Copeland	(Seal)
	David White	(Seal)

****

Thos. Newby
Petition to Liberate Negro Hannah
Rejected

To the Worshipfull Court of Pleas & Quarter sessions to be held in Hertford on The second Monday in Feby &c 1797. I Thomas Newby of the County of Perquimans and State of North Carolina Humbleth prayeth that Your Worships Will

Chapter 19: Perquimans County Records

take this my petition into Consideration, & Grant this the said Petition (to Wit) The Liberating of A Certain Negro Woman belonging to me Your Humble petitioner by the name of Hannah, for this my Reason In the first place, she being grown ould. And Can br Very little Service to me, as to any Hard Work or drudgery, & her being an Excellent Midwife Called on Every hand turn to Both White Women & Black and from account has performed her Duty with as Much Scill as any of that profession moreover She being a peaceable Negro Woman having lived in this place for the Space of forty years With on Certain Husband & Raised a Number of Children Which are at present Divided amongst the Heirs to Whom they fell, And I your Humble petitioner from being Satisfyed and Contented Withe the Services Which I have Rec'd from her the Sd. Hannah, Humbly Prayeth that your Worships May take in Consideration & Set the Sd. Negro free by your order & further your Petitioner prayeth not.

Thomas Newby

****

Tho. Newby Petition
1787
Rejected
Granted by the Majority of the Court
Freeing Slave

State of North Carolina

To the Inferior Court of Perqs. County
Now Sitting

The Petition of Thomas Newby humbly sheweth that whereas, I have under my care a Negro Girl Named Nacy, who as is as orderly as any that I have been acquainted with. & hath the character of being verry Trusty, and one that I should be willing to employ in my service as a hired Servant, (but being clearly convinced in my mind that It is wrong for me to hold her as a slave). Therefore beg that the Court would be pleased to Tolerate & confirm her freedom which favour will be greatfully acknowledged By Thomas Newby
Perquimans County
the 9th day 7th mo. 1787

****

Quaker Petition
for Negroe Peter

Petition to Perqs. Court

To the County Court now about to Sit in Perquimans

The Petition of several Subscribers Humbly Sheweth
That whereas Samuel Smith a few Years ago Manumitted a Servant Named Peter (Whose Mother was an Indian & Father a Negro) which said Servant Man hath not been taken up nor Sold by the Court; And as he hath hitherto Always been an orderly Servant & never that we know of been Accused of any Vilany, But on the Contrary Hath done Severak Meritorious Actions in Destroying Vermin Such as Bears Wolves Wild Cats & Foxes therefore we pray that the Court may take it into Consideration & order & adjudge that he may remain Free & unmolested as long as he behaves himself well And your Petitioners the several Subscribers, as in Duty Bound shall ever Pray &c

April 6th 1782   Samuel Smith
John Smith   Joseph Newby
Benjamin Smith   Demcy Elliot
Joseph Elliot Sener   James Settison[?]
Mordecai Elliot   Job Smith
Josiah Sanders

Chapter 19: Perquimans County Records

Joseph Sanders	
Joseph Elliot	William Sanders
Samuel Elliot	Gideon Newby
John Goodwin	John Roberts
Jacob Goodwin	Jacob Eason
Richard Goodwin	Joshua Sanders
	Samuel Williams

****

Petition
Negroe Dick by his
next friend

J Hamilton Counsel for Pet.
by the Leave of the Court

Unto the Worshipful the Justices of the County Court of Perquimans

The Petition of Negro Dick at present confined in the Common Gaol of the County by his next friend John Smith.

That your Petr. has been taken up by sundry Persons supposing him to have been a slave the property of John Smith one of the people called Quakers and illegally liberated by him.

That your Petr. is at present confined in Gaol under the acts of Assembly 1777 and 1779.

Sheweth that your Petr. Grandmother, Betty was an Indian, a free woman by the law of Nature.

May it therefore please your Worships to enquire into the fact of the natural freedom of your Petr. and to do further in the Premises as shall seem just & merciful.
In respect whereof &c

J Hamilton

Leave being first had from the worshipful Court to file the above Petition and directions received from the Chairman of the Court to proceed by Petition.
J Hamilton   Octob. Term 1788

****

Petition of Benja. Bundy
To the Worshipful Court of the County of Perqs. Now Siting Greeting &c
Whereas I have a Certain Negro Man Named Francis which Negroe I purchased about five Years Past Since which Time he hath demeaned himself as a faithful Servant and hath from his Infancy been of an orderly life his Knowledge & Skil in releasing the Brute Creation from many Complaints Which they are Insident to and his readiness to Serve The Citisen of his Neighborhood all taken in View I Consider Meritorious and Therefore Implore Your attention to this Particular Case -- believing that you will consider him worthy of that right which the Laws of our State allow in Certain Cases (which is Liberation. -- firmly believing that If he should meet with Your Sanction in this Case that he would be of Material Servise in the Neighborhood. I am desirous that You in Your good Wisdom may emansipate him the said franci & that his Name may be Caled Francis N. Bundy and as in duty Bound Your Petitioner will pray &c.
May 13th 1806 ---- Benjamin Bundy
The above Petition is Granted by the Court
[?] W. Blount

Chapter 19: Perquimans County Records

We the Subscribers being wel acquainted with the Within Named Frank do believe that it would be Great Justice for him to be emancipated as he is a Servisable Negroe in the Neighborhood and answers the description within mentioned.
Chas Nixon
Josiah Robinson
Thomas Church
Samuel [?] Jr.
Enoch Newby
Charles Overman
John Overman
Josiah Bundy

Bond £500
Benja. Bundy for Negroe
Francis N. Bundy
emancipation

State of North Carolina   } Know all men by these presents
Perqs. County   } that we Benjamin Bundy

and Elisha Henby are held and firmly Bound unto Isaac Barber Esquire and the rest of the Justices of the said County in the penal sum of Five Hundred Pounds for the which payment we bind ourselves & each of our Successors firmly by these presents dated this 13th day of May in the Year of our lord One thousand Eight Hundred & six 1806.

The condition of the above obligation is Such that whereas the above Bounden Benja. Bundy hath obtained an emancipation at this present May Term for a certain Negroe Man Named Francis N. Bundy) that if the said Francis shall from time to time and at all times during his Life demean himself as a good Citisen of this State Should do and also live Clear of any Charge to this County during his said Life then this obligation to be Void or else to remain in full force & Virtue.

Signed Sealed and Delivered   } Benjamin Bundy   (Seal)
in presents of   } Elisha Henby   (Seal)
Josiah Bundy

****

James Sumner
Petition to Liberate Phillis
1797
Granted

To the Worshipfull Court of Perquimans

We the Subscribers pray your Worships that Negroe Phillises freedom may be Established for Meritorious Services by the Court.
She first being Purchased by her Husband Doctor Tom & actually paid for also being verry Serviceable in the neighborhood both as a Midwife and Doctress & has Actually Performed Some Surprising Cures, & we your Petitioners as in Duty Bound Shall Ever pray.
Febry. 1797
Jas. Sumner   Fras. Newby
Robert Whedbee   William Borclift   Geo. Sutton
Joal kinyon   Joseph Peresher   Tho. Whedbee
John Miller   Wm Whedbee

****

Chapter 19: Perquimans County Records

Charles W Blount & others
Bond for the freedom of Negroe Jack
Frby. 1807
paid
Granted

State of North Carolina   }Know all men by these
Perqs. County   }presents that we Charles

W. Blount Myles Turner and John Sutton of the County aforesaid are held and firmly Bound unto Nathaniel Elexander Esqr. Governor of the State aforesaid in the sum of five hundred pounds Current money of the aforesd. State to be paid unto the said Nathl. Elexander or his successors in office on demand dated at Hertford in Perquimans County the 10th day of Feby. 1807.

     The Condition of the above obligation is such that if a Certain negro man Jack who is now in the possession of Charles W Blount shall in all things behave himself well conformable to the Laws of the State dureing his residence therein then the above obligation to be null and void otherwise to have full force given under our hands and seals the date and year above written.

Signed sealed and delivered   C.W. Blount   (Seal)
in presence of us   Myles Turner   (Seal)
William Jones   his
CWB ackd. before Thos. H. Harvey   John X Sutton   (Seal)
     mark

****

To the Court now seting at Hartford for the Countyof Perquimons

     The Petition of your Petitioner humbly Sheweth that having under him, a certain woman of Colour, Named Rose, and being desirous of setting her free, for her faithful services to him, humbly request that you will be pleased to grant to the said woman her freedom; and your clemency shall be acknowledged &c.
8th mo. 1805   By Caleb Winslow

We whose names are hereunto subscribed living near to, and being well acquainted with the above mentioned person, mai Inform on her behalf, that she is of an orderly life and conduct and that we are free the above request be granted.

Uriah Hudson
Jesse Rogerson
Langley Billups
Jacob Winslow
James Griffin
Elisha T[?]
Law Perry
John White
Thomas White Benj:
Seth Rodderick

The within Petition is granted on the Petitioner Entering into Bond and security for the within mention'd negroes good Behaviour and that she shall not become a publick Charge to this County.
Perqs. County Court August Term 1805

Caleb Winslow Senr. & Others
Bond for Negroe Rose

Chapter 19: Perquimans County Records

Set Free by Court
August 1805

State of North Carolina }
Perquimons County } Know all men by these presents that we Caleb Winslow, Thomas Hollowell & Josiah Townsend all of the County & State aforesaid are held and firmly Bound unto Francis Newby Esqr. Chairman of the Court of the aforesaid County in the just Sum of Five Hundred Dolars --- to be paid unto the said Francis Newby Esqr. or to his Successors in office firmly by these presents. Sealed with our Seals and dated this 13th day of August 1805.

The Condition of the above obligation is such That whereas a Negroe Woman Rose late the property of Caleb Winslow hath by & with the consent of the said Caleb being emancipated and set free according to Law   Now if the said Negroe Woman Rose shall from time to time & for ever after Keep the peace and be of her good behaviour & if the said Negroe Rose shall not at any time hereafter become Chargeable to the parish then the above obligation to be void & of no Effect.

Witness	Caleb Winslow	(Seal)
Tho. H. Harvey Clk	Josiah Townsend	(Seal)
	T. Hollowell	(Seal)

State of No. Carolina } Know all men by these presents
Perquimans County } that we John Sanders Esqr. & Willis

Riddick Esquire all of the County and State aforesaid are held and firmly bound unto Francis Newby Esqr. Chairman of the Court of the aforesaid County in the Just sum of five hundred dollars to be paid unto the said Francis Newby Esqr. or to his successors in office firmly by these presents Sealed with our Seals and dated this 12th day of Feby 1806.

The Condition of the above Obligation is Such that whereas a negro Woman Rose late the property of Caleb Winslow hath by and with the Consent of the said Caleb being emancipated and set free according to Law   Now if the said Negro Woman Rose Shall from time to time and forever after Keep the peace and be of her good behaviour and if the said Negro Rose Shall not at any time hereafter become Chargeable to the Parish then the above obligation to be Void and of no Effect.

Witness	his	
Thos. H. Harvey Clk	John X Sanders	(Seal)
	mark	
	Willis Riddick	(Seal)
	Jacob Winslow	(Seal)

****

To the County Court of Perquimons now Sitting -- The Petition of the subscriber Sheweth: That having under my Care a woman of Colour, Known by the name Cate, whome for her honesty and faithfull services, am desirous that she should Enjoy her freedom do wherefore Request that you would take it into consideration and grant her freedom, and your surety[?] therein will be acknowledged by your Petitioner.
John Sanders

We whose Names are here unto subscribed being acquainted with the above mentioned Person and Knowing her to be of a peaceable and orderly Conduct and pray the above request be granted.

Josiah Jordan	Caleb Winslow
Jesse Rogerson	James Wood Jr
	Thomas White
	Samuel White
	Joseph White

Chapter 19: Perquimans County Records

Thomas Whitt Bee
___

The within petition was granted on Mr. Sanders Entering Into Bond & security for the within ment'd negresses good Conduct & Behaviour and that she shall not become a County Charge February Term 1806 - in behalf of the Court
John Wood

****

To the Court Now Sitting at Hartford for the County of Perquimons

Your Petitioner Respectfully shewth that having under his Care a Certain person of Colour named Peter aged about forty Years, who for his Industry, honesty and orderly Conduct merits your humane Interferences, I therefore earnestly request that you will be pleased to take the matter under your serious Consideration, and your humanity will be acknowledged by your friend and well wishes.
8th mo. 14th 1809   Caleb Winslow

We whose names are hereunto subscribed being well acquainted with Peter a person of Coulor before mentioned and believing him to be an Industrious orderly & peaceable person request his behalf that the above petition be granted.

Jonathan White	Thos. White Benj.
Robert Reed	Uriah Hudson
Thomas White (of Josiah)	Josiah White
Seth Jones	Exum[?] S Bond
Caleb Newby	Thomas Moore
Jesse Stallings	Josiah Moore
John Colley	Samuel Wilson
Jesse White	Thomas Bogue
Demsey White	Wilkinson Hudson
his	Jacob Pery
John X Jones	
mark	
Chalkly Draper	N. Wood
Joseph Evans	Nathan Bogue
Mark Bogue	Aaron Bogue
Josiah Bagley	Joseph Bagley

___

Caleb Winslow to the Court
Emancipation for negro Peter
August Term 1809
fees Due 10s   paid

State of No. Carolina   } Know all men by these presents
Perquimans County   } that We Caleb Winslow Exum Newby
and Henry Hollowell our Held & firmly Bound unto The Justices of the County Court aforesaid in the Sum of One Hundred Pounds Current money - To the which payment well & truly to be made we Bind ourselves & Each of us our Heirs and assigns Jointly Severally & firmly By these presents sign'd with our seals & Dated the 15th of August 1809.

Condition of the Above is Such that Whereas the said Caleb Winslow Hath petitioned for & obtained the freedom of a Certain negro slave under His Direction Nam'd Peter - now if In Case the Said Caleb Winslow Do & shall Keep Harmless the parish of said County from any Expence that might Incur for the support & maintenance of the said Negro peter then the above To Be Void otherwise To Be & remain in full force & Effect

Sign'd Seal'd & Delivered   Caleb Winslow   (Seal)
In presence of   Exum Newby   (Seal)

Chapter 19: Perquimans County Records

John Wood Clk   Henry Hollowell   (Seal)

****

State of No. Carolina   }
     Vs.   } Bills of Cost
Negro Harey   }
                        WB

                         John Pritchard & Othrs
                           To The Court
                         Bond for the good
                      Behaviour of Negro Harey
                        August Term 1810

State of No Carolina   } Know all men by these presents
Perquimans County   } That we John Pritchard
James Jackson Elias Best Nathl. Brinkly & Wm Saunders are held & firmly bound unto Isaac Barber Esqr. Chairman of the County Court of Perquimans & the rest of the Justices assigned to Keep the peace for the said County in the Sum of Five Hundred Dollars to be paid to the said Justices or their Successors in office - to the which payment well & Truly to be made & Done we Bind ourselves & Each of us our & Each of our Heirs & assigns Jointly Severally & firmly By these presents   sign'd with our seals & Dated the 15th Day of August 1810.

     Condition of the above obligation Is Such that if a Certain negro man slave the property of John Pritchard shall from this Time Conduct Him self in A peaceable orderly manner & Be on His good Behaviour in Every respect To the Citisens of this said County of Perquimans for the space of Twelve months from this time agreeable to the sentence & Decree of the said Court then the Above obligation to be Void & of no Effect otherwise to be & remain in full force & Virtue.

Sign'd Seal'd & Delivered}   John Pritchard   (Seal)
In presence of   }   James Jackson   (Seal)
John Wood   Elias Best   (Seal)
                                      Nathl. Brinkly   (Seal)
Enterlin'd Before Signed   Wm Saunders   (Seal)

****

                          Cortny Newby Pto.
                     To The Court for Emancipation
                         August Term 1810

To the Court of Pleas & Quarter Sessions }
Of The County Of Perquimans   }

     This Petition of your Petitioner humbly sheweth that she is the sole possessor of a Negro man by the name of Christopher as will appear by a deed of gift give from & by Jacob Winslow Dec'd to me. And that from divers good offices done by sd. Christopher for me, I am desirous that he should have and enjoy his freedom as the just reward of Industry and honesty, Which your Petitioner humbly prayeth that the Court may grant, for whose prosperity your Petitioner will ever pray With Submission to the will and pleasure of the Court.
July 28th 1810   I remain your Humbl. Servt.
                                           her
                                  Cortney X Newby Alis Laurence
                                       mark
     This may Certify that we the undersigned have a long time known the Petitioner & the Petitioned that the former is a free woman who belonged to Exum Newby, and freed by the former Laws of Virga. that she has always been

Chapter 19: Perquimans County Records

of a good Caracter, and lives a peasible and a quiet life - That the latter is a negroe Man whom she in fact Purchased of Jacob Winslow dec'd but who was conveyed to her from him in a Deed of Gift, that he has always been the Caracter of an honest & Industrious Negroe submissive & orderly, And that from his studied efforts to become superior to others of his Colour in these respects we feal no hesitations in recommending him to the attention of the Court.

July 28th 1810

John Smith Jr	Exum Newby
John [?]	Restore Lamb
Matthew Jordain	John Bond
Josiah Bagley	his
[Faded] Perry	Pritlow + Bond
Joseph Gl[Torn]	mark
Jordan Winslow	Elias Albertson
Nathaniel [Torn]	David White
Josiah Jordan	Thomas White
John Bogue	[?] Parker
Thomas Granberry	Uriah Hudson
Thos. White of Benj.	
Isaac Witson[?]	

Peticion of Cortney Newby
for Negroe

August 14th 1810. The prayer of the Petitioner - Granted that the Petitioned have his freedom under the Act of Assembly
  by order of the Court
    Gabl. White

Cortny Newby &als.
To The Court
Bond for Emancipation
of Negro Christopher
August Term 1810
fees paid 10s

State of No Carolina } Know all men by these presents that
Perqs. County   } we Cortny Newby als. Laurence & Restore Lamb, Exum Newby
the younger all of the County & State aforesaid are Held & firmly Bound unto Isaac Barber Esqr. Chairman of the County Court aforesaid & the Rest of the Justices assigned To Keep the peace in the Sum of one Hundred pounds Currency of said State To be paid to the said Chairman & Justices aforesaid To the which payment Well & Truly to be made &c we Bind our selves & Each of us our & Each of our Heirs Extrs. admrs & assigns Jointly Severally by These presents. Signed with our Seals & Dated this the 13th Day of August 1810.

  Condition of the above is Such that whereas the Above Bound Cortney Newby als. Laurence Hath petitioned for & obtained the freedom & Liberation of A Certain Negro man slave in her possession By the name of Christopher, now if in Case the said Cortney shall Indemnify & save Harmless the parish of said County from any & Every Expence that may Hereafter incur Respecting the support & maintenance of the said Negro Christopher then this obligation to Be Void & of no Effect, otherwise to be & remain in full force & Virtue.

Sign'd Seal'd & Delivered}	Exum Newby	(Seal)
In presence of }	Restore Lamb	(Seal)

****

Chapter 19: Perquimans County Records

Harrison Douglas
Petition for Emancipation
April Term 1825
Extended in the Minutes

State of North Carolina Superior Court of Law
Perquimans County Ss April Term 1825

To the Honorable the Judge of the Superior Court of Law for the County aforesaid The Petition of Harrison Douglas a free person of Colour of Perquimans County humbly sheweth
That he hath lately intermarried with a negro girl slave named Annis, who at the time of such marriage was the property of Elizabeth L. Blair of Edenton -- that since the marriage the said Elizabeth in consideration of the excellent character & former services of the said slave has given to your Petitioner a Deed of Gift for the said girl Annis & with a hope that she might be liberated -- Your Petitioner sheweth that the said girl Annis has always supported an irreproachable character, has been remarkable for her moral & correct behaviour & industrious habits -- He therefore prays your Honor that he may be permitted to emancipate the said slave & as in Duty bound he will ever pray &c.
Ja Iredell
Atto. for H. Douglas

(Copy the Petition)

On hearing the forgoing Petition of Harrison Douglass & testimony in support of it It is considered & so adjudged by the Court that the said Harrison Douglas have permission to emancipate the said Woman Annis upon his entering into Bond as the Act of Assembly requires -- Whereupon the said Harrison Douglass entered into Bond as required by Law with Edward Wood & James Iredell as his securities which is approved by the Court -- and it is ordered that the Clerk deliver the said Bond to the Clerk of the County Court and the said Harrison ia accordingly permitted to emancipate the said woman Annis.
To be put on the minutes and a copy del'd Harrison with the Clks seal & Certificate

---

Harrison Douglas
Emancipation Bond
April Supr. Court 1825

State of North Carolina Ss.
Know all men by these presents that we Harrison Douglass, Edward Wood & James Iredell are held and firmly bound unto John Clary Chairman of the Court of Pleas and Quarter Sessions for the County of Perquimans in the sum of one hundred pounds to be paid to the said Chairman & his Successors in Office for the use of the Poor of the said County, to which payment well & truly to be made we bind ourselves, our & each of our Heirs Executors & administrators firmly by these presents Sealed with our Seals and dated this 21st day of April 1825.

The Condition of the above obligation is such that whereas the said Harrison Douglass hath been by the Superior Court of Law for the County of Perquimans at the present Term thereof permitted to emancipate a negro woman by the name of Annis, now if the said woman Annis after being emancipated in pursuance of the said permission shall never become chargeable to the said County of Perquimans or to the Wardens of the Poor thereof, then the above obligation to be void - otherwise to be in full force and effect.

Sealed & Delivered		his
In presence of	Harrison X Douglass (Seal)	
(the word "never" being	mark	
first interlined)	Jas Iredell (Seal)	
Francis Toms	Edw. Woods (Seal)	

****

Chapter 19: Perquimans County Records

William Bagley & als.
To} Peto. for freedom to
The Court
To Novr. Term 1812

State of No Carolina }
Perquimans County }

      To the worshipfull the Justices of the County Court of pleas & quarter Sessions for The County aforesaid now Sitting.
      The Petition of William Bagley Humbly Sheweth unto your worships That He Hath under his Care & Direction A Certain negro man slave by the name of Squire. And Being Desirous of Setting Him free for His faithfull Services To Him & Honest Conduct & Behaviour To others. Therefore pray your worships To Grant an order for the Freedom & Liberation of the said negro on your Petitioner Entering into Bond & Security according to An Act of the General Assembly in Such Case made & provided -- And your petitioner as in Duty Bound will Ever Pray &c &c
                                                  W Bagley

We Whose names are hereunto subscribed Being A long Time Acquainted with the said negro Whose freedom is Petition'd for & from His Conduct And Behaviour we Don't Conceive any Difficulty would Arise from His Being Liberated and are Therefore free & willing the Above petition should Be Granted.

Thomas Miers   }
Jno. Stafford Jr   }   John Wood
Thomas Bagley   }
C [?]   } Granted on the Petitioners Entering into Bond according
John [?]   } To act of Assembly
            Present } William Blount Gabriel White Jas. Whidbee

---

William Bagley
To} Emancipation Bond
The Court for Negro Squire
Novr. Term 1812

State of No Carolina   } Know All Men by these Presents that we
Perquimans County   } William Bagley & John Wood

are Held & firmly Bound unto the Chairman of the Court of The said County in the full & Just sum of One Hundred Pounds Current money To be paid to the said Chairman or To His Successors in office To the which payment well & Truly to be made we Bind our selves & Each of us our And Each of our Heirs Executors Administrators & assigns Jointly & Severally & firmly by these presents signed with our Seals & Dated this the 10th Day of Novr. 1812.

      Condition of the Above obligation is such that whereas The Above bounden William Bagley Hath petitioned for And obtained the Liberation & freedom of a Certain negro man slave By the name of Squire Now if the Said William Bagley shall secure & save Harmless The Parish of this said County from Any Expence that may Incur respecting the support & maintenance of the said negro Squire so Liberated & Set free the The Above to be Void & of no Effect otherwise to Be & remain in full force & Effect.

Sign'd Seal'd & Deliver'd }
In presence of   }   W Bagley   (Seal)
                                                    John Wood   (Seal)

***

James Perry
Bond for emancipation

Chapter 19: Perquimans County Records

of Negro Sipio
May 1819

fees due	
Entering & filing peto.	4/6
order on minutes	2
Imancipation Bond	6
Certificate of imancipation and Seal	5/
Due	17/6

State of No Carolina } Know all men by these presents
Perqs. County } That we James Perry & Mosses Roundtree Are Held & firmly bound to the wardains of the Poor for the said County in The sum of one Hundred pounds Currency of the said State To be paid to the said wardains or to Their successors In office To the which payment well & Truly to Be made we bind our selves & Each of us our And Each of our Heirs Executors Admnrs. & assigns Jointly & severally & firmly by these presents signed with our Seals & dated the 10th day of may 1819.
    Condition of the Above is such that whereas The said James Perry Did by petition to the Last Supr Court of said County obtain the Freedom or imancipation of A Certain negro man named Sipio formeryl the property of Benjamin Perry dec'd now therefore if the said James Perry or His Heirs &c shall save Harmless the Parish or wardains of the Poor of sd. County from any Expence which may hereafter occur as to the support And maintenance of the said negro Sipeo During life then the above obligation To be Void & of no Effect otherwise to Be & Remain in full force & Virtue.

Signed & ackn'd	}	James Perry	(Seal)
before me	}	Moses Rountree	(Seal)

***

To the County Court of Perquimans now Sitting

The Petition of the Subscriber Respectfully Sheweth That having under my care a Black man commonly Known by the name of Edward Gerrish whom for his faithfull Services, honesty, Industry and good Economy I am desirous should enjoy his freedom: do therefore request that you would take it into consideration and Grant that his freedom may be Established under the act of Assembly in that case made and provided.
    Your Lenity therein will be acknowledged by your Petitioner

                                    Josiah White

We whose names are hereunto Subscribed being acquainted with the Honest Peaceable and Industrious Character of the above mentioned person are free that the Petition be granted.

Caleb Winslow	Laurence Perry
Jesse Rogerson	Joseph White
Josiah Jordan	W. Jones
Caleb Elliot	Exum Newby
Uriah Hudson	

Petition in favour
of Edwd. Gerrish

The within petition on Mr. White Entering into Bond & Security that the within mention'd negro shall Conduct and Behave Live self in a peaceable Quiet manner and that He shall not become a County Charge. ----- in behalf of the Court
    John Wood

Josiah White & others
Bond for Edwd. gerrish
Set free by Court

Chapter 19: Perquimans County Records

Feby. Term 1806
fees paid

State of North Carolina } Know all men by these presents that we
Perquimans County   } Josiah White & Caleb Winslow

all of the Place aforesaid are held & firmly Bound unto Francis Newby Esquire Chairman of the Court of said County & to his Successors in Office in the full & Just of Five Hundred Pounds currency of the State aforesaid for the payment of which well & truly to be made we Bind ourselves, our Heirs, Exors. or admnrs. Jointly or Severally firmly by these presents Sealed with our Seals and Dated this 12th day of February 1806.

The Condition of the above Obligation is Such that whereas a Negro man Edward Gerrish late the property of Josiah White hath by and with the Consent of the said Josiah been emancipated and set free according to law now if the Said Negro man Edwd. shall from time to time and forever after keep the peace and be of good behaviour and shall not at any time hereafter Chargeable to the Parish then the above Obligation to be void and of no effect.

Witness	Josiah White	(Seal)
Thos. Harvey Clk	Caleb Winslow	(Seal)

****

A Petition on behalf
of Negro James
Granted

    To the Worshipfull the Justices of Perqs. County Court Now Sitting
The Petition of the Subscribers in Behalf of a certain Negro Man Named James formerly the Property of Thomas Newby of the County Aforesaid Humbly Sheweth.
    That some time in the Year 1776 the said Thomas Newby Manumitted the said Negro man James, That since that the Greater Part of his time he has been Employed as a Seaman, and has made several Voyages from this State & Virginia in the time of the Last War, and that he has Twice, or more been made Prisoner by the British, That he Embraced the Earliest opportunity in Making his Escape to Return to this Country being the Place of his Nativity, where he has a Wife & Children, That once during the War between America & Great Britain, he Entered hinself on board of one of the American Armed Vessels, , That During the Time of his Servitude with his said Master, he behaved himself as a faithfull Servant, and Rendered his Master great Services as a Seaman, and that since his freedom we have reasons to Believe he has Continued to behave Orderly and Honest, We are therefore willing to hope that on your Worships Maturely considering and Weighing every Particular, you will bee of opinion that the Poor fellow is Intitled to some small share of Merrit, If that should be your Worships Opinion, We earnestly Solicit (in the poor fellows behalf) that you Will Permit an Entry to be made on the Minutes of Your Court allowing the Fellow to have done Something Meritorious, and for that Reason you will give a Sanction to his freedom, that he may with safety Visit his Wife and Children, when It will be in his Power to Render further Services to this State, as an able Seaman, & Your Petitioners Shall ever Pray &c

                     Thos. Newby
                     Thomas Harvey
                     Robt. Derows[?]
                     [?] Bond
                     Thomas Sutton
                     Geo. Whidbee
                     John Creecy
                     Caleb Winslow
                     Samuel McClanahan

****

Chapter 19: Perquimans County Records

Pasquotank & Perquimans
SOUTHERN HISTORICAL COLLECTION
UNIVERSITY OF NORTH CAROLINA
MANUMISSION PAPERS
COLLECTION #1294

Personally appeared Josiah White, Caleb Trueblood, Mark Newby Being of the religious sect called quakers and solemnly affirmed that from the influence of conscientious motives, from a persuasion that Slavery was inconsistent with the divine law of the natural rights of mankind, certain of the Friends who were proprietors of negro Slaves were induced to manumit them without reserving to themselves any right of ownership or any claim to their future services. That in consequence of such manumissions the said negroes had set down in the full and free exercise of the freedom they had acquired paying a strict obedience to the laws of this state and pursuing various honest means for obtaining a subsistence, that at an Assembly held at Newbern on the eighth day of April 1777 which was subsequent to the said manumission an act passed entitled an Act to prevent domestick Insurrections and for other purposes, that by this act it is amongst other things enacted "that no Negro or Mulatto Slave shall hereafter be set free except for meritorious services to be adjudged of and allowed by the County court and licence first had and obtained thereupon. And when any Slave is or shall be set free by his or her Master or owner otherwise than is herein before directed it shall and may be lawful for any freeholder in this state to apprehend and take up such slave and deliver him or her to the Sheriff of the County who on receiving such slave shall give such Freeholder a receipt for the same and the Sheriff shall commit all such Slaves to the Gaol of the County there to remain until the next Court to be held for such County and the Court of the County shall order all such confined Slaves to be sold during the term to the highest bidder. That in consequence of such law passed certain negroes who had been the property of Thomas Newby and by him had been manumitted before the passing of this law viz Glasgow Tom Susanna Jack Cudjoe Patience Hannah Silla and certain other negroes viz James Ned Langa Phoebe which had been set free by Mark Newby who had heretofore held a property on them, and Jacob Will & Sibb manumitted by Benjamin White Peter by William White also Cuff and Rose and Hannah manumitted by Thomas White Rose by Joshua White Dick by Lydia White Jane by the said Thomas White Richard by Thomas Nicholson Jane Nicholas Nicholson Pompey by the said Thomas Nicholson, David by William Albertson Zelpha by Caleb White Violet and Fanny by Josiah White Duke by Isaac Lamb Abraham by Benjamin & Chalkley Albertson Judy by John Hasket Rose by Matthew White were seized and apprehended by certain Inhabitants of the County of Perquimans of the neighborhood thereof & by them delivered over to the Sheriff of the said County who by virtue of and obedience to several orders of the county Court of Perquimans founded as it has been suggested upon the Act of Assembly heretofore in part recited exposed the said Negroes at different times to publick vendue & sold the same to the highest bidder. The affirmants further say that the following Negroes viz Hannah who had been maunmitted previous to the passing of the said Act by Caleb Trueblood David by Charles Morgan Charles by Caleb Trueblood Toby by Matthew Pritchard Nero & Priscilla by Josiah Trueblood Rose by Thomas Newby Judith by Joseph Henley Jane by William Albertson Samuel by Mary Nixon Hagar by Charles Overman Ann by Mary Nixon & Sarah by Thomas Nicholson were in the County of Pasquotank seized by certain persons & by them delivered over to the Sheriff of the County of Pasquotank who in obedience to several orders of the Court of the same county exposed the same to publick Vendue & sold them to the highest bidder, that in consequence of such sale divers persons became purchasers who reside in different parts of this state and very remote from the places where the purchases were made, that the negroes were carried away and reduced to a state of Slavery and the Affirmants believe that in such condition they still remain in violation of the benevolent intentions of those who restored them to their natural freedom & thereby endeavoured to relieve themselves from their conscientious scruples at the justice of holding them in a state of Slavery - Thus circumtanced the affirmants further say that they have been advised by council learned in the laws & that it is their own opinion that such proceedings have been unjust illegal & extrajudicial, that such seizure detention & sale both in the County of Pasquotank & Perquimans has been an exercise of power without right & a gross infringement of the civil liberties of divers subjects of this state & in positive violation of the Bill of rights held and being part of the constitution of this State. That by the twenty fourth section of such Bill of rights it is declared that retrospective laws punishing facts committed before the existence of such laws and by them only declared criminal are oppressive unjust & incompatible with liberty wherefore no ex post facto law ought to be made. That at the Assembly of this state fully impressed with the truth of this and disposed strictly adhere to it had passed the act of Assembly heretofore in part recited intending it as a regulation of future manumission & not designed to operate upon any cases which had before the passing such act taken place. That notwithstanding such was the Spirit of the law & altho it could admit of no other legal interpretation as they are advised yet the County Courts of Pasquotank & Perquimans by forced construction and torturing expression have applied the penal operation thereof to the manumissions before mentioned, all of which took place previous to the

Chapter 19: Perquimans County Records

passing of the said Act & before the Affirmants knew or imagined that the Assembly of North Carolina had such law in Contemplation. The Affirmants further say that they are induced to think that upon a full disquision of the proceedings aforesaid before this Court it will appear that they have been both informal & substantially erroneous & a proper subject for the controlling Jurisdiction of this Court to consider & reverse & therefore the Affirmants pray that a Rule may be made as of this term for the Justices of the County Courts of Pasquotank & Perquimans to show Cause why a certiorari should not issue to them to certify to this court all records matters & things which have been made had or done relative to the seizure detention & sale of the said negroes by the said County Courts or the ministerial Officers thereof

Affirmed to, 5th May 1778   Caleb Trueblood
  before me   Mark Newby
    Saml. Ashe J' S.C.   Josiah White

***

To all to whom these presents May Come

    Know ye that we David White and Josiah Nicholson of Perquimans County North Carolina two of the Trustees of the yearly Meeting of Friends of North Carolina, have employed and do hereby Authorize and impower Charles H. Moore of Guilford County and State aforesaid, to take under his Care & Controll and Convey from this County to either or both of the Counties of Wayne and Washington in the State of Indiana Twenty One Negroes whose Names and ages are as follows (Viz) Judith Commonly Called Judith White aged about Sixty two years, and her Grand daughter Eliza aged about ten years: Peter, Called Peter Elliot aged about thirty two years; Penny, Called Penny Newby aged about thirty years and her three children, Tabitha aged about Eleven years, Catharine aged about Six years and Margaret aged about three years; Pharabe, Called Pharabe White aged about twenty six years and her four children, James aged about Eleven years, Simon Aged about eight years, Ellenor aged about five years and Murden, aged about two years: - Milton aged about Seventeen years Elias aged about fourteen years, Mavina aged About twelve years and Charlott aged About Nine years (the latter four being the children of Diver Watkins a Free Man of Colour:) Eliza aged about fifteen years Harrison Aged about thirteen years (the last two are the Children of Job Hurdle a Free man of Colour) Comfort, Called Comfort Albertson aged about thirty nine years, and her two Children Elvira aged about fourteen years and Moses aged about Seven Years Old All of which said Negroes are now in Our possession and one the Property of the Yearly Meeting of the Friends of North Carolina aforesaid as will appear on Record in Our said County of Perquimans; - And we the said David White and Josiah Nicholson Trustees as Aforesaid, through and by the Power and Authority Vested in us by said Yearly Meeting After the before Named Negroes shall Arrive in the State of Indiana do hereby by these presents Manumitt, Liberate and Set Free from Slavery each and every of the said Negroes Judith, Eliza, Peter Penny, Tabitha, Catharine, Margaret, Pharabe, James, Simon, Ellenor, Murden, Milton, Elias, Marina, Charlotte, Eliza, Harrison, Comfort, Elvira and Moses to be subject however to the existing laws of the State wherever they May be as other Free persons of Colour are.

    In Witness whereof we the said David White and Josiah Nicholson have hereunto set our hands and Seals the 25th day of the 4th Month 1829

Signed and Acknowledged
in presence of   David White   (Seal)
Nathan Winslow
Jonathan White   Josiah Nicholson   (Seal)

***

State of North Carolina }
Pasquotank County   } Before Me John R Bonnett

one of the Judges of the Superior Court of Law and Equity in the State of North Carolina, personally appeared Nathan Winslow one of the subscribing Witnesses to the forgoing Deed and Power of attorney and on his solemn Affirmation deposeth and Sayeth that he saw David White & Josiah Nicholson sign and acknowledge the same to be their Act and Deed, for the purposes therein Named; In testimony whereof I have hereunto Set my hand and Seal this 25th April 1829

        [?] Gale[?]

Chapter 19: Perquimans County Records

State of North Carolina }
Pasquotank County } I Samuel C. Moore Clerk of the Superior
Court of Law for the County aforesaid do hereby Certify that John
R Bonnett Esqr. is a Judge of the Superior Court of Law And Equity
for the State of North Carolina
Given under my hand and
Seal of office at Elza Coty
25th April 1829
Saml. C. Moore Clk

****

Martha Braxton
half sister of Michel Newby
Edmon Newby of Peola

Sely White grand
[?] of old Rose
Winslow

James Slanto[?]
Spring borough
Samuel Jones
Anna Copeland
Nathan Winslow

A List of the names
of the blacks

Richard Copeland
Judith White
Eliza White
Peter Elliot
Penny Newby
Tabitha Newby

Catharine Newby
Margaret Newby
Pharabe White
James White
Simon White
Ellenor White
Murden White
Diver Watkins

Milton }
Elias }
Merina } Watkins Children
Charlott }

Eliza [Marked Thru]
Job Hurdle

Chapter 19: Perquimans County Records

Huldah his wife
Elisha
Eliza
Harrison
Mary
Elsbery
Elisabeth
Ellenor
Richard Chappel
Comfort Albertson
Elvira
Moses

****

Day Book

Containing an account of the Expences of a Company of blacks Sent from Perquimans to Indiana Which started the 27th of the 4th mo. 1829

Chapter 20

Randolph County

NORTH CAROLINA STATE ARCHIVES
RANDOLPH COUNTY RECORDS
MISCELLANEOUS RECORDS
C.R.081.928.5

PETITION OF JOHN RIDING & JONATHAN RIDING

State of North Carolina } Superior Court of Law
Randolph County } Spring Term 1821

To the Honourable the Judge of the Superior Court of Law for Randolph County -- The Petition of John Riding & Jonathan Riding Sheweth unto Your Honour that Joseph Riding in his lifetime and at the time of his death Owned a negro man Slave by the name of Dick that the said Joseph Riding departed this life on the 10th day of January 1814 having first made and published his last Will and testament in Writing and Appointed your Petitioners his Executors Who proved his Said Will & took upon themselves the burthen of executing the Same - That the Said Joseph Riding by his Said Will bequeathed the Negro Slave Dick to his Wife Jane Riding during her lifetime - and then directed that the Said Negro Slave be emancipated and set free - The Said Jane Riding departed this life in the Month of September 1821 --Your Petitioners pray your Honour to grant them permission to emancipate the said Negro Slave Dick - He having performed meritorious Services - According to the directions of the aforesaid last Will & testament of their father the Said Joseph Riding Decd. And further pray your Honour to adjudge and decree that the Said Negro Dick be emancipated & Set free & be invested with all the rights privileges of a free Man of Colour.
And your Petitioners as in duty bound Will ever pray &c.
Signed   Jonathan Riding} Extr

ELIJAH SWEARINGEN & URIA TROGDEN'S BOND

Know all men by these presents that We Elijah Swearingen & Uria Trogden are held & firmly bound unto William Hogan Esqr Chairman of the Court of pleas and Quarter Sessions for Randolph County and his Successors in Office in the Sum of One hundred pounds Current Money of the State of North Carolina to Which payment well and truly to be made We bind Ourselves Our heirs &c jointly and Severally & firmly by these presents Sealed with our hands and dated this 4th of October AD 1824

The Condition of the Above Obligation is Such Whereas a Certain Man of Colour by the name of Dick Ridding hath been emancipated & set free by the Honourable the Superior Court of Law for Randolph County - now if the Said Dick Ridding Shall not become Chargeable to the County of Randolph for his Support & Maintenance at any period during his life then the above Obligation to be Void - In Testimony Whereof We have hereunto Set our hands & seals the day & date Above Written

Test	his	
Jno m Dick	Elijah X Swearingen	(Seal)
	mark	
	Uria Trogden	(Seal)

DICK RIDDING, ELIJAH SWEARINGEN & URIA TROGDEN'S BOND

Chapter 20: Randolph County Records

Know all men by these presents that We Dick Ridding Elijah Swearingen Uria Trogden are held and firmly bound unto his Excellency Gabriel Holmes Esqr. Governor of the State of North Carolina & his Successors in Office in the Sum of two hundred pounds Current Money of the State aforesaid to which payment well and truly to be made we bind Ourselves Our heirs &C jointly & Severally & firmly by these presents Sealed with Our Seals and dated this 4th day of October 1824.

The Condition of the Above Obligation is Such Whereas the Above Bounden Dick Ridding hath been emancipated and Set free by a Decree of the Honourable the Superior Court of Law for Randolph County - Now if the Said Dick Ridding Shall be of good behaviour to all the Citizens of North Carolina during his residence in Said State and shall Conduct himself as a peaceable and Orderly Citizen then the Above Obligation to be Void In testimony Whereof We have hereunto Set Our hands and Seals the day & date Above Written.

Test	his	
Jno m Dick	Dick X Ridding	(Seal)
	mark	
	his	
	Elijah X Swearingen	(Seal)
	mark	
	Uria Trogden	(Seal)

****

PETITION OF GEORGE FENTRIS

State of North Carolina }
Randolph County } November Sessions 1801

To the worshipfull the County Court of Randolph,

The petition of George Fentris humbly sheweth that he is the Owner of a Negro Woman Slave by the Name of Aliss Henly a female Child a daughter of Said Aliss by the Name of Cazy Which for the Meritorious Services of the Said Negro woman Which your petitioner is fully Satisfied and for Which prays that they the said Aliss and Caze may be liberated and Set free from their present State of Slavery as far as the law in that Case made and provided Shall and does direct and your petitioner will ever be thankfull.

Thereby request you Edward Fentriss to hand in A petition to the county court held at randolph courthouse the first monday in november in order to have Aliss and her child Caze mannumited as if I was present myself I say by me.

test	his	
Benjamin Hill	George X Fentriss	
	mark	

****

PETITION OF ZACHARIAH NICHOLSON & OTHERS

To the Honourable Court of pleas & quarter sessions of Randolph Now seting the petition of your petitioners Humbly Sheweth that having lawfully by a hereditery Right in our posession a negro man Named Mingo Pritchard, who hath Behaved himself Becomingly Honestly and Faithfully which we think Meritorious: therefore the petition of your petitioners is that you may Be pleased to Emancipate or manumit the above Said Slave Mingo Pritchard, So that he may be a free man agrable to Law, and your petitioners as in duty bound Shall Acknowledge &C: &C: this 3d Day of the Eleventh month 1801

Zachariah Nicholson
John Pritchard
Jesse Hill

Chapter 20: Randolph County Records

Joseph Pritchard

Sent from David Smith Senr. to John & Aaron Sanders of Loudon County Virginia Was proved by Bryan Smith Sr.

A Petition for a manamission Granted

****

PETITION OF WILLIAM BELL & JOSEPH DOOGAN

To the worshipfull the County Court of Pleas & quarter Sessions for the County of Randolph,
    The Petition of William Bell and Joseph Doogan of Said County Humbly Sheweth - that your petitioners have the right & titles to two Negroe slaves Named George and Margaret that the said Negroes are & have been Obedient orderly & industrious and in Consequence of the good behaviour of Said Slaves Your Petitioners some time since agreed to let them have their freedom provided they would pay to your petitioners the sum of five hundred & fifty Dollars which at that time was considered their value, that the said Slaves have by their own industry paid the whole of the aforesaid sum and Supported themselves decently during the time they were making the same   Your petitioners therefore are of the opinion said Slaves have acted Meritoriously & are entitled to their freedom   Your petitioners therefore prays your Worships to Emancipate said George & Margaret & grant them all those privileges that free persons of Colour are entitled to in this State & Your Petitioners as in duty bound will ever pray

Test A Gray
            Wm Bell
            Robert Walker[?]
            Joseph Doogan

The prayer of the Petitioners granted on the said Slaves giving bond & Security agreeable to Law
            E Mander[?] Ck

****

BOND OF JOSEPH HASKETT, PETER DICKS, & WILLIAM DENNIS

Know all men by these presents that we Joseph Haskett, Peter Dicks, William Dennis all of the County of Randolph and State of North Carolina are held & firmly bound unto Zebedee Wood Chairman of Randolph County Court & his Successors in Office for the use of the Poor of Randolph County in the just and full sum of one Hundred pounds Currency, for the which payment will & truly to be made & done we bind ourselves, & each of our heirs Executors & Admrs. Jointly & Severally - firmly by these presents sealed with our Seals & dated this 8th day of February 1814 -

    The Condition of the above obligation is such that whereas a Certain Negroe woman named Sarah & her Child named Paton the lately[**Marked thru**] the propert of Joseph Hasket Senr. hath been liberated and set free by an order of the County Court of Randolph at February Term 1814 - Now if the said Joseph Haskett, Peter Dicks & William Dennis shall well & truly keep the County of Randolph indemnified from the maintenance of the said Negro Sarah & her child Paton so that the said negro Sarah & child shall not become chargeable to the said County, then the above obligation shall be void & of none effect, else to remain in full force & virtue.

Interlined before signing	Joseph Haskett	(Seal)
Witness - Jesse Harper	Peter Dicks	(SeaL)
	Wm. Dennis	(Seal)

****

BOND OF MATTHEW SYMONS & ROBT. N [?]

State of North Carolina

    We the Subscribers acknowledge ourselves indebted to Zebedee Wood esquire Chairman of the County Court of Randolph & His Successors in office for the use of the Poor of said County in the sum of one hundred pounds to which

Chapter 20: Randolph County Records

payment we bind ourselves and our heirs - But to be Void if a certain Negro Named Pompy the property of Joseph Hasket and now liberated by the County Court of Randolph shall not become chargeable to the County Parish

Witness our hands and seals this 2nd of August 1803

Test	Robt. N [?]	(Seal)
A. Mbryde	Matthew Symons	(Seal)

Chapter 21: Rockingham County Records

chapter 21

Rockingham County

NORTH CAROLINA STATE ARCHIVES
ROCKINGHAM COUNTY RECORDS
MISCELLANEOUS RECORDS
C.R.084.928.3

        John Robertson Exor for Jarret Bowling
        Deed of Emancipation Joseph
        Registered in 2nd. Book R. Page 452

Know all men by these presents that I, John Robertson, Executor of the last will & Testament of Jarrat Bowling decd. late of the county of Rockingham & state of North Carolina, in obedience to the directions of the Testator in the said Will Contained, and with the permission of the Superior Court of Law for Rockingham County at the Fall Term thereof in the year 1852, have manumitted and set free from Slavery, and do hereby manumit and set free from Slavery a certain negro slave named Joseph, aged about thirty years, of yellow complexion, thick Curly hair, and near six feet in height, the said boy being a good boot and Shoe maker and a good Coarse harness maker

  And I do hereby give grant & release unto the said Joseph, all my right, title and claim of, in, and to the person, labor and services of the said Joseph as well as to all the estate and property which he may hereafter acquire or obtain.

  In witness whereof I John Robertson Exr. of the Last Will & Testament of Jarrat Bowling decd. have hereunto set my hand & affixed my seal This the 10th Day of January AD 1853.
John Robertson Exr. (Seal)
of Jarret Bowling Dcd.

State of North Carolina }
Rockingham County } In office of the clerk of the Court of pleas & Quarter Sessions for the County aforesaid.

I TB Wheeler Clerk of the Court of Pleas & Quarter Sessions for the County aforesaid hereby certify that the foregoing Deed of manumission from John Robertson Exor. to Slave Joseph was this day produced into my office & acknowledged by the said Robertson to be his Act & Deed. Therefore let the same be registered - Given under my hand this the 10th day of January AD 1853
    TB Wheeler CCC

State of North Carolina }
Rockingham County }

  I Abraham Perkins public register for said county certify that the foregoing deed of manumition was registered in the registers office for above said county in 2nd Book R Page 452. Given under my hand this 24th day of Jany AD 1853.
A Perkins P.R.
By E.W. House[?] DR

Chapter 22: Stokes County Records

chapter 22

Stokes County

NORTH CAROLINA STATE ARCHIVES
STOKES COUNTY RECORDS
MISCELLANEOUS RECORDS
C.R.090.928.13

To the Honorable the General Assembly
State of North Carolina, November Session 1810
  We the Citizens of Stokes County & State aforesaid Humbly sheweth that Richard a black Man formerly the Property of Mr. Noble Ladd, of said County, has lately purchased his Freedom of his Master Mr. Noble Ladd, that he has a free Woman to his Wife and several Children which they indeavour to bring up in an Orderly Manner together with some property that they have acquired by their Labor; We have known him for a Number of years beleaving him to be an honest, industerous Man, that he will still Support that Character and raise his family in repa[?], and free from Want. We Humbly solicit your Honorable body, that you will Liberate & set free the sd. Richard and your Petitioners will ever Pray &c.

Thomas Carr JP	Charles Angel	Thornton P. Guinn
J. Vaughn	Charles Dalton	William Barnett
Abel Lomax	John Ward	William Ward
Absalom Bostick	Jos. Winston	Samuel Garrod
Tho. L. Douglas	David Dalton	Adam Crawford
Isaac Dalton J.P.	Jn. Evans J.P.	Richard Gentry
Joel [?]angton	Peter Burton	Laurence Angel
Stokes County		

  I do certify that the above Named Negro, Richard has faithfully Served me since his childhood is Now about fifty years of Age Durring all which Time he Conducted himselfe as an honest industrous man and as he has fully satisfied me for the balence of his time or Life I pray the Gineral Assembly to pass a law giving him said Richard his freedom, by the name of Richard Ladd october 13th 1810
    Noble Ladd

Know all men by these Presents We Isaac Dalton Joseph Winston & Boling Fisher are firmly bound unto George Hauser Chairman of the County Court of Stokes in the full sum of One Hundred Pounds to be paid unto the said George Hauser Chairman as aforesaid or his Successors in Office To which we bind ourselves Our heirs Exrs & Admrs. jointly & severally by these presents sealed with our Seals & Dated the 14th March 1811.

  The Condition of this obligation is such that whereas Richard a man of Color belonging to Noble Ladd has been emancipated by the County Court of Stokes at March term 1811. Now if the said Isaac Dalton Joseph Winston & Boling Fisher shall well & truly Keep the said Richard from becoming Chargeable to the County aforesaid, then the above obligation to be Void, otherwise to remain in full force & Virtue

Test	Isaac Dalton	(Seal)
Tho. T. Armstrong DC	Jos. Winston	(Seal)
	Bolling Fisher	(Seal)

****

Chapter 22: Stokes County Records

Carolina Gazette more than six Weeks before the Sitting of this Court --

 Your Petitioner therefore prays Your Honor to Order and decree that Your Petitioner on giving the proper bonds be permitted to Emancipate Said Slaves according to the provisions of the Statutes in such Cases made and provided, and to Grant unto your Petitioner all such other and further relief as the Notice of his Case may require as in duty bound he will Ever Pray &C.
    John N. Gilmer
    Atto for Petitioner

    Thomas Vass Ex Parte
 Petition for Emancipation of Slaves James & Lucretia
    filed Fall Term 1842
   Isaac Gibson & Robert Walker, Surities
   J.N.G. Atto. my fee paid me by plf.
    J.N. Gilmer

State of North Carolina	} Superior Court of Law
Stokes County	} October Term 1842
Thomas Voss	} Petition to Emancipate
Ex Parte	} Slaves

 John L. Belting [?] that more than six weks before the Sitting of this Court, he Saw Affixed & Posted at the Court House Door of Stokes County, an advertisement substantially in the words and figures following towit
 "Emancipation of Slaves" By Virtue of a Act of the General Assembly of North Carolina Passed A.D. 1830 prescribing the manner of Emancipating Slaves, I shall file a Petition in the next Superior Court of Stokes County to be held at Germanton, for the purpose of Emancipating my Slaves, James and Lucretia.
August 15th 1842
    Thomas Voss
Or to that par post
J.L. Belting
Sworn to before
J. Estering C.S.C.

Col. Isaac Golding will make out a Copy of the Petition & the decree - and certify as follows --

State of N.C.	}
Stokes County	}

 I Isaac Golding Clerk &C. do hereby certify that the forgoing is a reue Copy & Exemplification of the record of our said Court in my Office in the application of Thomas Voss for the Emancipation of his two Slaves James & Lucretia.

In Testimony whereof I have hereunto Set my Official Seal at office this 10th day of October 1842 (Seal)
Test.

Stokes Superior Court of Law
Fall Term A.D. 1842

Thomas Voss	} Petition for Emancipation of Slaves
Ex Parte	} James & Lucretia

Chapter 22: Stokes County Records

This Case coming on to be heard on the reading of the Petition, the affidavit filed, the proofs offered, and it appearing to the satisfaction of the Court that due advertisement hath been made for six weeks previous to the Sitting of this Court in the Carolina Gazette and at the Court House Door & further the Petitioner having given bond in the penal sum of two thousand dollars with Isaac Gibson and Robert Walker his Securities, Conditioned that the Slaves James & Lucretia shall each honestly & correctly demean themselves, while they remain within the State of North Carolina, that they shall leave the State within ninety days, & never afterwards come within the same.

It is Considered ordered, adjudged and decreed by the Court that the Petitioner Thomas Voss have full power and authority to Emancipate his Slaves mentioned in the Petition James & Lucretia, & the said Slaves James & Lucretia are hereby Emancipated, & in all things invested with the rights of free persons of Colour.

Thomas Voss Ex Parte
Petition for Emancipation of Slaves James and Lucretia
Bond $2000
Isaac Gibson
Robert Walker
Sureties

Know all men by these presents - that we Thomas Voss, Isaac Gibson and Robert Walker are held & firmly bound unto the State of North Carolina in the sum of two thousand dollars, for the payment of which well and truly to be made and done, we bind ourselves our heirs &C jointly & severally firmly by these presents. Witness our hands & Seals this the 10th day of October A.D. 1842.

The Condition of the above obligation is such whereas the above bounden Thomas Voss hath obtained a decree of our Superior Court of Law for Stokes County to Emancipate his two slaves James and Lucretia, now if the said slave shall Each honestly and correctly demean themselves, while they remain within the State of North Carolina, and that the said Slaves Each James & Lucretia shall within ninety days from the date hereof leave the State of North Carolina, and Never Afterwards Come within the same then the above obligation to be void otherwise to remain in full force and Effect.

Syned Sealed and	Thos Voss	(Seal
delivered in the presence of	I. Gibson	(Seal)
Isaac Golding C.S.C.	Robert Walker	(Seal)

Chapter 23: Surry County Records

chapter 23

Surry County

NORTH CAROLINA STATE ARCHIVES
GENERAL ASSEMBLY SESSIONS RECORDS
NOV-DEC, 1802, BOX #1

Nov 5th 1802

The Honbl. the Gen'l Assembly

Your petitioner prays Your Honorable Body to take in consideration & pass an act to emancipate my Negro Slave Charles, whose long steady faithfull & Meritorious servitude entitles him to this my good will   Yours &c ever praying

Matthew Davis, senior

N:B the above named Charles prays your Honorable Body to give him the name of Charles Peters

---

In Senate Novembr 24th 1802
Read & refered to the Committee of Emancipation
By order   M Stokes Clk

The Report of the Committee on Emancipations On the Petition of Matthew Davis

The Committee of Emancipations to whom was refered the petition of Matthew Davis of Surry County praying that his negroe fellow Charles might be emancipated and that his name should henceforward be known by that of Charles Peters.
    Report that in the opinion of Your Committee it would be highly proper that the prayer of the petitioner should be granted, and that the said Charles should be Liberated; and henceforward known by the name of Charles Peters -- therefore recommend the Bill accompanying this report to be passed into Law.
        Submitted

In Senate 2 Decr 1802
    The foregoing report was read & concurred with.

By order   Jo Riddick S S
M Stokes Clk

In House of Commons 4 December 1802
Read & Concurred with
By order   S. Cabarrus Sp
J Hunt

A Bill to emancipate Charles, the property of Matthew Davis Senr. of the County of Surry
    Whereas it is the request of Matthew Davis Senr. of the County of Surry that his negroe man Charles should be emancipated and set free.

Chapter 23: Surry County Records

    Be it enacted by the General Assembly of the State of North Carolina and it is hereby enacted by the authority of the same That from and after the passing of this act, the said negroe man Charles, be emancipated and set free from slavery, and that he be henceforth called and known by the name of Charles Peters, under which name he shall be invested, and henceforward be entitled to possess and enjoy all the rights, privileges, and immunities of what kind or nature soever, and to all intents and purposes in as full and ample a manner as any free person of Colour, any thing to the contrary not withstanding

Chapter 24: Wake County Records

chapter 24

Wake County

NORTH CAROLINA STATE ARCHIVES
WAKE COUNTY RECORDS
MISCELLANEOUS RECORDS
C.R.099.928.12

Allen Rogers & others
Petition for Emancipation

State of North Carolina }
Wake County } Court of Pleas & Quarter Sessions

To the Worshipful the Justices of the Court of Pleas and Quarter Sessions for the County of Wake. The Petition of Allen Rogers and Henry Moring Executors of the last Will and Testament of Wilie Rogers decd. and Silah Rogers.

Respectfully represents that Willie Rogers died sometime in the year **[Blank]** possessed of a negro man slave by the name of Monday, and leaving a last Will and Testament in writing, in which the bequeathed the said negro to your petitioner Silah Rogers during her natural life, and directed the remainder or the said slave, together with other articles of property, to be disposed of at the discretion of the said Allen Rogers and Henry Moring his Executors -- Your petitioners are very desirous of having the said negro Monday emancipated on account of the late unexampled and meritorious conduct of the said negro whereby the lives of Isaac and Jonathan Lane, Hardy Burt, and your petitioner Allen, were saved. The facts are these - Some few weeks past, when the last mentioned Gentlemen were travelling in the State of Georgia with a number of negro fellows, seven of the fellows conspired together for the purpose of killing them and all the negroes who would not join in their conspiracy - In pursuance of that plot, the Fellows armed themselves with Clubs and at a dead hour of the night, whilst the Gentlemen were asleep, were upon the eve of executing their diabolical intention, when one of the fellows awoke Monday to assist them, & mentioned to him their intentions - Monday immediately threatened to inform against them, and in the confusion which their attempts to silence him produced, he run off and gave the information to your petitioner Allen, and thereby saved his life, as your petitioner believes, together with the lives of the other Gentlemen.

Your petitioner further states to your Worships that they have now in their possession, ample funds for the purpose of purchasing a younger & more valuable slave for the use of the legatees of the said Willie Rogers, in the event of Monday being emancipated. Your Petitioners therefore pray that on account of the above mentioned meritorious services performed by the said slave Monday, Your Worships will exercise the power vested in you by an Act of Assembly, and grant your license that he be emancipated and set free, and your petitioners will ever pray &c.

****

Wm. Andrews Petition

State of North Carolina } Court of Pleas & Quarter Sessions
Wake County } May Term AD 1819

To the worshipful the Justices of said Court the Petition of William Andrews -- Humbly sheweth unto your worships your Petitioner that he is the owner of a negro woman slave by the name of Rosetta, whom is anxious for her meritorious services to liberate & set free - Your Petitioner sheweth unto your Worships that the said Rosetta hath ever been an industrious faithful & obedient slave - & for her fidelity & attachment to your Petitioner, & humanity in the following instance has entitled herself to his lasting gratitude ---- A negro man slave owned by your Petitioner had

Chapter 24: Wake County Records

determined to avenge on your Petitioner, correction which she had justly received, by murdering Petitioners only child & to secure himself from detection & punishment he resolved to administer poison to the child. The diabolical plan became accidently known to Rosetta who immediately disclosed it to your Petitioner & thereby saved the life of his child -- the negro man was taken up & sent to the State of Georgia -- Your Petitioner prays your worships to exercise in favour of the said Rosetta, that power which the Legislature of our County has for wise & benevolent purposes entrusted to your hands by emancipating & seting her free - or by enabling your Petitioner to do so & as in duty bound he will ever pray &c

       F Nash for Petr.

****

Mark Childs & others
To
Wm Boylan
Chairman
Bond to indemnify Parish

North Carolina }
Wake County }

  Know all men by these presents that We Mark Childs & [Blank] are held & firmly bound unto William Boylan Chairman of the Court of said County & his successors to the use of the Poor of said County in the penal Sum of One Hundred Pounds - To which payment well & truly to be made We bind Ourselves & our Heirs.

  The Condition of the above obligation is such that Whereas the said Mark hath by his Petition in the Supr. Court of said County at Spring Term 1820 - procured the Liberation & Emancipation of a certain Slave named [Blank] the Wife of said Mark Now if the said Mark shall prevent the said [Blank] from becoming Chargeable to the Parish of said County then this obligation to be utterly null & Void, otherwise to remain in full force.

Signed & Sealed this 6th April 1825.   his
              Mark X Childs (Seal)
                mark
              Chas: Manly[?] (Seal)

****

Allen Jones
to the Court
Petition for the emancipation of Slaves
Filed Autumn Term A.D. 1829

To the Honorable the Judge of the Superior Court of the County of Wake.
  The Petition of Allen Jones a free man of Color, of the City of Raleigh humbly shews to your Honour, that he is the owner of several negro Slaves towit, Tempe, Munro, Bethena and Burham - that Tempe is the wife of your petitioner, and Munro, Bethena and Burham the children of your petitioner and the said Tempe - Your petitioner further shews unto your Honour, that the Character & deportment of the said slaves and more particularly of the said Tempe is fair & upright and their services toward your petitioner as well as towards her former owner has been diligent faithful & highly meritorious, in consideration of which your petitioner desires to emancipate & set free the said slaves, and humbly prays a license therefore from your Honour with such final order in the premises as may fully & completely effect your petitioners desire & the liberation of his said slaves and your petitioner as in duty bound will ever pray.

Sea[?]ell, Ruffin & Badg[?]
for the Petitioner

****

Cherry Malone & Edmund Malone

Chapter 24: Wake County Records

Emancipation By John Malone 1847

State of North Carolina
Wake County

    Know all Men by these presents that John Malone as principal and Wm H McKee James Edwards Sureties are held and firmly bound unto the State of North Carolina in the sum of Five Hundred Dollars to the payment of which we bind ourselves our Heirs and Assigns Witness our hands & seals this the sixth day of March AD 1847.

    The condition of the above obligation is as follows: that if Cherry Malone and Edmund Malone this day to be emancipated by John Malone according to the provisions of an Act of Assembly entitled "An Act authorizing John Malone a free man of color to emancipate his wife & son upon Conditions herein Mentioned" shall each be of good behaviour during his or her residence in the State and shall neither of them after their emancipation become chargeable to the County of Wake or any other parish or County in North Carolina and if the said John Malone shall renew his bond with approved Security when it shall be required at any time by the County Court of Wake County then the above obligation shall be void, but otherwise it shall be & remain in full force & virtue.

	his	
	John X Malone	(Seal)
Witness	mark	
James T. Marriott	W.H. McKee	(Seal)
	Jas Edwards	(Seal)

    This the March[?] at Wake County we the undersigned Justices of the Peace for Wake aforesaid do hereby approve of the foregoing bond and of the Sureties Merits to wit: Wm. H McKee and James Edwards -- and do direct & advise that the same shall be approved and taken by the Clerk of Wake County Court according to the provisions of Act of Assembly in such case made & passed at the Session of said General Assembly begun & held at Raleigh the 3rd Monday of November 1846 - Witness our hands & seals 6th March 1847.

Wm. H. Haywood Jr	JP	(Seal)
W.H. Holleman	JP	(Seal)

Clerks Office of Wake County Court

    John Malone this day tendered the foregoing bond to me and upon the approbation of Will H Haywood Jr & Wm. H. Holloman two Justices of the Peace for said County I have approved & accepted the same.

    And afterwards and upon the same day the said John Malone delivered his Deed emancipating the two slaves Cherry and Edmund in the words & figures following to wit:

A Copy

An Act Authorizing John Malone, a free man of Color, to emancipate his Wife and Son, upon certain conditions herein mentioned.Be it enacted by the General Assembly of the State of North Carolina, and it is hereby enacted by the authority of the same, That John Malone, a free Man of Color in the County of Wake, be, and he is hereby authorized to emancipate from Slavery, Cherry, his Wife, and Edmund his Son, who are the slaves of the said John Malone, and that the said Cherry, by the name of Cherry Malone, and the said Edmund, by the name of Edmund Malone, Shall henceforth be free, and have and enjoy the same rights and privileges as if they had been born free in this State, and may at their pleasures continue to reside in North Carolina, any law to the contrary notwithstanding: Provided, That the said Edmund Malone shall be, after his emancipation, considered in law the legitimate Son and heir of said John Malone, and capable in law to succeed as such to the property, real and personal, whereof the said John Malone may die seized and possessed, without devising it or otherwise conveying it to others in all respects as though the said Edmund had been born in lawful Wedlock, of the Body of the lawful Wife of the said John Malone: And Provided, further, That the said John Malone, shall in due form of law intermarry with said Cherry Malone, and make her his lawful Wife, on the same day that she shall be emancipated by him from slavery.
Be it further enacted, That before the said John Malone shall emancipate the said slaves, Cherry and Edmund, and as a precedent condition to give the said Act of emancipation effect in this State, the said John Malone shall give a bond in

Chapter 24: Wake County Records

the penal sum of five hundred dollars, payable to the State of North Carolina and conditioned, that the said two slaves, Cherry and Edmund, shall each be of good behaviour during his or her residence in the State, and that neither of them shall, after their emancipation, become chargeable to the County of Wake, or any parish or County in North Carolina, and further Conditioned that the said John Malone will renew the said bond, with approved security, when it shall at any time be required by the County Court of Wake, and the Clerk of the County Court of Wake, under the written approbation of any two Justices of the Peace, or the County Court of Wake County, may take the first bond, and the said John Malone shall give one or more good and approved Sureties to the said bond, as well as the one executed at first, as any other given in renewal thereof.

Ratified in General Assembly   }
on this 2nd. day of January 1847   }
Robt. B. Gilliam   Speaker of the House of Commons.
A. Joyner   Speaker of the Senate

State of North Carolina
    Office of the Secretary of State,
I William Hill Secretary of State in and for the State of North Carolina do hereby certify that the foregoing is a true copy of an act of the General Assembly of 1847, drawn off from the original which is on file in this Office.

Given under my hand this 15th day of January 1847.
Wm. Hill   Secretary of State

Know all Men by these presents that I John Malone of the City of Raleigh Wake County in pursuence of the power & authority Conferred by the Act of Assembly Whereof a Certified Copy is written on the two pages preceding do hereby emancipate and set free absolutely my two Slaves to wit   Cherry to be hereafter by the name of Cherry Malone and Edmund to be hereafter to be known by the name of Edmund Malone   And in further [?] of said Act I have this day & before the delivery of this my Deed given bond and Security as therein required which bond has been filed with the Clerk of the County Court of Wake aforesaid

In Witness Whereof I have hereto set my hand & seal the Sixth day of March 1847.

Witness   his
James T. Marriott   John X Malone   (Seal)
                                 mark

In Witness whereof I James T. Marriot have hereto set my hand & the seal of the County Court this Sixth day of March AD. 1847.
James T. Marriott Clerk
of the County Court of Wake County.

Chapter 25: Warren County Records

chapter 25

Warren County

NORTH CAROLINA STATE ARCHIVES
WARREN COUNTY RECORDS
MISCELLANEOUS RECORDS
C.R.100.928.3

Emancipation Bond

Bond for the emancipation of Polydore & Miranda two Slave late the Property of Wm. E. Johnson dec'd.

Warren County May Court 1811

This Bond was executed in open Court and on motion ordered to be recorded.
Test Wm Green CCo

State of No. Carolina
    Know all men by these Presents, that we James Turner, William Twitty and Buckner Davis all of the County of Warren, in the State aforesaid, are held and firmly bound unto Henry G. Williams, Chairman of the Court for the County of Warren and his Successors, in the sum of two hundred pounds, current money, to be paid to the said Henry G. Williams Chairman as aforesaid and his Successors, for the use and benefit of the poor of the County aforesaid; to which payment well and truly to be made, we bind ourselves, and each of us, each and every of our heirs, executors & administrators, jointly and severally, firmly by these presents
Seal'd with our seals, and dated the 29th day of May in the year of our Lord one thousand eighteen hundred and eleven--

    The Condition of the above obligation is such, that, Whereas at a Court held for the County of Warren, on the fourth Monday of May in the year eighteen hundred and eleven two negro[Marked Thru] Mulatto Slaves, to wit - one by the name of Polydore, a Man Slave, the other by the Name of Miranda, a female Slave, late the property of William Eaton Johnston dec'd, were liberated, manumitted and set free by and under the names of Polydore Johnston and Miranda Eaton upon the application of the aforesaid James Turner & William Twitty: Now if the said James Turner, William Twitty [and Buckner Davis] [The words "and Buckner Davis" are marked through] Shall well and truly indemnify and save harmles the Parish & County of Warren, from all costs and charges which may be imposed thereon either heretofore or hereafter forward on Account of the Negro Slaves So as aforesaid liberated, So that they do not become chargeable to the Parish or County aforesaid, then the above obligation to be void, otherwise to remain in full force and virtue.

Signed sealed and	James Turner	(Seal)
delivered in presence	Will: Twitty	(Seal)
of Wm. Green	B. Davis	(Seal)

****

SOUTHERN HISTORICAL COLLECTION
THE UNIVERSITY OF NORTH CAROLINA PRESS
MANUSCRIPT COLLECTION
HAWKINS FAMILY PAPERS
COLLECTION # 322

Chapter 25: Warren County Records

WARREN COUNTY

Box #1, Folder 6A

Will of Philemon Hawkins

I Philemon Hawkins Senior of the County of Warren and State of North Carolina of Sound and Perfect Memory do make and ordain my last Will and Testament in manner and form following.Imprimis, whereas I have heretofore given unto my Son John Hawkins more valuable lands than to either of my other Sons, also the more valuable of my Lots in the Town of Warrenton for which reason I do not wish or desire that he should have any more of my landed or real Estate than heretofore given him. I give to him my Son John the following Negro Slaves (Towit) Frank, Sukey and her child, Wordley and little Moses and their future increase, Two feather beds and furniture, Two Cows and Calves, my dark bay horse called Conner and Two yoke of Oxen to him and his heirs and assigns forever.--

My Son Philemon having found all the sawest Timbers and contributed otherwise in finding hands and having the Work executed in building my Sandy Creek Mill, I give and bequeath to him my said Son Philemon the Mill aforesaid and Two Thousand Acres of Land adjoining & including Said Mill and also Ball's Tract of Land to him his heirs and assigns forever, also the following Negro Slaves (Towit) Joe, my Miller at said Mill, his Wife Rhitte and her Children and their future increase, also Two feather beds & furniture, Ten Cows & Calves my blased face Sorrel Horse and two yoke of Oxen.

I give and devise to my Son Benjamin my manor plantation and all my lands adjoining thereto on the Waters of Fishing Creek and also a small Tract of Land adjoining his Roanoake Lands to him his heirs and assigns forever, and also the Negroes and their increase which he my said Son Benjamin has had entered on the records of Warren County Court as the property of my son Joseph dec'd and which he my Son Benjamin claims as formerly belonging to my said Son Joseph also Two feather beds and furniture & my large looking Glass which is placed over my Hall fire place, my Cloath's Press, and all my leathered bottomed chairs, Ten Cows and Calves, my Grey horse and Two yoke of Oxen.

I give to my Two Grandsons Benjamin Son of John and John D. Hawkins Son of Philemon Hawkins, the balance of my Lands on Sandy Creek, (except two hundred and fifty Acres on the South side of H. Ballads Tract to include Howells improvement) to them their heirs and assigns forever, I also give unto my said Grandson John D. Hawkins two negro Boys, one named Hopewell the other bud and to my said Grandson Benjamin One Hundred Pounds Virga. Money for the Purpose of Purchasing him Two negro Boys.

I give to my daughter Lucy Wife to my Son Philemon Two Negro Girls Sal & Rachell (children of Dorcas) and their future increase to wait on her and be at her own disposal.

I request and desire that my Son Benjamin give to my Grand Daughter Priscilla Cotton a Negro Girl between the age of Twelve and fifteen years.

It is my Will and desire that my Executors herein after named if in their Power prove the Emancipation of my old Waiting man Harry and old Jack and if they should be emancipated I give to each of them three Cows & Calves and Twenty five Barrels Of Corn and four hundred weight of Nitt Pork to each, But should my said Waiting Man not be emancipated then I give him to my Son Benjamin, with a request, which I know to be almost unnecessary that he should be well treated the Residue of his days.

I give and bequeath all the rest and residue of my Negroes to my Sons John and Philemon to be equally divided between them, to them and their heirs and assigns forever.

Whereas I am involved in a disagree Law Suit with my Grand Son Philemon Son of John and others respecting my Fishing Creek Lands and other Property being the lands which I have herein before Willed to my Son Benjamin, which property is claimed by defendants in said Suit by certain Deeds or Pretended Deeds of Gift obtained from me by fraud and Deceit. It is my desire that if the said Deeds should not be vacated and Set aside but should be held good, Then my Sons Benjamin and Philemon shall be indemnified and remunerated for their Loss of Property sustained thereby out of

Chapter 25: Warren County Records

my Son John's Part of my Estate, it being my intention to charge his part of my estate with the value of the said property contained in said Deeds in Case they should not be vacated and Set aside.

It is my desire that my son John lay out Money which he is indebted to me in the Purchase of Books for his son John.

As Part of my Estate is in Warren and Part in Granville County, It is my desire that General Thomas Eaton, Captain James Turner and Mr. Green Duke of Warren County and Colonel Joseph Taylor, Colonel Charles Eaton and Major James Vaughan of Granville County, or a Majority of them divide my Negroes between my Said Sons John and Philemon according to the foregoing Part of this Will and Settle any Disputes which may arise respecting my estate among the Legatees.

It is my desire that all the expenses of my law Suits with my Grand Son Philemon Son of John and with others should be deducted out of my Son John's Part of my Estate.

Teste   Phil. Hawkins   (Seal)
James Vaughan
W. Gilliam

It is my desire that the Balance of my Estate be sold at Six months Credit and after the Payments of my Debts and legacies the residue to be applied Towards the educating of and purchasing Books for my Grandson's John and Micajah Thomas Sons of my Son

John and Joseph, Benjamin, Philemon, Frank and George Washington Sons of my son Philemon.
I give and bequeath to my Son Philemon Hawkins in Trust for Phoebe Seagrove all the property which I had of John Seagrove also three Cows and Calves, Twenty Barrels of Corn and one Thousand Weight of Nett Pork and one Bed, It is my desire that she lives where she does now during her life or at some convenient place on the same Tract of Land where my Son Benjamin may choose.

I constitute and appoint my Son's John, Philemon and Benjamin and my friend Leonard Henderson Executors of this my last Will and Testament, with Power to act sell and divide property without rules or Orders of Court.

It is my desire that my old Negroes (Towit) Hannah, Jim, Doll, Robin, Moll, Nansey, and Lucy be Kept on my Manor Plantation and Supported at the joint expence of my three Sons, they doing Moderate Work or such as they are able. In Testimony Whereof I have hereunto Set my hand and affixed my Seal this Twenty Second Day of July Anno Dom. (1802) Eighteen hundred and two.
            Phil Hawkins   (Seal)
Signed Sealed published anddeclared by the Testator Phil. Hawkins Senior to be his last Will and Teatament in the presenceof us and Subscribed by us as Witnesses to his Will in his Presenceand at his Request
James Vaughan
W. Gilliam

I Philemon Hawkins Senior of the County of Warren and State of North Carolina do make and ordain this to be a Codicil to my last Will and Testament bearing date the Twenty Second Day of July 1801. **Whereas my Boy Matthew** has discovered an honest disposition in making Known to me many Circumstances relative to the Deeds of Gift which were obtained from me by fraud and imposition by my **Grand Son Philemon Son of John and negro Amy** and is very attentive to me in my sickness, It is my Desire that my Executors should do all in their Power to procure his Emancipation, provided, provided the Order for his Emancipation made by Warren County Court should be set aside and provided he should continue to behave himself well and there is no obstruction in the Way Towards the recovery of my Deeds from my Grand Son Philemon Son of John and others, I hereby give and bequeath to him two hundred and fifty acres of Land on the South Side of Ballards Tract including Howells improvement, one feather Bed and furniture; my bay Horse Saddle and Bridle, one hundred Pounds Virga. Currency, Two Cows and Calves, four Saws and pight, and fifty Barrels of Corn This Legacy to be void if he should hold the property contained in a Deed of Gift which it is alledged I have made to him at or about the Time it is alledged I made a Deed to my Grand Son Philemon Son of John It being my intention that he shall not Possess both this Legacy and the property contained in the said Deed.
In Witness whereof I have hereunto Set my Hand and affixed my Seal this Twenty Second Day of July Anno Dom.

Chapter 25: Warren County Records

1801.   Phil. Hawkins   (Seal)

Signed Sealed and declared to be his Codicil to his Will in presence of us
James Vaughan
W. Gilliam
Warren County --- February Court 1802.
This last Will and Testament of Philemon Hawkins dec'd together with the Codicil hereto was proved by the Oaths of James Vaughan and William Gilliam Subscribing Witnesses hereto and ordered to be recorded, whereupon John & Philemon Hawkins Executors named in Said Will qualified according and Letters Testamentary granted them.
    Test. M Duke Johnson CC
I William Green Clerk of Warren County Court do hereby certify that the forgoing Will and the Codicil to said Will are correct Copies from the Records in my office.
    Wm. Green C.W. Ct.
Warrenton
October 26. 1815

****

NORTH CAROLINA STATE ARCHIVES
WARREN COUNTY RECORDS
MISCELLANEOUS RECORDS
C.R.100.928.3

Bond of William Burroughs

Will. Burroughs to E.D. Drake Clerk
Delivery Bond &C for Rebecca Capps
Record page 51

State of North Carolina }
County of Warren   }

Know all men by these presents that we William Burroughs and James Somervill both of the County of Warren aforesaid, are held and firmly bound unto Edwin D. Drake Clerk of the Court of Pleas and Quarter Sessions of the County aforesaid, for the use of Rebecca Capps a woman of Colour, in the just and full sum of one thousand and five hundred dollars for which sum well & truly to be paid, we bind ourselves and our heirs, Executors and administrators firmly by these presents sealed with our seals and dated the 29th November 1834--

The Condition of the above obligation is such that whereas a suit is now pending in the Court of Pleas and Quarter Sessions of the said County of Warren, in which a Woman of Colour Calling herself by the above name of Rebecca Capps is Plaintiff and the above bound William Burroughs is Defendant, and whereas also the said William Burroughs claims to be the owner of the said Woman suing as aforesaid and claims the right to have the custody & possession of the said Woman, Now therefore, the object of the said suit being to try the question whether the said Woman of Colour suing as aforesaid is and of right ought to be free by the laws of this State, or whether she is by the laws aforesaid the slave of the said Burroughs, if the said William Burroughs shall well and truly produce the said woman of Colour before the said Court at each term while the said suit shall continue in the said Court, or in case of an appeal to the Superior Court of said County shall well and truly produce her at each Term of the said Superior Court, during the pending of said suit, and in the mean time & during the whole time while the said suit shall or pending between them shall treat the said woman with humanity - then the above obligation to be void otherwise to remain in full force and virtue.

WR Burroughs   (Seal)
Jas. Somervill   (Seal)
Witness
Peter R. Davies

Chapter 25: Warren County Records

Warren County - November Court 1834
This bond was duly executed in open Court and on motion ordered to be recorded
    Test   E.D. Drake Clk

****

Ivins's Bond to Chairman of the County Co.
Recorded

Warren County August Court 1806 This Bond was Executed in open Court and upon motion was Ordered to be Recorded.
Test Mr. Duke Johnson
Know all men by these presents that we Morning Ivins and Benjamin Kimbell are held & firmly bound unto Thomas Eaton Chairman of the County Court of Warren & his Successors in office in the full & Just Sum of One hundred pounds to which payment well and truly to be made we bind ourselves our heirs Exrs. &C jointly & severally firmly by these presents sealed with our seals and dated this 28th AD 1806
The Condition of the above obligation is such that whereas the above bounded Mourning Ivins hath obtained the emancipation of a Negro Man by the name of Nat, Now if the Said Mourning Ivins shall save harmles or free from Charge the parish or County; on account of the said emancipated man Nat then this obligation to be void otherwise to Remain in full force and virtue

Signed Sealed &c   }
in the presence of   }   her
                              Mourning X Ivins   (Seal)
                                        mark
                              Ben Kimbell   (Seal)

Chapter 26: Wayne County Records

chapter 26

Wayne County

NORTH CAROLINA STATE ARCHIVES
WAYNE COUNTY RECORDS
MISCELLANEOUS RECORDS
C.R.103.928.4

Petition of Simon Peacock

A Petition of Simon Peacock Citizen of the County of Wayne To the Court of Pleas & Quarter Sessions Now Siting Humbly sheweth that Your Petitioner has Under Care a Negro Man Named Cato whose honestly fidelity & General Conduct are Such as Your Petitioner Humbly Conceives Entitles him sd. Cato to the benefit of Emancipation - Your Petitioner therefore Requests On his behalf that You will Grant him the prayer of Your Petitioners & free him as the Law in such Case Directs.

I Remain in Submission
Yours &C Simon Peacock

****

Petition of Joseph Everett

The Petition of Joseph Everett Citizen of the County of Wayne to the Court of please & Quarter Sessions Now Sitting for Sd. County

Humbly Sheweth

Whereas your petitioner has under his Care three Negroes to wit Long Tom peggy & Lettice Whose Honesty & Industry are Truly Meritorious & Deserves the benefit of Emancipation & for as much as that Cannot be Compleat With out application to Court & Sanction thereof your petitioner therefore prays the Court to take this Case Into Consideration & Grant them Sd. Tom (Long) Peggy Lettice their liberty Which is said by the Constitution to be Right of all Man Kind.

Remain in Submission your Petr.
24th day 5th mt. - 1805   Jos. Everett

State of North Carolina   } Know all Men by these
Wayne County   } presents that We Joseph Everett Robert

Fellow and John McKinne all of the State and County aforesaid am held and firmly bound unto John C. Pender esquire Chairman of the County Court of Wayne or his Successors, in the sum of One Hundred Pounds to be paid to the said Chairman or his Successors to which payment well and truly to be made we bind ourselves our heirs Executors and administrators Jointly and Severally firmly by these presents Sealed with our Seals and dated this 24th day of May A.D. 1805.

The Condition of the above obligation is Such that the above bounden Joseph Everett Did at the term of May 1805 petition the County Court of Wayne to have a Certain Negro Man a Slave Named Tom emancipated. Now in Case the

Chapter 26: Wayne County Records

said Joseph Everett shall from time to time and at all times, Keep Said Negro Man Tom from becoming Chargeable on the parish or County then the above obligation to be void Otherwise to remain In full power and Virtue.

Signed Sealed & Acknowledged	}	Jos. Everett	(Seal)
In presence of	}	Robt. Fellow	(Seal)
Jas. Sasser Cc		John McKinne	(Seal)

State of North Carolina } Know all men by these presents
Wayne County } that We Joseph Everett, Robert

Fellow, & John McKinne all of the State and County aforesaid am held and firmly bound unto John C. Pender esquire Chairman of the County Court of Wayne or his Successors In the Sum of One Hundred pounds Current money to be paid to the said Chairman or his Successors to which payment well and truly to be made We bind ourselves our heirs Executors, and administrators Jointly and Severally firmly by these presents Sealed with our Seals and Dated this 24th day of May AD 1805.

The Condition of the above obligation is Such that the above bounden Joseph Everett did at the term of May 1805 petitioned the County Court of Wayne to have a Certain Negro Slave by the Name of Peggy Emancipated Now in Case the said Joseph Everett Shall from time to time and at all times Keep said Negro Woman Peggy from becoming Chargeable on the parish or County then the above Obligation to be Null and Void Otherwise to remain in full force and Virtue.

Signed Sealed and	}	Jos. Everitt	(Seal)
Acknowledged in presence of	}	Robt. Fellow	(Seal)
Jas. Sasser Cc		John McKinny	(Seal)

State of North Carolina } Know all men by these presents
Wayne County } that we Joseph Everett, Robert

Fellow & John McKinne all of the State and County aforesaid are held and firmly bound unto John C. Pender esquire Chairman of the County Court of Wayne or his Successors in the Sum of One Hundred pounds to be paid to the said Chairman or his Successors to Which payment Well and truly to be made We bind ourselves our heirs Executors and administrators Jointly and Severally firmly by these presents Sealed Withe our Seales and Dated this 24th day of May A.D. 1805.

The Condition of the above Obligation is Such that the above bounden Joseph Everett Did at the term of May 1805 petitioned the County Court of Wayne to have a Certain Negroe Woman a Slave Named Lettace emancipated Now in Case the said Joseph Everitt Shall from time to time and at all times, keep Said Negro Woman Lettace, from becoming Chargeable on the parish or County, then the above obligation to be Void Otherwise to remain In full force and Virtue.

Signed Sealed & Acknowledged	}	Jos. Everett	(Seal)
In presence of	}	Robt. Fellow	(Seal)
Jas. Sasser Cc		John McKinne	(Seal)

****

Petition of Thomas Outland

A Petition of Thomas Outland of the County of Wayne To the Ensuing Court of Pleas & Quarter Sessions To be Held at Waynesborough Humbly Presented
Whereas Your Petitioner is by Law Possessed of a negro Woman Named Hannah Whose Morals are So good that your Petitioner Conceives She is Justly Entitled the Benefit of Freedom but for as much as that Cannot be Compleat without Sanction of the Court therefore Your Petitioner Humbly Requests On her Behalf She may be Emancipated As the Law in Such Case Directs - Remain in Submission Your Friend & Petitioner &C

Chapter 26: Wayne County Records

the 10th Day of the [?] }   Thos. Outland
1799 }

****

Bond of William Outland

State of North Carolina } Know all men by these
Wayne County } presents that we John

Garland and Joshua Taylor of the State and County aforesaid are held and firmly bound to John C. Pender esquire Chairman of the County Court of Wayne and his Successors in the sum of One Hundred pounds Currency to which payment Well and truly to be made we bind ourselves our heirs Executors and administrators Jointly and Severally firmly by these presents Sealed with our Seales and dated this 19th day of February AD 1805.

The Condition of the above obligation is Such that William Outland applied to the County Court at this present term of February 1805 to have a Certain Negro Man Joe Emancipated now in Case the above Bounden John Garland and Joshua Taylor shall from time to time and at all times Keep the said Negro Man Joe from becoming Chargeable on the parish or County then the above obligation to be Void Otherwise to Remain in full fource and Virtue.

Signed Sealed and
Acknowledged in presence   John Garland   (Seal)
of Jas. Sasser Cc   Joshua Taylor   (Seal)

****

Petition of Benajah Herring

Petition of Benajah Herring for liberating Negro Man Willis

To Wayne Supr. Ct. Spring Term 1823

To the honorable the Judge of the Superior Court for the County of Wayne; the Petition of Benajah Herring of said County.

    Your Petitioner sheweth that he is the owner of a negro slave Willis, and is desirous of being permitted to emancipate him. Your Petitioner sheweth that the said slave was raised by Michael Herring formerly of said County and after the death of said Michael belonged for many years to Ichabod Herring now of said County - the said slave has been from his infancy up to this moment distinguished by his sobriety industry and faithfulness - that his services have uniformly been of the most meritorious kind - that he has been left in charge by his late master for months of his plantation and rural concerns and hath acquitted himself in the most exemplary manner - and that if slave be deserving of freedom your Petitioner believes that the said Willis is - Your Petitioner saith that the said Willis hath by his industry and economy paid to his late master a considerable sum as the price of his freedom, and having secured the payment of the residue a conveyance of the said slave hath been made to this Petitioner for the purpose of soliciting and endeavouring to effect his emancipation.
                                      Benajah Herring

Benajah Herring & N. Washington Bond for Negroe Willis

On hearing the Petition of Benajah Herring praying leave to emancipate his slave Willis, it being made satisfactorily to appear to the Court by the testimony of several witnesses that the said slave hath rendered meritorious services for which he deserves emancipation, and the Court having adjudged the same accordingly, it is ordered that a bond being given to the Chairman of the Court of Pleas and Quarter Sessions of Wayne County by the said Benajah Herring and Nicholas Washington his Security in the sum of one hundred pounds that the said Willis shall not become chargeable on the

Chapter 26: Wayne County Records

parish or County, as is required by law, the said slave Willis may be liberated; and it being shown to the Court that the bond aforesaid has been given, it is ordered that the said Willis be, and the said Willis hereby is liberated, and declared entitled to all the right and privelege of a freeborn negro.

Know all men by these presents that we Benajah Herring and Nicholas Washington are held and bound to Ezekiel Slocumb Esquire Chairmam of the Court of Pleas and Quarter Sessions for the County of Wayne and his Successors for the use of the poor of said County in the sum of one hundred pounds current money of the State of North Carolina to the which payment well and truly to be made and done we bind ourselves and our heirs jointly and severally firmly by these presents - april 3rd, 1823

   The Condition of the above obligation is such that whereas the said Benajah Herring hath been permitted by the Superior Court of Wayne to liberate the slave Willis and hath liberated him accordingly now if the said Willis shall not become chargeable on the parish or the County then the above obligation to be void, otherwise in force.

Delivered	}	Benajah Herring	(Seal)
		N. Washington	(Seal)
in presence of	}		
J. Hurst			

chapter 27

Wilkes County

NORTH CAROLINA STATE ARCHIVES
WILKES COUNTY RECORDS
MISCELLANEOUS RECORDS
C.R.104.928.6

Know all men by these presents that we Archibald Lovelace, James Wellborn, Eli Petty are held and firmly bound unto the State of North Carolina in the sum of One Thousand Dollars for which payment we bind ourselves Executors Administrators jointly severally firmly by These presents   Witness our hands and seals this 7th day of February 1839.

    The Condition of the above obligation is such whereas Caroline Cook and her four children Parmelia, Archibald T., James Ellis, and Martha Jane has been emancipated by an act of the Legislator of the State of North Carolina now if the said slaves shall humbly demean themselves as long as they shall remain in the State and shall not become a county charge, then the above obligation to be void otherwise to remain full & affect.

Test		
W.W. Peden	Archibald Lovelace	(S)
	Wellborn	(S)
	Eli Petty	(S)

Chapter 28: Acts of Emancipation

chapter 28

Acts of Emancipation by the General Assembly

The State Records of North Carolina
Volume XXIV, Laws 1777-1788
Edited by: Walter Clark
Nash Brothers Book and Job Printers
Goldsboro, N.C., 1906

Laws of N.C., 1784.
Page 639, Chapter LXX.
An Act for Enfranchising Ned Griffin, Late the Property of William Kitchen.
    I. Whereas, Ned Griffin, late the property of William Kitchen, of Edgecombe County, was promised the full enjoyments of his liberty, on condition that he, the said Ned Griffin, should faithfully serve as a soldier in the continental line of this State for and during the term of twelve months; and whereas the said Ned Griffin did faithfully on his part perform the condition, and whereas it is just and reasonable that the said Ned Griffin should receive the reward promised for the services which he performed;
    II. Be it therefore Enacted by the General Assembly of the State of North Carolina, and it is hereby Enacted by the Authority of the same, That the said Ned Griffin, late the property of William Kitchen, shall forever hereafter be in every respect declared to be a freeman; and he shall be, and he is hereby enfranchised and forever delivered and discharged from the yoke of slavery; any law, usage or custom to the contrary thereof in anywise notwithstanding.

****

The State Records of North Carolina
Volume XXIV
Laws, 1777-1788
Edited by: Walter Clark
Nash Brothers Book and Job Printers
Goldsboro, N.C., 1906

CHAPTER XLVIII. 1ST SESSION.
1786. **An Act to emancipate Caesar, formerly a Servant of Samuel Yeargen, Deceased. (Page 850).**
    Whereas by the last will and testament of Samuel Yeargen, deceased, late of the county of Warren, he did desire in his said will that a certain negro man of his property, should after the death of his daughter Anne Alston, wife to William Alston, of Chatham county, be set free, for and during the full term of fifty five years: And whereas the said Anne being now dead, it is thought just and right the said last will and testament should be adhered to:
    I. Be it therefore Enacted by the General Assembly, That from and after the passing of this Act, that the aforesaid Caesar shall and may be at his own liberty, for and during the term mentioned in his master's will, upon the same footing, and under the same restrictions as other free negroes are intitled to in this State, and shall be known and called by the name of Caesar Henry; any law to the contrary notwithstanding. (Passed Jan. 6, 1787).

****

The State Records of North Carolina
Volume XXIV

Chapter 28: Acts of Emancipation

Laws 1777-1788
Edited by: Walter Clark
Nash Brothers Book and Job Printers
Goldsboro, N.C., 1906

CHAPTER XXXV. 1ST SESSION.
1787. An Act to Emancipate Certain Persons therein mentioned. (Pages 929-930).

Whereas **Agerton Willis, late of Bladen county**, was in his lifetime possessed of a certain slave called **Joseph**, and in consideration of the services of him the said **Joseph**, and the particular obligations he conceived himself under to the said Joseph for his fidelity and attention, did by his last will and testament devise to the said **Joseph his freedom and emancipation**, and did also give unto the said Joseph a considerable property, both real and personal: And whereas the executor and next of kin to the said Joseph did in pursuance of the said will take counsel thereon, and were well advised that the same could not by any means take effect, but would be of prejudice to the said slave and subject him still as property of the said Agerton Willis; whereupon the said executor and next of kin, together with the heirs of the said Agerton Willis, deceased, did cause a fair and equal distribution of the said estate, as well to do equity and justice in the said case to the said Joseph, as in pursuance of their natural love and affection to the said Agerton, and did resolve on the freedom of the said Joseph and to give an equal proportion of the said estate: Wherefore,

I. Be it Enacted by the General Assembly of the State of North Carolina, and it is hereby Enacted by the authority of the same, That from and after the passing of this Act, the said Joseph shall and is hereby declared to be emancipated and set free; and from henceforward he be called and known by the name of Joseph Willis, by which name he may take, hold, occupy, possess and enjoy to him and his heirs forever, all and singular the property both real and personal so given him by the said distribution of the said executor, heirs and next of kin, and by the said name of Joseph Willis shall hencefoward be entitled to all the rights and privileges of a free person of mixed blood: Provided nevertheless, That this act shall not extend to enable the said Joseph by himself or attorney, or any other person in trust for him, in any manner to commence or prosecute any suit or suits for any other property but such as may be given him by this act or such as he may have acquired by his own industry, but this act may in all such cases be plead in bar, and the property therein given be considered as a full and ample consideration for the final accommodation and settlement of all doubts concerning the freedom and property either real, personal or mixed belonging or in any manner appertaining to the said Joseph.

And whereas it hath been made appear to the satisfaction of the General Assembly that Richard Dobbs Spaight, of Craven county, Esquire, hath consented and is desirous to liberate and set free a certain mulatto girl now his property, called or known by the name of Mary Long:

II. Be it therefore Enacted by the authority aforesaid, That from and after the passing of this act the before mentioned mulatto girl called Mary Long, now the property of Richard Dobbs Spaight, Esquire, shall be and continue liberated and set free, and shall thenceforward be entitled to all the rights and privileges of a free person of mixed blood in this State, and by the said name of Mary Long shall and may receive and hold, possess and enjoy any real and personal estate or property which she may hereafter acquire or become possessed of, in the same manner as any other person of mixed blood might or could acquire, and possess the same to all intents and purposes as if she had been born free.

Whereas it hath been represented to this General Assembly by the memorial of John Allen, a free man of mixed blood, that he hath purchased a mulatto woman named Betty and her child named Mary, which woman he has long lived with and considered as his wife, and praying that the General Assembly would be pleased to emancipate and set free the said mulatto woman and her child:

III. Be it therefore Enacted by the authority aforesaid, That the said mulatto woman named Betty and her child named Mary, shall be and they and each of them are hereby emancipated and made free, and they and each of them may hereafter take and use the surname of Allen, and are hereby declared to be able and capable in law to possess and enjoy every right, privilege and immunity in as full and ample manner as they could or might have done if they had been born free.

****

The State Records of North Carolina
Volume XXIV
Laws, 1777-1788
Edited by: Walter Clark

Chapter 28: Acts of Emancipation

Nash Brothers Book and Job Printers
Goldsboro, N.C., 1906

CHAPTER XVIII. 1ST SESSION.
1788. An Act to Emancipate a certain Negro Slave named Phillis, late the Property of George Jacobs, of the Town of Wilmington, Deceased. (Page 963)

Whereas it is represented to the General Assembly that the aforesaid George Jacobs, deceased, in his last illness, did earnestly request that his negro slave named Phillis should be liberated for her great attention to her said master during her continuance with him, and more especially for her care and assiduity in his last illness: In order therefore to carry into effect the dying request of the said George Jacobs, deceased:

I. Be it Enacted by the General Assembly of the State of North Carolina, and it is hereby Enacted by the authority of the same, That from and after the passing of this Act, the aforesaid negro woman named Phillis, shall be emancipated and forever discharged from her bondage, in as full and ample manner as if she had been born free; any law, usage or custom to the contrary notwithstanding: And the said negro woman shall forever hereafter be known by the name of Phillis Freeman.

****

The State Records of North Carolina
Volume XXV, Supplement, 1669-1771
Edited by: Walter Clark
Nash Brothers Book and Job Printers
Goldsboro, N.C., 1906

CHAPTER XXXV
1789. An Act to Emancipate Certain Negroes Therein Mentioned. (Page 37).

Whereas, it hath been represented to this General Assembly, that Robert Shaw, in his life-time, did receive a valuable consideration for the further services of a certain negro woman named Amelia, and has certified the same and declared her to be free: And by petition of Thomas Lovick, it appears to be his desire that a certain negro woman by the name of Betty, belonging to him, should be set free; also a petition of Monsieur Chaponel, desiring to have set free a mulatto slave belonging to him, by the name of Lucy, of three and half years old: And whereas, it appears by the petition of Ephraim Knight, of Halifax County, that he is desirous to emancipate two young mulatto men, called Richard and Alexander, the property of said Ephraim: And it hath also been represented to this Assembly by John Alderson, of Hyde County, that it is his desire to set free a mulatto boy belonging to him, called Sam: And whereas, it hath been made appear to this Assembly by the petition of Thomas Newman, of Fayetteville, that he hath a mulatto boy belonging to him, which he is desirous to emancipate, and known by the name of Thomas:

I. Be it enacted by the General Assembly of the State of North Carolina, and it is hereby enacted by the authority of the same, That the said negro women called Amelia and Betty, and the mulatto girl called Lucy, and the said mulatto men Richard and Alexander, and the mulatto boy called Sam, and the negro boy named Thomas Clinch, shall be, and each of them are hereby emancipated and declared free; and the said Richard and Alexander shall take and use the surname of Day, and the mulatto boy Sam shall be known and called by the name of Samuel Johnson; and the said slaves so liberated, and each of them, are hereby declared to be able and capable in law to posses and enjoy every right, privelege and immunity, in as full and ample manner as they could or might have done if they had been born free.

****

THE ACTS OF THE GENERAL ASSEMBLY OF THE STATE OF NORTH CAROLINA
PASSED DURING THE SESSIONS HELD IN THE YEARS 1791, 1792, 1793 AND 1794
BY: FRANCOIS XAVIER MARTIN
NEWBERN: FRANCOIS XAVIER MARTIN, 1795

CHAPTER XLVI.
1791. An Act to emancipate certain persons therein mentioned. (Page 27)

Whereas sundry petitions have been presented to this General Assembly, praying that Austin Curtis, a mulatto slave belonging to Willie Jones; Grace, and her children, to wit, Richard, Harriot, Samuel, Rebecca and Elizabeth,

Chapter 28: Acts of Emancipation

formerly the property of John Davis, deceased; Absalom Spicer, formerly the property of Benjamin Rush; and Rachel, formerly the property of Sarah Rush, deceased; Richard, Dolly, and her son Nathan, the property of George Merrick; and Linney, the property of John Spencer; and Richard and William, the property of the estate of Thomas Prichard, deceased, be liberated and set free:

I. Be it therefore enacted by the General Assembly of the State of North Carolina, and it is hereby enacted by the authority of the same, That the aforesaid Austin Curtis by and under the name of Austin Curtis Jones; and the aforesaid Grace, Richard, Harriot, Samuel, Rebecca and Elizabeth, by and under the names of Grace Davis, Richard Davis, Harriot Davis, Samuel Davis, Rebecca Davis and Elizabeth Davis; and the aforesaid Absalom Spicer and Rachel Spicer, by and under the names of Absalom Spicer and Rachel Spicer; and the aforesaid Richard, Dolly and Nathan, by and under the names of Richard Green, Dolly Green, and Nathan Green; and aforesaid Linney, under the name of Linney Charlton; and Richard and William above mentioned, under the name of Richard Prichard Morris, and William Prichard Morris, shall be, and they, and each and every of them, are hereby declared to be free, by and under the names aforesaid; and they, and each and every of them, shall from henceforward enjoy the protection of the laws and the benefits of the constitution of this state, in the same manner as others of their colour who were born free. Provided, nevertheless, That nothing herein contained shall be construed so as to affect the title or claime of any person or persons, other than the persons named in this act.

****

THE ACTS OF THE GENERAL ASSEMBLY OF THE STATE OF NORTH CAROLINA
PASSED DURING THE SESSIONS HELD IN THE YEARS 1791, 1792, 1793 AND 1794
BY: FRANCOIS XAVIER MARTIN
NEWBERN: FRANCOIS XAVIER MARTIN, 1795

CHAPTER XXXVIII.
1792. An Act to emancipate the persons therein named. (Page 61).

Whereas it hath been made appear to this General Assembly that Andrew, Peter and Juno, the illegitimate children of John Moore, of Craven County; Charlotte Green, the property of John Waite, of the town of Newbern, merchant; John Marshall, the property of Peter Thomeguex, of the same place, merchant; Rose, the property of Mary Clear, of the said place; Jack the property of Caleb White, of the County of Currituck; Peggy Handy, daughter of Nancy Handy, the property of Miss Betsy Vail, of the town of Newbern; Betsey and Jim, the property of Thomas Neale, of Brunswick County, should be liberated and set free:

I. Be it therefore enacted by the General Assembly of the State of North Carolina, and it is hereby enacted by the authority of the same, That the said Andrew, Peter, and Juno, under the names of Andrew Moore, Peter Moore and Juno Moore; Charlotte Green, under the name of Elizabeth Johnston; John Marshall, under the name of John Marshall; Rose, under the name of Rose Mary Clear; Jack, under the name of John Jasper White; Peggy Handy, under the name of Peggy Handy; Betsey and Jim, under the names of Elizabeth Phillips and James Phillips, shall be, and they and each and every of them, are hereby declared to be free by and under the names aforesaid; and they and each and every of them, shall from henceforward, enjoy the protection of the laws and the benefits of the constitution of this State, in the same manner as others of their colour who were born free.

****

THE ACTS OF THE GENERAL ASSEMBLY OF THE STATE OF NORTH CAROLINA
PASSED DURING THE SESSIONS HELD IN THE YEARS 1791, 1792, 1793 AND 1794
BY: FRANCOIS XAVIER MARTIN
NEWBERN: FRANCOIS XAVIER MARTIN, 1795

CHAPTER LXII.
1792. An Act to confirm the rights and privileges of a certain mulatto man called Frank, formerly the property of Thomas Lytle, late of Randolph County, and to confirm on him the name of Frank Lytle. (Page 160).

Whereas the court of the County of Randolph, at their session held in the month of November last, on the petition of Catherine Lytle, William Bell, John Beard and Samuel Millikin, the executors and legatees of the last will and testament of the said Thomas Lytle, deceased, did order that the said Frank should be at liberty, agreeable to an act of the General Assembly in such cases made and provided, for meritorious services done by him for the said Thomas

Chapter 28: Acts of Emancipation

Lytle in his lifetime: And whereas the said Catherine, William, John and Samuel have mentioned this this Assembly to pass an act to entitle the said Frank to be called and known by the name of Frank Lytle:

I. Be it therefore enacted by the General Assembly of the State of North Carolina, and it is hereby enacted by the authority of the same, That the said order of the court of Randolph County aforesaid, liberating the said Frank, be and is hereby ratified and confirmed; and by virtue thereof the said Frank, by and under the name of Frank Lytle, shall be and is hereby declared to be free, and shall henceforth enjoy the protection of the laws, and the benefit of the Constitution of this State, in the same manner as others of his colour who were born free, to evry intent and purpose.

****

THE ACTS OF THE GENERAL ASSEMBLY OF THE STATE OF NORTH CAROLINA
PASSED DURING THE SESSIONS HELD IN THE YEARS 1791, 1792, 1793 AND 1794
BY: FRANCOIS XAVIER MARTIN
NEWBERN: FRANCOIS XAVIER MARTIN, 1795

CHAPTER LXXVI.
1792. An Act to emancipate Jack, alias Jack Small, a person of colour. (Page 168).

Whereas Jemima Barrs, a free woman of mixed blood, hath represented to this General Assembly, that she hath purchased a certain Jack Small, for a valuable consideration, and since hath become his legal wife: And whereas the said Jemima Barrs hath petitioned this General Assembly to emancipate and set free her said husband, Jack Small aforesaid:

I. Be it therefore enacted by the General Assembly of the State of North Carolina, and it is hereby enacted by the authority of the same, That the aforesaid person of colour Jack Small, shall henceforth be emancipated and absolutely set free, by the name of Jack Small; and be entitled to all the privileges and immunities which free people of colour enjoy and possess in this state, any law to the contrary notwithstanding.

****

THE ACTS OF THE GENERAL ASSEMBLY OF THE STATE OF NORTH CAROLINA
PASSED DURING THE SESSIONS HELD IN THE YEARS 1791, 1792, 1793 AND 1794
BY: FRANCOIS XAVIER MARTIN
NEWBERN: FRANCOIS XAVIER MARTIN, 1795

CHAPTER XCIII.
1794. An Act to emancipate a mulatto girl named Mary, the property of Michael Beam, deceased, should be emancipated. (Page 177).

Whereas by the last will and testament of Michael Beam, deceased, late of Rowan County, it is devised that a mulatto girl, named Mary, the property of the said deceased, should be emancipated.

I. Be it therefore enacted by the General Assembly of the State of North Carolina, and it is hereby enacted by the authority of the same, That from and after the passing of this act, that the said mulatto girl named Mary, the property of the said deceased, be liberated and set free, and henceforward called and known by the name of Mary German; under which name she shall also henceforward be entitled to all the privileges of a free person of mixed blood in this state; and shall and may receive, hold, enjoy and possess all the real and personal property which she has or may hereafter acquire by the last will and testament of the said deceased, or which she may hereafter lawfully acquire, in as full and ample a matter as if she had been born free, any thing to the contrary notwithstanding.

****

STATE OF NORTH CAROLINA
LAWS OF THE STATE OF NORTH CAROLINA
1790-1802

CHAPTER XXXVIII.
1795. An Act to emancipate a mulatto boy by the name of Gustavus Adolphus Johnston, in the county of Chowan, and also a mulatto girl by the name of Amy Phillips, in the County of Brunswick. (Page 22).

Chapter 28: Acts of Emancipation

I. Be it enacted by the General Assembly of the State of North Carolina, and it is hereby enacted by the authority of the same, That from and after the passing of this act that the said mulatto boy, now aged about four years, by the name of Gustavus Adolphus Johnston, in the county of Chowan, shall be liberated and set free, and henceforward called and known by the said name; under which he shall henceforward be entitled to all the privileges of a free person of mixed blood in this state, and shall and may receive, hold, enjoy and possess any real or personal property which he may hereafter acquire by purchase or descent, in as full and ample manner as if he had been born free.

II. And be it further enacted, That Amy a mulatto girl, the property of Drury Allen, in the county of Brunswick, be also liberated and forever set free, and henceforward called and known by the name of Amy Phillips, under which name she shall henceforward be entitled to all the privileges of a free person of mixed blood in this state, and shall and may receive, hold and enjoy any real or personal estate which she may hereafter acquire by purchase or by descent, in as full and ample a manner as if she had been born free, any thing to the contrary notwithstanding.

****

STATE OF NORTH CAROLINA
LAWS OF THE STATE OF NORTH CAROLINA
1790-1802

CHAPTER XLI.
1795. An Act to emancipate Frank, a person of colour. (Page 23).

Whereas Milly Anderson, a free woman of colour, hath represented to this General Assembly that she hath purchased a certain negro man Frank, for a valuable consideration, and is his legal wife: And whereas the said Milly hath petitioned this General Assembly to emancipate and set free her said husband:

Be it therefore enacted by the General assembly of the State of North Carolina, and it is hereby enacted by the authority of the same, That the aforesaid person of colour, Frank, shall hereafter be emancipated and absolutely set free, by and under the name of Frank Anderson, and be entitled to all the privileges and immunities which free people of colour enjoy in this state.

****

STATE OF NORTH CAROLINA
LAWS OF THE STATE OF NORTH CAROLINA
1790-1802

CHAPTER XLVI.
1795. An Act to emancipate James, a mulatto man, the property of John Cunningham, of Gates County. (Page 24).

Whereas it is the request of John Cunningham, of Gates County, that a mulatto man called James, should be liberated and set free, for certain meritorious services:

I. Be it therefore enacted by the General Assembly of the State of North Carolina, and it is hereby enacted by the authority of the same, That from and after the passing of this act, the said mulatto man called James, the property of John Cunningham, be liberated and set free, and henceforward called and known by the name of James Cunningham, under which name he shall also henceforward be entitled to all the privileges of a free person of mixed blood in this state, and shall and may receive, hold, enjoy and possess all real and personal estate which he has now, or may hereafter lawfully acquire, either by purchase or by descent, in as full and ample manner, as if he had been born free, any thing to the contrary notwithstanding.

****

STATE OF NORTH CAROLINA
LAWS OF THE STATE OF NORTH CAROLINA
1790-1802

CHAPTER XLVII.
1795. An Act to emancipate a certain mulatto girl therein named. (Page 24).

Chapter 28: Acts of Emancipation

     I. Be it enacted by the General Assembly of the State of North Carolina, and it is hereby enacted by the authority of the same, That Sally, a mulatto girl, the property of William Person, by the name of Sally Pamilia, be and she is hereby declared to be free, by and under the name aforesaid: and she shall from henceforward enjoy the protection of the laws, and the benefits of the constitution of this state, in the same manners as others of her colour who were born free.

****

STATE OF NORTH CAROLINA
LAWS OF THE STATE OF NORTH CAROLINA
1790-1802

CHAPTER LXII.
1795. An Act to emancipate certain persons therein mentioned. (Page 28).
     Whereas Lemuel Hall, a free man of mixed blood, hath represented to this General Assembly, that he hath purchased a certain woman slave, called Jenny, for a valuable consideration, who hath since become his legal wife; and he hath had by his said wife Jenny three children, called Seth, Milley and Tabitha: And whereas the said Lemuel Hall hath petitioned the General Assembly to emancipate and set free his said wife and children aforesaid:
     I. Be it therefore enacted by the General Assembly of the State of North Carolina, and it is hereby enacted by the authority of the same, That the aforesaid persons, Jenny, Seth, Milley and Tabitha, shall henceforth be emancipated and absolutely set free, by the name of Jenny Hall, Seth Hall, Milley Hall and Tabitha Hall; and the said persons of colour so liberated, and each of them, are hereby declared to be entitled to all the privileges and immunities which free people of colour enjoy and possess in this state, any law to the contrary notwithstanding, That nothing contained in this act shall be so construed as to deprive any person or persons of his or their lawful claim, other than the said Lemuel Hall.

****

STATE OF NORTH CAROLINA
LAWS OF THE STATE OF NORTH CAROLINA
1790-1802

CHAPTER LIII.
1797. An Act to emancipate a mulatto girl Sally, formerly the property of John Ingram. (Page 19).
     Whereas the said John Ingram by his last will and testament, has requested that the said girl Sally should be emancipated:
     I. Be it enacted by the General Assembly of the State of North Carolina, and it is hereby enacted by the authority of the same, That the said girl Sally be, and she is hereby emancipated and declared free by the name of Sally Robinson; and hereby declared able and capable in law to possess and enjoy every right, privilege and immunity, in as full and able manner as she could or might have done had she been born free.

****

STATE OF NORTH CAROLINA
LAWS OF THE STATE OF NORTH CAROLINA
1790-1802

CHAPTER CXII.
1798. An Act to emancipate certain persons therein named. (Page 49).
     Whereas Alexander Stewart and Lydia his wife, have by deed under their hands and seals, given, granted and confirmed unto John Caruthers Stanly, a person of mixed blood, heretofore their slave, his freedom, as a reward for his meritorious services: And whereas the said John Caruthers Stanly is desirous of having his emancipation confirmed law. And whereas Amelia Green, a free woman of colour, has petitioned this General Assembly, to emancipate her daughter Princess Green;

Chapter 28: Acts of Emancipation

I. Be it therefore enacted by the General Assembly of the State of North Carolina, and it is hereby enacted by the authority of the same, That the said John Caruthers Stanly and Princess Green, by the said names, are hereby emancipated and set free: and the said persons hereby liberated, and each of them are hereby declared to be able and capable in law, to possess and enjoy every right, privilege and immunity, in as full and ample manner as they could or might have done if they had been born free.

****

STATE OF NORTH CAROLINA
LAWS OF THE STATE OF NORTH CAROLINA
1790-1802

Chapter CXIII.
1798. An Act to emancipate certain persons therein mentioned. (Page 49).

I. Be it enacted by the General Assembly of the State of North Carolina, and it is hereby enacted by the authority of the same, That from and after the passing of this act, Rose the wife of Lemuel Overton, and her two sons John, Burdock, a negro woman named Grace, and her son Harry, the property of Thomas Amis, deceased; a negro girl named Bett, and a negro boy named John, the property of Moses Parker; a mulatto girl named Nancy, and her child Eliza, the property of General Thomas Person, of Granville County; a negro woman named Crease; a negro fellow named Tom, and his wife Pris and her five children, to wit, Allen, Charity, Breny, Willie and Crease, the property of Samuel Williams, deceased, of the county of Warren, also the increase of the said Pris and her female children, since the date of the last Will of the said Williams; also one negro man Daniel, formerly the property of James Allen; and a negro man named Ginger, formerly the property of Mark Allen, of Montgomery County, be and they are hereby emancipated and set free, and hereafter shall be called and known by the following names, to wit: Rose Overton, John Overton, Burdock Overton, Grace Webb, Harry Webb, Betty Black, John Black, Nancy Hart, Eliza Hart, Crease Green, Tom Green, Pris Green, Allen Green, Charity Green, Breny Green, Willie Green, and Crease Green, and in increase of the said Priss and her female children as aforesaid, by their respective names, with the addition of Green, Daniel Shad and Ginger Pepper; and by the names aforesaid, they and each of them shall have, enjoy and possess all the rights, privileges and immunities which they would have been entitled to, had they been born free; any law to the contrary notwithstanding.

II. And be it further enacted, That a negro man the property of Ozborne Jeffries, named Sam, and a negro woman the property of Dixon Bogye, named Chelsea, shall be and they are hereby emancipated and set free, the said Sam by the name of Buffalo Sam, and the said Chelsea by the name of Chelsea Reed, and they shall be entitled to the same privileges, which persons of colour born free are entitled to.

****

STATE OF NORTH CAROLINA
LAWS OF THE STATE OF NORTH CAROLINA
1790-1802

CHAPTER LIII.
1799. An Act to emancipate certain persons therein named. (Page 23).

Whereas Joseph R. Gautier, of Elizabeth Town, in the County of Bladen, has by his petition represented to this General Assembly, that he is desirous of procuring the emancipation of two mulatto boys belonging to him; and that as their childhood would render fruitless a recourse to the county court, he prays the aid at the Legislature to establish by a law the freedom of the said boys:

I. Be it therefore enacted by the General Assembly of the State of North Carolina, and it is hereby enacted by the authority of the same, That the said mullato boys be emancipated and set free from slavery, and henceforward be called and known by the names of Thomas Sheridan and Louis Sheridan; under which names respectively they shall be, and are hereby invested with, and henceforward entitled to, every right and privilege they would have had they been severally born free; any law or usage to the contrary notwithstanding.

****

Chapter 28: Acts of Emancipation

STATE OF NORTH CAROLINA
LAWS OF THE STATE OF NORTH CAROLINA
1790-1802

CHAPTER XCVI.
1800. An Act to emancipate certain persons therein named. (Page 45).

Whereas by the last will and testament of Ephraim Knight, of the County of Halifax, he appeared to be desirous to emancipate two Mulatto girls belonging to him by the name of Sabina and Polly; and as the said Ephraim Knight died without making application to the General Assembly to pass a law to that effect,

Be it therefore enacted by the General Assembly of the State of North Carolina, and it is hereby enacted by the authority of the same, That the said Mulatto girls Sabina and Polly be emancipated and set free from slavery, and henceforward be called and known by the names of Sabina Curtis and Polly Curtis; under which names respectively they shall be, and are hereby invested with, and henceforward entitled to every right and privilege they would have, had they been severally born free, any law or usage to the contrary notwithstanding.

And whereas James Cunningham of Chowan, has, by his petition for that purpose, represented to this General Assembly, that he is desirous of procuring the emancipation of a mulatto woman slave named Betsey, belonging to him,

Be it therefore enacted by the authority aforesaid, That the said mulatto woman named Betsey, be emancipated and set free from slavery, and that she be henceforth called and known by the name of Elizabeth Cunningham, under which name she shall be and is hereby invested and henceforward shall be entitled to every right and privilege that she would have been entitled to, had she been born free, any law, usage or custom to the contrary notwithstanding.

****

STATE OF NORTH CAROLINA
LAWS OF THE STATE OF NORTH CAROLINA
1790-1802

CHAPTER XCIX.
1800. An Act to liberate and set free the persons therein named. (Page 46).

Whereas Daniel Shad is desirous of setting free a certain woman slave named Betty, his property, and her child Winny,

Be it therefore enacted by the General Assembly of the State of North Carolina, and it is hereby enacted by the authority of the same, that from and after the passing of this act, that Betty, a woman slave, the property and wife of Daniel Shad, and her child Winny, be and they are hereby liberated and set free, and shall be entitled to the same privileges of other free persons of colour in this State.

II. And be it further enacted, That hereafter the said Betty shall be called and known by the name of Winny Shad; and by those names respectively shall be entitled and enjoy all the privileges that they would or could have done, had they borne the said names from their nativity.

Read three times and ratified in the General Assembly, the 20th day of December Anno Domini 1800.
William White, Secretary   Joseph Riddick, S.S.
                                                        Stephen Cabarrus, S.H.C.

****

STATE OF NORTH CAROLINA
LAWS OF THE STATE OF NORTH CAROLINA
1790-1802

CHAPTER CXIII.
1802. An Act to emancipate Charles, the property of Matthew Davis, senior, of the county of Surry. (Page 48).

Whereas it is the request of Matthew Davis, senior, of the county of Surry, that his negro man Charles should be emancipated and set free.

Be it enacted by the General Assembly of the State of North Carolina, and it is hereby enacted by the authority of the same, That from and after the passing of this act, the said negro man Charles be emancipated and set free from slavery, and that he be henceforth be called and known by the name of Charles Peters, under which name he shall be

Chapter 28: Acts of Emancipation

invested, and henceforward be entitled to possess and enjoy all the rights, privileges and immunities of what kind or nature soever, and to all intents and purposes in as full and ample a manner, as any free person of colour; any thing to the contrary notwithstanding.

****

STATE OF NORTH CAROLINA
LAWS OF THE STATE OF NORTH CAROLINA
1803-1816

CHAPTER CIX.
1805. An Act to emancipate Isaac Jones and others, therein mentioned, of the County of Anson. (Page 45).

Be it enacted by the General Assembly of the State of North Carolina, and it is hereby enacted by the authority of the same, That Isaac Jones, Jacob Jones, John Jones, Thomas Jones, Abraham Jones, Lewis Jones, Sukey Jones, John Jones and Sally Jones, of the county of Anson, be, and they are hereby emancipated and set free, in as full as ample a manner, to all intents and purposes, as if they had been free from their nativity; any law, usage or custom to the contrary notwithstanding.

****

STATE OF NORTH CAROLINA
LAWS OF THE STATE OF NORTH CAROLINA
1803-1816

CHAPTER CXIX.
1808. An Act to emancipate Joseph Blackwell of the County of Brunswick. (Page 40).

Whereas it is represented to this General Assembly, that Blackwell M'Alister, of Brunswick County, was manumitted and set free for meritorious services by him rendered; and that he has purchased and paid for his grandson, Joseph Blackwell, and that he is desirous that the said Joseph should be emancipated by an act of this Legislature.

Be it therefore enacted by the General Assembly of the State of North Carolina, and it is hereby enacted by the authority of the same, That Joseph Blackwell, of the County of Brunswick, and he is hereby emancipated and set free, and declared to possess all the rights, privileges and advantages, in as full and ample manner as if he the said Joseph had been born free, any law to the contrary notwithstanding.

****

STATE OF NORTH CAROLINA
LAWS OF THE STATE OF NORTH CAROLINA
1803-1816

CHAPTER CXX.
1808. An Act to emancipate Charlotte Green of Chowan County. (Page 40).

Whereas it is represented to this General Assembly, that Rose, a free woman of colour, late the property of Angus Cabarrus, of Chowan County, was emancipated by the court of said county; and that the said Angus Cabarrus has since msde, to the said Rose, a deed of gift of her two children Charlotte and Leon,

Be it enacted by the General Assembly of the State of North Carolina, and it is hereby enacted by the authority of the same, That the negro slaves Charlotte and Leon, be, and each of them is hereby emancipated and set free; and they and each of them may hereafter take and use the surname of Green, and are hereby declared to be able and capable in law to possess and enjoy all the rights and privileges of free persons of mixed blood in this State, in as full and ample manner as the several laws heretofore enacted will permit.

****

STATE OF NORTH CAROLINA
LAWS OF THE STATE OF NORTH CAROLINA

Chapter 28: Acts of Emancipation

1803-1816

CHAPTER XCIV.
1811. An Act to emancipate certain persons therein mentioned. (Page 37).

Be it enacted by the General Assembly f the State of North Carolina, and it is hereby enacted by the authority of the same, That Prince, a negro man, formerly the property of James Baird, late of the county of Lincoln, and Rose, the wife of the said Prince, be, and the said slaves are hereby emancipated and made capable of exercising, holding and enjoying all such rights as if they and each of them had been born free, Provided always, That the property which any person or persons, other than such person or persons as claim by, from or through the said James Baird, shall not be impaired by this act, nor shall this act extend to defeat the creditors of the said James Baird of their just debts, but the said Prince shall remain liable to satisfy the same.

II. And be it further enacted, That this act shall not take effect, or be considered in force, until the heirs or representatives of the said James Baird shall enter into bond with security, payable to the Chairman of the county court of Lincoln, in such sum of money as may be by the said court required, to be void on condition that the negroes intended to be emancipated by this act, do never become a public charge; and that they shall also stand bound by the said bond for their good behaviour.

****

STATE OF NORTH CAROLINA
LAWS OF THE STATE OF NORTH CAROLINA
1803-1816

CHAPTER XCV.
1811. An Act to emancipate certain persons therein mentioned. (Page 37-38).

Be it enacted by the General Assembly of the State of North Carolina, and it is hereby enacted by the authority of the same, That the following Negroes, the property of William Williams, Esquire, of Martin County, to wit, Boson, Penny, and Freeman Hill, are hereby emancipated and made free, and shall be entitled to all the privileges of free persons of colour within the State, in the same manner and to all intents and purposes as if they had been born free: Provided, That the emancipation of the said Negroes shall not injure or prejudice the claim or claims which any person or persons, except William Williams of Martin, may have to the said Negroes.

II. And be it further enacted, That the said Boson and Penny be hereafter known by the name of Boson Hill and Penny Hill.

III. And be it further enacted, That this act shall not be in force until the said William Williams shall have entered into bond with sufficient security, to the Chairman of Bertie county court, in the sum of two hundred and fifty pounds, conditioned that the said Negroes nor either of them, shall become chargeable to the county of Bertie, or any county in the state.

****

STATE OF NORTH CAROLINA
LAWS OF THE STATE OF NORTH CAROLINA
1803-1816

CHAPTER XCVI.
1811. An Act to emancipate James, a man of colour of the county of Lenoir. (Page 38).

Be it enacted by the General Assembly of the State of North Carolina, and it is hereby enacted by the authority of the same, That James, a man of colour of the county of Lenoir, and the property of Richard W. Caswell, late of this State and now of the State of Tennessee, be, and the said James is hereby emancipated and set free, and made capable of taking, holding and disposing of property, and of enjoying all such privileges as persons of colour born free in this State, do enjoy; and that the said James shall hereafter be known by the name of James Charlton, Provided, always, That this act shall not operate so as to defeat the rights of any person or persons to the property in said James, except the right of the said Richard W. Caswell, and such persons as may claim by, through, from or under him.

II. And be it further enacted, That nothing in this act contained, shall be so construed as to authorise the emancipation of the said negro man James, until Francis Kilpatrick and James Bright, or one of them, shall have entered into bond in the sum of two hundred and fifty pounds, with good and sufficient security, made payable to the Chairman of the County Court of Lenoir and his successors in office, that the said James shall never become a charge to any of the counties in this State, and making themselves responsible for his good behaviour.

****

STATE OF NORTH CAROLINA
LAWS OF THE STATE OF NORTH CAROLINA
1803-1816

CHAPTER XCVIII.
1811. An Act to emancipate a Negro called Silvia. (Page 38).

    Be it enacted by the General Assembly of the State of North Carolina, and it is hereby enacted by the authority of the same, That a certain Negro girl named Silvia, belonging to the estate of Abraham Bass, late of the county of Nash, be, and she is hereby emancipated and made capable of taking, holding and possessing property of every kind, and of enjoying all such privileges as all other free persons of color.

    II. And be it further enacted, That the above named girl shall be known and called by the name of Silvia Spears: Provided always, That this act shall not affect the right which any person or persons may have to the service of and property in said girl Silvia, except such person or persons as may claim by, from or through the said Abraham Bass.

    III. And be it further enacted, That nothing in this act contained shall be construed so to authorise the emancipation of the said girl Silvia, until Thomas Hamilton shall have entered into bond with sufficient security, in the sum of two hundred and fifty pounds, made payable to the Chairman of the County Court of Nash and his successors in office, to be void on condition that the said Silvia will never become a charge or burthen to any of the counties of this State.

****

STATE OF NORTH CAROLINA
LAWS OF THE STATE OF NORTH CAROLINA
1803-1816

CHAPTER LXI.
1812. An Act to emancipate a Negro girl named Violet. (Page 24).

    Be it enacted by the General assembly of the State of North Carolina, and it is hereby enacted by the authority of the same, That a certain Negro Girl named Violet, late the property of Abraham Bass, late of the County of Nash, daughter of Silvia, who was emancipated by an act of the Legislature at its last session, be, and she is hereby emancipated and made capable of taking, holding and possessing property of every kind, and enjoying all such privileges as all other free persons of colour.

    II. And be it further enacted, That this act shall not Affect the right of which any person or persons may have to the service of, and property in said Girl Violet, except such person or persons as may claim by, from, and through the said Abraham Bass, deceased.

    III. And be it further enacted, That nothing in this act contained shall be so construed as to authorise the emancipation of the said Violet, until Thomas Hamilton shall have entered into bond with sufficient security in the sum of two hundred and fifty pounds, made payable to the Chairman of the County Court of Nash, and his successors in office, to be void on condition, that the said Violet never become a charge or burthen to any of the Counties in this State.

    IV. And be it further enacted, That the above named Negro Girl called Violet, shall be known and called by the name of Violet Spears.

****

STATE OF NORTH CAROLINA
LAWS OF THE STATE OF NORTH CAROLINA
1803-1816

CHAPTER LXII.

Chapter 28: Acts of Emancipation

1812. An Act to emancipate Isabella and Jane, two negro slaves belonging to the estate of James Allen, deceased. (Pages 24-25).

Be it enacted by the General Assembly of the State of North Carolina, and it is hereby enacted by the authority of the same, That Isabella and Jane, two female slaves belonging to the estate of the late James Allen of the town of Wilmington, be, and they are hereby emancipated and made free, by the names of Isabella Allen and Jane Allen; and they are hereby made able and capable in law to possess and enjoy all the rights and privileges which free persons of colour in this state are capable of possessing and enjoying: Provided always, That this act shall not be construed to effect the claim of any creditor of the said James Allen, if the personal estate of said Allen should be insufficient to discharge the demands which are against it; and Provided further, that this act shall not take effect until bond with good and sufficient security to be judged of, and approved by the Justices of the Court of Pleas and Quarter Sessions of the County of New Hanover, and payable to the Chairman thereof, be entered into, conditioned that neither of the persons liberated by this act shall ever become burdensome to the Parish in any County in this State; which bond may be put in suit without assignment by any Parish damnified by the breach thereof.

****

STATE OF NORTH CAROLINA
LAWS OF THE STATE OF NORTH CAROLINA
1803-1816

CHAPTER LXII.
1812. An Act to emancipate certain persons therein mentioned. (Page 25).

Be it enacted by the General Assembly of the State of North Carolina, and it is hereby enacted by the authority of the same, That three negro slaves by the names of Hannah, Peggy and Sally, the property of Jacob Spelman of the County of Currituck, be, and they are hereby emancipated and set free, by the names of Hannah Spelman, Peggy Spelman, and Sally Spelman; and the said persons are hereby invested with all the rights which free persons of colour are capable of enjoying by law; Provided, That before this act shall be of any force or effect, bond shall be entered into, in such sum and with such security as shall be approved by the Justices of the County Court of Currituck, and payable to the Chairman thereof, and his successors, conditioned, that neither of the persons hereby emancipated, shall ever become burdensome to the Parish in any County of this State; which bond may be put in suit without assignment, as often as any County in this State may be damnified by breach of the condition thereof.

****

STATE OF NORTH CAROLINA
LAWS OF THE STATE OF NORTH CAROLINA
1803-1816

CHAPTER CXXXI.
1816. An Act to emancipate Hannah Howe, Balaam Howe, John Howe and Sally Howe children of Balaam and Lucy Howe of the County of Brunswick. (Page 53).

Be it enacted by the General assembly of the State of North Carolina, and it is hereby enacted by the authority of the same, That Hannah Howe, John Howe, Balaam Howe and Sally Howe children of Balaam and Lucy his wife, of the County of Brunswick, be, and they are hereby emancipated and set free, and shall be entitled to all the rights and privileges of free persons of color within this state in as full and ample manner as if they had been born free.

****

Acts Passed by the General Assembly of the State
Of North Carolina at its Session
Commencing on the 17th of November, 1823
Raleigh: Printed by J. Gales & Son - State Printers. 1824

CHAPTER CLXVI.

Chapter 28: Acts of Emancipation

1823. An Act to emancipate Sally Zimmerman, a slave belonging to the estate of Andrew Caldcleugh, deceased, late of Rowan County. (Page 96)

Whereas the said Andrew Caldcluegh, in and by his last will, did devise that a female slave, called and known by the name of Sally Zimmerman, a child of tender years, should be emancipated and set free; and whereas the executors of the said Andrew Caldcleugh, by and with consent of the heirs at law, and residuary legatee of the said Andrew Caldcleugh, have petitioned this General Assembly to carry the will of the said Andrew into effect as it relates to the said slave:

Therefore be it enacted by the General Assembly of the State of North Carolina, and it is hereby enacted by the authority of the same, That from and after the ratification of this act, the said Sally shall be, and hereby is emancipated, and set free from slavery, fully and absolutely, and shall be called and known by the name of Sally Zimmerman.
Read three times and ratified in GeneralAssembly, this 31st day of Dec. 1823

        A. Moore, S.H.C.
        B. Yancy, S.S.

A true Copy,
        Wm. Hill, Secretary.

****

Acts Passed by the General Assembly
Of the State of North Carolina, at the Session of 1833-34
Raleigh: Printed by Lawrwence& Lemay
Printers to the State, 1834

CHAPTER CVIII.
1833-1834. An act to emancipate Joe, a slave. (Page 156).

Be it enacted by the General assembly of the State of North Carolina, and it is hereby enacted by the authority of the same, That Joe, a slave belonging to Sophia L. Smith, executrix of David Smith, deceased, late of Cumberland county, is hereby, with the consent and at the request of his said owner, emancipated and set free; and by the name of Joseph Hostler shall hereafter possess and exercise all the rights and privileges which are enjoyed by other free persons of color within this State: Provided, nevertheless, that before such slave shall be emancipated, the petitioner shall give bond and good security to the Governor and his successors in office, in the County Court of Cumberland county, that the said slave shall honestly and correctly demean himself as long as he shall remain in the State, and shall not become a parish charge; which bond may be sued upon in the name of the Governor for the time being, to the use of the parish and of any person injured by the malconduct of such slave.

****

Acts Passed by the General Assembly
of the State of North Carolina, at the Session of 1833-34
Raleigh: Printed by Lawrence & Lemay
Printers to the State, 1834

CHAPTER CIX.
1833-1834. An act to emancipate Ned Hyman, a slave. (Page 156-157).

Be it enacted by the General Assembly of the State of North Carolina, and it is hereby enacted by the authority of the same, That Ned Hyman, a slave belonging to Elizabeth Hagans, of Martin County, is hereby, with the consent and at the request of his said owner, emancipated and set free; and by the name of Ned Hyman, shall hereafter possess and exercise all the rights and privileges which are enjoyed by other free persons of color within this State: Provided, nevertheless, that before such slave shall be emancipated, the petitioner shall give bond and good security to the Governor and his Successors in office, in the County Court of Martin county, that the said slave shall honestly and correctly demean himself as long as he shall remain in the State, and shall not become a parish charge; which bond may be sued upon in the name of the Governor for the time being, to the use of the parish and of any person injured by the malconduct of such slave.

****

Chapter 28: Acts of Emancipation

Acts Passed by the General Assembly
of the State of North Carolina
at the Session of 1834-1835
Raleigh: Philo White, Printer to the State, 1835

CHAPTER CLXVI.
1834-1835. An Act to emancipate Daniel, a slave. (Page 91).
  Be it enacted by the General Assembly of the State of North Carolina, and it is hereby enacted by the authority of the same, That Daniel, a slave, the property of William Macay of Rowan County, be, and he is hereby, with the consent and at the request of his said owner, emancipated and set free; and by the name of Daniel Macay shall hereafter possess and exercise all the rights and privileges which are enjoyed by other free persons of color in this State: Provided, nevertheless, that before such slave shall be emancipated, the petitioner shall give bond and good security to the Governor and his successors in office in the county court of Rowan county, that the said slave shall honestly and correctly demean himself as long as he shall remain in the State, and shall not become a parish charge; which bond may be sued upon in the name of the Governor, for the time being to the use of the parish, and of any person injured by the malconduct of such slave.

****

Laws of the State of North Carolina
Passed by the General Assembly
At the Session of 1836-1837
Raleigh: Thomas J. Lemay, Printer, 1837.

CHAP. LXV.
1836-1837. An Act to emancipate Isaac, a slave. (Page 328).
  Be it enacted by the General Assembly of the State of North Carolina, and it is hereby enacted by the authority of the same, That Isaac, a slave, the property of Robert Belden, of the county of Cumberland, be, and he is hereby, with the consent and at the request of his said owner, emancipated and set free; and, by the name of Isaac Belden, shall hereafter possess and exercise all the rights and privileges which are enjoyed by other free persons of color in this State: Provided nevertheless, that before said slave shall be emancipated, his said master shall give bond and good security, to the Governor and his successors in office, in the county court of New Hanover county, that the said slave shall honestly and correctly demean himself as long as he shall remain in the State, and shall not become a parish charge; which bond may be sued upon, in the name of the Governor for the time being, to the use of the parish and of any person injured by the mal conduct of said slave.
[Ratified 14th December, 1836.]

****

Laws of the State of North Carolina
Passed by the General Assembly
At the Session of 1836-1837
Raleigh: Thomas J. Lemay, Printer, 1837.

CHAP. LXIV. EMANCIPATION.
1836-1837. An Act to emancipate Henry, Fanny and John, the slaves and children of Miles Howard. (Page 327).
  Be it enacted by the General Assembly of the State of North Carolina, and it is hereby enacted by the authority of the same, That Henry Howard, Fanny Howard and John Howard, children and slaves of Miles Howard, of Halifax county, at the special request of said Miles, be, and they are hereby emancipated and set free, and shall hereafter enjoy all the privileges of free persons of color.
[Ratified 10th December, 1836,].

****

Laws of the State of North Carolina

Chapter 28: Acts of Emancipation

Passed by the General Assembly
At the Session of 1838-1839
Raleigh: Printed by J. Gales and Son
Office of the Raleigh Register, 1839

CHAPTER XLVIII. MISCELLANEOUS.
1839. AN ACT to emancipate Caroline Cook and her four children, viz: Pamelia, Archibald T., James Ellis, and Martha Jane. (Page 157).

Be it enacted by the General Assembly of the State of North Carolina, and it is hereby enacted by the authority of the same, That Caroline Cook, wife of Joshua Cook, and her four children, viz: Pamelia, Archibald T., James Ellis, and Martha Jane, slaves the property of Archibald Lovelace, of the county of Wilkes, be, and they are hereby, with the consent and request of their said owner, emancipated and set free, and by their names of Caroline Cook, Pamelia Cook, Archibald T. Cook, James Ellis Cook, and Martha Jane Cook, shall hereafter possess and exercise all the rights and privileges which are enjoyed by other free persons of colour in this State: Provided, nevertheless, that before said slaves shall be emancipated, the said Joshua Cook, or their said Master, shall give bond and good security in the County Court of Wilkes County, that said slaves shall honestly demean themselves as long as they shall remain in the State, and shall not become a county charge, which said bond shall be made payable to the State of North Carolina, and may be sued upon in the name of the State, to the use of the county, and of any person injured by the mal-conduct of said slaves.
[Ratified 22d December, 1838].

***

Laws of the State of North Carolina
Passed by the General Assembly
At the Session of 1846-47
Raleigh: Thomas J. Lemay, Printer, 1847

EMANCIPATION
CHAPTER CLXII.
1846-47. An Act authorizing John Malone, a free man of color, to emancipate his wife and son, upon certain conditions herein mentioned. (Pages 297-298).

Sec. 1. Be it enacted by the General Assembly of the State of North Carolina, and it is hereby enacted by the authority of the same, That John Malone, a free man of color, in the county of Wake, be, and he is hereby authorized to emancipate from slavery, Cherry, his wife, and Edmond, his son, who are the slaves of the said John Malone; and that the said Cherry, by the name of Cherry Malone; and the said Edmond, by the name of Edmond Malone, shall thence forth be free and have and enjoy the same rights and privileges as if they had been born free in this State, and may at their pleasure continue to reside in North Carolina; any law to the contrary notwithstanding: Provided, that the said Edmond Malone shall be, after his emancipation, considered in law the legitimate son and heir of said John Malone, and capable in law to succeed as such to the property, real and personal, whereof the said John Malone may die seized and possessed, without devising it, or otherwise conveying it to others, in all respects, as though the said Edmond had been born in lawful wedlock of the body of the lawful wife of the said John Malone: and provided further, that the said John Malone shall in due form of law intermarry with the said Cherry Malone, and make her his lawful wife, on the same day that she shall be emancipated by him from slavery.

Sec. 2. Be it further enacted, That before the said John Malone shall emancipate the said slaves Cherry and Edmond, and as a precedent condition to give the said act of emancipation effect in this State, the said John Malone shall give a bond, in the penal sum of five hundred dollars, payable to the State of North Carolina, and conditioned that the said two slaves, Cherry and Edmond, shall each be of good behaviour during his or her residence in the State, and that neither of them shall, after their emancipation, become chargeable to the county or any parish or county in North Carolina; and further conditioned, that the said John Malone will renew the said bond, with approved security when it shall at any time be required by the county court of Wake, and the clerk of the county court of Wake, under the written approbation of any two justices of the peace or the county court of Wake, may take the first bond, and the said John Malone shall give one or more good and approved sureties to the said bond, as well as the one executed at first, as any other given in renewal thereof.
[Ratified 2nd of January 1847.]

Chapter 28: Acts of Emancipation

Laws of the State of North Carolina
Passed by the General Assembly
At the Session of 1846-47
Raleigh: Thomas J. Lemay, Printer, 1847

EMANCIPATION
CHAPTER CLXI.
1846-47. An Act to emancipate Abel Payne and his wife Patsey, slaves. (Page 297).
 Be it enacted by the General Assembly of the State of North Carolina, and it is hereby enacted by the authority of the same, That Abel Payne and his wife Patsey, the property of Joshua Carman, of the county of Cumberland, be, and they are hereby, with the consent and at the request of their said owner, emancipated and set free, and by the names of Abel and Patsey Payne, shall hereafter possess and exercise, all the rights and privileges which are enjoyed by other free persons of color in this State: Provided nevertheless, That before said slaves shall be emancipated, their said master, Joshua Carman, shall give bond and good security, in the sum of five hundred dollars, to the Governor and his successors in office, in the county court of Cumberland county, that the said slaves shall honestly and correctly demean themselves, as long as they shall remain in the State, and shall not become a parish charge, which bond may be sued upon, in the name of the Governor for the time being, to the use of the parish, or of any person injured by the malconduct of either of said slaves.
[Ratified 2d day of January, 1847]

****

Laws of the State of North Carolina
Passed by the General Assembly
At the Session of 1846-47
Raleigh: Thomas J. Lemay, Printer, 1847

EMANCIPATION.
CHAPTER CLX.
1846-47. An Act to emancipate Samuel Macky, a slave. (Pages 296-297)
 Be it enacted by the General Assembly of the State of North Carolina, and it is hereby enacted by the authority of the same, that Samuel Macky, a slave, the property of John S. Pearson, of Cumberland county, be, and he is hereby, with the consent and at the request of the said owner, emancipated and set free; and by the name of Samuel Macky, shall hereafter possess and exercise all the rights and privileges which are enjoyed by other free persons of color in this State: Provided nevertheless, That before said slave shall be emancipated, his said master shall give bond and good security to the Governor and his successors in office, in the court of Cumberland county, in the sum of five hundred dollars, that the said slave shall honestly and correctly demean himself as long as he shall remain in the State, and shall not become a parish charge; which bond may be sued upon, in the name of the Governor for the time being, to the use of the parish, and of any person injured by the mal conduct of such said slave.
[Ratified 7th of January, 1847.]

****

Laws of the State of North Carolina
Passed by the General Assembly
At the Session of 1850-51
Raleigh: T.J. Lemay, State Printer, 1851

MISCELLANEOUS
CHAPTER CCLII.
1850-51. An Act to emancipate Lucy, a slave, and her child Laura. (Pages 624-625).
 Sec. 1. Be it enacted by the General Assembly of the State of North Carolina, and it is hereby enacted by the authority of the same, That Lucy and her child Laura, the property of John Selph of Cumberland county, be, and they are hereby, with the consent, and at the request of the said owner, emancipated and set free, and by the names of Lucy Selph

Chapter 28: Acts of Emancipation

and Laura Selph, shall hereafter possess and exercise all the rights and privileges which are enjoyed by other free persons of color in this State: Provided, nevertheless, that before said slaves shall be emancipated, their said master shall give bond and good security to the Governor and his successors in office, in the county court of Cumberland county, in the sum of five hundred dollars, that the said slaves shall honestly and correctly demean themselves as long as they shall remain in the State; and shall not become a parish charge, which bond may be sued upon, in the name of the Governor for the time being, to the use of the parish and of any person injured by the malconduct of said slaves.
[Ratified 22nd January, 1851.]

****

Laws of the State of North Carolina
Passed by the General Assembly
At the Session of 1852
Published Agreeably to the Fifty-Ninth Chapter
Of the Revised Statutes
Raleigh: Wesley Whitaker Jr., Printer to the State

CHAPTER CLXXXII. EMANCIPATION OF SLAVES.
1852. An Act to emancipate James Langford, a Slave. (Page 667).

    Be it enacted by the General Assembly of the State of North Carolina, and it is hereby enacted by the authority of the same, That James Langford, the property of Jordan Beal, of the county of Northampton, be, and he is hereby, with the consent of said owner emancipated and set free, by the name of James Langford, shall hereafter possess and exercise all the rights and privileges which are enjoyed by other free persons of color in this State: Provided, nevertheless, That before the said slave shall be emancipated, he shall give bond and good security in the sum of five hundred dollars, payable to the State of North Carolina, conditioned that the said James Langford shall honestly and correctly demean himself, and shall not become a parish charge, which bond shall be approved by the court of pleas and quarter sessions of Northampton county and be deposited in the office of said court, which bond may be sued upon to the use of the parish, or of any person injured by the misconduct of said slave: And provided further, That if the said James Langford shall, at any time hereafter remove from the said county of Northampton, and remain out of said county for the space of thirty days, he shall forfeit his freedom.
[Read three times and ratified in General Assembly, this 22nd day of December, A.D., 1852.]

****

Private Laws of the State of North Carolina
Passed by the General Assembly
At its Session of 1854-55
Raleigh: Holden & Wilson, Printers to the State, 1855

CHAP. 111. EMANCIPATION.
1854-55. An Act to emancipate James G. Hostler, a slave. (Pages 90-91).

    Sec. 1. Be it enacted by the General assembly of the State of North Carolina, and it is hereby enacted by the authority of the same, That James G. Hostler, the property of James Anderson, William A. Wright, Armand J. DeRossett, Jr., Joshua G. Wright and Thomas C. Miller, of the town of Wilmington, be and he is hereby, with the consent of said owners, emancipated and set free, by the name of James G. Hostler, and shall hereafter possess and exercise all the rights and privileges which are enjoyed by free persons of color in this State: Provided, nevertheless, That before the said slave shall be emancipated, he shall give bond with good security in the sum of five hundred dollars, payable to the State of North Carolina, conditioned that the said James G. Hostler shall honestly and correctly demean himself, and shall not become a parish charge, which bond shall be approved by the court of pleas and quarter sessions of the county of New Hanover, and be deposited in the office of said court, and may be sued on to the use of any parish or person injured by the misconduct of said James G. Hostler.
[Ratified the 16th day of January, 1855.]

****

Public Laws of the State of North Carolina

Chapter 28: Acts of Emancipation

Passed by the General Assembly
At its Session of 1854-55
Raleigh: Holden & Wilson, Printers to the State, 1855

CHAP. 109. EMANCIPATION.
1854-55. An Act to emancipate Jerry, a slave. (Pages 89-90).
    Sec. 1. Be it enacted by the General Assembly of the State of North Carolina, and it is hereby enacted by the authority of the same, That Jerry, a slave, the property of H.B. Williams and S.A. Davis, of Mecklenburg county, be, and he is hereby, with the consent, and at the request of the said owners, emancipated and set free, and by the name of Jerry Bethel, shall hereafter possess and exercise all the rights and privileges which are enjoyed by other free persons of color in this State: Provided, nevertheless, That before the said slave is emancipated, the said Williams and Davis, or either of them, shall give bond and approved security, payable to the Governor and his successors in office, in the county court of Mecklenburg county, in the sum of one thousand dollars, that the said Jerry shall honestly and correctly demean himself as long as he shall remain in the State, and shall not become a county charge; which bond may be sued upon in the name of the Governor for the time being, to the use of said county, and of any person injured by the misconduct of the said slave hereby emancipated.
[Ratified the 8th day of January, 1855.]

****

Private Laws of the State of North Carolina
Passed by the General Assembly
At its Session of 1854-55
Raleigh: Holden & Wilson, Printers to the State, 1855

CHAP. 108. EMANCIPATION.
1854-55. An Act to emancipate Betty, a slave. (Page 89).
    Sec. 1. Be it enacted by the General Assembly of the State of North Carolina, and it is hereby enacted by the authority of the same, That Betty, a slave, the property of Joshua Carman, of Cumberland county, be and she is hereby emancipated and set free by the consent and at the request of her master, and by the name of Betty Beebee, shall possess and exercise all the rights and privileges of other free persons of color in this State: Provided, nevertheless, that before this act of emancipation shall take effect, the owner of the said slave Betty, or some person for him, shall file in the clerk's office of the court of pleas and quarter sessions of Cumberland county, a bond with good security, in the sum of five hundred dollars, payable to the Governor of the State and his successors in office, that the said Betty shall demean herself correctly while she remains in the State and not become a county charge, which bond may be put in suit in the name of the Governor for the time being, to the use of the county or person injured by a breach of its condition: Provided, That she do not reside out of the county aforesaid, more than thirty days at any one time; also that she give bond in such an amount as will be approved of by the county court, that she will not become a public charge.
[Ratified the 14th day of February, 1855.]

****

Acts Passed by the General Assembly
at it's Session of 1854-55
Raleigh, Holden & Wilson, Printers to the State, 1855

CHAP. 110. EMANCIPATION.
1854-55. An Act to emancipate John Good. (Page 90).
    Be it enacted by the General Assembly of the State of North Carolina, and it is hereby enacted by the authority of the same, That John Good, a slave, the property of George Bishop, of Craven county, be, and he is hereby, with the consent, and at the request of the said owner, emancipated and set free; and by the name of John Good, shall hereafter possess and exercise all the rights and privileges which are enjoyed by other free persons of color in this State: Provided, nevertheless, That before the said slave is emancipated, a good and sufficient bond, payable to the State of North Carolina, shall be given in the county court of Craven, in the sum of one thousand dollars, that the said John Good shall honestly and correctly demean himself as long as he shall remain in the State, and not become a county

Chapter 28: Acts of Emancipation

charge; which bond may be sued upon in the name of the State to the use of said county, or any other county of the State, and of any person injured by the misconduct of the said slave hereby emancipated.
[Ratified the 20th day of January, 1855.]

****

Private Laws of the State of North Carolina
Passed by the General Assembly
At its Session of 1854-55
Raleigh: Holden & Wilson, Printers to the State, 1855

CHAP. 113. EMANCIPATION.
1854-55. An Act to emancipate Louis, a slave, the property of James Dunn. (Pages 91-92).
 Sec. 1. Be it enacted by the General Assembly of the State of North Carolina, and it is hereby enacted by the authority of the same, That Louis, a slave, the property of James Dunn, of Cumberland county, be and he is hereby, emancipated and set free, and by the name of Louis Dunn shall hereafter possess and exercise all the rights and privileges which are enjoyed by other free persons of color in this State: Provided, nevertheless, That before said slave shall be emancipated, his said owner shall give bond with good sureties in the sum of five hundred dollars, payable to the Governor of the State and his successors in office, that the said slave shall honestly and correctly demean himself while he remains in this State, and not become a county charge; which bond shall be filed in the office of the clerk of the court of pleas and quarter sessions of Cumberland county, and may be sued upon in the name of the governor for the time being, to the use of the county or persons injured by a breach thereof.
[Ratified the 16th day of February, 1855.]

****

Private Laws of the State of North Carolina
Passed by the General Assembly
At its Session of 1854-55
Raleigh: Holden & Wilson, Printers to the State, 1855

CHAP. 112. EMANCIPATION.
1854-55. A Bill to emancipate Albert, a slave, the property of John Hockody. (Page 91).
 Sec. 1. Be it enacted by the General Assembly of the State of North Carolina, and it is hereby enacted by the authority of the same, That Albert, a slave, the property of John Hockody, be and he is hereby, with the consent and at the request of said owner, emancipated and set free, and by the name of Albert Hockody shall hereafter possess and exercise all the rights and privileges which are enjoyed by other free persons of color in the State: Provided, nevertheless, That before the said slave Albert is emancipated, the said John Hockody shall give bond and approved security, payable to the governor and his successors in office, in the county court of Halifax, in the sum of one thousand dollars, that the said Albert shall honestly and correctly demean himself as long as he shall remain in the State, and shall not become a county charge; which bond may be sued on in the name of the governor for the time being, to the use of the said county, and of any person injured by the misconduct of the said slave hereby emancipated.
[Ratified the 16th day of February, 1855.]

Appendix A: Emancipation Laws

appendix A

Emancipation Laws

NORTH CAROLINA EMANCIPATION LAWS

The State Records of North Carolina
Volume XXIII., 1715-1776
Edited by: Walter Clark
Nash Brothers Book and Job Printers
Goldsboro, North Carolina, 1904

CHAPTER XLVI.
1715. An Act Concerning Servants & Slaves. (Repealed by Act 4 April, 1741, ch. 24.). (Pages 62-66)
    XVIII. And Be It Further Enacted by the Authority aforesaid that no person within this Government shall make any contract with his or their Negro or Negroes for his or their freedom or Liberty that are Runaways or Refractory Negroes. Provided that this Act shall not hinder any man from setting his Negro free as a Reward for his, or their honest & Faithful service. And Provided that such Negro depart the Government within Six Months after his Freedom But if any Negro set free as aforesaid shall not within the time Limitted & according to the true Intent & Meaning of this Act depart the Government then such Negro or Negroes shall by the precinct Court be sold for Five Years to such person or Persons as shall give security for their Transportation & the Moneys arising by such sale shall be paid into the Publick Treasury.

CHAPTER V.
1723. An Act for an additional Tax on all free Negroes, Mulattoes, Mustees, and such Persons, Male and Female, as now are, or hereafter shall be, intermarried with any such Persons, resident in this Government. (Pages 106-107).
    IV. And forasmuch as divers of the Inhabitants of this Government, for Causes them thereunto moving, have set free Slaves of Sundry kinds, who are, all by Law, obliged to depart the Government in Six Months after their being so freed, otherwise they are liable to be sold to such Person or Persons as shall give security for transporting them out of this Government; notwithstanding the said Law, and contrary to the true Intent and Meaning thereof, many of such freed Negroes, and Slaves of other Kinds, after having departed this Government for a Little Time, Have returned again, deeming themselves Inhabitants of this Government by such Departure and Return: For the Prevention whereof for the future;
    V. Be it therefore Enacted, by the Authority of the aforesaid, That all Slaves, of what kind soever, which shall hereafter be set free, that shall be obliged to depart this Government within Six Months after being so freed, according to the Direction of the aforesaid Act, and shall not return into this Government, under the Penalties and Pains hereafter expressed: And if any Slave or Slaves being so freed and set at Liberty, having departed as before directed, shall presume to return back into this Province, it shall and may be lawful for any Person or Persons whatsoever to apprehend and take up such Slave or Slaves so offending, and carry him or them before some Magistrate, who is hereby authorized and empowered, upon due proof made, to commit such Person or Persons so offending, to the Provost Marshall of the County where such offender or offenders shall be apprehended, till the next General Court, to be held for this Government, and shall then sell him or them for Seven Years, at Public Vendue, to the highest Bidder; and the Money arising by the said Sale, after Charges paid, shall be applied, the one Half to the Apprehender, and the other Half towards defraying the contingent charges of the Government; and at the End and Expiration of the said Seven Years, the said Slave or Slaves so set free, shall, and are hereby compelled to depart this Government, within Six Months after being so freed: And if any such Person or Persons so departing shall presume to return a Second Time, they are hereby made liable to be apprehended, taken up, and sold, as aforesaid.
    VI. And be it further Enacted, by the Authority aforesaid, That after such Sale is made as aforesaid, if any Person or Persons, Inhabitants of this Government, shall presume to harbour, conceal, or detain any such Negroe or Slave set free, upon pretence of Debt, or otherwise, such Person or Persons so offending shall forfeit and pay One

Appendix A: Emancipation Laws

Hundred Pounds Current Money; shall sue for the same: to be recovered by Bill, Plaint, or Information, in any Court of record within this Government; wherein no Injunction, or Wager of Law, shall be allowed or admitted of.

CHAPTER XXIV.
1741. An Act Concerning Servants and Slaves. (Pages 191-204).

   LVI. And be it further Enacted, by the Authority aforesaid, That no Negro or Mulatto Slaves shall be set free, upon any pretence whatsoever, except for meritorious Services, to be adjudged and allowed of by the County Court, and Licence thereupon first had and obtained; And that where any Slave shall be set free by his or her Master or Owner, otherwise than is hereinbefore directed, it shall and may be lawful for the Church Wardens of the Parish wherein such Negro, Mulatto or Indian shall be found, at the Expiration of Six Months, next after his or her being set free, and they are hereby authorized and required, to take up and sell the said Negro, Mulatto or Indian as a Slave, at the next Court to be held for the said County at Public Vendue; and the Monies arising by such Sale, shall be applied to the Use of the Parish, by the Vestry thereof: And if any Negro, Mulatto or Indian Slave, set free otherwise than is herein directed, shall depart this Province within Six Months next after his or her Freedom, and shall afterwards return into this Government, it shall and may be lawful for the Church Wardens of the Parish where such Negro or Mulatto shall be found, at the Expiration of one Month, next after his or her return into this Government, to take up such Negro or Mulatto, and sell him or them, as Slaves at the next Court to be held for the County, at Public Vendue; and the Monies arising thereby, to be applied, by the Vestry, to the Use of the Parish, as aforesaid.

   LVII. And be it further Enacted, by the Authority aforesaid, That until this Act shall be printed, it shall be publicly read, Yearly, and every Year, Two several Times in the year, in every County within this Government, by the Clerk of each County, in open Court, that is to say, at the Courts in or next to the Months of April and September; under the Penalty of Twenty Shillings, Proclamation Money, for every such Omission and Neglect; to be levied by a Warrant from any Justice of the Peace, and applied to the Use of the Parish where the Offence shall be committed: and the Church Wardens of every Parish are hereby required to provide a Copy of this Act, at the Charge of the Parish.

   LVIII. And be it further Enacted, by the Authority aforesaid, That all and every other Act and Acts, and every Clause and Article thereof heretofore made, so far as relates to Servants and Slaves, or to any other Matter or Thing whatsoever, within the Purview of this Act, is and are hereby repealed and made void, to all Intents and Purposes, as if the same had never been made.

The State Records of North Carolina
Volume XXIV., 1777-1788
Edited by: Walter L. Clark
Nash Brothers Book and Job Printers
Goldsboro, N.C., 1906

CHAPTER VI.
1777. An Act to prevent domestic Insurrections, and for other Purposes. (Pages 14-15).

   I. Whereas the evil and pernicious Practice of freeing Slaves in this State, ought at this alarming and critical Time to be guarded against by every friend and Wellwisher to his Country:

   II. Be it therefore enacted by the General Assembly of the State of North Carolina, and by the authority of the same, That no Negro or Mulatto Slave shall hereafter be set free, except for meritorious Services, to be adjudged of and allowed by the County Court, and License first had and obtained thereupon. And when any Slave is or shall be set free by his or her Master or Owner otherwise than is herein before directed, it shall and may be lawful for any Free holder in this State, to apprehend and take up such Slave, and deliver him or her to the Sheriff of the County, who, on receiving such Slave, shall give such Freeholder a Receipt for the same; and the Sheriff shall committ all such Slaves to the Gaol of the County, there to remain untill the next Court to be held for such County; and the Court of the County shall order all such confined Slaves to be sold during the Term to the highest Bidder.

   III. Provided always, That the Sheriff, upon committing any such Slave or Slaves, shall at least five Days before such Sale, give Notice in Writing to the last Owner or Owners, or the reputed Owner or Owners of such Slave or Slaves, of the Time and Place of Sale, and of the Name and Names of such Slaves, to the End that such Owner or Owners may, if he or they think proper, make his or their Claim to the same; but if such Owner or Owners shall neglect or refuse to appear on the Day of Sale (due Proof of the Service of such Notice being made to the Satisfaction of the Court) such Owner or owners, so neglecting or refusing, shall be forever barred from making any Claim to such Slaves.

Appendix A: Emancipation Laws

IV. And be it further enacted by the Authority aforesaid, That the net Proceeds of the Money arising by such Sale shall be disposed of in the following Manner, that is to say, That one-fifth Part thereof shall be paid to the Takers up of such Negroes or Mulattoes, and that the remaining Part of such Money be paid into the Hands of the Public Treasurers, to defray the contingent Charges of Government, and to no other Intent, Use or Purpose, whatsoever.

V. And be it enacted by the Authority aforesaid, That if any Slave or Slaves shall hereafter be allowed by his or her Master, Mistress, or Overseer, or other Person having the Care of such Slave or Slaves, to hire out him or herself, such Slave may be taken up by any Magistrate or Freeholder, and kept to hard Labour, for the Use of the Poor of the County, for any Time not exceeding Twenty Days; any Law, Usage, or Custom, to the contrary notwithstanding.

CHAPTER XII. 3RD SESSION.
1778. An Act for Apprehending and selling certain Slaves set free contrary to Law and for Confirming the Sales of Others, and for other purposes. (Page 221).

I. Whereas, by an Act entitled an Act to prevent Domestick Insurrections & for other purposes, it is provided, that no person shall liberate his or her slave except for meritorious Services, to be judged of and allowed by the County Court, and by the said Act, it is Directed in what Manner and for what purposes such liberated slaves shall be apprehended and sold; and whereas, before the passing of the said Act, and since the sixteenth day of April, one thousand seven hundred and seventy five, divers evil minded persons, intending to disturb the public peace, did liberate and set free their slaves, notwithstanding the same was especially contrary to the Laws of this State and the County Courts of Perquimans and Pasquotank, conceiving they had power to proceed against all such liberated slaves, did order them to be sold to the highest bidder, and whereas, doubts have now arisen whether the purchasers of such slaves have good and legal title thereto, for remedy whereof,

II. Be it Enacted by the General Assembly of the State of North Carolina, and it is hereby Enacted by the Authority of the same, that all such sales made bona fide and for valuable consideration shall be deemed good and valid to all intents and purposes, and as many negroes are now going at large to the terror of the good People of this State, who were liberated in manner aforesaid previous to the passing of the said recited Act,

III. Be it further enacted by the Authority aforesaid, That the same Proceeding shall and may be had against all such illegally liberated slaves as is directed in the said recited Act intitled, An Act to prevent domestic insurrections, and for other purposes, in the same manner as if such negro slaves had been set free after the passing of the same; Provided, that nothing herein contained shall deprive of Liberty any Slave who having been liberated & not sold by order of any Court has inlisted in the service of this or the United States previous to the passing of this Act.

CHAPTER XX. 1ST SESSION.
1788. An Act to Amend an Act Entitled "An Act to Prevent Domestic Insurrections." (Page 964).

Whereas by the before recited Act it is Enacted, that no person shall liberate or set free his or her slave except for meritorious services to be adjudged and allowed of by the county court, and by the said Act it is directed in what manner and for what purpose slaves illegally liberated shall be apprehended and sold: And whereas divers persons from religious motives, in violation of the said law, continue to liberate their slaves, who are now going at large to the terror of the people of this State: And whereas the mode prescribed for apprehending such slave or slaves is found by experience not to answer the good purposes by the said Act intended, the power of apprehending liberated slaves being confined to freeholders only, and optional in them whether they will exercise the authority or not; and it appearing the said law is not fully adequate to the good purposes intended: Therefore,

I. Be it Enacted by the General Assembly of the State of North Carolina, and it is hereby Enacted by the authority of the same, That from and after the passing of this Act, if any slave hath been liberated contrary to the before recited Act, should be still be within the limits of this State, and all slaves liberated after the passing of this Act should be known or suspected to be lurking in any of the uninhabited parts thereof, then and in such case, on information made to any justice of the peace by any freeman of such liberated slave or slaves going at large or lurking about, contrary to the true intent and meaning of the said Act, then and in such case the justice to whom such information is made, is hereby impowered and required immediately to issue his warrant, directed to the sheriff of the county, commanding him to make diligent search and to apprehend all such slave or slaves, and to commit him, her or them to the gaol of the county, there to remain until the next succeeding court of the county, on which warrant all proceedings shall be regulated in the same manner as is directed by the before recited Act; and that the person or persons apprehending any such slave or slaves by virtue of any such warrant, shall be entitled to the emoluments as is allowed to freeholders by the before recited Act. Provided nevertheless, That nothing in this Act shall be construed to debar any freeholder or freeholders from stepping forward in the execution of said law in the usual manner, or to divest them of the emoluments given by the said Act.

Appendix A: Emancipation Laws

Laws of the State of North Carolina
Revised, Under the Authority of the General Assembly
Volume I.
Henry Potter
Raleigh: Printed and Sold by J. Gales, 1821

CHAP. 444.
1795. An act to prevent any person who may emigrate from any of the West India or Bahama islands, or the French, Dutch, or Spanish settlements on the southern coast of America, from bringing slaves into this state, an also for imposing certain restrictions on free persons of colour who may hereafter come into this state. (See act of Congress, 20th April, 1818, c. 86.). (Pages 786-788).

    1. Be it enacted, &c. That from and after the first day of April next, it shall not be lawful for any person coming into this state, with an intent to settle or otherwise, from any of the West India or Bahama islands, or the settlements on the southern coasts of America, to land any negro or negroes, or people of colour, over the age of fifteen years, under the penalty of one hundred pounds for each and every such slave or persons of colour, to be recovered before any jurisdiction having cognizance of the same, one fifth to the use of the informer, and the other four fifths to the use of the state.

    2. And be it further enacted, That it shall be the duty of such person or persons bringing in any such negro or negroes, or people of colour, under the age of fifteen years, to prove the age of the same by his own oath, or the oath of some other person, before some justice of the peace, if the same be required.

    3. And be it further enacted, That if any free person of colour shall come into this state, by land or water, or any slave shall hereafter be emancipated, **(See 1788, c. 289, and the acts there referred to.)** he, she or they shall be compelled to give bond and security to the sheriff, payable to the governor for the use of the state, in the sum of two hundred pounds, for his, her or their good behaviour, during the time he, she or they may remain in this state; and it is hereby declared to be the duty of the sheriff to apply to the above described persons, and take from them a bond as aforesaid; and if any person so applied to should refuse to give such bond, the sheriff of the county where the person so applied to for the time being resides, shall be and is hereby authorised and directed, to take him, her or them into custody, and confine them and every of them in the gaol of the county, until the ensuing court, when it shall be the duty of the said court to empannel a jury to enquire whether the person so confined comes within the meaning and purview of this act; and if the said jury shall find that such person does come within the meaning of this act, then and in that case the court shall compel such person to give bond as aforesaid for his, her or their good behaviour, and upon failing so to do, the court shall order such person to be sold, for the benefit of the state, at public auction.

    4. And be it further enacted, That it shall be the duty of the severall county courts in the state, to charge the grand juries of the respective counties to make presentments of all such free persons of colour as conduct themselves so as to become dangerous to the peace and good order of the state and county, upon which the said presentments, it shall be the duty of the court to whom the same is made, to issue an order to the sheriff to take into custody the person so presented, and him safely keep until the next county court, when a jury shall be empannelled, as before directed in this act, and a trial agreeably thereto had; and if any person shall be found guilty on such trial, he shall be compelled to give bond and security, as in cases of persons coming into this state contrary to this act; and in case of failure of the person so found guilty to give bond, he, she or they shall be sold for the use and in the manner aforementioned.

    5. And be it further enacted, That when any number of negroes, or other slaves, or free people of colour, shall collect together in arms, and be going about the country, committing thefts, and alarming the inhabitants of any county, it shall be the duty of the commanding officer of such county, or captain of a troop of horse, upon three or more justices of the peace requiring the same, **(See 1802, c. 618, s. 7, 8.)** immediately to call out a sufficient number to suppress such depredations or insurrections; which detachment of militia shall be under the same rules and regulations, as in cases of invasion and Insurrection, and shall be entitled to receive the same pay and rations as the troops of the United States, when in actual service; and if any person shall be wounded or disabled in suppressing such insurrection, he shall be provided for at the public expense, in the same manner as heretofore practised in this state. Provided nevertheless, That if the officer above mentioned shall fail or neglect to order out a detachment of the militia in the above directed cases, his superior officer may, upon sufficient proof being made of the necessity of such a measure, order him or any other officer under his command, to suppress such depredation or insurrection, and if the person so ordered shall fail to obey the same, they shall suffer as in cases of insurrection or invasion.

Laws of the State of North Carolina
Revised Under the Authority of the General Assembly

Appendix A: Emancipation Laws

Volume II
Henry Potter
Raleigh: Printed and Sold by J. Gales, 1821

CHAP. 453.
1796. An act to amend, strengthen and confirm the several acts of Assembly of this State against the emancipation of slaves. (Page 801). (See 1777, c. 109, s. 1.).

Whereas doubts have arisen in the construction of the said acts, as to the extent of the liberation powers vested in the county courts, by an act passed in the year one thousand seven hundred and seventy-seven, chapter sixth, entitled, "An act to prevent domestic insurrection," and another act passed in the year one thousand seven hundred and forty-one, chapter twenty-nine:

1. Be it further enacted, &c. That no slave shall be set free in any case, or under any pretence whatever, except for meritorious services, to adjudged of and allowed by the county court, and license first had and obtained therefor; and that such liberation when entered of record, shall vest in the said slave, so as aforesaid liberated, all the right and privilege of a free born negro, any thing in the said act to the contrary notwithstanding.

CHAP. 584.
1801. An act to compel persons who are permitted to have their slaves liberated, to give bond and security for keeping such slaves from becoming a public or county charge, and other purposes. (Pages 947-948). (See 1777, c. 109, s. 2, & 1796, c. 453.).

Whereas it has been represented to this General Assembly, it frequently happens that slaves or negroes emancipated by their owners, become a county charge: For remedy whereof, Be it enacted, &c. That from and after the passing of this act, all persons who are permitted to liberate their slaves or negroes, either by an act of the General Assembly, or by the county courts within this state, it shall be their express duty to enter into bond in the sum of one hundred pounds for each slave so liberated, with approved security; which bond shall be made payable to the chairman of the court and his successors, for the use of the poor of the county in which the slave or negro may reside, that such slave or negro shall not become chargeable on the parish or county, previous to his having the same effected; and every person or persons who shall fail for six months after the said slave or slaves shall be so set free, to enter into bond and security as above directed, shall forfeit and pay the sum of three hundred pounds to the wardens of the poor of the county, for the benefit of the poor of the county in which such slave or slaves shall be so liberated, to be recovered by an action of debt in any court having cognizance of the same.

2. And be it further enacted, That the wardens of the poor in the several counties in this state, or any one of them, shall have power and authority, on application to them made, that any person or persons are about to remove themselves out of the county, and have any slave or slaves that are likely to become a county charge, to issue their or his warrant to bring such person or persons before him or them, and take such security by bond as may be deemed sufficient to indemnify the parish or county; which bond shall be made payable to the chairman of the county court and his successors. And in case such person or persons shall refuse to give bond as is herein directed, he shall have power and authority to commit the said person or persons, and keep him or them committed until he or they shall enter into such bonds, or remove the slave or slaves so about to be left, usage or custom to the contrary notwithstanding.

Acts Passed by the General Assembly
Of the State of North Carolina at the Session of 1830-1831
Raleigh: Printed by Lawrence & Lemay
Printers to the State. 1831

CHAPTER IX.
1830-1831. An act to regulate the emancipation of slaves in this State. (Pages 12-14).

Be it enacted by the General Assembly of the State of North Carolina, and it is hereby enacted by the authority of the same, That hereafter any inhabitant of this State, desirous to emancipate a slave or slaves, shall file a petition in writing in some one of the Superior Courts of this State, setting forth, as near as may be, the name, sex and age of each slave intended to be emancipated, and praying permission to emancipate the same; and the court before whom such petition shall be filed, shall grant the prayer thereof on the following conditions, and not otherwise, That the petitioner shall show that he has given public notice of his intention to file such petition at the court house of the county and in the State Gazette for at least six weeks before before the hearing of such petition; and that the petitioner shall enter into

Appendix A: Emancipation Laws

bond, with two securities, each to be good and sufficient, payable to the Governor of the State and his successors in office, in the sum of one thousand dollars for each slave named in the petition, conditioned that the said slave or slaves shall honestly and correctly demean him, her, or themselves, while he, she or they shall remain within the State of North Carolina; and that he, she or they will, within ninety days after granting the prayer of the petitioner to emancipate him, her or them, leave the State of North Carolina, and never afterwards come within the same: Provided, nevertheless, that no such emancipation shall in any manner whatever invalidate the or affect the rights or claims of any creditor of such petitioner.

II. And be it further enacted, That any emancipation hereafter granted to any slave or slaves, as herein directed, shall be upon the express condition that he, she or they will leave the STate within ninety days from the granting thereof, and will never return within the State afterwards.

III. And be it further enacted, That it shall hereafter be lawful for any person, by his or her last will and testament, to direct and authorise his or her executor or executors to cause to be emancipated any slave or slaves, pursuant to this act; and such bequest or authority shall be good and avaliable in law and equity, and shall justify said executor or executors in emancipating such slave or slaves at any time thereafter, provided he, she or they file his, her or their petition, and pursue the directions of this act in the same manner as if he, she or they were the absolute owners of such slave or slaves: and provided further, that nothing herein contained shall be taken or held to interfere with the claims of creditors, or exempt any slave directed to be emancipated from liability to the claims of creditors: and provided further, that any slave, emancipated by an executor, pursuant to the directors of the testator, shall be emancipated on the same conditions, and under the same liabilities, as herein before set forth: Provided further, that no permission shall be granted to any executor or executors to emancipate any slave or slaves under the directions of the last will and testament of his or their testator, before the expiration of two years from and after the probate of said last will and testament, unless the said executor or executors shall enter into bond, with approved security, to the Governor of the State for the time being, in double the value of the slave or slaves proposed to be emancipated, conditioned to be answerable to the creditors of his, her or their testator for the value of the said slave or slaves.

IV. And be it further enacted, That it may be lawful at any time hereafter to emancipate, upon petition filed and under the order of any Superior Court of Law in this State, any slave over the age of fifty years, provided his or her owner shall prove by their own oath or otherwise to the satisfaction of the court and jury that said slave has performed meritorious services, (which meritorious services must consist in more than mere general performance of duty:) Provided, nevertheless, that the petitioner shall swear that he or she has not received in money or otherwise the price or value, or any part thereof, of said slave, or been induced to petition for his or her emancipation in consideration for any price paid therefore or to be paid: And provided further, that before such slave shall be emancipated, the petitioner shall give bond and good security in the sum of five hundred dollars, payable to the Governor and his successors in office, that said slave shall honestly and correctly demean him or herself so long as she or he shall remain in the State, and shall not become a parish charge; which bond may be sued upon in the name of the Governor for the time being, to the use of the parish or of any person injured by the mal conduct of such slave.

V. And be it further enacted, That if any slave shall refuse or neglect to leave the State within ninety days after permission to emancipate him or her has been granted as aforesaid by any Superior Court, or shall ever come within the State after having left it, it shall be the duty of any justice of the peace of any county wherein said slave may be found, to issue a warrant to arrest said slave, and shall, upon proper proof being made of his or her having violated the provisions of this act, commit him or her to the jail of the county, there to remain until the next ensuing term of the Court of Pleas and Quarter Sessions where an issue shall be made up and immediately tried, whether the accused has violated the provisions of this act; and upon the finding of the jury that said accused has violated the provisions of this act, he, she or they shall by the said Court of Pleas and Quarter Sessions be ordered to be sold; which sale shall vest an absolute right of property in the purchaser in and to the accused, and the proceeds thereof be equally divided between the informer and the wardens of the poor of the county.

VI. And be it further enacted, That if any slave shall refuse or neglect to leave the State as aforesaid, or shall ever come within the same after having left it, it shall and may be lawful for any person to bring suit in the name of the Governor, for the joint use of himself and the wardens of the poor of the county, and to be applied by them to the support of the poor of said county, upon the bond which may have been given in pursuance of the provisions of this act.

VII. Be it further enacted, That it shall be the duty of all grand juries within the State to make presentment of all slaves who may hereafter be emancipated, who may violate the provisions of this act of Assembly; and upon such presentment it shall be the duty of the prosecuting officer of the county wherein the presentment may be made, to prosecute such slave as herein before provided.

VIII. Be it further enacted, That all laws and clauses of laws heretofore passed relative to the emancipation of slaves, be, and the same are hereby replaced.

Appendix A: Emancipation Laws

Revised Statutes of North Carolina
Passed by the General Assembly at the Session of 1836-7
Revised Under an Act of the General Assembly, Passed
At the Session of 1833-4, Volume I.
Raleigh: Published by Turner and Hughes, 1837

CHAPTER 111. SLAVES AND FREE PERSONS OF COLOR.
An Act Concerning Slaves And Free Persons Of Color. (Pages 571-593).

57. Any inhabitant of this State, desirous to emancipate any slave or slaves, shall file a petition in writing in some one of the superior courts of this State, setting forth, as near as may be, the name, sex and age of such slave intended to be emancipated, and praying permission to emancipate the same; and the court, before whom such petition shall be filed, shall grant the prayer thereof on the following conditions and not otherwise, viz: That the petitioner shall shew that he has given public notice of his intention to file such petition, as the court house of the county, and in the State Gazette, for at least six weeks before the hearing of such petition, and that the petitioner shall enter into bond with two securities, each to be good and sufficient, payable to the State of North Carolina, in the sum of one thousand dollars for each slave named in the petition, conditioned that the said slave or slaves shall honestly and correctly demean him, her or themselves, while he, she or they shall remain within the State of North Carolina, and that he, she or they will, within ninety days after granting the prayer of the petitioner to emancipate him, her or them, leave the State of North Carolina, and never afterwards come within the same: Provided nevertheless, that no such emancipation shall, in any manner whatever, invalidate or affect the rights of claims of any creditor of such petitioner. **(Reference: 1830, c. 9, s. 1.).**

58. Any emancipation granted to any slave or slaves, as herein directed, shall be upon the express condition, that he, she or they will leave the State, within ninety days from the granting thereof, and never will return within the State afterwards. **(Reference: 1830, c. 9, s. 2.).**

59. It shall be lawful for any person, by his or her last will and testament, to direct and authorize his or her executor or executors, to cause to be emancipated any slave or slaves pursuant to this act; and such bequest or authority shall be good and available in law and equity, and shall justify said executor or executors in emancipating such slave or slaves at any time thereafter: Provided, he, she or they file his, her or their petition, and pursue the directions of this act, in the same manner as if he, she or they were the absolute owners of such slave or slaves: And provided further, that nothing herein contained shall be taken or held to interfere with the claims of creditors, or exempt any slave, directed to be emancipated, from liability to the claims of creditors: And provided further, that any slave emancipated by an executor, pursuant to the directions of the testator, shall be emancipated on the same conditions and under the same liabilities as herein before set forth: Provided further, that no permission shall be granted to any executor or executors to emancipate any slave or slaves, under the directions of the last will and testament of his or their testator, before the expiration of two years from and after the probate of said last will and testament, unless the said executor or executors shall enter into bond, with approved security, to the State of North Carolina, in double the value of the slave or slaves, proposed to be emancipated, conditioned to be answerable to the creditors of his, her or their testator for the value of the said slave or slaves. **(Reference: 1830, c. 9, s. 3.).**

60. It may be lawful to emancipate, upon the petition filed and under the order of any superior court of law in this State, any slave over the age of fifty years. Provided, his or her owner shall prove, by his own oath or otherwise, to the satisfaction of the court and jury, that said slave has performed meritorious services (which meritorious services must consist in more than mere general performance of duty:) Provided nevertheless, that the petitioner shall swear that he or she has not received, in money or otherwise, the price or value, or any part thereof, of said slave, or been induced to petition for his or her emancipation in consideration of any price paid therefor or to be paid: And provided further, that before such slave shall be emancipated, the petitioner shall give bond and good security, in the sum of five hundred dollars, payable to the State of North Carolina, that said slave shall honestly and correctly demean him or herself, so long as he or she shall remain in the State, and shall not become a parish charge; which bond may be sued upon, in the name of the State, to the use of the poor, or of any person injured by the malconduct of such slave. **(Reference: 1830, c. 9, s. 4.).**

61. If any slave, other than such as may be emancipated under the sixtieth section of the act, shall refuse or neglect to leave the State, within ninety days after permission to emancipate him or her has been granted, as aforesaid, by any superior court, or shall ever come within the State after having left it, it shall be the duty of any justice of the peace of any county, wherein said slave may be found, to issue a warrant to arrest said slave; and he shall, upon proper proof being made of his or her having violated the provisions of this act, commit him or her to the jail of the county, there to remain until the next ensuing term of the court of pleas and quarter sessions, where an issue shall be made up

Appendix A: Emancipation Laws

and immediately tried, whether the accused has violated the provisions of this act; and upon the finding of the jury that the accused has so done, he, she or they shall, by the said court of pleas and quarter sessions, be ordered to be sold, which sale shall vest an absolute right of property in the purchaser in and to the accused, and the proceeds thereof be equally divided between the informer and the wardens of the poor of the county. **(Reference: 1830, c. 9, s. 5.).**

62. If any slave shall refuse or neglect to leave the State as aforesaid, or shall ever come within the same after having left it, it shall and may be lawful for any person to bring suit, in the name of the State, for the joint use of himself and the wardens of the poor of the county, and to be applied by them to the support of the poor of the county, upon the bond which may have been given, in pursuance of the provisions of this act. **(Reference: 1830, c. 9, s. 6.).**

63. It shall be the duty of all grand juries within this State to make presentment of all slaves, who may hereafter be emancipated, who may violate the provisions of this act; and upon such presentment, it shall be the duty of the prosecuting officer of the county, wherein the presentment may be made, to prosecute such slave as herein before provided. **(Reference: 1830, c. 9, s. 7.).**

64. No slave shall be set free but according to the provisions of this act. **(Reference: 1830, c. 9, s. 8.).**

Public Laws of the State of North Carolina
Passed by the General Assembly
At its Session of 1860-61
Raleigh: John Spelman, Printer to the State, 1861.

CHAPTER 37.
1860-61. An Act to Prohibit the Emancipation of Slaves by Will. (Page 69).

Be it enacted by the General Assembly of the State of North Carolina, and it is hereby enacted by the authority of the same, That no Slave in this State shall hereafter be emancipated by last will and testament, or deed, or other instrument or conveyance to take effect as to said emancipation after the death of the testator or person executing or making such deed, or other instrument or conveyance, but that all such wills, deeds or other instruments or conveyance in so far as they purport to effect such emancipation, shall be null and void; and no slave so attempted to be emancipated, shall pass under any general residuary clause in any last will and testament, but the testator shall be deemed and taken to have died intestate as to such slave.

[Ratified the 31st day of January, 1861.]

Appendix B: Quaker Documents

appendix B

Quaker Documents

NORTH CAROLINA STATE ARCHIVES
PASQUOTANK COUNTY
RECORDS OF SLAVES AND FREE PERSONS OF COLOR
C.R.075.928.10

Edenton District
October Term 1793

    the Grand Jurors for the aforesaid District Present as a Grievance, the Distressing Inconvenience, the good people of the district lay under from the Inefficiency of the Laws intended to restrict the Emancipation of Slaves. That the people called Quakers in other respect good Citizens, have by their Conduct, made that Species of property not only of Small Value, but have Rendered it dangerous to the personal Safety of the proprietors of Negroes, and those who live in the Vicinity of them, by enfranchising their own Slaves and Sowing discontent and disobedience in the minds of their Neighbors Slaves. That it is now become Necessary for the preservation of good Order and the Security of the Citizens of this district that Measures Shoud be Taken to put a stop to this Evil.

    It is not for the Grand Jury to point out the remedial Laws, but to declare a Necessity for them; They therefore require their Representatives in the next general Assembly; to lay this their presentment before the Legislature - In whose Wisdom they Confide, and whose protection as Citizens they Demand trusting that Measures will be taken so to modify the religious Enthusiasm which pervades their Quaker Neighbors: that the Citizens of this District may Enjoy a full participation of a Constitution which they have Assisted to raise. Vizt. a protection of their Personal Liberties and properties.

1. Woolsey Hathaway foreman
2. William Satterfield
3. Thomas E. Hare
4. J.H. Ward
5. Thomas Simons
6. Enoch Dauge
7. Thomas Davis
8. John Burn
9. saml. W. Johnston
10. Enoch Darley
11. Jos. Banks
12. Willis Roberts
13. Joseph Tarkington
14. Spencer Thach
15. James Temple
16. John Campbell
17. John Jones

NORTH CAROLINA STATE ARCHIVES
PASQUOTANK COUNTY
RECORDS OF SLAVES AND FREE PERSONS OF COLOR
C.R.075.928.10

Presentment
Grand Jury of Pasquotank County

North Carolina   }
Pasquotank County   } Ss December Term 1795

The Jurors for the State and County afforesaid, do present, that the County of Pasquotank is reduced to a Situation of great perril and danger, in consequence of the proceedings of the Society of people called Quakers. That the Idea of emancipations, amongst Slaves is publicly held out to them, and encouraged by the Conduct of the Quakers; that the

Appendix B: Quaker Documents

Minds of the Slaves are not only greatly corrupted, and Allienated from the Service of their Masters, in consequence of Such conduct, But runaways are protected, harbored, and encourag'd by them - Arsons, are even committed, without a possibility of discovery -- The grand Jury, are So perfectly Sensible, of the infatuated enthusiasm of the Quakers, As to partial & generall emancipations, that they See a present alarm amongst the Minds of the people, and forsee a prospect of iminent danger to impend by the influence and designing attempts of the Quakers to this purpose; which unless prevented in due time, must burst with destruction, around the Cittizens of the State.

The Grand Jurry reflecting upon the Miserable havock and Massacres which have lately taken place in the West Indies, in consequence of emancipation; Knowing the opinion of the Northern States; of the many hundred thousand Slaves around them; and of the infatuated enthusiasm of Men Calling themselves religious, who are amongst them; Conceive it a duty Which they owe to themselves, their families, and their Country, to present this existing, and alarming evil, and to present the people Called Quakers and their Abettors, As the Authors of the Common mischiefs, in this Quarter of the World; Where Independent of foreign opinion, emancipation is publicly held out by the Quakers, to the Negroes, and private funds established in Suport of it

The Grand Jurry present that speedy & resolute Measures ought to be adopted, by the good sence and Spirrit of the people, in order to prevent, that common Appeal to Arms, in their own defence, which at present appears to be allmost, if not alltogether Necessary

True Bill   Henry Lankater
                         foreman

NORTH CAROLINA STATE ARCHIVES
CHOWAN COUNTY MISCELLANEOUS RECORDS
C.R.X., BOX #4
BEAUFORT-ROWAN
1699-1865

Presentment
Grand Jury of Chowan
Emancipation of the Blacks 1795

North Carolina }
Chowan County } Decem Term 1795

The jurors for the State & County aforesaid present that the Country is reduced to a situation of great peril & danger in Consequence of the proceedings of the Society of people called Quakers - that the idea of Emancipation amongst Slaves is publickly held out to them & encouraged by the Conduct of the Quakers - that the minds of the Slaves are not only greatly corrupted & alienated from the Service of their Masters But run aways are protected, harboured & encouraged by them. Arsons are committed without a possibility of Discovery

The Grand Jury are so Perfectly sensible of the infatuated enthusiasm of the Quakers as to partial & general Emancipation, that they see a present alarm amongst the minds of the people & forsee a prospect of imminent Danger to impend by the influence & [?] attempts of the Quakers to this purpose, which unless presented in due time, must [?] with destruction around the Citizens of the State.

The Grand Jury reflecting upon the miserable havoc & Massacres
which have lately taken place in the West Indies in Consequence of Emancipation; knowing the opinion of the Northern States; of the many hundred thousand slaves around them ; & of the infatuated enthusiasm of Men calling themselves religious, who are amongst them, conceive it a Duty which they owe to themselves, their familys & their Country to present this existing & alarming evil & to present the people called Quakers & their Abettors as the authors of the common Mischief in this quarter of the State where independent of foreign Opinion; emancipation is publickly held out by the Quakers to the Negroes & private funds established in support of it.

The Grand Jury present that speedy & resolute Measures ought to be adopted by the good sensed Spirit of the people, in order to prevent that common appeal to arms in their own Defense which at present appears to be almost, if not altogether necessary.

Appendix B: Quaker Documents

John Little foreman
Josiah Herdell
Robert Egan
James Woodward
Chs. Laughren

Masan Miller
Wm. Jones
John Badham
Wm. Goodwin

James Bond
JP [?]
Willis Wilder
Joshua White

****

AMERICAN STATE PAPERS
DOCUMENTS
LEGISLATIVE AND EXECUTIVE
OF THE
CONGRESS OF THE UNITED STATES
FROM THE FIRST SESSION OF THE FIRST TO THE SECOND SESSION OF THE TENTH CONGRESS, INCLUSIVE:
COMMENCING MARCH 3, 1789, AND ENDING MARCH 3, 1809
SELECTED AND EDTIED, UNDER THE AUTHORITY OF CONGRESS,
BY WALTER LOWRIE, Secretary of the Senate,
AND
WALTER S. FRANKLIN, Clerk of the House of Representatives.
WASHINGTON: PUBLISHED BY GALES AND SEATON, 1834.

CLASS X.
MISCELLANEOUS
VOLUME I.

Pp. 163-165

FREE NEGROES IN NORTH CAROLINA

LAWS OF NORTH CAROLINA RELATIVE TO FREE NEGROES

COMMUNICATED TO THE HOUSE OF REPRESENTATIVES, JANUARY 29, 1798

Mr. Sitgreaves, from the committee to whom was referred the memorial and address of the people called Quakers, from their yearly meeting, held in Philadelphia, in the month of September last, made the following report:

That, inasmuch as the said memorial and address present, in general terms only, certain subjects to the consideration of the Legislature, without containing any definite state of facts, or any specific application for its interposition, the memorialists were desired to exhibit a particular view of the grievances of which they complained, in order that the attention of the House might be directed to precise objects, and that it might be better discerned whether the complaints of the memorialists were of a nature to justify legislative interference:

That, in consequence of this request, the memorialists laid before the committee the representation and documents which accompany this report:

That, on the subject of this representation, the memorialists were invited to confer with the committee, and were solicited to suggest the remedy which they conceived it to be in the power of Congress to apply to the case as stated by them:

That the committee, after several conferences with the memorialists, and an attentive consideration of the subject, are very clearly of opinion that the facts disclosed in the said representation are exclusively of judicial cognizance; and that it is not competent to the legislative authority of Congress to do any act in relation to the matter thereof.

Wherefore, the committee recommend the following resolution:

Resolved, That the memorialists have leave to withdraw the said memorial and address.

To the Senate and House of Representatives of the United States, in Congress assembled: The Memorial and address of the people called Quakers, from their yearly meeting, held in Philadelphia, by adjournment, from the 25th of the 9th month, to the 29th of the same, inclusive, 1797, respectfully showeth:

Appendix B: Quaker Documents

That being convened, at our annual solemnity, for the promotion of the cause of truth and righteousness, we have been favored to experience religious weight to attend our minds, and an anxious desire to follow after those things which make for peace. Among other investigations, the oppressed state of our brethren of the African race has been brought into view, and particularly the circumstances of one hundred and thirty four in North Carolina, and many others whose cases have not so fully come to our knowledge, who were set free by members of our religious society, and again reduced into cruel bondage, under the authority of existing retrospective laws; husbands, and wives, and children, separated from one another, which we apprehend to be an abominable tragedy; and, with other acts of a similar nature, practised in other States, has a tendency to bring down the judgments of a righteous God upon our land.

This City and neighborhood, and some other parts, have been visited with an awful calamity, which ought to excite an inquiry into the cause and endeavor to do away those things which occasion the heavy clouds that hang over us. It is easy with the Almighty to bring down the loftiness of men, by diversified judgments, and make them fear the rod, and him that hath appointed it.

We wish to revive in your view the solemn engagement of Congress, made in the year 1774, as follows:

"And therefore we do for ourselves, and the inhabitants of the several colonies, whom we represent, firmly agree and associate, under the sacred ties of virtue, honor, and love of our country, as follows:

"Art. 2. We will neither import nor purchase any slaves imported after the 1st day of December next; after which time we will wholly discontinue the slave trade; and will neither be concerned in it ourselves, nor will we hire our vessels, nor sell our commodities or manufactures to those who are concerned in it."

"Art. 8. And will discountenance and discourage every species of extravagance and dissipation, especially all horse racing, and all kinds of gaming, cock fighting, exhibitions of shows, plays, and other expensive diversions and entertainments."

This was a solemn league and covenant with the Almighty in an hour of distress, and he is now calling upon you to perform and fulfill it. But how has this solemn covenant been contravened by the wrongs and cruelties practised upon the poor African race; the increase of dissipation and luxury, the countenance and encouragement given to play houses, and other vain amusements! And how grossly is the Almighty affronted on the day of the celebration of independence! What rioting and drunkeness, chambering and wantoness! To the great grief of sober inhabitants, and the disgrace of our national character.

National evils produce judgments; we therefore fervently pray the Governor of the universe may enlighten your understandings and influence your minds, so as to engage you to use every exertion in your power to have these things redressed.

With sincere desires for your happiness here and hereafter, and that when you come to close this life you may individually be able to appeal as a ruler did formerly -- *"Remember now, O Lord, I beseech thee, how I have walked before thee, in truth, and with a perfect heart, and have done that which is good in thy sight:"*

We remain your friends and fellow citizens.

Signed in and on behalf of the said meeting, by

Jonathan Evans
Clerk to the meeting this year

To the committee of Congress to whom was referred the memorial of the people called Quakers.

In the latter part of the year 1776, several of the people called Quakers, residing within the counties of Perquimons and Pasquotank, in the State of North Carolina, liberated their negroes; as it was then clear there was no existing law to prevent their so doing, for the law of 1741 could not, at that time, be carried into effect; and they were suffered to remain free until a law was passed in the spring of 1777, under which they were taken up and sold, contrary to the bill of rights recognised in the constitution of that State as a part thereof, and to which it was annexed.

In the spring of 1777, when the General Assembly met for the first time, a law was enacted to prevent slaves from being manumitted, except for meritorious services, &c., to be judged of by the county courts or the General Assembly; and ordering that, if any shall be manumitted in any other manner, they be taken up, and the county courts, within whose jurisdiction they are apprehended, order them to be sold. Under this law, the county courts of Perquimons and Pasquotank, in the year 1777, ordered a large number of persons to be sold who were free at the time the law was made. In the year 1778, several of those cases were, by *certiorari*, brought before the superior court for the district of Edenton, where the decisions of the county courts were reversed, the superior court declaring "that the said county courts, in such their proceedings, have exceeded their jurisdiction, violated the rights of the subjects, and acted in direct opposition to the bill of rights of this State, considered justly as part of the constitution thereof, by giving a law, not

Appendix B: Quaker Documents

intended to affect this case, a retrospective operation; thereby to deprive free men of this State of their liberty contrary to the laws of the land."

In consequence of this decree, several of the negroes were again set at liberty, but the next General Assembly, early in 1779, passed a law, wherein they mention that *doubts have arisen* whether the purchasers of such *slaves* have a good and legal title thereto, and confirm the same, under which they were again taken up by the purchaser and reduced to slavery.

Being much affected with this enormity, we believed it right to spread it before you. We wish not to give unnecessary trouble, but being persuaded that righteousness exalteth a nation, and promotes the peace and happiness of the people, it is the fervent concern of our minds that it may more and more prevail; and having discharged our duty in this matter at this time, we leave the subject with you, and the event to Him who hath the hearts of all men in his hands; and are,

Respectfully, your friends,

Signed, on behalf of the committee of our yearly meeting:

John Parrish
Nicholas Waln
Thomas Morris
Warner Mifflin
Jonathan Evans
Thomas Stewardson

Philadelphia, 22d of 1st month, 1798.

A list of emancipated blacks taken up and sold by order of the county courts of Pasquotank, Perquimons, and Chowan, in consequence of several acts of the General Assembly of the State of North Carolina, since the passing of the first act, in the year 1777, to the present time.

David, emancipated by William Albertson; parted from his wife and children.
Abram, by Benjamin and Chalkly Albertson; carried to South Carolina from his wife and children.
Joan, by William Albertson.
Tom, Jem, Jacob, and Harry, by John Anderson.
Caesar and Jupiter, by Elihu Albertson.
Dublin and Cuffee, by Jeremiah Cannon.
Candace, by Samuel Charles.
Jack, by Isaac Elliot.
Pleasant and three children, by James Elliot and wife; carried into the back country.
Tom, by William Griffin.
Mingo and Juda, by John Haskitt.
Rose, by Joseph Jones.
Sarah, by Josiah Jordan.
Dick, by Isaac Lamb
Candace, by George and Sarah Metcalfe.
Anna and child, by Samuel Moore; said child born after its mother was manumitted.
David, by Charles Morgan.
Esther and child, rebekah and children, Joab and penny, by Aaron Morris, Jun.
Ben, by Zachariah Newby.
Sam, by Thomas Newby, of Pasquotank.
Hannah, by Keziah Nixon.
Glasgow, Jack, Cudgo, Tom and wife, Susanna, Patience, Hannah, and Priscilla, by Thomas Newby, of Perquimons; Glasgow and Jack carried a very considerable distance from their wives and children; Tom and wife sold from their children.
David, Peggy, Priscilla, and Jenny, by Robert Newby.
Jem, Zango, Ned, and Phoebe, by Mark Newby.

Appendix B: Quaker Documents

Samuel, Ann, and Hagar, by Mary Nixon.
Francis, by Zachariah Nixon.
Charity, Francis, Sarah, Richard, and Pompey, by Thomas Nicholson; Richard carried into the back country from his children
Dill and child, and Jenny, by Nicholas Nicholson; Jenny carried into the back country from her children.
Rose, by Thomas Newby, of Pasquotank.
Jonas, by Christopher Nicholson.
Bosor, Job, and Hagar, by Charles Overman; Hagar carried to South Carolina from her husband and children.
Toby, by Matthew Pritchard.
Tamar and child, by Henry Palin.
Hagar, Fanny, and Job, by William Robinson.
Dick, by Samuel Smith.
Patience, by John Saunders.
Dick, Lemuel, Frank, Ruth and child, and Dorcas, by John Smith.
Easter, by Jesse Symons.
Ephraim and Hagar, by Elizabeth Symons.
Jenny and child, by William Townsend.
Aaron, by Joseph Thornton.
Judah, by John Trueblood.
Sampson and Nero, by Josiah Trueblood.
Moses, Charles, and Benjamin, by Caleb Trueblood.
Sawney, by Aaron Trueblood.
Jacob, William, Sibba, and Hagar, by Benjamin White.
Cuffee, Hannah, Rose, Jane, Ruth, and Candace, by Thomas White.
Luke, Zilpha, Nancy, Priscilla, and Mingo, by Caleb White.
Lyddai, Peter, Robin, and Patience, by William White.
Cancer, by Margaret White.
Ned, Violet, Fanny, and Quea, by Josiah White.
Rebeka, by Benjamin Winslow.
Jane and Rose, by Matthew White.
Robin and Dinah, by Jacob Wilson.
Dick and Judah, by Lydia White.
Dick, by Rachael Williams.
Dol, by Caleb Winslow.
Nancy, by Jacob Winslow.
Rose, by Joshua White.
Dinah, By George Walton.
Jenny and child, by Matthew White.

Perquimons County, *July term, at Hereford*, A.D. 1777.

These may certify, that it was then and there ordered, that the sheriff of this county, tomorrow morning, at 10 o'clock, expose to sale to the highest bidder, for ready money, at the court house door, the several negroes taken up as free, and in his custody, agreeable to law.

Test: W. SKINNER, *Clerk pro tem*.

A true copy: 25th August, 1791.
Test: J. HARVEY, *Clerk*.

Pasquotank County, *September, County Court*, &c. 1777.

Present, the worshipful Thomas Boyd, Timothy Hixon, John Pailin, Edmund Chancy, Joseph Reding, and Thomas Reese, esquires, justices.

It was then and there ordered that Thomas Reding, Esquire, take the free negroes taken up under an act to prevent domestic insurrection and other purposes, and expose the same to the best bidder at public vendue, for ready money, and be accountable for the same, agreeable to the aforesaid act, and make return to this or the next succeeding court of his proceedings.

A copy: ENOCH REESE, *C. C.*

State of North Carolina:

Appendix B: Quaker Documents

At a superior court of law, begun and held at the court house in Edenton, for the district of Edenton, the first day of May, in the year of our Lord one thousand seven hundred and seventy eight, before the honorable Samuel Ashe, Samuel Spence, and James Iredell, esquires, justices.

On motion of William Hooper, esquire, attorney at law, in behalf of the following negroes, viz: Glasgow, Tom, Susanna, Jack, Cudgo, Patience, Hannah, Silla, James, Ned, Langa, Phoebe, Jacob, Will, Sibb, Cuff, Rose, Hannah, Peter, Rose, Dick, Jane, Richard, Jane, Pompey, David, Zilpha, Violet, Fanny, Dick, Abraham, Judy, Rose, Hannah, David, Charles, Toby, Nero, Priscilla, Rose, Judith, Jane, Samuel, Hagar, Ann, Sarah, on a suggestion that the said persons, though free subjects of the State, were sold and enslaved, by order of the county courts of Perquimons and Pasquotank, in express violation of the constitution of this State, and contrary to natural justice, and that there are manifest errors and irregularities in the said proceedings: *Ordered*, That a *certiorari* issue, unless sufficient cause to the contrary be shown within the three first days of the next term.

And at the superior court of law, begun and held at Edenton court house, for the district of Edenton, on the second day of November, one thousand seven hundred and seventy eight, before the honorable Samuel Spence, esquire, one of the justices of the said court:

On motion that the rule to show cause, granted last term, why a writ of *certiorari* should not issue, directed to the justices of Perquimons county, to remove all the orders and proceedings of the court of the said county, relating to the sale and enslaving of the following negroes, to wit: Glasgow, Tom, Susanna, Jack, Cudgo, Patience, Hannah, Silla, James, Ned, Langa, Phoebe, Jacob, Will, Sibb, Peter, Cuff, Rose, Hannah, Rose, Dick, Jane, Richard, James, Pompey, David, Zilpha, Violet, Fanny, Dick, Abraham, Judy, Rose, might be made absolute, affidavit having been made of the due service of the said rule upon the said justices in open court, and they failing to show cause; and it is further ordered, that a writ of *Certiorari* issue, *instanter*, directed to the clerk of the said county court, commanding him to certify a transcript of the said orders and proceedings immediately: *Ordered*, That such a writ of *Certiorari* should issue to the said clerk accordingly.

On motion that a writ of *certiorari* should issue to the justices of Pasquotank county, to remove all the orders and proceedings of the court of the said county relating to the sale and enslaving of the following persons, or either of them, viz: Hannah, David, Charles, Toby, Pritchard, Nero, and Priscilla, Rose, Judith, Jane Albertson, Samuel, Hagar, Ann, and Sarah, on the suggestion that the said persons, though free subjects of the State, were sold and enslaved by order of the said court, in express violation of the constitution of this State, and contrary to natural justice, and that there are manifest errors and irregularities in the said proceedings: *Ordered*, That a *certiorari* issue accordingly, unless sufficient cause to the contrary be shown within the three first days of the next term.

On motion that a writ of *certiorari* should issue to the justices of Perquimons county, to remove all the orders and proceedings of the court of the said county, relating to the sale and enslaving of the following persons, or either of them, viz: Dinah, Robin, Luke, and Nancy, on a suggestion that the said persons, though free subjects of the State, were sold and enslaved by order of the said court, in express violation of the constitution of this State, and contrary to natural justice, and that there are manifest errors and irregularities in the said proceedings:

ANNALS OF THE CONGRESS OF THE UNITED STATES, 4TH CONGRESS, 2ND SESSION, VOLUME 6 (WASHINGTON: GALES & SEATON, 1849) 2015-2024

MANUMITTED SLAVES

Mr. Swanwick presented the following petition:
To the President, Senate, and House of Representatives.

The Petition and Representation of the under-named Freemen, respectively showeth:

That, being of African descent, late inhabitants and natives of North Carolina, to you only, under God, can we apply with any hope of effect, for redress of our grievances, having been compelled to leave the State wherein we had a right of residence, as freemen liberated under the hand and seal of humane and conscientious masters, the validity of which act of Justice, in restoring us to our native right of freedom, was confirmed by judgment of the Superior Court of North Carolina, wherein it was brought to trial; yet, not long after this decision, a law of that State was enacted, under which men of cruel disposition, and void of just principle, received countenance and authority in violently seizing, imprisoning, and selling into slavery, such as had been so emancipated; whereby we were reduced to the necessity of separating from some of our nearest and most tender connexions, and of seeking refuge in such parts of the Union where more regard is paid to the public declaration in favor of liberty and the common right of men, several hundreds, under

Appendix B: Quaker Documents

our circumstances, having, in consequence of the said law, been hunted day and night, like beasts of the forest, by armed men with dogs, and made a prey of as free and lawful plunder. Among others thus exposed, I, Jupiter Nicholson, of Perquimans county, North Carolina, after being set free by my master, Thomas Nicholson, and having been about two years employed as a seaman in the service of Zachary Nickson, on coming on shore, was pursued by men with dog and arms; but was favored to escape by night to Virginia, with my wife, who was manumitted by Gabriel Cosand, where I resided about four years in the town of Portsmouth, chiefly employed in sawing boards and scantling; from thence I removed with my wife to Philadelphia, where I have been employed, at times, by water, working along shore, or sawing wood. I left behind me a father and mother, who were manumitted by Thomas Nicholson and Zachary Dickson; they have been since taken up, with a beloved brother, and sold into cruel bondage.

I, Jacob Nicholson, also of North Carolina, being set free by my master, Joseph Nicholson, but continuing to live with him till, being pursued day and night, I was obliged to leave my abode, sleep in the woods, and stacks in the fields, &c., to escape the hands of violent men who, induced by the profit afforded them by law, followed this course as a business; at length, by night, I made my escape, leaving a mother, one child, and two brothers, to see whom I dare not return.

I, Job Albert, manumitted by Benjamin Albertson, who was my careful guardian to protect me from being afterwards taken and sold, providing me with a house to accommodate me and my wife, who was liberated by William Robertson; but we were night and day hunted by men armed with guns, swords, and pistols, accompanied with mastiff dogs; from whose violence, being one night apprehensive of immediate danger, I left my dwelling, locked and barred, and fastened with a chain, being at some distance from it, while my wife was by my kindmaster locked up under his roof. I heard them break into my house, where, not finding their prey, they got but a small booty, a handkerchief of about a dollar value, and some provisions; but, not long after, I was discovered and seized by Alexander Stafford, William Stafford, and Thomas Creesy, who were armed with guns and clubs. After binding me with my hands behind me, and a rope around my arms and body, they took me about four miles to Hartford prison, where I lay four weeks, suffering much for want of provision; from thence, with the assistance of a fellow prisoner, (a white man,) I made my escape, and for three dollars was conveyed, with my wife, by a humane person, in a covered wagon by night, to Virginia, where in the neighborhood of Portsmouth, I continued unmolested about four years, being chiefly engaged in sawing boards and plank. On being advised to move Northward, I came with my wife to Philadelphia, where I have labored for a livelihood upwards of two years, in Summer mostly, along shore in vessels and stores, and sawing wood in the Winter. My mother was set free by Phineas Nickson, my sister by John Trueblood, and both taken up and sold into slavery, myself deprived of the consolation of seeing them, without being exposed to the like grievous oppression.

I, Thomas Pritchet, was set free by my master Thomas Pritchet, who furnished me with land to raise provisions for my use, where I built myself a house, cleared a sufficient spot of woodland to produce ten bushels of corn; the second year about fifteen, and the third, had as much planted as I suppose would have produced thirty bushels; this I was obliged to leave about one month before it was fit for gathering, being threatened by Holland Lockwood, who married my said master's widow, that if I would not come and serve him, he would apprehend me, and send me to the west Indies; Enoch Ralph also threatening to send me to jail, and sell me for the good of the country: being thus in jeopardy, I left my little farm, with my small stock and utensils, and my corn standing, and escaped by night into Virginia, where shipping myself for Boston, I was, through stress of weather landed in New York, where I served as a waiter for seventeen months; but my mind being distressed on account of the situation of my wife and children, I returned to Norfolk in Virginia, with a hope of at least seeing them, if I could not obtain their freedom; but finding I was advertised in the newspaper, twenty dollars the reward for apprehending me, my dangerous situation obliged me to leave Virginia, disappointed of seeing my wife and children, coming to Philadelphia, where I resided in the employment of a waiter upward of two years.

In addition to the hardship of our on case, as above set forth, we believe ourselves warranted, on the present occasion, in offering to your consideration the singular case of a fellow black now confined in the jail of this city, under sanction of the act of General Government, called the Fugitive Law, as it appears to us a flagrant proof how far human beings, merely on account of color and complexion, are, through prevailing prejudice, outlawed and excluded from common justice and common humanity, by the operation of such partial laws in support of habits and customs cruelly oppressive. This man, having been many years past manumitted by his master in North Carolina, was under the authority of the aforementioned law of that State, sold again into slavery, and, after having served his purchaser upwards of six years, made his escape to Philadelphia, where he has resided eleven years, having a wife and children; and, by an agent of the Carolina claimer, has been lately apprehended and committed to prison, his said claimer, soon after the man's escaping from him, having advertised him, offering a reward of ten silver dollars to any person that would bring him back, or five times that sum to any person that would make due proof of his being killed, and no questions asked by whom.

Appendix B: Quaker Documents

We beseech your impartial attention to our hard condition, not only with respect to our personal sufferings, as freemen, but as a class of that people who, distinguished by color, are therefore with a degrading partiality, considered by many, even of those in eminent stations, as unentitled to that public justice and protection which is the great object of Government. We indulge not a hope, or presume to ask for the interposition of your honorable body, beyond the extent of your Constitutional power or influence, yet are willing to believe your serious, disinterested, and candid consideration of the premises, under the benign impressions of equity and mercy, may not be without some salutary effect, both for our relief as a people, and towards the removal of obstructions to public order and well being.

If, notwithstanding all that has been publicly avowed as essential principles respecting the extent of human right to freedom; notwithstanding we have had that right restored to us, so far as was in the power of those by whom we were held as slaves, we cannot claim the privilege of representation in your councils, yet we trust we may address you as fellow men, who, under God, the sovereign Ruler of the Universe, are intrusted with the distribution of justice, for the terror of evil doers, the encouragement and protection of the innocent, not doubting that you are men of liberal minds, susceptible of benevolent feelings and clear conception of rectitude to a catholic extent, who can admit that black people (servile as their condition generally is throughout this Continent) have natural affections, social and domestic attachments and sensibilities; and that, therefore, we may hope for a share in your sympathetic attention while we represent that the unconstitutional bondage in which multitudes of our fellows in complexion are held, is to us a subject sorrowfully affecting; for we cannot conceive their condition (more especially those who have been emancipated and tasted the sweets of liberty, and again reduced to slavery by kidnappers and man stealers) to be less afflicting or deplorable than the situation of citizens of the United States, captured and enslaved through the unrighteous policy prevalent in Algiers. We are far from considering all those who retain slaves as wilful oppressors, being well assured that numbers in the State from whence we are exiles, hold their slaves in bondage, not of choice, but possessing them them by inheritance, feel their minds burdened under the slavish restraint of legal impediments to doing thst justice which they are convinced is due to fellow rationals. May we not be allowed to consider this stretch of power, morally and politically, a Governmental defect, if not a direct violation of the declared fundamental principles of the Constitution; and finally, is not some remedy for an evil of such magnitude highly worthy of the deep inquiry and unfeigned zeal of the supreme Legislative body of a free and enlightened people? Submitting our cause to God, and humbly craving your best aid and influence, as you may be favored and directed by that wisdom which is from above, where with that you may be eminently dignified and rendered conspicuously, in the view of nations, a blessing to the people you represent, is the sincere prayer of your petitioners.

JACOB NICHOLSON
JUPITER NICHOLSON, his mark
JOB ALBERT, his mark
THOMAS PRITCHET, his mark

Philadelphia, January 23, 1797.

The petition being read--

Mr. Swanwick said, he hoped it would be referred to a select committee.

Mr. Blount hoped it would not even be received by the House. Agreeably to a law of the State of North Carolina, he said they were slaves, and could, of course, be seized as such.

Mr. Thatcher thought the petition ought to be referred to the Committee on the Fugitive Law. he conceived the gentleman much mistaken in asserting these petitioners to be absolute slaves. They state that they *were* slaves, but that their masters manumitted them, and that their manumissions were sanctioned by a law of that State, but that a subsequent law of the same State, subjected them to slavery; and even if there was a law that allowed them to be taken and sold into slavery again, he could not see any propriety in refusing their petition in that House--they certainly (said Mr. T.) are free people. It appeared they were taken under the fugitive act, which he thought ought not to affect them; they now came and prayed the House so to model that fugitive act, as to prevent its affecting persons of their description. He therefore saw great propriety in referring their petition to the committe appointed to amend that act in another part; they could as well consider its relation to the present case. He could not see how there would be a propriety in rejecting their petition; they had an undoubted right to petition the House, and to be heard.

Mr. Swanwick was surprised at the gentleman from North Carolina [Mr. Blount] desiring to reject this petition; he could not have thought, nor could he indulge the suspicion now, that the gentleman was so far from acknowledging the rights of man, as to prevent any class of men from petitioning. If men were aggrieved, and conceive they have claim to attention, petitioning was their sacred right, and that right should never suffer innovation; whether the House ought to grant, was another question. The subject of their petition had a claim to the attention of the House. They state they

Appendix B: Quaker Documents

were freed from slavery, but that they were much injured under a law of the United States. If a law was ever made that bore hard on any class of people, Mr. S. hoped that the door would never be shut to their complaints. If the circumstance respecting these people was as they stated, their case was very hard. He animadverted on the atrocity of that reward of ten dollars offered for one of them if taken alive, but that fifty should be given if found dead, and no questions asked. Was not this, he said, encouragement to put a period to that man's existence? Horrid reward! Could gentlemen hear it and not shudder?

Mr. Blount said, the gentlemen last up was mistaken in calling the petitioners free men; the laws of North Carolina, as he observed before, did not suffer individuals to emancipate their slaves, and he should wish to know what evidence there was to prove these men free, and except that was proved, the House had no right to attend to the petition.

Mr. Sitgreaves, in answer to the gentleman last up, said he would reverse his question, and ask what evidence he had to prove that these men are not freemen; can he prove they are slaves? They have stated that a law has been made in North Carolina with a view to affect their case, and bring them again into a worse slavery than before; they want to know whether they cannot obtain relief by their application to the Government of the United States. Under these circumstances, Mr. S. wished to know why their petition should not be taken into consideration? Was there anything in these men, he asked, that should prevent every kind of assistance being bestowed on them? Had they not an equal right to be heard with other petitioners? He hoped the House would not only give them a hearing, but afford them all the consolation of which their unfortunate case was susceptible. If the House were obliged, through a want of power to extend to the case, to object compliance with the prayers, yet, he hoped it would be done with all due tenderness; before hearing them, he thought it would be exceedingly unjust to decide. These people may produce documents sufficient to obtain favorable attention; therefore, it was impossible before they were heard to conceive whether the House could constitutionally grant relief or not. He could see no impropriety in referring it; the object of referring a case, was to inquire into facts; thus, the committee prepared the way for discussion in the House; and why the House should refuse to deliberate and discuss this case, he knew not.

Mr. Heath was clearly convinced these people were slaves, and therefore hoped their petition would lie on the table. He would remind the gentlemen that, if they undertook this business, they would soon have petitions enough of the same kind, and public business would be thereby prevented. It appeared to him to be more within the jurisdiction of the Legislature of that State; indeed, the United States had nothing to do with it.

Mr. Madison said, he should be sorry to reject any petition whatever, in which it became the business of the House to attend; but he thought this case had no claim on their attention. Yet, if it did not come within the purview of the Legislative body, he thought, it might be suffered to lie on the table. He thought it a Judicial case, and could obtain its due in a Court of Appeal in that State. If they are free by the laws of North Carolina, they ought to apply to those laws, and have their privilege established. If they are slaves, the Constitution gives them no hopes of being heard here. A law has been passed to prevent the owners of those slaves emancipating them; it is therefore impossible that any relief can be granted. The petitioner are under the laws of North Carolina, and those laws cannot be the interpreters of the laws of the United States.

Mr. Sitgreaves said, he was not prepared to deny that this petition is in the situation the gentleman from Virginia [Mr. Madison] states; nor was he prepared to prove that it came under the power of the General Government, but he could see no kind of reason why it should not be sent to a committee who should examine the case and report whether it required Legislative interference, or whether it was a subject of Judicial authority in the country whence the petitioners came. May petitions, he said, were sent to the House, who referred them for investigation to a committee, and many had been reported as being under Judicial power only, and as such been rejected here. If this underwent the same order, and should be found to be of a Judicial nature, the committee would report so, and the House would honorably refuse it. This he thought the only just method.

Mr. Rutherford concurred with the gentleman from Pennsylvania, that this memorial ought to be referred to a committee who would report whether these people had been emancipated according to a law of the State of North Carolina, or not. The circumstances attending this case, he said, demanded a just and full investigation, and if a law did exist either to emancipate, or send these poor people into slavery, the house would then know. He doubted not, every thing just and proper would be done, but he hoped every due respect would be paid to the petition. In short, he was assured every member in the House would wish to act consistently. This case, from the great hardships represented in the petition, applied closely to the nicest feelings of the heart, and he hoped humanity would dictate a just decision.

Mr. Gilbert hoped the petition would be referred to the committee proposed; he thought it laid claim to the humanity of the House. He thought every just satisfaction should be given, and attention paid, to every class of persons who appeal for decision to the House.

Mr. W. Smith said, the practice of a former time, in a similar case, was, that the petition was sealed up and sent back to the petitioners, not being allowed even to remain on the files of the office. This method, he said, ought to be

Appendix B: Quaker Documents

pursued with respect to the present petition. It was not a matter that claimed the attention of the Legislature of the United States. he thoght it of such an improper nature, as to be surprised any gentleman would present a petition of the kind. These men are slaves, and, he thought, not entitled to attention from that body; to encourage slaves to petition the House would have a tendency to invite continual applications. Indeed it would tend to spread an alarm throughout the Southern States; it would act as an "entering wedge," whose consequences could not be forseen. This is a kind of property on which the House has no power to legislate. He hoped it would not be committed at all; it was not a proper subject for Legislative attention. He was not of the opinion of some gentlemen, that the House were bound to sit on every question recommended to their notice. He thought particular attention ought to be paid to the lateness of the session; if this subject were to be considered, too much time of the House would be devoured which was much wanted on important business.

Mr. Thatcher said, he was in favor of referring this petition. He could see no reason which had been adduced to prove the impropriety of receiving a petition from these people. The gentleman from North Carolina [Mr. Blount] is of the opinion that these people being slaves, the House ought not to pay attention to their prayer. This, he said, was quite new language--a system of conduct which he never saw the House practise, and hoped he never should. That the House should not receive a petition without evidence to prove it was from a free man. This was a language which opposed the Constitutional freedom of every State where the Declaration of Rights had been made; they all declare that every man is born equally free, and that each have an equal right to petition if aggrieved--this doctrine he never heard objected to.

The gentlemen from Virginia [Mr. Madison and Mr. Heath] had said, it was a Judicial and not a Legislative question; they say the petition proves it, and that it ought not to be attended to. Mr. T. said, he saw no proof whatever of the impropriety of the House receiving it. There might be some Judicial question growing out of the case; but that was no reason, because it might possibly undergo a Judicial course, that the General Government were not to be petitioned. The gentleman from South Carolina [Mr. Smith] had said, "that this was a kind of property on which the House could not legislate;" but he would answer, this was a kind of property on which they were bound to legislate. The fugitive act could prove this authority; if petitions were not to be received they would have to legislate in the dark. It appeared plainly that these men were manumitted by their masters; and because a number of men who called themselves legislators should, after they had the actual enjoyment of their liberty, come forward and say that these men should not remain at liberty, and actually authorize their re-captivity, he thought it exceedingly unjust to deprive them of the right of petitioning to have their injuries redressed. These were a set of men on whom the fugitive law had no power, and he thought they claimed protection under the power of that House, which always ought to lean towards freedom. Though they could not give freedom to slaves, yet he hoped gentlemen would never refuse to lend their aid to secure freemen in their rights against tyrannical imposition.

Mr. Christie thought no part of the fugitive act operated against freedom. He thought no good could be derived from sending the petition to a committee; they could not prove whether they were slaves or not. He was much surprised any gentlemen in the House should present such a petition. Mr. C. said, he was of the same opinion with the gentleman from South Carolina [Mr. Smith] that the petition ought to be sent back again. He hoped the gentleman from Pennsylvania [Mr. Swanwick] would never hand such another petition into the House.

Mr. Holland said, the gentleman from Massachusetts [Mr. Thatcher] said, "the House ought to lean towards freedom." Did he mean to set all slaves at liberty, or receive petitions from all? Sure he was, that if this was received, it would not be long before the table would be filled with similar complaints, and the House might sit for no other purpose than to hear them. It was a Judicial question, and the House ought not to pretend to determine the point; why, then, should they take time upon it? To put an end to it he hoped, it would be ordered to lie on the table.

Mr. Macon said, he had hearkened very closely to the observations of Gentlemen on the subject, and could see no reason to alter his desire that it would not be committed. No man, he said, wished to encourage petitions more than himself and no man had considered this subject more. These men could not receive any aid from the General Government; but by application to the State, justice would be done them. Trials of this kind had very frequently been brought on in all the different Courts of that State, and had very often ended in freedom of slaves; the appeal was fair, and justice was done. Mr. M. thought it a very delicate subject for the General Government to act on; he hoped it would not be committed; but he should not be sorry if the proposition of a gentleman [Mr. Smith] was to take place, that it was to be sent back again.

Mr. W. Smith observed, that a gentleman [Mr. Thatcher] had uttered a wish to draw these people from their state of slavery to liberty. Mr. S. did not think they were sent there to take up the subject of emancipation. When subjects of this kind are brought up in the House they ought to be deprecated as dangerous. They tended to produce very uncomfortable circumstances.

Appendix B: Quaker Documents

Mr. Varnum said, the petitioners had received injury under a law of the United States, (the fugitive act) and not merely a law of North Carolina, and therefore, he thought, they had an undoubted right to the attention of the General Government if that act bore hard on them. They stated themselves to be freemen, and he did not see any opposition of force to convince the House they were not; surely it could not be said that color alone should designate them as slaves. If these people had been free, and yet were taken up under a law of the United States, and put into prison, then it appeared plainly the duty of the House to inquire whether that act had such an unjust tendency, and if it had, proper amendments should be made to it to prevent the like consequences in future. It required nothing more under that act than that the person suspected should be brought before a single magistrate, and evidence given that he is a slave, which evidence the magistrate could not know if distant from the State; the person may be a freeman, for it would not be easy to know whether the evidence was good, at a distance from the State; the poor man is then sent to his State in slavery. Mr. V. hoped the House would take all possible care that freemen should not be made slaves; to be deprived of liberty was more important than to be deprived of property. He could not think why gentlemen should be against having the fact examined; if it appears that they are slaves, the petition will of course be dismissed, but if it should appear they are free, and receive injury under the fugitive act, the United States ought to amend it, so that justice should be done.

Mr. Blount said, admitting those persons who had been taken up were sent back to North Carolina, they would then have permission to apply to any of the Courts in the State for a fair trial of their plea; there are very few Courts in which some negroes have not tried this cause, and obtained their liberty. He agreed with the gentleman from Massachusetts, on the freedom of these men to procure their rights; it did not appear to him that they were free; true they had been set free, but that manumission was from their masters, who had not a right to set them free without permission of the Legislature.

Mr. Kitchell could not see what objection could obtain to prevent these people being heard. The question was not now, whether they are or are not slaves, but it is on a law of the United States. They assert that this law does act injurious to them; the question is, therefore, whether a committee shall be appointed to inquire on the improper force of this law on the case of these men; if they are freemen, he said, they ought not to be sent back from the most distant part of the United States to North Carolina, to have justice done them, but they ought to receive it from the General Government who made the law they complain of.

Mr. K. said, he had not examined the force of the law on the subject, and was not prepared to decide; there could be no evil in referring it for examination, when the committee would report their opinion of the subject and gentlemen be prepared to act on it.

On the question for receiving the petition being put, it was negatived--ayes 33, noes 50.

Index

[

[Torn] Charles, 196
[Torn] Davis, 196
[Torn] Donald, 196
[Torn] Jackson, 196
[Torn] lassey, 196
[Torn] Metcalfe, 196
[Torn] Sikes, 196
[Torn] White, 196
[Torn]amin White, 196

A

Aaron
   Ismael, 117
   Polly, 116, 117
   Polly, a slave, 116
Aarons
   Ismael, 117
Abbot
   Henry, 3
   Mr. Henry, 3
Abolitionists, 143
   Goodell, viii
   Wilberforce, ix
   William Jay, ix
Ackess
   Thos., 208
Ackis
   Thos, 199
Acre
   John, 32
Acrey
   John, 32
Africa, ix
African Race, 322
Albert
   Job, 327
Albertson
   A, 240
   Aaron, 240
   B:, 194
   Benja, 191
   Benjamin, 191, 259, 323, 326
   Chalkley, 259
   Chalkly, 323
   Comfort, 262
   Elias, 200, 245, 246, 254
   Elihu, 323
   Jane. *See* Slaves
   William, 259, 323
Alderson
   John, 293

Alexander
   Nathaniel, 50, 52, 53, 54, 80
Algiers, 327
Allan
   John, 181, 182
Allen
   Abram M R, 96
   Drury, 296
   Isabella, 179, 303
   James, 298, 303
   Jane, 179, 303
   Jas V, 169
   John, 292
   Mark, 298
   Nath., 13
   V, 77
Alston
   Anne, 291
   William, 291
American Colonization Society, ix
American State Papers, 321
Amis
   Thomas, 298
Anderson
   Frank, 296
   James, 308
   John, 323
   Milly, free woman of colour, 296
   W.J., 130
   William J., 130
Andrews
   William, 275
   Wm., 275
Angel
   Charles, 269
   Laurence, 269
Anti-Slavery Societies, 143
Armstrong
   Coll. James, 137
   Colo. James, 138
   Colo:, 138
   James, 137
   Tho. T., 269
Arthur
   Asa, 62, 63
   Hannah, 62
   John, 62, 63
Ash
   Jennie, 1
   Jenny, 1, 2. *See* Indians
   Jenny, an Indian or Mulatto, 1
   Nancy, an Indian. *See* Indians
Ashe
   Saml., 260
   Samuel, 181, 325
Ashley
   Miles, 35

Atkins
   William E., 182
Attorneys
   Blair
      W, 198
      Will, 198
      Wm, 194
   Gil[?] & Shober, 160
   Jas. Norfleet, 232
Austin
   Thomas, 84
   Thos., 84, 85
Avery
   Robert, 222

B

Badham
   John, 12, 321
Bagley
   Joseph, 252
   Josiah, 245, 252, 254
   Thomas, 256
   W, 256
   William, 256
Bailey
   Benja, 201
   Benja., 235
   Gabl., 197, 230
   J.L., 242
   Jno. L., 242
   Robert, 197
Baily
   John, 199
Baird
   J., 173
   James, 173, 301
   James C., 173
   John, 173
Baker
   John W., Jr, 131
   Mr Joseph, 9
Ballads
   H., 280
Ballard
   Thomas, 150
   Thos. W., 150
Ballards Tract, 281
Ballinger
   Jehu, 165, 166
Banks
   Adam[?] G, 239
   J, 196, 199
   John, 197
   Jon., 217
   Jonathan, 209, 221

Index

Jos., 319
Thomas, 233, 239, 244
Thos., 244
W, 192, 222
W., 192
Wm, 199
Wm., 210
Barber
  Isaac, 245, 249, 253, 254
Barnes
  Stephen, 199
Barnett
  William, 269
Barns
  Stephen, 222
Barnwell
  John, viii
  Thomas, 18, 19
  Thomas, free person of color, 18
  Thos., 19
Barrow
  Saml, 52
  Saml., 52
  Saml. G., 53
  Saml. G. Barrow, 53
  Wm, 200
Barrs
  Jemima, 295
  Jemima, a free woman, 295
Bass
  Abraham, 302
Battle
  Joel, 141
  Mr., 139
Battles
  Battle of Guilford, 138
Batts
  Jno., 140
Bautz[?]
  Adam, 62
Beal
  Jordan, 308
Beam
  Michael, 295
Beaseley
  John, 32
Beasely
  James, 32
Beasley
  Francis, 12
  John, 12, 20
Beasly
  Jn., 20, 21
Beebee
  Betty, 309
Belden
  Isaac, 179
  R.C., 180
  Robert, 179, 180, 305
Bell
  John, 193, 208

Tho., 193
William, 265, 294
Wm., 265
Belting
  J.L., 270
  John L., 270
Ben
  Free Negro, 30
Benbury
  Tho., 139
Benners
  John, 46
Bent
  J.R., 24, 25, 26
  James, 25
  James R., 23, 24, 25
Bent[**Burt?**]
  James R., 24
Benton
  Devotion, 213
  James, 199
Berry
  John, 222
  William, 173, 174, 175
  Wm., 173, 174, 175
Bess
  A Mullatoe Girl, 3
Best
  Elias, 253
Bethel
  Jerry, 309
Bevell
  Henry, 162
Bevill
  [?]Bert, 163
  Edward, 163
  Henry, 163
Beville
  Henry, 162, 163
Billups
  Langley, 250
Binum
  Joel, 34
Biriam
  Isaac Junr., 34
Birkhead
  Abraham, 38
  James, 38
Bishop
  George, 309
Bissett
  Charles, 21
  Thos, 12
Black
  Betty, 298
  John, 298
Blackinal
  William, 144
Blackledge
  Will T, 104
  Will., 75, 76

Blacknall
  Thomas, 144, 145
Blacksmith, 236, 238
Blackwell
  Joseph, 300
Blair
  Elizabeth L., 255
  G.W., 21
  Geo, 21
  W, 198
  Will, 198, 199
  William, 20
  Wm, 194
Blake
  Thomas C., 129, 130
Blaney
  Bn., 182
Blany
  Ben, 182
  Benjamin, 182
Bledsoe
  Joseph, 147
Blinn
  Ann, 39
Blount
  ann, 32
  Ann, 47
  C.W., 250
  Charles W, 250
  Charles W., 250
  Jn. B., 17
  John, 17, 18
  John B., 17
  Jos., 14, 231
  Mr., 327, 328, 329, 330
  T M, 241
  Tho. M, 241
  Thomas M, 241, 242
  Thos. M., 242
  W., 248
  William, 256
  Wilson, 47, 48
Bogue
  Aaron, 252
  John, 245, 254
  Mark, 252
  Nathan, 252
  Thomas, 252
Bogye
  Dixon, 298
Boling
  Rebecca, 7, 8
Bollinger
  Jehu, 165, 166
Bombrough
  Wm., 31
Bond
  Exum[?] S, 252
  James, 12, 321
  John, 16, 18, 19, 254
  Jos. D., 30

Index

Joseph, 29, 30
Joseph D., 29
Nat., 21
Pritlow, 254
Saml. T., 29
Bondfield
   Charles, 195
Bonner
   George, 17, 243
Bonners
   George, 243
Bonnett
   John R, 260, 261
Borclift
   William, 249
Borden
   Benja, 46
   Benja., 46
   Benjamin, 84
Bordin
   Benja., 84, 85
Borritz
   James, 24, 25, 26
Bostick
   Absalom, 269
Boston, viii, 326
Boswell
   Abraham, 198
Boush
   John, 27
   William, 27
Bowe
   Tully and Betty
      free persons, 192
Bowling
   Jarrat, 267
   Jarret, 267
Boyd
   Frances, 153
   James, 175, 176
   John, 175, 176, 222, 223, 224, 225
   John Snr., 176
   Thomas, 324
   William, 153
Boylan
   William, 276
   Wm, 276
Bozman
   Joseph, 12, 21
Br[?]
   Wm, 203
Bracken
   Joseph, 8
Bragg
   John, 62
   John Jur., 50
   Thomas, 132
Branch
   John, 71, 97, 99, 100, 101, 113
Brantley
   Blake, 9

Brantly
   William, 9
   Wm, 9
Braveboy
   John, 11
Braxton
   Martha, 261
Brewer
   Wm, 200
Brewster[?]
   J.H., 180
Brice
   Francis, 127
Brickell
   JSM, 113
   WW, 168
Bridgers
   Ann, 140
Bridges
   Newbegun Bridge, 220
Bright
   E., 55, 56, 57, 58, 59, 60
   James, 301
   John, 52
Brimer
   J., 78
Brimson
   Dorcas, 42
Brinkly
   Nathl., 253
Brister[?]
   Jarvis B, 99, 100
British, x
British Prisoners, 258
Brittain
   Jos., 71
   Joseph, 70, 71
Britton
   Wm., 4
Brodie
   John, 147, 153
Brosher
   Cesar, 237
   Jno., 209, 222
   Jno. L., 224
   Jo. L., 209
   John L, 224
   John L., 224
   Jos. L., 214, 226
   Joseph L., 214, 225
   Simon, 222, 236
   Simon L, 236
Broshers
   Cesar, 236
Brother
   [Faded], 199
   Jno, 199
   Joseph, 199
   Joshua, 199
Brothers
   Briant, 197, 235

Enoch, 198
John, 198
Joshua, 197
Richard, 198
William, 229, 230
William T, 229
Brougham
   Mr., 28
Brown
   Aaron, 45
   Evelina, 126
   Jesse, 3
   Joel, 3
   John, 221
   John, Man of Colour, 221
   Miss Evelina, 126
   Mr., 3
   Mr. Joel, 2
   Nathl, 125, 126
   Parthena, 221
   Perthena, 221
   Rose, 221
   Silvester, 125
Browne
   Henry, 152, 153
   Wm. C., 211
Browning
   T M, 169
   W, 169
Brownrigg
   George, 141
   Thomas, 20, 21, 22
Browns
   Jesse, 3
Bru[?]
   Wm, 198
   Wm., 196
Bryan
   James W, 122
   James W., 82, 122, 123
   Jas W., 122
   Jenny, 118
   Jenny, a slave, 118
   Jn H, 101, 118, 123
   Jn. H., 117, 118, 119, 122, 123
   John H, 122, 123
   Lewis, 44
   Nathan, 44
   William, 44
   William G, 103
   Wm G., 102
   Wm., 44
Buchanan
   John
      A free man, 30
   John, a free yellow man, 30
Buffalo Sam, 298
Bullock
   Elizabeth, 153
   Jno, 154
   John, 154

Index

Micajah, 155
William, 153, 154
Wm., 153
Bundy
  Benja, 249
  Benja., 248, 249
  Benjamin, 248, 249
  Enoch, 222
  Francis N., 248, 249. *See* Slaves, Francis
  John, 195
  Jonathan, 199
  Joseph, 205
  Joshua, 201
  Josiah, 201, 233, 234, 249
  Samll[?], 195
Bunting
  Saml R., 180
Burges
  Jeremiah, 194
  Nancy
    a Free Woman of Colour, 194
Burgess
  Jas B, 168
Burgioyse
  G H, 108, 109, 110
Burgwin
  Geo. HB, 82
  George, 87
  George HB, 82
Burkhead
  Eliazar, 38
Burkitt
  Christopher, 27
  Christopher, a free man of Color, 26
Burlingham
  Willm., 147
Burn
  John, 319
burney
  William, 157
Burney
  Burney, 157
  William, 157
Burroughs
  Will., 282
  William, 282
  WR, 282
Burrow
  Wm, 199
Burt
  Hardy, 275
Burt[?]
  Jacob, 63
Burton
  A.M., 175
  G., 156
  Hutchins, 116
  Hutchins G., 118, 122, 177
  Peter, 269

R.H., 176
Robt. H., 172
Bush
  William, 27
Butler
  Sam, 12
Butts
  Jas, 169
Byriam
  Isaac Junr., 34
  James, 34

C

Cabarrus
  A., 13, 16, 20
  Aguste, 20
  Angus, 300
  Aug., 16
  Augt., 15
  August, 16
  Auguste, 13, 15, 16, 20
  Augustus, 20
  S., 4, 13, 16, 273
  Stephen, 13, 15, 16, 17, 299
  Stephen Esqr., 13
Cain
  Peter, 30, 31
  Peter, a free negro, 30
  William, 186, 187
  Wm., 186
Caldcleugh
  Andrew, 304
Caldcluegh
  Andrew, 304
Caldwell
  Jno, 163, 164
  Judge, 170
  Tho., 160, 166
  Thos., 165
Callaway
  Elijah, 51, 52, 69, 70
  Reuben, 52, 69, 70
  Reuben, free man of color, 68
  Reubin, 70
Calloway
  Elijah, 51
Cameron
  Dun., 188
Campbell
  John, 319
Cannon
  Jeremiah, 323
Cape Fear, x
Capps
  Rebecca, 282
  Rebecca, free woman of Colour, 282
Carey
  Miles, 151

Carlisle
  John H, 169
Carman
  Joshua, 307, 309
Carmon
  Joshua, 130
Carney
  John, 40
Carpenter, 221
  Richd, 168
  Stephen, 12
Carr
  Thomas, 269
Carter
  Jesse, 168
  Mary, 45
  W, 235, 236, 237
  William, 1, 2, 237
Carthagene, 42
Carthy
  Catharine, 68
  Dan, 68
  Daniel, 68
  Danl., 68
  Elizabeth, 68
Cartwright
  Ch[?], 222
  Chris, 217
  Christopher, 221
  Clement, 213
  eph, 222
  Hezekiah, 221
  Job, 216
  John, 242
  Mc., 224
  McKeel, 224
  Thomas, 222, 228
  Thos, 228
  Thos., 228
  William, 222
Cartwrite
  Clem, 199
  Jas, 199
Carver
  James, 213, 219
  Jobe, 199
Casey
  Thomas, 72, 73
Caspillis[?]
  Samuel, 69
Caswell
  R, 139
  Richard W., 301
Chadwick
  Cha[?], 126
  Mrs., 125
Chalke
  Wm., 222
Chancey
  Micajah, 220
Chancy

Index

Edmund, 324
Chapman
  Bell, 48
  Catharine, 61, 62
  H.L., 61, 62
  Isabella, 48
  s, 51
  S, 47
  Saml, 50, 80
  Saml., 43, 46, 51, 53, 80, 81
Chaponel
  Monsieur, 293
Chappel
  Gabriel, 34
  Richard, 262
Charles
  Samuel, 323
  Stephen, 233
Charlton
  James, 301
  Linney, 4, 294
Chase
  Samuel, 37
Cheshire
  henry, 12
  Jno, 12
  Jntn., 21
Child
  Frances, 187
Childs
  Mark, 276
Chowan, 323
Chowan County
  grand juries of, x
  Grand Jury, 320
Christie
  Mr., 329
Church
  Thomas, 249
Civil War, vii
Clark
  Captain John, 43
  Elijah, 69
  ET, 169
  James, 152
  John, 43, 152
  John Jnr., 77
  John Jr, 77
  Mr., 152
  Mrs., 152
  Watkins, 169
  William, 14, 15, 42
  Wm., 15
Clarke
  Sarah, 151, 153
Clary
  John, 255
Clear
  Mary, 294
  Mr., 42
  Rose Mary, 294

Timothy, 42
CN Counties
  New London, 43
CN Towns
  Lyme, 43
  New Haven, 43
Cobb
  Mark, 242
  Samuel, 199
  Tho R., 243
  Thomas R, 242
  Thos R, 242
Cogdell
  R, 42
Coleman
  Charles, 5
Colley
  John, 252
Colonization Society in Virginia, ix
Colton
  Lt., 137
Coltraine
  John, 160, 161, 162
  Joseph, 160, 161, 162
Commander
  Jno., 201
  John, 199, 202, 204, 243
  Sarah, 243
Congress of the United States, 321
Conigland[?]
  Edwd., 170
Conner
  Geo AL, 224
  George AL, 223
  John, 212
  William, 220
Conway
  Robert W, 114
  Robert W, a slave, 114
  William, 87, 88, 89
  Wm., 88, 89
Cook
  Archibald T., 306
  Caroline, 289, 306
  Harry, 156
  Harry, free negro, 155
  James Ellis, 306
  James G., 129, 132
  Jas G, 133
  Jas. C., 130
  John, 229, 231, 239
  Joshua, 306
  Martha Jane, 306
  Pamelia, 306
  Rachel, free negro, 155
  Rachiel, 156
Cooke
  John, 220
  Silas, 37
Cooper, 214
  Geo, 84, 85

Geo., 85
George, 85
Copeland
  Anna, 261
  Jesse, 246
  Joseph Junr., 35
  Richard, 261
Cosand
  Gabriel, 326
Cotton
  Priscilla, 280
  Samuel
    Will of, 1
Counties
  Loudon County, Virginia, 265
  Washington County, Indiana, 260
  Wayne County, Indiana, 260
Counts
  M.R.[?], 21
Courtney
  William, 186
  Wm., 186
Cowper
  Wiles, 149, 150
  Wills, 150
Cox
  John, 31
Crawford
  Adam, 269
  Masten D., 160
  Virgil, 86
Crecy
  J.C., 21
Creecy
  Frederick, 32
  John, 258
  T., 22
Creeks
  Fishing Creek, 280
  Newbegun Creek, 220
  Sandy Creek, 280
  Symons, 215
Creesy
  Thomas, 326
Crocker
  John, 199
Crutch
  William, 233
Crutch[?]
  William, 231
Cunningham
  Elizabeth, 299
  James, 296, 299
  John, 16, 296
Curtis
  Austin, 294
  Austin, a mulatto, 293
  Austin, a Mullato Slave, 4
  Polly, 299
  Sabina, 299
Cusick

Index

J, 158
Jedediah, 157, 158
Jediah, 158
William, 158
Cuttar
  William, 182

D

Daggett
  Henry, 43
Daivrou[?]
  Jno B, 102
Dalton
  Charles, 269
  David, 269
  Isaac, 269
Daly
  Ann G., 41
  JN., 53, 54
  John, 41, 42, 43, 53, 54
  Sidney M., 41
  Sidney Maria, 41
Dameron
  Oney, 199
Daniel
  Sarah, 149
  W.W., 168
Darley
  Enoch, 319
Dauge
  Enoch, 319
Daves
  T.H., 94, 95
  Thomas H, 94
Daves[?]
  Thomas H., 101
Davie
  Dolphus A., 10
Davies
  Peter R., 282
Davis
  [Torn]rd, 199
  Adam[?], 235
  Archd, 201
  Archd., 199
  B., 279
  Bailey, 198, 208, 235
  Buckner, 279
  Devotion, 197
  Devotion Junr, 203
  Devotion Senr., 203
  Devotion Sinr., 197
  Durant, 197, 199, 203, 215
  Elizabeth, 4, 294
  Grace, 4, 294
  Harriot, 4, 294
  I., 174
  Isaac, 174, 175
  Jesse, 5

John, 4, 236, 294
Jos, 203
Kelcy, 82
Matthew, 273
Matthew senior, 273
Matthew Senr., 273
Matthew, senior, 299
Miles, 197, 235, 236
Rebecca, 4, 294
Richard, 4, 294
S.A., 309
Samuel, 4, 294
Thomas, 9, 10, 229, 230, 231, 235, 236, 319
Thomas Jr., 10
Thos F, 181
Thos., 197
William, 222
Dawson
  Jno B., 103
  John B., 103
Declaration of Rights, 329
Dellinger
  David, 172
delon
  William, 210
Delon
  Mark, 198
Dennis
  William, 265
  Wm., 265
Denson
  J., 146
  Jordan, 146
DeRossett
  Armand J. Jr., 308
Derows[?]
  Robt., 258
Devaney
  A., 147
Devereaux
  John, 112
  Mr, 111
  Mr John, 111
Devereux
  John, 112
Dick
  Jno, 263, 264
  Jno [?], 158
Dickey
  Alexander, 177, 178
  Alexr, 177, 178
Dickinson
  Davy, 29, 30
  John, 31
  S., 13
  Samuel, 13, 17, 33
Dicks
  Peter, 265
  Zachariah, 187, 188
Dickson

John, 132
  Zachary, 326
Digges
  Robt., 138, 139
Dillinger
  David, 172
Dingle
  Dick, 35
Dingley
  Deek, 33
  Dick, 33, 34, 35
  Dick, a free person of color, 33
Dingly
  Dick, 35
Divoux
  F., 115
  Fr., 77
  Frederick, 77, 78, 115
Doctor Tom
  A Free Man of Color, 249
  Husband of Phillis. *See*
    Slaves:Phillis
Doherty
  Mary, 187
Dominick
  Mr., 31
Donaldson
  [?]C., 31
  Robert, 33
Donell
  Robert, 41
Donnell
  Elisa, 41
  Jn, 75, 76, 97, 98
  John R, 75, 76
  Robert, 37, 41
Doogan
  Joseph, 265
Douglas
  H., 255
  Harrison, 255
  Harrison, a free person of Colour, 255
  Tho. L., 269
Douglass
  Harrison, 255
Dove
  Mary, 38. *See* East Indians
  Mary Dove, an East Indian or Madagascarian, 38
  Mary, sued for freedom, 38
Dowden
  Ann, 110, 111
  William, 110
Downs
  John, 90, 91, 93, 94
Dowrey
  William, 38. *See* East Indians
  William, an East Indian, 37
Dowry
  William, 37, 38

Index

Doyal
  JW, 170
Drake
  E.D., 282, 283
  Edwin D., 282
Draper
  Chalkly, 252
Dubberly
  Sacker, 66, 67, 68
Dudley
  Edward B., 181
Dudly
  Edward B, 179
Dukais[?]
  Jonathan, 211
Duke
  Mr. Green, 281
Duncan
  William, 135
Dunn
  David D., 51
  James, 132, 310
  Jas, 132
  Louis, 132, 310
Duvall
  G, 37
  G., 37, 39

E

Eaker
  Christian, 171, 172
Eason
  Jacob, 248
East Indian, 38
East Indians, viii
  Alexander Sands, 38
  Indian Sawony, 38
  Malaga Moll or Mary, 38
  Mary Dove, 38
  William Dowrey, 38
Eaton
  Colonel Charles, 281
  General Thomas, 281
  Miranda, 279
  Thomas, 283
Eccles
  Jno.D., 127
Edenton, 325
  District of, 322
Edenton District, 194, 319
Edwards
  James, 277
  Jas, 277
  John, 32
Eelbeck
  Henry, 14
  Joseph, 14
  Major, a slave, 14
Egan
  Robert, 12, 321
Ehringhaus
  John, 237
  John C, 193, 236, 237
  John C., 237
Elexander
  Nathaniel, 250
  Nathl., 250
Elizabeth Town, 298
Elliot
  B., 31
  Ca[?] Jr, 245
  Demcy, 247
  Gabriel, 34
  Isaac, 323
  James, 194, 323
  Joseph, 248
  Joseph Senr, 247
  Mordecai, 247
  Peter, 261
  Samuel, 248
  Solomon, 17, 18
Ellis
  A., 77
  Amaryllis, 117
  Geo., 50
  George, 50
  Judge, 169
  Michael, 85
Elmesly
  Alexander, 151
Emancipation
  Grand Jury statement, 12
Emancipation Laws
  Act of 1715, 311
  Act of 1723, 311
  Act of 1741, 312
  Act of 1777, 312
  Act of 1778, 313
  Act of 1788, 313
  Act of 1795, 314
  Act of 1796, 315
  Act of 1801, 315
  Act of 1830-1831, 315
  Act of 1833-4, 317
  Act of 1860-61, 318
Ernul
  Aaron, 51, 69
  Moses, 51
Estering
  J., 270
Etheridge
  Sarah, 18
Eures
  Mills, 150
Evans
  Bartholomew, 191
  Evan, 192
  Jn., 269
  Jonathan, 322, 323
  Joseph, 252
Everett
  Jos., 285, 286
  Joseph, 285, 286
Evergain
  Colo. Edward, 235
  Ruth, 210, 232
Evergan
  Col. Edward, 211
  Colo., 210, 213
  Colo. Edward, 209
  Hester, 209
  Tony, 213
Evergans
  Colo. Edward, 199
  Ruth, 232
Everigain
  Edward, 194
Everitt
  Jos., 286
  Joseph, 286

F

Fain
  Jacob, 153, 154
  James, 154
  Sally, 154
Farang
  William, 210
Farange
  William, 210, 225
  Wm, 209, 225
Farange[?]
  Wm, 204
Faslane[?]
  John W., 31
Faucett
  Wm D, 168
Fell[?]
  Edwd, 169
Fellow
  Robert, 285, 286
  Robt., 286
Felton
  Richard, 34
Fennel
  Jack, 41
Fennell
  Jack, 41
Fenner
  Wm E, 168
Fentris
  George, 264
Fentriss
  Edward, 264
  George, 264
Ferrand
  Stephen L., 61, 115, 116
  Stephn. L., 61, 62
  Will. P., 61, 62

Index

William P., 61
Ferris
  John, 199
Finley
  Thos., 110
Fisher
  Boling, 269
Fite
  John, 12
Fletcher
  Frederick, 235
Flowers
  Thomas, 133
Flury[?]
  Henry, 29
Fonville
  Lewis, 54
Forbes
  Stephen B, 101, 102
  Stephen B., 102
  Stephn. B., 102
  Stepn. B., 77, 102
Forrest
  J.H., 158
Fort
  Joseph, 138
Foster
  C., 147
fourhand
  thomas, 35
Fox
  Jos., 222
  William, 222
Foy
  James, 181
Franklin
  John, 89, 90, 91, 93, 94
  John Hope, viii
  Walter S., 321
Free people of color
  Rights of, ix
Freeman
  EB, 170
  Phillis, 293
  Robert, 187
  Robt., 187
Freshwater
  T, 209, 214, 218, 221, 231, 233, 239
  T., 231
  Thaddeus, 218
  Thads, 221
  Thads., 214
  W.W., 242
  William W., 242
Friday
  Billi, 172
  Billy, 172
  Billy, free man of color, 172
Friends of North Carolina, 260
Fugitive Law, 326, 327, 329

Fulenwider
  Henry, 172
  John, 172
Fullinton
  John, 34
Fundamental Constitutions, 1669, viii

G

Gardiner
  John, 1
Gardner
  James, 1, 2
  John, 1, 2
  Mr. John, 1
Garland
  John, 287
garrett
  Ser[?], 35
Garrod
  Samuel, 269
Gaskin
  Adam, 69
Gaskins
  Thomas, 218
  William, 218
  Wm, 199, 221
Gaston
  Will:, 114, 116
Gatlin
  A.M., 28
  Alfred M., 28, 29
  W., 78
Gautier
  Joseph R., 298
Gaynor
  Jenny, 118
  Jenny, a slave, 118
General Assembly Session Records, x
Gentry
  Richard, 269
George
  David, 194, 210
  Mr., 213
  William C, 220, 231
German
  Mary, 295
Gerock
  Charles, 75
  Chas., 75
  Samuel, 37
gerrish
  Edwd., 257
Gerrish
  Edward, 258
  Edward, a Black man, 257
  Edwd., 257
Gibbes
  William, 39
  Willm., 40

Gibson
  I., 271
  Isaac, 270, 271
  Joseph, 164, 165, 166
Gilbert
  Mr., 328
Gillespie
  B.C., 75, 76, 90, 91
  Borthwick C, 90
  Bothwick, 90
Gilliam
  H., 150
  Henry, 150
  Robt. B., 278
  W., 281, 282
  William, 282
Gilmer
  J.N., 270
  John A, 161
  John N., 270
Gipson
  Davis, 210
Gl[Torn]
  Joseph, 254
God[?]
  Peter, 85
Godett
  Peter, 47
Godrich
  Elizer, 43
Golding
  Col. Isaac, 270
  Isaac, 270, 271
Good
  B.C., 115
  John, 309
  William, 50
Goodin
  Thomas, 35
Goodman
  Frank, 241, 242
  William, 149
Goodwin
  Jacob, 248
  John, 248
  Richard, 248
  Wm., 12, 321
Goss
  Elijah, 155
  Fanny, 155
  T, 154
  Thomas, 155
Gossett
  Abram, 160
  John O., 160, 161
  Thomas, 161, 162
    Free Man of Color, 160
Grace
  Thomas, 72, 73
  Thos, 73
Graham

Index

E, 111
E., 87
Edward, 46, 48
Edwd., 99
William A., 130
Granberry
   Thomas, 254
Grand Jury
   Presentment Against Quakers in Chowan County, 320
Gray
   A., 265
   Stevens, 2
Great Britain
   War with, 258
Green
   Allen, 298
   Amelia, 48, 49
   Amelia, a free woman of colour, 297
   Amelia, free woman of color, 48
   Breny, 298
   Capt, 145
   Capt William, 145
   Captain Wm., 145
   Charity, 298
   Charlotte, 98, 294, 300
   Crease, 298
   Dolly, 4, 294
   Harriet, 49
   James S, 180
   James S., 180
   James Y, 87, 95, 96, 99, 100
   James Y., 99, 100
   James York, 86, 87, 89
   Jas. Y., 100
   Jno S, 96, 97
   John, 69, 89, 95
   John R., 76, 116
   Leon, 300
   M.E., 89
   Mingo, 146
   Nancy, 48
   Nathan, 4, 294
   Princess, 48, 298
   Pris, 298
   Richard, 4, 45, 98, 181, 294
   Richd, 181
   Rich'd, 181
   Tho A, 89
   Tom, 298
   William, 182, 282
   William B, 89, 90
   William B., 89, 90
   Willie, 298
   Wm, 279
   Wm., 279, 282
   Wm. B., 89
Gregory
   Isaac, 3
   Wm, 235, 236

Grey
   Thos W, 168
Grice
   Charles, 216, 225, 233, 234, 241
Grifess[?]
   [Faded], 199
Griffin
   Brinkley, 34
   Edwd, 137
   Edwin, 137
   Humphrey, 34
   James, 213, 250
   Ned, 137, 138, 139, 291
      a free man, 137
      Continental Service of, 138
      man of mixed Blood, 138
      Mollatoe or Mustee, 137
   William, 137, 138, 323
   Willis, 34
Griffis
   William, 138, 139
Griffith
   Edward, 53, 54
   Mr., 2
Grigg
   Jas Grigg, 170
   Jas M., 170
Grover
   Susannah, 2
Groves
   Sol., 7
   Solomon, 7, 8
Grymes
   Maria, 131, 132
   Thomas, 131, 132
Guin
   Christopher, 140
   Mr., 140
Guinn
   Thornton P., 269
Guion
   Jno. W., 76
   John W., 76
Gun Permit, 222
Gunn
   Griffin, 8
Guthrie
   William, 9
Guyer[?]
   Wm., 241
Gwinn
   Jno., 37

H

Hagans
   Elizabeth, 304
Halifax
   District of, 137
Hall

   Edward, 140, 141
   Edwd., 140
   Jehu, 240
   Jenny, 297
   Lamuel and Jenny free born, 193
   Lemuel, 297
   Lemuel & Jenny free persons of color, 192
   Lemuel, a free man, 297
   Milley, 297
   Seth, 297
   Tabitha, 297
   Thomas, 140
   William, 14, 15
   Wm., 15
Hallings
   Henry, 245
Hamilton
   Col John, 222
   J, 243, 248
   Jn, 222
   Thomas, 302
Hammon
   Edward, 103
Hammons
   Edward, 102, 103
Hampton, 159
   John, 159
Hancock
   W., 92
Handcock
   W., 69, 92
   William, 91, 92
   William H., 103
   Wm, 91
Handy
   Nancy, 49
   Nancy, a free person of Color, 49
   Peggy, 294
Hankins
   John, 210, 213
Hanner
   J, 158
   J., 157
Hardee
   John, 169
Hare
   Thomas E., 319
Hargett
   Abner, 65, 66
   Alfred, 65, 66
Harper
   Jesse, 265
Harrell
   Mary, 2, 3
Harrington
   Thomas, 9
Harris
   JW, 169
   Stephen, 66, 104

Index

Hart
  Col. Henry, 139
  Eliza, 298
  Henry, 139, 140
  Nancy, 298
Hartford Prison, 326
Harval
  John, 34
Harvey
  Caesar, 236
  J., 324
  Mary, 117
  Tho. H., 251
  Thomas, 258
  Thos., 258
  Thos. H., 250, 251
Harvy
  Colo. Thos., 235
Hasket
  John, 259
  Joseph, 266
  Joseph Senr., 265
Haskett
  Joseph, 265
Haskitt
  John, 323
Haslen
  Margaret, 121, 122
  Margt., 121, 122
Haslin
  Margaret, 121
  Mrs., 121
  Mrs. Margaret, 121
Hassel
  B[?], 31
Hatch
  D., 94, 95
  Durant, 94, 95
Hathaway
  Jas., 12, 21, 31
  Thomas V., 30
  Woolsey, 319
Hathcock
  Ave, 188
Haughton
  John, 32
  Jonathan Junr., 32
  Nat, 27
Hauser
  George, 269
Havannah, 42
Hawkins
  Benjamin, 280, 281
  Frank, 281
  George Washington, 281
  John, 280, 281, 282
  John D., 144, 146, 147, 280
  Joseph, 280, 281
  Lucy, 280
  Phil, 281
  Phil., 281, 282

  Philemon, 281, 282
  Philemon Senior, 280
  William, 61, 62, 64, 65, 66, 67, 68, 78, 89, 91, 114
Hawks
  Fran., 100
  Francis, 77
  Frans., 100
  Jno S, 125
Hayes
  Mary, 151, 153
Hayti, ix
Haywood
  John, 139, 147
  Will H, Jr., 277
  Wm. H., Jr., 277
Hazell
  Job, 127
  Job, free man of color, 127
  Mary Ann, 127
  Polly, 127
Heath
  Mr., 328, 329
Heathcock
  Ave, 188
Henby
  Elisha, 249
Henderson
  A, 100
  A., 100
  Alexander, 100
  J.P., 172
  L., 153
  Leonard, 153, 281
  Lwn, 178
  Lwn., 172, 174, 175, 177, 178
  P., 186
  Pleasant, 186
  Richard, 187
  Richd., 152, 187
  Wallace A., 176
Hendley
  Joseph, 194
Henley
  Ann, 217
  George R., 220, 231
  Joseph, 259
  Stephen, 217
Henly
  Aliss, 264
  W, 222
Henry
  Caesar, 291
  E., 52, 53, 54, 55, 56, 57, 58, 59, 60, 77
  Eliz., 55
  Eliza., 56, 57, 59, 60
  Elizabeth, 52, 53, 54, 55, 56, 57, 58, 59, 60
Herdell
  Josiah, 12, 321

Herndon
  Pomfrett, 185, 186
Herring
  Benajah, 287, 288
  Ichabod, 287
  Michael, 287
Herritage
  William M, 42
  William M., 43
  Wm. M., 43
Hester
  Marcus C, 46
Hill
  Aaron, 245
  Benjamin, 264
  Boson, 301
  C.A., 147
  Jesse, 264
  Mr., 139
  Penny, 301
  W., 4
  William, 4, 278
  Wm., 278, 304
Hixon
  Timothy, 324
Hockody
  Albert, 310
  John, 310
Hodges
  Thomas, 140
Hogan
  William, 263
Hogg
  Francis, 185
  John, 182, 185
Holder
  Isaac, 187
Holland
  I., 173
  Isaac, 173
  Mr., 329
  William, 70, 71
Holleman
  W.H., 277
Holliman
  Micajah, 152, 153
Hollister
  Tom, 119
  Tom, a slave, 119
  William, 113, 119, 120, 121
  Wm, 112, 113, 120
  Wm., 93, 120, 121
Hollowell
  Abner, 34
  Henry, 252, 253
  John, 34
  Luke, 34
  Moses, 34
  T., 251
  Thomas, 251
Holls

Index

Moses, 35
Holmes
   Gabriel, 119, 123, 124, 264
Hoobs
   Ruben, 35
Hooper
   A.M., 184
   G., 182
   George, 181
   William, 325
Horn
   Wm., 2, 3
Horniblow
   Elizabeth, 28
   Mrs., 28
Horton
   Betty, 79
Hosener
   Sylvester, 225
Hoskins
   Edm, 21
   Edm., 28
   Edmd., 12, 15, 31
   Edmond, 29
   Nathaniel, 14, 15
   Nathl., 15
   Richd., 21
   Saml., 12
   William, 14, 15
   Wm., 15
Hostler
   James G, 180
   James G., 180, 308
   JG, 180
   Joseph, 128, 129, 304
   Joseph, a man of Colour, 128
House
   E.W., 267
   James, 144, 145
   Jas., 144
   Mr., 3
   Reubin, 3
House of Representatives, 321
Houser
   James, 144, 145
Howard
   Elizabeth, 77
   Fanny, 305
   Henry, 305
   John, 46, 47, 305
   Luke, 205
   Miles, 305
Howe
   Balaam, 303
   Hannah, 303
   John, 303
   Lucy, 303
   Sally, 303
   William, 48
   William T, 49
   Wm T, 49

Howel
   John, 163
Howel[Harvel?]
   John, 158
Howell
   John, 157
Howells improvement, 281
Hoyle
   Andrew, 172
   Peter, 173, 176, 177
Hubbard
   Jacob, 166
Hudgins
   Hy, 150
Hudson
   Uriah, 245, 250, 252, 254
   Wilkinson, 252
Hughes
   Willis, 149
Humphrys
   Henry, 164
   Humphrys, 165
Hunt
   E.F., 132
   J, 139, 273
   Nat, 147
   Nathan, 158, 159, 160
   Nathan Jnr., 159, 160
   Nathan Jun., 160
   Nathan Junior, 158, 159, 160
   Nathan Senior, 158, 159, 160
   Nathan Snr., 159
   William, 156
   Wm, 156
   Wm., 156
Hurdle
   Abraham, 245
   Harmon, 245
   Job, 261
   Job, a Man of Colour, 245
   Job, Free Man of Colour, 260
Hurst
   J., 288
Huske
   James, 128
   John N., 129
Hussey
   Thomas, 159
Hussy
   Thomas, 158, 159
   Thos., 159
Hyman
   Ned, 304

I

Indian
   Women and children as slaves, viii
Indian Slavery, 14
Indian War, 14

Indiana, ix
Indianna
   State of, 159
Indians, 1, 140, 141
   Beck, an Indian woman, 140
   Betty, a Free Indian, 248
   East Indians, viii
   Held as Slaves
      Jenny Ash, 1
   Held as slaves, or illegally held as slaves, viii
   Indian Moll, 151
   Indian Sarah, 151, 153
   Jenny Ash, a mustee, 1
   Jenny, mother of Beck, 140
   Listed as indentured servants, viii
   Listed as slaves, viii
   Moll, an Indian wench, 151
   Moll, from Cape Fear, 151
   Nancy Ash, 1
   Peter, 247
   Sarah, a Cape Fear Indian, 151
   Sarah, daughter of a free Indian, 152
   Sarah, descended from an Indian, 152
Ingram
   Jeremiah, 147
   John, 297
   Willis P., 147
Irby
   Thomas, 168
Iredell
   Ja, 255
   Ja., 18, 21, 22
   James, 20, 21, 73, 74, 108, 109, 110, 119, 120, 255, 325
   Jas, 255
   Thos., 12
Ivins
   Morning, 283
   Mourning, 283

J

Jackson
   Asa, 235
   Bailey, 231
   Jacob, 208
   James, 225, 253
   Jas, 233
   Jas., 226
   Joab, 197, 210
   Miles, 228
   Moses jur., 196
   Nat[?], 236
   Natha, 235
   Sam, 202
   Saml., 202
   Samuel, 202

Index

Zachariah, 199
Jacobs
  George, 293
Jamaica, 42
James
  William, 244
Slaves, 301
Jarves
  Mrs. Liddia, 240
Jay
  William. *See* Abolitionists
Jeffries
  Ozborne, 298
Jenkins
  W.A., 170
  Wm A, 170
Jennings
  Demcey, 222
  Fred, 221
  John, 236
  Lemuel, 201
Jervis
  John, 221
Jesop
  William, 82, 83, 85
Jessop
  William, 83, 84, 85, 86
  Wm., 84
John Braveboy, 11
Johnson
  Amos, 141
  Augustus, 23
  B, 37
  G.A., 24, 25, 26
  Gustavus A., 24, 25
  Gustavus Adolphus, 23, 24, 25
  Gustavus Adolphus, free man of Color, 24
  John, 84, 85
  M Duke, 282
  Mr. Duke, 283
  Thomas, 197
  Wm. E., 279
  WS, 169
Johnston
  Elizabeth alias Charlotte Green, 294
  Gustavus Adolphus, 296
  Jacob, 188
  Polydore, 279
  Saml, 42
  Saml. W., 319
  Samuel, 42
  William Eaton, 279
  Wm, 49
  Wm., 50
Jones
  Abraham, 300
  Allen, 276
  Allen, free man of Color, 276
  Arthur, 31

  Asa, 61, 71, 72, 78, 93, 115, 124, 125
  Austin Curtis, 294
  Caleb, 252
  Dick, 150
  Elizabeth M., 23
  Evan, 70
  Frederick, 71, 91, 92, 124, 125
  Fredk., 71, 72, 92, 124
  Fredr., 91
  G., 84
  Gideon, 83, 84, 105, 106
  Isaac, 300
  Jacob, 300
  James C., 146
  Jas., 21
  John, 69, 77, 90, 92, 93, 124, 125, 252, 300, 319
  Joseph, 323
  Lewis, 300
  Lovick, 61, 71, 83, 84
  Mary, 90, 91
  R P, 69
  Reuben P., 84
  Sally, 300
  Saml, 233, 234
  Samuel, 261
  Seth, 245
  Sukey, 300
  Thomas, 300
  William, 250
  William Watts, 22, 23, 182
  Willie, 4
  Wm., 12, 246, 321
  Wm. G., 147
  Wm. Watts, 23, 183
Jordain
  Matthew, 254
Jordan
  Abram, 201
  J.A., 199
  JA, 200
  Jacob, 14
  Jchabod, 35
  Jochabod, 33, 34, 35
  John A., 212
  Jordan, 245
  Joseph, 35
  Josiah, 35, 251, 254, 257, 323
  M, 245
  Mr. Jochabod, 34
  Robt B, 201
  Tho., 216
  Thomas, 199, 202, 203, 205, 208, 211, 212, 217, 231, 233, 234, 235
  Thomas Junier, 235
  Thomas Junr., 234
  Thomas Senr., 205
  Thos., 213
  William, 230, 231, 233, 234

Jordin
  Abram, 213
Joyner
  A., 278
Justice
  John, 69, 78, 113
Justus
  Peter, 185

K

Kean
  P, 68
keaton
  [**Keaton**], 199
  Jos. L., 231
Keaton
  Beno, 233
  Henry, 222
  Isaac, 222
  J, 209
  John Junr., 222
  Jos. Z., 231
  Reu, 213
  Reub, 209, 210
  Reub., 199
  Saml, 197
  Stephen, 220, 222, 233
  W, 197
  W., 218, 221
Keith, 159
  Wm., 159
Kello
  Isaac, 153
  S., 151
  Sam, 151
  Samuel, 152, 153
Kilpatrick
  Francis, 301
Kimbell
  Ben, 283
  Benjamin, 283
King
  Hen., 22, 26, 31
  Henry, 26, 31
  Miles, 152
kinyon
  Joel, 249
Kitchell
  Mr., 330
Kitchen
  William, 137, 138, 139, 291
  Wm., 138
Knight
  Abel, 159
  Ephraim, 293, 299
Knights
  Thomas, 236
Knox
  ambrose, 243

Index

Ambrose, 192, 220, 231, 233
Andrew, 21, 210, 231
Ferebee, 223
H., 232
Harey, 223
Harry, 223, 224, 231, 232
Hugh, 204, 210, 213, 222, 223, 227, 228, 231, 232, 233
Primus, 231
Koen
  Col John, 222
  J, 222

L

Lacy
  Joseph, 222
Ladd
  Mr. Noble, 269
  Noble, 269
  Richard, 269
Lamb
  Isaac, 259, 323
  Restore, 254
Lancaster
  J.W., 170
Lane
  Caroline, 115, 116
  Caroline, a slave, 115, 116
  Isaac, 275
  J, 197, 203, 208, 216
  Jack, 201
  Jn, 196
  John T, 103, 104
  John T., 104
  Jonathan, 275
  Wm, 197, 199, 204, 208
  Wm., 213
Langford
  James, 308
Lankater
  Henry, 320
Laughren
  Chs., 13, 321
Laurance
  Peter P, 12
Laurence
  Wm, 77
Laws
  Emancipation laws, x
  Missing laws, x
  Statute of 1715, x
  Statute of 1723, x
  Statute of 1741, x
  Statute of 1777, x
  Statute of 1778, x
  Statute of 1788, x
  Statute of 1796, xi
  Statute of 1801, xi
  Statute of 1818, xi

Statute of 1830, xi
Statute of 1861, xi
Lea
  William, 7
Leary
  Job, 21
Leatherman, 159
  Jonas, 159
  Nancy, 159
  Scipio, 159
Leech
  Joseph, 45
Legett
  James, 33, 34
  Mr. James, 35
Leggett
  James, 169
Leigh
  William, 141
Lemay
  Thomas J., 4
Lenah, alias Tenah, 43
Lenoir
  Wm., 4
Lente
  Michl H., 77
Leonard
  Benjamin, 209
  Benjn., 217
  London, 213, 214
  London, a person of color, 214
Letchworth
  Dorcas, 2
  Elizabeth, 2
  Joseph, 2
  Tabitha, 2
Lewes
  Joshua, 83, 84
Lewes[?]
  Owen Stanton, 83
Lewis
  David, 69
  Eli, 169
  Jno., 154
  Michael, 85
  Seniah, 85
  Simon, 84
  Sinah, 85
Liberia, ix
Lindsey
  Jona., 240
  Jonathan, 240
Lisbon
  Bob, 114
  Robert, 77, 78, 114, 115
  Robert, formerly a slave, 114
  Robert, free man of color, 77
  Robt., 77, 114
Little
  John, 12, 26, 321
Littlejohn

Elizabeth M., 22, 23
J.W., 21, 23, 28, 31
John W., 22, 28, 29
Mr. William, 31
William, 23
Wm. A., 15, 17
Wm:, 31
Lockwood
  Halld., 199, 201
  Holland, 326
Loftin
  Leonard, 66, 67
Lomax
  Abel, 269
Long
  Mary, 292
  Mr. Reuben, 12
  NM, 169
  Reuben, 11, 12
Louisiana, ix
Loury
  Ben, 233, 236
Louthorp
  Fr., 50
  Francis, 50
Lovelace
  Archibald, 289, 306
Lovick
  Thomas, 293
Low
  Thomas, 227
  Thos., 227
Lowe[?]
  Joshua, 236
Lowrie
  Walter, 321
Lowry
  Benj, 222
  J, 199
  Robt., 222
Luis
  George, 85, 86
  Isaac, 83
  Simon, 84
Luten
  [?], 221
  Anna, 18
  Const., 199, 222
  John, 12
  King, 14, 15, 31
Luydam
  James, 64
Lytle
  Catherine, 294
  frank, 295
  Frank, 294, 295
  John, 294
  Thomas, 294, 295

Index

M

M'Alister
  Blackwell, 300
Macauslan
  John, 182, 183
Macay
  Daniel, 305
  William, 305
Macky
  Samuel, 307
Maclin
  Eliza, 153
  James, 153
Macon
  Mr., 329
MacRae
  Alex, 179
Madagascar, viii, 38
Maddux
  Benjn., 222
Madison
  Mr., 328, 329
Madkins
  Richard, 221
Magellan
  Tobias. *See* Slaves:Tobias
  Tobias Ballinger. *See* Tobias, a Slave
Malone
  Cherry, 276, 277, 278, 306
  Edmond, 306
  Edmund, 276, 277
  John, 277, 278, 306
  John, free man of Color, 277, 306
Man
  Thomas, 222
Mander[?]
  E., 265
Manley
  Nancy, 191
  Sarah
    born of free parents, 191
Manly
  John, 197
  Judge, 169
  M.E., 102, 103
  Matthias E, 102, 103
  Matthias E., 102, 103
Manly[?]
  Chas:, 276
Manns
  Abraham, 186
Manumitted Slave
  Albert
    Job, 326
  Nicholson
    Jacob, 326
    Jupiter, 326
  Pritchet

    Thomas, 326
Markam
  Thos., 204, 213, 218
Markham
  Anthony, 242
  Charles, 218, 221
  Robert, 222
  Thomas, 221
Marrick
  George, 4
Marriot
  James T., 278
Marriott
  James T., 277, 278
Marshall
  Capt., 151
  Capt. Humphry, 151
  John, 294
Marsteller
  L H, 179
  L.H., 179
  LH, 180
Martin
  Alexander, 44
  B H, 49
  B.H., 135
  Benjm., 49
  F X, 41, 80
  F.X., 44
  FX, 49, 51, 52
  L., 21
  TN, 39
Maryland Counties
  Anne arundel, 38
Massachusetts, 329, 330
Massey
  Adkins, 199, 213
Mastin
  J., 89
Mathews
  S., 243
Matthews
  Samuel, 242
Mauney
  Peter, 171
Maxwell
  James, 147
Mbryde
  A., 266
McAdam
  Jas., 235
McAddams
  Joseph, 196
McAustan
  John, 182
McBee
  V., 176
  Vardry, 173
McCassan
  David, 5
McClanahan

  Samuel, 258
McClennan
  Harry, 141
McDonald
  D., 22, 24, 27, 31
  Duncan, 30
  J, 199
  Jno, 227
  Jno., 200, 204, 208, 213, 220, 225, 227, 233, 236
  John, 196, 209, 210, 211, 221, 222, 224, 225, 226, 231
  L., 21
McKee
  W.H., 277
  Wm H, 277
  Wm. H, 277
McKey
  Saml., 131
  Samuel, 131
McKinley
  James, 50
  Jas., 50
McKinne
  John, 285, 286
McLean
  A., 130
  Archd. Jr., 128, 129, 130
  Archibald Jun., 128
McLellan
  John, 181, 182
Mclin
  Jno. S., 78
  Tho., 72
  Thomas, 72
McLin
  Jno. J., 64, 114
  John, 114
  John J, 64, 114
  John J., 114
  Thomas, 72
McMorine
  Robert, 235
McPherson
  Daniel, 193
McRae
  Alexander, 179
Meeds
  Benjamin, 222
  John, 222
Merrick
  George, 45, 294
Metcalfe
  George, 323
  Sarah, 323
Michell
  Richard, 219
Midwife, 214, 235
Miers
  Thomas, 32, 256
Mifflin

Index

Warner, 323
Miller
  Alexr, 12
  James T., 179
  Jno., 5
  John, 249
  Masan, 12, 321
  Thomas C., 308
  William, 70, 72, 75, 79, 86, 92, 93, 94, 95, 96, 98, 115
    Governor, 157
Mills
  Captn., 137
  Sandy Creek Mill, 280
Ming
  Wiley, 35
Mitchel
  Adam, 164
  Kiziah, 165
Mitchell
  A, 120, 121
  Adam, 163, 164
  Jno., 146, 147
  John, 147, 226, 227
  John, a free man of Colour, 146
  Kiziah
    Free Woman, 165
  Mitchell, 164
  William, 87, 88
  Wm., 88, 89
Moffatt
  James, 28, 29
Molatto
  Bess, Free Born, 2
  Slaves, 229
Montford
  Donnum, 73, 74
  Donum, 95, 96
Moody
  Epps, 146
  Mr., 146
Moore
  A., 304
  Andrew, 294
  Augustus, 242
  B, 169
  Charles H., 260
  David, 96, 97
  James, 181
  James Jr., viii
  John, 294
  Josiah, 252
  Juno, 294
  Margaret, a free negro, 41
  Peter, 294
  Saml. C., 261
  Samuel, 323
  Samuel C., 261
  Thomas, 252
Morehead
  J.M., 166

Morgan
  Charles, 259, 323
  Geo, 12, 31
Moring
  Henry, 275
Morris
  [?] Senr, 201
  A Junior, 208
  Aaron, 207, 208, 211, 212, 239, 243
  Aaron Jun., 323
  Aaron Junr, 204
  Aaron Junr., 243
  Aaron Senior, 239
  Aaron Senr, 239
  Aaron Senr., 220, 238, 239
  Betty, 193
  Emanuel, 216
  Job, 211
  John, 192, 193, 197
    a free man, 193
  John S, 123, 124
  John S., 123
  Joshua Senr., 210
  Mordecai, 208
  Nathan, 208
  Rachel, 192
  Rd., 226
  Rd. P., 226
  Richard P., 226
  Richard Prichard, 4, 294
  Thomas, 210, 213, 323
  Thomas Nicholson, 207
  William Prichard, 4, 294
Moses, a free negro, 240
Mulatoes
  Bess
    Alias Betty Tootle, 2
Mulattoes
  Child of Dorcas Tootle, 2
Mullin
  Stephn, 235
Mumford
  Donum, 66
Muray
  Antonio, a free Negro, 42
Murden
  Robert, 209
Murphey
  Alex., 7, 8
  Alexander, 7
Murphy
  A., 8
  A.D., 189
Muse
  Mrs., 243
  Richard, 229, 231, 234, 235, 236, 238, 239, 240
  Richd., 232
  Will
    T., 193

  Will T., 200, 201, 202, 203, 204, 205, 206, 207, 208, 209, 211, 213, 215, 224, 227, 228, 233, 235
  Will. T., 17, 204, 207, 208, 209, 210, 211, 212, 213, 214, 215, 216, 218, 219, 220, 223, 224, 225, 226, 228, 229, 230, 231, 233, 234, 236, 237, 238, 239, 243, 244
  Will. T. Muse, 201
  William, 223
  William T, 223, 229, 232, 236, 238
  William T., 17, 226, 229, 234, 235, 236, 238, 239, 243
  William Templeman, 193, 225
  Willm. T., 238
  Wm T., 223
  Wm., 238
  Wm. T., 17, 226, 228, 236, 238, 243

N

N.C. Counties
  Bertie, 32
  Martin, 31
  New Hanover, 48
  Pitt, 137
N.C. Towns
  Edenton, 22, 23, 26, 30, 31, 32
  Germonton, 270
  Halifax Town, 167
  Hillsborough, 186
  Louisburg, 145
  Martinborough, 137, 138
  Newbern, 37, 38, 39, 44, 48, 81, 259
  Newvern, 137
  Pittsborough, 9
  Raleigh, 276, 278
  Waynesborough, 286
  Wilmington, 22, 182, 185, 308
Nash
  A, 121, 122
  Ann, 121
  Demsey, 199
  F, 82, 276
  Frederick, 82, 87
  Solomon, 180
  Solomon W., 129, 130
NC Counties
  Carteret, 194
  Currituck County, 240
  Gates County, 222
  Jones County, 201
  Perquimans, 206
  Perquimons County, 217
  Randolph County, 217

Index

NC County
  Chatham, 103
NC Towns
  Edenton, 241, 255
  Elizabeth City, 241, 242
  New Bern, 107
  Newbern, 102, 116, 124
  Nixiton, 210
  Nixonton, 200, 201
Neale
  Benjamin, 49, 50
  Philip Junior, 49
  Philip Junr., 49, 50
  Philip Senr., 49
  Philip Sr., 50
  Thomas, 294
Nealy
  Chris, 44
Negroes
  Twenty one to Indiana, 260
Nelson
  Benjamin, 91
  Danl, 91
  John S, 91
New Garden Boarding School, 161
New York, 119, 326
Newbern, North Carolina, x
Newbould
  S, 228
  Samuel, 227
Newby
  Caleb, 252
  Catharine, 261
  Cortney, 254
  Cortney Alis Laurence, 253
  Cortney, former Slave of Exum Newby, 253. *See* Newby:Cortny
  Cortny, 253, 254
  Edmon, 261
  Enoch, 249
  Exum, 252, 253, 254
  Francis, 251, 258
  Fras., 249
  Gideon, 248
  Joseph, 247
  Margaret, 261
  Mark, 259, 260, 323
  Michel, 261
  Newby, 254
  Penny, 261
  Robert, 323
  Tabitha, 261
  Tho., 247
  Thomas, 246, 247, 258, 259, 323, 324
  Thos., 246, 258
  Zachariah, 323
Newlin
  John, 188, 189, 190
Newman
  Thomas, 293

Newspapers
  Carolina Gazette, 270, 271
  Evening Star, 144
  N. York Courier, 144
  N.C. Gazette, 4
  Raleigh Register, 104
  Star, 4
Newton
  Macklin, 113
  Macklin, a slave, 113
  Thomas, 111, 112, 113
  Tom, 112
  Tom, a slave, 112
Nicholson
  Christopher, 202, 324
  Cr, 204, 208
  Cr., 197
  Henley, 212, 213, 222
  Jacob, 327
  Jno, 197
  Jno., 200
  Joseph, 326
  Josiah, 260
  Jupiter, 327
  Mary, 212
  Nicholas, 259, 324
  Rose White, 204, 208
  Thomas, 203, 204, 207, 208, 209, 212, 259, 324, 326
  Thos, 204, 230
  Thos., 207
  William, 212
  Wm., 222
  Zachariah, 264
Nickson
  Phineas, 326
  Zachary, 326
Niel
  Flono[?], 12
  H., 16
  H:, 31
  Honore, 16
Nixon
  Chas, 249
  James, 196, 201, 204, 208, 228, 245
  Jas., 197, 200, 204, 208, 228
  John, 203
  Keziah, 323
  Mary, 259, 324
  Robert, 182
  Thomas, 206
  Z Junr, 197
  Zachariah, 324
Nixons
  James, 208
Norcom
  E., 32
  Frederick, 32
  Ja., 19, 20, 21
  James, 18, 19

  John, 21
  Martin, 31
Norfleet
  E., 33, 35
  Elisha, 33, 35
  J, 18
  James, 20
  Jas., 17, 20, 149, 232
  Will., 22
Norfolk, 326
Norfolk, Virginia, ix
Norris
  A, 216
Norsworthy
  Rachael, 151, 153
North Carolina, 322, 325, 326, 327, 328, 329, 330
North Carolina Courts
  Courts of Pleas and Quarter Sessions, vii
  Superior Courts, vii
North Carolina Courts of Pleas and Quarter Sessions, x
North Carolina General Assembly
  Private Acts of Emancipation, vii
North Carolina Indians
  Grievances of, viii
North Carolina Manumission Society, ix
North Carolina State Archives
  "miscellaneous records", vii
  "slave papers", vii
  "slaves and free Negroes, vii
  "slaves and free persons of color", vii
North Carolina Superior Courts, x
Northern States, 12, 195
Norwan[?]
  Jn, 28
Norwood
  Wm., 185, 186
NY Towns
  New York, 43

O

Oats
  William, 177, 178
  Wm., 177
Occupations
  Tanner, 158
Ochiltree
  D., 132
  David, 131, 132
O'Hanlan
  A.J., 132
O'Hanlon
  A.J., 133
Ohio, ix
Oliver

Index

Jno, 65
Jno., 65, 93
John, 64, 65
Joseph, 65
Saml., 93, 112, 113, 119, 120, 121
William W., 64, 65
Wm. W., 65
Omalley
   Myles, 12
O'malley[Torn]yler, 31
Osborne
   John C, 114
Ott
   George, 237
Ousby
   Wm C, 169
Outland
   Thomas, 286
   Thos., 287
   William, 287
Overman
   Benj, 199
   Charles, 259, 324
   Henry P., 231
   Isaac, 199, 234
   John, 249
   N., 209
   Nathan, 222, 231
   Overman, 249
   Ozios, 221
   Sam., 209
   Thomas, 220
   Thos., 220
Overton
   Abbey, 192
   Abby, 192
   Braddock, 191, 193
   Burdock, 298
   Jane, 191
   Jeffrey, 191
     free born person, 191
   John, 191, 192, 193, 298
   John, free man of Colour, 191
   Lamuel, 191
   Lemuel, 298
   Molly, 192
   Moly, 193
   Rachael
     a free Person of Colour, 193
   Roas, 191
   Rose, 191, 298
   Thamar, 191
Owen
   John, 75, 76, 102, 117
Owens
   John, 174

P

Pailin
   John, 324
Palin
   [?], 201
   Henery, 200
   Hennery, 200
   Henry, 199, 210, 324
Palmer
   Benjamin, 221
   Jeremiah, 217
   John, 222
   Robert, 218
Pamilia
   Sally, 297
Pamphlet
   David Walker's Appeal, viii
Parish of St. James, 183
Parker
   [?], 254
   Africa, 186
   Enuck, 35
   Job, 35
   John, 35
   Jos., 229, 239
   Miles, 149
   Moses, 298
   Richd B, 169
   Samuel, 34
Parkes
   Jonathan, 166
Parks
   Robert, 8
   S., 8
   Solomon, 7, 8
Parrish
   John, 323
Parsons
   Thomas, 42
Pasquotank, 322, 323, 324, 325
Pasquotank County, 324, 325
   grand juries of, x
   Grand Jury, 319
Pasteur
   Abner, 75, 82, 102, 126
Patterson
   G., 148
   J., 146
   N., 145
   Rachel, 240
   Rachel, Woman of Colour, 240
Payne
   Abel, 130, 307
   Michl., 12
   Patsey, 130, 307
Peacock
   Simon, 285
Pearce
   Abner, 69
   David, 52
Pearson
   EA, 169
   Jenney, 235
   Jenny, 235, 236
   John S, 131
   John S., 131, 307
   Rebekah, 217
   Richard, 235
   William, 217
Peden
   W.W., 289
Pender
   John C., 285, 286, 287
Pendleton
   Andrew, 217
   Benja., 225
   Benjamin, 225, 226
   G.W., 233
   J, 199
   J[?], 199
   John, 197
   Lemuel, 199
   Nehe., 231
   Nehemiah, 222
   Peleg, 209
   Sarah, 226
Pendlton
   Jos, 199
Penn
   J, 152
   Mr. John, 152
Pennsylvania, 328, 329
Pennsylvania Legislature
   Law against importation of Indian slaves, viii
Pepper
   Ginger, 298
Peresher
   Joseph, 249
Perkins
   A, 267
   Abraham, 267
Perquimans County, 326
Perquimons, 322, 323, 325
Perquimons County, 324, 325
Perry
   Benjamin, 257
   David, 227
   James, 256, 257
   John, 35
   Josiah, 227
   Laurence, 257
   Law, 250
   Samuel, 35
   Willie, 147
Person
   General Thomas, 298
   J., 145, 146
   Jesse, 145, 146
   John, 146
   Judge Samuel, 169
   P.C., 147
   William, 297
Pery

Index

Jacob, 252
Peters
   Charles, 273, 274, 299
Petition
   Manumitted Slaves to Congress, 325
Petty
   Eli, 289
Pettyjohn
   Job, 32
Philadelphia, ix, 321, 323, 326, 327
Phillips
   Amy, 296
   Elizabeth, 294
   James, 294
Physioc
   Jos., 83
   Joseph, 83
   William, 83, 105, 106
   Wm, 83, 85, 105, 106
   Wm., 83, 85, 86
Pickett
   James, 159, 160
Pierce
   A B, 169
   Leroy, 169
Pilot, 220
Pittard
   J, 169
   Jesse, 168
Pittman
   MW, 169
Places
   Bacons Bridge, 137
   Brittons X Roads, 4
   Cumberland Settlement, 32
   Norflets ferry, 3
   Parish of St. James, 179
   Peola, 261
   Springborough, 261
Plummer
   Henry, 146
Pool
   J.M., 191
   James, 161, 222
   John, 221
   John Senr., 235
   Joseph B., 222
   Joshua A., 192
   Robert, 222
   Solomon, 240
   Thos, 236
Poor
   W.P., 5
Poore
   William P., 5
Popelston
   John, 21, 22, 31
Port of New Haven, 43
Portsmouth, 326
Potter

John, 152
William, 152
Powels Point, 240
Powers
   Benja., 191
   Mr Benja., 193
Price
   John, 196, 197, 200, 201, 208, 210, 220
   Jona., 212
   Jonathan, 98, 211, 212
   William, 197
Prichard
   Hannah, 28
   Thomas, 4, 294
Primrose
   Robert, 102
   Robert H, 102
Pritchard
   B, 200
   Benjamin, 206, 219, 220, 239
   David, 220, 229, 232, 234, 235, 236, 237, 238, 239, 240
   Hannah, 28
   John, 199, 201, 253, 264
   Joseph, 265
   Matthew, 259, 324
   Mingo, 264
   Miss, 28
   Thomas, 197, 201, 213
   Thos., 201
Pritchet, 327
   Hannah, 29
   Thomas, 326
Pritchit
   H., 28
   Hannah, 28
Proby
   William, 226, 227
   Wm, 227
Pugh
   Francis, 147
Pugh[?]
   William, 181
Purkins
   Joshua, 32

Q

Quakers, ix, x, 12, 18, 248, 259, 319, 320, 321, 322
   Memorial to Congress, 321
   Memorial to House of Representatives in 1798, xi
   Petition of 1778, x
   Petition of 1779, x
   Yearly Meeting, ix
Quince
   Richard, 181

R

Raleigh Register, ix
Ralph
   Enoch, 326
Ramsaur
   Jacob, 171
Ramsour
   Jacob, 171
Ransom
   Wm., 147
Ratcliff
   Cornelious, 151, 153
Ratlieff
   Ritchard, 30
Rea
   Thos., 32
Read
   Jno. L., 154
   Samuel, 93, 94
   Silas, 105
Reding
   Joseph, 324
   Thomas, 199
   Thomas, Esquire, 324
   Thos, 201
Reece
   Southy J, 40
Reed
   Chelsea, 298
   Robert, 252
   Silas, 105
Rees
   John, 51
   Levi, 51, 69
Reese
   Enoch, C.C., 324
   Thomas, 324
Reiley[?]
   Edward, 12
Relfe
   Abner, Boy of Colour, 207
   Enoch, 199, 202, 219, 229
   Joseph, 199
   Mary, 192
   Pleasant, 192, 219
      free Person of Colour, 192
   Stephen, 192
   Thomas T, 199
   Thos. T., 209, 213
Revolutionary War, x
Reynolds
   Peter, 124, 125
   Peter, a slave, 124
Rhoades
   Thos., 3
Rhodes
   Thomas, 3
Richard
   Peter, 105, 106

Index

Richards
  George, 146
Richardson
  Benj., 5
  Benjamin, 5
  Dan, 11
  Richd., 96, 97
  Valentine, 96
  Valt, 96
  Valtn, 97
Richmond County, N.C., 159
Richmond, Virginia, ix
Riddick
  Isaiah, 245
  Jo, 222, 273
  Job, 245
  Joseph, 222
  Tobi[?], 35
  Willis, 251
Riddicks
  Joseph, 222
Ridding
  Dick, 263, 264
  Jesse, 199
Riddix
  Rueben, 245
Ridgeley
  Mrs., 37
Ridgely
  Ann, 38
  Anne, 37
Riding
  Colo., 230
  Jane, 263
  Jesse, 200, 230
  John, 263
  Jonathan, 263
  Joseph, 263
Righton
  Mr. William, 27
  Mr. Wm., 22
  Will, 195
  William, 22, 27
  Wm., 21, 22, 27
Rivers
  Tar River, 2, 139
  Yadkin, 38
Roach
  Charles Jr, 53
  Charles Jr., 53
  Charles Junr, 54
  Charles Junr., 54
  Ivey, 215
Robarts
  Joshua, 221
Roberson
  Abner, 138
Roberts
  Capt., 42
  Chas., 12, 33, 35
  Jno., 22
  John, 248
  Willis, 319
Robertson
  J, 222
  John, 267
  William, 326
Robinson
  C.E., 31
  Chas., 30
  Hagar, 206
  James, 208
  Josiah, 249
  Sally, 297
  Tom, 211
  William, 205, 206, 211, 324
  Wm, 206
  Wm., 211
Roch
  Cattron, 215
Rodderick
  Seth, 250
Rogers
  Allen, 275
  Sarah, 141
  Silah, 275
  Wilie, 275
  Willie, 275
Rogerson
  Jesse, 250, 251, 257
Rombough
  Wm., 12
Rose, a free woman of colour, 300
Rosser
  Will, 10
Roundtree
  Mosses, 257
Rountree
  Moses, 257
Rowan
  John, 147
Rowan County, N.C., 159
Ruffin
  L, 138
  Sea[?]ell, 276
  Thomas, 7
Runaway Slaves, 195
Rush
  Benjamin, 4, 294
  Sarah, 4, 294
Russel
  John, 12
Russell
  John, 212
  William, 44
Rutherford
  Mr., 328

S

Sackwood[?]
  Holld., 210
Saley[?]
  John, 188
Sallings
  John, 35
Sampson
  David, 198
  Jeffrey, 46
  John, 209
  Lovey
    a Free woman of Colour, 198
Sanderlin
  Asa, 236
  Wilson, 193
Sanders
  aaron, 265
  Benja., 30
  Charles, 12, 119
  John, 14, 251, 265
  Joseph, 248
  Joshua, 248
  Josiah, 247
  Mr., 252
  Romulus, 7, 8
  W, 222
  William, 248
Sands
  Alexander, an East Indian, 38
Sasser
  Jas., 286, 287
Satterfield
  Thos., 12
  William, 319
  Wm., 12
Saunders
  John, 14, 324
  Judge, 169
  Wm, 221, 253
Sawyer
  Benja., 220
  Benjamin, 210
  Dr, 212
  Enoch, 236
  Fred. B., 197, 199, 200, 209
  Griffith, 211
  John, 151, 153, 196
  M., 22
  Spencer, 244
Scerlock
  Harry, 10
Scott
  Elijah, 72, 78, 98, 107
  Jos., 199
  Joseph, 245
  Joseph Junr., 35
  Joseph Senr., 34
  Joshua, 119
  Stephen, 233
Scott[?]
  Hiram, 169
Scurlock

Index

Harry, 10
Joseph, 10
Sea
  Doctr., 3
  Dr., 3
Seagrove
  John, 281
  Phoebe, 281
Searcy
  Asa, 152
  Reuben, 152
Sears
  Jn, 41
  Jno., 41
  John, 41
Seawell
  James, 128
Seay
  Docter, 2, 3
  Docter James, 2, 3
Selph
  John, 307
  Laura, 308
  Lucy, 307
Sessums
  Alexander, 140
  Isaac, 138
Settison[?]
  James, 247
Sexton
  Samuel, 193
Shackelford
  D., 119
  David, 119
Shad
  Daniel, 298, 299
  Winny, 299
Shanawoolf
  S B, 111
  S.B, 111
Shannanhous
  Thos. L., 191
Shannawoolf
  S B, 110
Shannonhouse
  J.S., 206
  James L., 219, 235
  James S, 206
  Jas. L., 199, 209, 210, 219, 229, 230, 231
  Jas. S, 207
  Thos, 233, 234
  Thos L., 193
Sharp
  Mary, 117, 118
Sharrod
  Mr. Jonathan, 30
Shaw
  Ann, 48
  John, 231, 233, 234
  Robert, 293

Sheffield
  Jos. E., 87
Shekell
  Frances, 38
  John, 38
Shepard
  WB, 28
  William, 43
Shepherd
  [?], 208
Sheridan
  Louis, 298
  Thomas, 298
Sherwood
  Daniel, 180
Shields
  Wm H, 168
Shinley
  Danl., 199, 201
Simmons
  Bacchus, 86, 87
  James, 167, 168
  Jas, 169
Simn
  Backhaus, 79
Simons
  Bacchus, 79
  Backhaus, 79
  John Senr., 32
  Reuben, 15
  Thomas, 319
Simpson
  Exum, 22, 24, 25, 26, 27, 28
Sine
  Dominick, 32
Singleton
  Thomas G., 107
  Thos. G., 107, 108
Sitgreaves
  Mr., 321, 328
Skiner
  Mr. Eaven, 14
Skinner
  Evan, 14
  John, 21
  Jos. B., 21, 23
  Joseph B., 22
  W., 324
  W.R., 30
Slade
  E., 32
  Mr. Ebenezer, 31
  W., 12, 21, 33, 34, 202
Slanto[?]
  James, 261
Slave
  Negro Scipio, 160
  Scipio, 160
Slaves
  Aaron, 200, 209, 324
  Abba, 198

Abel, 130
Abel Payne, 130
Abner, 207
Abraham, 95, 186, 259, 325
Abraham Manns, 186
Abraham Moody Russell Allen, 95
Abram, 54, 56, 57, 323
Abram M. R Allen, 95
Absalom Spicer, 4, 294
Adam, 135
Affrica, 186
Africa, 186, 187
Africa Parker, 186
Albert, 310
Albertson, 194
Alexander, 293
Alexander Day, 293
Alford, 79
Alfred, 79
Alice, 53, 54, 96
Aliss, 264
Aliss Henly, 264
Allen, 298
Alsey, 96, 97
Amelia, 293
Amereto, 200
Amey, 81
Amos, 8
Amy, 79, 80, 81, 281, 296
Amy Phillips, 295
Andrew, 294
Ann, 23, 25, 130, 194, 259, 324, 325
Anna, 323
Annaretta, 198
Annis, 255
Anthony, 45
Antonio, 42
Archibald T., 289, 306
Archibald T. Cook, 306
Asa, 18, 19
Austin Curtis, 4, 293
Austin Curtis Jones, 4
Bachus, 87, 88
Backus, 87
Balaam Howe, 303
Beck an Indian, 140
Ben, 49, 54, 59, 226, 323
Ben, mother was an Indian, 152
Benja. Vicery[?], 152
Benjamin, 226, 324
Benny, 44
Bet, 51
Bet (Elizabeth), 140
Bethena, 276
Betsey, 49, 294, 299
Bett, 298
Betty, 22, 23, 24, 106, 107, 110, 211, 223, 292, 293, 299, 309
Betty Beebee, 309
Billy, 187

Index

Binah, 46
Boson, 301
Bosor, 324
Boston, 106, 108, 109
Boston Fr[?]uson, 76
Braveboy
   John, 11
Breny, 298
Bridget, 162, 163
Brister, 106, 109
bud, 280
Bunyer, 68
Burdock, 298
Burham, 276
Caesar, 43, 71, 236, 291, 323
Caesar Henry, 291
Cambridge, 155
Cancer, 324
Candace, 323, 324
Candis, 157, 158
Cannon, 67, 68
Caroline Cook, 306
Caroline Lane, 115
Cate, 251
Catharine, 260
Catharine Newby, 261
Cato, 285
Cattron, 215
Caty, 122
Caty Webber, 122, 123
Caze, 264
Cazy, 264
Chandis, 158
Charity, 27, 243, 298, 324
Charles, 23, 25, 26, 31, 194, 237, 259, 273, 274, 299, 324, 325
Charles Peters, 273
Charlott, 260, 261
Charlotte, 98, 218, 219, 260, 300
Charlotte Green, 98, 300
Chelsea, 54, 55, 298
Cherry, 277, 278, 306
Cherry Malone, 277
Chloe, 219
Christopher, 253, 254
Cloe, 218
Comfort, 215, 216, 260
Comfort Albertson, 260
Crease, 298
Cudgo, 323, 325
Cudjoe, 259
Cuff, 259, 325
Cuffee, 323, 324
Daniel, 91, 187, 298, 305
Daniel Macay, 305
Dave, 165, 171, 196
Davice, 210
David, 194, 198, 200, 201, 227, 259, 323, 325
Davis, 207, 210
Davy, 29

Davy Dickinson, 29
Delia, 123, 124
Derry, 177, 178
Dick, 9, 18, 50, 167, 168, 169, 236, 248, 259, 263, 323, 324, 325
Dick Dingley, 33
Dick Jones, 150
Dick Ridding, 263
Dick, whose Grandmother was a free Indian, 248
Dill, 324
Dinah, 324, 325
Doctor Jack, 230
Doctr Jack, 229
Dol, 324
Doll, 281
Dolly, 4, 14, 15, 294
Dorcas, 280, 324
Douglas, 66
Dublin, 323
Duke, 259
Easter, 197, 324
Easther, 197
Edith, 214
Edmond, 306
Edmund, 92, 93, 277, 278, 306
Edmund Malone, 277
Edny, 125, 126
Edward, 104. *See* Edward Hammons
Elias, 260, 261
Elisabeth, 262
Elisha, 262
Eliza, 260, 261, 262, 298
Eliza White, 261
Elizabeth, 4, 23, 24, 181, 182, 293
Ellenor, 260, 262
Ellenor White, 261
Elsbery, 262
Elvira, 260, 262
Emancipation of, 320
Emanuel, 52, 53, 243
Emiline, 130
Ephraim, 324
Esther, 323
Eunice Carruthers, 46
Evelina, 114, 115
Fanny, 38, 187, 216, 259, 305, 324, 325
Fanny Whitted, 187
Fereba, 223
Ferebee, 223, 224
Francis, 248, 324
Francis Hogg, 185
Frank, 185, 241, 280, 294, 295, 296, 324. *See* Slaves, Francis
Frank Goodman, 242
Fred, 86, 87
Freeman Hill, 301
Geoffrey, 20, 21

George, 17, 82, 203, 211, 212, 221, 265
George Bonner, 17
George Lewis, 86
George Luis, 86
Gerrish
   Edward, 257
Gilbert, 217
Ginger, 298
Glasgow, 259, 323, 325
Grace, 4, 293, 298
Gustavus Adolphus Johnston, 295
Hagai, 194
Hagar, 206, 259, 324, 325
Hanna, 171
Hannah, 47, 48, 54, 56, 79, 194, 207, 214, 246, 247, 259, 281, 286, 303, 323, 324, 325
Hannah Howe, 303
Hannah, a Midwife, 247
Hanneh, 79
Hannibal, 232
Hanson, 155
Harey, 253
Harriet, 4, 49
Harriet Green, 49
Harriot, 4, 293
Harrison, 260, 262
Harry, 9, 10, 21, 22, 52, 156, 228, 280, 298, 323
Harry Scerlock, 10
Harry Tredwell, 21
Henry, 53, 167, 168, 169, 305
Hester, 208, 209
Hicksy, 146
Higgins, 82
Hopewell, 280
Horace, 168
Huldah, 262
Ichabod, 202
Indian Sarah. *See* Indians
Isaac, 82, 83, 180, 217, 228, 305
Isaac Belden, 305
Isabella, 179, 303
Isabella Allen, 179
Ivey, 215
Jack, 32, 33, 149, 193, 201, 202, 230, 239, 244, 250, 259, 280, 294, 295, 323, 325
Jack Fennel, 41
Jacob, 94, 153, 188, 207, 259, 323, 324, 325
Jacob Fain, 153
Jacob Johnston, 188
Jacob McClure, 94, 95
Jacob Stevenson, 199
James, 16, 20, 45, 154, 208, 212, 217, 218, 258, 259, 260, 270, 271, 296, 301, 302, 325
James Ellis, 289, 306
James Ellis Cook, 306

Index

James G. Hostler, 180
James Langford, 308
James White, 261
James York Green, 89, 90
James, a Seaman, 258
James, Manumitted by Thomas Newby, 258
Jane, 179, 193, 194, 259, 303, 324, 325
Jane Albertson, 325
Jane Allen, 179
Jean, 227
Jeffery, 157
Jeffrey, 46
Jem, 323
Jenny, 21, 22, 75, 117, 118, 217, 297, 323, 324
Jeoffrey, 61
Jerry, 39, 40, 198, 309
Jerry Bethel, 309
Jesse, 168, 205
Jim, 20, 281, 294
Jim Williams, 20
Jinny, 21, 22
Jno Stanly, 40
Joab, 323
Joan, 198, 323
Job, 245, 246, 324
Job Hurdle, 245
Joe, 129, 215, 238, 280, 287, 304
John, 11, 40, 45, 62, 77, 79, 100, 101, 205, 221, 298, 305
John Downs, 90
John Good, 309
John Green, 100
John Howe, 303
John Marshall, 294
Jolly, 141
Jonah, 208
Jonas, 202, 232, 233, 324
Joseph, 233, 238, 267, 292
Joseph Blackwell, 300
Joseph Hostler, 128
Joshua, 82
Joshua Lewes, 83, 84
Juda, 323
Judah, 224, 324
Judey, 70
Judith, 194, 259, 260, 325
Judith White, 260, 261
Judy, 259, 325
Julia, 168
June, 50
Juno, 294
Jupiter, 323
Kelcy, 82
Kelcy Davis, 82
Kelsey, 79
Kelso, 81, 82
Ketty, 46, 79
Ketty Green Stanly, 46

Keziah, 205
Kitty, 79
Kiziah, 164, 165
Lanah, 46
Langa, 259, 325
Laura, 307
Laura Selph, 308
Lemuel, 324
Lenah, 43
Leon, 300
Lettace, 286
Lettice, 101, 102, 285
Limeric, 141
Limeric, a Mullato Man, 141
Limeric, Mother was an Indian, 141
Linney, 4, 294
London, 209, 210
Long Tom, 285
Louis, 132, 310
Louis Dunn, 132
Louisa, 49, 133
Lucretia, 270, 271
Lucy, 130, 281, 293, 307
Lucy Selph, 307
Luke, 203, 205, 324, 325
Lyda, 193
Lyddai, 324
Lydia, 46, 86, 87, 167, 168, 169
Mack, 168
Macklin Newton, 113
Major, 14
Margaret, 181, 182, 260, 265
Margaret Newby, 261
Maria, 97, 98, 131, 181, 182
Maria Grymes, 131
Mariah, 97
Marina, 260
Mark, 242
Martha Jane, 289, 306
Martha Jane Cook, 306
Martial, 44
Martial, a Mustee, 44
Mary, 23, 25, 31, 38, 41, 86, 87, 119, 120, 121, 181, 182, 262, 292, 295
Mary Ann, 127, 128
Mary Ann Hazell, 127, 128
Mary Dove, 38
Mary Long, 292
Mary, daughter of John Daly, 41
Matthew, 281
Mavina, 260
Merina, 261
Milley, 297
Mills, 246
Milly, 173, 174, 175, 240, 241
Milton, 260, 261
Mingo, 14, 15, 145, 146, 323, 324
  a Baptist preacher, 145
Mingo Green, 145

Mingo Pritchard, 264
Miranda, 279
Miranda Eaton, 279
Miriam, 215
Moll, 151, 281
Molly, 28, 29, 229, 230
Monday, 275
Money, 106, 107, 108
Mony, 107
Moses, 40, 119, 197, 220, 260, 262, 280, 324
Munro, 276
Murden, 260
Murden White, 261
Myrtilla, 77, 78
Myrtylla, 77
Nacy, 247
Nancy, 18, 19, 27, 48, 198, 298, 324, 325
Nancy Green, 48
Nancy Handy, 294
Nansey, 281
Nat, 283
Nathan, 4, 61, 62, 188, 294
Ned, 224, 225, 259, 323, 324, 325
Ned Griffin, 138
Ned Hyman, 304
Negro Man Scipio, 159
negro Philip, 163
Negro Philip, 163, 164
Negro Scipio, 159
Negro, Mulatto, or Indian, x
Nelson, 73, 74
Nero, 194, 259, 324, 325
Old George, 46
Page, 182
Pamelia, 306
Pamelia Cook, 306
Parmelia, 289
Parthena, 221
Patience, 188, 194, 259, 323, 324, 325
Patience Brawer[?], 188
Paton, 265
Patsey, 130
Patsey Payne, 130
Peggy, 27, 54, 60, 74, 285, 286, 303, 323
Peggy Handy, 294
Peleg, 243
penny, 323
Penny, 26, 63, 225, 260, 301
Penny Newby, 260, 261
Perthena, 221
peter, 252
Peter, 54, 55, 65, 66, 104, 105, 106, 124, 185, 247, 252, 259, 260, 294, 324, 325
Peter Elliot, 260, 261
Peter Godett, 47
Peter Justus, 185

352

Index

Peter Reynolds, 124
Peter, Whose Mother was an Indian, 247
Pharabe, 260
Pharabe White, 260, 261
Philip, 163, 164
Phillis, 43, 47, 228, 229, 249, 293
Phillis Freeman, 293
Phillis, a Midwife, 249
Phoebe, 121, 122, 259, 323, 325
Phyllis, 43
Pleasant, 204, 219, 246, 323
Plesant, 193
Plesent, 193
Polly, 127, 128, 146, 147, 299
Polly Aaron, 116
Polly Hazell, 127, 128
Polydore, 279
Polydore Johnston, 279
Pomona, 77
Pompey, 259, 324, 325
Pompy, 214, 266
Primus, 231, 232
Prince, 173, 301
Princess, 48
Princess Green, 48, 297
Pris, 298
Priscilla, 130, 259, 323, 324, 325
Priss, 298
Prissilla, 194
Pritchard, 194, 325
Quea, 324
Rachael, 4, 79, 156, 187, 205
Rachel, 79, 121, 187, 205, 294
Rachell, 280
Rachiel, 156
Rebecca, 4, 7, 8, 293
Rebeka, 324
rebekah, 323
Removed to free State, 169
Reuben, 51, 52
Rhitte, 280
Richard, 4, 98, 150, 219, 220, 235, 259, 269, 293, 294, 324, 325
Richard Copeland, 261
Richard Day, 293
Richard Green, 98
Richard Ladd, 269
Rigdon, 99, 100
Rigdon Green, 99
Ritter, 167, 168, 169
Robbin, 71, 72
Robert W Conway, 114
Robin, 281, 324, 325
Rosa, 237
Rosanna, 54, 57
Rose, 15, 16, 54, 59, 60, 173, 194, 208, 221, 224, 225, 226, 237, 250, 251, 259, 261, 294, 298, 301, 323, 324, 325
Rosetta, 275, 276

Ruth, 69, 205, 210, 324
Sabina, 299
Sal, 150, 280
Sal, an East Indian, 38
Sally, 64, 78, 154, 172, 297, 303, 304
Sally Howe, 303
Sally Zimmerman, 304
Saly, 9
Sam, 197, 201, 293, 298, 323
Sampson, 324
Samuel, 4, 194, 197, 259, 293, 324, 325
Samuel Johnson, 293
Samuel Macky, 307
Samuel McKey, 131
Saphey, 72
Sarah, 75, 76, 93, 94, 111, 112, 151, 152, 192, 194, 200, 259, 265, 323, 324, 325
Sawney, 324
Scipio, 158, 159, 160
Sely White, 261
sesar, 2, 222
Sesar, 222
Seth, 297
Sibb, 259, 325
Sibba, 324
Silas, 104, 105, 240
Silla, 259, 325
Silva, 218
Silvia, 13, 302
Silvia Lorint, 13
Simon, 73, 82, 84, 260
Simon White, 261
Sinah, 82, 85
Sinath, 85
Sipeo, 257
Sipio, 257
Sipo, 159
Solomon, 242
Solomon Nash, 181
Sophia, 78
Squire, 256
Stephen, 46, 212
Sukey, 87, 88, 89, 187, 280
Susan, 86, 87
Susanna, 259, 323, 325
Sylvester, 39
Sylvia, 219
Tabitha, 260, 297
Tabitha Newby, 261
Taffey, 30
Tamar, 235, 324
Tamer, 233, 234
Tempe, 91, 92, 276
Tenah, 43, 54, 58
Thomas, 18, 19, 26, 65, 119, 120, 144, 145, 160, 161, 207, 234, 293
    a Servant at New Garden, 161

Thomas Blacknall, 144
Thomas Clinch, 293
Thomas Gossett, 160, 161
Thomas Gossett, a Slave, 161, 162
Thomas K Green, 65
Thomas Newton, 111
Tobias, 165, 166
Toby, 165, 194, 259, 324, 325
Tom, 167, 168, 169, 182, 183, 211, 230, 231, 233, 234, 259, 285, 286, 298, 323, 325
Tom (Long), 285
Toney, 80, 195, 213
Tony, 213
Transported to free states, ix
Venus, 114, 181, 218, 219
Violet, 99, 100, 101, 171, 259, 302, 324, 325
Virchey, 86, 87
Virchy, 87
Virgil, 82, 86, 87
Weeks, 224
Welcom, 11, 12
Weldon, 168
Will, 79, 157, 158, 259, 325
Will, an East Indian, 38
William, 4, 181, 182, 207, 294, 324
Willie, 298
Willis, 287, 288
Winney, 155
Winny, 155, 299
Wordley, 280
York, 110, 111, 175, 176
Young Tom, 230
Zango, 323
Zelpha, 259
Zilpha, 324, 325
Slocumb
    Ezekiel, 288
Small
    Jack, 295
    Jack, a person of colour, 295
Smith
    Benjamin, 63, 66, 87, 88, 90, 112, 247
    Betsy, 244
    Betty, 244
    David, 304
    David Senr., 265
    James, 152
    Jn. F., 66
    Jno F, 65
    Jno. F., 39
    Job, 247
    John, 14, 247, 248, 324
    John F, 64, 65, 66, 67, 68, 69, 70, 71, 72, 73, 74, 75, 76, 78, 79, 88, 89, 90, 92, 93, 94, 95, 96, 97, 98, 99, 100, 101, 102, 113, 115, 116, 117, 124, 125

Index

John F., 39, 61, 63, 64, 65, 67, 78, 87, 108, 109, 110, 113, 114, 118, 120, 121, 123
John Jr, 254
Mr., 329
Mr. W., 328, 329
Mrs. Sophia L., 129
Na, 117
Nathaniel, 116, 117
Richard, a mulatto, 119
Samuel, 247, 324
Sarah, 154
Sophia L., 129, 304
Wm H, 168
Smithson
  J, 197, 200
  Jno. junior, 201
  John, 223, 224, 225, 226, 227, 228
Snead
  Jno, 75
  Jno., 75, 98
  John, 75, 92, 93
Sneed
  J, 155
  Jas., 153
  Step K, 155
  William M., 155, 156
  Wm M, 155
Snow
  James S, 170
Snowdon
  Henry A, 222
Society of Friends, ix, 234
Society of Friends of North Carolina, 233
Somervell
  John, 155
Somervill
  James, 282
  Jas., 282
Somerville
  J., 155
  John, 155
  Tho., 155
Soren[**Toren?**]
  Thomas, 35
South Carolina, 323, 324, 329
Spaight
  Mary Jones, 75, 76
  R D, 101
  Rd D, 101
  Richard D, 97, 100, 101
  Richard Dobbs, 129, 292
  Richd, 97
  Richd D, 98, 101
Spartan[?]
  Wm. S., 98
Spears
  Silvia, 302
  Violet, 302
Speller
  Henry, 11
  patience, 11
Spelman
  Hannah, 303
  Jacob, 303
  Peggy, 303
  Sally, 303
Spence
  Hen[?], 192
  Samuel, 325
  Wm, 229
  Wm., 226
Spence[?]
  Wm, 231
Spencer
  John, 4, 294
  Mr., 2
  Mr. John, 3
  Thomas, 2
  Thos., 2
  Wm., 220
Spencer[?]
  William, 231
  Wm, 223
Spicer
  Absalom, 4, 294
  Rachael, 4
  Rachel, 4, 294
Spivey
  John T, 169
Stafford
  Alexander, 326
  Jno. Jr, 256
  William, 326
Stalker
  aaron, 162
  Aaron, 161, 162
Stallings
  Elias, 34
  Jesse, 252
  Miles, 34
  Zachariah, 35
Stamp
  Thomas R, 232
Stand[?]
  Hend., 12
Standin
  Henderson, 18, 19
  Hendn., 18, 19, 21, 31
  Hendn. J., 19, 20
  Joseph, 32
  Mr., 18
Stanley
  John C, 72
Stanly
  Edw., 82
  Edward, 82
  J, 74, 108, 109, 110
  J C, 56
  J G, 53, 54, 55, 56, 57, 58, 59, 60, 65, 66, 71, 77, 90, 91, 94, 95, 96, 99, 100, 124
  J., 69, 77, 96, 115
  J.C., 45, 55
  J.G., 103
  J.S., 119
  James G., 82
  JC, 57, 58, 59, 60
  Jn C., 108
  Jn. C., 81, 86, 107, 108, 109, 110
  Jno, 40, 78
  Jno C, 59, 60, 72, 74, 91, 97, 118, 121, 122
  Jno C., 79, 122
  Jno G, 116
  Jno Stuart, 118
  Jno., 46
  Jno. C, 58, 77
  Jno. C., 45, 51, 54, 55, 56, 57, 58, 59, 60, 80, 81, 82, 97, 107, 123
  John, 74, 108, 109, 110
  John C, 54, 55, 56, 57, 58, 59, 60, 68, 72, 74, 77, 78, 79, 86, 87, 91, 92, 93, 97, 98, 108, 114, 117
  John C., 45, 46, 50, 51, 54, 68, 80, 81, 82, 86, 106, 107, 108, 109, 110, 114
  John Caruthers, 297, 298
  John Stewart, 73, 74
  M. C., 107
  W C, 92
Stanton
  Owen, 82, 104, 105, 106
Starre[?]
  John, 193
State of Virginia, 233
Staten
  WD, 169
States
  Alabama, 146
  Connecticut, 43
  Georgia, 275, 276
  Indiana, 260, 262
  Maryland, 37, 38
    Annapolis, 37
  New York, 43, 106
  South Carolina, 1
  Virginia, 1, 30, 151, 152, 153, 265
Stedman
  N. A, 103
Stephens
  M. C, 113
  M.C, 112
  M.C., 77
  M.E, 89, 93, 112
  M.E., 69
  Marcus C, 113
  Marcus C., 112
Stephenson

Index

Jacob, 199
Jno., 155
Stevenson
  Jacob, 199. *See* Slaves
  John, 199
  Joseph, 238
Stewardson
  Thomas, 323
Stewart
  Alex., 40
  Alexander, 40, 297
  Alexr., 40
  L., 121, 122
  Lydia, 40, 47, 50, 51, 80, 81, 297
  Mrs., 81, 82
Stiron
  Wallace, 40
Stock[?]
  Hyram, 168
Stokes
  M, 273
Stone
  David, 61, 62, 105, 111, 112, 121, 187
Stott
  Thomas, 221
  William, 197, 199, 222
Street
  Jn, 102
  Saml., 123, 124
  Samuel, 123, 124
  Wm R, 69
Strong
  Bela W., 131
Stroup
  Moses, 178
Sullivan
  Daniel, 176
Sumner
  J., 149
  James, 249
  Jas., 249
  Jethro, 149
Superior Court of North Carolina, 325
Supreme Court
  Appeal to, 170
Sutton
  David, 1
  Geo., 249
  James, 32
  John, 250
  Thomas, 258
Swain
  David L., 128, 129
  George, 160
  William, 2
Swaine
  Stephen, 11
Swann
  Penelope, 232

Swanwick
  Mr., 327, 329
Swearingen
  Elijah, 263, 264
Sylvester
  Abba, 198
  Annaretta, 198
  Jerry, 198
  Joan, 198
  Nancy, 198
  Thomas
    a free man of Colour, 198
Symon's Creek Bridge, 195
Symonds
  Elizabeth, 201
  Jera., 200
Symons
  Anne, 195
  Benj., 197
  Benjamin, 208
  Elizabeth, 324
  Jeremiah, 196, 198, 200
  Jesse, 196, 200, 324
  John, 195
  Matthew, 265, 266
  Reuben, 14
  Sarah, 209
  Thos., 195
  William, 209
  Wm., 222

T

Tadlock
  James, 218
Taggart
  Joseph, 37
Taler
  Daniel, 34
Tarkington
  Joseph, 319
Tatem
  David, 196, 197, 200, 204
Tatlock
  James, 218
Taylor
  Col. Thomas, 156
  Colo. Thomas, 156
  Colonel Joseph, 281
  George, 103
  Hannah, 214
  J., 187
  John, 42, 187
  John, a Sailor, 42
  Joshua, 287
  Pompy, 214
  Taylor, 214
Telfair
  Jno, 182
  John, 182

Temple
  James, 319
Templeton
  Jno, 114
  Jno., 79, 98, 111, 115
  John, 78, 79, 98, 111, 114
Tenah, alias Lenah, 43
Tenah, free negroe, 42
Tennessee, 301
Terrell
  Hezekiah, 147
  John, 147
  Tobs., 147
  Tolliver, 147
Terry
  Eli, 159, 160
Tettor
  Tettor, 245
Thach
  Spencer, 319
Thackry
  Olliver, 199
Thatcher
  Mr., 327, 329
Thomas
  A Servant, 161
  Francis, 37, 38
  John, 146
  Leonard, 38
  Micajah, 281
  Mr., 37
  Thomas, 38
Thomeguex
  Peter, 294
Thomejeaux
  Peter, 44
Thomejuex
  Peter, 44
Thomlinson
  Thomas, 50
Thornton
  Joseph, 324
Tignor
  William, 111
  Wm, 111
Tillman
  John, 51, 53, 54, 55, 56, 57, 58, 59, 60, 62, 80, 81, 82, 83, 84, 85, 86, 105, 106, 111, 112, 121
Tinker
  Euphronia, 39
  Stephen, 42, 43
Toms
  Benjnm., 245
  Francis, 255
  John A, 245
Tooley
  Adam, 39
  James, 39
  Jams., 39
Tooly

Index

Adam, 39
Tootle
  Absalom, 2
  Betty, 2, 3
  Dorcas, 2
  Elizabeth, 3
  Mr., 2
Totle
  Dorcas, 2
Town of Edenton, 18
Town of Warrenton, 280
Townsend
  Josiah, 251
  William, 324
Tredwell
  Saml., 12, 21, 22, 31
  Samuel, 22
Trogden
  Uria, 263, 264
Trott
  J, 200
Trotter
  W.D., 162
  WD, 161
Trublood
  Josiah, 215
Trueblood
  Aaron, 324
  Caleb, 204, 259, 260, 324
  Jesse, 221, 222
  John, 324, 326
  Joshua, 220, 233, 234, 240
  Josiah, 215, 259, 324
  N., 240
  Nathan, 233, 234, 239, 240
  Samuel, 235
  Timy, 197
Turner
  Ann, 191
    free Woman of Colour, 191
  Captain James, 281
  Harriet, 191
  James, 46, 50, 52, 279
  John P., 169
  Myles, 250
  Simon, 1
Tuscarora Indians, viii
Tuscarora War
  Governor Hyde of North Carolina, viii
  James Moore Jr. of South Carolina, viii
  John Barnwell of South Carolina, viii
  Slaves and captives taken, viii
  Tuscaroras enslaved, viii
Twitty
  Will:, 279
  William, 279

U

United States, 327
  Legislature of, 329
United States Congress
  Tenth Congress, 321
United States House of Representatives
  Petition to in 1797 by four slaves, xi
United States Senate, 321
Unthank
  Joseph, 158, 159, 160
  Josiah, 158, 159, 160
Urquhart
  Henry, 181, 182

V

VA Counties
  Isle of Wight, 151, 153
  Isle of Wight County, 230
  Nansemond, 151
  South Hampton, 152
  Southampton, 153
Vail
  B, 63
  B., 64
  Benners, 45, 46, 63
  Miss Betsy, 294
  Mrs. Betsey, 49
  T., 32, 33
  Thomas, 33
Valet
  Francis, 31
Varnum
  Mr., 330
Vass
  Thomas, 270
Vaughan
  James, 281, 282
  Major James Vaughan, 281
Vaughn
  J., 269
Vermont Legislature, 1826, viii
Vessels
  Indian Chief, ix
  Sloop Catherine, 43
Vickory
  Benjamin. See Indians
Vicory
  Benjamin. See Indians
Virginia, ix, 234, 258, 326, 328, 329
Voss
  Thomas, 270, 271
  Thos, 271

W

Waddell
  F.N., 181
  Francis N., 181
  John, 181
  John Jr., 181
Wadsworth
  Thomas, 77, 89
Waff[?]
  Jos T., 30
Waite
  John, 294
Walker
  David, viii
  James W., 182
  John, 163
  Richard H, 168
  Robert, 265, 270, 271
Wallace
  Benj, 63, 64
  Benjamin, 63, 64
  Joseph, 72, 73
  Rebecca, 117
Waln
  Nicholas, 323
Walton
  George, 324
  lewis, 162
  Lewis, 160, 161, 162
Ward
  Denby, 34
  Harden, 35
  J.H., 319
  Jacob, 34
  James, 11, 34
  John, 269
  Josias, 34
  Mr. James, 11
  Nathan, 245
  Thos., 35
  William, 35, 269
Warner
  John, a free person of Colour, 235
Warren
  Samuel, 229, 230
  Th. D., 30
  Tho. D., 29
  W.C., 30
  Wm. C., 29
Warrin
  Henry, 51
Washington
  N., 287, 288
  Nicholas, 287, 288
Washington, D.C., ix
Watkins
  Diver, 261
  Diver, Free Man of Colour, 260
Watson

Index

Thos. C., 4
We[?]
  Hiram C., 197
Weatherbee
  Willis, 169
Webb
  Demsey, 35
  Grace, 298
  Harry, 298
  James, 187
  Wilson, 32
  Z., 32
  Zachariah, 14, 15
  Zackariah, 32, 33
  Zackeriah, 33
Webber
  Caty, 122
  Caty, a slave, 122
  T, 47
  Thomas, 47
Weeks
  Emily, 167
  Emily Caroline, 168
  Jno D, 167
  John D, 167, 170
  John D., 170
Weir
  Thomas, 177
Welch
  David, 35
  Edward, 34
Wellborn
  James, 289
Wells
  John, 38
West
  Joshua, 221
West Indies, 119, 320, 326
  Emancipation in, 12
  Massacres in, 320
Whedbee
  Robert, 249
  Tho., 249
  Wm, 249
Wheeler
  TB, 267
Whidbee
  Geo., 258
  Jas., 256
Whitaker
  FH, 169
  James H., 170
White
  Aaron, 239
  Benja., 227
  Benjamin, 197, 227, 259, 324
  Benjn., 227
  Caleb, 218, 219, 259, 294, 324
  Comfort, 216
  David, 245, 246, 254, 260
  Demsey, 252

Devotion, 199
Edm., 202, 204
Edmund, 202
Eliza, 261
Ellenor, 261
Francis, 215, 216
Frs., 215, 216
Gab., 245
Gabl., 254
Gabriel, 256
James, 192, 212, 261
Jefrey, 34
Jesse, 252
John, 250
John Jasper, 294
Jonathan, 252, 260
Joseph, 251, 257
Joshua, 12, 259, 321, 324
Josiah, 231, 252, 257, 258, 259, 260, 324
Judith, 261
Lydia, 259, 324
Margaret, 324
Matthew, 259, 324
Mr James, 192
Mr., 216, 257
Murden, 261
P.F., 31
Pharabe, 261
S.S., 245
Saml. S., 245
Samuel, 195, 246, 251
Samuel S., 245, 246
Simon, 261
Thomas, 210, 250, 251, 254, 259, 324
Thomas, (of Josiah), 252
Thos., 3, 252
Thos. of Benj., 254
William, 259, 299, 324
WhiteEdward, 204
Whitehead
  Abner, 85, 86
  Jno., 85, 86
Whitehurst
  Fredk., 244
Whitfield
  Thomas, 151
Whitford
  D, 69
  D., 69
  David, 51, 52, 69
  John, 51, 52, 69
Whitt Bee
  Thomas, 252
Whitted
  Fanny, 187
  Jehu, 187
  Levi, 187
  Levy, 187
Wiggins

M.S., 169
Wilder
  Willis, 12, 321
Wilkes County, viii
Wilkins
  Eli, 31
  Eli, a person of colour, 31
  Geo., 32
  Tamer, 31, 32
Wilkinson
  Geo., 12
Willcox
  Jeremiah, 217
  M A, 169
Williams
  Abner, 191
  Benjamin, 46, 47, 49, 54, 55, 56, 57, 58, 59, 60, 77, 83, 84, 85, 151
  Chas., 51
  Davd., 220
  David, 235
  David L, 235
  FNM, 167
  H.B., 309
  Henry G., 279
  J.B., 12
  James, 141, 218
  James, a slave, 20
  Jim, 20
  Jim, a slave, 20
  John P., 181
  M, 169
  Owen, 242
  Rachael, 324
  Richard, 46, 47
  Samuel, 248, 298
  Thos, 154
  Thos S, 154
  William, 301
Willie
  Tho A, 154
  Tho H, 154
Willis
  Agerton, 292
  Ephraim, 51
  Ezre, 162
  Hezekiah, 70
  Isaac, 51
  Joseph, 292
  Joshua, 51
  Major, 69
  Norman, 51, 69
  Richd, 69
  Richd., 51
Wills
  Henry, 21, 24, 25, 26
  James, 31
Willson
  Mary, 151, 153
  William J., 173

Index

Wilmington, 303
Wilmington, North Carolina, viii
Wilson
   Francis, 239
   George, 107
   Jacob, 324
   Jos., 205, 209
   Joseph, 205, 209, 210
   Mrs. Winney, 107
   Samuel, 252
   Thos, 201
   William, 199, 224, 226
   William J., 174, 175
   Winefred, 107
   Wm, 213, 220, 222, 231
   Wm., 208, 209, 210, 212, 225, 226, 227, 228, 231, 233
   Wm. J., 173, 174, 175
   Wm.J., 174
Winslow
   Benjamin, 324
   caleb, 246
   Caleb, 246, 250, 251, 252, 257, 258, 324
   E.L., 128
   Edward L., 128
   Edward Lee, 128
   Jacob, 250, 251, 253, 254, 324
   John, 127, 129, 227
   Jordan, 254
   Miss Elizabeth, 131
   Nathan, 260, 261
   William, 34
Winston
   Jos., 269
   Joseph, 269

Witson[?]
   Isaac, 254
Wood
   Edward, 255
   James Jr, 251
   John, 246, 252, 253, 256, 257
   John H, 169
   Mr, 111
   N., 252
   Sarah, 112
   Seth, 35
   Thomas, 222
   Zebedee, 265
Woods
   Benjamin, 111
   Edw., 255
   Sarah, 112
Woodward
   James, 12, 321
Wooton
   Charles, 222
Wright
   Jno. W., 131
   John W., 131
   Joshua G., 308
   JW, 131
   William A., 179, 180, 308
   William E., 199
   Wm A, 180
   Wm. A., 179, 180
Wrights
   Wm. A., 179

Y

Yancey
   Thornton, 152
Yancy
   B., 304
Yarborough
   James, 144
Yarbrough
   James, 144, 145
Yeargen
   Samuel, 291
Yearly Meeting of friends, x
York
   Jas. Y, 99
Young
   Elisabeth, 40
   Elizabeth, 40

Z

Zimmerman
   Sally, 304
Zollicoffer
   George, 170
   George B, 168, 170
   Jerome, 170
   Jerome B, 168, 170
   Julius, 168
   Julius H, 167, 168, 169, 170
   Julius H., 170
Zolliecoffer
   George, 167
   George B, 167, 168
   Jerome B, 167, 168
   Julius, 167
   Julius H, 167

www.ingramcontent.com/pod-product-compliance
Lightning Source LLC
Chambersburg PA
CBHW081148290426
44108CB00018B/2480